TURING 图灵原版数学·统计学系

CW01618932

Introduction Series and Forecasting

时间序列与预测

（英文版·第2版）

[美] Peter J. Brockwell
Richard A. Davis 著

人民邮电出版社
北 京

图书在版编目（CIP）数据

时间序列与预测＝Introduction to Time Series and Forecasting：第2版：英文/（美）布罗克韦尔（Brockwell, P. J.），（美）戴维斯（Davis, R. A.）著. —北京：人民邮电出版社，2009.3

（图灵原版数学 · 统计学系列）

ISBN 978-7-115-19682-8

I. 时… II. ①布… ②戴… III. 时间序列分析－英文 IV. O211.61

中国版本图书馆CIP数据核字（2009）第011822号

内 容 提 要

本书全面介绍了经济学、工程学、自然科学和社会科学中所用的时间序列和预测方法，核心内容是平稳过程、ARMA过程、ARIMA过程、多变量时间序列、状态空间模型和谱分析. 另外，本书还介绍了Burg算法、Hannan-Rissanen算法、EM算法、结构模型、指数平滑、转移函数模型、非线性模型、连续时间模型和长记忆模型等. 每章的末尾都有大量习题，供读者巩固所学概念和方法. 本书强调方法和数据集的分析，配有时间序列软件包ITSM2000的学生版.

本书适合作为各专业学生时间序列入门课程的教材，也适合其他有兴趣的科研工作者阅读.

图灵原版数学 · 统计学系列

时间序列与预测（英文版 · 第2版）

◆ 著　[美] Peter J. Brockwell　Richard A. Davis

责任编辑　明永玲

◆ 人民邮电出版社出版发行　北京市崇文区夕照寺街14号

邮编　100061　电子函件　315@ptpress.com.cn

网址　http://www.ptpress.com.cn

北京铭成印刷有限公司印刷

◆ 开本：700 × 1000　1/16

印张：28.25

字数：450 千字　2009年 3 月第 1 版

印数：1-2 000 册　2009年 3 月北京第 1 次印刷

著作权合同登记号　图字：01-2008-5816 号

ISBN 978-7-115-19682-8/O1

定价：69.00元

读者服务热线：（010）88593802　印装质量热线：（010）67129223

反盗版热线：（010）67171154

版 权 声 明

Introduction to Time Series and Forecasting, Second Edition by Peter J. Brockwell, Richard A. Davis, ISBN: 978-0-387-95351-9.

To Pam and Patti

Preface

This book is aimed at the reader who wishes to gain a working knowledge of time series and forecasting methods as applied in economics, engineering and the natural and social sciences. Unlike our earlier book, *Time Series: Theory and Methods*, referred to in the text as TSTM, this one requires only a knowledge of basic calculus, matrix algebra and elementary statistics at the level (for example) of Mendenhall, Wackerly and Scheaffer (1990). It is intended for upper-level undergraduate students and beginning graduate students.

The emphasis is on methods and the analysis of data sets. The student version of the time series package ITSM2000, enabling the reader to reproduce most of the calculations in the text (and to analyze further data sets of the reader's own choosing), is included on the CD-ROM[①] which accompanies the book. The data sets used in the book are also included. The package requires an IBM-compatible PC operating under Windows 95, NT version 4.0, or a later version of either of these operating systems. The program ITSM can be run directly from the CD-ROM or installed on a hard disk as described at the beginning of Appendix D, where a detailed introduction to the package is provided.

Very little prior familiarity with computing is required in order to use the computer package. Detailed instructions for its use are found in the on-line help files which are accessed, when the program ITSM is running, by selecting the menu option `Help>Contents` and selecting the topic of interest. Under the heading `Data` you will find information concerning the data sets stored on the CD-ROM. The book can also be used in conjunction with other computer packages for handling time series. Chapter 14 of the book by Venables and Ripley (1994) describes how to perform many of the calculations using S-plus.

There are numerous problems at the end of each chapter, many of which involve use of the programs to study the data sets provided.

To make the underlying theory accessible to a wider audience, we have stated some of the key mathematical results without proof, but have attempted to ensure that the logical structure of the development is otherwise complete. (References to proofs are provided for the interested reader.)

---

① 该CD-ROM上的内容可以从图灵网站www.turingbook.com下载. ——编者注

Since the upgrade to ITSM2000 occurred after the first edition of this book appeared, we have taken the opportunity, in this edition, to coordinate the text with the new software, to make a number of corrections pointed out by readers of the first edition and to expand on several of the topics treated only briefly in the first edition.

Appendix D, the software tutorial, has been rewritten in order to be compatible with the new version of the software.

Some of the other extensive changes occur in (i) Section 6.6, which highlights the role of the innovations algorithm in generalized least squares and maximum likelihood estimation of regression models with time series errors, (ii) Section 6.4, where the treatment of forecast functions for ARIMA processes has been expanded and (iii) Section 10.3, which now includes GARCH modeling and simulation, topics of considerable importance in the analysis of financial time series. The new material has been incorporated into the accompanying software, to which we have also added the option `Autofit`. This streamlines the modeling of time series data by fitting maximum likelihood ARMA(p, q) models for a specified range of (p, q) values and automatically selecting the model with smallest AICC value.

There is sufficient material here for a full-year introduction to univariate and multivariate time series and forecasting. Chapters 1 through 6 have been used for several years in introductory one-semester courses in univariate time series at Colorado State University and Royal Melbourne Institute of Technology. The chapter on spectral analysis can be excluded without loss of continuity by readers who are so inclined.

We are greatly indebted to the readers of the first edition and especially to Matthew Calder, coauthor of the new computer package, and Anthony Brockwell for their many valuable comments and suggestions. We also wish to thank Colorado State University, the National Science Foundation, Springer-Verlag and our families for their continuing support during the preparation of this second edition.

Fort Collins, Colorado
August 2001

Peter J. Brockwell
Richard A. Davis

Contents

1 Introduction

In this chapter we introduce some basic ideas of time series analysis and stochastic processes. Of particular importance are the concepts of stationarity and the autocovariance and sample autocovariance functions. Some standard techniques are described for the estimation and removal of trend and seasonality (of known period) from an observed time series. These are illustrated with reference to the data sets in Section 1.1. The calculations in all the examples can be carried out using the time series package ITSM, the student version of which is supplied on the enclosed CD. The data sets are contained in files with names ending in .TSM. For example, the Australian red wine sales are filed as WINE.TSM. Most of the topics covered in this chapter will be developed more fully in later sections of the book. The reader who is not already familiar with random variables and random vectors should first read Appendix A, where a concise account of the required background is given.

1.1 Examples of Time Series

A **time series** is a set of observations x_t, each one being recorded at a specific time t. A *discrete-time time series* (the type to which this book is primarily devoted) is one in which the set T_0 of times at which observations are made is a discrete set, as is the

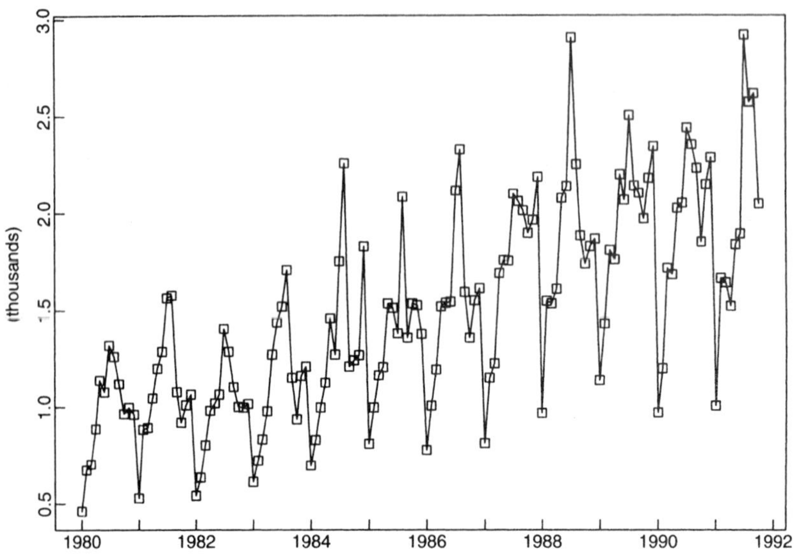

Figure 1-1 The Australian red wine sales, Jan. '80 – Oct. '91.

case, for example, when observations are made at fixed time intervals. *Continuous-time time series* are obtained when observations are recorded continuously over some time interval, e.g., when $T_0 = [0, 1]$.

Example 1.1.1 Australian red wine sales; WINE.TSM

Figure 1.1 shows the monthly sales (in kiloliters) of red wine by Australian winemakers from January 1980 through October 1991. In this case the set T_0 consists of the 142 times {(Jan. 1980), (Feb. 1980), ...,(Oct. 1991)}. Given a set of n observations made at uniformly spaced time intervals, it is often convenient to rescale the time axis in such a way that T_0 becomes the set of integers $\{1, 2, \ldots, n\}$. In the present example this amounts to measuring time in months with (Jan. 1980) as month 1. Then T_0 is the set $\{1, 2, \ldots, 142\}$. It appears from the graph that the sales have an upward trend and a seasonal pattern with a peak in July and a trough in January. To plot the data using ITSM, run the program by double-clicking on the ITSM icon and then select the option `File>Project>Open>Univariate`, click OK, and select the file WINE.TSM. The graph of the data will then appear on your screen. □

Example 1.1.2 All-star baseball games, 1933–1995

Figure 1.2 shows the results of the all-star games by plotting x_t, where

$$x_t = \begin{cases} 1 & \text{if the National League won in year } t, \\ -1 & \text{if the American League won in year } t. \end{cases}$$

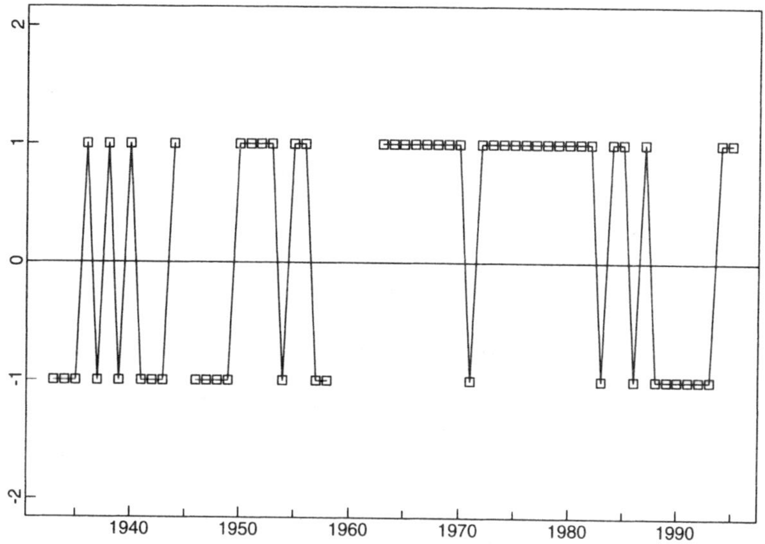

Figure 1-2 Results of the all-star baseball games, 1933–1995.

This is a series with only two possible values, ± 1. It also has some missing values, since no game was played in 1945, and two games were scheduled for each of the years 1959–1962. □

Example 1.1.3 Accidental deaths, U.S.A., 1973–1978; DEATHS.TSM

Like the red wine sales, the monthly accidental death figures show a strong seasonal pattern, with the maximum for each year occurring in July and the minimum for each year occurring in February. The presence of a trend in Figure 1.3 is much less apparent than in the wine sales. In Section 1.5 we shall consider the problem of representing the data as the sum of a trend, a seasonal component, and a residual term. □

Example 1.1.4 A signal detection problem; SIGNAL.TSM

Figure 1.4 shows simulated values of the series

$$X_t = \cos\left(\frac{t}{10}\right) + N_t, \quad t = 1, 2, \ldots, 200,$$

where $\{N_t\}$ is a sequence of independent normal random variables, with mean 0 and variance 0.25. Such a series is often referred to as *signal plus noise*, the signal being the smooth function, $S_t = \cos(\frac{t}{10})$ in this case. Given only the data X_t, how can we determine the unknown signal component? There are many approaches to this general problem under varying assumptions about the signal and the noise. One simple approach is to *smooth* the data by expressing X_t as a sum of sine waves of various frequencies (see Section 4.2) and eliminating the high-frequency components. If we do this to the values of $\{X_t\}$ shown in Figure 1.4 and retain only the lowest

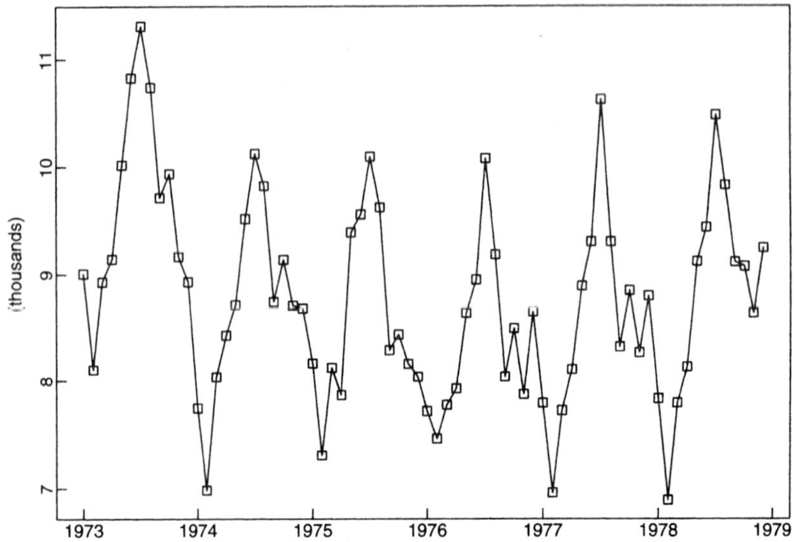

Figure 1-3 The monthly accidental deaths data, 1973–1978.

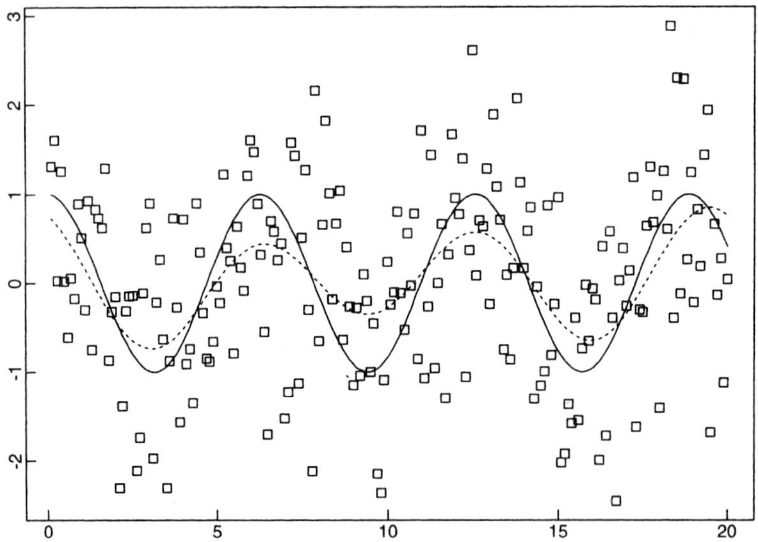

Figure 1-4 The series $\{X_t\}$ of Example 1.1.4.

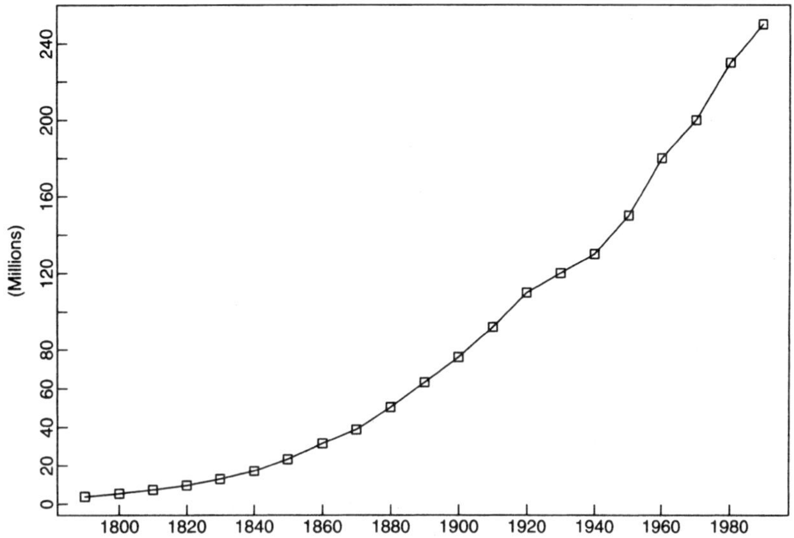

Figure 1-5 Population of the U.S.A. at ten-year intervals, 1790–1990.

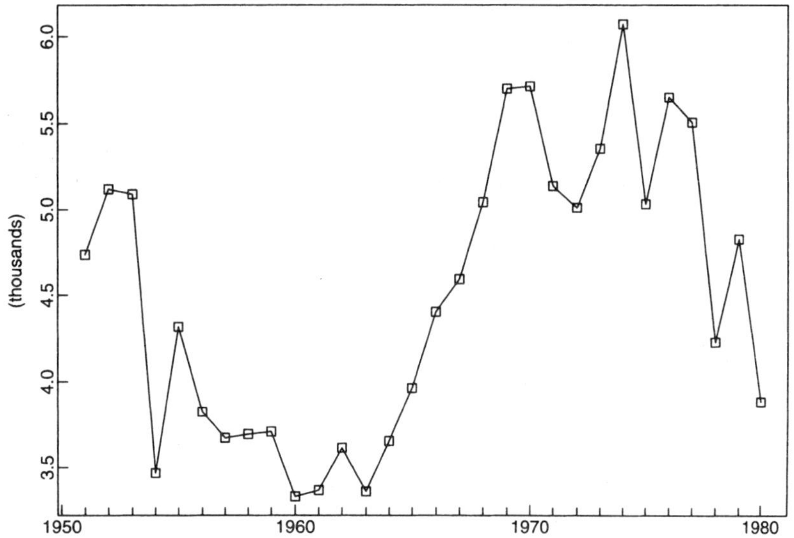

Figure 1-6 Strikes in the U.S.A., 1951–1980.

3.5% of the frequency components, we obtain the estimate of the signal also shown in Figure 1.4. The waveform of the signal is quite close to that of the true signal in this case, although its amplitude is somewhat smaller. □

Example 1.1.5 Population of the U.S.A., 1790–1990; USPOP.TSM

The population of the U.S.A., measured at ten-year intervals, is shown in Figure 1.5. The graph suggests the possibility of fitting a quadratic or exponential trend to the data. We shall explore this further in Section 1.3. □

Example 1.1.6 Number of strikes per year in the U.S.A., 1951–1980; STRIKES.TSM

The annual numbers of strikes in the U.S.A. for the years 1951–1980 are shown in Figure 1.6. They appear to fluctuate erratically about a slowly changing level. □

1.2 Objectives of Time Series Analysis

The examples considered in Section 1.1 are an extremely small sample from the multitude of time series encountered in the fields of engineering, science, sociology, and economics. Our purpose in this book is to study techniques for drawing inferences from such series. Before we can do this, however, it is necessary to set up a hypothetical probability model to represent the data. After an appropriate family of models has been chosen, it is then possible to estimate parameters, check for goodness of fit to the data, and possibly to use the fitted model to enhance our understanding of the mechanism generating the series. Once a satisfactory model has been developed, it may be used in a variety of ways depending on the particular field of application.

The model may be used simply to provide a compact description of the data. We may, for example, be able to represent the accidental deaths data of Example 1.1.3 as the sum of a specified trend, and seasonal and random terms. For the interpretation of economic statistics such as unemployment figures, it is important to recognize the presence of seasonal components and to remove them so as not to confuse them with long-term trends. This process is known as **seasonal adjustment**. Other applications of time series models include separation (or filtering) of noise from signals as in Example 1.1.4, prediction of future values of a series such as the red wine sales in Example 1.1.1 or the population data in Example 1.1.5, testing hypotheses such as global warming using recorded temperature data, predicting one series from observations of another, e.g., predicting future sales using advertising expenditure data, and controlling future values of a series by adjusting parameters. Time series models are also useful in simulation studies. For example, the performance of a reservoir depends heavily on the random daily inputs of water to the system. If these are modeled as a time series, then we can use the fitted model to simulate a large number of independent sequences of daily inputs. Knowing the size and mode of operation of the reservoir, we can determine the fraction of the simulated input sequences that cause the reservoir to run out of water in a given time period. This fraction will then be an estimate of the probability of emptiness of the reservoir at some time in the given period.

1.3 Some Simple Time Series Models

An important part of the analysis of a time series is the selection of a suitable probability model (or class of models) for the data. To allow for the possibly unpredictable nature of future observations it is natural to suppose that each observation x_t is a realized value of a certain random variable X_t.

Definition 1.3.1

A **time series model** for the observed data $\{x_t\}$ is a specification of the joint distributions (or possibly only the means and covariances) of a sequence of random variables $\{X_t\}$ of which $\{x_t\}$ is postulated to be a realization.

Remark. We shall frequently use the term *time series* to mean both the data and the process of which it is a realization. □

A complete probabilistic time series model for the sequence of random variables $\{X_1, X_2, \ldots\}$ would specify all of the **joint distributions** of the random vectors $(X_1, \ldots, X_n)'$, $n = 1, 2, \ldots$, or equivalently all of the probabilities

$$P[X_1 \leq x_1, \ldots, X_n \leq x_n], \quad -\infty < x_1, \ldots, x_n < \infty, \quad n = 1, 2, \ldots.$$

Such a specification is rarely used in time series analysis (unless the data are generated by some well-understood simple mechanism), since in general it will contain far too many parameters to be estimated from the available data. Instead we specify only the **first-** and **second-order moments** of the joint distributions, i.e., the expected values EX_t and the expected products $E(X_{t+h}X_t)$, $t = 1, 2, \ldots$, $h = 0, 1, 2, \ldots$, focusing on properties of the sequence $\{X_t\}$ that depend only on these. Such properties of $\{X_t\}$ are referred to as **second-order properties**. In the particular case where all the joint distributions are multivariate normal, the second-order properties of $\{X_t\}$ completely determine the joint distributions and hence give a complete probabilistic characterization of the sequence. In general we shall lose a certain amount of information by looking at time series "through second-order spectacles"; however, as we shall see in Chapter 2, the theory of minimum mean squared error linear prediction depends only on the second-order properties, thus providing further justification for the use of the second-order characterization of time series models.

Figure 1.7 shows one of many possible realizations of $\{S_t, t = 1, \ldots, 200\}$, where $\{S_t\}$ is a sequence of random variables specified in Example 1.3.3 below. In most practical problems involving time series we see only *one* realization. For example, there is only one available realization of Fort Collins's annual rainfall for the years 1900–1996, but we imagine it to be one of the many sequences that *might* have occurred. In the following examples we introduce some simple time series models. One of our goals will be to expand this repertoire so as to have at our disposal a broad range of models with which to try to match the observed behavior of given data sets.

1.3.1 Some Zero-Mean Models

Example 1.3.1 iid noise

Perhaps the simplest model for a time series is one in which there is no trend or seasonal component and in which the observations are simply independent and identically distributed (iid) random variables with zero mean. We refer to such a sequence of random variables $X_1, X_2, \ldots$ as iid noise. By definition we can write, for any positive integer n and real numbers $x_1, \ldots, x_n$,

$$P[X_1 \le x_1, \ldots, X_n \le x_n] = P[X_1 \le x_1] \cdots P[X_n \le x_n] = F(x_1) \cdots F(x_n),$$

where $F(\cdot)$ is the cumulative distribution function (see Section A.1) of each of the identically distributed random variables $X_1, X_2, \ldots$. In this model there is no dependence between observations. In particular, for all $h \ge 1$ and all $x, x_1, \ldots, x_n$,

$$P[X_{n+h} \le x | X_1 = x_1, \ldots, X_n = x_n] = P[X_{n+h} \le x],$$

showing that knowledge of $X_1, \ldots, X_n$ is of no value for predicting the behavior of X_{n+h}. Given the values of $X_1, \ldots, X_n$, the function f that minimizes the mean squared error $E\left[(X_{n+h} - f(X_1, \ldots, X_n))^2\right]$ is in fact identically zero (see Problem 1.2). Although this means that iid noise is a rather uninteresting process for forecasters, it plays an important role as a building block for more complicated time series models. □

Example 1.3.2 A binary process

As an example of iid noise, consider the sequence of iid random variables $\{X_t, t = 1, 2, \ldots,\}$ with

$$P[X_t = 1] = p, \quad P[X_t = -1] = 1 - p,$$

where $p = \frac{1}{2}$. The time series obtained by tossing a penny repeatedly and scoring $+1$ for each head and -1 for each tail is usually modeled as a realization of this process. A priori we might well consider the same process as a model for the all-star baseball games in Example 1.1.2. However, even a cursory inspection of the results from 1963–1982, which show the National League winning 19 of 20 games, casts serious doubt on the hypothesis $P[X_t = 1] = \frac{1}{2}$. □

Example 1.3.3 Random walk

The random walk $\{S_t, t = 0, 1, 2, \ldots\}$ (starting at zero) is obtained by cumulatively summing (or "integrating") iid random variables. Thus a random walk with zero mean is obtained by defining $S_0 = 0$ and

$$S_t = X_1 + X_2 + \cdots + X_t, \quad \text{for } t = 1, 2, \ldots,$$

where $\{X_t\}$ is iid noise. If $\{X_t\}$ is the binary process of Example 1.3.2, then $\{S_t, t = 0, 1, 2, \ldots, \}$ is called a **simple symmetric random walk**. This walk can be viewed as the location of a pedestrian who starts at position zero at time zero and at each integer time tosses a fair coin, stepping one unit to the right each time a head appears and one unit to the left for each tail. A realization of length 200 of a simple symmetric random walk is shown in Figure 1.7. Notice that the outcomes of the coin tosses can be recovered from $\{S_t, t = 0, 1, \ldots\}$ by differencing. Thus the result of the tth toss can be found from $S_t - S_{t-1} = X_t$. □

1.3.2 Models with Trend and Seasonality

In several of the time series examples of Section 1.1 there is a clear trend in the data. An increasing trend is apparent in both the Australian red wine sales (Figure 1.1) and the population of the U.S.A. (Figure 1.5). In both cases a zero-mean model for the data is clearly inappropriate. The graph of the population data, which contains no apparent periodic component, suggests trying a model of the form

$$X_t = m_t + Y_t,$$

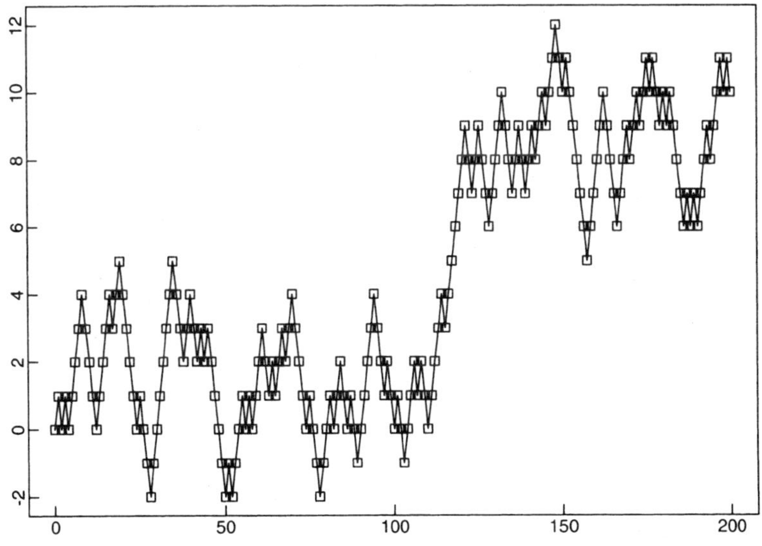

Figure 1-7 One realization of a simple random walk $\{S_t, t = 0, 1, 2, \ldots, 200\}$

where m_t is a slowly changing function known as the **trend component** and Y_t has zero mean. A useful technique for estimating m_t is the method of least squares (some other methods are considered in Section 1.5).

In the least squares procedure we attempt to fit a parametric family of functions, e.g.,

$$m_t = a_0 + a_1 t + a_2 t^2, \tag{1.3.1}$$

to the data $\{x_1, \ldots, x_n\}$ by choosing the parameters, in this illustration a_0, a_1, and a_2, to minimize $\sum_{t=1}^{n}(x_t - m_t)^2$. This method of curve fitting is called **least squares regression** and can be carried out using the program ITSM and selecting the `Regression` option.

Example 1.3.4 Population of the U.S.A., 1790–1990

To fit a function of the form (1.3.1) to the population data shown in Figure 1.5 we relabel the time axis so that $t = 1$ corresponds to 1790 and $t = 21$ corresponds to 1990. Run ITSM, select `File>Project>Open>Univariate`, and open the file USPOP.TSM. Then select `Regression>Specify`, choose `Polynomial Regression` with order equal to 2, and click OK. Then select `Regression>Estimation>Least Squares`, and you will obtain the following estimated parameter values in the model (1.3.1):

$$\hat{a}_0 = 6.9579 \times 10^6,$$

$$\hat{a}_1 = -2.1599 \times 10^6,$$

and

$$\hat{a}_2 = 6.5063 \times 10^5.$$

A graph of the fitted function is shown with the original data in Figure 1.8. The estimated values of the noise process Y_t, $1 \le t \le 21$, are the residuals obtained by subtraction of $\hat{m}_t = \hat{a}_0 + \hat{a}_1 t + \hat{a}_2 t^2$ from x_t.

The estimated trend component $\hat{m}_t$ furnishes us with a natural predictor of future values of X_t. For example, if we estimate the noise Y_{22} by its mean value, i.e., zero, then (1.3.1) gives the estimated U.S. population for the year 2000 as

$$\hat{m}_{22} = 6.9579 \times 10^6 - 2.1599 \times 10^6 \times 22 + 6.5063 \times 10^5 \times 22^2 = 274.35 \times 10^6.$$

However, if the residuals $\{Y_t\}$ are highly correlated, we may be able to use their values to give a better estimate of Y_{22} and hence of the population X_{22} in the year 2000. □

Example 1.3.5 Level of Lake Huron 1875–1972; LAKE.DAT

A graph of the level in feet of Lake Huron (reduced by 570) in the years 1875–1972 is displayed in Figure 1.9. Since the lake level appears to decline at a roughly linear rate, ITSM was used to fit a model of the form

$$X_t = a_0 + a_1 t + Y_t, \quad t = 1, \ldots, 98 \tag{1.3.2}$$

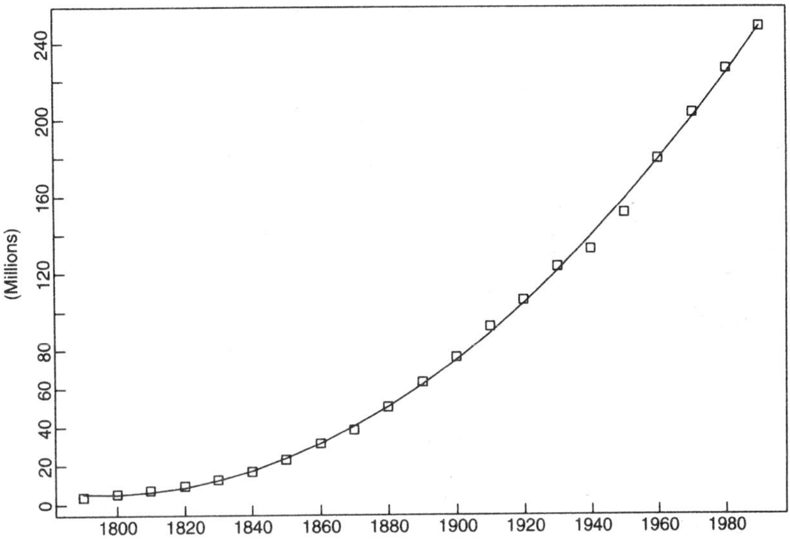

Figure 1-8 Population of the U.S.A. showing the quadratic trend fitted by least squares.

(with the time axis relabeled as in Example 1.3.4). The least squares estimates of the parameter values are

$$\hat{a}_0 = 10.202 \quad \text{and} \quad \hat{a}_1 = -.0242.$$

(The resulting least squares line, $\hat{a}_0 + \hat{a}_1 t$, is also displayed in Figure 1.9.) The estimates of the noise, Y_t, in the model (1.3.2) are the residuals obtained by subtracting the least squares line from x_t and are plotted in Figure 1.10. There are two interesting

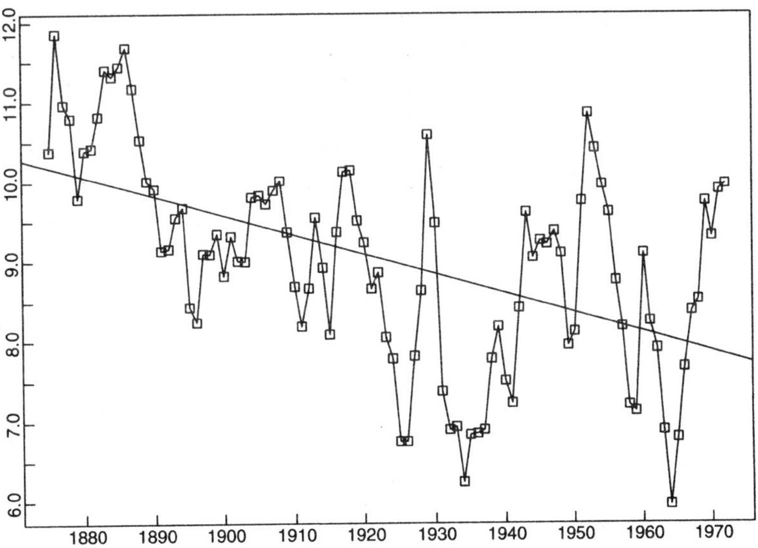

Figure 1-9 Level of Lake Huron 1875–1972 showing the line fitted by least squares.

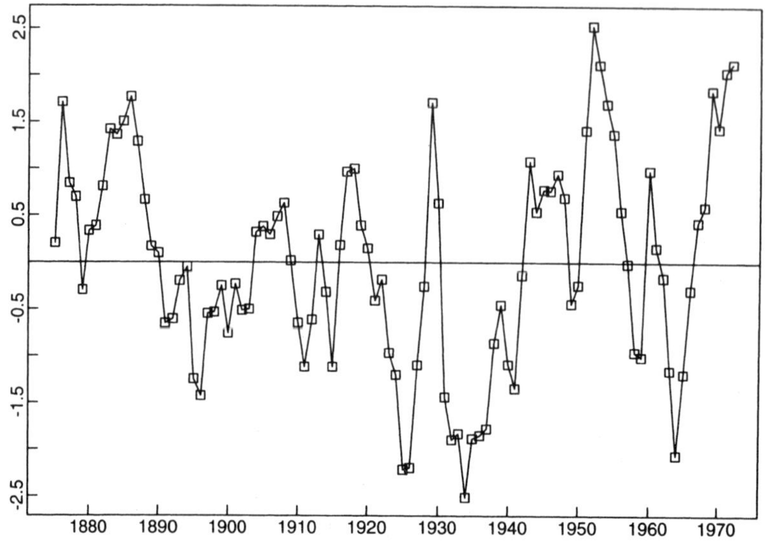

Figure 1-10 Residuals from fitting a line to the Lake Huron data in Figure 1.9.

features of the graph of the residuals. The first is the absence of any discernible trend. The second is the smoothness of the graph. (In particular, there are long stretches of residuals that have the same sign. This would be very unlikely to occur if the residuals were observations of iid noise with zero mean.) Smoothness of the graph of a time series is generally indicative of the existence of some form of dependence among the observations.

Such dependence can be used to advantage in forecasting future values of the series. If we were to assume the validity of the fitted model with iid residuals $\{Y_t\}$, then the minimum mean squared error predictor of the next residual (Y_{99}) would be zero (by Problem 1.2). However, Figure 1.10 strongly suggests that Y_{99} will be positive.

How then do we quantify dependence, and how do we construct models for forecasting that incorporate dependence of a particular type? To deal with these questions, Section 1.4 introduces the autocorrelation function as a measure of dependence, and stationary processes as a family of useful models exhibiting a wide variety of dependence structures. □

Harmonic Regression

Many time series are influenced by seasonally varying factors such as the weather, the effect of which can be modeled by a periodic component with fixed known period. For example, the accidental deaths series (Figure 1.3) shows a repeating annual pattern with peaks in July and troughs in February, strongly suggesting a seasonal factor with period 12. In order to represent such a seasonal effect, allowing for noise but assuming no trend, we can use the simple model,

$$X_t = s_t + Y_t,$$

where s_t is a periodic function of t with period d ($s_{t-d} = s_t$). A convenient choice for s_t is a sum of harmonics (or sine waves) given by

$$s_t = a_0 + \sum_{j=1}^{k} (a_j \cos(\lambda_j t) + b_j \sin(\lambda_j t)), \tag{1.3.3}$$

where $a_0, a_1, \ldots, a_k$ and $b_1, \ldots, b_k$ are unknown parameters and $\lambda_1, \ldots, \lambda_k$ are fixed frequencies, each being some integer multiple of $2\pi/d$. To carry out harmonic regression using ITSM, select `Regression>Specify` and check `Include intercept term` and `Harmonic Regression`. Then specify the number of harmonics (k in (1.3.3)) and enter k integer-valued Fourier indices $f_1, \ldots, f_k$. For a sine wave with period d, set $f_1 = n/d$, where n is the number of observations in the time series. (If n/d is not an integer, you will need to delete a few observations from the beginning of the series to make it so.) The other $k - 1$ Fourier indices should be positive integer multiples of the first, corresponding to harmonics of the fundamental sine wave with period d. Thus to fit a single sine wave with period 365 to 365 daily observations we would choose $k = 1$ and $f_1 = 1$. To fit a linear combination of sine waves with periods $365/j$, $j = 1, \ldots, 4$, we would choose $k = 4$ and $f_j = j$, $j = 1, \ldots, 4$. Once k and $f_1, \ldots, f_k$ have been specified, click OK and then select `Regression>Estimation >Least Squares` to obtain the required regression coefficients. To see how well the fitted function matches the data, select `Regression>Show fit`.

Example 1.3.6 Accidental deaths

To fit a sum of two harmonics with periods twelve months and six months to the monthly accidental deaths data $x_1, \ldots, x_n$ with $n = 72$, we choose $k = 2$, $f_1 =$

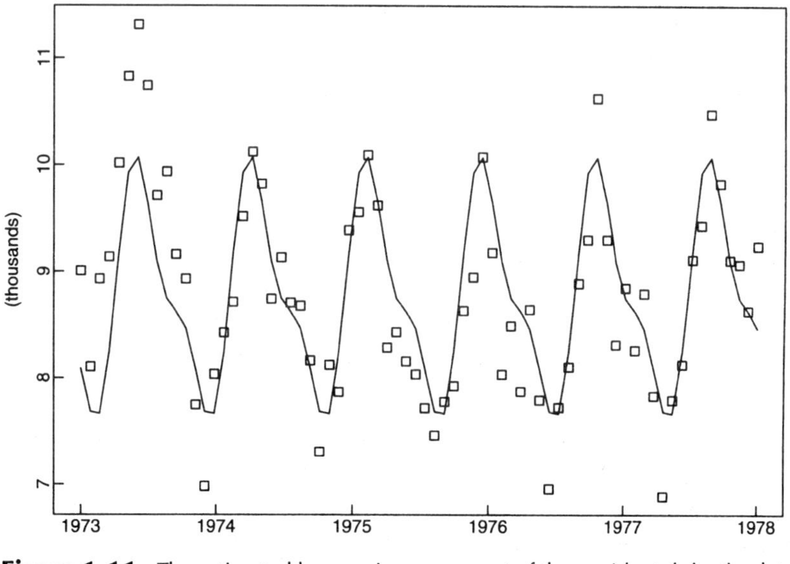

Figure 1-11 The estimated harmonic component of the accidental deaths data from ITSM.

$n/12 = 6$, and $f_2 = n/6 = 12$. Using ITSM as described above, we obtain the fitted function shown in Figure 1.11. As can be seen from the figure, the periodic character of the series is captured reasonably well by this fitted function. In practice, it is worth experimenting with several different combinations of harmonics in order to find a satisfactory estimate of the seasonal component. The program ITSM also allows fitting a linear combination of harmonics and polynomial trend by checking both `Harmonic Regression` and `Polynomial Regression` in the `Regression>Specification` dialog box. Other methods for dealing with seasonal variation in the presence of trend are described in Section 1.5. □

1.3.3 A General Approach to Time Series Modeling

The examples of the previous section illustrate a general approach to time series analysis that will form the basis for much of what is done in this book. Before introducing the ideas of dependence and stationarity, we outline this approach to provide the reader with an overview of the way in which the various ideas of this chapter fit together.

- Plot the series and examine the main features of the graph, checking in particular whether there is
  (a) a trend,
  (b) a seasonal component,
  (c) any apparent sharp changes in behavior,
  (d) any outlying observations.
- Remove the trend and seasonal components to get *stationary* residuals (as defined in Section 1.4). To achieve this goal it may sometimes be necessary to apply a preliminary transformation to the data. For example, if the magnitude of the fluctuations appears to grow roughly linearly with the level of the series, then the transformed series $\{\ln X_1, \ldots, \ln X_n\}$ will have fluctuations of more constant magnitude. See, for example, Figures 1.1 and 1.17. (If some of the data are negative, add a positive constant to each of the data values to ensure that all values are positive before taking logarithms.) There are several ways in which trend and seasonality can be removed (see Section 1.5), some involving estimating the components and subtracting them from the data, and others depending on *differencing* the data, i.e., replacing the original series $\{X_t\}$ by $\{Y_t := X_t - X_{t-d}\}$ for some positive integer d. Whichever method is used, the aim is to produce a stationary series, whose values we shall refer to as residuals.
- Choose a model to fit the residuals, making use of various sample statistics including the sample autocorrelation function to be defined in Section 1.4.
- Forecasting will be achieved by forecasting the residuals and then inverting the transformations described above to arrive at forecasts of the original series $\{X_t\}$.

- An extremely useful alternative approach touched on only briefly in this book is to express the series in terms of its Fourier components, which are sinusoidal waves of different frequencies (cf. Example 1.1.4). This approach is especially important in engineering applications such as signal processing and structural design. It is important, for example, to ensure that the resonant frequency of a structure does not coincide with a frequency at which the loading forces on the structure have a particularly large component.

1.4 Stationary Models and the Autocorrelation Function

Loosely speaking, a time series $\{X_t, t = 0, \pm 1, \ldots\}$ is said to be stationary if it has statistical properties similar to those of the "time-shifted" series $\{X_{t+h}, t = 0, \pm 1, \ldots\}$, for each integer h. Restricting attention to those properties that depend only on the first- and second-order moments of $\{X_t\}$, we can make this idea precise with the following definitions.

Definition 1.4.1

Let $\{X_t\}$ be a time series with $E(X_t^2) < \infty$. The **mean function** of $\{X_t\}$ is

$$\mu_X(t) = E(X_t).$$

The **covariance function** of $\{X_t\}$ is

$$\gamma_X(r, s) = \mathrm{Cov}(X_r, X_s) = E[(X_r - \mu_X(r))(X_s - \mu_X(s))]$$

for all integers r and s.

Definition 1.4.2

$\{X_t\}$ is **(weakly) stationary** if

(i) $\mu_X(t)$ is independent of t,

and

(ii) $\gamma_X(t+h, t)$ is independent of t for each h.

Remark 1. Strict stationarity of a time series $\{X_t, t = 0, \pm 1, \ldots\}$ is defined by the condition that $(X_1, \ldots, X_n)$ and $(X_{1+h}, \ldots, X_{n+h})$ have the same joint distributions for all integers h and $n > 0$. It is easy to check that if $\{X_t\}$ is strictly stationary and $EX_t^2 < \infty$ for all t, then $\{X_t\}$ is also weakly stationary (Problem 1.3). Whenever we use the term *stationary* we shall mean weakly stationary as in Definition 1.4.2, unless we specifically indicate otherwise. □

Remark 2. In view of condition (ii), whenever we use the term covariance function with reference to a *stationary* time series $\{X_t\}$ we shall mean the function γ_X of *one* variable, defined by

$$\gamma_X(h) := \gamma_X(h, 0) = \gamma_X(t+h, t).$$

The function $\gamma_X(\cdot)$ will be referred to as the autocovariance function and $\gamma_X(h)$ as its value at *lag* h. □

Definition 1.4.3

Let $\{X_t\}$ be a stationary time series. The **autocovariance function** (ACVF) of $\{X_t\}$ at lag h is

$$\gamma_X(h) = \mathrm{Cov}(X_{t+h}, X_t).$$

The **autocorrelation function** (ACF) of $\{X_t\}$ at lag h is

$$\rho_X(h) \equiv \frac{\gamma_X(h)}{\gamma_X(0)} = \mathrm{Cor}(X_{t+h}, X_t).$$

In the following examples we shall frequently use the easily verified **linearity property of covariances**, that if $\mathrm{E}X^2 < \infty$, $\mathrm{E}Y^2 < \infty$, $\mathrm{E}Z^2 < \infty$ and a, b, and c are any real constants, then

$$\mathrm{Cov}(aX + bY + c, Z) = a\,\mathrm{Cov}(X, Z) + b\,\mathrm{Cov}(Y, Z).$$

Example 1.4.1 iid noise

If $\{X_t\}$ is iid noise and $E(X_t^2) = \sigma^2 < \infty$, then the first requirement of Definition 1.4.2 is obviously satisfied, since $E(X_t) = 0$ for all t. By the assumed independence,

$$\gamma_X(t+h, t) = \begin{cases} \sigma^2, & \text{if } h = 0, \\ 0, & \text{if } h \neq 0, \end{cases}$$

which does not depend on t. Hence iid noise with finite second moment is stationary. We shall use the notation

$$\{X_t\} \sim \mathrm{IID}\left(0, \sigma^2\right)$$

to indicate that the random variables X_t are independent and identically distributed random variables, each with mean 0 and variance σ^2. □

Example 1.4.2 White noise

If $\{X_t\}$ is a sequence of uncorrelated random variables, each with zero mean and variance σ^2, then clearly $\{X_t\}$ is stationary with the same covariance function as the iid noise in Example 1.4.1. Such a sequence is referred to as **white noise** (with mean 0 and variance σ^2). This is indicated by the notation

$$\{X_t\} \sim \mathrm{WN}\left(0, \sigma^2\right).$$

Clearly, every IID$(0, \sigma^2)$ sequence is WN$(0, \sigma^2)$ but not conversely (see Problem 1.8 and the ARCH(1) process of Section 10.3). □

Example 1.4.3 The random walk

If $\{S_t\}$ is the random walk defined in Example 1.3.3 with $\{X_t\}$ as in Example 1.4.1, then $ES_t = 0$, $E(S_t^2) = t\sigma^2 < \infty$ for all t, and, for $h \geq 0$,

$$\begin{aligned}\gamma_S(t+h, t) &= \text{Cov}(S_{t+h}, S_t) \\ &= \text{Cov}(S_t + X_{t+1} + \cdots + X_{t+h}, S_t) \\ &= \text{Cov}(S_t, S_t) \\ &= t\sigma^2.\end{aligned}$$

Since $\gamma_S(t+h, t)$ depends on t, the series $\{S_t\}$ is *not* stationary. □

Example 1.4.4 First-order moving average or MA(1) process

Consider the series defined by the equation

$$X_t = Z_t + \theta Z_{t-1}, \quad t = 0, \pm 1, \ldots, \tag{1.4.1}$$

where $\{Z_t\} \sim \text{WN}\left(0, \sigma^2\right)$ and θ is a real-valued constant. From (1.4.1) we see that $EX_t = 0$, $EX_t^2 = \sigma^2(1+\theta^2) < \infty$, and

$$\gamma_X(t+h, t) = \begin{cases} \sigma^2\left(1+\theta^2\right), & \text{if } h = 0, \\ \sigma^2\theta, & \text{if } h = \pm 1, \\ 0, & \text{if } |h| > 1. \end{cases}$$

Thus the requirements of Definition 1.4.2 are satisfied, and $\{X_t\}$ is stationary. The autocorrelation function of $\{X_t\}$ is

$$\rho_X(h) = \begin{cases} 1, & \text{if } h = 0, \\ \theta/\left(1+\theta^2\right), & \text{if } h = \pm 1, \\ 0, & \text{if } |h| > 1. \end{cases}$$ □

Example 1.4.5 First-order autoregression or AR(1) process

Let us *assume* now that $\{X_t\}$ is a stationary series satisfying the equations

$$X_t = \phi X_{t-1} + Z_t, \quad t = 0, \pm 1, \ldots, \tag{1.4.2}$$

where $\{Z_t\} \sim \text{WN}(0, \sigma^2)$, $|\phi| < 1$, and Z_t is uncorrelated with X_s for each $s < t$. (We shall show in Section 2.2 that there is in fact exactly one such solution of (1.4.2).) By taking expectations on each side of (1.4.2) and using the fact that $EZ_t = 0$, we see at once that

$$EX_t = 0.$$

To find the autocorrelation function of $\{X_t\}$ we multiply each side of (1.4.2) by X_{t-h} $(h > 0)$ and then take expectations to get

$$\begin{aligned}\gamma_X(h) &= \mathrm{Cov}(X_t, X_{t-h}) \\ &= \mathrm{Cov}(\phi X_{t-1}, X_{t-h}) + \mathrm{Cov}(Z_t, X_{t-h}) \\ &= \phi\gamma_X(h-1) + 0 = \cdots = \phi^h \gamma_X(0).\end{aligned}$$

Observing that $\gamma(h) = \gamma(-h)$ and using Definition 1.4.3, we find that

$$\rho_X(h) = \frac{\gamma_X(h)}{\gamma_X(0)} = \phi^{|h|}, \quad h = 0, \pm 1, \ldots.$$

It follows from the linearity of the covariance function in each of its arguments and the fact that Z_t is uncorrelated with X_{t-1} that

$$\gamma_X(0) = \mathrm{Cov}(X_t, X_t) = \mathrm{Cov}(\phi X_{t-1} + Z_t, \phi X_{t-1} + Z_t) = \phi^2\gamma_X(0) + \sigma^2$$

and hence that $\gamma_X(0) = \sigma^2 / \left(1 - \phi^2\right)$. □

1.4.1 The Sample Autocorrelation Function

Although we have just seen how to compute the autocorrelation function for a few simple time series models, in practical problems we do not start with a model, but with *observed data* $\{x_1, x_2, \ldots, x_n\}$. To assess the degree of dependence in the data and to select a model for the data that reflects this, one of the important tools we use is the **sample autocorrelation function** (sample ACF) of the data. If we believe that the data are realized values of a stationary time series $\{X_t\}$, then the sample ACF will provide us with an estimate of the ACF of $\{X_t\}$. This estimate may suggest which of the many possible stationary time series models is a suitable candidate for representing the dependence in the data. For example, a sample ACF that is close to zero for all nonzero lags suggests that an appropriate model for the data might be iid noise. The following definitions are natural *sample* analogues of those for the autocovariance and autocorrelation functions given earlier for stationary time series *models*.

Definition 1.4.4

Let $x_1, \ldots, x_n$ be observations of a time series. The **sample mean** of $x_1, \ldots, x_n$ is

$$\bar{x} = \frac{1}{n}\sum_{t=1}^{n} x_t.$$

The **sample autocovariance function** is

$$\hat{\gamma}(h) := n^{-1}\sum_{t=1}^{n-|h|}(x_{t+|h|} - \bar{x})(x_t - \bar{x}), \qquad -n < h < n.$$

The **sample autocorrelation function** is

$$\hat{\rho}(h) = \frac{\hat{\gamma}(h)}{\hat{\gamma}(0)}, \qquad -n < h < n.$$

Remark 3. For $h \geq 0$, $\hat{\gamma}(h)$ is approximately equal to the sample covariance of the $n-h$ pairs of observations $(x_1, x_{1+h}), (x_2, x_{2+h}), \ldots, (x_{n-h}, x_n)$. The difference arises from use of the divisor n instead of $n-h$ and the subtraction of the *overall* mean, $\bar{x}$, from each factor of the summands. Use of the divisor n ensures that the sample covariance matrix $\hat{\Gamma}_n := [\hat{\gamma}(i-j)]_{i,j=1}^{n}$ is nonnegative definite (see Section 2.4.2). □

Remark 4. Like the sample covariance matrix defined in Remark 3, the sample correlation matrix $\hat{R}_n := [\hat{\rho}(i-j)]_{i,j=1}^{n}$ is nonnegative definite. Each of its diagonal elements is equal to 1, since $\hat{\rho}(0) = 1$. □

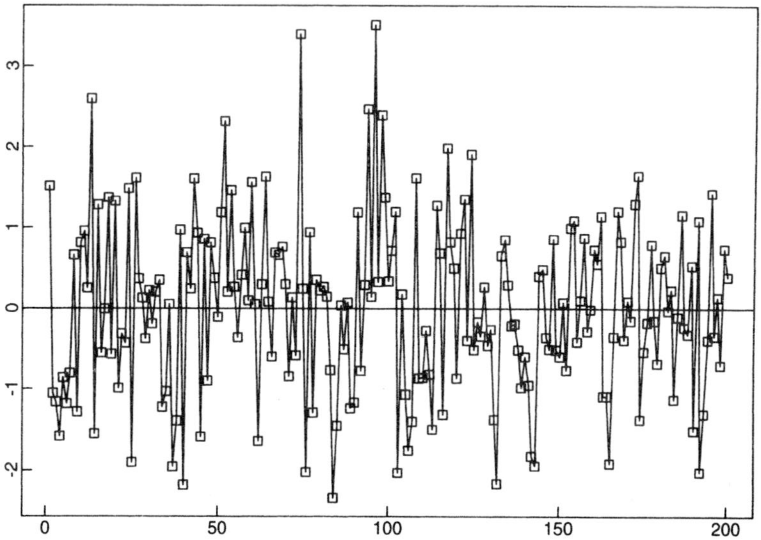

Figure 1-12 200 simulated values of iid N(0,1) noise.

Example 1.4.6

Figure 1.12 shows 200 simulated values of normally distributed iid (0, 1), denoted by IID N(0, 1), noise. Figure 1.13 shows the corresponding sample autocorrelation function at lags 0, 1, ..., 40. Since $\rho(h) = 0$ for $h > 0$, one would also expect the corresponding sample autocorrelations to be near 0. It can be shown, in fact, that for iid noise with finite variance, the sample autocorrelations $\hat{\rho}(h)$, $h > 0$, are approximately IID N(0, $1/n$) for n large (see TSTM p. 222). Hence, approximately 95% of the sample autocorrelations should fall between the bounds $\pm 1.96/\sqrt{n}$ (since 1.96 is the .975 quantile of the standard normal distribution). Therefore, in Figure 1.13 we would expect roughly $40(.05) = 2$ values to fall outside the bounds. To simulate 200 values of IID N(0, 1) noise using ITSM, select `File>Project>New>Univariate` then `Model>Simulate`. In the resulting dialog box, enter 200 for the required `Number of Observations`. (The remaining entries in the dialog box can be left as they are, since the model assumed by ITSM, until you enter another, is IID N(0, 1) noise. If you wish to reproduce exactly the same sequence at a later date, record the `Random Number Seed` for later use. By specifying different values for the random number seed you can generate independent realizations of your time series.) Click on `OK` and you will see the graph of your simulated series. To see its sample autocorrelation function together with the autocorrelation function of the model that generated it, click on the third yellow button at the top of the screen and you will see the two graphs superimposed (with the latter in red.) The horizontal lines on the graph are the bounds $\pm 1.96/\sqrt{n}$. □

Remark 5. The sample autocovariance and autocorrelation functions can be computed for *any* data set $\{x_1, \ldots, x_n\}$ and are not restricted to observations from a

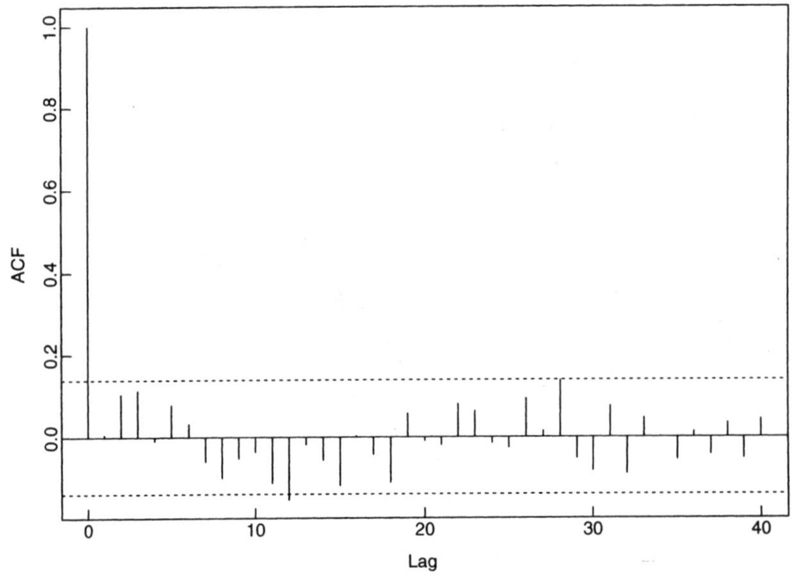

Figure 1-13 The sample autocorrelation function for the data of Figure 1.12 showing the bounds $\pm 1.96/\sqrt{n}$.

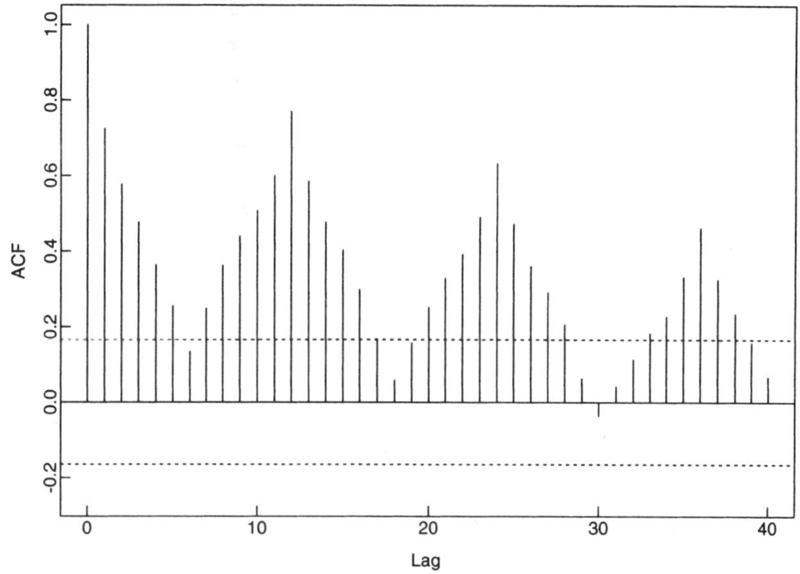

Figure 1-14 The sample autocorrelation function for the Australian red wine sales showing the bounds $\pm 1.96/\sqrt{n}$.

stationary time series. For data containing a trend, $|\hat{\rho}(h)|$ will exhibit slow decay as h increases, and for data with a substantial deterministic periodic component, $|\hat{\rho}(h)|$ will exhibit similar behavior with the same periodicity. (See the sample ACF of the Australian red wine sales in Figure 1.14 and Problem 1.9.) Thus $\hat{\rho}(\cdot)$ can be useful as an indicator of nonstationarity (see also Section 6.1). □

1.4.2 A Model for the Lake Huron Data

As noted earlier, an iid noise model for the residuals $\{y_1, \ldots, y_{98}\}$ obtained by fitting a straight line to the Lake Huron data in Example 1.3.5 appears to be inappropriate. This conclusion is confirmed by the sample ACF of the residuals (Figure 1.15), which has three of the first forty values well outside the bounds $\pm 1.96/\sqrt{98}$.

The roughly geometric decay of the first few sample autocorrelations (with $\hat{\rho}(h+1)/\hat{\rho}(h) \approx 0.7$) suggests that an AR(1) series (with $\phi \approx 0.7$) might provide a reasonable model for these residuals. (The form of the ACF for an AR(1) process was computed in Example 1.4.5.)

To explore the appropriateness of such a model, consider the points (y_1, y_2), $(y_2, y_3), \ldots, (y_{97}, y_{98})$ plotted in Figure 1.16. The graph does indeed suggest a linear relationship between y_t and y_{t-1}. Using simple least squares estimation to fit a straight line of the form $y_t = ay_{t-1}$, we obtain the model

$$Y_t = .791Y_{t-1} + Z_t, \tag{1.4.3}$$

where $\{Z_t\}$ is iid noise with variance $\sum_{t=2}^{98}(y_t - .791y_{t-1})^2/97 = .5024$. The sample ACF of the estimated noise sequence $z_t = y_t - .791y_{t-1}, t = 2, \ldots, 98$, is slightly

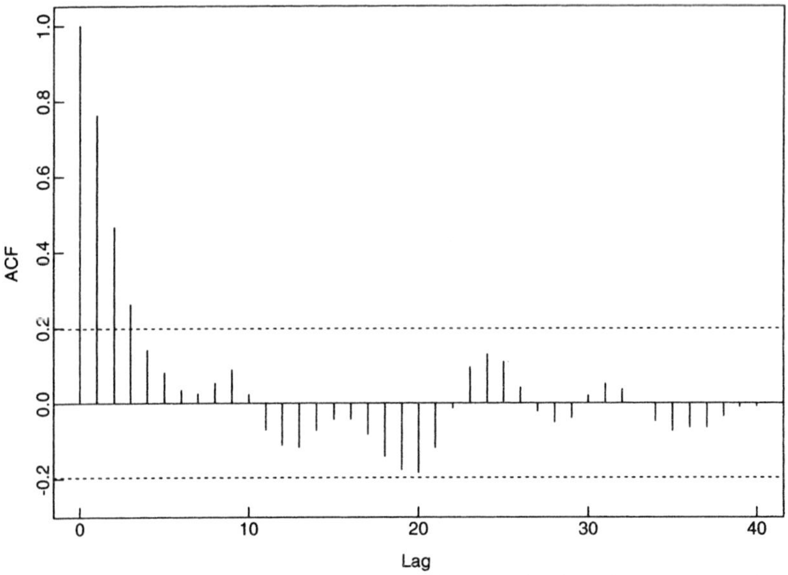

Figure 1-15 The sample autocorrelation function for the Lake Huron residuals of Figure 1.10 showing the bounds $\pm 1.96/\sqrt{n}$.

outside the bounds $\pm 1.96/\sqrt{97}$ at lag 1 ($\hat{\rho}(1) = .216$), but it is inside the bounds for all other lags up to 40. This check that the estimated noise sequence is consistent with the iid assumption of (1.4.3) reinforces our belief in the fitted model. More *goodness of fit* tests for iid noise sequences are described in Section 1.6. The estimated noise sequence $\{z_t\}$ in this example passes them all, providing further support for the model (1.4.3).

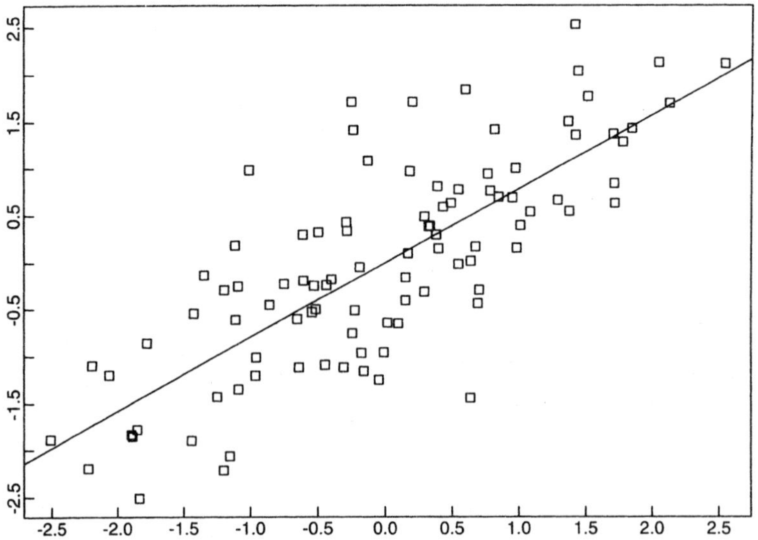

Figure 1-16 Scatter plot of (y_{t-1}, y_t), $t = 2, \ldots, 98$, for the data in Figure 1.10 showing the least squares regression line $y = .791x$.

A better fit to the residuals in equation (1.3.2) is provided by the second-order autoregression

$$Y_t = \phi_1 Y_{t-1} + \phi_2 Y_{t-2} + Z_t, \tag{1.4.4}$$

where $\{Z_t\}$ is iid noise with variance σ^2. This is analogous to a linear model in which Y_t is regressed on the previous *two* values Y_{t-1} and Y_{t-2} of the time series. The least squares estimates of the parameters ϕ_1 and ϕ_2, found by minimizing $\sum_{t=3}^{98}(y_t - \phi_1 y_{t-1} - \phi_2 y_{t-2})^2$, are $\hat{\phi}_1 = 1.002$ and $\hat{\phi}_2 = -.2834$. The estimate of σ^2 is $\hat{\sigma}^2 = \sum_{t=3}^{98}(y_t - \hat{\phi}_1 y_{t-1} - \hat{\phi}_2 y_{t-2})^2/96 = .4460$, which is approximately 11% smaller than the estimate of the noise variance for the AR(1) model (1.4.3). The improved fit is indicated by the sample ACF of the estimated residuals, $y_t - \hat{\phi}_1 y_{t-1} - \hat{\phi}_2 y_{t-2}$, which falls well within the bounds $\pm 1.96/\sqrt{96}$ for *all* lags up to 40.

1.5 Estimation and Elimination of Trend and Seasonal Components

The first step in the analysis of any time series is to plot the data. If there are any apparent discontinuities in the series, such as a sudden change of level, it may be advisable to analyze the series by first breaking it into homogeneous segments. If there are outlying observations, they should be studied carefully to check whether there is any justification for discarding them (as for example if an observation has been incorrectly recorded). Inspection of a graph may also suggest the possibility of representing the data as a realization of the process (the **classical decomposition** model)

$$X_t = m_t + s_t + Y_t, \tag{1.5.1}$$

where m_t is a slowly changing function known as a **trend component**, s_t is a function with known period d referred to as a **seasonal component**, and Y_t is a **random noise component** that is stationary in the sense of Definition 1.4.2. If the seasonal and noise fluctuations appear to increase with the level of the process, then a preliminary transformation of the data is often used to make the transformed data more compatible with the model (1.5.1). Compare, for example, the red wine sales in Figure 1.1 with the transformed data, Figure 1.17, obtained by applying a logarithmic transformation. The transformed data do not exhibit the increasing fluctuation with increasing level that was apparent in the original data. This suggests that the model (1.5.1) is more appropriate for the transformed than for the original series. In this section we shall assume that the model (1.5.1) is appropriate (possibly after a preliminary transformation of the data) and examine some techniques for estimating the components m_t, s_t, and Y_t in the model.

Our aim is to estimate and extract the deterministic components m_t and s_t in the hope that the residual or noise component Y_t will turn out to be a stationary time series. We can then use the theory of such processes to find a satisfactory probabilistic

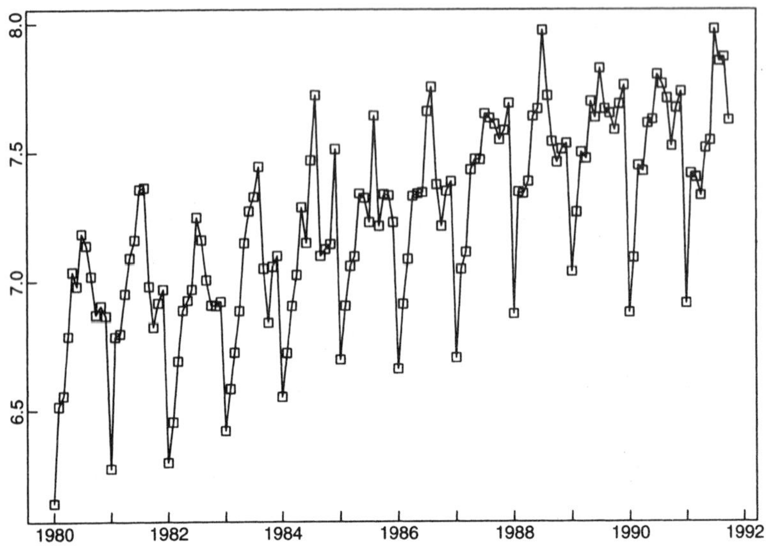

Figure 1-17 The natural logarithms of the red wine data.

model for the process Y_t, to analyze its properties, and to use it in conjunction with m_t and s_t for purposes of prediction and simulation of $\{X_t\}$.

Another approach, developed extensively by Box and Jenkins (1976), is to apply differencing operators repeatedly to the series $\{X_t\}$ until the differenced observations resemble a realization of some stationary time series $\{W_t\}$. We can then use the theory of stationary processes for the modeling, analysis, and prediction of $\{W_t\}$ and hence of the original process. The various stages of this procedure will be discussed in detail in Chapters 5 and 6.

The two approaches to trend and seasonality removal, (1) by estimation of m_t and s_t in (1.5.1) and (2) by differencing the series $\{X_t\}$, will now be illustrated with reference to the data introduced in Section 1.1.

1.5.1 Estimation and Elimination of Trend in the Absence of Seasonality

In the absence of a seasonal component the model (1.5.1) becomes the following.

Nonseasonal Model with Trend:

$$X_t = m_t + Y_t, \quad t = 1, \ldots, n, \tag{1.5.2}$$

where $EY_t = 0$.

(If $EY_t \neq 0$, then we can replace m_t and Y_t in (1.5.2) with $m_t + EY_t$ and $Y_t - EY_t$, respectively.)

Method 1: Trend Estimation

Moving average and spectral smoothing are essentially nonparametric methods for trend (or signal) estimation and not for model building. Special smoothing filters can also be designed to remove periodic components as described under Method S1 below. The choice of smoothing filter requires a certain amount of subjective judgment, and it is recommended that a variety of filters be tried in order to get a good idea of the underlying trend. Exponential smoothing, since it is based on a moving average of *past* values only, is often used for forecasting, the smoothed value at the present time being used as the forecast of the next value.

To construct a *model* for the data (with no seasonality) there are two general approaches, both available in ITSM. One is to fit a polynomial trend (by least squares) as described in Method 1(d) below, then to subtract the fitted trend from the data and to find an appropriate stationary time series model for the residuals. The other is to eliminate the trend by differencing as described in Method 2 and then to find an appropriate stationary model for the differenced series. The latter method has the advantage that it usually requires the estimation of fewer parameters and does not rest on the assumption of a trend that remains fixed throughout the observation period. The study of the residuals (or of the differenced series) is taken up in Section 1.6.

(a) *Smoothing with a finite moving average filter.* Let q be a nonnegative integer and consider the two-sided moving average

$$W_t = (2q+1)^{-1}\sum_{j=-q}^{q} X_{t-j} \tag{1.5.3}$$

of the process $\{X_t\}$ defined by (1.5.2). Then for $q+1 \le t \le n-q$,

$$W_t = (2q+1)^{-1}\sum_{j=-q}^{q} m_{t-j} + (2q+1)^{-1}\sum_{j=-q}^{q} Y_{t-j} \approx m_t, \tag{1.5.4}$$

assuming that m_t is approximately linear over the interval $[t-q, t+q]$ and that the average of the error terms over this interval is close to zero (see Problem 1.11).

The moving average thus provides us with the estimates

$$\hat{m}_t = (2q+1)^{-1}\sum_{j=-q}^{q} X_{t-j}, \quad q+1 \le t \le n-q. \tag{1.5.5}$$

Since X_t is not observed for $t \le 0$ or $t > n$, we cannot use (1.5.5) for $t \le q$ or $t > n-q$. The program ITSM deals with this problem by defining $X_t := X_1$ for $t < 1$ and $X_t := X_n$ for $t > n$.

Example 1.5.1

The result of applying the moving-average filter (1.5.5) with $q = 2$ to the strike data of Figure 1.6 is shown in Figure 1.18. The estimated noise terms $\hat{Y}_t = X_t - \hat{m}_t$ are shown in Figure 1.19. As expected, they show no apparent trend. To apply this filter using ITSM, open the project STRIKES.TSM, select `Smooth>Moving Average`, specify

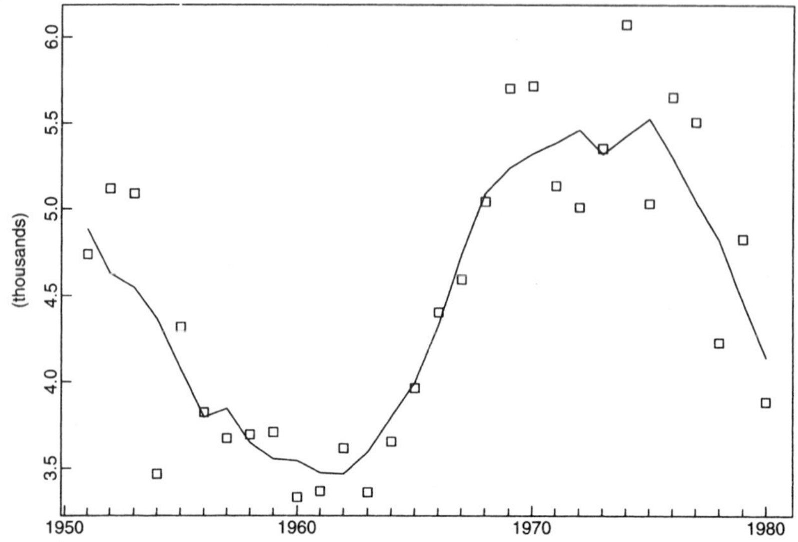

Figure 1-18 Simple 5-term moving average $\hat{m}_t$ of the strike data from Figure 1.6.

2 for the filter order, and enter the weights 1,1,1 for Theta(0), Theta(1), and Theta(2) (these are automatically normalized so that the sum of the weights is one). Then click OK. □

It is useful to think of $\{\hat{m}_t\}$ in (1.5.5) as a process obtained from $\{X_t\}$ by application of a linear operator or linear filter $\hat{m}_t = \sum_{j=-\infty}^{\infty} a_j X_{t-j}$ with weights $a_j = (2q+1)^{-1}$, $-q \le j \le q$. This particular filter is a **low-pass** filter in the sense that it takes the

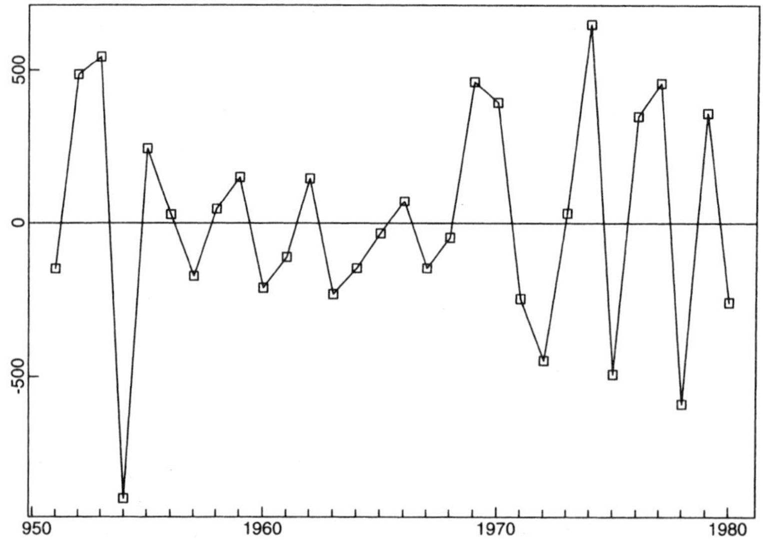

Figure 1-19 Residuals $\hat{Y}_t = X_t - \hat{m}_t$ after subtracting the 5-term moving average from the strike data.

Figure 1-20 Smoothing with a low-pass linear filter.

data $\{X_t\}$ and removes from it the rapidly fluctuating (or high frequency) component $\{\hat{Y}_t\}$ to leave the slowly varying estimated trend term $\{\hat{m}_t\}$ (see Figure 1.20).

The particular filter (1.5.5) is only one of many that could be used for smoothing. For large q, provided that $(2q+1)^{-1}\sum_{j=-q}^{q} Y_{t-j} \approx 0$, it not only will attenuate noise but at the same time will allow linear trend functions $m_t = c_0 + c_1 t$ to pass without distortion (see Problem 1.11). However, we must beware of choosing q to be too large, since if m_t is not linear, the filtered process, although smooth, will not be a good estimate of m_t. By clever choice of the weights $\{a_j\}$ it is possible (see Problems 1.12–1.14 and Section 4.3) to design a filter that will not only be effective in attenuating noise in the data, but that will also allow a larger class of trend functions (for example all polynomials of degree less than or equal to 3) to pass through without distortion. The Spencer 15-point moving average is a filter that passes polynomials of degree 3 without distortion. Its weights are

$$a_j = 0, \quad |j| > 7,$$

with

$$a_j = a_{-j}, \quad |j| \le 7,$$

and

$$[a_0, a_1, \ldots, a_7] = \frac{1}{320}[74, 67, 46, 21, 3, -5, -6, -3]. \tag{1.5.6}$$

Applied to the process (1.5.2) with $m_t = c_0 + c_1 t + c_2 t^2 + c_3 t^3$, it gives

$$\sum_{j=-7}^{7} a_j X_{t-j} = \sum_{j=-7}^{7} a_j m_{t-j} + \sum_{j=-7}^{7} a_j Y_{t-j} \approx \sum_{j=-7}^{7} a_j m_{t-j} = m_t,$$

where the last step depends on the assumed form of m_t (Problem 1.12). Further details regarding this and other smoothing filters can be found in Kendall and Stuart (1976), Chapter 46.

(b) *Exponential smoothing.* For any fixed $\alpha \in [0, 1]$, the one-sided moving averages $\hat{m}_t$, $t = 1, \ldots, n$, defined by the recursions

$$\hat{m}_t = \alpha X_t + (1-\alpha)\hat{m}_{t-1}, \quad t = 2, \ldots, n, \tag{1.5.7}$$

and

$$\hat{m}_1 = X_1 \tag{1.5.8}$$

can be computed using ITSM by selecting `Smooth>Exponential` and specifying the value of α. Application of (1.5.7) and (1.5.8) is often referred to as exponential smoothing, since the recursions imply that for $t \geq 2$, $\hat{m}_t = \sum_{j=0}^{t-2} \alpha(1-\alpha)^j X_{t-j} + (1-\alpha)^{t-1} X_1$, a weighted moving average of $X_t, X_{t-1}, \ldots$, with weights decreasing exponentially (except for the last one).

(c) *Smoothing by elimination of high-frequency components.* The option `Smooth>FFT` in the program ITSM allows us to smooth an arbitrary series by elimination of the high-frequency components of its Fourier series expansion (see Section 4.2). This option was used in Example 1.1.4, where we chose to retain the fraction $f = .035$ of the frequency components of the series in order to estimate the underlying signal. (The choice $f = 1$ would have left the series unchanged.)

Example 1.5.2

In Figures 1.21 and 1.22 we show the results of smoothing the strike data by exponential smoothing with parameter $\alpha = 0.4$ (see (1.5.7)) and by high-frequency elimination with $f = 0.4$, i.e., by eliminating a fraction 0.6 of the Fourier components at the top of the frequency range. These should be compared with the simple 5-term moving average smoothing shown in Figure 1.18. Experimentation with different smoothing parameters can easily be carried out using the program ITSM. The exponentially smoothed value of the last observation is frequently used to forecast the next data value. The program automatically selects an optimal value of α for this purpose if α is specified as -1 in the exponential smoothing dialog box. □

(d) *Polynomial fitting.* In Section 1.3.2 we showed how a trend of the form $m_t = a_0 + a_1 t + a_2 t^2$ can be fitted to the data $\{x_1, \ldots, x_n\}$ by choosing the parameters

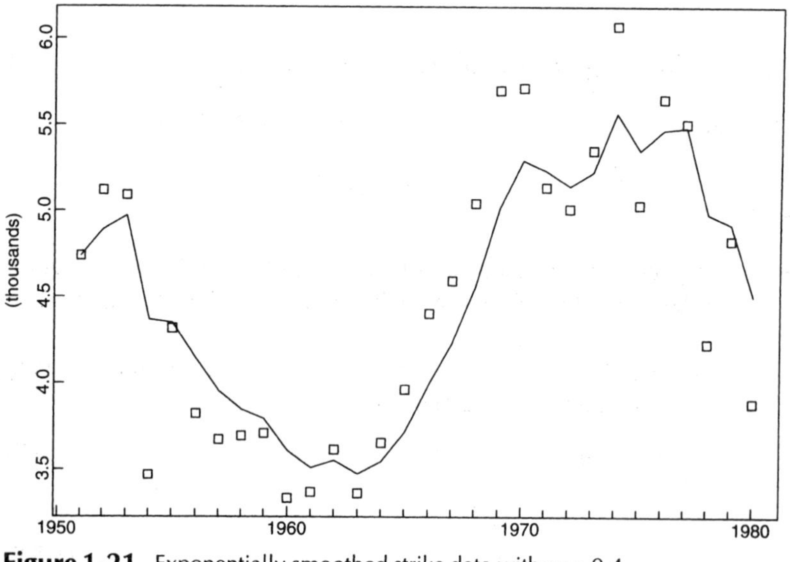

Figure 1-21 Exponentially smoothed strike data with $\alpha = 0.4$.

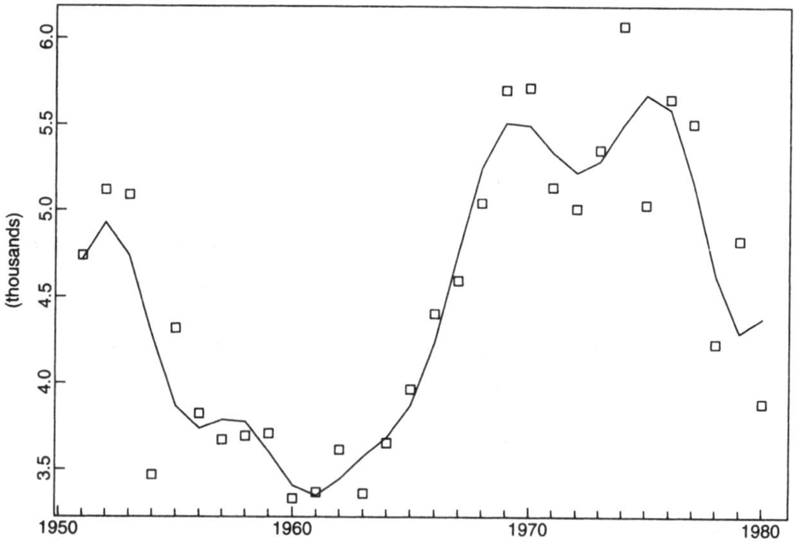

Figure 1-22 Strike data smoothed by elimination of high frequencies with $f = 0.4$.

a_0, a_1, and a_2 to minimize the sum of squares, $\sum_{t=1}^{n}(x_t - m_t)^2$ (see Example 1.3.4). The method of least squares estimation can also be used to estimate higher-order polynomial trends in the same way. The `Regression` option of ITSM allows least squares fitting of polynomial trends of order up to 10 (together with up to four harmonic terms; see Example 1.3.6). It also allows generalized least squares estimation (see Section 6.6), in which correlation between the residuals is taken into account.

Method 2: Trend Elimination by Differencing

Instead of attempting to remove the noise by smoothing as in Method 1, we now attempt to eliminate the trend term by differencing. We define the lag-1 difference operator ∇ by

$$\nabla X_t = X_t - X_{t-1} = (1 - B)X_t, \tag{1.5.9}$$

where B is the backward shift operator,

$$BX_t = X_{t-1}. \tag{1.5.10}$$

Powers of the operators B and ∇ are defined in the obvious way, i.e., $B^j(X_t) = X_{t-j}$ and $\nabla^j(X_t) = \nabla(\nabla^{j-1}(X_t))$, $j \geq 1$, with $\nabla^0(X_t) = X_t$. Polynomials in B and ∇ are manipulated in precisely the same way as polynomial functions of real variables. For example,

$$\begin{aligned}\nabla^2 X_t &= \nabla(\nabla(X_t)) = (1 - B)(1 - B)X_t = (1 - 2B + B^2)X_t \\ &= X_t - 2X_{t-1} + X_{t-2}.\end{aligned}$$

If the operator ∇ is applied to a linear trend function $m_t = c_0 + c_1 t$, then we obtain the constant function $\nabla m_t = m_t - m_{t-1} = c_0 + c_1 t - (c_0 + c_1(t-1)) = c_1$. In the same way any polynomial trend of degree k can be reduced to a constant by application of the operator ∇^k (Problem 1.10). For example, if $X_t = m_t + Y_t$, where $m_t = \sum_{j=0}^{k} c_j t^j$ and Y_t is stationary with mean zero, application of ∇^k gives

$$\nabla^k X_t = k! c_k + \nabla^k Y_t,$$

a stationary process with mean $k!c_k$. These considerations suggest the possibility, given any sequence $\{x_t\}$ of data, of applying the operator ∇ repeatedly until we find a sequence $\{\nabla^k x_t\}$ that can plausibly be modeled as a realization of a stationary process. It is often found in practice that the order k of differencing required is quite small, frequently one or two. (This relies on the fact that many functions can be well approximated, on an interval of finite length, by a polynomial of reasonably low degree.)

Example 1.5.3

Applying the operator ∇ to the population values $\{x_t, t = 1, \ldots, 20\}$ of Figure 1.5, we find that two differencing operations are sufficient to produce a series with no apparent trend. (To carry out the differencing using ITSM, select `Transform>Difference`, enter the value 1 for the differencing lag, and click `OK`.) This replaces the original series $\{x_t\}$ by the once-differenced series $\{x_t - x_{t-1}\}$. Repetition of these steps gives the twice-differenced series $\nabla^2 x_t = x_t - 2x_{t-1} + x_{t-2}$, plotted in Figure 1.23. Notice that the magnitude of the fluctuations in $\nabla^2 x_t$ increases with the value of x_t. This effect can be suppressed by first taking natural logarithms, $y_t = \ln x_t$, and then applying the operator ∇^2 to the series $\{y_t\}$. (See also Figures 1.1 and 1.17.) □

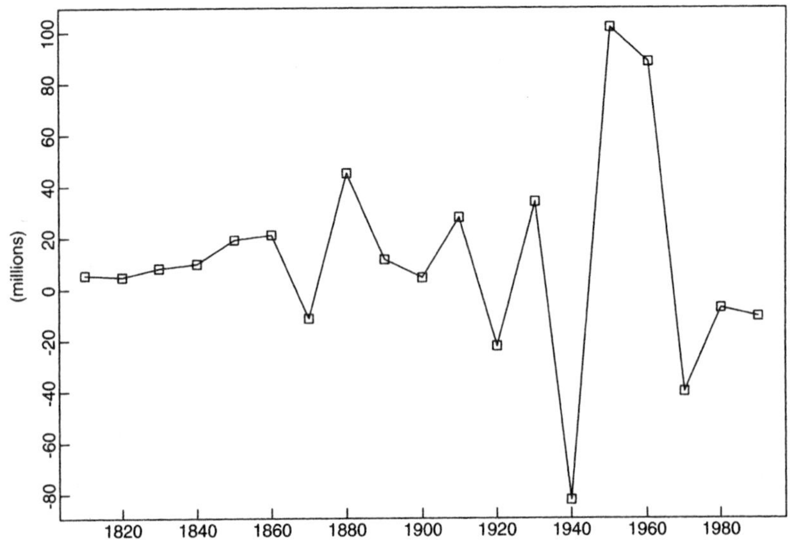

Figure 1-23 The twice-differenced series derived from the population data of Figure 1.5.

1.5.2 Estimation and Elimination of Both Trend and Seasonality

The methods described for the estimation and elimination of trend can be adapted in a natural way to eliminate both trend and seasonality in the general model, specified as follows.

Classical Decomposition Model

$$X_t = m_t + s_t + Y_t, \quad t = 1, \ldots, n, \tag{1.5.11}$$

where $EY_t = 0$, $s_{t+d} = s_t$, and $\sum_{j=1}^{d} s_j = 0$.

We shall illustrate these methods with reference to the accidental deaths data of Example 1.1.3, for which the period d of the seasonal component is clearly 12.

Method S1: Estimation of Trend and Seasonal Components

The method we are about to describe is used in the `Transform>Classical` option of ITSM.

Suppose we have observations $\{x_1, \ldots, x_n\}$. The trend is first estimated by applying a moving average filter specially chosen to eliminate the seasonal component and to dampen the noise. If the period d is even, say $d = 2q$, then we use

$$\hat{m}_t = (0.5x_{t-q} + x_{t-q+1} + \cdots + x_{t+q-1} + 0.5x_{t+q})/d, \quad q < t \le n - q. \tag{1.5.12}$$

If the period is odd, say $d = 2q + 1$, then we use the simple moving average (1.5.5).

The second step is to estimate the seasonal component. For each $k = 1, \ldots, d$, we compute the average w_k of the deviations $\{(x_{k+jd} - \hat{m}_{k+jd}), q < k + jd \le n - q\}$. Since these average deviations do not necessarily sum to zero, we estimate the seasonal component s_k as

$$\hat{s}_k = w_k - d^{-1} \sum_{i=1}^{d} w_i, \quad k = 1, \ldots, d, \tag{1.5.13}$$

and $\hat{s}_k = \hat{s}_{k-d}$, $k > d$.

The *deseasonalized* data is then defined to be the original series with the estimated seasonal component removed, i.e.,

$$d_t = x_t - \hat{s}_t, \quad t = 1, \ldots, n. \tag{1.5.14}$$

Finally, we reestimate the trend from the deseasonalized data $\{d_t\}$ using one of the methods already described. The program ITSM allows you to fit a least squares polynomial trend $\hat{m}$ to the deseasonalized series. In terms of this reestimated trend and the estimated seasonal component, the estimated noise series is then given by

$$\hat{Y}_t = x_t - \hat{m}_t - \hat{s}_t, \quad t = 1, \ldots, n.$$

The reestimation of the trend is done in order to have a parametric form for the trend that can be extrapolated for the purposes of prediction and simulation.

Example 1.5.4

Figure 1.24 shows the deseasonalized accidental deaths data obtained from ITSM by reading in the series DEATHS.TSM, selecting `Transform>Classical`, checking *only* the box marked `Seasonal Fit`, entering 12 for the period, and clicking `OK`. The estimated seasonal component $\hat{s}_t$, shown in Figure 1.25, is obtained by selecting `Transform>Show Classical Fit`. (Except for having a mean of zero, this estimate is very similar to the harmonic regression function with frequencies $2\pi/12$ and $2\pi/6$ displayed in Figure 1.11.) The graph of the deseasonalized data suggests the presence of an additional quadratic trend function. In order to fit such a trend to the deseasonalized data, select `Transform>Undo Classical` to retrieve the original data and then select `Transform>Classical` and check the boxes marked `Seasonal Fit` and `Polynomial Trend`, entering 12 for the period and selecting `Quadratic` for the trend. Then click OK and you will obtain the trend function

$$\hat{m}_t = 9952 - 71.82t + 0.8260t^2, \quad 1 \le t \le 72.$$

At this point the data stored in ITSM consists of the estimated noise

$$\hat{Y}_t = x_t - \hat{m}_t - \hat{s}_t, \quad t = 1, \ldots, 72,$$

obtained by subtracting the estimated seasonal and trend components from the original data. □

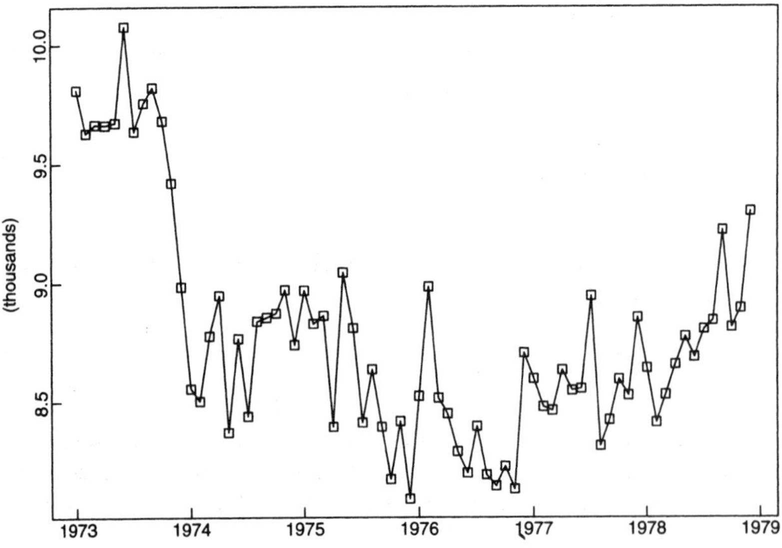

Figure 1-24 The deseasonalized accidental deaths data from ITSM.

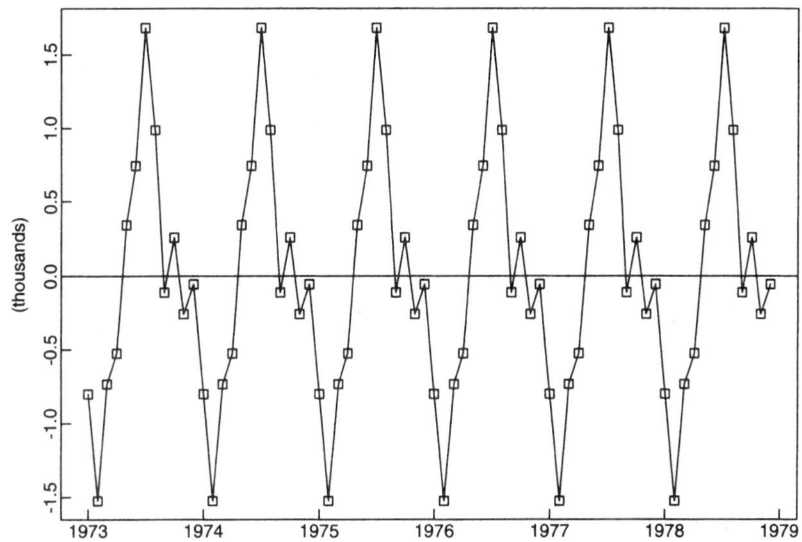

Figure 1-25 The estimated seasonal component of the accidental deaths data from ITSM.

Method S2: Elimination of Trend and Seasonal Components by Differencing
The technique of differencing that we applied earlier to nonseasonal data can be adapted to deal with seasonality of period d by introducing the lag-d differencing operator ∇_d defined by

$$\nabla_d X_t = X_t - X_{t-d} = (1 - B^d)X_t. \tag{1.5.15}$$

(This operator should not be confused with the operator $\nabla^d = (1 - B)^d$ defined earlier.)

Applying the operator ∇_d to the model

$$X_t = m_t + s_t + Y_t,$$

where $\{s_t\}$ has period d, we obtain

$$\nabla_d X_t = m_t - m_{t-d} + Y_t - Y_{t-d},$$

which gives a decomposition of the difference $\nabla_d X_t$ into a trend component $(m_t - m_{t-d})$ and a noise term $(Y_t - Y_{t-d})$. The trend, $m_t - m_{t-d}$, can then be eliminated using the methods already described, in particular by applying a power of the operator ∇.

Example 1.5.5

Figure 1.26 shows the result of applying the operator ∇_{12} to the accidental deaths data. The graph is obtained from ITSM by opening DEATHS.TSM, selecting `Transform>Difference`, entering lag 12, and clicking `OK`. The seasonal component evident in Figure 1.3 is absent from the graph of $\nabla_{12}x_t$, $13 \le t \le 72$. However, there still appears to be a nondecreasing trend. If we now apply the operator ∇ to $\{\nabla_{12}x_t\}$ by again selecting `Transform>Difference`, this time with lag one, we obtain the graph

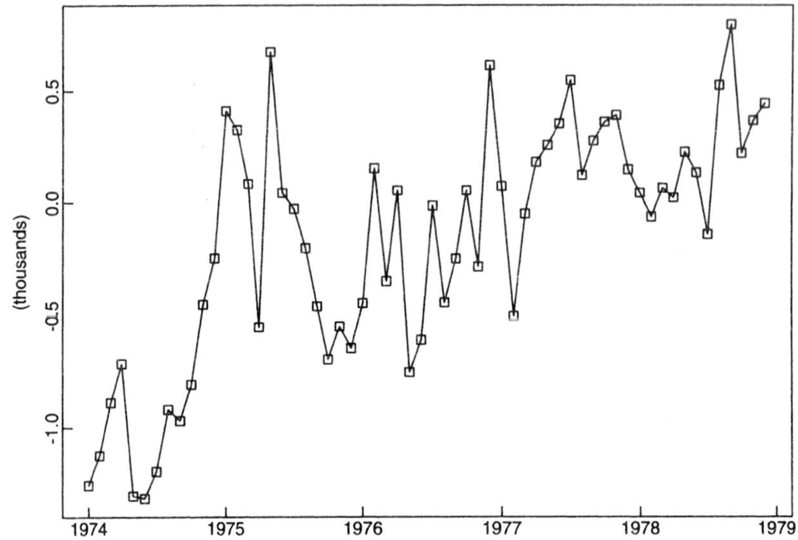

Figure 1-26 The differenced series $\{\nabla_{12}x_t, t = 13, \ldots, 72\}$ derived from the monthly accidental deaths $\{x_t, t = 1, \ldots, 72\}$.

of $\nabla\nabla_{12}x_t$, $14 \le t \le 72$, shown in Figure 1.27, which has no apparent trend or seasonal component. In Chapter 5 we shall show that this doubly differenced series can in fact be well represented by a stationary time series model. □

In this section we have discussed a variety of methods for estimating and/or removing trend and seasonality. The particular method chosen for any given data set will depend on a number of factors including whether or not estimates of the

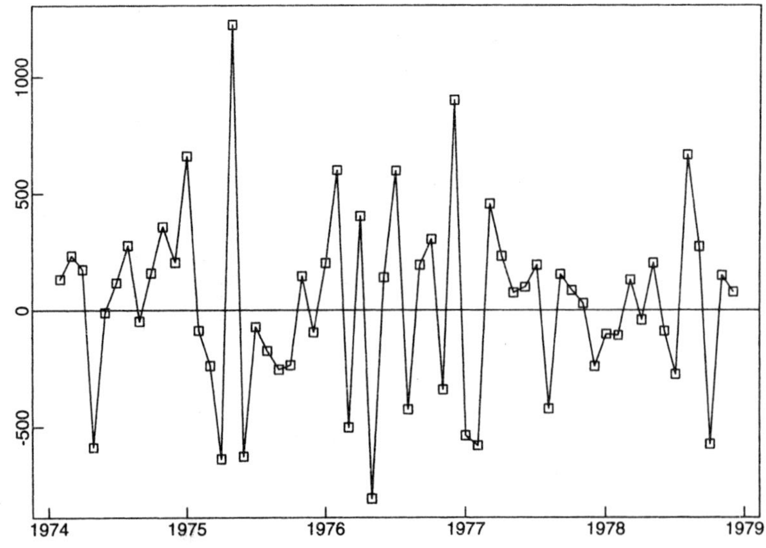

Figure 1-27 The differenced series $\{\nabla\nabla_{12}x_t, t = 14, \ldots, 72\}$ derived from the monthly accidental deaths $\{x_t, t = 1, \ldots, 72\}$.

components of the series are required and whether or not it appears that the data contain a seasonal component that does not vary with time. The program ITSM allows two options under the `Transform` menu:

1. "classical decomposition," in which trend and/or seasonal components are estimated and subtracted from the data to generate a noise sequence, and
2. "differencing," in which trend and/or seasonal components are removed from the data by repeated differencing at one or more lags in order to generate a noise sequence.

A third option is to use the `Regression` menu, possibly after applying a Box–Cox transformation. Using this option we can (see Example 1.3.6)

3. fit a sum of harmonics and a polynomial trend to generate a noise sequence that consists of the residuals from the regression.

In the next section we shall examine some techniques for deciding whether or not the noise sequence so generated differs significantly from iid noise. If the noise sequence *does* have sample autocorrelations significantly different from zero, then we can take advantage of this serial dependence to forecast future noise values in terms of past values by modeling the noise as a stationary time series.

1.6 Testing the Estimated Noise Sequence

The objective of the data transformations described in Section 1.5 is to produce a series with no apparent deviations from stationarity, and in particular with no apparent trend or seasonality. Assuming that this has been done, the next step is to model the estimated noise sequence (i.e., the **residuals** obtained either by differencing the data or by estimating and subtracting the trend and seasonal components). If there is no dependence among between these residuals, then we can regard them as observations of independent random variables, and there is no further modeling to be done except to estimate their mean and variance. However, if there is significant dependence among the residuals, then we need to look for a more complex stationary time series model for the noise that accounts for the dependence. This will be to our advantage, since dependence means in particular that past observations of the noise sequence can assist in predicting future values.

In this section we examine some simple tests for checking the hypothesis that the residuals from Section 1.5 are observed values of independent and identically distributed random variables. If they are, then our work is done. If not, then we must use the theory of stationary processes to be developed in later chapters to find a more appropriate model.

(a) *The sample autocorrelation function.* For large n, the sample autocorrelations of an iid sequence $Y_1, \ldots, Y_n$ with finite variance are approximately iid with distribution $N(0, 1/n)$ (see TSTM p. 222). Hence, if $y_1, \ldots, y_n$ is a realization of such an iid sequence, about 95% of the sample autocorrelations should fall between the bounds $\pm 1.96/\sqrt{n}$. If we compute the sample autocorrelations up to lag 40 and find that more than two or three values fall outside the bounds, or that one value falls far outside the bounds, we therefore reject the iid hypothesis. The bounds $\pm 1.96/\sqrt{n}$ are automatically plotted when the sample autocorrelation function is computed by the program ITSM.

(b) *The portmanteau test.* Instead of checking to see whether each sample autocorrelation $\hat{\rho}(j)$ falls inside the bounds defined in (a) above, it is also possible to consider the single statistic

$$Q = n \sum_{j=1}^{h} \hat{\rho}^2(j).$$

If $Y_1, \ldots, Y_n$ is a finite-variance iid sequence, then by the same result used in (a), Q is approximately distributed as the sum of squares of the independent $N(0, 1)$ random variables, $\sqrt{n}\hat{\rho}(j)$, $j = 1, \ldots, h$, i.e., as chi-squared with h degrees of freedom. A large value of Q suggests that the sample autocorrelations of the data are too large for the data to be a sample from an iid sequence. We therefore reject the iid hypothesis at level α if $Q > \chi^2_{1-\alpha}(h)$, where $\chi^2_{1-\alpha}(h)$ is the $1 - \alpha$ quantile of the chi-squared distribution with h degrees of freedom. The program ITSM conducts a refinement of this test, formulated by Ljung and Box (1978), in which Q is replaced by

$$Q_{LB} = n(n+2) \sum_{j=1}^{h} \hat{\rho}^2(j)/(n-j),$$

whose distribution is better approximated by the chi-squared distribution with h degrees of freedom.

Another portmanteau test, formulated by McLeod and Li (1983), can be used as a further test for the iid hypothesis, since if the data are iid, then the squared data are also iid. It is based on the same statistic used for the Ljung–Box test, except that the sample autocorrelations of the data are replaced by the sample autocorrelations of the *squared* data, $\hat{\rho}_{WW}(h)$, giving

$$Q_{ML} = n(n+2) \sum_{k=1}^{h} \hat{\rho}^2_{WW}(k)/(n-k).$$

The hypothesis of iid data is then rejected at level α if the observed value of Q_{ML} is larger than the $1 - \alpha$ quantile of the $\chi^2(h)$ distribution.

(c) *The turning point test.* If $y_1, \ldots, y_n$ is a sequence of observations, we say that there is a turning point at time i, $1 < i < n$, if $y_{i-1} < y_i$ and $y_i > y_{i+1}$ or if $y_{i-1} > y_i$ and $y_i < y_{i+1}$. If T is the number of turning points of an iid sequence of length n, then, since the probability of a turning point at time i is $\frac{2}{3}$, the expected value of T is

$$\mu_T = E(T) = 2(n-2)/3.$$

It can also be shown for an iid sequence that the variance of T is

$$\sigma_T^2 = \text{Var}(T) = (16n - 29)/90.$$

A large value of $T - \mu_T$ indicates that the series is fluctuating more rapidly than expected for an iid sequence. On the other hand, a value of $T - \mu_T$ much smaller than zero indicates a positive correlation between neighboring observations. For an iid sequence with n large, it can be shown that

$$T \text{ is approximately } \mathrm{N}\left(\mu_T, \sigma_T^2\right).$$

This means we can carry out a test of the iid hypothesis, rejecting it at level α if $|T - \mu_T|/\sigma_T > \Phi_{1-\alpha/2}$, where $\Phi_{1-\alpha/2}$ is the $1-\alpha/2$ quantile of the standard normal distribution. (A commonly used value of α is .05, for which the corresponding value of $\Phi_{1-\alpha/2}$ is 1.96.)

(d) *The difference-sign test.* For this test we count the number S of values of i such that $y_i > y_{i-1}$, $i = 2, \ldots, n$, or equivalently the number of times the differenced series $y_i - y_{i-1}$ is positive. For an iid sequence it is clear that

$$\mu_S = ES = \frac{1}{2}(n-1).$$

It can also be shown, under the same assumption, that

$$\sigma_S^2 = \text{Var}(S) = (n+1)/12,$$

and that for large n,

$$S \text{ is approximately } \mathrm{N}\left(\mu_S, \sigma_S^2\right).$$

A large positive (or negative) value of $S - \mu_S$ indicates the presence of an increasing (or decreasing) trend in the data. We therefore reject the assumption of no trend in the data if $|S - \mu_S|/\sigma_S > \Phi_{1-\alpha/2}$.

The difference-sign test must be used with caution. A set of observations exhibiting a strong cyclic component will pass the difference-sign test for randomness, since roughly half of the observations will be points of increase.

(e) *The rank test.* The rank test is particularly useful for detecting a linear trend in the data. Define P to be the number of pairs (i, j) such that $y_j > y_i$ and $j > i$, $i = 1, \ldots, n-1$. There is a total of $\binom{n}{2} = \frac{1}{2}n(n-1)$ pairs (i, j) such that $j > i$. For an iid sequence $\{Y_1, \ldots, Y_n\}$, each event $\{Y_j > Y_i\}$ has probability $\frac{1}{2}$, and the mean of P is therefore

$$\mu_P = \frac{1}{4}n(n-1).$$

It can also be shown for an iid sequence that the variance of P is

$$\sigma_P^2 = n(n-1)(2n+5)/72$$

and that for large n,

$$P \text{ is approximately } \mathrm{N}\left(\mu_P, \sigma_P^2\right)$$

(see Kendall and Stuart, 1976). A large positive (negative) value of $P - \mu_P$ indicates the presence of an increasing (decreasing) trend in the data. The assumption that $\{y_j\}$ is a sample from an iid sequence is therefore rejected at level $\alpha = 0.05$ if $|P - \mu_P|/\sigma_P > \Phi_{1-\alpha/2} = 1.96$.

(f) *Fitting an autoregressive model.* A further test that can be carried out using the program ITSM is to fit an autoregressive model to the data using the Yule–Walker algorithm (discussed in Section 5.1.1) and choosing the order which minimizes the AICC statistic (see Section 5.5). A selected order equal to zero suggests that the data is white noise.

(g) *Checking for normality.* If the noise process is Gaussian, i.e., if all of its joint distributions are normal, then stronger conclusions can be drawn when a model is fitted to the data. The following test enables us to check whether it is reasonable to assume that observations from an iid sequence are also Gaussian.

Let $Y_{(1)} < Y_{(2)} < \cdots < Y_{(n)}$ be the order statistics of a random sample $Y_1, \ldots, Y_n$ from the distribution $\mathrm{N}(\mu, \sigma^2)$. If $X_{(1)} < X_{(2)} < \cdots < X_{(n)}$ are the order statistics from a N(0, 1) sample of size n, then

$$EY_{(j)} = \mu + \sigma m_j,$$

where $m_j = EX_{(j)}$, $j = 1, \ldots, n$. The graph of the points $\left(m_1, Y_{(1)}\right), \ldots, \left(m_n, Y_{(n)}\right)$ is called a Gaussian **qq plot**) and can be displayed in ITSM by clicking on the yellow button labeled QQ. If the normal assumption is correct, the Gaussian qq plot should be approximately linear. Consequently, the squared correlation of the points $(m_i, Y_{(i)})$, $i = 1, \ldots, n$, should be near 1. The assumption of normality is therefore rejected if the squared correlation R^2 is sufficiently small. If we approximate m_i by $\Phi^{-1}((i-.5)/n)$ (see Mage, 1982 for some alternative approximations), then R^2 reduces to

$$R^2 = \frac{\left(\sum_{i=1}^n (Y_{(i)} - \overline{Y})\Phi^{-1}\left(\frac{i-.5}{n}\right)\right)^2}{\sum_{i=1}^n (Y_{(i)} - \overline{Y})^2 \sum_{i=1}^n \left(\Phi^{-1}\left(\frac{i-.5}{n}\right)\right)^2},$$

where $\overline{Y} = n^{-1}(Y_1 + \cdots + Y_n)$. Percentage points for the distribution of R^2, assuming normality of the sample values, are given by Shapiro and Francia (1972) for sample sizes $n < 100$. For $n = 200$, $P(R^2 < .987) = .05$ and $P(R^2 < .989) = .10$. For larger values of n the Jarque-Bera test for normality can be used (see Section 5.3.3).

Example 1.6.1

If we did not know in advance how the signal plus noise data of Example 1.1.4 were generated, we might suspect that they came from an iid sequence. We can check this hypothesis with the aid of the tests (a)–(f) introduced above.

(a) The sample autocorrelation function (Figure 1.28) is obtained from ITSM by opening the project SIGNAL.TSM and clicking on the second yellow button at the top of the ITSM window. Observing that 25% of the autocorrelations are outside the bounds $\pm 1.96/\sqrt{200}$, we reject the hypothesis that the series is iid.

The remaining tests (b), (c), (d), (e), and (f) are performed by choosing the option `Statistics>Residual Analysis>Tests of Randomness`. (Since no model has been fitted to the data, the residuals are the same as the data themselves.)

(b) The sample value of the Ljung–Box statistic Q_{LB} with $h = 20$ is 51.84. Since the corresponding p-value (displayed by ITSM) is $.00012 < .05$, we reject the iid hypothesis at level .05. The p-value for the McLeod–Li statistic Q_{ML} is 0.717. The McLeod–Li statistic does therefore not provide sufficient evidence to reject the iid hypothesis at level .05.

(c) The sample value of the turning-point statistic T is 138, and the asymptotic distribution under the iid hypothesis (with sample size $n = 200$) is N(132, 35.3). Thus $|T - \mu_T|/\sigma_T = 1.01$, corresponding to a computed p-value of .312. On the basis of the value of T there is therefore not sufficient evidence to reject the iid hypothesis at level .05.

(d) The sample value of the difference-sign statistic S is 101, and the asymptotic distribution under the iid hypothesis (with sample size $n = 200$) is N(99.5, 16.7). Thus $|S - \mu_S|/\sigma_S = 0.38$, corresponding to a computed p-value of 0.714. On the basis of the value of S there is therefore not sufficient evidence to reject the iid hypothesis at level .05.

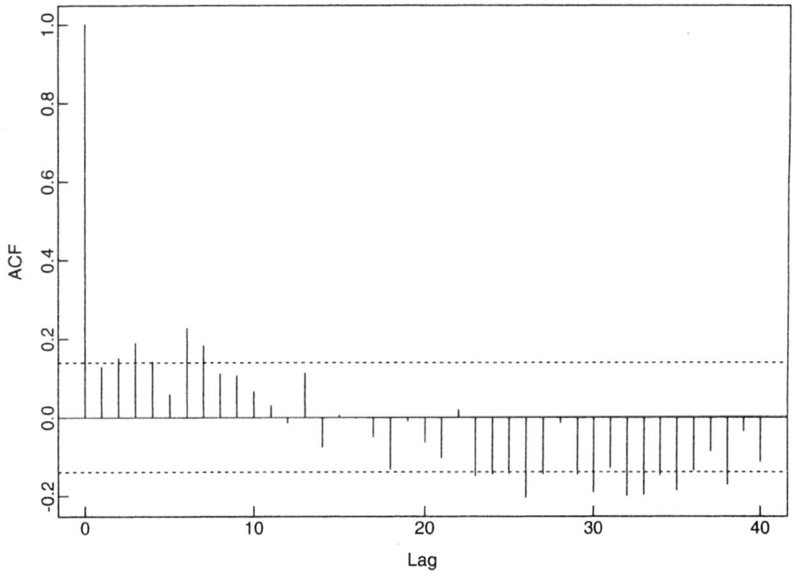

Figure 1-28 The sample autocorrelation function for the data of Example 1.1.4 showing the bounds $\pm 1.96/\sqrt{n}$.

(e) The sample value of the rank statistic P is 10310, and the asymptotic distribution under the iid hypothesis (with $n = 200$) is $N(9950, 2.239 \times 10^5)$. Thus $|P - \mu_P|/\sigma_P = 0.76$, corresponding to a computed p-value of 0.447. On the basis of the value of P there is therefore not sufficient evidence to reject the iid hypothesis at level .05.

(f) The minimum-AICC Yule–Walker autoregressive model for the data is of order seven, supporting the evidence provided by the sample ACF and Ljung–Box tests against the iid hypothesis.

Thus, although not all of the tests detect significant deviation from iid behavior, the sample autocorrelation, the Ljung–Box statistic, and the fitted autoregression provide strong evidence against it, causing us to reject it (correctly) in this example. □

The general strategy in applying the tests described in this section is to check them all and to proceed with caution if any of them suggests a serious deviation from the iid hypothesis. (Remember that as you increase the number of tests, the probability that *at least one* rejects the null hypothesis when it is true increases. You should therefore not necessarily reject the null hypothesis on the basis of one test result only.)

Problems

1.1. Let X and Y be two random variables with $E(Y) = \mu$ and $EY^2 < \infty$.

a. Show that the constant c that minimizes $E(Y - c)^2$ is $c = \mu$.

b. Deduce that the random variable $f(X)$ that minimizes $E\big[(Y - f(X))^2|X\big]$ is

$$f(X) = E[Y|X].$$

c. Deduce that the random variable $f(X)$ that minimizes $E(Y - f(X))^2$ is also

$$f(X) = E[Y|X].$$

1.2. (Generalization of Problem 1.1.) Suppose that $X_1, X_2, \ldots$ is a sequence of random variables with $E(X_t^2) < \infty$ and $E(X_t) = \mu$.

a. Show that the random variable $f(X_1, \ldots, X_n)$ that minimizes $E\big[(X_{n+1} - f(X_1, \ldots, X_n))^2|X_1, \ldots, X_n\big]$ is

$$f(X_1, \ldots, X_n) = E[X_{n+1}|X_1, \ldots, X_n].$$

b. Deduce that the random variable $f(X_1, \ldots, X_n)$ that minimizes $E\big[(X_{n+1} - f(X_1, \ldots, X_n))^2\big]$ is also

$$f(X_1, \ldots, X_n) = E[X_{n+1}|X_1, \ldots, X_n].$$

c. If $X_1, X_2, \ldots$ is iid with $E(X_i^2) < \infty$ and $EX_i = \mu$, where μ is known, what is the minimum mean squared error predictor of X_{n+1} in terms of $X_1, \ldots, X_n$?

d. Under the conditions of part (c) show that the best linear unbiased estimator of μ in terms of $X_1, \ldots, X_n$ is $\bar{X} = \frac{1}{n}(X_1 + \cdots + X_n)$. ($\hat{\mu}$ said to be an unbiased estimator of μ if $\mathrm{E}\hat{\mu} = \mu$ for all μ.)

e. Under the conditions of part (c) show that $\bar{X}$ is the best linear predictor of X_{n+1} that is unbiased for μ.

f. If $X_1, X_2, \ldots$ is iid with $E(X_i^2) < \infty$ and $EX_i = \mu$, and if $S_0 = 0$, $S_n = X_1 + \cdots + X_n$, $n = 1, 2, \ldots$, what is the minimum mean squared error predictor of S_{n+1} in terms of $S_1, \ldots, S_n$?

1.3. Show that a strictly stationary process with $E(X_i^2) < \infty$ is weakly stationary.

1.4. Let $\{Z_t\}$ be a sequence of independent normal random variables, each with mean 0 and variance σ^2, and let a, b, and c be constants. Which, if any, of the following processes are stationary? For each stationary process specify the mean and autocovariance function.

a. $X_t = a + bZ_t + cZ_{t-2}$

b. $X_t = Z_1 \cos(ct) + Z_2 \sin(ct)$

c. $X_t = Z_t \cos(ct) + Z_{t-1} \sin(ct)$

d. $X_t = a + bZ_0$

e. $X_t = Z_0 \cos(ct)$

f. $X_t = Z_t Z_{t-1}$

1.5. Let $\{X_t\}$ be the moving-average process of order 2 given by

$$X_t = Z_t + \theta Z_{t-2},$$

where $\{Z_t\}$ is WN(0, 1).

a. Find the autocovariance and autocorrelation functions for this process when $\theta = .8$.

b. Compute the variance of the sample mean $(X_1 + X_2 + X_3 + X_4)/4$ when $\theta = .8$.

c. Repeat (b) when $\theta = -.8$ and compare your answer with the result obtained in (b).

1.6. Let $\{X_t\}$ be the AR(1) process defined in Example 1.4.5.

a. Compute the variance of the sample mean $(X_1 + X_2 + X_3 + X_4)/4$ when $\phi = .9$ and $\sigma^2 = 1$.

b. Repeat (a) when $\phi = -.9$ and compare your answer with the result obtained in (a).

1.7. If $\{X_t\}$ and $\{Y_t\}$ are uncorrelated stationary sequences, i.e., if X_r and Y_s are uncorrelated for every r and s, show that $\{X_t + Y_t\}$ is stationary with autocovariance function equal to the sum of the autocovariance functions of $\{X_t\}$ and $\{Y_t\}$.

1.8. Let $\{Z_t\}$ be IID N(0, 1) noise and define

$$X_t = \begin{cases} Z_t, & \text{if } t \text{ is even,} \\ (Z_{t-1}^2 - 1)/\sqrt{2}, & \text{if } t \text{ is odd.} \end{cases}$$

a. Show that $\{X_t\}$ is WN(0, 1) but not iid(0, 1) noise.

b. Find $E(X_{n+1}|X_1, \ldots, X_n)$ for n odd and n even and compare the results.

1.9. Let $\{x_1, \ldots, x_n\}$ be observed values of a time series at times $1, \ldots, n$, and let $\hat{\rho}(h)$ be the sample ACF at lag h as in Definition 1.4.4.

a. If $x_t = a + bt$, where a and b are constants and $b \neq 0$, show that for each fixed $h \geq 1$,

$$\hat{\rho}(h) \to 1 \text{ as } n \to \infty.$$

b. If $x_t = c\cos(\omega t)$, where c and ω are constants ($c \neq 0$ and $\omega \in (-\pi, \pi]$), show that for each fixed h,

$$\hat{\rho}(h) \to \cos(\omega h) \text{ as } n \to \infty.$$

1.10. If $m_t = \sum_{k=0}^{p} c_k t^k$, $t = 0, \pm 1, \ldots$, show that ∇m_t is a polynomial of degree $p-1$ in t and hence that $\nabla^{p+1} m_t = 0$.

1.11. Consider the simple moving-average filter with weights $a_j = (2q+1)^{-1}$, $-q \leq j \leq q$.

a. If $m_t = c_0 + c_1 t$, show that $\sum_{j=-q}^{q} a_j m_{t-j} = m_t$.

b. If Z_t, $t = 0, \pm 1, \pm 2, \ldots$, are independent random variables with mean 0 and variance σ^2, show that the moving average $A_t = \sum_{j=-q}^{q} a_j Z_{t-j}$ is "small" for large q in the sense that $EA_t = 0$ and $\text{Var}(A_t) = \sigma^2/(2q+1)$.

1.12. a. Show that a linear filter $\{a_j\}$ passes an arbitrary polynomial of degree k without distortion, i.e., that

$$m_t = \sum_j a_j m_{t-j}$$

for all kth-degree polynomials $m_t = c_0 + c_1 t + \cdots + c_k t^k$, if and only if

$$\begin{cases} \sum_j a_j = 1 & \text{and} \\ \sum_j j^r a_j = 0, & \text{for } r = 1, \ldots, k. \end{cases}$$

b. Deduce that the Spencer 15-point moving-average filter $\{a_j\}$ defined by (1.5.6) passes arbitrary third-degree polynomial trends without distortion.

1.13. Find a filter of the form $1 + \alpha B + \beta B^2 + \gamma B^3$ (i.e., find α, β, and γ) that passes linear trends without distortion and that eliminates arbitrary seasonal components of period 2.

1.14. Show that the filter with coefficients $[a_{-2}, a_{-1}, a_0, a_1, a_2] = \frac{1}{9}[-1, 4, 3, 4, -1]$ passes third-degree polynomials and eliminates seasonal components with period 3.

1.15. Let $\{Y_t\}$ be a stationary process with mean zero and let a and b be constants.

a. If $X_t = a + bt + s_t + Y_t$, where s_t is a seasonal component with period 12, show that $\nabla\nabla_{12}X_t = (1 - B)(1 - B^{12})X_t$ is stationary and express its autocovariance function in terms of that of $\{Y_t\}$.

b. If $X_t = (a + bt)s_t + Y_t$, where s_t is a seasonal component with period 12, show that $\nabla_{12}^2 X_t = (1 - B^{12})^2 X_t$ is stationary and express its autocovariance function in terms of that of $\{Y_t\}$.

1.16. (Using ITSM to smooth the strikes data.) Double-click on the ITSM icon, select `File>Project>Open>Univariate`, click OK, and open the file STRIKES. TSM. The graph of the data will then appear on your screen. To smooth the data select `Smooth>Moving Ave`, `Smooth>Exponential`, or `Smooth>FFT`. Try using each of these to reproduce the results shown in Figures 1.18, 1.21, and 1.22.

1.17. (Using ITSM to plot the deaths data.) In ITSM select `File>Project>Open>Univariate`, click OK, and open the project DEATHS.TSM. The graph of the data will then appear on your screen. To see a histogram of the data, click on the sixth yellow button at the top of the ITSM window. To see the sample autocorrelation function, click on the second yellow button. The presence of a strong seasonal component with period 12 is evident in the graph of the data and in the sample autocorrelation function.

1.18. (Using ITSM to analyze the deaths data.) Open the file DEATHS.TSM, select `Transform>Classical`, check the box marked `Seasonal Fit`, and enter 12 for the period. Make sure that the box labeled `Polynomial Fit` is not checked, and click, `OK`. You will then see the graph (Figure 1.24) of the deseasonalized data. This graph suggests the presence of an additional quadratic trend function. To fit such a trend to the deseasonalized data, select `Transform>Undo Classical` to retrieve the original data. Then select `Transform>Classical` and check the boxes marked `Seasonal Fit` and `Polynomial Trend`, entering 12 for the period and `Quadratic` for the trend. Click `OK` and you will obtain the trend function

$$\hat{m}_t = 9952 - 71.82t + 0.8260t^2, \quad 1 \le t \le 72.$$

At this point the data stored in ITSM consists of the estimated noise

$$\hat{Y}_t = x_t - \hat{m}_t - \hat{s}_t, \quad t = 1, \ldots, 72,$$

obtained by subtracting the estimated seasonal and trend components from the original data. The sample autocorrelation function can be plotted by clicking on the second yellow button at the top of the ITSM window. Further tests for dependence can be carried out by selecting the options `Statistics>Residual Analysis>Tests of Randomness`. It is clear from these that there is substantial dependence in the series $\{Y_t\}$.

To forecast the data without allowing for this dependence, select the option `Forecasting>ARMA`. Specify 24 for the number of values to be forecast, and the program will compute forecasts based on the assumption that the estimated seasonal and trend components are true values and that $\{Y_t\}$ is a white noise sequence with zero mean. (This is the default model assumed by ITSM until a more complicated stationary model is estimated or specified.) The original data are plotted with the forecasts appended.

Later we shall see how to improve on these forecasts by taking into account the dependence in the series $\{Y_t\}$.

1.19. Use a text editor, e.g., WORDPAD or NOTEPAD, to construct and save a text file named TEST.TSM, which consists of a single column of 30 numbers, $\{x_1, \ldots, x_{30}\}$, defined by

$$x_1, \ldots, x_{10} : 486, 474, 434, 441, 435, 401, 414, 414, 386, 405;$$

$$x_{11}, \ldots, x_{20} : 411, 389, 414, 426, 410, 441, 459, 449, 486, 510;$$

$$x_{21}, \ldots, x_{30} : 506, 549, 579, 581, 630, 666, 674, 729, 771, 785.$$

This series is in fact the sum of a quadratic trend and a period-three seasonal component. Use the program ITSM to apply the filter in Problem 1.14 to this time series and discuss the results.

(Once the data have been typed, they can be imported directly into ITSM by coping and pasting to the clipboard, and then in ITSM selecting `File>Project>New>Univariate`, clicking on OK and selecting `File>Import Clipboard.)`

2 Stationary Processes

A key role in time series analysis is played by processes whose properties, or some of them, do not vary with time. If we wish to make predictions, then clearly we must assume that *something* does not vary with time. In extrapolating deterministic functions it is common practice to assume that either the function itself or one of its derivatives is constant. The assumption of a constant first derivative leads to linear extrapolation as a means of prediction. In time series analysis our goal is to predict a series that typically is not deterministic but contains a random component. If this random component is stationary, in the sense of Definition 1.4.2, then we can develop powerful techniques to forecast its future values. These techniques will be developed and discussed in this and subsequent chapters.

2.1 Basic Properties

In Section 1.4 we introduced the concept of stationarity and defined the autocovariance function (ACVF) of a stationary time series $\{X_t\}$ as

$$\gamma(h) = \mathrm{Cov}(X_{t+h}, X_t), \quad h = 0, \pm 1, \pm 2, \ldots.$$

The autocorrelation function (ACF) of $\{X_t\}$ was defined similarly as the function $\rho(\cdot)$ whose value at lag h is

$$\rho(h) = \frac{\gamma(h)}{\gamma(0)}.$$

The ACVF and ACF provide a useful measure of the degree of dependence among the values of a time series at different times and for this reason play an important role when we consider the prediction of future values of the series in terms of the past and present values. They can be estimated from observations of $X_1, \ldots, X_n$ by computing the *sample* ACVF and ACF as described in Section 1.4.1.

The role of the autocorrelation function in prediction is illustrated by the following simple example. Suppose that $\{X_t\}$ is a stationary Gaussian time series (see Definition A.3.2) and that we have observed X_n. We would like to find the function of X_n that gives us the best predictor of X_{n+h}, the value of the series after another h time units have elapsed. To define the problem we must first say what we mean by "best." A natural and computationally convenient definition is to specify our required predictor to be the function of X_n with minimum mean squared error. In this illustration, and indeed throughout the remainder of this book, we shall use this as our criterion for "best." Now by Proposition A.3.1 the conditional distribution of X_{n+h} given that $X_n = x_n$ is

$$\mathrm{N}\big(\mu + \rho(h)(x_n - \mu), \sigma^2\big(1 - \rho(h)^2\big)\big),$$

where μ and σ^2 are the mean and variance of $\{X_t\}$. It was shown in Problem 1.1 that the value of the constant c that minimizes $E(X_{n+h} - c)^2$ is $c = E(X_{n+h})$ and that the function m of X_n that minimizes $E(X_{n+h} - m(X_n))^2$ is the conditional mean

$$m(X_n) = E(X_{n+h}|X_n) = \mu + \rho(h)(X_n - \mu). \tag{2.1.1}$$

The corresponding mean squared error is

$$E(X_{n+h} - m(X_n))^2 = \sigma^2\big(1 - \rho(h)^2\big). \tag{2.1.2}$$

This calculation shows that at least for stationary Gaussian time series, prediction of X_{n+h} in terms of X_n is more accurate as $|\rho(h)|$ becomes closer to 1, and in the limit as $\rho \to \pm 1$ the best predictor approaches $\mu \pm (X_n - \mu)$ and the corresponding mean squared error approaches 0.

In the preceding calculation the assumption of joint normality of X_{n+h} and X_n played a crucial role. For time series with nonnormal joint distributions the corresponding calculations are in general much more complicated. However, if instead of looking for the best function of X_n for predicting X_{n+h}, we look for the best **linear predictor**, i.e., the best predictor of the form $\ell(X_n) = aX_n + b$, then our problem becomes that of finding a and b to minimize $E(X_{n+h} - aX_n - b)^2$. An elementary calculation (Problem 2.1), shows that the best predictor of this form is

$$\ell(X_n) = \mu + \rho(h)(X_n - \mu) \tag{2.1.3}$$

with corresponding mean squared error

$$E(X_{n+h} - \ell(X_n))^2 = \sigma^2(1 - \rho(h)^2). \tag{2.1.4}$$

Comparison with (2.1.1) and (2.1.3) shows that for Gaussian processes, $\ell(X_n)$ and $m(X_n)$ are the same. In general, of course, $m(X_n)$ will give smaller mean squared error than $\ell(X_n)$, since it is the best of a larger class of predictors (see Problem 1.8). However, the fact that the best linear predictor depends only on the mean and ACF of the series $\{X_t\}$ means that it can be calculated without more detailed knowledge of the joint distributions. This is extremely important in practice because of the difficulty of estimating all of the joint distributions and because of the difficulty of computing the required conditional expectations even if the distributions were known.

As we shall see later in this chapter, similar conclusions apply when we consider the more general problem of predicting X_{n+h} as a function not only of X_n, but also of $X_{n-1}, X_{n-2}, \ldots$. Before pursuing this question we need to examine in more detail the properties of the autocovariance and autocorrelation functions of a stationary time series.

Basic Properties of $\gamma(\cdot)$:

$$\gamma(0) \geq 0,$$

$$|\gamma(h)| \leq \gamma(0) \text{ for all } h,$$

and $\gamma(\cdot)$ is even, i.e.,

$$\gamma(h) = \gamma(-h) \text{ for all } h.$$

Proof

The first property is simply the statement that $\mathrm{Var}(X_t) \geq 0$, the second is an immediate consequence of the fact that correlations are less than or equal to 1 in absolute value (or the Cauchy–Schwarz inequality), and the third is established by observing that

$$\gamma(h) = \mathrm{Cov}(X_{t+h}, X_t) = \mathrm{Cov}(X_t, X_{t+h}) = \gamma(-h). \quad \blacksquare$$

Autocovariance functions have another fundamental property, namely that of nonnegative definiteness.

Definition 2.1.1

A real-valued function κ defined on the integers is **nonnegative definite** if

$$\sum_{i,j=1}^{n} a_i \kappa(i - j) a_j \geq 0 \tag{2.1.5}$$

for all positive integers n and vectors $\mathbf{a} = (a_1, \ldots, a_n)'$ with real-valued components a_i.

Theorem 2.1.1

A real-valued function defined on the integers is the autocovariance function of a stationary time series if and only if it is even and nonnegative definite.

Proof

To show that the autocovariance function $\gamma(\cdot)$ of any stationary time series $\{X_t\}$ is nonnegative definite, let $\mathbf{a}$ be any $n \times 1$ vector with real components $a_1, \ldots, a_n$ and let $\mathbf{X}_n = (X_n, \ldots, X_1)'$. Then by equation (A.2.5) and the nonnegativity of variances,

$$\mathrm{Var}(\mathbf{a}'\mathbf{X}_n) = \mathbf{a}'\Gamma_n\mathbf{a} = \sum_{i,j=1}^{n} a_i\gamma(i-j)a_j \geq 0,$$

where Γ_n is the covariance matrix of the random vector $\mathbf{X}_n$. The last inequality, however, is precisely the statement that $\gamma(\cdot)$ is nonnegative definite. The converse result, that there exists a stationary time series with autocovariance function κ if κ is even, real-valued, and nonnegative definite, is more difficult to establish (see TSTM, Theorem 1.5.1 for a proof). A slightly stronger statement can be made, namely, that under the specified conditions there exists a stationary *Gaussian* time series $\{X_t\}$ with mean 0 and autocovariance function $\kappa(\cdot)$. ∎

Remark 1. An autocorrelation function $\rho(\cdot)$ has all the properties of an autocovariance function and satisfies the additional condition $\rho(0) = 1$. In particular, we can say that $\rho(\cdot)$ is the autocorrelation function of a stationary process if and only if $\rho(\cdot)$ is an ACVF with $\rho(0) = 1$. □

Remark 2. To verify that a given function is nonnegative definite it is often simpler to find a stationary process that has the given function as its ACVF than to verify the conditions (2.1.5) directly. For example, the function $\kappa(h) = \cos(\omega h)$ is nonnegative definite, since (see Problem 2.2) it is the ACVF of the stationary process

$$X_t = A\cos(\omega t) + B\sin(\omega t),$$

where A and B are uncorrelated random variables, both with mean 0 and variance 1. Another illustration is provided by the following example. □

Example 2.1.1 We shall show now that the function defined on the integers by

$$\kappa(h) = \begin{cases} 1, & \text{if } h = 0, \\ \rho, & \text{if } h = \pm 1, \\ 0, & \text{otherwise,} \end{cases}$$

is the ACVF of a stationary time series if and only if $|\rho| \leq \frac{1}{2}$. Inspection of the ACVF of the MA(1) process of Example 1.4.4 shows that κ is the ACVF of such a process if we can find real θ and nonnegative σ^2 such that

$$\sigma^2(1 + \theta^2) = 1$$

and

$$\sigma^2\theta = \rho.$$

If $|\rho| \leq \frac{1}{2}$, these equations give solutions $\theta = (2\rho)^{-1}\left(1 \pm \sqrt{1-4\rho^2}\right)$ and $\sigma^2 = \left(1+\theta^2\right)^{-1}$. However, if $|\rho| > \frac{1}{2}$, there is no real solution for θ and hence no MA(1) process with ACVF κ. To show that there is no *stationary* process with ACVF κ, we need to show that κ is not nonnegative definite. We shall do this directly from the definition (2.1.5). First, if $\rho > \frac{1}{2}$, $K = [\kappa(i-j)]_{i,j=1}^n$, and $\mathbf{a}$ is the n-component vector $\mathbf{a} = (1, -1, 1, -1, \ldots)'$, then

$$\mathbf{a}'K\mathbf{a} = n - 2(n-1)\rho < 0 \text{ for } n > 2\rho/(2\rho - 1),$$

showing that $\kappa(\cdot)$ is not nonnegative definite and therefore, by Theorem 2.1.1, is not an autocovariance function. If $\rho < -\frac{1}{2}$, the same argument with $\mathbf{a} = (1, 1, 1, 1, \ldots)'$ again shows that $\kappa(\cdot)$ is not nonnegative definite.

If $\{X_t\}$ is a (weakly) stationary time series, then the vector $(X_1, \ldots, X_n)'$ and the time-shifted vector $(X_{1+h}, \ldots, X_{n+h})'$ have the same mean vectors and covariance matrices for every integer h and positive integer n. A strictly stationary sequence is one in which the joint distributions of these two vectors (and not just the means and covariances) are the same. The precise definition is given below. □

Definition 2.1.2

$\{X_t\}$ is a **strictly stationary time series** if

$$(X_1, \ldots, X_n)' \stackrel{d}{=} (X_{1+h}, \ldots, X_{n+h})'$$

for all all integers h and $n \geq 1$. (Here $\stackrel{d}{=}$ is used to indicate that the two random vectors have the same joint distribution function.)

For reference, we record some of the elementary properties of strictly stationary time series.

Properties of a Strictly Stationary Time Series $\{X_t\}$:

a. The random variables X_t are identically distributed.

b. $(X_t, X_{t+h})' \stackrel{d}{=} (X_1, X_{1+h})'$ for all integers t and h.

c. $\{X_t\}$ is weakly stationary if $E(X_t^2) < \infty$ for all t.

d. Weak stationarity does not imply strict stationarity.

e. An iid sequence is strictly stationary.

Proof

Properties (a) and (b) follow at once from Definition 2.1.2. If $EX_t^2 < \infty$, then by (a) and (b) EX_t is independent of t and $\text{Cov}(X_t, X_{t+h}) = \text{Cov}(X_1, X_{1+h})$, which is also independent of t, proving (c). For (d) see Problem 1.8. If $\{X_t\}$ is an iid sequence of random variables with common distribution function F, then the joint distribution function of $(X_{1+h}, \ldots, X_{n+h})'$ evaluated at $(x_1, \ldots, x_n)'$ is $F(x_1) \cdots F(x_n)$, which is independent of h. ■

One of the simplest ways to construct a time series $\{X_t\}$ that is strictly stationary (and hence stationary if $EX_t^2 < \infty$) is to "filter" an iid sequence of random variables. Let $\{Z_t\}$ be an iid sequence, which by (e) is strictly stationary, and define

$$X_t = g(Z_t, Z_{t-1}, \ldots, Z_{t-q}) \tag{2.1.6}$$

for some real-valued function $g(\cdot, \ldots, \cdot)$. Then $\{X_t\}$ is strictly stationary, since $(Z_{t+h}, \ldots, Z_{t+h-q})' \stackrel{d}{=} (Z_t, \ldots, Z_{t-q})'$ for all integers h. It follows also from the defining equation (2.1.6) that $\{X_t\}$ is ***q*-dependent**, i.e., that X_s and X_t are independent whenever $|t - s| > q$. (An iid sequence is 0-dependent.) In the same way, adopting a second-order viewpoint, we say that a stationary time series is ***q*-correlated** if $\gamma(h) = 0$ whenever $|h| > q$. A white noise sequence is then 0-correlated, while the MA(1) process of Example 1.4.4 is 1-correlated. The moving-average process of order q defined below is q-correlated, and perhaps surprisingly, the converse is also true (Proposition 2.1.1).

The MA(q) Process:

$\{X_t\}$ is a **moving-average process of order q** if

$$X_t = Z_t + \theta_1 Z_{t-1} + \cdots + \theta_q Z_{t-q}, \tag{2.1.7}$$

where $\{Z_t\} \sim \text{WN}(0, \sigma^2)$ and $\theta_1, \ldots, \theta_q$ are constants.

It is a simple matter to check that (2.1.7) defines a stationary time series that is strictly stationary if $\{Z_t\}$ is iid noise. In the latter case, (2.1.7) is a special case of (2.1.6) with g a linear function.

The importance of MA(q) processes derives from the fact that *every* q-correlated process is an MA(q) process. This is the content of the following proposition, whose proof can be found in TSTM, Section 3.2. The extension of this result to the case $q = \infty$ is essentially Wold's decomposition (see Section 2.6).

Proposition 2.1.1

If $\{X_t\}$ is a stationary q-correlated time series with mean 0, then it can be represented as the MA(q) *process in (2.1.7).*

2.2 Linear Processes

The class of linear time series models, which includes the class of autoregressive moving-average (ARMA) models, provides a general framework for studying stationary processes. In fact, every second-order stationary process is either a linear process or can be transformed to a linear process by subtracting a *deterministic* component. This result is known as Wold's decomposition and is discussed in Section 2.6.

Definition 2.2.1

The time series $\{X_t\}$ is a **linear process** if it has the representation

$$X_t = \sum_{j=-\infty}^{\infty} \psi_j Z_{t-j}, \tag{2.2.1}$$

for all t, where $\{Z_t\} \sim \mathrm{WN}(0, \sigma^2)$ and $\{\psi_j\}$ is a sequence of constants with $\sum_{j=-\infty}^{\infty} |\psi_j| < \infty$.

In terms of the backward shift operator B, (2.2.1) can be written more compactly as

$$X_t = \psi(B) Z_t, \tag{2.2.2}$$

where $\psi(B) = \sum_{j=-\infty}^{\infty} \psi_j B^j$. A linear process is called a **moving average** or **MA(∞)** if $\psi_j = 0$ for all $j < 0$, i.e., if

$$X_t = \sum_{j=0}^{\infty} \psi_j Z_{t-j}.$$

Remark 1. The condition $\sum_{j=-\infty}^{\infty} |\psi_j| < \infty$ ensures that the infinite sum in (2.2.1) converges (with probability one), since $E|Z_t| \le \sigma$ and

$$E|X_t| \le \sum_{j=-\infty}^{\infty} \left(|\psi_j| E|Z_{t-j}|\right) \le \left(\sum_{j=-\infty}^{\infty} |\psi_j|\right) \sigma < \infty.$$

It also ensures that $\sum_{j=-\infty}^{\infty} \psi_j^2 < \infty$ and hence (see Appendix C, Example C.1.1) that the series in (2.2.1) converges in mean square, i.e., that X_t is the mean square limit of the partial sums $\sum_{j=-n}^{n} \psi_j Z_{t-j}$. The condition $\sum_{j=-n}^{n} |\psi_j| < \infty$ also ensures convergence in both senses of the more general series (2.2.3) considered in Proposition 2.2.1 below. In Section 10.5 we consider a more general class of linear processes, the fractionally integrated ARMA processes, for which the coefficents are not absolutely summable but only square summable. □

The operator $\psi(B)$ can be thought of as a linear filter, which when applied to the white noise "input" series $\{Z_t\}$ produces the "output" $\{X_t\}$ (see Section 4.3). As established in the following proposition, a linear filter, when applied to any stationary input series, produces a stationary output series.

Proposition 2.2.1

Let $\{Y_t\}$ be a stationary time series with mean 0 and covariance function γ_Y. If $\sum_{j=-\infty}^{\infty} |\psi_j| < \infty$, then the time series

$$X_t = \sum_{j=-\infty}^{\infty} \psi_j Y_{t-j} = \psi(B)Y_t \tag{2.2.3}$$

is stationary with mean 0 and autocovariance function

$$\gamma_X(h) = \sum_{j=-\infty}^{\infty} \sum_{k=-\infty}^{\infty} \psi_j \psi_k \gamma_Y(h+k-j). \tag{2.2.4}$$

In the special case where $\{X_t\}$ is a linear process,

$$\gamma_X(h) = \sum_{j=-\infty}^{\infty} \psi_j \psi_{j+h} \sigma^2. \tag{2.2.5}$$

Proof

The argument used in Remark 1, with σ replaced by $\sqrt{\gamma_Y(0)}$, shows that the series in (2.2.3) is convergent. Since $EY_t = 0$, we have

$$E(X_t) = E\left(\sum_{j=-\infty}^{\infty} \psi_j Y_{t-j}\right) = \sum_{j=-\infty}^{\infty} \psi_j E(Y_{t-j}) = 0$$

and

$$\begin{aligned} E(X_{t+h}X_t) &= E\left[\left(\sum_{j=-\infty}^{\infty} \psi_j Y_{t+h-j}\right)\left(\sum_{k=-\infty}^{\infty} \psi_k Y_{t-k}\right)\right] \\ &= \sum_{j=-\infty}^{\infty} \sum_{k=-\infty}^{\infty} \psi_j \psi_k E(Y_{t+h-j} Y_{t-k}) \\ &= \sum_{j=-\infty}^{\infty} \sum_{k=-\infty}^{\infty} \psi_j \psi_k \gamma_Y(h-j+k), \end{aligned}$$

which shows that $\{X_t\}$ is stationary with covariance function (2.2.4). (The interchange of summation and expectation operations in the above calculations can be justified by the absolute summability of ψ_j.) Finally, if $\{Y_t\}$ is the white noise sequence $\{Z_t\}$ in (2.2.1), then $\gamma_Y(h-j+k) = \sigma^2$ if $k = j-h$ and 0 otherwise, from which (2.2.5) follows. ■

Remark 2. The absolute convergence of (2.2.3) implies (Problem 2.6) that filters of the form $\alpha(B) = \sum_{j=-\infty}^{\infty} \alpha_j B^j$ and $\beta(B) = \sum_{j=-\infty}^{\infty} \beta_j B^j$ with absolutely summable coefficients can be applied successively to a stationary series $\{Y_t\}$ to generate a new stationary series

$$W_t = \sum_{j=-\infty}^{\infty} \psi_j Y_{t-j},$$

where

$$\psi_j = \sum_{k=-\infty}^{\infty} \alpha_k \beta_{j-k} = \sum_{k=-\infty}^{\infty} \beta_k \alpha_{j-k}. \tag{2.2.6}$$

These relations can be expressed in the equivalent form

$$W_t = \psi(B) Y_t,$$

where

$$\psi(B) = \alpha(B)\beta(B) = \beta(B)\alpha(B), \tag{2.2.7}$$

and the products are defined by (2.2.6) or equivalently by multiplying the series $\sum_{j=-\infty}^{\infty} \alpha_j B^j$ and $\sum_{j=-\infty}^{\infty} \beta_j B^j$ term by term and collecting powers of B. It is clear from (2.2.6) and (2.2.7) that the order of application of the filters $\alpha(B)$ and $\beta(B)$ is immaterial. □

Example 2.2.1 An AR(1) process

In Example 1.4.5, an AR(1) process was defined as a stationary solution $\{X_t\}$ of the equations

$$X_t - \phi X_{t-1} = Z_t, \tag{2.2.8}$$

where $\{Z_t\} \sim \text{WN}(0, \sigma^2)$, $|\phi| < 1$, and Z_t is uncorrelated with X_s for each $s < t$. To show that such a solution exists and is the unique stationary solution of (2.2.8), we consider the linear process defined by

$$X_t = \sum_{j=0}^{\infty} \phi^j Z_{t-j}. \tag{2.2.9}$$

(The coefficients ϕ^j for $j \geq 0$ are absolutely summable, since $|\phi| < 1$.) It is easy to verify directly that the process (2.2.9) is a solution of (2.2.8), and by Proposition 2.2.1 it is also stationary with mean 0 and ACVF

$$\gamma_X(h) = \sum_{j=0}^{\infty} \phi^j \phi^{j+h} \sigma^2 = \frac{\sigma^2 \phi^h}{1 - \phi^2},$$

for $h \geq 0$.

To show that (2.2.9) is the *only* stationary solution of (2.2.8) let $\{Y_t\}$ be *any* stationary solution. Then, iterating (2.2.8), we obtain

$$\begin{aligned} Y_t &= \phi Y_{t-1} + Z_t \\ &= Z_t + \phi Z_{t-1} + \phi^2 Y_{t-2} \\ &= \cdots \\ &= Z_t + \phi Z_{t-1} + \cdots + \phi^k Z_{t-k} + \phi^{k+1} Y_{t-k-1}. \end{aligned}$$

If $\{Y_t\}$ is stationary, then EY_t^2 is finite and independent of t, so that

$$E(Y_t - \sum_{j=0}^{k} \phi^j Z_{t-j})^2 = \phi^{2k+2} E(Y_{t-k-1})^2$$

$$\to 0 \text{ as } k \to \infty.$$

This implies that Y_t is equal to the mean square limit $\sum_{j=0}^{\infty} \phi^j Z_{t-j}$ and hence that the process defined by (2.2.9) is the unique stationary solution of the equations (2.2.8).

It the case $|\phi| > 1$, the series in (2.2.9) does not converge. However, we can rewrite (2.2.8) in the form

$$X_t = -\phi^{-1} Z_{t+1} + \phi^{-1} X_{t+1}. \tag{2.2.10}$$

Iterating (2.2.10) gives

$$\begin{aligned} X_t &= -\phi^{-1} Z_{t+1} - \phi^{-2} Z_{t+2} + \phi^{-2} X_{t+2} \\ &= \cdots \\ &= -\phi^{-1} Z_{t+1} - \cdots - \phi^{-k-1} Z_{t+k+1} + \phi^{-k-1} X_{t+k+1}, \end{aligned}$$

which shows, by the same arguments used above, that

$$X_t = -\sum_{j=1}^{\infty} \phi^{-j} Z_{t+j} \tag{2.2.11}$$

is the unique stationary solution of (2.2.8). This solution should not be confused with the nonstationary solution $\{X_t\}$ of (2.2.8) obtained when X_0 is any specified random variable that is uncorrelated with $\{Z_t\}$.

The solution (2.2.11) is frequently regarded as unnatural, since X_t as defined by (2.2.11) is correlated with *future* values of Z_s, contrasting with the solution (2.2.9), which has the property that X_t is uncorrelated with Z_s for all $s > t$. It is customary therefore in modeling stationary time series to restrict attention to AR(1) processes with $|\phi| < 1$. Then X_t has the representation (2.2.8) in terms of $\{Z_s, s \le t\}$, and we say that $\{X_t\}$ is a **causal** or **future-independent** function of $\{Z_t\}$, or more concisely that $\{X_t\}$ is a causal autoregressive process. It should be noted that every AR(1) process with $|\phi| > 1$ can be reexpressed as an AR(1) process with $|\phi| < 1$ and a new white noise sequence (Problem 3.8). From a second-order point of view, therefore, nothing is lost by eliminating AR(1) processes with $|\phi| > 1$ from consideration.

If $\phi = \pm 1$, there is no stationary solution of (2.2.8) (see Problem 2.8). □

Remark 3. It is worth remarking that when $|\phi| < 1$ the unique stationary solution (2.2.9) can be found immediately with the aid of (2.2.7). To do this let $\phi(B) = 1 - \phi B$ and $\pi(B) = \sum_{j=0}^{\infty} \phi^j B^j$. Then

$$\psi(B) := \phi(B)\pi(B) = 1.$$

Applying the operator $\pi(B)$ to both sides of (2.2.8), we obtain

$$X_t = \pi(B)Z_t = \sum_{j=0}^{\infty} \phi^j Z_{t-j}$$

as claimed. □

2.3 Introduction to ARMA Processes

In this section we introduce, through an example, some of the key properties of an important class of linear processes known as ARMA (autoregressive moving average) processes. These are defined by linear difference equations with constant coefficients. As our example we shall consider the ARMA(1,1) process. Higher-order ARMA processes will be discussed in Chapter 3.

Definition 2.3.1

The time series $\{X_t\}$ is an **ARMA(1, 1) process** if it is stationary and satisfies (for every t)

$$X_t - \phi X_{t-1} = Z_t + \theta Z_{t-1}, \tag{2.3.1}$$

where $\{Z_t\} \sim \mathrm{WN}(0, \sigma^2)$ and $\phi + \theta \neq 0$.

Using the backward shift operator B, (2.3.1) can be written more concisely as

$$\phi(B)X_t = \theta(B)Z_t, \tag{2.3.2}$$

where $\phi(B)$ and $\theta(B)$ are the linear filters

$$\phi(B) = 1 - \phi B \text{ and } \theta(B) = 1 + \theta B,$$

respectively.

We first investigate the range of values of ϕ and θ for which a stationary solution of (2.3.1) exists. If $|\phi| < 1$, let $\chi(z)$ denote the power series expansion of $1/\phi(z)$, i.e., $\sum_{j=0}^{\infty} \phi^j z^j$, which has absolutely summable coefficients. Then from (2.2.7) we conclude that $\chi(B)\phi(B) = 1$. Applying $\chi(B)$ to each side of (2.3.2) therefore gives

$$X_t = \chi(B)\theta(B)Z_t = \psi(B)Z_t,$$

where

$$\psi(B) = \sum_{j=0}^{\infty} \psi_j B^j = \left(1 + \phi B + \phi^2 B^2 + \cdots\right)(1 + \theta B).$$

By multiplying out the right-hand side or using (2.2.6), we find that

$$\psi_0 = 1 \text{ and } \psi_j = (\phi + \theta)\phi^{j-1} \text{ for } j \geq 1.$$

As in Example 2.2.1, we conclude that the MA(∞) process

$$X_t = Z_t + (\phi + \theta)\sum_{j=1}^{\infty}\phi^{j-1}Z_{t-j} \tag{2.3.3}$$

is the unique stationary solution of (2.3.1).

Now suppose that $|\phi| > 1$. We first represent $1/\phi(z)$ as a series of powers of z with absolutely summable coefficients by expanding in powers of z^{-1}, giving (Problem 2.7)

$$\frac{1}{\phi(z)} = -\sum_{j=1}^{\infty}\phi^{-j}z^{-j}.$$

Then we can apply the same argument as in the case where $|\phi| < 1$ to obtain the unique stationary solution of (2.3.1). We let $\chi(B) = -\sum_{j=1}^{\infty}\phi^{-j}B^{-j}$ and apply $\chi(B)$ to each side of (2.3.2) to obtain

$$X_t = \chi(B)\theta(B)Z_t = -\theta\phi^{-1}Z_t - (\theta + \phi)\sum_{j=1}^{\infty}\phi^{-j-1}Z_{t+j}. \tag{2.3.4}$$

If $\phi = \pm 1$, there is no stationary solution of (2.3.1). Consequently, there is no such thing as an ARMA(1,1) process with $\phi = \pm 1$ according to our definition.

We can now summarize our findings about the existence and nature of the stationary solutions of the ARMA(1,1) recursions (2.3.2) as follows:

- A stationary solution of the ARMA(1,1) equations exists if and only if $\phi \neq \pm 1$.
- If $|\phi| < 1$, then the unique stationary solution is given by (2.3.3). In this case we say that $\{X_t\}$ is **causal** or a causal function of $\{Z_t\}$, since X_t can be expressed in terms of the current and past values Z_s, $s \le t$.
- If $|\phi| > 1$, then the unique stationary solution is given by (2.3.4). The solution is **noncausal**, since X_t is then a function of Z_s, $s \ge t$.

Just as causality means that X_t is expressible in terms of Z_s, $s \le t$, the dual concept of invertibility means that Z_t is expressible in terms of X_s, $s \le t$. We show now that the ARMA(1,1) process defined by (2.3.1) is invertible if $|\theta| < 1$. To demonstrate this, let $\xi(z)$ denote the power series expansion of $1/\theta(z)$, i.e., $\sum_{j=0}^{\infty}(-\theta)^j z^j$, which has absolutely summable coefficients. From (2.2.7) it therefore follows that $\xi(B)\theta(B) = 1$, and applying $\xi(B)$ to each side of (2.3.2) gives

$$Z_t = \xi(B)\phi(B)X_t = \pi(B)X_t,$$

where

$$\pi(B) = \sum_{j=0}^{\infty}\pi_j B^j = \left(1 - \theta B + (-\theta)^2B^2 + \cdots\right)(1 - \phi B).$$

By multiplying out the right-hand side or using (2.2.6), we find that

$$Z_t = X_t - (\phi + \theta)\sum_{j=1}^{\infty}(-\theta)^{j-1}X_{t-j}. \tag{2.3.5}$$

Thus the ARMA(1,1) process is **invertible**, since Z_t can be expressed in terms of the present and past values of the process X_s, $s \le t$. An argument like the one used to show noncausality when $|\phi| > 1$ shows that the ARMA(1,1) process is **noninvertible** when $|\theta| > 1$, since then

$$Z_t = -\phi\theta^{-1}X_t + (\theta + \phi)\sum_{j=1}^{\infty}(-\theta)^{-j-1}X_{t+j}. \tag{2.3.6}$$

We summarize these results as follows:

- If $|\theta| < 1$, then the ARMA(1,1) process is **invertible**, and Z_t is expressed in terms of $X_s, s \le t$, by (2.3.5).
- If $|\theta| > 1$, then the ARMA(1,1) process is **noninvertible**, and Z_t is expressed in terms of $X_s, s \ge t$, by (2.3.6).

Remark 1. In the cases $\theta = \pm 1$, the ARMA(1,1) process is invertible in the more general sense that Z_t is a mean square limit of finite linear combinations of X_s, $s \le t$, although it cannot be expressed explicitly as an infinite linear combination of X_s, $s \le t$ (see Section 4.4 of TSTM). In this book the term *invertible* will always be used in the more restricted sense that $Z_t = \sum_{j=0}^{\infty} \pi_j X_{t-j}$, where $\sum_{j=0}^{\infty} |\pi_j| < \infty$. □

Remark 2. If the ARMA(1,1) process $\{X_t\}$ is noncausal or noninvertible with $|\theta| > 1$, then it is possible to find a new white noise sequence $\{W_t\}$ such that $\{X_t\}$ is a causal and noninvertible ARMA(1,1) process relative to $\{W_t\}$ (Problem 4.10). Therefore, from a second-order point of view, nothing is lost by restricting attention to causal and invertible ARMA(1,1) models. This last sentence is also valid for higher-order ARMA models. □

2.4 Properties of the Sample Mean and Autocorrelation Function

A stationary process $\{X_t\}$ is characterized, at least from a second-order point of view, by its mean μ and its autocovariance function $\gamma(\cdot)$. The estimation of μ, $\gamma(\cdot)$, and the autocorrelation function $\rho(\cdot) = \gamma(\cdot)/\gamma(0)$ from observations $X_1, \ldots, X_n$ therefore plays a crucial role in problems of inference and in particular in the problem of constructing an appropriate model for the data. In this section we examine some of the properties of the sample estimates $\bar{x}$ and $\hat{\rho}(\cdot)$ of μ and $\rho(\cdot)$, respectively.

2.4.1 Estimation of μ

The moment estimator of the mean μ of a stationary process is the sample mean

$$\bar{X}_n = n^{-1}(X_1 + X_2 + \cdots + X_n). \tag{2.4.1}$$

It is an unbiased estimator of μ, since

$$E(\bar{X}_n) = n^{-1}(EX_1 + \cdots + EX_n) = \mu.$$

The mean squared error of $\bar{X}_n$ is

$$\begin{aligned}
E(\bar{X}_n - \mu)^2 &= \mathrm{Var}(\bar{X}_n) \\
&= n^{-2} \sum_{i=1}^{n} \sum_{j=1}^{n} \mathrm{Cov}(X_i, X_j) \\
&= n^{-2} \sum_{i-j=-n}^{n} (n - |i-j|)\gamma(i-j) \\
&= n^{-1} \sum_{h=-n}^{n} \left(1 - \frac{|h|}{n}\right) \gamma(h).
\end{aligned} \tag{2.4.2}$$

Now if $\gamma(h) \to 0$ as $h \to \infty$, the right-hand side of (2.4.2) converges to zero, so that $\bar{X}_n$ converges in mean square to μ. If $\sum_{h=-\infty}^{\infty} |\gamma(h)| < \infty$, then (2.4.2) gives $\lim_{n\to\infty} n\mathrm{Var}(\bar{X}_n) = \sum_{|h|<\infty} \gamma(h)$. We record these results in the following proposition.

Proposition 2.4.1

If $\{X_t\}$ is a stationary time series with mean μ and autocovariance function $\gamma(\cdot)$, then as $n \to \infty$,

$$\mathrm{Var}(\bar{X}_n) = E(\bar{X}_n - \mu)^2 \to 0 \qquad \text{if } \gamma(n) \to 0,$$

$$nE(\bar{X}_n - \mu)^2 \to \sum_{|h|<\infty} \gamma(h) \qquad \text{if } \sum_{h=-\infty}^{\infty} |\gamma(h)| < \infty.$$

To make inferences about μ using the sample mean $\bar{X}_n$, it is necessary to know the distribution or an approximation to the distribution of $\bar{X}_n$. If the time series is Gaussian (see Definition A.3.2), then by Remark 2 of Section A.3 and (2.4.2),

$$n^{1/2}(\bar{X}_n - \mu) \sim \mathrm{N}\left(0, \sum_{|h|<n} \left(1 - \frac{|h|}{n}\right) \gamma(h)\right).$$

It is easy to construct exact confidence bounds for μ using this result if $\gamma(\cdot)$ is known, and approximate confidence bounds if it is necessary to estimate $\gamma(\cdot)$ from the observations.

For many time series, in particular for linear and ARMA models, $\bar{X}_n$ is approximately normal with mean μ and variance $n^{-1}\sum_{|h|<\infty}\gamma(h)$ for large n (see TSTM, p. 219). An approximate 95% confidence interval for μ is then

$$\left(\bar{X}_n - 1.96v^{1/2}/\sqrt{n},\, \bar{X}_n + 1.96v^{1/2}/\sqrt{n}\right), \tag{2.4.3}$$

where $v = \sum_{|h|<\infty}\gamma(h)$. Of course, v is not generally known, so it must be estimated from the data. The estimator computed in the program ITSM is $\hat{v} = \sum_{|h|<\sqrt{n}}(1 - |h|/n)\hat{\gamma}(h)$. For ARMA processes this is a good approximation to v for large n.

Example 2.4.1 An AR(1) model

Let $\{X_t\}$ be an AR(1) process with mean μ, defined by the equations

$$X_t - \mu = \phi(X_{t-1} - \mu) + Z_t,$$

where $|\phi| < 1$ and $\{Z_t\} \sim \text{WN}(0, \sigma^2)$. From Example 2.2.1 we have $\gamma(h) = \phi^{|h|}\sigma^2/(1-\phi^2)$ and hence $v = \left(1+2\sum_{h=1}^{\infty}\phi^h\right)\sigma^2/\left(1-\phi^2\right) = \sigma^2/(1-\phi)^2$. Approximate 95% confidence bounds for μ are therefore given by $\bar{x}_n \pm 1.96\sigma n^{-1/2}/(1-\phi)$. Since ϕ and σ are unknown in practice, they must be replaced in these bounds by estimated values. □

2.4.2 Estimation of $\gamma(\cdot)$ and $\rho(\cdot)$

Recall from Section 1.4.1 that the sample autocovariance and autocorrelation functions are defined by

$$\hat{\gamma}(h) = n^{-1}\sum_{t=1}^{n-|h|}\left(X_{t+|h|} - \bar{X}_n\right)\left(X_t - \bar{X}_n\right) \tag{2.4.4}$$

and

$$\hat{\rho}(h) = \frac{\hat{\gamma}(h)}{\hat{\gamma}(0)}. \tag{2.4.5}$$

Both the estimators $\hat{\gamma}(h)$ and $\hat{\rho}(h)$ are biased even if the factor n^{-1} in (2.4.4) is replaced by $(n-h)^{-1}$. Nevertheless, under general assumptions they are nearly unbiased for large sample sizes. The sample ACVF has the desirable property that for each $k \geq 1$ the k-dimensional sample covariance matrix

$$\hat{\Gamma}_k = \begin{bmatrix} \hat{\gamma}(0) & \hat{\gamma}(1) & \cdots & \hat{\gamma}(k-1) \\ \hat{\gamma}(1) & \hat{\gamma}(0) & \cdots & \hat{\gamma}(k-2) \\ \vdots & \vdots & \cdots & \vdots \\ \hat{\gamma}(k-1) & \hat{\gamma}(k-2) & \cdots & \hat{\gamma}(0) \end{bmatrix} \tag{2.4.6}$$

is nonnegative definite. To see this, first note that if $\hat{\Gamma}_m$ is nonnegative definite, then $\hat{\Gamma}_k$ is nonnegative definite for all $k < m$. So assume $k \geq n$ and write

$$\hat{\Gamma}_k = n^{-1}TT',$$

where T is the $k \times 2k$ matrix

$$T = \begin{bmatrix} 0 & \cdots & 0 & 0 & Y_1 & Y_2 & \cdots & Y_k \\ 0 & \cdots & 0 & Y_1 & Y_2 & \cdots & Y_k & 0 \\ \vdots & & & & & & & \vdots \\ 0 & Y_1 & Y_2 & \cdots & Y_k & 0 \cdots & 0 & \end{bmatrix},$$

$Y_i = X_i - \bar{X}_n$, $i = 1, \ldots, n$, and $Y_i = 0$ for $i = n+1, \ldots, k$. Then for any real $k \times 1$ vector $\mathbf{a}$ we have

$$\mathbf{a}'\hat{\Gamma}_k\mathbf{a} = n^{-1}(\mathbf{a}'T)(T'\mathbf{a}) \geq 0, \tag{2.4.7}$$

and consequently the sample autocovariance matrix $\hat{\Gamma}_k$ and sample autocorrelation matrix

$$\hat{R}_k = \hat{\Gamma}_k/\gamma(0) \tag{2.4.8}$$

are nonnegative definite. Sometimes the factor n^{-1} is replaced by $(n-h)^{-1}$ in the definition of $\hat{\gamma}(h)$, but the resulting covariance and correlation matrices $\hat{\Gamma}_n$ and $\hat{R}_n$ may not then be nonnegative definite. We shall therefore use the definitions (2.4.4) and (2.4.5) of $\hat{\gamma}(h)$ and $\hat{\rho}(h)$.

Remark 1. The matrices $\hat{\Gamma}_k$ and $\hat{R}_k$ are in fact nonsingular if there is at least one nonzero Y_i, or equivalently if $\hat{\gamma}(0) > 0$. To establish this result, suppose that $\hat{\gamma}(0) > 0$ and $\hat{\Gamma}_k$ is singular. Then there is equality in (2.4.7) for some nonzero vector $\mathbf{a}$, implying that $\mathbf{a}'T = 0$ and hence that the rank of T is less than k. Let Y_i be the first nonzero value of $Y_1, Y_2, \ldots, Y_k$, and consider the $k \times k$ submatrix of T consisting of columns $(i+1)$ through $(i+k)$. Since this matrix is lower right triangular with each diagonal element equal to Y_i, its determinant has absolute value $|Y_i|^k \neq 0$. Consequently, the submatrix is nonsingular, and T must have rank k, a contradiction. □

Without further information beyond the observed data $X_1, \ldots, X_n$, it is impossible to give reasonable estimates of $\gamma(h)$ and $\rho(h)$ for $h \geq n$. Even for h slightly smaller than n, the estimates $\hat{\gamma}(h)$ and $\hat{\rho}(h)$ are unreliable, since there are so few pairs (X_{t+h}, X_t) available (only one if $h = n-1$). A useful guide is provided by Box and Jenkins (1976), p. 33, who suggest that n should be at least about 50 and $h \leq n/4$.

The sample ACF plays an important role in the selection of suitable models for the data. We have already seen in Example 1.4.6 and Section 1.6 how the sample ACF can be used to test for iid noise. For systematic inference concerning $\rho(h)$, we need the sampling distribution of the estimator $\hat{\rho}(h)$. Although the distribution of $\hat{\rho}(h)$ is intractable for samples from even the simplest time series models, it can usually be well approximated by a normal distribution for large sample sizes. For linear models and in particular for ARMA models (see Theorem 7.2.2 of TSTM for exact conditions) $\hat{\rho}_k = (\hat{\rho}(1), \ldots, \hat{\rho}(k))'$ is approximately distributed for large n as

$N(\rho_k, n^{-1}W)$, i.e.,

$$\hat{\rho} \approx N\big(\rho, n^{-1}W\big), \tag{2.4.9}$$

where $\rho = (\rho(1), \ldots, \rho(k))'$, and W is the covariance matrix whose (i, j) element is given by **Bartlett's formula**

$$w_{ij} = \sum_{k=-\infty}^{\infty} \big\{\rho(k+i)\rho(k+j) + \rho(k-i)\rho(k+j) + 2\rho(i)\rho(j)\rho^2(k)$$
$$- 2\rho(i)\rho(k)\rho(k+j) - 2\rho(j)\rho(k)\rho(k+i)\big\}.$$

Simple algebra shows that

$$w_{ij} = \sum_{k=1}^{\infty} \{\rho(k+i) + \rho(k-i) - 2\rho(i)\rho(k)\}$$
$$\times \{\rho(k+j) + \rho(k-j) - 2\rho(j)\rho(k)\}, \tag{2.4.10}$$

which is a more convenient form of w_{ij} for computational purposes.

Example 2.4.2 iid Noise

If $\{X_t\} \sim \text{IID}\big(0, \sigma^2\big)$, then $\rho(h) = 0$ for $|h| > 0$, so from (2.4.10) we obtain

$$w_{ij} = \begin{cases} 1 & \text{if } i = j, \\ 0 & \text{otherwise.} \end{cases}$$

For large n, therefore, $\hat{\rho}(1), \ldots, \hat{\rho}(h)$ are approximately independent and identically distributed normal random variables with mean 0 and variance n^{-1}. This result is the basis for the test that data are generated from iid noise using the sample ACF described in Section 1.6. (See also Example 1.4.6.) □

Example 2.4.3 An MA(1) process

If $\{X_t\}$ is the MA(1) process of Example 1.4.4, i.e., if

$$X_t = Z_t + \theta Z_{t-1}, \quad t = 0, \pm 1, \ldots,$$

where $\{Z_t\} \sim \text{WN}(0, \sigma^2)$, then from (2.4.10)

$$w_{ii} = \begin{cases} 1 - 3\rho^2(1) + 4\rho^4(1), & \text{if } i = 1, \\ 1 + 2\rho^2(1), & \text{if } i > 1, \end{cases}$$

is the approximate variance of $n^{-1/2}(\hat{\rho}(i) - \rho(i))$ for large n. In Figure 2.1 we have plotted the sample autocorrelation function $\hat{\rho}(k)$, $k = 0, \ldots, 40$, for 200 observations from the MA(1) model

$$X_t = Z_t - .8Z_{t-1}, \tag{2.4.11}$$

where $\{Z_t\}$ is a sequence of iid N(0, 1) random variables. Here $\rho(1) = -.8/1.64 = -.4878$ and $\rho(h) = 0$ for $h > 1$. The lag-one sample ACF is found to be $\hat{\rho}(1) =$

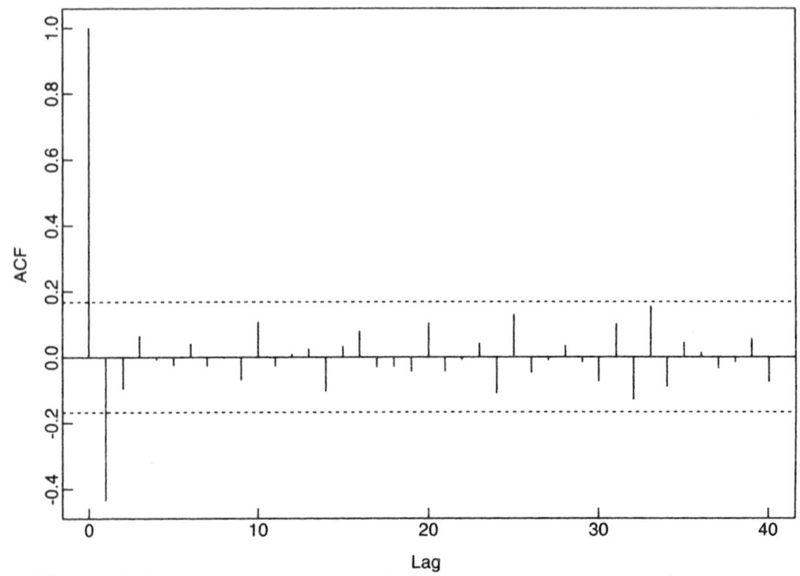

Figure 2-1 The sample autocorrelation function of $n = 200$ observations of the MA(1) process in Example 2.4.3, showing the bounds $\pm 1.96n^{-1/2}(1 + 2\hat{\rho}^2(1))^{1/2}$.

$-.4333 = -6.128n^{-1/2}$, which would cause us (in the absence of our prior knowledge of $\{X_t\}$) to reject the hypothesis that the data are a sample from an iid noise sequence. The fact that $|\hat{\rho}(h)| \leq 1.96n^{-1/2}$ for $h = 2, \ldots, 40$ strongly suggests that the data are from a model in which observations are uncorrelated past lag 1. In Figure 2.1 we have plotted the bounds $\pm 1.96n^{-1/2}(1+2\rho^2(1))^{1/2}$, indicating the compatibility of the data with the model (2.4.11). Since, however, $\rho(1)$ is not normally known in advance, the autocorrelations $\hat{\rho}(2), \ldots, \hat{\rho}(40)$ would in practice have been compared with the more stringent bounds $\pm 1.96n^{-1/2}$ or with the bounds $\pm 1.96n^{-1/2}(1+2\hat{\rho}^2(1))^{1/2}$ in order to check the hypothesis that the data are generated by a moving-average process of order 1. Finally, it is worth noting that the lag-one correlation $-.4878$ is well inside the 95% confidence bounds for $\rho(1)$ given by $\hat{\rho}(1) \pm 1.96n^{-1/2}(1 - 3\hat{\rho}^2(1) + 4\hat{\rho}^4(1))^{1/2} = -.4333 \pm .1053$. This further supports the compatibility of the data with the model $X_t = Z_t - 0.8Z_{t-1}$. □

Example 2.4.4 An AR(1) process

For the AR(1) process of Example 2.2.1,

$$X_t = \phi X_{t-1} + Z_t,$$

where $\{Z_t\}$ is iid noise and $|\phi| < 1$, we have, from (2.4.10) with $\rho(h) = \phi^{|h|}$,

$$\begin{aligned} w_{ii} &= \sum_{k=1}^{i} \phi^{2i}\left(\phi^{-k} - \phi^{k}\right)^2 + \sum_{k=i+1}^{\infty} \phi^{2k}\left(\phi^{-i} - \phi^{i}\right)^2 \\ &= \left(1 - \phi^{2i}\right)\left(1 + \phi^2\right)\left(1 - \phi^2\right)^{-1} - 2i\phi^{2i}, \end{aligned} \tag{2.4.12}$$

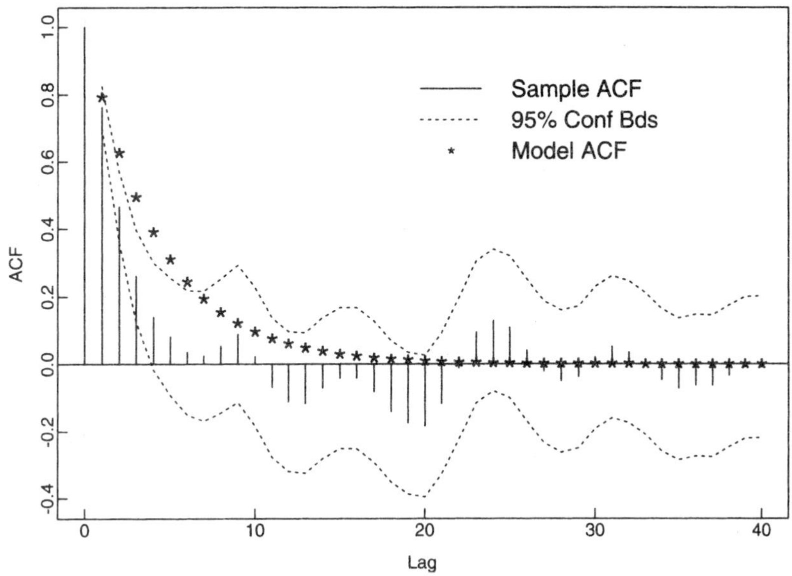

Figure 2-2 The sample autocorrelation function of the Lake Huron residuals of Figure 1.10 showing the bounds $\hat{\rho}(i) \pm 1.96n^{-1/2}w_{ii}^{1/2}$ and the model ACF $\rho(i) = (.791)^i$.

$i = 1, 2, \ldots$. In Figure 2.2 we have plotted the sample ACF of the Lake Huron residuals $y_1, \ldots, y_{98}$ from Figure 1.10 together with 95% confidence bounds for $\rho(i)$, $i = 1, \ldots, 40$, assuming that data are generated from the AR(1) model

$$Y_t = .791Y_{t-1} + Z_t \tag{2.4.13}$$

(see equation (1.4.3)). The confidence bounds are computed from $\hat{\rho}(i) \pm 1.96n^{-1/2} w_{ii}^{1/2}$, where w_{ii} is given in (2.4.12) with $\phi = .791$. The model ACF, $\rho(i) = (.791)^i$, is also plotted in Figure 2.2. Notice that the model ACF lies just outside the confidence bounds at lags 2–6. This suggests some incompatibility of the data with the model (2.4.13). A much better fit to the residuals is provided by the second-order autoregression defined by (1.4.4). □

2.5 Forecasting Stationary Time Series

We now consider the problem of predicting the values X_{n+h}, $h > 0$, of a stationary time series with known mean μ and autocovariance function γ in terms of the values $\{X_n, \ldots, X_1\}$, up to time n. Our goal is to find the *linear combination* of $1, X_n, X_{n-1}, \ldots, X_1$, that forecasts X_{n+h} with minimum mean squared error. The best linear predictor in terms of $1, X_n, \ldots, X_1$ will be denoted by P_nX_{n+h} and clearly has the form

$$P_nX_{n+h} = a_0 + a_1X_n + \cdots + a_nX_1. \tag{2.5.1}$$

It remains only to determine the coefficients $a_0, a_1, \ldots, a_n$, by finding the values that minimize

$$S(a_0, \ldots, a_n) = E(X_{n+h} - a_0 - a_1 X_n - \cdots - a_n X_1)^2. \tag{2.5.2}$$

(We already know from Problem 1.1 that $P_0 Y = E(Y)$.) Since S is a quadratic function of $a_0, \ldots, a_n$ and is bounded below by zero, it is clear that there is at least one value of $(a_0, \ldots, a_n)$ that minimizes S and that the minimum $(a_0, \ldots, a_n)$ satisfies the equations

$$\frac{\partial S(a_0, \ldots, a_n)}{\partial a_j} = 0, \quad j = 0, \ldots, n. \tag{2.5.3}$$

Evaluation of the derivatives in equations (2.5.3) gives the equivalent equations

$$E\left[X_{n+h} - a_0 - \sum_{i=1}^{n} a_i X_{n+1-i}\right] = 0, \tag{2.5.4}$$

$$E\left[(X_{n+h} - a_0 - \sum_{i=1}^{n} a_i X_{n+1-i})X_{n+1-j}\right] = 0, \quad j = 1, \ldots, n. \tag{2.5.5}$$

These equations can be written more neatly in vector notation as

$$a_0 = \mu\left(1 - \sum_{i=1}^{n} a_i\right) \tag{2.5.6}$$

and

$$\Gamma_n \mathbf{a}_n = \gamma_n(h), \tag{2.5.7}$$

where

$$\mathbf{a}_n = (a_1, \ldots, a_n)', \qquad \Gamma_n = [\gamma(i-j)]_{i,j=1}^{n},$$

and

$$\gamma_n(h) = (\gamma(h), \gamma(h+1), \ldots, \gamma(h+n-1))'.$$

Hence,

$$P_n X_{n+h} = \mu + \sum_{i=1}^{n} a_i (X_{n+1-i} - \mu), \tag{2.5.8}$$

where $\mathbf{a}_n$ satisfies (2.5.7). From (2.5.8) the expected value of the prediction error $X_{n+h} - P_n X_{n+h}$ is zero, and the mean square prediction error is therefore

$$\begin{aligned} E(X_{n+h} - P_n X_{n+h})^2 &= \gamma(0) - 2\sum_{i=1}^{n} a_i \gamma(h+i-1) + \sum_{i=1}^{n}\sum_{j=1}^{n} a_i \gamma(i-j) a_j \\ &= \gamma(0) - \mathbf{a}_n' \gamma_n(h), \end{aligned} \tag{2.5.9}$$

where the last line follows from (2.5.7).

Remark 1. To show that equations (2.5.4) and (2.5.5) determine $P_n X_{n+h}$ uniquely, let $\{a_j^{(1)}, j = 0, \ldots, n\}$ and $\{a_j^{(2)}, j = 0, \ldots, n\}$ be two solutions and let Z be the difference between the corresponding predictors, i.e.,

$$Z = a_0^{(1)} - a_0^{(2)} + \sum_{j=1}^{n} \left(a_j^{(1)} - a_j^{(2)}\right) X_{n+1-j}.$$

Then

$$Z^2 = Z \left(a_0^{(1)} - a_0^{(2)} + \sum_{j=1}^{n} \left(a_j^{(1)} - a_j^{(2)}\right) X_{n+1-j} \right).$$

But from (2.5.4) and (2.5.5) we have $EZ = 0$ and $E(ZX_{n+1-j}) = 0$ for $j = 1, \ldots, n$. Consequently, $E(Z^2) = 0$ and hence $Z = 0$. □

Properties of $P_n X_{n+h}$:

1. $P_n X_{n+h} = \mu + \sum_{i=1}^{n} a_i (X_{n+1-i} - \mu)$, where $\mathbf{a}_n = (a_1, \ldots, a_n)'$ satisfies (2.5.7).
2. $E(X_{n+h} - P_n X_{n+h})^2 = \gamma(0) - \mathbf{a}_n' \gamma_n(h)$, where $\gamma_n(h) = (\gamma(h), \ldots, \gamma(h+n-1))'$.
3. $E(X_{n+h} - P_n X_{n+h}) = 0$.
4. $E[(X_{n+h} - P_n X_{n+h})X_j] = 0,\ j = 1, \ldots, n$.

Remark 2. Notice that properties 3 and 4 are exactly equivalent to (2.5.4) and (2.5.5). They can be written more succinctly in the form

$$E[(\text{Error}) \times (\text{PredictorVariable})] = 0. \tag{2.5.10}$$

Equations (2.5.10), one for each predictor variable, therefore uniquely determine $P_n X_{n+h}$. □

Example 2.5.1 One-step prediction of an AR(1) series

Consider now the stationary time series defined in Example 2.2.1 by the equations

$$X_t = \phi X_{t-1} + Z_t, \quad t = 0, \pm 1, \ldots,$$

where $|\phi| < 1$ and $\{Z_t\} \sim \text{WN}(0, \sigma^2)$. From (2.5.7) and (2.5.8), the best linear predictor of X_{n+1} in terms of $\{1, X_n, \ldots, X_1\}$ is (for $n \geq 1$)

$$P_n X_{n+1} = \mathbf{a}_n' \mathbf{X}_n,$$

where $\mathbf{X}_n = (X_n, \ldots, X_1)'$ and

$$\begin{bmatrix} 1 & \phi & \phi^2 & \cdots & \phi^{n-1} \\ \phi & 1 & \phi & \cdots & \phi^{n-2} \\ \vdots & \vdots & \vdots & \vdots & \vdots \\ \phi^{n-1} & \phi^{n-2} & \phi^{n-3} & \cdots & 1 \end{bmatrix} \begin{bmatrix} a_1 \\ a_2 \\ \vdots \\ a_n \end{bmatrix} = \begin{bmatrix} \phi \\ \phi^2 \\ \vdots \\ \phi^n \end{bmatrix}. \tag{2.5.11}$$

A solution of (2.5.11) is clearly

$$\mathbf{a}_n = (\phi, 0, \ldots, 0)',$$

and hence the best linear predictor of X_{n+1} in terms of $\{X_1, \ldots, X_n\}$ is

$$P_n X_{n+1} = \mathbf{a}_n' \mathbf{X}_n = \phi X_n,$$

with mean squared error

$$E(X_{n+1} - P_n X_{n+1})^2 = \gamma(0) - \mathbf{a}_n' \gamma_n(1) = \frac{\sigma^2}{1 - \phi^2} - \phi \gamma(1) = \sigma^2.$$

A simpler approach to this problem is to guess, by inspection of the equation defining X_{n+1}, that the best predictor is ϕX_n. Then to verify this conjecture, it suffices to check (2.5.10) for each of the predictor variables $1, X_n, \ldots, X_1$. The prediction error of the predictor ϕX_n is clearly $X_{n+1} - \phi X_n = Z_{n+1}$. But $E(Z_{n+1} Y) = 0$ for $Y = 1$ and for $Y = X_j$, $j = 1, \ldots, n$. Hence, by (2.5.10), ϕX_n is the required best linear predictor in terms of $1, X_1, \ldots, X_n$. □

Prediction of Second-Order Random Variables

Suppose now that Y and $W_n, \ldots, W_1$ are *any* random variables with finite second moments and that the means $\mu = EY$, $\mu_i = EW_i$ and covariances $\mathrm{Cov}(Y, Y)$, $\mathrm{Cov}(Y, W_i)$, and $\mathrm{Cov}(W_i, W_j)$ are all known. It is convenient to introduce the random vector $\mathbf{W} = (W_n, \ldots, W_1)'$, the corresponding vector of means $\boldsymbol{\mu}_W = (\mu_n, \ldots, \mu_1)'$, the vector of covariances

$$\boldsymbol{\gamma} = \mathrm{Cov}(Y, \mathbf{W}) = (\mathrm{Cov}(Y, W_n), \mathrm{Cov}(Y, W_{n-1}), \ldots, \mathrm{Cov}(Y, W_1))',$$

and the covariance matrix

$$\Gamma = \mathrm{Cov}(\mathbf{W}, \mathbf{W}) = \left[\mathrm{Cov}(W_{n+1-i}, W_{n+1-j})\right]_{i,j=1}^{n}.$$

Then by the same arguments used in the calculation of $P_n X_{n+h}$, the best linear predictor of Y in terms of $\{1, W_n, \ldots, W_1\}$ is found to be

$$P(Y|\mathbf{W}) = \mu_Y + \mathbf{a}'(\mathbf{W} - \boldsymbol{\mu}_W), \tag{2.5.12}$$

where $\mathbf{a} = (a_1, \ldots, a_n)'$ is any solution of

$$\Gamma \mathbf{a} = \boldsymbol{\gamma}. \tag{2.5.13}$$

The mean squared error of the predictor is

$$E\left[(Y - P(Y|\mathbf{W}))^2\right] = \mathrm{Var}(Y) - \mathbf{a}'\boldsymbol{\gamma}. \tag{2.5.14}$$

Example 2.5.2 Estimation of a missing value

Consider again the stationary series defined in Example 2.2.1 by the equations

$$X_t = \phi X_{t-1} + Z_t, \quad t = 0, \pm 1, \ldots,$$

where $|\phi| < 1$ and $\{Z_t\} \sim \mathrm{WN}(0, \sigma^2)$. Suppose that we observe the series at times 1 and 3 and wish to use these observations to find the linear combination of $1, X_1$, and X_3 that estimates X_2 with minimum mean squared error. The solution to this problem can be obtained directly from (2.5.12) and (2.5.13) by setting $Y = X_2$ and $\mathbf{W} = (X_1, X_3)'$. This gives the equations

$$\begin{bmatrix} 1 & \phi^2 \\ \phi^2 & 1 \end{bmatrix} \mathbf{a} = \begin{bmatrix} \phi \\ \phi \end{bmatrix},$$

with solution

$$\mathbf{a} = \frac{1}{1+\phi^2} \begin{bmatrix} \phi \\ \phi \end{bmatrix}.$$

The best estimator of X_2 is thus

$$P(X_2|\mathbf{W}) = \frac{\phi}{1+\phi^2}(X_1 + X_3),$$

with mean squared error

$$E[(X_2 - P(X_2|\mathbf{W}))^2] = \frac{\sigma^2}{1-\phi^2} - \mathbf{a}' \begin{bmatrix} \dfrac{\phi\sigma^2}{1-\phi^2} \\ \dfrac{\phi\sigma^2}{1-\phi^2} \end{bmatrix} = \frac{\sigma^2}{1+\phi^2}. \quad \square$$

The Prediction Operator $P(\cdot|\mathbf{W})$

For any given $\mathbf{W} = (W_n, \ldots, W_1)'$ and Y with finite second moments, we have seen how to compute the best linear predictor $P(Y|\mathbf{W})$ of Y in terms of $1, W_n, \ldots, W_1$ from (2.5.12) and (2.5.13). The function $P(\cdot|\mathbf{W})$, which converts Y into $P(Y|\mathbf{W})$, is called a **prediction operator**. (The operator P_n defined by equations (2.5.7) and (2.5.8) is an example with $\mathbf{W} = (X_n, X_{n-1}, \ldots, X_1)'$.) Prediction operators have a number of useful properties that can sometimes be used to simplify the calculation of best linear predictors. We list some of these below.

Properties of the Prediction Operator $P(\cdot|\mathbf{W})$:

Suppose that $EU^2 < \infty$, $EV^2 < \infty$, $\Gamma = \text{cov}(\mathbf{W}, \mathbf{W})$, and $\beta, \alpha_1, \ldots, \alpha_n$ are constants.

1. $P(U|\mathbf{W}) = EU + \mathbf{a}'(\mathbf{W} - E\mathbf{W})$, where $\Gamma\mathbf{a} = \text{cov}(U, \mathbf{W})$.
2. $E[(U - P(U|\mathbf{W}))\mathbf{W}] = \mathbf{0}$ and $E[U - P(U|\mathbf{W})] = 0$.
3. $E[(U - P(U|\mathbf{W}))^2] = \text{var}(U) - \mathbf{a}'\text{cov}(U, \mathbf{W})$.
4. $P(\alpha_1 U + \alpha_2 V + \beta|\mathbf{W}) = \alpha_1 P(U|\mathbf{W}) + \alpha_2 P(V|\mathbf{W}) + \beta$.
5. $P\left(\sum_{i=1}^n \alpha_i W_i + \beta|\mathbf{W}\right) = \sum_{i=1}^n \alpha_i W_i + \beta$.
6. $P(U|\mathbf{W}) = EU$ if $\text{cov}(U, \mathbf{W}) = \mathbf{0}$.
7. $P(U|\mathbf{W}) = P(P(U|\mathbf{W}, \mathbf{V})|\mathbf{W})$ if $\mathbf{V}$ is a random vector such that the components of $E(\mathbf{V}\mathbf{V}')$ are all finite.

Example 2.5.3 One-step prediction of an AR(p) series

Suppose now that $\{X_t\}$ is a stationary time series satisfying the equations

$$X_t = \phi_1 X_{t-1} + \cdots + \phi_p X_{t-p} + Z_t, \quad t = 0, \pm 1, \ldots,$$

where $\{Z_t\} \sim \text{WN}(0, \sigma^2)$ and Z_t is uncorrelated with X_s for each $s < t$. Then if $n > p$, we can apply the prediction operator P_n to each side of the defining equations, using properties (4), (5), and (6) to get

$$P_n X_{n+1} = \phi_1 X_n + \cdots + \phi_p X_{n+1-p}.$$

□

Example 2.5.4 An AR(1) series with nonzero mean

The time series $\{Y_t\}$ is said to be an AR(1) process with mean μ if $\{X_t = Y_t - \mu\}$ is a zero-mean AR(1) process. Defining $\{X_t\}$ as in Example 2.5.1 and letting $Y_t = X_t + \mu$, we see that Y_t satisfies the equation

$$Y_t - \mu = \phi(Y_{t-1} - \mu) + Z_t. \tag{2.5.15}$$

If $P_n Y_{n+h}$ is the best linear predictor of Y_{n+h} in terms of $\{1, Y_n, \ldots, Y_1\}$, then application of P_n to (2.5.15) with $t = n+1, n+2, \ldots$ gives the recursions

$$P_n Y_{n+h} - \mu = \phi(P_n Y_{n+h-1} - \mu), \quad h = 1, 2, \ldots.$$

Noting that $P_n Y_n = Y_n$, we can solve these equations recursively for $P_n Y_{n+h}$, $h = 1, 2, \ldots$, to obtain

$$P_n Y_{n+h} = \mu + \phi^h (Y_n - \mu). \tag{2.5.16}$$

The corresponding mean squared error is (from (2.5.14))

$$E(Y_{n+h} - P_n Y_{n+h})^2 = \gamma(0)[1 - \mathbf{a}_n' \rho_n(h)]. \tag{2.5.17}$$

From Example 2.2.1 we know that $\gamma(0) = \sigma^2/(1-\phi^2)$ and $\rho(h) = \phi^h, h \geq 0$. Hence, substituting $\mathbf{a}_n = (\phi^h, 0, \ldots, 0)'$ (from (2.5.16)) into (2.5.17) gives

$$E(Y_{n+h} - P_n Y_{n+h})^2 = \sigma^2(1-\phi^{2h})/(1-\phi^2). \tag{2.5.18}$$

□

Remark 3. In general, if $\{Y_t\}$ is a stationary time series with mean μ and if $\{X_t\}$ is the zero-mean series defined by $X_t = Y_t - \mu$, then since the collection of all linear combinations of $1, Y_n, \ldots, Y_1$ is the same as the collection of all linear combinations of $1, X_n, \ldots, X_1$, the linear predictor of any random variable W in terms of $1, Y_n, \ldots, Y_1$ is the same as the linear predictor in terms of $1, X_n, \ldots, X_1$. Denoting this predictor by $P_n W$ and applying P_n to the equation $Y_{n+h} = X_{n+h} + \mu$ gives

$$P_n Y_{n+h} = \mu + P_n X_{n+h}. \tag{2.5.19}$$

Thus the best linear predictor of Y_{n+h} can be determined by finding the best linear predictor of X_{n+h} and then adding μ. Note from (2.5.8) that since $E(X_t) = 0$, $P_n X_{n+h}$ is the same as the best linear predictor of X_{n+h} in terms of $X_n, \ldots, X_1$ only. □

2.5.1 The Durbin–Levinson Algorithm

In view of Remark 3 above, we can restrict attention from now on to zero-mean stationary time series, making the necessary adjustments for the mean if we wish to predict a stationary series with nonzero mean. If $\{X_t\}$ is a zero-mean stationary series with autocovariance function $\gamma(\cdot)$, then in principle the equations (2.5.12) and (2.5.13) completely solve the problem of determining the best linear predictor $P_n X_{n+h}$ of X_{n+h} in terms of $\{X_n, \ldots, X_1\}$. However, the direct approach requires the determination of a solution of a system of n linear equations, which for large n may be difficult and time-consuming. In cases where the process is defined by a system of linear equations (as in Examples 2.5.2 and 2.5.3) we have seen how the linearity of P_n can be used to great advantage. For more general stationary processes it would be helpful if the one-step predictor $P_n X_{n+1}$ based on n previous observations could be used to simplify the calculation of $P_{n+1} X_{n+2}$, the one-step predictor based on $n+1$ previous observations. Prediction algorithms that utilize this idea are said to be **recursive**. Two important examples are the Durbin–Levinson algorithm, discussed in this section, and the innovations algorithm, discussed in Section 2.5.2 below.

We know from (2.5.12) and (2.5.13) that if the matrix Γ_n is nonsingular, then

$$P_n X_{n+1} = \phi_n' \mathbf{X}_n = \phi_{n1} X_n + \cdots + \phi_{nn} X_1,$$

where

$$\phi_n = \Gamma_n^{-1} \gamma_n,$$

$\gamma_n = (\gamma(1), \ldots, \gamma(n))'$, and the corresponding mean squared error is

$$v_n := E(X_{n+1} - P_n X_{n+1})^2 = \gamma(0) - \phi_n' \gamma_n.$$

A useful sufficient condition for nonsingularity of *all* the autocovariance matrices $\Gamma_1, \Gamma_2, \ldots$ is $\gamma(0) > 0$ and $\gamma(h) \to 0$ as $h \to \infty$. (For a proof of this result see TSTM, Proposition 5.1.1.)

The Durbin–Levinson Algorithm:

The coefficients $\phi_{n1}, \ldots, \phi_{nn}$ can be computed recursively from the equations

$$\phi_{nn} = \left[\gamma(n) - \sum_{j=1}^{n-1} \phi_{n-1,j}\gamma(n-j)\right] v_{n-1}^{-1}, \tag{2.5.20}$$

$$\begin{bmatrix} \phi_{n1} \\ \vdots \\ \phi_{n,n-1} \end{bmatrix} = \begin{bmatrix} \phi_{n-1,1} \\ \vdots \\ \phi_{n-1,n-1} \end{bmatrix} - \phi_{nn} \begin{bmatrix} \phi_{n-1,n-1} \\ \vdots \\ \phi_{n-1,1} \end{bmatrix} \tag{2.5.21}$$

and

$$v_n = v_{n-1}\left[1 - \phi_{nn}^2\right], \tag{2.5.22}$$

where $\phi_{11} = \gamma(1)/\gamma(0)$ and $v_0 = \gamma(0)$.

Proof The definition of ϕ_{11} ensures that the equation

$$R_n \phi_n = \rho_n \tag{2.5.23}$$

(where $\rho_n = (\rho(1), \ldots, \rho(n))'$) is satisfied for $n = 1$. The first step in the proof is to show that ϕ_n, defined recursively by (2.5.20) and (2.5.21), satisfies (2.5.23) for all n. Suppose this is true for $n = k$. Then, partitioning R_{k+1} and defining

$$\rho_k^{(r)} := (\rho(k), \rho(k-1), \ldots, \rho(1))'$$

and

$$\phi_k^{(r)} := (\phi_{kk}, \phi_{k,k-1}, \ldots, \phi_{k1})',$$

we see that the recursions imply

$$\begin{aligned} R_{k+1}\phi_{k+1} &= \begin{bmatrix} R_k & \rho_k^{(r)} \\ \rho_k^{(r)\prime} & 1 \end{bmatrix} \begin{bmatrix} \phi_k - \phi_{k+1,k+1}\phi_k^{(r)} \\ \phi_{k+1,k+1} \end{bmatrix} \\ &= \begin{bmatrix} \rho_k - \phi_{k+1,k+1}\rho_k^{(r)} + \phi_{k+1,k+1}\rho_k^{(r)} \\ \rho_k^{(r)\prime}\phi_k - \phi_{k+1,k+1}\rho_k^{(r)\prime}\phi_k^{(r)} + \phi_{k+1,k+1} \end{bmatrix} \\ &= \rho_{k+1}, \end{aligned}$$

as required. Here we have used the fact that if $R_k\phi_k = \rho_k$, then $R_k\phi_k^{(r)} = \rho_k^{(r)}$. This is easily checked by writing out the component equations in reverse order. Since (2.5.23) is satisfied for $n = 1$, it follows by induction that the coefficient vectors ϕ_n defined recursively by (2.5.20) and (2.5.21) satisfy (2.5.23) for all n.

It remains only to establish that the mean squared errors

$$v_n := E(X_{n+1} - \phi_n'\mathbf{X}_n)^2$$

satisfy $v_0 = \gamma(0)$ and (2.5.22). The fact that $v_0 = \gamma(0)$ is an immediate consequence of the definition $P_0X_1 := E(X_1) = 0$. Since we have shown that $\phi_n'\mathbf{X}_n$ is the best linear predictor of X_{n+1}, we can write, from (2.5.9) and (2.5.21),

$$v_n = \gamma(0) - \phi_n'\gamma_n = \gamma(0) - \phi_{n-1}'\gamma_{n-1} + \phi_{nn}\phi_{n-1}^{(r)\prime}\gamma_{n-1} - \phi_{nn}\gamma(n).$$

Applying (2.5.9) again gives

$$v_n = v_{n-1} + \phi_{nn}\left(\phi_{n-1}^{(r)\prime}\gamma_{n-1} - \gamma(n)\right),$$

and hence, by (2.5.20),

$$v_n = v_{n-1} - \phi_{nn}^2(\gamma(0) - \phi_{n-1}'\gamma_{n-1}) = v_{n-1}\left(1 - \phi_{nn}^2\right).$$

■

Remark 4. Under the conditions of the proposition, the function defined by $\alpha(0) = 1$ and $\alpha(n) = \phi_{nn}$, $n = 1, 2, \ldots$, is known as the **partial autocorrelation function** (PACF) of $\{X_t\}$. It will be discussed further in Section 3.2. Of particular interest is equation (2.5.22), which shows the relation between $\alpha(n)$ and the reduction in the one-step mean squared error as the number of predictors is increased from $n - 1$ to n. □

2.5.2 The Innovations Algorithm

The recursive algorithm to be discussed in this section is applicable to *all* series with finite second moments, regardless of whether they are stationary or not. Its application, however, can be simplified in certain special cases.

Suppose then that $\{X_t\}$ is a zero-mean series with $E|X_t|^2 < \infty$ for each t and

$$E(X_iX_j) = \kappa(i, j). \tag{2.5.24}$$

It will be convenient to introduce the following notation for the best one-step predictors and their mean squared errors:

$$\hat{X}_n = \begin{cases} 0, & \text{if } n = 1, \\ P_{n-1}X_n, & \text{if } n = 2, 3, \ldots, \end{cases}$$

and

$$v_n = E(X_{n+1} - P_nX_{n+1})^2.$$

We shall also introduce the **innovations**, or one-step prediction errors,

$$U_n = X_n - \hat{X}_n.$$

In terms of the vectors $\mathbf{U}_n = (U_1, \ldots, U_n)'$ and $\mathbf{X}_n = (X_1, \ldots, X_n)'$ the last equations can be written as

$$\mathbf{U}_n = A_n \mathbf{X}_n, \tag{2.5.25}$$

where A_n has the form

$$A_n = \begin{bmatrix} 1 & 0 & 0 & \cdots & 0 \\ a_{11} & 1 & 0 & \cdots & 0 \\ a_{22} & a_{21} & 1 & \cdots & 0 \\ \vdots & \vdots & \vdots & \ddots & 0 \\ a_{n-1,n-1} & a_{n-1,n-2} & a_{n-1,n-3} & \cdots & 1 \end{bmatrix}.$$

(If $\{X_t\}$ is stationary, then $a_{ij} = -a_j$ with a_j as in (2.5.7) with $h = 1$.) This implies that A_n is nonsingular, with inverse C_n of the form

$$C_n = \begin{bmatrix} 1 & 0 & 0 & \cdots & 0 \\ \theta_{11} & 1 & 0 & \cdots & 0 \\ \theta_{22} & \theta_{21} & 1 & \cdots & 0 \\ \vdots & \vdots & \vdots & \ddots & 0 \\ \theta_{n-1,n-1} & \theta_{n-1,n-2} & \theta_{n-1,n-3} & \cdots & 1 \end{bmatrix}.$$

The vector of one-step predictors $\hat{\mathbf{X}}_n := (X_1, P_1X_2, \ldots, P_{n-1}X_n)'$ can therefore be expressed as

$$\hat{\mathbf{X}}_n = \mathbf{X}_n - \mathbf{U}_n = C_n\mathbf{U}_n - \mathbf{U}_n = \Theta_n \left(\mathbf{X}_n - \hat{\mathbf{X}}_n\right), \tag{2.5.26}$$

where

$$\Theta_n = \begin{bmatrix} 0 & 0 & 0 & \cdots & 0 \\ \theta_{11} & 0 & 0 & \cdots & 0 \\ \theta_{22} & \theta_{21} & 0 & \cdots & 0 \\ \vdots & \vdots & \vdots & \ddots & 0 \\ \theta_{n-1,n-1} & \theta_{n-1,n-2} & \theta_{n-1,n-3} & \cdots & 0 \end{bmatrix}$$

and $\mathbf{X}_n$ itself satisfies

$$\mathbf{X}_n = C_n \left(\mathbf{X}_n - \hat{\mathbf{X}}_n\right). \tag{2.5.27}$$

Equation (2.5.26) can be rewritten as

$$\hat{X}_{n+1} = \begin{cases} 0, & \text{if } n = 0, \\ \displaystyle\sum_{j=1}^{n} \theta_{nj} \left(X_{n+1-j} - \hat{X}_{n+1-j}\right), & \text{if } n = 1, 2, \ldots, \end{cases} \tag{2.5.28}$$

from which the one-step predictors $\hat{X}_1, \hat{X}_2, \ldots$ can be computed recursively once the coefficients θ_{ij} have been determined. The following algorithm generates these coefficients and the mean squared errors $v_i = E\left(X_{i+1} - \hat{X}_{i+1}\right)^2$, starting from the covariances $\kappa(i, j)$.

The Innovations Algorithm:

The coefficients $\theta_{n1}, \ldots, \theta_{nn}$ can be computed recursively from the equations

$$v_0 = \kappa(1, 1),$$

$$\theta_{n,n-k} = v_k^{-1}\left(\kappa(n+1, k+1) - \sum_{j=0}^{k-1} \theta_{k,k-j}\theta_{n,n-j}v_j\right), \qquad 0 \le k < n,$$

and

$$v_n = \kappa(n+1, n+1) - \sum_{j=0}^{n-1} \theta_{n,n-j}^2 v_j.$$

(It is a trivial matter to solve first for v_0, then successively for $\theta_{11}, v_1; \theta_{22}, \theta_{21}, v_2; \theta_{33}, \theta_{32}, \theta_{31}, v_3; \ldots$.)

Proof See TSTM, Proposition 5.2.2. ■

Remark 5. While the Durbin–Levinson recursion gives the coefficients of $X_n, \ldots, X_1$ in the representation $\hat{X}_{n+1} = \sum_{j=1}^{n} \phi_{nj} X_{n+1-j}$, the innovations algorithm gives the coefficients of $\left(X_n - \hat{X}_n\right), \ldots, \left(X_1 - \hat{X}_1\right)$, in the expansion $\hat{X}_{n+1} = \sum_{j=1}^{n} \theta_{nj}\left(X_{n+1-j} - \hat{X}_{n+1-j}\right)$. The latter expansion has a number of advantages deriving from the fact that the innovations are uncorrelated (see Problem 2.20). It can also be greatly simplified in the case of ARMA(p, q) series, as we shall see in Section 3.3. An immediate consequence of (2.5.28) is the innovations representation of X_{n+1} itself. Thus (defining $\theta_{n0} := 1$),

$$X_{n+1} = X_{n+1} - \hat{X}_{n+1} + \hat{X}_{n+1} = \sum_{j=0}^{n} \theta_{nj}\left(X_{n+1-j} - \hat{X}_{n+1-j}\right), \qquad n = 0, 1, 2, \ldots. \quad \square$$

Example 2.5.5 Recursive prediction of an MA(1)

If $\{X_t\}$ is the time series defined by

$$X_t = Z_t + \theta Z_{t-1}, \{Z_t\} \sim \text{WN}\left(0, \sigma^2\right),$$

then $\kappa(i, j) = 0$ for $|i - j| > 1$, $\kappa(i, i) = \sigma^2\left(1 + \theta^2\right)$, and $\kappa(i, i+1) = \theta\sigma^2$. Application of the innovations algorithm leads at once to the recursions

$$\theta_{nj} = 0, 2 \le j \le n,$$

$$\theta_{n1} = v_{n-1}^{-1}\theta\sigma^2,$$

$$v_0 = (1 + \theta^2)\sigma^2,$$

and

$$v_n = \left[1 + \theta^2 - v_{n-1}^{-1}\theta^2\sigma^2\right]\sigma^2.$$

For the particular case

$$X_t = Z_t - 0.9Z_{t-1}, \quad \{Z_t\} \sim \text{WN}(0, 1),$$

the mean squared errors v_n of $\hat{X}_{n+1}$ and coefficients θ_{nj}, $1 \le j \le n$, in the innovations representation

$$\hat{X}_{n+1} = \sum_{j=1}^{n} \theta_{nj}\left(X_{n+1-j} - \hat{X}_{n+1-j}\right) = \theta_{n1}\left(X_n - \hat{X}_n\right)$$

are found from the recursions to be as follows:

$$\begin{array}{lllll}
v_0 = 1.8100, & & & & \\
\theta_{11} = -.4972, & v_1 = 1.3625, & & & \\
\theta_{21} = -.6606, & \theta_{22} = 0, & v_2 = 1.2155, & & \\
\theta_{31} = -.7404, & \theta_{32} = 0, & \theta_{33} = 0, & v_3 = 1.1436, & \\
\theta_{41} = -.7870, & \theta_{42} = 0, & \theta_{43} = 0, & \theta_{44} = 0, & v_4 = 1.1017.
\end{array}$$

If we apply the Durbin–Levinson algorithm to the same problem, we find that the mean squared errors v_n of $\hat{X}_{n+1}$ and coefficients ϕ_{nj}, $1 \le j \le n$, in the representation

$$\hat{X}_{n+1} = \sum_{j=1}^{n} \phi_{nj} X_{n+1-j}$$

are as follows:

$$\begin{array}{lllll}
v_0 = 1.8100, & & & & \\
\phi_{11} = -.4972, & v_1 = 1.3625, & & & \\
\phi_{21} = -.6606, & \phi_{22} = -.3285, & v_2 = 1.2155, & & \\
\phi_{31} = -.7404, & \phi_{32} = -.4892, & \phi_{33} = -.2433, & v_3 = 1.1436, & \\
\phi_{41} = -.7870, & \phi_{42} = -.5828, & \phi_{43} = -.3850, & \phi_{44} = -.1914, & v_4 = 1.1017.
\end{array}$$

Notice that as n increases, v_n approaches the white noise variance and θ_{n1} approaches θ. These results hold for any MA(1) process with $|\theta| < 1$. The innovations algorithm is particularly well suited to forecasting MA(q) processes, since for them $\theta_{nj} = 0$ for $n - j > q$. For AR(p) processes the Durbin–Levinson algorithm is usually more convenient, since $\phi_{nj} = 0$ for $n - j > p$. □

Recursive Calculation of the h-Step Predictors

For h-step prediction we use the result

$$P_n(X_{n+k} - P_{n+k-1}X_{n+k}) = 0, \quad k \ge 1. \tag{2.5.29}$$

This follows from (2.5.10) and the fact that

$$E[(X_{n+k} - P_{n+k-1}X_{n+k} - 0)X_{n+j-1}] = 0, \quad j = 1, \ldots, n.$$

Hence,

$$\begin{aligned} P_n X_{n+h} &= P_n P_{n+h-1} X_{n+h} \\ &= P_n \hat{X}_{n+h} \\ &= P_n \left(\sum_{j=1}^{n+h-1} \theta_{n+h-1,j} \left(X_{n+h-j} - \hat{X}_{n+h-j} \right) \right). \end{aligned}$$

Applying (2.5.29) again and using the linearity of P_n we find that

$$P_n X_{n+h} = \sum_{j=h}^{n+h-1} \theta_{n+h-1,j} \left(X_{n+h-j} - \hat{X}_{n+h-j} \right), \tag{2.5.30}$$

where the coefficients θ_{nj} are determined as before by the innovations algorithm. Moreover, the mean squared error can be expressed as

$$\begin{aligned} E(X_{n+h} - P_n X_{n+h})^2 &= E X_{n+h}^2 - E(P_n X_{n+h})^2 \\ &= \kappa(n+h, n+h) - \sum_{j=h}^{n+h-1} \theta_{n+h-1,j}^2 v_{n+h-j-1}. \end{aligned} \tag{2.5.31}$$

2.5.3 Prediction of a Stationary Process in Terms of Infinitely Many Past Values

It is often useful, when many past observations $X_m, \ldots, X_0, X_1, \ldots, X_n$ ($m < 0$) are available, to evaluate the best linear predictor of X_{n+h} in terms of $1, X_m, \ldots, X_0, \ldots, X_n$. This predictor, which we shall denote by $P_{m,n} X_{n+h}$, can easily be evaluated by the methods described above. If $|m|$ is large, this predictor can be approximated by the sometimes more easily calculated mean square limit

$$\tilde{P}_n X_{n+h} = \lim_{m \to -\infty} P_{m,n} X_{n+h}.$$

We shall refer to $\tilde{P}_n$ as the **prediction operator based on the infinite past, $\{X_t, -\infty < t \le n\}$**. Analogously we shall refer to P_n as the **prediction operator based on the finite past,** $\{X_1, \ldots, X_n\}$. (Mean square convergence of random variables is discussed in Appendix C.)

Determination of $\tilde{P}_n X_{n+h}$

Like $P_n X_{n+h}$, the best linear predictor $\tilde{P}_n X_{n+h}$ when $\{X_n\}$ is a zero-mean stationary process with autocovariance function $\gamma(\cdot)$ is characterized by the equations

$$E\left[\left(X_{n+h} - \tilde{P}_n X_{n+h} \right) X_{n+1-i} \right] = 0, \quad i = 1, 2, \ldots.$$

If we can find a solution to these equations, it will necessarily be the uniquely defined predictor $\tilde{P}_n X_{n+h}$. An approach to this problem that is often effective is to *assume* that $\tilde{P}_n X_{n+h}$ can be expressed in the form

$$\tilde{P}_n X_{n+h} = \sum_{j=1}^{\infty} \alpha_j X_{n+1-j},$$

in which case the preceding equations reduce to

$$E\left[\left(X_{n+h} - \sum_{j=1}^{\infty} \alpha_j X_{n+1-j}\right) X_{n+1-i}\right] = 0, \quad i = 1, 2, \ldots,$$

or equivalently,

$$\sum_{j=1}^{\infty} \gamma(i-j)\alpha_j = \gamma(h+i-1), \quad i = 1, 2, \ldots.$$

This is an infinite set of linear equations for the unknown coefficients α_i that determine $\tilde{P}_n X_{n+h}$, *provided that the resulting series converges.*

Properties of $\tilde{P}_n$:

Suppose that $EU^2 < \infty$, $EV^2 < \infty$, a, b, and c are constants, and $\Gamma = \text{Cov}(\mathbf{W}, \mathbf{W})$.

1. $E[(U - \tilde{P}_n(U))X_j] = 0$, $j \le n$.
2. $\tilde{P}_n(aU + bV + c) = a\tilde{P}_n(U) + b\tilde{P}_n(V) + c$.
3. $\tilde{P}_n(U) = U$ if U is a limit of linear combinations of X_j, $j \le n$.
4. $\tilde{P}_n(U) = EU$ if $\text{Cov}(U, X_j) = 0$ for all $j \le n$.

These properties can sometimes be used to simplify the calculation of $\tilde{P}_n X_{n+h}$, notably when the process $\{X_t\}$ is an ARMA process.

Example 2.5.7

Consider the causal invertible ARMA(1,1) process $\{X_t\}$ defined by

$$X_t - \phi X_{t-1} = Z_t + \theta Z_{t-1}, \quad \{Z_t\} \sim \text{WN}(0, \sigma^2).$$

We know from (2.3.3) and (2.3.5) that we have the representations

$$X_{n+1} = Z_{n+1} + (\phi + \theta) \sum_{j=1}^{\infty} \phi^{j-1} Z_{n+1-j}$$

and

$$Z_{n+1} = X_{n+1} - (\phi + \theta) \sum_{j=1}^{\infty} (-\theta)^{j-1} X_{n+1-j}.$$

Applying the operator $\tilde{P}_n$ to the second equation and using the properties of $\tilde{P}_n$ gives

$$\tilde{P}_n X_{n+1} = (\phi + \theta) \sum_{j=1}^{\infty} (-\theta)^{j-1} X_{n+1-j}.$$

Applying the operator $\tilde{P}_n$ to the first equation and using the properties of $\tilde{P}_n$ gives

$$\tilde{P}_n X_{n+1} = (\phi + \theta) \sum_{j=1}^{\infty} \phi^{j-1} Z_{n+1-j}.$$

Hence,

$$X_{n+1} - \tilde{P}_n X_{n+1} = Z_{n+1},$$

and so the mean squared error of the predictor $\tilde{P}_n X_{n+1}$ is $EZ_{n+1}^2 = \sigma^2$. □

2.6 The Wold Decomposition

Consider the stationary process

$$X_t = A\cos(\omega t) + B\sin(\omega t),$$

where $\omega \in (0, \pi)$ is constant and A, B are uncorrelated random variables with mean 0 and variance σ^2. Notice that

$$X_n = (2\cos\omega)X_{n-1} - X_{n-2} = \tilde{P}_{n-1}X_n, \quad n = 0, \pm 1, \ldots,$$

so that $X_n - \tilde{P}_{n-1}X_n = 0$ for all n. Processes with the latter property are said to be **deterministic**.

The Wold Decomposition:

If $\{X_t\}$ is a nondeterministic stationary time series, then

$$X_t = \sum_{j=0}^{\infty} \psi_j Z_{t-j} + V_t, \tag{2.6.1}$$

where

1. $\psi_0 = 1$ and $\sum_{j=0}^{\infty} \psi_j^2 < \infty$,
2. $\{Z_t\} \sim \mathrm{WN}\left(0, \sigma^2\right)$,
3. $\mathrm{Cov}(Z_s, V_t) = 0$ for all s and t,
4. $Z_t = \tilde{P}_t Z_t$ for all t,
5. $V_t = \tilde{P}_s V_t$ for all s and t, and
6. $\{V_t\}$ is deterministic.

Here as in Section 2.5, $\tilde{P}_t Y$ denotes the best predictor of Y in terms of linear combinations, or limits of linear combinations of $1, X_s, -\infty < s \leq t$. The sequences $\{Z_t\}$, $\{\psi_j\}$, and $\{V_t\}$ are unique and can be written explicitly as $Z_t = X_t - \tilde{P}_{t-1}X_t$, $\psi_j = E(X_t Z_{t-j})/E(Z_t^2)$, and $V_t = X_t - \sum_{j=0}^{\infty} \psi_j Z_{t-j}$. (See TSTM, p. 188.) For most of the zero-mean stationary time series dealt with in this book (in particular for all ARMA processes) the deterministic component V_t is 0 for all t, and the series is then said to be **purely nondeterministic**.

Example 2.6.1

If $X_t = U_t + Y$, where $\{U_t\} \sim \text{WN}\left(0, \nu^2\right)$, $E(U_t Y) = 0$ for all t, and Y has mean 0 and variance τ^2, then $\tilde{P}_{t-1}X_t = Y$, since Y is the mean square limit as $s \to \infty$ of $[X_{t-1} + \cdots + X_{t-s}]/s$, and $E[(X_t - Y)X_s] = 0$ for all $s \leq t-1$. Hence the sequences in the Wold decomposition of $\{X_t\}$ are given by $Z_t = U_t$, $\psi_0 = 1$, $\psi_j = 0$ for $j > 0$, and $V_t = Y$. □

Problems

2.1. Suppose that $X_1, X_2, \ldots,$ is a stationary time series with mean μ and ACF $\rho(\cdot)$. Show that the best predictor of X_{n+h} of the form $aX_n + b$ is obtained by choosing $a = \rho(h)$ and $b = \mu(1 - \rho(h))$.

2.2. Show that the process

$$X_t = A\cos(\omega t) + B\sin(\omega t), \quad t = 0, \pm 1, \ldots$$

(where A and B are uncorrelated random variables with mean 0 and variance 1 and ω is a fixed frequency in the interval $[0, \pi]$), is stationary and find its mean and autocovariance function. Deduce that the function $\kappa(h) = \cos(\omega h)$, $h = 0, \pm 1, \ldots,$ is nonnegative definite.

2.3. a. Find the ACVF of the time series $X_t = Z_t + .3Z_{t-1} - .4Z_{t-2}$, where $\{Z_t\} \sim \text{WN}(0, 1)$.

b. Find the ACVF of the time series $Y_t = \tilde{Z}_t - 1.2\tilde{Z}_{t-1} - 1.6\tilde{Z}_{t-2}$, where $\{\tilde{Z}_t\} \sim \text{WN}(0, .25)$. Compare with the answer found in (a).

2.4. It is clear that the function $\kappa(h) = 1, h = 0, \pm 1, \ldots,$ is an autocovariance function, since it is the autocovariance function of the process $X_t = Z, t = 0, \pm 1, \ldots,$ where Z is a random variable with mean 0 and variance 1. By identifying appropriate sequences of random variables, show that the following functions are also autocovariance functions:

(a) $\kappa(h) = (-1)^{|h|}$

(b) $\kappa(h) = 1 + \cos\left(\frac{\pi h}{2}\right) + \cos\left(\frac{\pi h}{4}\right)$

(c) $\kappa(h) = \begin{cases} 1, & \text{if } h = 0, \\ 0.4, & \text{if } h = \pm 1, \\ 0, & \text{otherwise.} \end{cases}$

2.5. Suppose that $\{X_t, t = 0, \pm 1, \ldots\}$ is stationary and that $|\theta| < 1$. Show that for each fixed n the sequence

$$S_m = \sum_{j=1}^{m} \theta^j X_{n-j}$$

is convergent absolutely and in mean square (see Appendix C) as $m \to \infty$.

2.6. Verify equations (2.2.6).

2.7. Show, using the geometric series $1/(1-x) = \sum_{j=0}^{\infty} x^j$ for $|x| < 1$, that $1/(1 - \phi z) = -\sum_{j=1}^{\infty} \phi^{-j} z^{-j}$ for $|\phi| > 1$ and $|z| \geq 1$.

2.8. Show that the autoregressive equations

$$X_t = \phi_1 X_{t-1} + Z_t, \quad t = 0, \pm 1, \ldots,$$

where $\{Z_t\} \sim \mathrm{WN}(0, \sigma^2)$ and $|\phi| = 1$, have *no stationary solution*. HINT: Suppose there does exist a stationary solution $\{X_t\}$ and use the autoregressive equation to derive an expression for the variance of $X_t - \phi_1^{n+1} X_{t-n-1}$ that contradicts the stationarity assumption.

2.9. Let $\{Y_t\}$ be the AR(1) plus noise time series defined by

$$Y_t = X_t + W_t,$$

where $\{W_t\} \sim \mathrm{WN}(0, \sigma_w^2)$, $\{X_t\}$ is the AR(1) process of Example 2.2.1, i.e.,

$$X_t - \phi X_{t-1} = Z_t, \{Z_t\} \sim \mathrm{WN}\left(0, \sigma_z^2\right),$$

and $E(W_s Z_t) = 0$ for all s and t.

a. Show that $\{Y_t\}$ is stationary and find its autocovariance function.

b. Show that the time series $U_t := Y_t - \phi Y_{t-1}$ is 1-correlated and hence, by Proposition 2.1.1, is an MA(1) process.

c. Conclude from (b) that $\{Y_t\}$ is an ARMA(1,1) process and express the three parameters of this model in terms of ϕ, σ_w^2, and σ_z^2.

2.10. Use the program ITSM to compute the coefficients ψ_j and π_j, $j = 1, \ldots, 5$, in the expansions

$$X_t = \sum_{j=0}^{\infty} \psi_j Z_{t-j}$$

and

$$Z_t = \sum_{j=0}^{\infty} \pi_j X_{t-j}$$

for the ARMA(1,1) process defined by the equations

$$X_t - 0.5X_{t-1} = Z_t + 0.5Z_{t-1}, \quad \{Z_t\} \sim \text{WN}\left(0, \sigma^2\right).$$

(Select `File>Project>New>Univariate`, then `Model>Specify`. In the resulting dialog box enter 1 for the AR and MA orders, specify $\phi(1) = \theta(1) = 0.5$, and click `OK`. Finally, select `Model>AR/MA Infinity>Default lag` and the values of ψ_j and π_j will appear on the screen.) Check the results with those obtained in Section 2.3.

2.11. Suppose that in a sample of size 100 from an AR(1) process with mean μ, $\phi = .6$, and $\sigma^2 = 2$ we obtain $\bar{x}_{100} = .271$. Construct an approximate 95% confidence interval for μ. Are the data compatible with the hypothesis that $\mu = 0$?

2.12. Suppose that in a sample of size 100 from an MA(1) process with mean μ, $\theta = -.6$, and $\sigma^2 = 1$ we obtain $\bar{x}_{100} = .157$. Construct an approximate 95% confidence interval for μ. Are the data compatible with the hypothesis that $\mu = 0$?

2.13. Suppose that in a sample of size 100, we obtain $\hat{\rho}(1) = .438$ and $\hat{\rho}(2) = .145$.

a. Assuming that the data were generated from an AR(1) model, construct approximate 95% confidence intervals for both $\rho(1)$ and $\rho(2)$. Based on these two confidence intervals, are the data consistent with an AR(1) model with $\phi = .8$?

b. Assuming that the data were generated from an MA(1) model, construct approximate 95% confidence intervals for both $\rho(1)$ and $\rho(2)$. Based on these two confidence intervals, are the data consistent with an MA(1) model with $\theta = .6$?

2.14. Let $\{X_t\}$ be the process defined in Problem 2.2.

a. Find $P_1 X_2$ and its mean squared error.

b. Find $P_2 X_3$ and its mean squared error.

c. Find $\tilde{P}_n X_{n+1}$ and its mean squared error.

2.15. Suppose that $\{X_t, t = 0, \pm 1, \ldots\}$ is a stationary process satisfying the equations

$$X_t = \phi_1 X_{t-1} + \cdots + \phi_p X_{t-p} + Z_t,$$

where $\{Z_t\} \sim \mathrm{WN}(0, \sigma^2)$ and Z_t is uncorrelated with X_s for each $s < t$. Show that the best linear predictor $P_n X_{n+1}$ of X_{n+1} in terms of $1, X_1, \ldots, X_n$, assuming $n > p$, is

$$P_n X_{n+1} = \phi_1 X_n + \cdots + \phi_p X_{n+1-p}.$$

What is the mean squared error of $P_n X_{n+1}$?

2.16. Use the program ITSM to plot the sample ACF and PACF up to lag 40 of the sunspot series $D_t, t = 1, 100$, contained in the ITSM file SUNSPOTS.TSM. (Open the project SUNSPOTS.TSM and click on the second yellow button at the top of the screen to see the graphs. Repeated clicking on this button will toggle between graphs of the sample ACF, sample PACF, and both. To see the numerical values, right-click on the graph and select `Info`.) Fit an AR(2) model to the mean-corrected data by selecting `Model>Estimation>Preliminary` and click `Yes` to subtract the sample mean from the data. In the dialog box that follows, enter 2 for the AR order and make sure that the MA order is zero and that the `Yule-Walker` algorithm is selected *without* AICC minimization. Click `OK` and you will obtain a model of the form

$$X_t = \phi_1 X_{t-1} + \phi_2 X_{t-2} + Z_t, \qquad \text{where } \{Z_t\} \sim \mathrm{WN}\left(0, \sigma^2\right),$$

for the mean-corrected series $X_t = D_t - 46.93$. Record the values of the estimated parameters ϕ_1, ϕ_2, and σ^2. Compare the model and sample ACF and PACF by selecting the third yellow button at the top of the screen. Print the graphs by right-clicking and selecting `Print`.

2.17. Without exiting from ITSM, use the model found in the preceding problem to compute forecasts of the next ten values of the sunspot series. (Select `Forecasting>ARMA`, make sure that the number of forecasts is set to 10 and the box `Add the mean to the forecasts` is checked, and then click `OK`. You will see a graph of the original data with the ten forecasts appended. Right-click on the graph and then on `Info` to get the numerical values of the forecasts. Print the graph as described in Problem 2.16.) The details of the calculations will be taken up in Chapter 3 when we discuss ARMA models in detail.

2.18. Let $\{X_t\}$ be the stationary process defined by the equations

$$X_t = Z_t - \theta Z_{t-1}, \quad t = 0, \pm 1, \ldots,$$

where $|\theta| < 1$ and $\{Z_t\} \sim \mathrm{WN}(0, \sigma^2)$. Show that the best linear predictor $\tilde{P}_n X_{n+1}$ of X_{n+1} based on $\{X_j, -\infty < j \le n\}$ is

$$\tilde{P}_n X_{n+1} = -\sum_{j=1}^{\infty} \theta^j X_{n+1-j}.$$

What is the mean squared error of the predictor $\tilde{P}_n X_{n+1}$?

2.19. If $\{X_t\}$ is defined as in Problem 2.18 and $\theta = 1$, find the best linear predictor $P_n X_{n+1}$ of X_{n+1} in terms of $X_1, \ldots, X_n$. What is the corresponding mean squared error?

2.20. In the innovations algorithm, show that for each $n \ge 2$, the innovation $X_n - \hat{X}_n$ is uncorrelated with $X_1, \ldots, X_{n-1}$. Conclude that $X_n - \hat{X}_n$ is uncorrelated with the innovations $X_1 - \hat{X}_1, \ldots, X_{n-1} - \hat{X}_{n-1}$.

2.21. Let X_1, X_2, X_4, X_5 be observations from the MA(1) model

$$X_t = Z_t + \theta Z_{t-1}, \quad \{Z_t\} \sim \mathrm{WN}\left(0, \sigma^2\right).$$

a. Find the best linear estimate of the missing value X_3 in terms of X_1 and X_2.

b. Find the best linear estimate of the missing value X_3 in terms of X_4 and X_5.

c. Find the best linear estimate of the missing value X_3 in terms of X_1, X_2, X_4, and X_5.

d. Compute the mean squared errors for each of the estimates in (a), (b), and (c).

2.22. Repeat parts (a)–(d) of Problem 2.21 assuming now that the observations X_1, X_2, X_4, X_5 are from the causal AR(1) model

$$X_t = \phi X_{t-1} + Z_t, \quad \{Z_t\} \sim \mathrm{WN}\left(0, \sigma^2\right).$$

3 ARMA Models

In this chapter we introduce an important parametric family of stationary time series, the autoregressive moving-average, or ARMA, processes. For a large class of autocovariance functions $\gamma(\cdot)$ it is possible to find an ARMA process $\{X_t\}$ with ACVF $\gamma_X(\cdot)$ such that $\gamma(\cdot)$ is well approximated by $\gamma_X(\cdot)$. In particular, for any positive integer K, there exists an ARMA process $\{X_t\}$ such that $\gamma_X(h) = \gamma(h)$ for $h = 0, 1, \ldots, K$. For this (and other) reasons, the family of ARMA processes plays a key role in the modeling of time series data. The linear structure of ARMA processes also leads to a substantial simplification of the general methods for linear prediction discussed earlier in Section 2.5.

3.1 ARMA(p, q) Processes

In Section 2.3 we introduced an ARMA(1,1) process and discussed some of its key properties. These included existence and uniqueness of stationary solutions of the defining equations and the concepts of causality and invertibility. In this section we extend these notions to the general ARMA(p, q) process.

Definition 3.1.1

$\{X_t\}$ is an **ARMA(p,q) process** if $\{X_t\}$ is stationary and if for every t,

$$X_t - \phi_1 X_{t-1} - \cdots - \phi_p X_{t-p} = Z_t + \theta_1 Z_{t-1} + \cdots + \theta_q Z_{t-q}, \qquad (3.1.1)$$

where $\{Z_t\} \sim \mathrm{WN}(0, \sigma^2)$ and the polynomials $(1 - \phi_1 z - \ldots - \phi_p z^p)$ and $(1 + \theta_1 z + \ldots + \theta_q z^q)$ have no common factors.

The process $\{X_t\}$ is said to be an **ARMA(p, q) process with mean μ** if $\{X_t - \mu\}$ is an ARMA(p, q) process.

It is convenient to use the more concise form of (3.1.1)

$$\phi(B)X_t = \theta(B)Z_t, \tag{3.1.2}$$

where $\phi(\cdot)$ and $\theta(\cdot)$ are the pth and qth-degree polynomials

$$\phi(z) = 1 - \phi_1 z - \cdots - \phi_p z^p$$

and

$$\theta(z) = 1 + \theta_1 z + \cdots + \theta_q z^q,$$

and B is the backward shift operator ($B^j X_t = X_{t-j}$, $B^j Z_t = Z_{t-j}$, $j = 0, \pm 1, \ldots$). The time series $\{X_t\}$ is said to be an **autoregressive process of order p** (or AR(p)) if $\theta(z) \equiv 1$, and a **moving-average process of order q** (or MA(q)) if $\phi(z) \equiv 1$.

An important part of Definition 3.1.1 is the requirement that $\{X_t\}$ be stationary. In Section 2.3 we showed, for the ARMA(1,1) equations (2.3.1), that a stationary solution exists (and is unique) if and only if $\phi_1 \neq \pm 1$. The latter is equivalent to the condition that the autoregressive polynomial $\phi(z) = 1 - \phi_1 z \neq 0$ for $z = \pm 1$. The analogous condition for the general ARMA(p, q) process is $\phi(z) = 1 - \phi_1 z - \cdots - \phi_p z^p \neq 0$ for all complex z with $|z| = 1$. (Complex z is used here, since the zeros of a polynomial of degree $p > 1$ may be either real or complex. The region defined by the set of complex z such that $|z| = 1$ is referred to as the unit circle.) If $\phi(z) \neq 0$ for all z on the unit circle, then there exists $\delta > 0$ such that

$$\frac{1}{\phi(z)} = \sum_{j=-\infty}^{\infty} \chi_j z^j \text{ for } 1 - \delta < |z| < 1 + \delta,$$

and $\sum_{j=-\infty}^{\infty} |\chi_j| < \infty$. We can then define $1/\phi(B)$ as the linear filter with absolutely summable coefficients

$$\frac{1}{\phi(B)} = \sum_{j=-\infty}^{\infty} \chi_j B^j.$$

Applying the operator $\chi(B) := 1/\phi(B)$ to both sides of (3.1.2), we obtain

$$X_t = \chi(B)\phi(B)X_t = \chi(B)\theta(B)Z_t = \psi(B)Z_t = \sum_{j=-\infty}^{\infty} \psi_j Z_{t-j}, \tag{3.1.3}$$

where $\psi(z) = \chi(z)\theta(z) = \sum_{j=-\infty}^{\infty} \psi_j z^j$. Using the argument given in Section 2.3 for the ARMA(1,1) process, it follows that $\psi(B)Z_t$ is the unique stationary solution of (3.1.1).

Existence and Uniqueness:

A stationary solution $\{X_t\}$ of equations (3.1.1) exists (and is also the unique stationary solution) if and only if

$$\phi(z) = 1 - \phi_1 z - \cdots - \phi_p z^p \neq 0 \quad \text{for all } |z| = 1. \tag{3.1.4}$$

In Section 2.3 we saw that the ARMA(1,1) process is causal, i.e., that X_t can be expressed in terms of Z_s, $s \le t$, if and only if $|\phi_1| < 1$. For a general ARMA(p, q) process the analogous condition is that $\phi(z) \neq 0$ for $|z| \le 1$, i.e., the zeros of the autoregressive polynomial must all be greater than 1 in absolute value.

Causality:

An ARMA(p, q) process $\{X_t\}$ is **causal**, or a **causal function of $\{Z_t\}$**, if there exist constants $\{\psi_j\}$ such that $\sum_{j=0}^{\infty} |\psi_j| < \infty$ and

$$X_t = \sum_{j=0}^{\infty} \psi_j Z_{t-j} \text{ for all } t. \tag{3.1.5}$$

Causality is equivalent to the condition

$$\phi(z) = 1 - \phi_1 z - \cdots - \phi_p z^p \neq 0 \text{ for all } |z| \le 1. \tag{3.1.6}$$

The proof of the equivalence between causality and (3.1.6) follows from elementary properties of power series. From (3.1.3) we see that $\{X_t\}$ is causal if and only if $\chi(z) := 1/\phi(z) = \sum_{j=0}^{\infty} \chi_j z^j$ (assuming that $\phi(z)$ and $\theta(z)$ have no common factors). But this, in turn, is equivalent to (3.1.6).

The sequence $\{\psi_j\}$ in (3.1.5) is determined by the relation $\psi(z) = \sum_{j=0}^{\infty} \psi_j z^j = \theta(z)/\phi(z)$, or equivalently by the identity

$$\left(1 - \phi_1 z - \cdots - \phi_p z^p\right)(\psi_0 + \psi_1 z + \cdots) = 1 + \theta_1 z + \cdots + \theta_q z^q.$$

Equating coefficients of z^j, $j = 0, 1, \ldots$, we find that

$$\begin{aligned} 1 &= \psi_0, \\ \theta_1 &= \psi_1 - \psi_0 \phi_1, \\ \theta_2 &= \psi_2 - \psi_1 \phi_1 - \psi_0 \phi_2, \\ &\vdots \end{aligned}$$

or equivalently,

$$\psi_j - \sum_{k=1}^{p} \phi_k \psi_{j-k} = \theta_j, \quad j = 0, 1, \ldots, \tag{3.1.7}$$

where $\theta_0 := 1, \theta_j := 0$ for $j > q$, and $\psi_j := 0$ for $j < 0$.

Invertibility, which allows Z_t to be expressed in terms of X_s, $s \le t$, has a similar characterization in terms of the moving-average polynomial.

Invertibility:

An ARMA(p,q) process $\{X_t\}$ is **invertible** if there exist constants $\{\pi_j\}$ such that $\sum_{j=0}^{\infty} |\pi_j| < \infty$ and

$$Z_t = \sum_{j=0}^{\infty} \pi_j X_{t-j} \text{ for all } t.$$

Invertibility is equivalent to the condition

$$\theta(z) = 1 + \theta_1 z + \cdots + \theta_q z^q \neq 0 \text{ for all } |z| \le 1.$$

Interchanging the roles of the AR and MA polynomials, we find from (3.1.7) that the sequence $\{\pi_j\}$ is determined by the equations

$$\pi_j + \sum_{k=1}^{q} \theta_k \pi_{j-k} = -\phi_j, \quad j = 0, 1, \ldots, \tag{3.1.8}$$

where $\phi_0 := -1, \phi_j := 0$ for $j > p$, and $\pi_j := 0$ for $j < 0$.

Example 3.1.1 An ARMA(1,1) process

Consider the ARMA(1,1) process $\{X_t\}$ satisfying the equations

$$X_t - .5X_{t-1} = Z_t + .4Z_{t-1}, \quad \{Z_t\} \sim \text{WN}\left(0, \sigma^2\right). \tag{3.1.9}$$

Since the autoregressive polynomial $\phi(z) = 1 - .5z$ has a zero at $z = 2$, which is located outside the unit circle, we conclude from (3.1.4) and (3.1.6) that there exists a unique ARMA process satisfying (3.1.9) that is also causal. The coefficients $\{\psi_j\}$ in the MA(∞) representation of $\{X_t\}$ are found directly from (3.1.7):

$$\psi_0 = 1,$$

$$\psi_1 = .4 + .5,$$

$$\psi_2 = .5(.4 + .5),$$

$$\psi_j = .5^{j-1}(.4 + .5), \quad j = 1, 2, \ldots.$$

The MA polynomial $\theta(z) = 1 + .4z$ has a zero at $z = -1/.4 = -2.5$, which is also located outside the unit circle. This implies that $\{X_t\}$ is invertible with coefficients

$\{\pi_j\}$ given by (see (3.1.8))

$$\pi_0 = 1,$$
$$\pi_1 = -(.4 + .5),$$
$$\pi_2 = -(.4 + .5)(-.4),$$
$$\pi_j = -(.4 + .5)(-.4)^{j-1}, \quad j = 1, 2, \ldots.$$

(A direct derivation of these formulas for $\{\psi_j\}$ and $\{\pi_j\}$ was given in Section 2.3 without appealing to the recursions (3.1.7) and (3.1.8).) □

Example 3.1.2 An AR(2) process

Let $\{X_t\}$ be the AR(2) process

$$X_t = .7X_{t-1} - .1X_{t-2} + Z_t, \quad \{Z_t\} \sim \mathrm{WN}\left(0, \sigma^2\right).$$

The autoregressive polynomial for this process has the factorization $\phi(z) = 1 - .7z + .1z^2 = (1 - .5z)(1 - .2z)$, and is therefore zero at $z = 2$ and $z = 5$. Since these zeros lie outside the unit circle, we conclude that $\{X_t\}$ is a causal AR(2) process with coefficients $\{\psi_j\}$ given by

$$\psi_0 = 1,$$
$$\psi_1 = .7,$$
$$\psi_2 = .7^2 - .1,$$
$$\psi_j = .7\psi_{j-1} - .1\psi_{j-2}, \quad j = 2, 3, \ldots.$$

While it is a simple matter to calculate ψ_j numerically for any j, it is possible also to give an explicit solution of these difference equations using the theory of linear difference equations (see TSTM, Section 3.6). □

The option `Model>Specify` of the program ITSM allows the entry of any causal ARMA(p, q) model with $p < 28$ and $q < 28$. This option contains a causality check and will immediately let you know if the entered model is noncausal. (A causal model can be obtained by setting all the AR coefficients equal to .001.) Oncc a causal model has been entered, the coefficients ψ_j in the MA(∞) representation of the process can be computed by selecting `Model>AR/MA Infinity`. This option will also compute the AR(∞) coefficients π_j, provided that the model is invertible.

Example 3.1.3 An ARMA(2,1) process

Consider the ARMA(2,1) process defined by the equations

$$X_t - .75X_{t-1} + .5625X_{t-2} = Z_t + 1.25Z_{t-1}, \quad \{Z_t\} \sim \mathrm{WN}\left(0, \sigma^2\right).$$

The AR polynomial $\phi(z) = 1 - .75z + .5625z^2$ has zeros at $z = 2\left(1 \pm i\sqrt{3}\right)/3$, which lie outside the unit circle. The process is therefore causal. On the other hand, the MA polynomial $\theta(z) = 1 + 1.25z$ has a zero at $z = -.8$, and hence $\{X_t\}$ is not invertible. □

Remark 1. It should be noted that causality and invertibility are properties not of $\{X_t\}$ alone, but rather of the relationship between the two processes $\{X_t\}$ and $\{Z_t\}$ appearing in the defining ARMA equations (3.1.1). □

Remark 2. If $\{X_t\}$ is an ARMA process defined by $\phi(B)X_t = \theta(B)Z_t$, where $\theta(z) \neq 0$ if $|z| = 1$, then it is always possible (see TSTM, p. 127) to find polynomials $\tilde{\phi}(z)$ and $\tilde{\theta}(z)$ and a white noise sequence $\{W_t\}$ such that $\tilde{\phi}(B)X_t = \tilde{\theta}(B)W_t$ and $\tilde{\theta}(z)$ and $\tilde{\phi}(z)$ are nonzero for $|z| \leq 1$. However, if the original white noise sequence $\{Z_t\}$ is iid, then the new white noise sequence will not be iid unless $\{Z_t\}$ is Gaussian. □

In view of the preceding remark, we will focus our attention principally on causal and invertible ARMA processes.

3.2 The ACF and PACF of an ARMA(*p*, *q*) Process

In this section we discuss three methods for computing the autocovariance function $\gamma(\cdot)$ of a causal ARMA process $\{X_t\}$. The autocorrelation function is readily found from the ACVF on dividing by $\gamma(0)$. The partial autocorrelation function (PACF) is also found from the function $\gamma(\cdot)$.

3.2.1 Calculation of the ACVF

First we determine the ACVF $\gamma(\cdot)$ of the causal ARMA(p, q) process defined by

$$\phi(B)X_t = \theta(B)Z_t, \quad \{Z_t\} \sim \mathrm{WN}\left(0, \sigma^2\right), \tag{3.2.1}$$

where $\phi(z) = 1 - \phi_1 z - \cdots - \phi_p z^p$ and $\theta(z) = 1 + \theta_1 z + \cdots + \theta_q z^q$. The causality assumption implies that

$$X_t = \sum_{j=0}^{\infty} \psi_j Z_{t-j}, \tag{3.2.2}$$

where $\sum_{j=0}^{\infty} \psi_j z^j = \theta(z)/\phi(z)$, $|z| \leq 1$. The calculation of the sequence $\{\psi_j\}$ was discussed in Section 3.1.

First Method. From Proposition 2.2.1 and the representation (3.2.2), we obtain

$$\gamma(h) = E(X_{t+h}X_t) = \sigma^2 \sum_{j=0}^{\infty} \psi_j \psi_{j+|h|}. \tag{3.2.3}$$

Example 3.2.1 The ARMA(1,1) process

Substituting from (2.3.3) into (3.2.3), we find that the ACVF of the process defined by

$$X_t - \phi X_{t-1} = Z_t + \theta Z_{t-1}, \quad \{Z_t\} \sim \text{WN}\left(0, \sigma^2\right), \tag{3.2.4}$$

with $|\phi| < 1$ is given by

$$\begin{aligned}
\gamma(0) &= \sigma^2 \sum_{j=0}^{\infty} \psi_j^2 \\
&= \sigma^2 \left[1 + (\theta + \phi)^2 \sum_{j=0}^{\infty} \phi^{2j} \right] \\
&= \sigma^2 \left[1 + \frac{(\theta + \phi)^2}{1 - \phi^2} \right], \\
\gamma(1) &= \sigma^2 \sum_{j=0}^{\infty} \psi_{j+1} \psi_j \\
&= \sigma^2 \left[\theta + \phi + (\theta + \phi)^2 \phi \sum_{j=0}^{\infty} \phi^{2j} \right] \\
&= \sigma^2 \left[\theta + \phi + \frac{(\theta + \phi)^2 \phi}{1 - \phi^2} \right],
\end{aligned}$$

and

$$\gamma(h) = \phi^{h-1} \gamma(1), \quad h \geq 2.$$

□

Example 3.2.2 The MA(q) process

For the process

$$X_t = Z_t + \theta_1 Z_{t-1} + \cdots + \theta_q Z_{t-q}, \quad \{Z_t\} \sim \text{WN}\left(0, \sigma^2\right),$$

equation (3.2.3) immediately gives the result

$$\gamma(h) = \begin{cases} \sigma^2 \sum_{j=0}^{q-|h|} \theta_j \theta_{j+|h|}, & \text{if } |h| \leq q, \\ 0, & \text{if } |h| > q, \end{cases}$$

where θ_0 is defined to be 1. The ACVF of the MA(q) process thus has the distinctive feature of vanishing at lags greater than q. Data for which the sample ACVF is small for lags greater than q therefore suggest that an appropriate model might be a moving average of order q (or less). Recall from Proposition 2.1.1 that *every* zero-mean stationary process with correlations vanishing at lags greater than q can be represented as a moving-average process of order q or less. □

Second Method. If we multiply each side of the equations

$$X_t - \phi_1 X_{t-1} - \cdots - \phi_p X_{t-p} = Z_t + \theta_1 Z_{t-1} + \cdots + \theta_q Z_{t-q},$$

by X_{t-k}, $k = 0, 1, 2, \ldots$, and take expectations on each side, we find that

$$\gamma(k) - \phi_1\gamma(k-1) - \cdots - \phi_p\gamma(k-p) = \sigma^2 \sum_{j=0}^{\infty} \theta_{k+j}\psi_j, \quad 0 \le k < m, \tag{3.2.5}$$

and

$$\gamma(k) - \phi_1\gamma(k-1) - \cdots - \phi_p\gamma(k-p) = 0, \quad k \ge m, \tag{3.2.6}$$

where $m = \max(p, q+1)$, $\psi_j := 0$ for $j < 0$, $\theta_0 := 1$, and $\theta_j := 0$ for $j \notin \{0, \ldots, q\}$. In calculating the right-hand side of (3.2.5) we have made use of the expansion (3.2.2). Equations (3.2.6) are a set of homogeneous linear difference equations with constant coefficients, for which the solution is well known (see, e.g., TSTM, Section 3.6) to be of the form

$$\gamma(h) = \alpha_1\xi_1^{-h} + \alpha_2\xi_2^{-h} + \cdots + \alpha_p\xi_p^{-h}, \quad h \ge m - p, \tag{3.2.7}$$

where $\xi_1, \ldots, \xi_p$ are the roots (assumed to be distinct) of the equation $\phi(z) = 0$, and $\alpha_1, \ldots, \alpha_p$ are arbitrary constants. (For further details, and for the treatment of the case where the roots are not distinct, see TSTM, Section 3.6.) Of course, we are looking for the solution of (3.2.6) that also satisfies (3.2.5). We therefore substitute the solution (3.2.7) into (3.2.5) to obtain a set of m linear equations that then uniquely determine the constants $\alpha_1, \ldots, \alpha_p$ and the $m - p$ autocovariances $\gamma(h)$, $0 \le h < m - p$.

Example 3.2.3 The ARMA(1,1) process

For the causal ARMA(1,1) process defined in Example 3.2.1, equations (3.2.5) are

$$\gamma(0) - \phi\gamma(1) = \sigma^2(1 + \theta(\theta + \phi)) \tag{3.2.8}$$

and

$$\gamma(1) - \phi\gamma(0) = \sigma^2\theta. \tag{3.2.9}$$

Equation (3.2.6) takes the form

$$\gamma(k) - \phi\gamma(k-1) = 0, \quad k \ge 2. \tag{3.2.10}$$

The solution of (3.2.10) is

$$\gamma(h) = \alpha\phi^h, \quad h \ge 1.$$

Substituting this expression for $\gamma(h)$ into the two preceding equations (3.2.8) and (3.2.9) gives two linear equations for α and the unknown autocovariance $\gamma(0)$. These equations are easily solved, giving the autocovariances already found for this process in Example 3.2.1. □

Example 3.2.4 The general AR(2) process

For the causal AR(2) process defined by

$$\left(1-\xi_1^{-1}B\right)\left(1-\xi_2^{-1}B\right)X_t = Z_t, \quad |\xi_1|, |\xi_2| > 1, \xi_1 \neq \xi_2,$$

we easily find from (3.2.7) and (3.2.5) using the relations

$$\phi_1 = \xi_1^{-1} + \xi_2^{-1}$$

and

$$\phi_2 = -\xi_1^{-1}\xi_2^{-1}$$

that

$$\gamma(h) = \frac{\sigma^2\xi_1^2\xi_2^2}{(\xi_1\xi_2 - 1)(\xi_2 - \xi_1)}\left[(\xi_1^2-1)^{-1}\xi_1^{1-h} - (\xi_2^2-1)^{-1}\xi_2^{1-h}\right]. \qquad (3.2.11)$$

Figures 3.1–3.4 illustrate some of the possible forms of $\gamma(\cdot)$ for different values of ξ_1 and ξ_2. Notice that in the case of complex conjugate roots $\xi_1 = re^{i\theta}$ and $\xi_2 = re^{-i\theta}$, $0 < \theta < \pi$, we can write (3.2.11) in the more illuminating form

$$\gamma(h) = \frac{\sigma^2 r^4 \cdot r^{-h}\sin(h\theta + \psi)}{(r^2-1)(r^4 - 2r^2\cos 2\theta + 1)\sin\theta}, \qquad (3.2.12)$$

where

$$\tan\psi = \frac{r^2+1}{r^2-1}\tan\theta \qquad (3.2.13)$$

and $\cos\psi$ has the same sign as $\cos\theta$. Thus in this case $\gamma(\cdot)$ has the form of a damped sinusoidal function with damping factor r^{-1} and period $2\pi/\theta$. If the roots are close to the unit circle, then r is close to 1, the damping is slow, and we obtain a nearly sinusoidal autocovariance function. □

Third Method. The autocovariances can also be found by solving the first $p+1$ equations of (3.2.5) and (3.2.6) for $\gamma(0)\ldots,\gamma(p)$ and then using the subsequent equations to solve successively for $\gamma(p+1), \gamma(p+2), \ldots$. This is an especially convenient method for numerical determination of the autocovariances $\gamma(h)$ and is used in the option `Model>ACF/PACF>Model` of the program ITSM.

Example 3.2.5

Consider again the causal ARMA(1,1) process of Example 3.2.1. To apply the third method we simply solve (3.2.8) and (3.2.9) for $\gamma(0)$ and $\gamma(1)$. Then $\gamma(2), \gamma(3), \ldots$

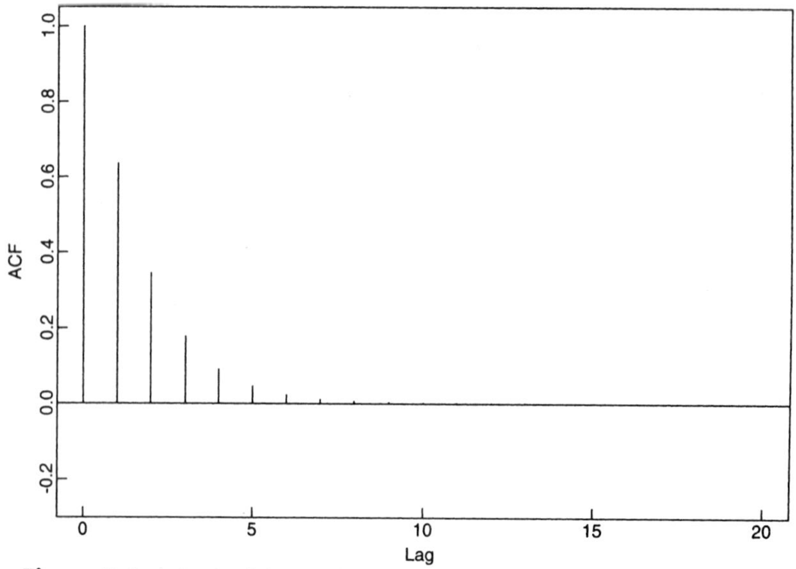

Figure 3-1 The model ACF of the AR(2) series of Example 3.2.4 with $\xi_1 = 2$ and $\xi_2 = 5$.

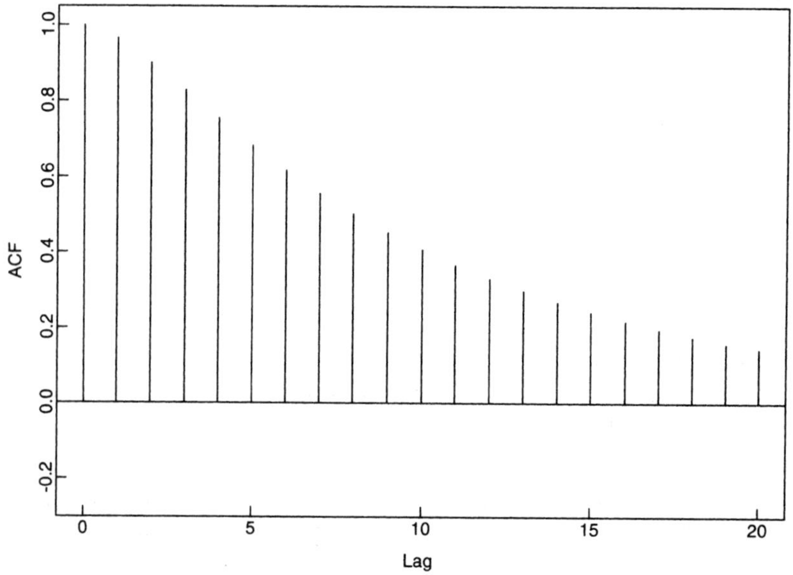

Figure 3-2 The model ACF of the AR(2) series of Example 3.2.4 with $\xi_1 = 10/9$ and $\xi_2 = 2$.

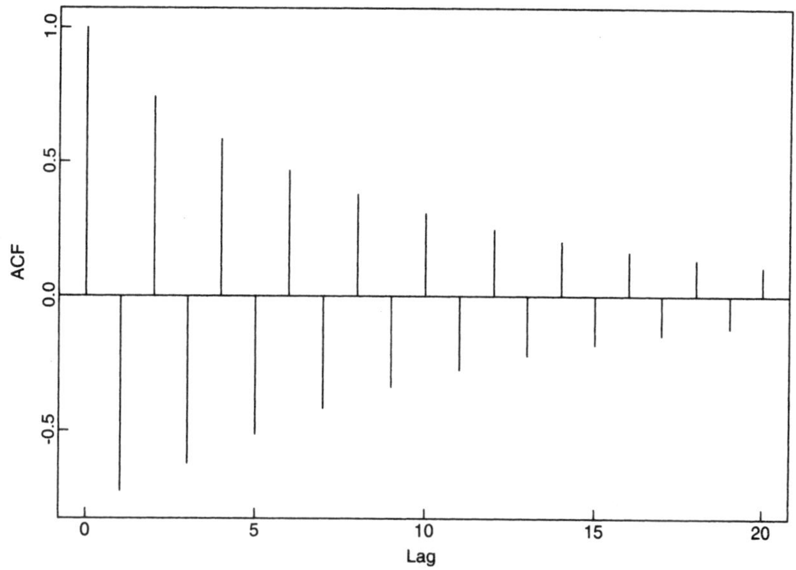

Figure 3-3 The model ACF of the AR(2) series of Example 3.2.4 with $\xi_1 = -10/9$ and $\xi_2 = 2$.

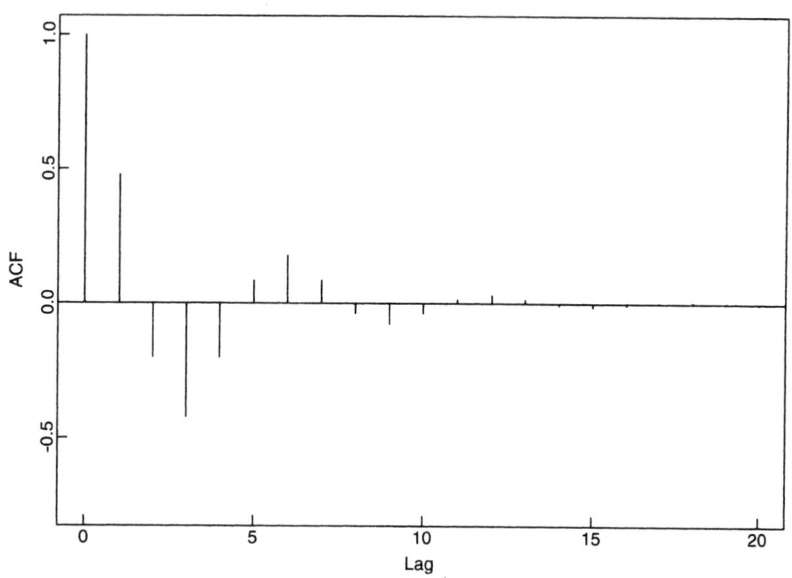

Figure 3-4 The model ACF of the AR(2) series of Example 3.2.4 with $\xi_1 = 2(1 + i\sqrt{3})/3$ and $\xi_2 = 2(1 - i\sqrt{3})/3$.

can be found successively from (3.2.10). It is easy to check that this procedure gives the same results as those obtained in Examples 3.2.1 and 3.2.3. □

3.2.2 The Autocorrelation Function

Recall that the ACF of an ARMA process $\{X_t\}$ is the function $\rho(\cdot)$ found immediately from the ACVF $\gamma(\cdot)$ as

$$\rho(h) = \frac{\gamma(h)}{\gamma(0)}.$$

Likewise, for any set of observations $\{x_1, \ldots, x_n\}$, the sample ACF $\hat{\rho}(\cdot)$ is computed as

$$\hat{\rho}(h) = \frac{\hat{\gamma}(h)}{\hat{\gamma}(0)}.$$

The Sample ACF of an MA(q) Series. Given observations $\{x_1, \ldots, x_n\}$ of a time series, one approach to the fitting of a model to the data is to match the sample ACF of the data with the ACF of the model. In particular, if the sample ACF $\hat{\rho}(h)$ is significantly different from zero for $0 \le h \le q$ and negligible for $h > q$, Example 3.2.2 suggests that an MA(q) model might provide a good representation of the data. In order to apply this criterion we need to take into account the random variation expected in the sample autocorrelation function before we can classify ACF values as "negligible." To resolve this problem we can use Bartlett's formula (Section 2.4), which implies that for a large sample of size n from an MA(q) process, the sample ACF values at lags greater than q are approximately normally distributed with means 0 and variances $w_{hh}/n = \left(1+2\rho^2(1)+\cdots+2\rho^2(q)\right)/n$. This means that if the sample is from an MA(q) process and if $h > q$, then $\hat{\rho}(h)$ should fall between the bounds $\pm 1.96\sqrt{w_{hh}/n}$ with probability approximately 0.95. In practice we frequently use the more stringent values $\pm 1.96/\sqrt{n}$ as the bounds between which sample autocovariances are considered "negligible." A more effective and systematic approach to the problem of model selection, which also applies to ARMA(p, q) models with $p > 0$ and $q > 0$, will be discussed in Section 5.5.

3.2.3 The Partial Autocorrelation Function

The **partial autocorrelation function (PACF)** of an ARMA process $\{X_t\}$ is the function $\alpha(\cdot)$ defined by the equations

$$\alpha(0) = 1$$

and

$$\alpha(h) = \phi_{hh}, \quad h \ge 1,$$

where ϕ_{hh} is the last component of

$$\boldsymbol{\phi}_h = \Gamma_h^{-1}\boldsymbol{\gamma}_h, \tag{3.2.14}$$

$\Gamma_h = [\gamma(i-j)]_{i,j=1}^h$, and $\boldsymbol{\gamma}_h = [\gamma(1), \gamma(2), \ldots, \gamma(h)]'$.

For any set of observations $\{x_1, \ldots, x_n\}$ with $x_i \neq x_j$ for some i and j, the **sample PACF** $\hat{\alpha}(h)$ is given by

$$\hat{\alpha}(0) = 1$$

and

$$\hat{\alpha}(h) = \hat{\phi}_{hh}, \quad h \geq 1,$$

where $\hat{\phi}_{hh}$ is the last component of

$$\hat{\boldsymbol{\phi}}_h = \hat{\Gamma}_h^{-1}\hat{\boldsymbol{\gamma}}_h. \tag{3.2.15}$$

We show in the next example that the PACF of a causal AR(p) process is zero for lags greater than p. Both sample and model partial autocorrelation functions can be computed numerically using the program ITSM. Algebraic calculation of the PACF is quite complicated except when q is zero or p and q are both small.

It can be shown (TSTM, p. 171) that ϕ_{hh} is the correlation between the prediction errors $X_h - P(X_h|X_1, \ldots, X_{h-1})$ and $X_0 - P(X_0|X_1, \ldots, X_{h-1})$.

Example 3.2.6 The PACF of an AR(p) process

For the causal AR(p) process defined by

$$X_t - \phi_1 X_{t-1} - \cdots - \phi_p X_{t-p} = Z_t, \quad \{Z_t\} \sim \mathrm{WN}\left(0, \sigma^2\right),$$

we know (Problem 2.15) that for $h \geq p$ the best linear predictor of X_{h+1} in terms of $1, X_1, \ldots, X_h$ is

$$\hat{X}_{h+1} = \phi_1 X_h + \phi_2 X_{h-1} + \cdots + \phi_p X_{h+1-p}.$$

Since the coefficient ϕ_{hh} of X_1 is ϕ_p if $h = p$ and 0 if $h > p$, we conclude that the PACF $\alpha(\cdot)$ of the process $\{X_t\}$ has the properties

$$\alpha(p) = \phi_p$$

and

$$\alpha(h) = 0 \text{ for } h > p.$$

For $h < p$ the values of $\alpha(h)$ can easily be computed from (3.2.14). For any specified ARMA model the PACF can be evaluated numerically using the option `Model>ACF/PACF>Model` of the program ITSM. □

Example 3.2.7 The PACF of an MA(1) process

For the MA(1) process, it can be shown from (3.2.14) (see Problem 3.12) that the PACF at lag h is

$$\alpha(h) = \phi_{hh} = -(-\theta)^h / \left(1 + \theta^2 + \cdots + \theta^{2h}\right). \qquad \square$$

The Sample PACF of an AR(p) Series. If $\{X_t\}$ is an AR(p) series, then the sample PACF based on observations $\{x_1, \ldots, x_n\}$ should reflect (with sampling variation) the properties of the PACF itself. In particular, if the sample PACF $\hat{\alpha}(h)$ is significantly different from zero for $0 \le h \le p$ and negligible for $h > p$, Example 3.2.6 suggests that an AR(p) model might provide a good representation of the data. To decide what is meant by "negligible" we can use the result that for an AR(p) process the sample PACF values at lags greater than p are approximately independent $N(0, 1/n)$ random variables. This means that roughly 95% of the sample PACF values beyond lag p should fall within the bounds $\pm 1.96/\sqrt{n}$. If we observe a sample PACF satisfying $|\hat{\alpha}(h)| > 1.96/\sqrt{n}$ for $0 \le h \le p$ and $|\hat{\alpha}(h)| < 1.96/\sqrt{n}$ for $h > p$, this suggests an AR(p) model for the data. For a more systematic approach to model selection, see Section 5.5.

3.2.4 Examples

Example 3.2.8

The time series plotted in Figure 3.5 consists of 57 consecutive daily *overshorts* from an underground gasoline tank at a filling station in Colorado. If y_t is the measured amount of fuel in the tank at the end of the tth day and a_t is the measured amount sold minus the amount delivered during the course of the tth day, then the overshort at the end of day t is defined as $x_t = y_t - y_{t-1} + a_t$. Due to the error in measuring the current amount of fuel in the tank, the amount sold, and the amount delivered to the station, we view y_t, a_t, and x_t as observed values from some set of random variables Y_t, A_t, and X_t for $t = 1, \ldots, 57$. (In the absence of any measurement error and any leak in the tank, each x_t would be zero.) The data and their ACF are plotted in Figures 3.5 and 3.6. To check the plausibility of an MA(1) model, the bounds $\pm 1.96\left(1 + 2\hat{\rho}^2(1)\right)^{1/2} / n^{1/2}$ are also plotted in Figure 3.6. Since $\hat{\rho}(h)$ is well within these bounds for $h > 1$, the data appear to be compatible with the model

$$X_t = \mu + Z_t + \theta Z_{t-1}, \quad \{Z_t\} \sim \text{WN}\left(0, \sigma^2\right). \tag{3.2.16}$$

The mean μ may be estimated by the sample mean $\bar{x}_{57} = -4.035$, and the parameters θ, σ^2 may be estimated by equating the sample ACVF with the model ACVF at lags 0 and 1, and solving the resulting equations for θ and σ^2. This estimation procedure is known as the method of moments, and in this case gives the equations

$$(1 + \theta^2)\sigma^2 = \hat{\gamma}(0) = 3415.72,$$

$$\theta\sigma^2 = \hat{\gamma}(1) = -1719.95.$$

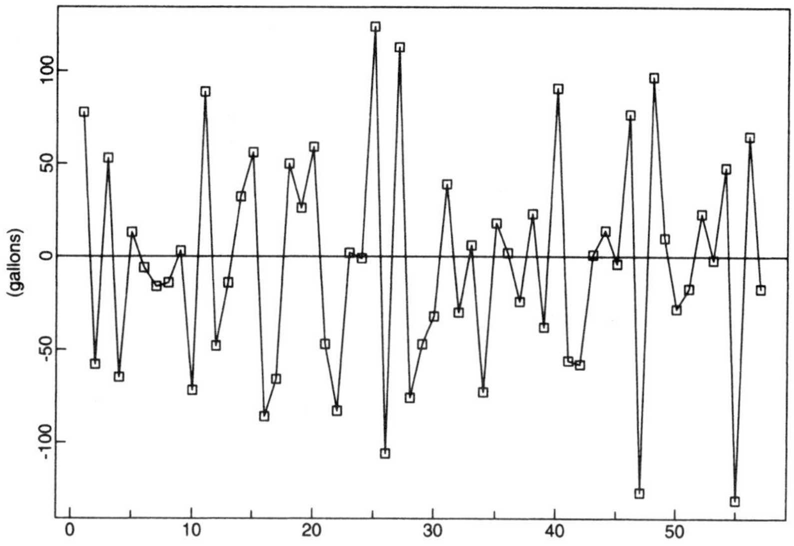

Figure 3-5 Time series of the overshorts in Example 3.2.8.

Using the approximate solution $\theta = -1$ and $\sigma^2 = 1708$, we obtain the noninvertible MA(1) model

$$X_t = -4.035 + Z_t - Z_{t-1}, \quad \{Z_t\} \sim \text{WN}(0, 1708).$$

Typically, in time series modeling we have little or no knowledge of the underlying physical mechanism generating the data, and the choice of a suitable class of models

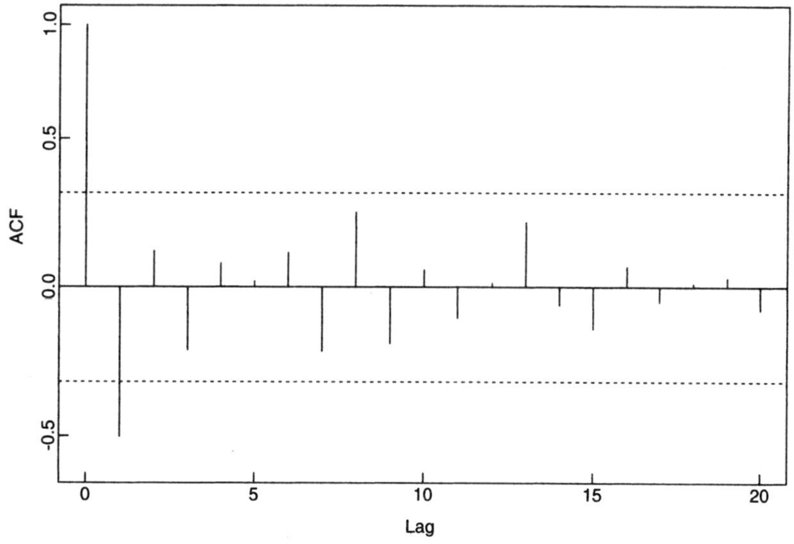

Figure 3-6 The sample ACF of the data in Figure 3.5 showing the bounds $\pm 1.96 n^{-1/2}\left(1 + 2\hat{\rho}^2(1)\right)^{1/2}$ assuming an MA(1) model for the data.

is entirely data driven. For the time series of overshorts, the data, through the graph of the ACF, lead us to the MA(1) model. Alternatively, we can attempt to model the mechanism generating the time series of overshorts using a *structural model*. As we will see, the structural model formulation leads us again to the MA(1) model. In the structural model setup, write Y_t, the observed amount of fuel in the tank at time t, as

$$Y_t = y_t^* + U_t, \tag{3.2.17}$$

where y_t^* is the true (or actual) amount of fuel in the tank at time t (not to be confused with y_t above) and U_t is the resulting *measurement error*. The variable y_t^* is an idealized quantity that in principle cannot be observed even with the most sophisticated measurement devices. Similarly, we assume that

$$A_t = a_t^* + V_t, \tag{3.2.18}$$

where a_t^* is the actual amount of fuel sold minus the actual amount delivered during day t, and V_t is the associated measurement error. We further assume that $\{U_t\} \sim \text{WN}(0, \sigma_U^2)$, $\{V_t\} \sim \text{WN}(0, \sigma_V^2)$, and that the two sequences $\{U_t\}$ and $\{V_t\}$ are uncorrelated with one another ($E(U_t V_s) = 0$ for all s and t). If the change of level per day due to leakage is μ gallons ($\mu < 0$ indicates leakage), then

$$y_t^* = \mu + y_{t-1}^* - a_t^*. \tag{3.2.19}$$

This equation relates the actual amounts of fuel in the tank at the end of days t and $t-1$, adjusted for the actual amounts that have been sold and delivered during the day. Using (3.2.17)–(3.2.19), the model for the time series of overshorts is given by

$$X_t = Y_t - Y_{t-1} + A_t = \mu + U_t - U_{t-1} + V_t.$$

This model is stationary and 1-correlated, since

$$EX_t = E(\mu + U_t - U_{t-1} + V_t) = \mu$$

and

$$\begin{aligned}\gamma(h) &= E[(X_{t+h} - \mu)(X_t - \mu)] \\ &= E[(U_{t+h} - U_{t+h-1} + V_{t+h})(U_t - U_{t-1} + V_t)] \\ &= \begin{cases} 2\sigma_U^2 + \sigma_V^2, & \text{if } h = 0, \\ -\sigma_U^2, & \text{if } |h| = 1, \\ 0, & \text{otherwise.} \end{cases}\end{aligned}$$

It follows from Proposition 2.1.1 that $\{X_t\}$ is the MA(1) model (3.2.16) with

$$\rho(1) = \frac{\theta_1}{1+\theta_1^2} = \frac{-\sigma_U^2}{2\sigma_U^2 + \sigma_V^2}.$$

From this equation we see that the measurement error associated with the adjustment $\{A_t\}$ is zero (i.e., $\sigma_V^2 = 0$) if and only if $\rho(1) = -.5$ or, equivalently, if and only if $\theta_1 = -1$. From the analysis above, the moment estimator of θ_1 for the overshort data is in fact -1, so that we conclude that there is relatively little measurement error associated with the amount of fuel sold and delivered.

We shall return to a more general discussion of structural models in Chapter 8. □

Example 3.2.9 The sunspot numbers

Figure 3.7 shows the sample PACF of the sunspot numbers $S_1, \ldots, S_{100}$ (for the years 1770 – 1869) as obtained from ITSM by opening the project SUNSPOTS.TSM and clicking on the second yellow button at the top of the screen. The graph also shows the bounds $\pm 1.96/\sqrt{100}$. The fact that all of the PACF values beyond lag 2 fall within the bounds suggests the possible suitability of an AR(2) model for the mean-corrected data set $X_t = S_t - 46.93$. One simple way to estimate the parameters ϕ_1, ϕ_2, and σ^2 of such a model is to require that the ACVF of the model at lags 0, 1, and 2 should match the sample ACVF at those lags. Substituting the sample ACVF values

$$\hat{\gamma}(0) = 1382.2, \quad \hat{\gamma}(1) = 1114.4, \quad \hat{\gamma}(2) = 591.73,$$

for $\gamma(0)$, $\gamma(1)$, and $\gamma(2)$ in the first three equations of (3.2.5) and (3.2.6) and solving for ϕ_1, ϕ_2, and σ^2 gives the fitted model

$$X_t - 1.318X_{t-1} + 0.634X_{t-2} = Z_t, \quad \{Z_t\} \sim \mathrm{WN}(0, 289.2). \tag{3.2.20}$$

(This method of model fitting is called Yule–Walker estimation and will be discussed more fully in Section 5.1.1.) □

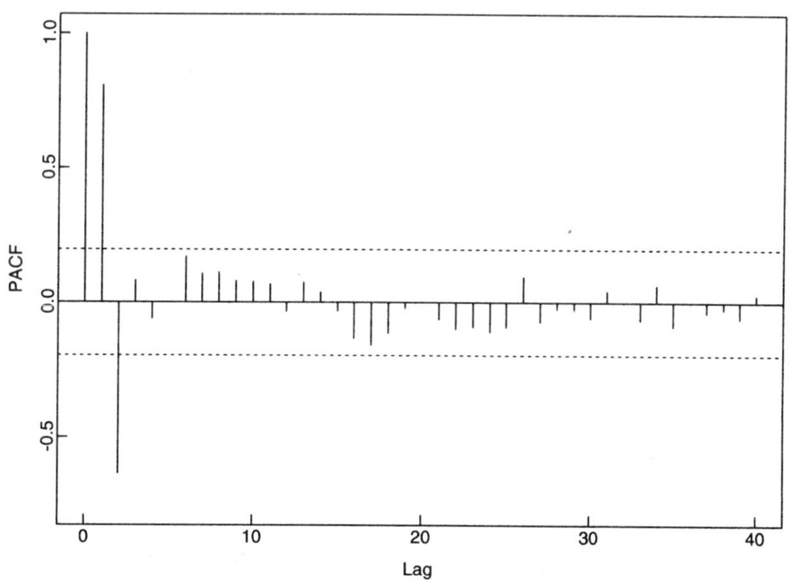

Figure 3-7 The sample PACF of the sunspot numbers with the bounds $\pm 1.96/\sqrt{100}$.

3.3 Forecasting ARMA Processes

The innovations algorithm (see Section 2.5.2) provided us with a recursive method for forecasting second-order zero-mean processes that are not necessarily stationary. For the causal ARMA process

$$\phi(B)X_t = \theta(B)Z_t, \quad \{Z_t\} \sim \mathrm{WN}\left(0, \sigma^2\right),$$

it is possible to simplify the application of the algorithm drastically. The idea is to apply it not to the process $\{X_t\}$ itself, but to the transformed process (cf. Ansley, 1979)

$$\begin{cases} W_t = \sigma^{-1}X_t, & t = 1, \ldots, m, \\ W_t = \sigma^{-1}\phi(B)X_t, & t > m, \end{cases} \tag{3.3.1}$$

where

$$m = \max(p, q). \tag{3.3.2}$$

For notational convenience we define $\theta_0 := 1$ and $\theta_j := 0$ for $j > q$. We shall also assume that $p \geq 1$ and $q \geq 1$. (There is no loss of generality in these assumptions, since in the analysis that follows we may take any of the coefficients ϕ_i and θ_i to be zero.)

The autocovariance function $\gamma_X(\cdot)$ of $\{X_t\}$ can easily be computed using any of the methods described in Section 3.2.1. The autocovariances $\kappa(i, j) = E(W_i W_j)$, $i, j \geq 1$, are then found from

$$\kappa(i,j) = \begin{cases} \sigma^{-2}\gamma_X(i-j), & 1 \leq i, j \leq m \\ \sigma^{-2}\left[\gamma_X(i-j) - \sum_{r=1}^{p}\phi_r\gamma_X(r-|i-j|)\right], & \min(i,j) \leq m < \max(i,j) \leq 2m, \\ \sum_{r=0}^{q}\theta_r\theta_{r+|i-j|}, & \min(i,j) > m, \\ 0, & \text{otherwise.} \end{cases} \tag{3.3.3}$$

Applying the innovations algorithm to the process $\{W_t\}$ we obtain

$$\begin{cases} \hat{W}_{n+1} = \sum_{j=1}^{n}\theta_{nj}(W_{n+1-j} - \hat{W}_{n+1-j}), & 1 \leq n < m, \\ \hat{W}_{n+1} = \sum_{j=1}^{q}\theta_{nj}(W_{n+1-j} - \hat{W}_{n+1-j}), & n \geq m, \end{cases} \tag{3.3.4}$$

where the coefficients θ_{nj} and the mean squared errors $r_n = E\left(W_{n+1} - \hat{W}_{n+1}\right)^2$ are found recursively from the innovations algorithm with κ defined as in (3.3.3). The notable feature of the predictors (3.3.4) is the vanishing of θ_{nj} when both $n \geq m$ and

$j > q$. This is a consequence of the innovations algorithm and the fact that $\kappa(r, s) = 0$ if $r > m$ and $|r - s| > q$.

Observe now that equations (3.3.1) allow each X_n, $n \geq 1$, to be written as a linear combination of W_j, $1 \leq j \leq n$, and, conversely, each W_n, $n \geq 1$, to be written as a linear combination of X_j, $1 \leq j \leq n$. This means that the best linear predictor of any random variable Y in terms of $\{1, X_1, \ldots, X_n\}$ is the same as the best linear predictor of Y in terms of $\{1, W_1, \ldots, W_n\}$. We shall denote this predictor by $P_n Y$. In particular, the one-step predictors of W_{n+1} and X_{n+1} are given by

$$\hat{W}_{n+1} = P_n W_{n+1}$$

and

$$\hat{X}_{n+1} = P_n X_{n+1}.$$

Using the linearity of P_n and equations (3.3.1) we see that

$$\begin{cases} \hat{W}_t = \sigma^{-1} \hat{X}_t, & t = 1, \ldots, m, \\ \hat{W}_t = \sigma^{-1} \left[\hat{X}_t - \phi_1 X_{t-1} - \cdots - \phi_p X_{t-p} \right], & t > m, \end{cases} \tag{3.3.5}$$

which, together with (3.3.1), shows that

$$X_t - \hat{X}_t = \sigma \left[W_t - \hat{W}_t \right] \quad \text{for all } t \geq 1. \tag{3.3.6}$$

Replacing $(W_j - \hat{W}_j)$ by $\sigma^{-1}(X_j - \hat{X}_j)$ in (3.3.3) and then substituting into (3.3.4), we finally obtain

$$\hat{X}_{n+1} = \begin{cases} \sum_{j=1}^{n} \theta_{nj} \left(X_{n+1-j} - \hat{X}_{n+1-j} \right), & 1 \leq n < m, \\ \phi_1 X_n + \cdots + \phi_p X_{n+1-p} + \sum_{j=1}^{q} \theta_{nj} \left(X_{n+1-j} - \hat{X}_{n+1-j} \right), & n \geq m, \end{cases} \tag{3.3.7}$$

and

$$E \left(X_{n+1} - \hat{X}_{n+1} \right)^2 = \sigma^2 E \left(W_{n+1} - \hat{W}_{n+1} \right)^2 = \sigma^2 r_n, \tag{3.3.8}$$

where θ_{nj} and r_n are found from the innovations algorithm with κ as in (3.3.3). Equations (3.3.7) determine the one-step predictors $\hat{X}_2, \hat{X}_3, \ldots$ recursively.

Remark 1. It can be shown (see TSTM, Problem 5.6) that if $\{X_t\}$ is invertible, then as $n \to \infty$,

$$E \left(X_n - \hat{X}_n - Z_n \right)^2 \to 0,$$

$$\theta_{nj} \to \theta_j, \; j = 1, \ldots, q,$$

and

$$r_n \to 1.$$

Algebraic calculation of the coefficients θ_{nj} and r_n is not feasible except for very simple models, such as those considered in the following examples. However, numerical implementation of the recursions is quite straightforward and is used to compute predictors in the program ITSM. □

Example 3.3.1 Prediction of an AR(p) process

Applying (3.3.7) to the ARMA(p, 1) process with $\theta_1 = 0$, we easily find that

$$\hat{X}_{n+1} = \phi_1 X_n + \cdots + \phi_p X_{n+1-p}, \quad n \geq p. \qquad \square$$

Example 3.3.2 Prediction of an MA(q) process

Applying (3.3.7) to the ARMA($1, q$) process with $\phi_1 = 0$ gives

$$\hat{X}_{n+1} = \sum_{j=1}^{\min(n,q)} \theta_{nj} \left(X_{n+1-j} - \hat{X}_{n+1-j} \right), \quad n \geq 1,$$

where the coefficients θ_{nj} are found by applying the innovations algorithm to the covariances $\kappa(i, j)$ defined in (3.3.3). Since in this case the processes $\{X_t\}$ and $\{\sigma^{-1} W_t\}$ are identical, these covariances are simply

$$\kappa(i, j) = \sigma^{-2} \gamma_X(i - j) = \sum_{r=0}^{q-|i-j|} \theta_r \theta_{r+|i-j|}. \qquad \square$$

Example 3.3.3 Prediction of an ARMA(1,1) process

If

$$X_t - \phi X_{t-1} = Z_t + \theta Z_{t-1}, \quad \{Z_t\} \sim \mathrm{WN}\left(0, \sigma^2\right),$$

and $|\phi| < 1$, then equations (3.3.7) reduce to the single equation

$$\hat{X}_{n+1} = \phi X_n + \theta_{n1}(X_n - \hat{X}_n), \quad n \geq 1.$$

To compute θ_{n1} we first use Example 3.2.1 to find that $\gamma_X(0) = \sigma^2 \left(1 + 2\theta\phi + \theta^2\right) / (1 - \phi^2)$. Substituting in (3.3.3) then gives, for $i, j \geq 1$,

$$\kappa(i, j) = \begin{cases} \left(1 + 2\theta\phi + \theta^2\right) / \left(1 - \phi^2\right), & i = j = 1, \\ 1 + \theta^2, & i = j \geq 2, \\ \theta, & |i - j| = 1, i \geq 1, \\ 0, & \text{otherwise.} \end{cases}$$

With these values of $\kappa(i, j)$, the recursions of the innovations algorithm reduce to

$$\begin{aligned} r_0 &= \left(1 + 2\theta\phi + \theta^2\right) / \left(1 - \phi^2\right), \\ \theta_{n1} &= \theta / r_{n-1}, \\ r_n &= 1 + \theta^2 - \theta^2 / r_{n-1}, \end{aligned} \tag{3.3.9}$$

which can be solved quite explicitly (see Problem 3.13). □

Example 3.3.4 Numerical prediction of an ARMA(2,3) process

In this example we illustrate the steps involved in numerical prediction of an ARMA(2,3) process. Of course, these steps are shown for illustration only. The calculations are all carried out automatically by ITSM in the course of computing predictors for any specified data set and ARMA model. The process we shall consider is the ARMA process defined by the equations

$$X_t - X_{t-1} + 0.24X_{t-2} = Z_t + 0.4Z_{t-1} + 0.2Z_{t-2} + 0.1Z_{t-3}, \tag{3.3.10}$$

where $\{Z_t\} \sim \mathrm{WN}(0, 1)$. Ten values of $X_1, \ldots, X_{10}$ simulated by the program ITSM are shown in Table 3.1. (These were produced using the option `Model>Specify` to specify the order and parameters of the model and then `Model>Simulate` to generate the series from the specified model.)

The first step is to compute the covariances $\gamma_X(h)$, $h = 0, 1, 2$, which are easily found from equations (3.2.5) with $k = 0, 1, 2$ to be

$$\gamma_X(0) = 7.17133, \quad \gamma_X(1) = 6.44139, \quad \text{and} \quad \gamma_X(2) = 5.0603.$$

From (3.3.3) we find that the symmetric matrix $K = [\kappa(i, j)]_{i,j=1,2,\ldots}$ is given by

$$K = \begin{bmatrix} 7.1713 & & & & & & & & \\ 6.4414 & 7.1713 & & & & & & & \\ 5.0603 & 6.4414 & 7.1713 & & & & & & \\ 0.10 & 0.34 & 0.816 & 1.21 & & & & & \\ 0 & 0.10 & 0.34 & 0.50 & 1.21 & & & & \\ 0 & 0 & 0.10 & 0.24 & 0.50 & 1.21 & & & \\ \cdot & 0 & 0 & 0.10 & 0.24 & 0.50 & 1.21 & & \\ \cdot & \cdot & 0 & 0 & 0.10 & 0.24 & 0.50 & 1.21 & \\ \cdot & \cdot & \cdot & \cdot & \cdot & \cdot & \cdot & \cdot & \cdot \end{bmatrix}.$$

The next step is to solve the recursions of the innovations algorithm for θ_{nj} and r_n using these values for $\kappa(i, j)$. Then

$$\hat{X}_{n+1} = \begin{cases} \displaystyle\sum_{j=1}^{n} \theta_{nj} \left(X_{n+1-j} - \hat{X}_{n+1-j}\right), & n = 1, 2, \\ \displaystyle X_n - 0.24X_{n-1} + \sum_{j=1}^{3} \theta_{nj} \left(X_{n+1-j} - \hat{X}_{n+1-j}\right), & n = 3, 4, \ldots, \end{cases}$$

and

$$E\left(X_{n+1} - \hat{X}_{n+1}\right)^2 = \sigma^2 r_n = r_n.$$

The results are shown in Table 3.1. □

h-Step Prediction of an ARMA(p, q) Process

As in Section 2.5, we use $P_n Y$ to denote the best linear predictor of Y in terms of $X_1, \ldots, X_n$ (which, as pointed out after (3.3.4), is the same as the best linear predictor of Y in terms of $W_1, \ldots, W_n$). Then from (2.5.30) we have

$$P_n W_{n+h} = \sum_{j=h}^{n+h-1} \theta_{n+h-1,j}\left(W_{n+h-j} - \hat{W}_{n+h-j}\right) = \sigma^2 \sum_{j=h}^{n+h-1} \theta_{n+h-1,j}\left(X_{n+h-j} - \hat{X}_{n+h-j}\right).$$

Using this result and applying the operator P_n to each side of equations (3.3.1), we conclude that the h-step predictors $P_n X_{n+h}$ satisfy

$$P_n X_{n+h} = \begin{cases} \displaystyle\sum_{j=h}^{n+h-1} \theta_{n+h-1,j}\left(X_{n+h-j} - \hat{X}_{n+h-j}\right), & 1 \le h \le m-n, \\ \displaystyle\sum_{i=1}^{p} \phi_i P_n X_{n+h-i} + \sum_{j=h}^{n+h-1} \theta_{n+h-1,j}\left(X_{n+h-j} - \hat{X}_{n+h-j}\right), & h > m-n. \end{cases} \tag{3.3.11}$$

If, as is almost always the case, $n > m = \max(p, q)$, then for all $h \ge 1$,

$$P_n X_{n+h} = \sum_{i=1}^{p} \phi_i P_n X_{n+h-i} + \sum_{j=h}^{q} \theta_{n+h-1,j}\left(X_{n+h-j} - \hat{X}_{n+h-j}\right). \tag{3.3.12}$$

Once the predictors $\hat{X}_1, \ldots \hat{X}_n$ have been computed from (3.3.7), it is a straightforward calculation, with n fixed, to determine the predictors $P_n X_{n+1}, P_n X_{n+2}, P_n X_{n+3}, \ldots$

Table 3.1 $\hat{X}_{n+1}$ for the ARMA(2,3) Process of Example 3.3.4.

n	X_{n+1}	r_n	θ_{n1}	θ_{n2}	θ_{n3}	$\hat{X}_{n+1}$
0	1.704	7.1713	0			
1	0.527	1.3856	0.8982	1.5305		
2	1.041	1.0057	1.3685	0.7056	−0.1710	
3	0.942	1.0019	0.4008	0.1806	0.0139	1.2428
4	0.555	1.0019	0.3998	0.2020	0.0732	0.7443
5	−1.002	1.0005	0.3992	0.1995	0.0994	0.3138
6	−0.585	1.0000	0.4000	0.1997	0.0998	−1.7293
7	0.010	1.0000	0.4000	0.2000	0.0998	−0.1688
8	−0.638	1.0000	0.4000	0.2000	0.0999	0.3193
9	0.525	1.0000	0.4000	0.2000	0.1000	−0.8731
10	1.0000	0.4000	0.2000	0.1000	1.0638	
11	1.0000	0.4000	0.2000	0.1000		
12	1.0000	0.4000	0.2000	0.1000		

recursively from (3.3.12) (or (3.3.11) if $n \le m$). The calculations are performed automatically in the Forecasting>ARMA option of the program ITSM.

Example 3.3.5 *h*-step prediction of an ARMA(2,3) process

To compute h-step predictors, $h = 1, \ldots, 10$, for the data of Example 3.3.4 and the model (3.3.10), open the project E334.TSM in ITSM and enter the model using the option `Model>Specify`. Then select `Forecasting>ARMA` and specify 10 for the number of forecasts required. You will notice that the white noise variance is automatically set by ITSM to an estimate based on the sample. To retain the model value of 1, you must reset the white noise variance to this value. Then click `OK` and you will see a graph of the original series with the ten predicted values appended. If you right-click on the graph and select `Info`, you will see the numerical results shown in the following table as well as prediction bounds based on the assumption that the series is Gaussian. (Prediction bounds are discussed in the last paragraph of this chapter.) The mean squared errors are calculated as described below. Notice how the predictors converge fairly rapidly to the mean of the process (i.e., zero) as the lead time h increases. Correspondingly, the one-step mean squared error increases from the white noise variance (i.e., 1) at $h = 1$ to the variance of X_t (i.e., 7.1713), which is virtually reached at $h = 10$. □

The Mean Squared Error of $P_n X_{n+h}$

The mean squared error of $P_n X_{n+h}$ is easily computed by ITSM from the formula

$$\sigma_n^2(h) := E(X_{n+h} - P_n X_{n+h})^2 = \sum_{j=0}^{h-1} \left(\sum_{r=0}^{j} \chi_r \theta_{n+h-r-1,j-r} \right)^2 v_{n+h-j-1}, \quad (3.3.13)$$

Table 3.2 *h*-step predictors for the ARMA(2,3) Series of Example 3.3.4.

h	$P_{10}X_{10+h}$	$\sqrt{MSE}$
1	1.0638	1.0000
2	1.1217	1.7205
3	1.0062	2.1931
4	0.7370	2.4643
5	0.4955	2.5902
6	0.3186	2.6434
7	0.1997	2.6648
8	0.1232	2.6730
9	0.0753	2.6761
10	0.0457	2.6773

where the coefficients χ_j are computed recursively from the equations $\chi_0 = 1$ and

$$\chi_j = \sum_{k=1}^{\min(p,j)} \phi_k \chi_{j-k}, \quad j = 1, 2, \ldots. \tag{3.3.14}$$

Example 3.3.6 *h*-step prediction of an ARMA(2,3) process

We now illustrate the use of (3.3.12) and (3.3.13) for the h-step predictors and their mean squared errors by manually reproducing the output of ITSM shown in Table 3.2. From (3.3.12) and Table 3.1 we obtain

$$\begin{aligned} P_{10}X_{12} &= \sum_{i=1}^{2} \phi_i P_{10}X_{12-i} + \sum_{j=2}^{3} \theta_{11,j}\left(X_{12-j} - \hat{X}_{12-j}\right) \\ &= \phi_1 \hat{X}_{11} + \phi_2 X_{10} + 0.2\left(X_{10} - \hat{X}_{10}\right) + 0.1\left(X_9 - \hat{X}_9\right) \\ &= 1.1217 \end{aligned}$$

and

$$\begin{aligned} P_{10}X_{13} &= \sum_{i=1}^{2} \phi_i P_{10}X_{13-i} + \sum_{j=3}^{3} \theta_{12,j}\left(X_{13-j} - \hat{X}_{13-j}\right) \\ &= \phi_1 P_{10}X_{12} + \phi_2 \hat{X}_{11} + 0.1\left(X_{10} - \hat{X}_{10}\right) \\ &= 1.0062. \end{aligned}$$

For $k > 13$, $P_{10}X_k$ is easily found recursively from

$$P_{10}X_k = \phi_1 P_{10}X_{k-1} + \phi_2 P_{10}X_{k-2}.$$

To find the mean squared errors we use (3.3.13) with $\chi_0 = 1$, $\chi_1 = \phi_1 = 1$, and $\chi_2 = \phi_1\chi_1 + \phi_2 = 0.76$. Using the values of θ_{nj} and $v_j(= r_j)$ in Table 3.1, we obtain

$$\sigma_{10}^2(2) = E(X_{12} - P_{10}X_{12})^2 = 2.960$$

and

$$\sigma_{10}^2(3) = E(X_{13} - P_{10}X_{13})^2 = 4.810,$$

in accordance with the results shown in Table 3.2. □

Large-Sample Approximations

Assuming as usual that the ARMA(p, q) process defined by $\phi(B)X_t = \theta(B)Z_t$, $\{Z_t\} \sim \mathrm{WN}\left(0, \sigma^2\right)$, is causal and invertible, we have the representations

$$X_{n+h} = \sum_{j=0}^{\infty} \psi_j Z_{n+h-j} \tag{3.3.15}$$

and

$$Z_{n+h} = X_{n+h} + \sum_{j=1}^{\infty} \pi_j X_{n+h-j}, \tag{3.3.16}$$

where $\{\psi_j\}$ and $\{\pi_j\}$ are uniquely determined by equations (3.1.7) and (3.1.8), respectively. Let $\tilde{P}_n Y$ denote the best (i.e., minimum mean squared error) approximation to Y that is a linear combination or limit of linear combinations of X_t, $-\infty < t \le n$, or equivalently (by (3.3.15) and (3.3.16)) of Z_t, $-\infty < t \le n$. The properties of the operator $\tilde{P}_n$ were discussed in Section 2.5.3. Applying $\tilde{P}_n$ to each side of equations (3.3.15) and (3.3.16) gives

$$\tilde{P}_n X_{n+h} = \sum_{j=h}^{\infty} \psi_j Z_{n+h-j} \tag{3.3.17}$$

and

$$\tilde{P}_n X_{n+h} = -\sum_{j=1}^{\infty} \pi_j \tilde{P}_n X_{n+h-j}. \tag{3.3.18}$$

For $h = 1$ the jth term on the right of (3.3.18) is just X_{n+1-j}. Once $\tilde{P}_n X_{n+1}$ has been evaluated, $\tilde{P}_n X_{n+2}$ can then be computed from (3.3.18). The predictors $\tilde{P}_n X_{n+3}$, $\tilde{P}_n X_{n+4}, \ldots$ can then be computed successively in the same way. Subtracting (3.3.17) from (3.3.15) gives the h-step prediction error as

$$X_{n+h} - \tilde{P}_n X_{n+h} = \sum_{j=0}^{h-1} \psi_j Z_{n+h-j},$$

from which we see that the mean squared error is

$$\tilde{\sigma}^2(h) = \sigma^2 \sum_{j=0}^{h-1} \psi_j^2. \tag{3.3.19}$$

The predictors obtained in this way have the form

$$\tilde{P}_n X_{n+h} = \sum_{j=0}^{\infty} c_j X_{n-j}. \tag{3.3.20}$$

In practice, of course, we have only observations $X_1, \ldots, X_n$ available, so we must truncate the series (3.3.20) after n terms. The resulting predictor is a useful approximation to $P_n X_{n+h}$ if n is large and the coefficients c_j converge to zero rapidly as j increases. It can be shown that the mean squared error (3.3.19) of $\tilde{P}_n X_{n+h}$ can also be obtained by letting $n \to \infty$ in the expression (3.3.13) for the mean squared error of $P_n X_{n+h}$, so that $\tilde{\sigma}^2(h)$ is an easily calculated approximation to $\sigma_n^2(h)$ for large n.

Prediction Bounds for Gaussian Processes

If the ARMA process $\{X_t\}$ is driven by Gaussian white noise (i.e., if $\{Z_t\} \sim$ IID $N(0, \sigma^2)$), then for each $h \geq 1$ the prediction error $X_{n+h} - P_n X_{n+h}$ is normally distributed with mean 0 and variance $\sigma_n^2(h)$ given by (3.3.19).

Consequently, if $\Phi_{1-\alpha/2}$ denotes the $(1-\alpha/2)$ quantile of the standard normal distribution function, it follows that X_{n+h} lies between the bounds $P_n X_{n+h} \pm \Phi_{1-\alpha/2}\sigma_n(h)$ with probability $(1-\alpha)$. These bounds are therefore called $(1-\alpha)$ prediction bounds for X_{n+h}.

Problems

3.1. Determine which of the following ARMA processes are causal and which of them are invertible. (In each case $\{Z_t\}$ denotes white noise.)

a. $X_t + 0.2X_{t-1} - 0.48X_{t-2} = Z_t$.

b. $X_t + 1.9X_{t-1} + 0.88X_{t-2} = Z_t + 0.2Z_{t-1} + 0.7Z_{t-2}$.

c. $X_t + 0.6X_{t-1} = Z_t + 1.2Z_{t-1}$.

d. $X_t + 1.8X_{t-1} + 0.81X_{t-2} = Z_t$.

e. $X_t + 1.6X_{t-1} = Z_t - 0.4Z_{t-1} + 0.04Z_{t-2}$.

3.2. For those processes in Problem 3.1 that are causal, compute and graph their ACF and PACF using the program ITSM.

3.3. For those processes in Problem 3.1 that are causal, compute the first six coefficients $\psi_0, \psi_1, \ldots, \psi_5$ in the causal representation $X_t = \sum_{j=0}^{\infty} \psi_j Z_{t-j}$ of $\{X_t\}$.

3.4. Compute the ACF and PACF of the AR(2) process

$$X_t = .8X_{t-2} + Z_t, \quad \{Z_t\} \sim \text{WN}\left(0, \sigma^2\right).$$

3.5. Let $\{Y_t\}$ be the ARMA plus noise time series defined by

$$Y_t = X_t + W_t,$$

where $\{W_t\} \sim \text{WN}\left(0, \sigma_w^2\right)$, $\{X_t\}$ is the ARMA(p, q) process satisfying

$$\phi(B)X_t = \theta(B)Z_t, \quad \{Z_t\} \sim \text{WN}\left(0, \sigma_z^2\right),$$

and $E(W_s Z_t) = 0$ for all s and t.

a. Show that $\{Y_t\}$ is stationary and find its autocovariance in terms of σ_W^2 and the ACVF of $\{X_t\}$.

b. Show that the process $U_t := \phi(B)Y_t$ is r-correlated, where $r = \max(p, q)$ and hence, by Proposition 2.1.1, is an MA(r) process. Conclude that $\{Y_t\}$ is an ARMA(p, r) process.

3.6. Show that the two MA(1) processes

$$X_t = Z_t + \theta Z_{t-1}, \quad \{Z_t\} \sim \text{WN}\left(0, \sigma^2\right)$$

$$Y_t = \tilde{Z}_t + \frac{1}{\theta}\tilde{Z}_{t-1}, \quad \{\tilde{Z}_t\} \sim \text{WN}\left(0, \sigma^2\theta^2\right),$$

where $0 < |\theta| < 1$, have the same autocovariance functions.

3.7. Suppose that $\{X_t\}$ is the noninvertible MA(1) process

$$X_t = Z_t + \theta Z_{t-1}, \quad \{Z_t\} \sim \text{WN}\left(0, \sigma^2\right),$$

where $|\theta| > 1$. Define a new process $\{W_t\}$ as

$$W_t = \sum_{j=0}^{\infty}(-\theta)^{-j}X_{t-j}$$

and show that $\{W_t\} \sim \text{WN}\left(0, \sigma_W^2\right)$. Express σ_W^2 in terms of θ and σ^2 and show that $\{X_t\}$ has the *invertible* representation (in terms of $\{W_t\}$)

$$X_t = W_t + \frac{1}{\theta}W_{t-1}.$$

3.8. Let $\{X_t\}$ denote the unique stationary solution of the autoregressive equations

$$X_t = \phi X_{t-1} + Z_t, \quad t = 0, \pm 1, \ldots,$$

where $\{Z_t\} \sim \text{WN}(0, \sigma^2)$ and $|\phi| > 1$. Then X_t is given by the expression (2.2.11). Define the new sequence

$$W_t = X_t - \frac{1}{\phi}X_{t-1},$$

show that $\{W_t\} \sim \text{WN}\left(0, \sigma_W^2\right)$, and express σ_W^2 in terms of σ^2 and ϕ. These calculations show that $\{X_t\}$ is the (unique stationary) solution of the *causal* AR equations

$$X_t = \frac{1}{\phi}X_{t-1} + W_t, \quad t = 0, \pm 1, \ldots.$$

3.9. a. Calculate the autocovariance function $\gamma(\cdot)$ of the stationary time series

$$Y_t = \mu + Z_t + \theta_1 Z_{t-1} + \theta_{12}Z_{t-12}, \quad \{Z_t\} \sim \text{WN}\left(0, \sigma^2\right).$$

b. Use the program ITSM to compute the sample mean and sample autocovariances $\hat{\gamma}(h)$, $0 \le h \le 20$, of $\{\nabla\nabla_{12}X_t\}$, where $\{X_t, t = 1, \ldots, 72\}$ is the accidental deaths series DEATHS.TSM of Example 1.1.3.

c. By equating $\hat{\gamma}(1)$, $\hat{\gamma}(11)$, and $\hat{\gamma}(12)$ from part (b) to $\gamma(1)$, $\gamma(11)$, and $\gamma(12)$, respectively, from part (a), find a model of the form defined in (a) to represent $\{\nabla\nabla_{12}X_t\}$.

3.10. By matching the autocovariances and sample autocovariances at lags 0 and 1, fit a model of the form

$$X_t - \mu = \phi(X_{t-1} - \mu) + Z_t, \quad \{Z_t\} \sim \mathrm{WN}(0, \sigma^2),$$

to the data STRIKES.TSM of Example 1.1.6. Use the fitted model to compute the best predictor of the number of strikes in 1981. Estimate the mean squared error of your predictor and construct 95% prediction bounds for the number of strikes in 1981 assuming that $\{Z_t\} \sim$ iid $\mathrm{N}(0, \sigma^2)$.

3.11. Show that the value at lag 2 of the partial ACF of the MA(1) process

$$X_t = Z_t + \theta Z_{t-1}, \quad t = 0, \pm 1, \ldots,$$

where $\{Z_t\} \sim \mathrm{WN}(0, \sigma^2)$, is

$$\alpha(2) = -\theta^2 / \left(1 + \theta^2 + \theta^4\right).$$

3.12. For the MA(1) process of Problem 3.11, the best linear predictor of X_{n+1} based on $X_1, \ldots, X_n$ is

$$\hat{X}_{n+1} = \phi_{n,1} X_n + \cdots + \phi_{n,n} X_1,$$

where $\phi_n = \left(\phi_{n1}, \ldots, \phi_{nn}\right)'$ satisfies $R_n \phi_n = \rho_n$ (equation (2.5.23)). By substituting the appropriate correlations into R_n and ρ_n and solving the resulting equations (starting with the last and working up), show that for $1 \le j < n$, $\phi_{n,n-j} = (-\theta)^{-j}\left(1 + \theta^2 + \cdots + \theta^{2j}\right)\phi_{nn}$ and hence that the PACF $\alpha(n) := \phi_{nn} = -(-\theta)^n / \left(1 + \theta^2 + \cdots + \theta^{2n}\right)$.

3.13. The coefficients θ_{nj} and one-step mean squared errors $v_n = r_n \sigma^2$ for the general causal ARMA(1,1) process in Example 3.3.3 can be found as follows:

a. Show that if $y_n := r_n / (r_n - 1)$, then the last of equations (3.3.9) can be rewritten in the form

$$y_n = \theta^{-2} y_{n-1} + 1, \quad n \ge 1.$$

b. Deduce that $y_n = \theta^{-2n} y_0 + \sum_{j=1}^{n} \theta^{-2(j-1)}$ and hence determine r_n and θ_{n1}, $n = 1, 2, \ldots$.

c. Evaluate the limits as $n \to \infty$ of r_n and θ_{n1} in the two cases $|\theta| < 1$ and $|\theta| \ge 1$.

4 Spectral Analysis

This chapter can be omitted without any loss of continuity. The reader with no background in Fourier or complex analysis should go straight to Chapter 5. The spectral representation of a stationary time series $\{X_t\}$ essentially decomposes $\{X_t\}$ into a sum of sinusoidal components with uncorrelated random coefficients. In conjunction with this decomposition there is a corresponding decomposition into sinusoids of the autocovariance function of $\{X_t\}$. The spectral decomposition is thus an analogue for stationary processes of the more familiar Fourier representation of deterministic functions. The analysis of stationary processes by means of their spectral representation is often referred to as the "frequency domain analysis" of time series or "spectral analysis." It is equivalent to "time domain" analysis based on the autocovariance function, but provides an alternative way of viewing the process, which for some applications may be more illuminating. For example, in the design of a structure subject to a randomly fluctuating load, it is important to be aware of the presence in the loading force of a large sinusoidal component with a particular frequency to ensure that this is not a resonant frequency of the structure. The spectral point of view is also particularly useful in the analysis of multivariate stationary processes and in the analysis of linear filters. In Section 4.1 we introduce the spectral density of a stationary process $\{X_t\}$, which specifies the frequency decomposition of the autocovariance function, and the closely related spectral representation (or frequency decomposition) of the process $\{X_t\}$ itself. Section 4.2 deals with the periodogram, a sample-based function from which we obtain estimators of the spectral density. In Section 4.3 we discuss time-invariant linear filters from a spectral point of view and in Section 4.4 we use the results to derive the spectral density of an arbitrary ARMA process.

4.1 Spectral Densities

Suppose that $\{X_t\}$ is a zero-mean stationary time series with autocovariance function $\gamma(\cdot)$ satisfying $\sum_{h=-\infty}^{\infty} |\gamma(h)| < \infty$. The **spectral density** of $\{X_t\}$ is the function $f(\cdot)$ defined by

$$f(\lambda) = \frac{1}{2\pi} \sum_{h=-\infty}^{\infty} e^{-ih\lambda} \gamma(h), \quad -\infty < \lambda < \infty, \tag{4.1.1}$$

where $e^{i\lambda} = \cos(\lambda) + i \sin(\lambda)$ and $i = \sqrt{-1}$. The summability of $|\gamma(\cdot)|$ implies that the series in (4.1.1) converges absolutely (since $\left|e^{ih\lambda}\right|^2 = \cos^2(h\lambda) + \sin^2(h\lambda) = 1$). Since cos and sin have period 2π, so also does f, and it suffices to confine attention to the values of f, on the interval $(-\pi, \pi]$.

Basic Properties of f:

(a) f is even, i.e., $f(\lambda) = f(-\lambda)$, (4.1.2)

(b) $f(\lambda) \geq 0$ for all $\lambda \in (-\pi, \pi]$, (4.1.3)

and

(c) $\gamma(k) = \int_{-\pi}^{\pi} e^{ik\lambda} f(\lambda)\, d\lambda = \int_{-\pi}^{\pi} \cos(k\lambda) f(\lambda)\, d\lambda.$ (4.1.4)

Proof

Since $\sin(\cdot)$ is an odd function and $\cos(\cdot)$ and $\gamma(\cdot)$ are even functions, we have

$$\begin{aligned} f(\lambda) &= \frac{1}{2\pi} \sum_{h=-\infty}^{\infty} (\cos(h\lambda) - i \sin(h\lambda))\gamma(h) \\ &= \frac{1}{2\pi} \sum_{h=-\infty}^{\infty} \cos(-h\lambda)\gamma(h) + 0 \\ &= f(-\lambda). \end{aligned}$$

For each positive integer N define

$$f_N(\lambda) = \frac{1}{2\pi N} E\left(\left|\sum_{r=1}^{N} X_r e^{-ir\lambda}\right|^2\right)$$

$$= \frac{1}{2\pi N} E\left(\sum_{r=1}^{N} X_r e^{-ir\lambda} \sum_{s=1}^{N} X_s e^{is\lambda}\right)$$

$$= \frac{1}{2\pi N} \sum_{|h|<N} (N - |h|) e^{-ih\lambda} \gamma(h),$$

where $\Gamma_N = [\gamma(i-j)]_{i,j=1}^{N}$. Clearly, the function f_N is nonnegative for each N, and since $f_N(\lambda) \to \frac{1}{2\pi}\sum_{h=-\infty}^{\infty} e^{-ih\lambda}\gamma(h) = f(\lambda)$ as $N \to \infty$, f must also be nonnegative. This proves (4.1.3). Turning to (4.1.4),

$$\int_{-\pi}^{\pi} e^{ik\lambda} f(\lambda)\, d\lambda = \int_{-\pi}^{\pi} \frac{1}{2\pi} \sum_{h=-\infty}^{\infty} e^{i(k-h)\lambda} \gamma(h)\, d\lambda$$

$$= \frac{1}{2\pi} \sum_{h=-\infty}^{\infty} \gamma(h) \int_{-\pi}^{\pi} e^{i(k-h)\lambda}\, d\lambda$$

$$= \gamma(k),$$

since the only nonzero summand in the second line is the one for which $h = k$ (see Problem 4.1). ■

Equation (4.1.4) expresses the autocovariances of a stationary time series with absolutely summable ACVF as the Fourier coefficients of the nonnegative even function on $(-\pi, \pi]$ defined by (4.1.1). However, even if $\sum_{h=-\infty}^{\infty} |\gamma(h)| = \infty$, there may exist a corresponding spectral density defined as follows.

Definition 4.1.1

A function f is the **spectral density** of a stationary time series $\{X_t\}$ with ACVF $\gamma(\cdot)$ if

(i) $f(\lambda) \ge 0$ for all $\lambda \in (0, \pi]$,

(ii) $\gamma(h) = \int_{-\pi}^{\pi} e^{ih\lambda} f(\lambda)\, d\lambda$ for all integers h.

Remark 1. Spectral densities are essentially unique. That is, if f and g are two spectral densities corresponding to the autocovariance function $\gamma(\cdot)$, i.e., $\gamma(h) = \int_{-\pi}^{\pi} e^{ih\lambda} f(\lambda)\, d\lambda = \int_{-\pi}^{\pi} e^{ih\lambda} g(\lambda)\, d\lambda$ for all integers h, then f and g have the same Fourier coefficients and hence are equal (see, for example, TSTM, Section 2.8). □

The following proposition characterizes spectral densities.

Proposition 4.1.1

A real-valued function f defined on $(-\pi, \pi]$ is the spectral density of a stationary process if and only if

(i) $f(\lambda) = f(-\lambda)$,

(ii) $f(\lambda) \geq 0$, *and*

(iii) $\int_{-\pi}^{\pi} f(\lambda)\, d\lambda < \infty$.

Proof

If $\gamma(\cdot)$ is absolutely summable, then (i)–(iii) follow from the basic properties of f, (4.1.2)–(4.1.4). For the argument in the general case, see TSTM, Section 4.3.

Conversely, suppose f satisfies (i)–(iii). Then it is easy to check, using (i), that the function defined by

$$\gamma(h) = \int_{-\pi}^{\pi} e^{ih\lambda} f(\lambda)\, d\lambda$$

is even. Moreover, if $a_r \in \mathbb{R}$, $r = 1, \ldots, n$, then

$$\begin{aligned}\sum_{r,s=1}^{n} a_r \gamma(r-s) a_s &= \int_{-\pi}^{\pi} \sum_{r,s=1}^{n} a_r a_s e^{i\lambda(r-s)} f(\lambda)\, d\lambda \\ &= \int_{-\pi}^{\pi} \left| \sum_{r=1}^{n} a_r e^{i\lambda r} \right|^2 f(\lambda)\, d\lambda \\ &\geq 0,\end{aligned}$$

so that $\gamma(\cdot)$ is also nonnegative definite and therefore, by Theorem 2.1.1, is an autocovariance function. ■

Corollary 4.1.1

An absolutely summable function $\gamma(\cdot)$ is the autocovariance function of a stationary time series if and only if it is even and

$$f(\lambda) = \frac{1}{2\pi} \sum_{h=-\infty}^{\infty} e^{-ih\lambda} \gamma(h) \geq 0, \quad \textit{for all } \lambda \in (-\pi, \pi], \tag{4.1.5}$$

in which case $f(\cdot)$ is the spectral density of $\gamma(\cdot)$.

Proof

We have already established the necessity of (4.1.5). Now suppose (4.1.5) holds. Applying Proposition 4.1.1 (the assumptions are easily checked) we conclude that f is the spectral density of some autocovariance function. But this ACVF must be $\gamma(\cdot)$, since $\gamma(k) = \int_{-\pi}^{\pi} e^{ik\lambda} f(\lambda)\, d\lambda$ for all integers k. ■

Example 4.1.1

Using Corollary 4.1.1, it is a simple matter to show that the function defined by

$$\kappa(h) = \begin{cases} 1, & \text{if } h = 0, \\ \rho, & \text{if } h = \pm 1, \\ 0, & \text{otherwise,} \end{cases}$$

is the ACVF of a stationary time series if and only if $|\rho| \leq \frac{1}{2}$ (see Example 2.1.1). Since $\kappa(\cdot)$ is even and nonzero only at lags $0, \pm 1$, it follows from the corollary that

κ is an ACVF if and only if the function

$$f(\lambda) = \frac{1}{2\pi} \sum_{h=-\infty}^{\infty} e^{-ih\lambda}\gamma(h) = \frac{1}{2\pi}[1 + 2\rho\cos\lambda]$$

is nonnegative for *all* $\lambda \in [-\pi, \pi]$. But this occurs if and only if $|\rho| \le \frac{1}{2}$. □

As illustrated in the previous example, Corollary 4.1.1 provides us with a powerful tool for checking whether or not an absolutely summable function on the integers is an autocovariance function. It is much simpler and much more informative than direct verification of nonnegative definiteness as required in Theorem 2.1.1.

Not all autocovariance functions have a spectral density. For example, the stationary time series

$$X_t = A\cos(\omega t) + B\sin(\omega t), \tag{4.1.6}$$

where A and B are uncorrelated random variables with mean 0 and variance 1, has ACVF $\gamma(h) = \cos(\omega h)$ (Problem 2.2), which is not expressible as $\int_{-\pi}^{\pi} e^{ih\lambda} f(\lambda)d\lambda$, with f a function on $(-\pi, \pi]$. Nevertheless, $\gamma(\cdot)$ can be written as the Fourier transform of the discrete distribution function

$$F(\lambda) = \begin{cases} 0 & \text{if } \lambda < -\omega, \\ 0.5 & \text{if } -\omega \le \lambda < \omega, \\ 1.0 & \text{if } \lambda \ge \omega, \end{cases}$$

i.e.,

$$\cos(\omega h) = \int_{(-\pi,\pi]} e^{ih\lambda} dF(\lambda),$$

where the integral is as defined in Section A.1. As the following theorem states (see TSTM, p. 117), every ACVF is the Fourier transform of a (generalized) distribution function on $[-\pi, \pi]$. This representation is called the **spectral representation of the ACVF**.

Theorem 4.1.1

(Spectral Representation of the ACVF) *A function $\gamma(\cdot)$ defined on the integers is the ACVF of a stationary time series if and only if there exists a right-continuous, nondecreasing, bounded function F on $[-\pi,\pi]$ with $F(-\pi) = 0$ such that*

$$\gamma(h) = \int_{(-\pi,\pi]} e^{ih\lambda} dF(\lambda) \tag{4.1.7}$$

for all integers h. (For real-valued time series, F is symmetric in the sense that $\int_{(a,b]} dF(x) = \int_{[-b,-a)} dF(x)$ for all a and b such that $0 < a < b$.)

Remark 2. The function F is a **generalized distribution function** on $[-\pi, \pi]$ in the sense that $G(\lambda) = F(\lambda)/F(\pi)$ is a probability distribution function on $[-\pi, \pi]$.

Note that since $F(\pi) = \gamma(0) = \text{Var}(X_1)$, the ACF of $\{X_t\}$ has spectral representation

$$\rho(h) = \int_{(-\pi,\pi]} e^{ih\lambda} dG(\lambda).$$

The function F in (4.1.7) is called the **spectral distribution function** of $\gamma(\cdot)$. If $F(\lambda)$ can be expressed as $F(\lambda) = \int_{-\pi}^{\lambda} f(y)\,dy$ for all $\lambda \in [-\pi, \pi]$, then f is the **spectral density function** and the time series is said to have a **continuous spectrum**. If F is a discrete distribution (i.e., if G is a discrete probability distribution), then the time series is said to have a **discrete spectrum**. The time series (4.1.6) has a discrete spectrum. □

Example 4.1.2 Linear combination of sinusoids

Consider now the process obtained by adding uncorrelated processes of the type defined in (4.1.6), i.e.,

$$X_t = \sum_{j=1}^{k} (A_j \cos(\omega_j t) + B_j \sin(\omega_j t)), \quad 0 < \omega_1 < \cdots < \omega_k < \pi, \tag{4.1.8}$$

where $A_1, B_1, \ldots, A_k, B_k$ are uncorrelated random variables with $E(A_j) = 0$ and $\text{Var}(A_j) = \text{Var}(B_j) = \sigma_j^2$, $j = 1, \ldots, k$. By Problem 4.5, the ACVF of this time series is $\gamma(h) = \sum_{j=1}^{k} \sigma_j^2 \cos(\omega_j h)$ and its spectral distribution function is $F(\lambda) = \sum_{j=1}^{k} \sigma_j^2 F_j(\lambda)$, where

$$F_j(\lambda) = \begin{cases} 0 & \text{if } \lambda < -\omega_j, \\ 0.5 & \text{if } -\omega_j \le \lambda < \omega_j, \\ 1.0 & \text{if } \lambda \ge \omega_j. \end{cases}$$

A sample path of this time series with $k = 2$, $\omega_1 = \pi/4$, $\omega_2 = \pi/6$, $\sigma_1^2 = 9$, and $\sigma_2^2 = 1$ is plotted in Figure 4.1. Not surprisingly, the sample path closely approximates a sinusoid with frequency $\omega_1 = \pi/4$ (and period $2\pi/\omega_1 = 8$). The general features of this sample path could have been deduced from the spectral distribution function (see Figure 4.2), which places 90% of its total mass at the frequencies $\pm\pi/4$. This means that 90% of the variance of X_t is contributed by the term $A_1 \cos(\omega_1 t) + B_1 \cos(\omega_1 t)$, which is a sinusoid with period 8. □

The remarkable feature of Example 4.1.2 is that *every* zero-mean stationary process can be expressed as a superposition of uncorrelated sinusoids with frequencies $\omega \in [0, \pi]$. In general, however, a stationary process is a superposition of infinitely many sinusoids rather than a finite number as in (4.1.8). The required generalization of (4.1.8) that allows for this is called a stochastic integral, written as

$$X_t = \int_{(-\pi,\pi]} e^{ih\lambda} dZ(\lambda), \tag{4.1.9}$$

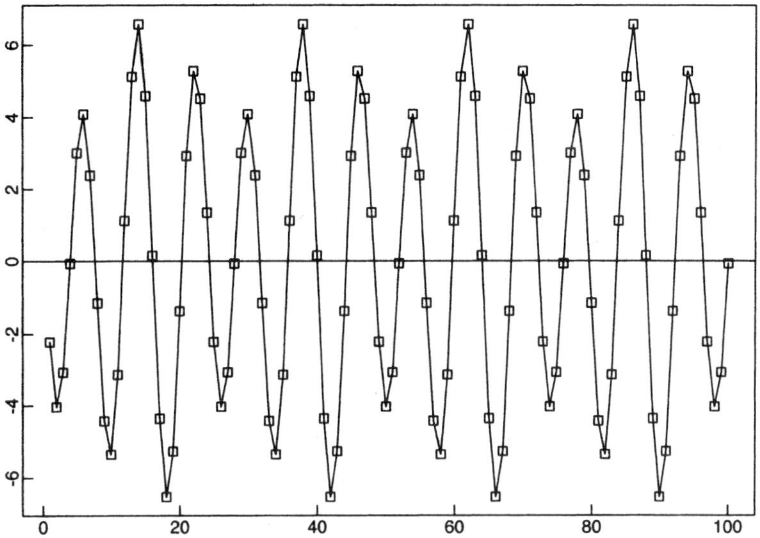

Figure 4-1 A sample path of size 100 from the time series in Example 4.1.2.

where $\{Z(\lambda), -\pi < \lambda \le \pi\}$ is a complex-valued process with orthogonal (or uncorrelated) increments. The representation (4.1.9) of a zero-mean stationary process $\{X_t\}$ is called the **spectral representation of the process** and should be compared with the corresponding spectral representation (4.1.7) of the autocovariance function $\gamma(\cdot)$. The underlying technical aspects of stochastic integration are beyond the scope of this book; however, in the simple case of the process (4.1.8) it is not difficult to

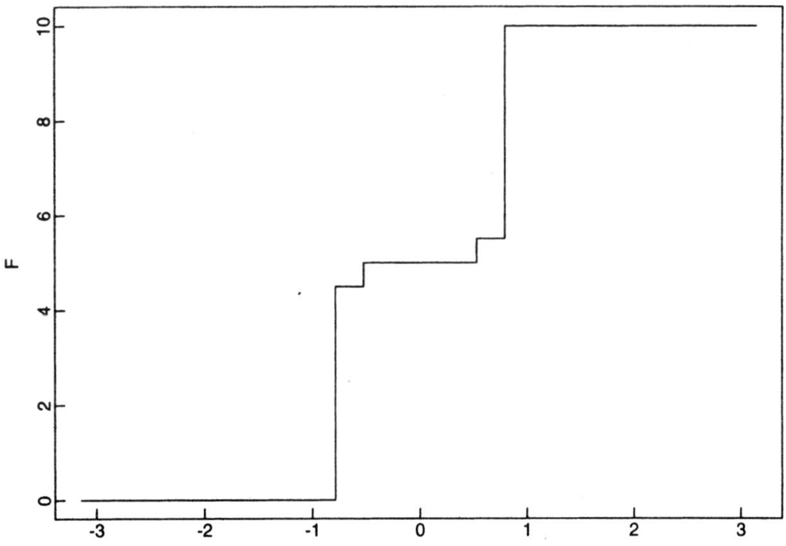

Figure 4-2 The spectral distribution function $F(\lambda)$, $-\pi \le \lambda \le \pi$, of the time series in Example 4.1.2.

see that it can be reexpressed in the form (4.1.9) by choosing

$$dZ(\lambda) = \begin{cases} \dfrac{A_j + iB_j}{2}, & \text{if } \lambda = -\omega_j \text{ and } j \in \{1, \ldots, k\}, \\ \dfrac{A_j - iB_j}{2}, & \text{if } \lambda = \omega_j \text{ and } j \in \{1, \ldots, k\}, \\ 0, & \text{otherwise.} \end{cases}$$

For this example it is also clear that

$$E(dZ(\lambda)\overline{dZ(\lambda)}) = \begin{cases} \dfrac{\sigma_j^2}{2}, & \text{if } \lambda = \pm\omega_j, \\ 0, & \text{otherwise.} \end{cases}$$

In general, the connection between $dZ(\lambda)$ and the spectral distribution function of the process can be expressed symbolically as

$$E(dZ(\lambda)\overline{dZ(\lambda)}) = \begin{cases} F(\lambda) - F(\lambda-), & \text{for a discrete spectrum,} \\ f(\lambda)d\lambda, & \text{for a continuous spectrum.} \end{cases} \tag{4.1.10}$$

These relations show that a large jump in the spectral distribution function (or a large peak in the spectral density) at frequency $\pm\omega$ indicates the presence in the time series of strong sinusoidal components at (or near) ω. The period of a sinusoid with frequency ω radians per unit time is $2\pi/\omega$.

Example 4.1.3 White noise

If $\{X_t\} \sim \text{WN}\left(0, \sigma^2\right)$, then $\gamma(0) = \sigma^2$ and $\gamma(h) = 0$ for all $|h| > 0$. This process has a flat spectral density (see Problem 4.2)

$$f(\lambda) = \frac{\sigma^2}{2\pi}, \quad -\pi \le \lambda \le \pi.$$

A process with this spectral density is called **white noise**, since each frequency in the spectrum contributes equally to the variance of the process. □

Example 4.1.4 The spectral density of an AR(1) process

If

$$X_t = \phi X_{t-1} + Z_t,$$

where $\{Z_t\} \sim \text{WN}(0, \sigma^2)$, then from (4.1.1), $\{X_t\}$ has spectral density

$$\begin{aligned} f(\lambda) &= \frac{\sigma^2}{2\pi(1-\phi^2)}\left(1+\sum_{h=1}^{\infty}\phi^h\left(e^{-ih\lambda}+e^{ih\lambda}\right)\right) \\ &= \frac{\sigma^2}{2\pi(1-\phi^2)}\left(1+\frac{\phi e^{i\lambda}}{1-\phi e^{i\lambda}}+\frac{\phi e^{-i\lambda}}{1-\phi e^{-i\lambda}}\right) \\ &= \frac{\sigma^2}{2\pi}\left(1-2\phi\cos\lambda+\phi^2\right)^{-1}. \end{aligned}$$

Graphs of $f(\lambda)$, $0 \le \lambda \le \pi$, are displayed in Figures 4.3 and 4.4 for $\phi = .7$ and $\phi = -.7$. Observe that for $\phi = .7$ the density is large for low frequencies and small for high frequencies. This is not unexpected, since when $\phi = .7$ the process has a positive ACF with a large value at lag one (see Figure 4.5), making the series smooth with relatively few high-frequency components. On the other hand, for $\phi = -.7$ the ACF has a large negative value at lag one (see Figure 4.6), producing a series that fluctuates rapidly about its mean value. In this case the series has a large contribution from high-frequency components as reflected by the size of the spectral density near frequency π. □

Example 4.1.5 Spectral density of an MA(1) process

If

$$X_t = Z_t + \theta Z_{t-1},$$

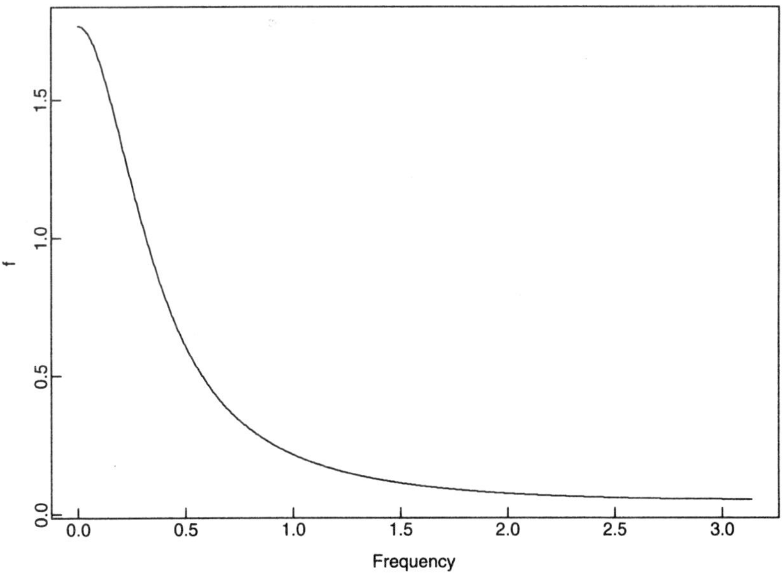

Figure 4-3 The spectral density $f(\lambda)$, $0 \le \lambda \le \pi$, of $X_t = .7X_{t-1} + Z_t$, where $\{Z_t\} \sim \text{WN}(0, \sigma^2)$.

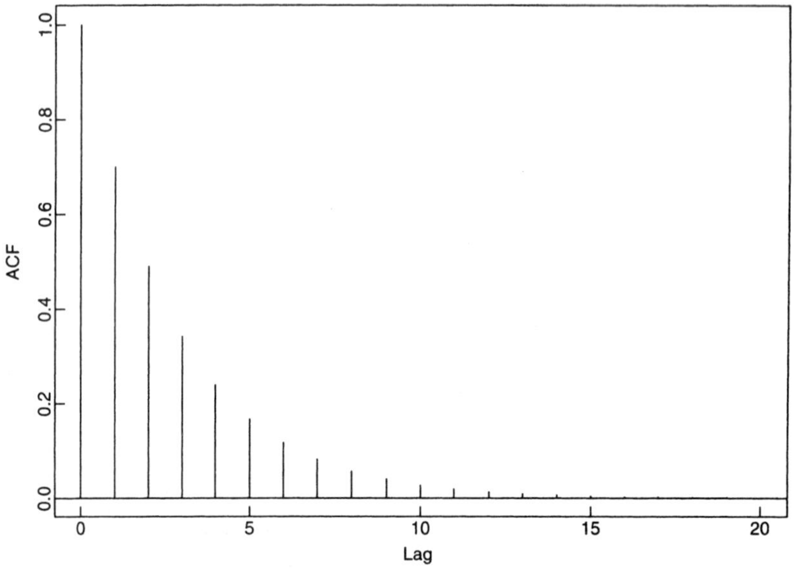

Figure 4-4 The spectral density $f(\lambda)$, $0 \le \lambda \le \pi$, of $X_t = -.7X_{t-1} + Z_t$, where $\{Z_t\} \sim \mathrm{WN}\left(0, \sigma^2\right)$.

where $\{Z_t\} \sim \mathrm{WN}(0, \sigma^2)$, then from (4.1.1),

$$f(\lambda) = \frac{\sigma^2}{2\pi}\left(1 + \theta^2 + \theta\left(e^{-i\lambda} + e^{i\lambda}\right)\right) = \frac{\sigma^2}{2\pi}\left(1 + 2\theta\cos\lambda + \theta^2\right).$$

This function is shown in Figures 4.7 and 4.8 for the values $\theta = .9$ and $\theta = -.9$. Interpretations of the graphs analogous to those in Example 4.1.4 can again be made. □

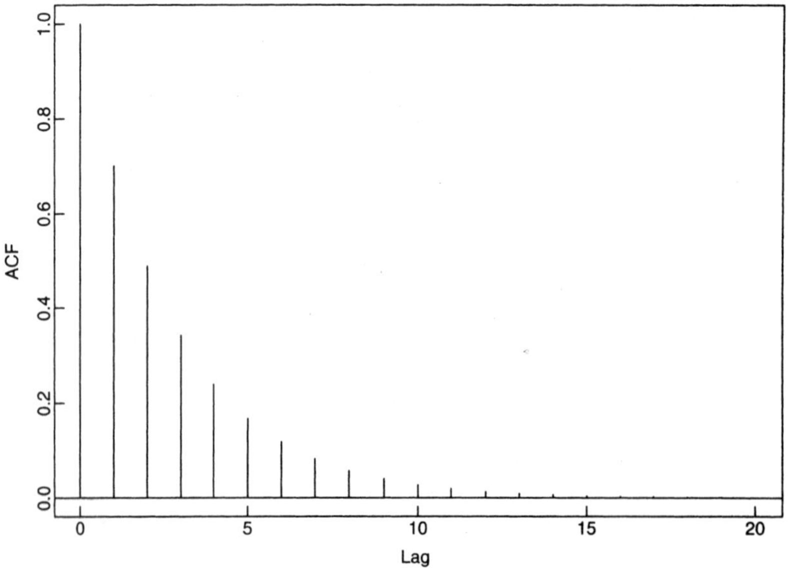

Figure 4-5 The ACF of the AR(1) process $X_t = .7X_{t-1} + Z_t$.

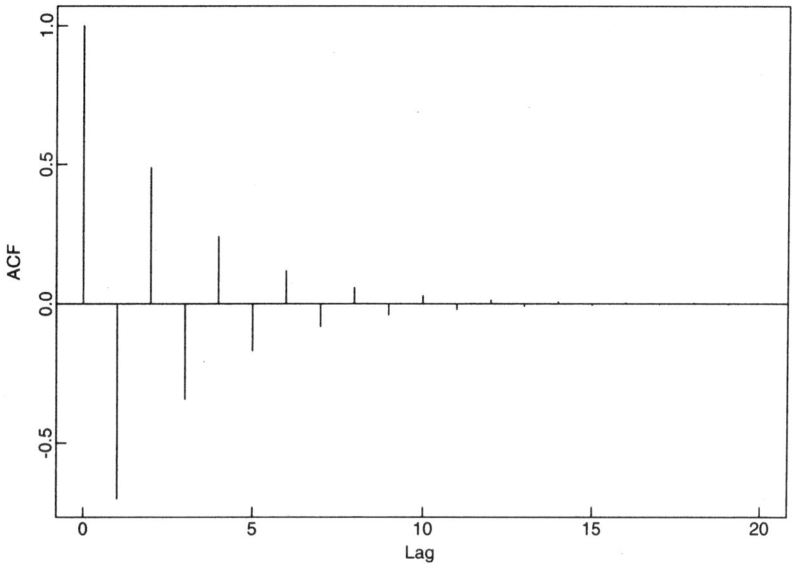

Figure 4-6 The ACF of the AR(1) process $X_t = -.7X_{t-1} + Z_t$.

4.2 The Periodogram

If $\{X_t\}$ is a stationary time series $\{X_t\}$ with ACVF $\gamma(\cdot)$ and spectral density $f(\cdot)$, then just as the sample ACVF $\hat{\gamma}(\cdot)$ of the observations $\{x_1, \ldots, x_n\}$ can be regarded as a sample analogue of $\gamma(\cdot)$, so also can the periodogram $I_n(\cdot)$ of the observations be regarded as a sample analogue of $2\pi f(\cdot)$.

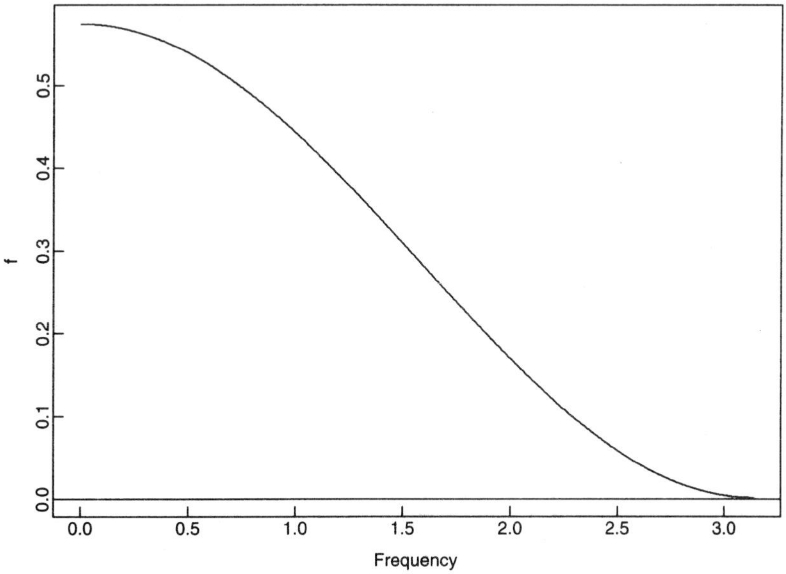

Figure 4-7 The spectral density $f(\lambda)$, $0 \le \lambda \le \pi$, of $X_t = Z_t + .9Z_{t-1}$ where $\{Z_t\} \sim \text{WN}\left(0, \sigma^2\right)$.

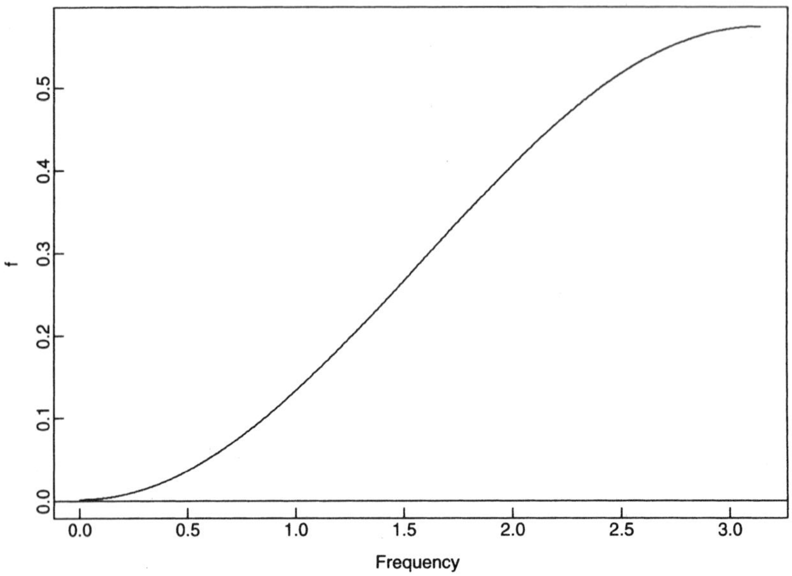

Figure 4-8 The spectral density $f(\lambda)$, $0 \le \lambda \le \pi$, of $X_t = Z_t - .9Z_{t-1}$ where $\{Z_t\} \sim \mathrm{WN}\left(0, \sigma^2\right)$.

To introduce the periodogram, we consider the vector of complex numbers

$$\mathbf{x} = \begin{bmatrix} x_1 \\ x_2 \\ \vdots \\ x_n \end{bmatrix} \in \mathbb{C}^n,$$

where $\mathbb{C}^n$ denotes the set of all column vectors with complex-valued components. Now let $\omega_k = 2\pi k/n$, where k is any integer between $-(n-1)/2$ and $n/2$ (inclusive), i.e.,

$$\omega_k = \frac{2\pi k}{n}, \quad k = -\left[\frac{n-1}{2}\right], \ldots, \left[\frac{n}{2}\right], \tag{4.2.1}$$

where $[y]$ denotes the largest integer less than or equal to y. We shall refer to the set F_n of these values as the **Fourier frequencies** associated with sample size n, noting that F_n is a subset of the interval $(-\pi, \pi]$. Correspondingly, we introduce the n vectors

$$\mathbf{e}_k = \frac{1}{\sqrt{n}} \begin{bmatrix} e^{i\omega_k} \\ e^{2i\omega_k} \\ \vdots \\ e^{ni\omega_k} \end{bmatrix}, \qquad k = -\left[\frac{n-1}{2}\right], \ldots, \left[\frac{n}{2}\right]. \tag{4.2.2}$$

Now $\mathbf{e}_1, \ldots, \mathbf{e}_n$ are **orthonormal** in the sense that

$$\mathbf{e}_j{}^*\mathbf{e}_k = \begin{cases} 1, & \text{if } j = k, \\ 0, & \text{if } j \neq k, \end{cases} \tag{4.2.3}$$

where $\mathbf{e}_j{}^*$ denotes the row vector whose kth component is the complex conjugate of the kth component of $\mathbf{e}_j$ (see Problem 4.3). This implies that $\{\mathbf{e}_1, \ldots, \mathbf{e}_n\}$ is a basis for $\mathbb{C}^n$, so that any $\mathbf{x} \in \mathbb{C}^n$ can be expressed as the sum of n components,

$$\mathbf{x} = \sum_{k=-[(n-1)/2]}^{[n/2]} a_k \mathbf{e}_k. \tag{4.2.4}$$

The coefficients a_k are easily found by multiplying (4.2.4) on the left by $\mathbf{e}_k{}^*$ and using (4.2.3). Thus,

$$a_k = \mathbf{e}_k{}^*\mathbf{x} = \frac{1}{\sqrt{n}} \sum_{t=1}^{n} x_t e^{-it\omega_k}. \tag{4.2.5}$$

The sequence $\{a_k\}$ is called the **discrete Fourier transform** of the sequence $\{x_1, \ldots, x_n\}$.

Remark 1. The tth component of (4.2.4) can be written as

$$x_t = \sum_{k=-[(n-1)/2]}^{[n/2]} a_k[\cos(\omega_k t) + i \sin(\omega_k t)], \quad t = 1, \ldots, n, \tag{4.2.6}$$

showing that (4.2.4) is just a way of representing x_t as a linear combination of sine waves with frequencies $\omega_k \in F_n$. □

Definition 4.2.1

The **periodogram** of $\{x_1, \ldots, x_n\}$ is the function

$$I_n(\lambda) = \frac{1}{n} \left| \sum_{t=1}^{n} x_t e^{-it\lambda} \right|^2. \tag{4.2.7}$$

Remark 2. If λ is one of the Fourier frequencies ω_k, then $I_n(\omega_k) = |a_k|^2$, and so from (4.2.4) and (4.2.3) we find at once that the squared length of $\mathbf{x}$ is

$$\sum_{t=1}^{n} |x_t|^2 = \mathbf{x}^*\mathbf{x} = \sum_{k=-[(n-1)/2]}^{[n/2]} |a_k|^2 = \sum_{k=-[(n-1)/2]}^{[n/2]} I_n(\omega_k).$$

The value of the periodogram at frequency ω_k is thus the contribution to this sum of squares from the "frequency ω_k" term $a_k\mathbf{e}_k$ in (4.2.4). □

The next proposition shows that $I_n(\lambda)$ can be regarded as a sample analogue of $2\pi f(\lambda)$. Recall that if $\sum_{h=-\infty}^{\infty} |\gamma(h)| < \infty$, then

$$2\pi f(\lambda) = \sum_{h=-\infty}^{\infty} \gamma(h)e^{-ih\lambda}, \quad \lambda \in (-\pi, \pi]. \tag{4.2.8}$$

Proposition 4.2.1

If $x_1, \ldots, x_n$ are any real numbers and ω_k is any of the nonzero Fourier frequencies $2\pi k/n$ in $(-\pi, \pi]$, then

$$I_n(\omega_k) = \sum_{|h|<n} \hat{\gamma}(h)e^{-ih\omega_k}, \tag{4.2.9}$$

where $\hat{\gamma}(h)$ is the sample ACVF of $x_1, \ldots, x_n$.

Proof

Since $\sum_{t=1}^{n} e^{-it\omega_k} = 0$ if $\omega_k \neq 0$, we can subtract the sample mean $\bar{x}$ from x_t in the defining equation (4.2.7) of $I_n(\omega_k)$. Hence,

$$\begin{aligned} I_n(\omega_k) &= n^{-1} \sum_{s=1}^{n} \sum_{t=1}^{n} (x_s - \bar{x})(x_t - \bar{x})e^{-i(s-t)\omega_k} \\ &= \sum_{|h|<n} \hat{\gamma}(h)e^{-ih\omega_k}. \end{aligned}$$

■

In view of the similarity between (4.2.8) and (4.2.9), a natural estimate of the spectral density $f(\lambda)$ is $I_n(\lambda)/(2\pi)$. For a very large class of stationary time series $\{X_t\}$ with strictly positive spectral density, it can be shown that for any fixed frequencies $\lambda_1, \ldots, \lambda_m$ such that $0 < \lambda_1 < \cdots < \lambda_m < \pi$, the joint distribution function $F_n(x_1, \ldots, x_m)$ of the periodogram values $(I_n(\lambda_1), \ldots, I_n(\lambda_m))$ converges, as $n \to \infty$, to $F(x_1, \ldots, x_m)$, where

$$F(x_1, \ldots, x_m) = \begin{cases} \prod_{i=1}^{m} \left(1 - \exp\left\{\dfrac{-x_i}{2\pi f(\lambda_i)}\right\}\right), & \text{if } x_1, \ldots, x_m > 0, \\ 0, & \text{otherwise.} \end{cases} \tag{4.2.10}$$

Thus for large n the periodogram ordinates $(I_n(\lambda_1), \ldots, I_n(\lambda_m))$ are approximately distributed as independent exponential random variables with means $2\pi f(\lambda_1), \ldots, 2\pi f(\lambda_m)$, respectively. In particular, for each fixed $\lambda \in (0, \pi)$ and $\epsilon > 0$,

$$P[|I_n(\lambda) - 2\pi f(\lambda)| > \epsilon] \to p > 0, \text{ as } n \to \infty,$$

so the probability of an estimation error larger than ϵ cannot be made arbitrarily small by choosing a sufficiently large sample size n. Thus, $I_n(\lambda)$ is not a *consistent* estimator of $2\pi f(\lambda)$.

Since for large n the periodogram ordinates at fixed frequencies are approximately independent with variances changing only slightly over small frequency intervals, we might hope to construct a consistent estimator of $f(\lambda)$ by averaging the periodogram estimates in a small frequency interval containing λ, provided that we can choose the interval in such a way that its width decreases to zero while at the same time the number of Fourier frequencies in the interval increases to ∞ as $n \to \infty$. This can indeed be done, since the number of Fourier frequencies in any *fixed* frequency interval increases approximately linearly with n. Consider, for example, the estimator

$$\tilde{f}(\lambda) = \frac{1}{2\pi} \sum_{|j| \le m} (2m+1)^{-1} I_n(g(n,\lambda) + 2\pi j/n), \tag{4.2.11}$$

where $m = \sqrt{n}$ and $g(n,\lambda)$ is the multiple of $2\pi/n$ closest to λ. The number of periodogram ordinates being averaged is approximately $2\sqrt{n}$, and the width of the frequency interval over which the average is taken is approximately $4\pi/\sqrt{n}$. It can be shown (see TSTM, Section 10.4) that this estimator is consistent for the spectral density f. The argument in fact establishes the consistency of a whole class of estimators defined as follows.

Definition 4.2.2

A **discrete spectral average estimator** of the spectral density $f(\lambda)$ has the form

$$\hat{f}(\lambda) = \frac{1}{2\pi} \sum_{|j| \le m_n} W_n(j) I_n(g(n,\lambda) + 2\pi j/n), \tag{4.2.12}$$

where the **bandwidths** m_n satisfy

$$m_n \to \infty \text{ and } m_n/n \to 0 \text{ as } n \to \infty, \tag{4.2.13}$$

and the **weight functions** $W_n(\cdot)$ satisfy

$$W_n(j) = W_n(-j),\ W_n(j) \ge 0 \text{ for all } j, \tag{4.2.14}$$

$$\sum_{|j| \le m_n} W_n(j) = 1, \tag{4.2.15}$$

and

$$\sum_{|j| \le m_n} W_n^2(j) \to 0 \text{ as } n \to \infty. \tag{4.2.16}$$

Remark 3. The conditions imposed on the sequences $\{m_n\}$ and $\{W_n(\cdot)\}$ ensure consistency of $\hat{f}(\lambda)$ for $f(\lambda)$ for a very large class of stationary processes (see TSTM, Theorem 10.4.1) including all the ARMA processes considered in this book. The conditions (4.2.13) simply mean that the number of terms in the weighted average (4.2.12) goes to ∞ as $n \to \infty$ while at the same time the width of the *frequency* interval over which the average is taken goes to zero. The conditions on $\{W_n(\cdot)\}$ ensure that the mean and variance of $\hat{f}(\lambda)$ converge as $n \to \infty$ to $f(\lambda)$ and 0, respectively. Under the conditions of TSTM, Theorem 10.4.1, it can be shown, in fact, that

$$\lim_{n\to\infty} E\hat{f}(\lambda) = f(\lambda)$$

and

$$\lim_{n\to\infty}\left(\sum_{|j|\le m_n} W_n^2(j)\right)^{-1}\operatorname{Cov}(\hat{f}(\lambda),\hat{f}(\nu)) = \begin{cases} 2f^2(\lambda) & \text{if } \lambda=\nu=0 \text{ or } \pi,\\ f^2(\lambda) & \text{if } 0<\lambda=\nu<\pi,\\ 0 & \text{if } \lambda\ne\nu. \end{cases}$$

□

Example 4.2.1

For the simple moving average estimator with $m_n = \sqrt{n}$ and $W_n(j) = (2m_n + 1)^{-1}$, $|j| \le m_n$, Remark 3 gives

$$(2\sqrt{n}+1)\operatorname{Var}\left(\hat{f}(\lambda)\right) \to \begin{cases} 2f^2(\lambda) & \text{if } \lambda = 0 \text{ or } \pi,\\ f^2(\lambda) & \text{if } 0<\lambda<\pi. \end{cases}$$

□

In practice, when the sample size n is a fixed finite number, the choice of m and $\{W(\cdot)\}$ involves a compromise between achieving small bias and small variance for the estimator $\hat{f}(\lambda)$. A weight function that assigns roughly equal weights to a broad band of frequencies will produce an estimate of $f(\lambda)$ that, although smooth, may have a large bias, since the estimate of $f(\lambda)$ depends on the values of I_n at frequencies distant from λ. On the other hand, a weight function that assigns most of its weight to a narrow frequency band centered at zero will give an estimator with relatively small bias, but with a larger variance. In practice it is advisable to experiment with a range

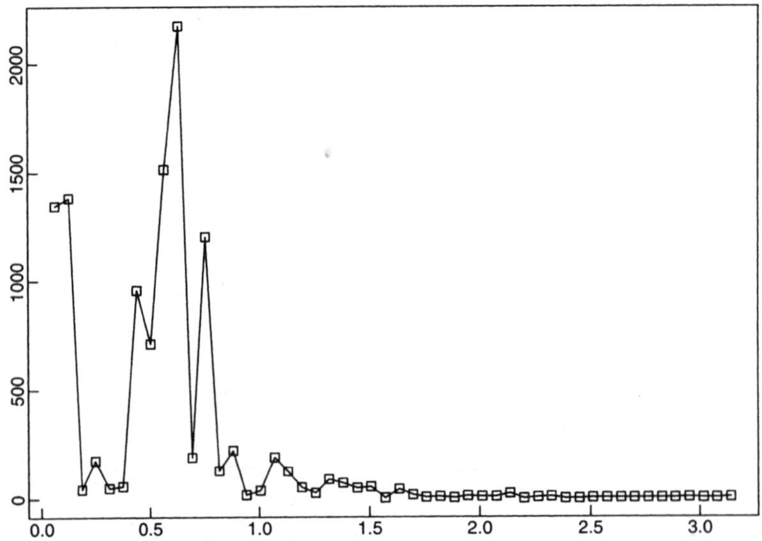

Figure 4-9 The spectral density estimate, $I_{100}(\lambda)/(2\pi)$, $0 < \lambda \le \pi$, of the sunspot numbers, 1770–1869.

of weight functions and to select the one that appears to strike a satisfactory balance between bias and variance.

The option `Spectrum>Smoothed Periodogram` in the program ITSM allows the user to apply up to 50 successive discrete spectral average filters with weights $W(j) = 1/(2m+1),\ j = -m, -m+1, \ldots, m$, to the periodogram. The value of m for each filter can be specified arbitrarily, and the weights of the filter corresponding to the combined effect (the **convolution** of the component filters) is displayed by the program. The program computes the corresponding discrete spectral average estimators $\hat{f}(\lambda), 0 \le \lambda \le \pi$.

Example 4.2.2 The sunspot numbers, 1770–1869

Figure 4.9 displays a plot of $(2\pi)^{-1}$ times the periodogram of the annual sunspot numbers (obtained by opening the project SUNSPOTS.TSM in ITSM and selecting `Spectrum>Periodogram`). Figure 4.10 shows the result of applying the discrete spectral weights $\left\{\frac{1}{3}, \frac{1}{3}, \frac{1}{3}\right\}$ (corresponding to $m = 1$, $W(j) = 1/(2m+1)$, $|j| \le m$). It is obtained from ITSM by selecting `Spectrum>Smoothed Periodogram`, entering 1 for the number of Daniell filters, 1 for the order m, and clicking on `Apply`. As expected, with such a small value of m, not much smoothing of the periodogram occurs. If we change the number of Daniell filters to 2 and set the order of the first filter to 1 and the order of the second filter to 2, we obtain a combined filter with a more dispersed set of weights, $W(0) = W(1) = \frac{3}{15}$, $W(2) = \frac{2}{15}$, $W(3) = \frac{1}{15}$. Clicking on `Apply` will then give the smoother spectral estimate shown in Figure 4.11. When you are satisfied with the smoothed estimate click `OK`, and the dialog box will close. All three spectral density estimates show a well-defined peak at the frequency $\omega_{10} = 2\pi/10$ radians per year, in keeping with the suggestion from the graph of the data itself that the sunspot series contains an approximate cycle with period around 10 or 11 years. □

4.3 Time-Invariant Linear Filters

In Section 1.5 we saw the utility of time-invariant linear filters for smoothing the data, estimating the trend, eliminating the seasonal and/or trend components of the data, etc. A linear process is the output of a time-invariant linear filter (TLF) applied to a white noise input series. More generally, we say that the process $\{Y_t\}$ is the output of a linear filter $C = \{c_{t,k}, t, k = 0 \pm 1, \ldots\}$ applied to an input process $\{X_t\}$ if

$$Y_t = \sum_{k=-\infty}^{\infty} c_{t,k} X_k, \quad t = 0, \pm 1, \ldots. \tag{4.3.1}$$

The filter is said to be **time-invariant** if the weights $c_{t,t-k}$ are independent of t, i.e., if

$$c_{t,t-k} = \psi_k.$$

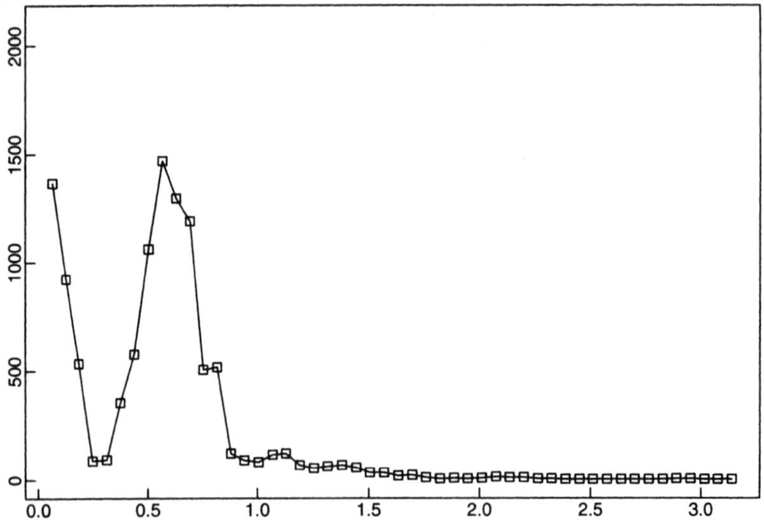

Figure 4-10 The spectral density estimate, $\hat{f}(\lambda)$, $0 < \lambda \leq \pi$, of the sunspot numbers, 1770–1869, with weights $\left\{\frac{1}{3}, \frac{1}{3}, \frac{1}{3}\right\}$.

In this case,

$$Y_t = \sum_{k=-\infty}^{\infty} \psi_k X_{t-k}$$

and

$$Y_{t-s} = \sum_{k=-\infty}^{\infty} \psi_k X_{t-s-k},$$

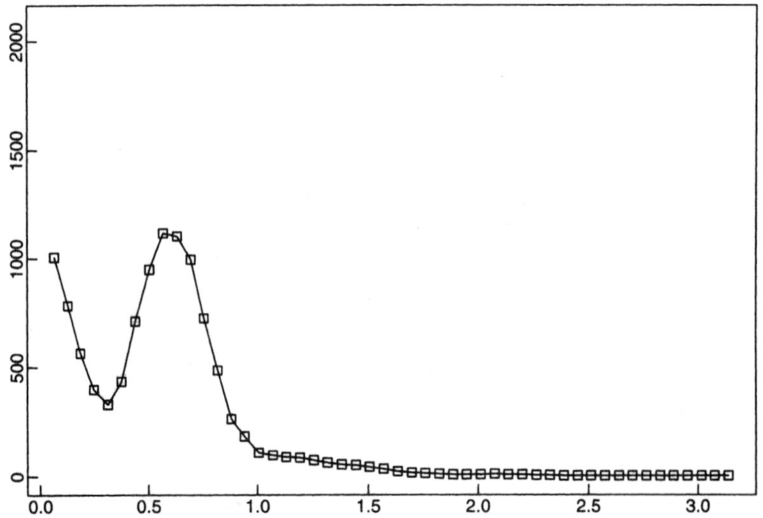

Figure 4-11 The spectral density estimate, $\hat{f}(\lambda)$, $0 < \lambda \leq \pi$, of the sunspot numbers, 1770–1869, with weights $\left\{\frac{1}{15}, \frac{2}{15}, \frac{3}{15}, \frac{3}{15}, \frac{3}{15}, \frac{2}{15}, \frac{1}{15}\right\}$.

so that the time-shifted process $\{Y_{t-s}, t = 0, \pm 1, \ldots\}$ is obtained from $\{X_{t-s}, t = 0, \pm 1, \ldots\}$ by application of the same linear filter $\Psi = \{\psi_j, j = 0, \pm 1, \ldots\}$. The TLF Ψ is said to be **causal** if

$$\psi_j = 0 \text{ for } j < 0,$$

since then Y_t is expressible in terms only of X_s, $s \le t$.

Example 4.3.1 The filter defined by

$$Y_t = aX_{-t}, \quad t = 0, \pm 1, \ldots,$$

is linear but not time-invariant, since $c_{t,t-k} = 0$ except when $2t = k$. Thus, $c_{t,t-k}$ depends on the value of t. □

Example 4.3.2 The simple moving average

The filter

$$Y_t = (2q + 1)^{-1} \sum_{|j| \le q} X_{t-j}$$

is a TLF with $\psi_j = (2q + 1)^{-1}$, $j = -q, \ldots, q$, and $\psi_j = 0$ otherwise. □

Spectral methods are particularly valuable in describing the behavior of time-invariant linear filters as well as in designing filters for particular purposes such as the suppression of high-frequency components. The following proposition shows how the spectral density of the output of a TLF is related to the spectral density of the input—a fundamental result in the study of time-invariant linear filters.

Proposition 4.3.1

Let $\{X_t\}$ be a stationary time series with mean zero and spectral density $f_X(\lambda)$. Suppose that $\Psi = \{\psi_j, j = 0, \pm 1, \ldots\}$ is an absolutely summable TLF (i.e., $\sum_{j=-\infty}^{\infty} |\psi_j| < \infty$). Then the time series

$$Y_t = \sum_{j=-\infty}^{\infty} \psi_j X_{t-j}$$

is stationary with mean zero and spectral density

$$f_Y(\lambda) = \left|\Psi\left(e^{-i\lambda}\right)\right|^2 f_X(\lambda) = \Psi\left(e^{-i\lambda}\right)\Psi\left(e^{i\lambda}\right) f_X(\lambda),$$

where $\Psi(e^{-i\lambda}) = \sum_{j=-\infty}^{\infty} \psi_j e^{-ij\lambda}$. (The function $\Psi\left(e^{-i\cdot}\right)$ is called the **transfer function** *of the filter, and the squared modulus $\left|\Psi\left(e^{-i\cdot}\right)\right|^2$ is referred to as the* **power transfer function** *of the filter.)*

Proof

Applying Proposition 2.2.1, we see that $\{Y_t\}$ is stationary with mean 0 and ACVF

$$\gamma_Y(h) = \sum_{j,k=-\infty}^{\infty} \psi_j \psi_k \gamma_X(h + k - j). \tag{4.3.2}$$

Since $\{X_t\}$ has spectral density $f_X(\lambda)$, we have

$$\gamma_X(h+k-j) = \int_{-\pi}^{\pi} e^{i(h-j+k)\lambda} f_X(\lambda)\,d\lambda, \tag{4.3.3}$$

which, by substituting (4.3.3) into (4.3.2), gives

$$\begin{aligned}\gamma_Y(h) &= \sum_{j,k=-\infty}^{\infty} \psi_j \psi_k \int_{-\pi}^{\pi} e^{i(h-j+k)\lambda} f_X(\lambda)\,d\lambda \\ &= \int_{-\pi}^{\pi} \left(\sum_{j=-\infty}^{\infty} \psi_j e^{-ij\lambda}\right)\left(\sum_{k=-\infty}^{\infty} \psi_k e^{ik\lambda}\right) e^{ih\lambda} f_X(\lambda)\,d\lambda \\ &= \int_{-\pi}^{\pi} e^{ih\lambda} \left|\sum_{j=-\infty}^{\infty} \psi_j e^{-ij\lambda}\right|^2 f_X(\lambda)\,d\lambda.\end{aligned}$$

The last expression immediately identifies the spectral density function of $\{Y_t\}$ as

$$f_Y(\lambda) = \left|\Psi\left(e^{-i\lambda}\right)\right|^2 f_X(\lambda) = \Psi\left(e^{-i\lambda}\right)\Psi\left(e^{i\lambda}\right) f_X(\lambda).$$ ■

Remark 1. Proposition 4.3.1 allows us to analyze the net effect of applying one or more filters in succession. For example, if the input process $\{X_t\}$ with spectral density f_X is operated on sequentially by two absolutely summable TLFs Ψ_1 and Ψ_2, then the net effect is the same as that of a TLF with transfer function $\Psi_1\left(e^{-i\lambda}\right)\Psi_2\left(e^{-i\lambda}\right)$ and the spectral density of the output process

$$W_t = \Psi_1(B)\Psi_2(B)X_t$$

is $\left|\Psi_1\left(e^{-i\lambda}\right)\Psi_2\left(e^{-i\lambda}\right)\right|^2 f_X(\lambda)$. (See also Remark 2 of Section 2.2.) □

As we saw in Section 1.5, differencing at lag s is one method for removing a seasonal component with period s from a time series. The transfer function for this filter is $1 - e^{-is\lambda}$, which is zero for all frequencies that are integer multiples of $2\pi/s$ radians per unit time. Consequently, this filter has the desired effect of removing all components with period s.

The simple moving-average filter in Example 4.3.2 has transfer function

$$\Psi\left(e^{-i\lambda}\right) = D_q(\lambda),$$

where $D_q(\lambda)$ is the Dirichlet kernel

$$D_q(\lambda) = (2q+1)^{-1} \sum_{|j|\le q} e^{-ij\lambda} = \begin{cases} \dfrac{\sin[(q+.5)\lambda]}{(2q+1)\sin(\lambda/2)}, & \text{if } \lambda \ne 0, \\ 1, & \text{if } \lambda = 0. \end{cases}$$

A graph of D_q is given in Figure 4.12. Notice that $|D_q(\lambda)|$ is near 1 in a neighborhood of 0 and tapers off to 0 for large frequencies. This is an example of a low-pass filter.

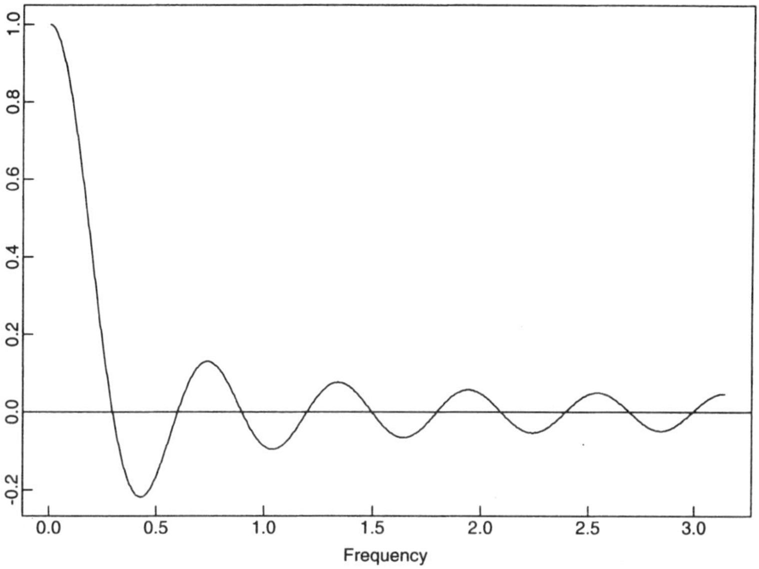

Figure 4-12 The transfer function $D_{10}(\lambda)$ for the simple moving-average filter.

The ideal low-pass filter would have a transfer function of the form

$$\Psi(e^{-i\lambda}) = \begin{cases} 1, & \text{if } |\lambda| \le \omega_c, \\ 0, & \text{if } |\lambda| > \omega_c, \end{cases}$$

where ω_c is a predetermined cutoff value. To determine the corresponding linear filter, we expand $\Psi\left(e^{-i\lambda}\right)$ as a Fourier series,

$$\Psi\left(e^{-i\lambda}\right) = \sum_{j=-\infty}^{\infty} \psi_j e^{-ij\lambda}, \tag{4.3.4}$$

with coefficients

$$\psi_j = \frac{1}{2\pi}\int_{-\omega_c}^{\omega_c} e^{ij\lambda}\, d\lambda = \begin{cases} \dfrac{\omega_c}{\pi}, & \text{if } j = 0, \\ \dfrac{\sin(j\omega_c)}{j\pi}, & \text{if } |j| > 0. \end{cases}$$

We can approximate the ideal low-pass filter by truncating the series in (4.3.4) at some large value q, which may depend on the length of the observed input series. In Figure 4.13 the transfer function of the ideal low-pass filter with $w_c = \pi/4$ is plotted with the approximations $\Psi^{(q)}\left(e^{-i\lambda}\right) = \sum_{j=-q}^{q} \psi_j e^{-ij\lambda}$ for $q = 2$ and $q = 10$. As can be seen in the figure, the approximations do not mirror Ψ very well near the cutoff value ω_c and behave like damped sinusoids for frequencies greater than ω_c. The poor approximation in the neighborhood of ω_c is typical of Fourier series approximations to functions with discontinuities, an effect known as the **Gibbs phenomenon**. Convergence factors may

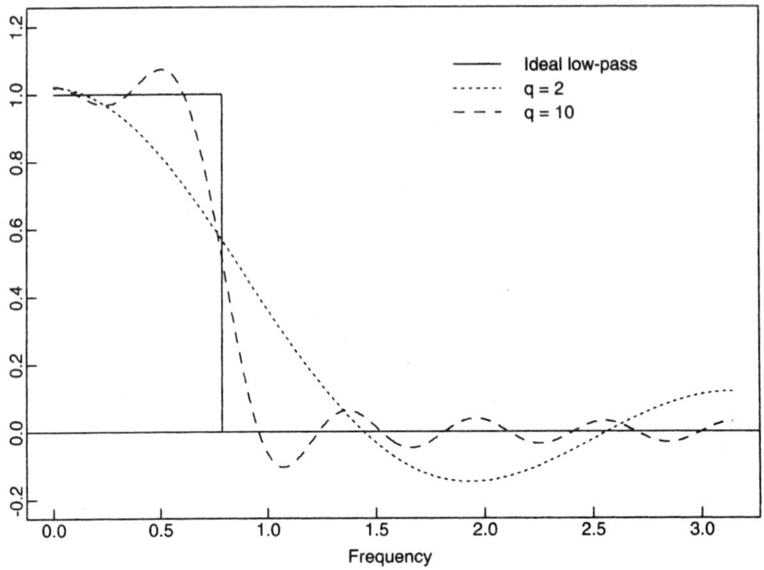

Figure 4-13 The transfer function for the ideal low-pass filter and truncated Fourier approximations $\Psi^{(q)}$ for $q = 2, 10$.

be employed to help mitigate the overshoot problem at ω_c and to improve the overall approximation of $\Psi^{(q)}(e^{-i\cdot})$ to $\Psi(e^{-i\cdot})$ (see Bloomfield, 2000).

4.4 The Spectral Density of an ARMA Process

In Section 4.1 the spectral density was computed for an MA(1) and for an AR(1) process. As an application of Proposition 4.3.1, we can now easily derive the spectral density of an arbitrary ARMA(p, q) process.

Spectral Density of an ARMA(p, q) Process:

If $\{X_t\}$ is a causal ARMA(p, q) process satisfying $\phi(B)X_t = \theta(B)Z_t$, then

$$f_X(\lambda) = \frac{\sigma^2}{2\pi} \frac{\left|\theta\left(e^{-i\lambda}\right)\right|^2}{\left|\phi\left(e^{-i\lambda}\right)\right|^2}, \qquad -\pi \le \lambda \le \pi. \tag{4.4.1}$$

Because the spectral density of an ARMA process is a ratio of trigonometric polynomials, it is often called a **rational spectral density**.

Proof

From (3.1.3), $\{X_t\}$ is obtained from $\{Z_t\}$ by application of the TLF with transfer function

$$\Psi\left(e^{-i\lambda}\right) = \frac{\theta\left(e^{-i\lambda}\right)}{\phi\left(e^{-i\lambda}\right)}.$$

Since $\{Z_t\}$ has spectral density $f_Z(\lambda) = \sigma^2/(2\pi)$, the result now follows from Proposition 4.3.1. ■

For any specified values of the parameters $\phi_1, \ldots, \phi_p, \theta_1, \ldots, \theta_q$ and σ^2, the `Spectrum>Model` option of ITSM can be used to plot the model spectral density.

Example 4.4.1 The spectral density of an AR(2) process

For an AR(2) process (4.4.1) becomes

$$f_X(\lambda) = \frac{\sigma^2}{2\pi\left(1 - \phi_1 e^{-i\lambda} - \phi_2 e^{-2i\lambda}\right)\left(1 - \phi_1 e^{i\lambda} - \phi_2 e^{2i\lambda}\right)}$$

$$= \frac{\sigma^2}{2\pi\left(1 + \phi_1^2 + 2\phi_2 + \phi_2^2 + 2(\phi_1\phi_2 - \phi_1)\cos\lambda - 4\phi_2\cos^2\lambda\right)}.$$

Figure 4.14 shows the spectral density, found from the `Spectrum>Model` option of ITSM, for the model (3.2.20) fitted to the mean-corrected sunspot series. Notice the well-defined peak in the model spectral density. The frequency at which this peak occurs can be found by differentiating the denominator of the spectral density with respect to $\cos\lambda$ and setting the derivative equal to zero. This gives

$$\cos\lambda = \frac{\phi_1\phi_2 - \phi_1}{4\phi_2} = 0.849.$$

The corresponding frequency is $\lambda = 0.556$ radians per year, or equivalently $c = \lambda/(2\pi) = 0.0885$ cycles per year, and the corresponding period is therefore $1/0.0885 = 11.3$ years. The model thus reflects the approximate cyclic behavior of

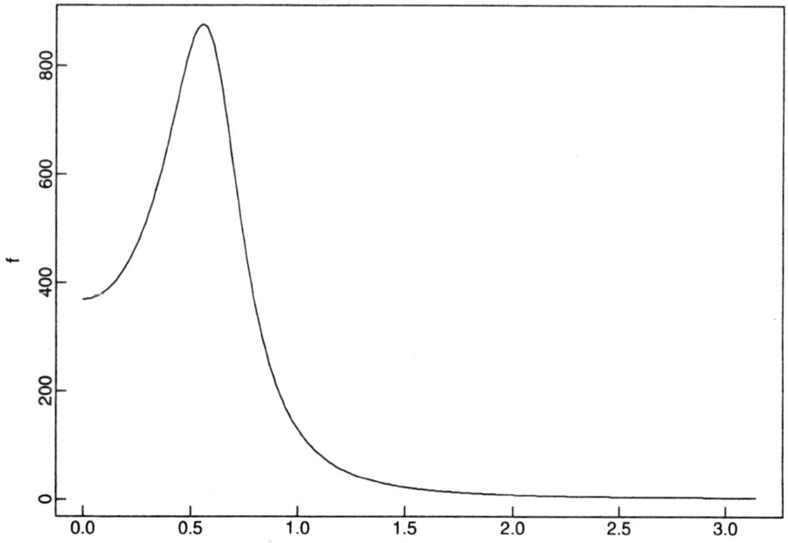

Figure 4-14 The spectral density $f_X(\lambda), 0 \leq \lambda \leq \pi$ of the AR(2) model (3.2.20) fitted to the mean-corrected sunspot series.

the data already pointed out in Example 4.2.2. The model spectral density in Figure 4.14 should be compared with the rescaled periodogram of the data and the nonparametric spectral density estimates of Figures 4.9–4.11. □

Example 4.4.2 The ARMA(1,1) process

In this case the expression (4.4.1) becomes

$$f_X(\lambda) = \frac{\sigma^2(1+\theta e^{i\lambda})(1+\theta e^{-i\lambda})}{2\pi(1-\phi e^{i\lambda})(1-\phi e^{-i\lambda})} = \frac{\sigma^2(1+\theta^2+2\theta\cos\lambda)}{2\pi(1+\phi^2-2\phi\cos\lambda)}.$$

□

Rational Spectral Density Estimation

An alternative to the spectral density estimator of Definition 4.2.2 is the estimator obtained by fitting an ARMA model to the data and then computing the spectral density of the fitted model. The spectral density shown in Figure 4.14 can be regarded as such an estimate, obtained by fitting an AR(2) model to the mean-corrected sunspot data.

Provided that there is an ARMA model that fits the data satisfactorily, this procedure has the advantage that it can be made systematic by selecting the model according (for example) to the AICC criterion (see Section 5.5.2). For further information see TSTM, Section 10.6.

Problems

4.1. Show that

$$\int_{-\pi}^{\pi} e^{i(k-h)\lambda}\, d\lambda = \begin{cases} 2\pi, & \text{if } k = h, \\ 0, & \text{otherwise.} \end{cases}$$

4.2. If $\{Z_t\} \sim \mathrm{WN}(0, \sigma^2)$, apply Corollary 4.1.1 to compute the spectral density of $\{Z_t\}$.

4.3. Show that the vectors $\mathbf{e}_1, \ldots, \mathbf{e}_n$ are orthonormal in the sense of (4.2.3).

4.4. Use Corollary 4.1.1 to establish whether or not the following function is the autocovariance function of a stationary process $\{X_t\}$:

$$\gamma(h) = \begin{cases} 1 & \text{if } h = 0, \\ -0.5 & \text{if } h = \pm 2, \\ -0.25 & \text{if } h = \pm 3, \\ 0 & \text{otherwise.} \end{cases}$$

4.5. If $\{X_t\}$ and $\{Y_t\}$ are uncorrelated stationary processes with autocovariance functions $\gamma_X(\cdot)$ and $\gamma_Y(\cdot)$ and spectral distribution functions $F_X(\cdot)$ and $F_Y(\cdot)$, respectively, show that the process $\{Z_t = X_t + Y_t\}$ is stationary with autocovariance function $\gamma_Z = \gamma_X + \gamma_Y$ and spectral distribution function $F_Z = F_X + F_Y$.

4.6. Let $\{X_t\}$ be the process defined by

$$X_t = A\cos(\pi t/3) + B\sin(\pi t/3) + Y_t,$$

where $Y_t = Z_t + 2.5Z_{t-1}$, $\{Z_t\} \sim \text{WN}(0, \sigma^2)$, A and B are uncorrelated with mean 0 and variance ν^2, and Z_t is uncorrelated with A and B for each t. Find the autocovariance function and spectral distribution function of $\{X_t\}$.

4.7. Let $\{X_t\}$ denote the sunspot series filed as SUNSPOTS.TSM and let $\{Y_t\}$ denote the mean-corrected series $Y_t = X_t - 46.93$, $t = 1, \ldots, 100$. Use ITSM to find the Yule–Walker AR(2) model

$$Y_t = \phi_1 Y_{t-1} + \phi_2 Y_{t-2} + Z_t, \quad \{Z_t\} \sim \text{WN}\left(0, \sigma^2\right),$$

i.e., find ϕ_1, ϕ_2, and σ^2. Use ITSM to plot the spectral density of the fitted model and find the frequency at which it achieves its maximum value. What is the corresponding period?

4.8. a. Use ITSM to compute and plot the spectral density of the stationary series $\{X_t\}$ satisfying

$$X_t - 0.99X_{t-3} = Z_t, \quad \{Z_t\} \sim \text{WN}(0, 1).$$

b. Does the spectral density suggest that the sample paths of $\{X_t\}$ will exhibit approximately oscillatory behavior? If so, then with what period?

c. Use ITSM to simulate a realization of $X_1, \ldots, X_{60}$ and plot the realization. Does the graph of the realization support the conclusion of part (b)? Save the generated series as X.TSM by clicking on the window displaying the graph, then on the red EXP button near the top of the screen. Select `Time Series` and `File` in the resulting dialog box and click `OK`. You will then be asked to provide the file name, X.TSM.

d. Compute the spectral density of the filtered process

$$Y_t = \frac{1}{3}(X_{t-1} + X_t + X_{t+1})$$

and compare the numerical values of the spectral densities of $\{X_t\}$ and $\{Y_t\}$ at frequency $\omega = 2\pi/3$ radians per unit time. What effect would you expect the filter to have on the oscillations of $\{X_t\}$?

e. Open the project X.TSM and use the option `Smooth>Moving Ave.` to apply the filter of part (d) to the realization generated in part (c). Comment on the result.

4.9. The spectral density of a real-valued time series $\{X_t\}$ is defined on $[0, \pi]$ by

$$f(\lambda) = \begin{cases} 100, & \text{if } \pi/6 - .01 < \lambda < \pi/6 + .01, \\ 0, & \text{otherwise,} \end{cases}$$

and on $[-\pi, 0]$ by $f(\lambda) = f(-\lambda)$.

a. Evaluate the ACVF of $\{X_t\}$ at lags 0 and 1.

b. Find the spectral density of the process $\{Y_t\}$ defined by

$$Y_t := \nabla_{12} X_t = X_t - X_{t-12}.$$

c. What is the variance of Y_t?

d. Sketch the power transfer function of the filter ∇_{12} and use the sketch to explain the effect of the filter on sinusoids with frequencies (i) near zero and (ii) near $\pi/6$.

4.10. Suppose that $\{X_t\}$ is the noncausal and noninvertible ARMA(1,1) process satisfying

$$X_t - \phi X_{t-1} = Z_t + \theta Z_{t-1}, \quad \{Z_t\} \sim \mathrm{WN}\left(0, \sigma^2\right),$$

where $|\phi| > 1$ and $|\theta| > 1$. Define $\tilde{\phi}(B) = 1 - \frac{1}{\phi} B$ and $\tilde{\theta}(B) = 1 + \frac{1}{\theta} B$ and let $\{W_t\}$ be the process given by

$$W_t := \tilde{\theta}^{-1}(B) \tilde{\phi}(B) X_t.$$

a. Show that $\{W_t\}$ has a constant spectral density function.

b. Conclude that $\{W_t\} \sim \mathrm{WN}\left(0, \sigma_w^2\right)$. Give an explicit formula for σ_w^2 in terms of ϕ, θ, and σ^2.

c. Deduce that $\tilde{\phi}(B) X_t = \tilde{\theta}(B) W_t$, so that $\{X_t\}$ is a causal and invertible ARMA(1,1) process relative to the white noise sequence $\{W_t\}$.

5 Modeling and Forecasting with ARMA Processes

The determination of an appropriate ARMA(p, q) model to represent an observed stationary time series involves a number of interrelated problems. These include the choice of p and q (order selection) and estimation of the mean, the coefficients $\{\phi_i, i = 1, \ldots, p\}$, $\{\theta_i, i = 1, \ldots, q\}$, and the white noise variance σ^2. Final selection of the model depends on a variety of goodness of fit tests, although it can be systematized to a large degree by use of criteria such as minimization of the AICC statistic as discussed in Section 5.5. (A useful option in the program ITSM is `Model>Estimation>Autofit`, which automatically minimizes the AICC statistic over all ARMA(p, q) processes with p and q in a specified range.)

This chapter is primarily devoted to the problem of estimating the parameters $\boldsymbol{\phi} = (\phi_i, \ldots, \phi_p)h'$, $\boldsymbol{\theta} = (\theta_i, \ldots, \theta_q)h'$, and σ^2 when p and q are assumed to be known, but the crucial issue of order selection is also considered. It will be assumed throughout (unless the mean is believed a priori to be zero) that the data have been "mean-corrected" by subtraction of the sample mean, so that it is appropriate to fit a zero-mean ARMA model to the adjusted data $x_1, \ldots, x_n$. If the model fitted to the mean-corrected data is

$$\phi(B)X_t = \theta(B)Z_t, \quad \{Z_t\} \sim \text{WN}\left(0, \sigma^2\right),$$

then the corresponding model for the original stationary series $\{Y_t\}$ is found on replacing X_t for each t by $Y_t - \overline{y}$, where $\overline{y} = n^{-1} \sum_{j=1}^{n} y_j$ is the sample mean of the original data, treated as a fixed constant.

When p and q are known, good estimators of $\boldsymbol{\phi}$ and $\boldsymbol{\theta}$ can be found by imagining the data to be observations of a stationary Gaussian time series and maximizing the likelihood with respect to the $p + q + 1$ parameters $\phi_1, \ldots, \phi_p, \theta_1, \ldots, \theta_q$ and σ^2. The estimators obtained by this procedure are known as maximum likelihood (or maximum Gaussian likelihood) estimators. Maximum likelihood estimation is discussed in Section 5.2 and can be carried out in practice using the ITSM option `Model>Estimation>Max likelihood`, after first specifying a preliminary model to initialize the maximization algorithm. Maximization of the likelihood and selection of the minimum AICC model over a specified range of p and q values can also be carried out using the option `Model>Estimation>Autofit`.

The maximization is nonlinear in the sense that the function to be maximized is not a quadratic function of the unknown parameters, so the estimators cannot be found by solving a system of linear equations. They are found instead by searching numerically for the maximum of the likelihood surface. The algorithm used in ITSM requires the specification of initial parameter values with which to begin the search. The closer the preliminary estimates are to the maximum likelihood estimates, the faster the search will generally be.

To provide these initial values, a number of preliminary estimation algorithms are available in the option `Model>Estimation>Preliminary` of ITSM. They are described in Section 5.1. For pure autoregressive models the choice is between Yule–Walker and Burg estimation, while for models with $q > 0$ it is between the innovations and Hannan–Rissanen algorithms. It is also possible to begin the search with an arbitrary causal ARMA model by using the option `Model>Specify` and entering the desired parameter values. The initial values are chosen automatically in the option `Model>Estimation>Autofit`.

Calculation of the exact Gaussian likelihood for an ARMA model (and in fact for *any* second-order model) is greatly simplified by use of the innovations algorithm. In Section 5.2 we take advantage of this simplification in discussing maximum likelihood estimation and consider also the construction of confidence intervals for the estimated coefficients.

Section 5.3 deals with goodness of fit tests for the chosen model and Section 5.4 with the use of the fitted model for forecasting. In Section 5.5 we discuss the theoretical basis for some of the criteria used for order selection.

For an overview of the general strategy for model-fitting see Section 6.2.

5.1 Preliminary Estimation

In this section we shall consider four techniques for preliminary estimation of the parameters $\boldsymbol{\phi} = (\phi_1, \ldots, \phi_p)'$, $\boldsymbol{\theta} = (\theta_1, \ldots, \phi_p)'$, and σ^2 from observations $x_1, \ldots, x_n$

of the causal ARMA(p,q) process defined by

$$\phi(B)X_t = \theta(B)Z_t, \quad \{Z_t\} \sim \mathrm{WN}(0,\sigma^2). \tag{5.1.1}$$

The Yule–Walker and Burg procedures apply to the fitting of pure autoregressive models. (Although the former can be adapted to models with $q > 0$, its performance is less efficient than when $q = 0$.) The innovation and Hannan–Rissanen algorithms are used in ITSM to provide preliminary estimates of the ARMA parameters when $q > 0$.

For pure autoregressive models Burg's algorithm usually gives higher likelihoods than the Yule–Walker equations. For pure moving-average models the innovations algorithm frequently gives slightly higher likelihoods than the Hannan–Rissanen algorithm (we use only the first two steps of the latter for preliminary estimation). For mixed models (i.e., those with $p > 0$ and $q > 0$) the Hannan–Rissanen algorithm is usually more successful in finding causal models (which are required for initialization of the likelihood maximization).

5.1.1 Yule–Walker Estimation

For a pure autoregressive model the moving-average polynomial $\theta(z)$ is identically 1, and the causality assumption in (5.1.1) allows us to write X_t in the form

$$X_t = \sum_{j=0}^{\infty} \psi_j Z_{t-j}, \tag{5.1.2}$$

where, from Section 3.1, $\psi(z) = \sum_{j=0}^{\infty} \psi_j z^j = 1/\phi(z)$. Multiplying each side of (5.1.1) by X_{t-j}, $j = 0, 1, 2, \ldots, p$, taking expectations, and using (5.1.2) to evaluate the right-hand side of the first equation, we obtain the Yule–Walker equations

$$\Gamma_p \boldsymbol{\phi} = \boldsymbol{\gamma}_p \tag{5.1.3}$$

and

$$\sigma^2 = \gamma(0) - \boldsymbol{\phi}'\boldsymbol{\gamma}_p, \tag{5.1.4}$$

where Γ_p is the covariance matrix $[\gamma(i-j)]_{i,j=1}^{p}$ and $\boldsymbol{\gamma}_p = (\gamma(1), \ldots, \gamma(p))'$. These equations can be used to determine $\gamma(0), \ldots, \gamma(p)$ from σ^2 and $\boldsymbol{\phi}$.

On the other hand, if we replace the covariances $\gamma(j)$, $j = 0, \ldots, p$, appearing in (5.1.3) and (5.1.4) by the corresponding sample covariances $\hat{\gamma}(j)$, we obtain a set of equations for the so-called Yule–Walker estimators $\hat{\boldsymbol{\phi}}$ and $\hat{\sigma}^2$ of $\boldsymbol{\phi}$ and σ^2, namely,

$$\hat{\Gamma}_p \hat{\boldsymbol{\phi}} = \hat{\boldsymbol{\gamma}}_p \tag{5.1.5}$$

and

$$\hat{\sigma}^2 = \hat{\gamma}(0) - \hat{\boldsymbol{\phi}}'\hat{\boldsymbol{\gamma}}_p, \tag{5.1.6}$$

where $\hat{\Gamma}_p = \left[\hat{\gamma}(i-j)\right]_{i,j=1}^{p}$ and $\hat{\boldsymbol{\gamma}}_p = \left(\hat{\gamma}(1), \ldots, \hat{\gamma}(p)\right)'$.

If $\hat{\gamma}(0) > 0$, then $\hat{\Gamma}_m$ is nonsingular for every $m = 1, 2, \ldots$ (see TSTM, Problem 7.11), so we can rewrite equations (5.1.5) and (5.1.6) in the following form:

Sample Yule–Walker Equations:

$$\hat{\phi} = \left(\hat{\phi}_1, \ldots, \hat{\phi}_p\right)' = \hat{R}_p^{-1}\hat{\rho}_p \tag{5.1.7}$$

and

$$\hat{\sigma}^2 = \hat{\gamma}(0)\left[1 - \hat{\rho}_p'\hat{R}_p^{-1}\hat{\rho}_p\right], \tag{5.1.8}$$

where $\hat{\rho}_p = \left(\hat{\rho}(1), \ldots, \hat{\rho}(p)\right)' = \hat{\gamma}_p/\hat{\gamma}(0)$.

With $\hat{\phi}$ as defined by (5.1.7), it can be shown that $1 - \hat{\phi}_1 z - \cdots - \hat{\phi}_p z^p \neq 0$ for $|z| \leq 1$ (see TSTM, Problem 8.3). Hence the fitted model

$$X_t - \hat{\phi}_1 X_{t-1} - \cdots - \hat{\phi}_p X_{t-p} = Z_t, \quad \{Z_t\} \sim \mathrm{WN}\left(0, \hat{\sigma}^2\right)$$

is causal. The autocovariances $\gamma_F(h)$, $h = 0, \ldots, p$, of the fitted model therefore satisfy the $p + 1$ linear equations

$$\gamma_F(h) - \hat{\phi}_1\gamma_F(h-1) - \cdots - \hat{\phi}_p\gamma_F(h-p) = \begin{cases} 0, & h = 1, \ldots, p, \\ \hat{\sigma}^2, & h = 0. \end{cases}$$

However, from (5.1.5) and (5.1.6) we see that the solution of these equations is $\gamma_F(h) = \hat{\gamma}(h)$, $h = 0, \ldots, p$, so that the autocovariances of the fitted model at lags $0, 1, \ldots, p$ coincide with the corresponding sample autocovariances.

The argument of the preceding paragraph shows that for *every* nonsingular covariance matrix of the form $\Gamma_{p+1} = [\gamma(i-j)]_{i,j=1}^{p+1}$ there is an AR(p) process whose autocovariances at lags $0, \ldots, p$ are $\gamma(0), \ldots, \gamma(p)$. (The required coefficients and white noise variance are found from (5.1.7) and (5.1.8) on replacing $\hat{\rho}(j)$ by $\gamma(j)/\gamma(0)$, $j = 0, \ldots, p$, and $\hat{\gamma}(0)$ by $\gamma(0)$.) There may not, however, be an MA(p) process with this property. For example, if $\gamma(0) = 1$ and $\gamma(1) = \gamma(-1) = \beta$, the matrix Γ_2 is a nonsingular covariance matrix for all $\beta \in (-1, 1)$. Consequently, there is an AR(1) process with autocovariances 1 and β at lags 0 and 1 for all $\beta \in (-1, 1)$. However, there is an MA(1) process with autocovariances 1 and β at lags 0 and 1 if and only if $|\beta| \leq \frac{1}{2}$. (See Example 2.1.1.)

It is often the case that moment estimators, i.e., estimators that (like $\hat{\phi}$) are obtained by equating theoretical and sample moments, have much higher variances than estimators obtained by alternative methods such as maximum likelihood. However, the Yule–Walker estimators of the coefficients $\phi_1, \ldots, \phi_p$ of an AR(p) process have approximately the same distribution for large samples as the corresponding maximum likelihood estimators. For a precise statement of this result see TSTM, Section 8.10. For our purposes it suffices to note the following:

Large-Sample Distribution of Yule–Walker Estimators:

For a large sample from an AR(p) process,

$$\hat{\phi} \approx N\left(\phi, n^{-1}\sigma^2\Gamma_p^{-1}\right).$$

If we replace σ^2 and Γ_p by their estimates $\hat{\sigma}^2$ and $\hat{\Gamma}_p$, we can use this result to find large-sample confidence regions for ϕ and each of its components as in (5.1.12) and (5.1.13) below.

Order Selection

In practice we do not know the true order of the model generating the data. In fact, it will usually be the case that there is *no* true AR model, in which case our goal is simply to find one that represents the data optimally in some sense. Two useful techniques for selecting an appropriate AR model are given below. The second is more systematic and extends beyond the narrow class of pure autoregressive models.

- Some guidance in the choice of order is provided by a large-sample result (see TSTM, Section 8.10), which states that if $\{X_t\}$ is the causal AR(p) process defined by (5.1.1) with $\{Z_t\} \sim \text{iid}\left(0, \sigma^2\right)$ and if we fit a model with order $m > p$ using the Yule–Walker equations, i.e., if we fit a model with coefficient vector

  $$\hat{\phi}_m = \hat{R}_m^{-1}\hat{\rho}_m, \quad m > p,$$

  then the *last component*, $\hat{\phi}_{mm}$, of the vector $\hat{\phi}_m$ is approximately normally distributed with mean 0 and variance $1/n$. Notice that $\hat{\phi}_{mm}$ is exactly the sample partial autocorrelation at lag m as defined in Section 3.2.3.

  Now, we already know from Example 3.2.6 that for an AR(p), process the partial autocorrelations ϕ_{mm}, $m > p$, are zero. By the result of the previous paragraph, if an AR(p) model is appropriate for the data, then the values $\hat{\phi}_{kk}$, $k > p$, should be compatible with observations from the distribution N(0, $1/n$). In particular, for $k > p$, $\hat{\phi}_{kk}$ will fall between the bounds $\pm 1.96n^{-1/2}$ with probability close to 0.95. This suggests using as a preliminary estimator of p the smallest value m such that $\left|\hat{\phi}_{kk}\right| < 1.96n^{-1/2}$ for $k > m$.

  The program ITSM plots the sample PACF $\left\{\hat{\phi}_{mm}, m = 1, 2, \ldots\right\}$ together with the bounds $\pm 1.96/\sqrt{n}$. From this graph it is easy to read off the preliminary estimator of p defined above.

- A more systematic approach to order selection is to find the values of p and ϕ_p that minimize the AICC statistic (see Section 5.5.2 below)

  $$\text{AICC} = -2\ln L(\phi_p, S(\phi_p)/n) + 2(p+1)n/(n-p-2),$$

where L is the Gaussian likelihood defined in (5.2.9) and S is defined in (5.2.11). The `Preliminary Estimation` dialog box of ITSM (opened by pressing the blue PRE button) allows you to search for the minimum AICC Yule–Walker (or Burg) models by checking `Find AR model with min AICC`. This causes the program to fit autoregressions of orders $0, 1, \ldots, 27$ and to return the model with smallest AICC value.

Definition 5.1.1

The **fitted Yule–Walker AR(m) model** is

$$X_t - \hat{\phi}_{m1} X_{t-1} - \cdots - \hat{\phi}_{mm} X_{t-m} = Z_t, \quad \{Z_t\} \sim \mathrm{WN}\left(0, \hat{v}_m\right), \tag{5.1.9}$$

where

$$\hat{\phi}_m = \left(\hat{\phi}_{m1}, \ldots, \hat{\phi}_{mm}\right)' = \hat{R}_m^{-1} \hat{\rho}_m \tag{5.1.10}$$

and

$$\hat{v}_m = \hat{\gamma}(0)\left[1 - \hat{\rho}_m' \hat{R}_m^{-1} \hat{\rho}_m\right]. \tag{5.1.11}$$

For both approaches to order selection we need to fit AR models of gradually increasing order to our given data. The problem of solving the Yule–Walker equations with gradually increasing orders has already been encountered in a slightly different context in Section 2.5.1, where we derived a recursive scheme for solving the equations (5.1.3) and (5.1.4) with p successively taking the values $1, 2, \ldots$. Here we can use exactly the same scheme (the Durbin–Levinson algorithm) to solve the Yule–Walker equations (5.1.5) and (5.1.6), the only difference being that the covariances in (5.1.3) and (5.1.4) are replaced by their sample counterparts. This is the algorithm used by ITSM to perform the necessary calculations.

Confidence Regions for the Coefficients

Under the assumption that the order p of the fitted model is the correct value, we can use the asymptotic distribution of $\hat{\phi}_p$ to derive approximate large-sample confidence regions for the true coefficient vector ϕ_p and for its individual components ϕ_{pj}. Thus, if $\chi^2_{1-\alpha}(p)$ denotes the $(1-\alpha)$ quantile of the chi-squared distribution with p degrees of freedom, then for large sample-size n the region

$$\left\{\phi \in \mathbf{R}^p : \left(\hat{\phi}_p - \phi\right)' \hat{\Gamma}_p \left(\hat{\phi}_p - \phi\right) \le n^{-1} \hat{v}_p \chi^2_{1-\alpha}(p)\right\} \tag{5.1.12}$$

contains ϕ_p with probability close to $(1-\alpha)$. (This follows from Problem A.7 and the fact that $\sqrt{n}(\hat{\phi}_p - \phi_p)$ is approximately normally distributed with mean $\mathbf{0}$ and covariance matrix $\hat{v}_p \hat{\Gamma}_p^{-1}$.) Similarly, if $\Phi_{1-\alpha}$ denotes the $(1-\alpha)$ quantile of the standard normal distribution and $\hat{v}_{jj}$ is the jth diagonal element of $\hat{v}_p \hat{\Gamma}_p^{-1}$, then for large n the interval bounded by

$$\hat{\phi}_{pj} \pm \Phi_{1-\alpha/2} n^{-1/2} \hat{v}_{jj}^{1/2} \tag{5.1.13}$$

contains ϕ_{pj} with probability close to $(1-\alpha)$.

Example 5.1.1 The Dow Jones Utilities Index, Aug. 28–Dec. 18, 1972; DOWJ.TSM

The very slowly decaying positive sample ACF of the time series contained in the file DOWJ.TSM this time series suggests differencing at lag 1 before attempting to fit a stationary model. One application of the operator $(1-B)$ produces a new series $\{Y_t\}$ with no obvious deviations from stationarity. We shall therefore try fitting an AR process to this new series

$$Y_t = D_t - D_{t-1}$$

using the Yule–Walker equations. There are 77 values of Y_t, which we shall denote by $Y_1, \ldots, Y_{77}$. (We ignore the unequal spacing of the original data resulting from the five-day working week.) The sample autocovariances of the series $y_1, \ldots, y_{77}$ are $\hat{\gamma}(0) = 0.17992$, $\hat{\gamma}(1) = 0.07590$, $\hat{\gamma}(2) = 0.04885$, etc.

Applying the Durbin–Levinson algorithm to fit successively higher-order autoregressive processes to the data, we obtain

$$\hat{\phi}_{11} = \hat{\rho}(1) = 0.4219,$$

$$\hat{v}_1 = \hat{\gamma}(0)\left[1 - \hat{\rho}^2(1)\right] = 0.1479,$$

$$\hat{\phi}_{22} = \left[\hat{\gamma}(2) - \hat{\phi}_{11}\hat{\gamma}(1)\right]/\hat{v}_1 = 0.1138,$$

$$\hat{\phi}_{21} = \hat{\phi}_{11} - \hat{\phi}_{11}\hat{\phi}_{22} = 0.3739,$$

$$\hat{v}_2 = \hat{v}_1\left[1 - \hat{\phi}_{22}^2\right] = 0.1460.$$

The sample ACF and PACF of the data can be displayed by pressing the second yellow button at the top of the ITSM window. They are shown in Figures 5.1 and 5.2, respectively. Also plotted are the bounds $\pm 1.96/\sqrt{77}$. Since the PACF values at lags greater than 1 all lie between the bounds, the first order-selection criterion described above indicates that we should fit an AR(1) model to the data set $\{Y_t\}$. Unless we wish to assume that $\{Y_t\}$ is a zero-mean process, we should subtract the sample mean from the data before attempting to fit a (zero-mean) AR(1) model. When the blue PRE (preliminary estimation) button at the top of the ITSM window is pressed, you will be given the option of subtracting the mean from the data. In this case (as in most) click `Yes` to obtain the new series

$$X_t = Y_t - 0.1336.$$

You will then see the `Preliminary Estimation` dialog box. Enter 1 for the AR order, zero for the MA order, select `Yule-Walker`, and click `OK`. We have already computed $\hat{\phi}_{11}$ and $\hat{v}_1$ above using the Durbin–Levinson algorithm. The Yule–Walker AR(1) model obtained by ITSM for $\{X_t\}$ is therefore (not surprisingly)

$$X_t - 0.4219X_{t-1} = Z_t, \quad \{Z_t\} \sim \text{WN}(0, 0.1479), \tag{5.1.14}$$

and the corresponding model for $\{Y_t\}$ is

$$Y_t - 0.1336 - 0.4219(Y_{t-1} - 0.1336) = Z_t, \quad \{Z_t\} \sim \text{WN}(0, 0.1479). \tag{5.1.15}$$

Assuming that our observed data really are generated by an AR process with $p = 1$, (5.1.13) gives us approximate 95% confidence bounds for the autoregressive coefficient ϕ,

$$0.4219 \pm \frac{(1.96)(.1479)}{(.17992)\sqrt{77}} = (0.2194, 0.6244).$$

Besides estimating the autoregressive coefficients, ITSM computes and prints out the ratio of each coefficient to 1.96 times its estimated standard deviation. From these numbers large-sample 95% confidence intervals for each of the coefficients are easily obtained. In this particular example there is just one coefficient estimate, $\hat{\phi}_1 = 0.4219$, with ratio of coefficient to $1.96\times$standard error equal to 2.0832. Hence the required 95% confidence bounds are $0.4219 \pm 0.4219/2.0832 = (0.2194, 0.6244)$, as found above.

A useful technique for preliminary autoregressive estimation that incorporates automatic model selection (i.e., choice of p) is to minimize the AICC (see equation (5.5.4)) over all fitted autoregressions of orders 0 through 27. This is achieved by selecting *both* `Yule-Walker` and `Find AR model with min AICC` in the `Prelim-`

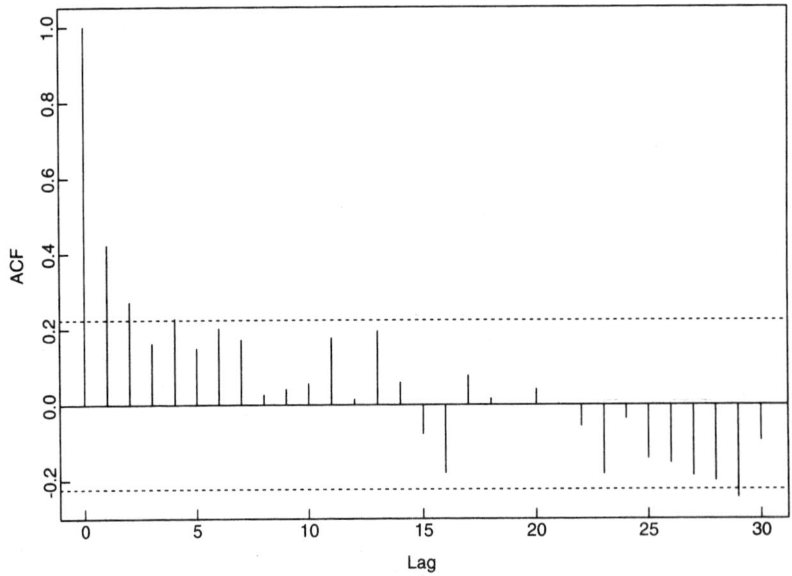

Figure 5-1 The sample ACF of the differenced series $\{Y_t\}$ in Example 5.1.1.

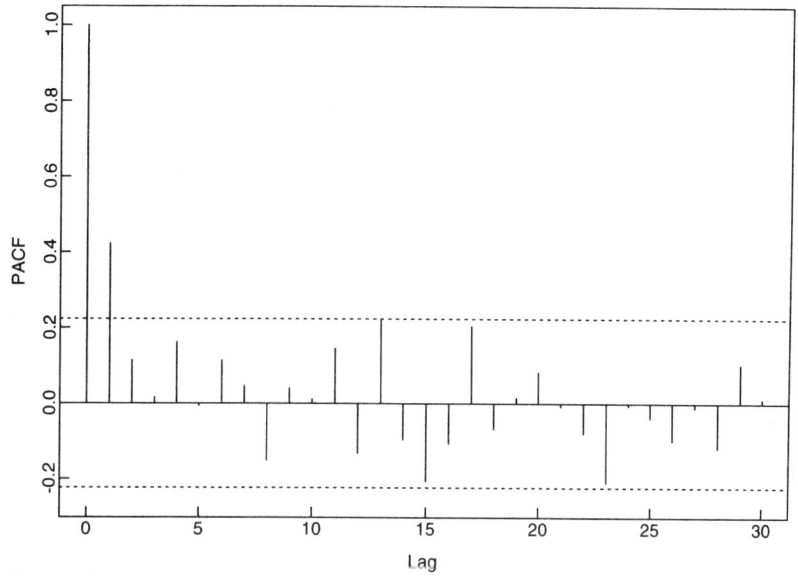

Figure 5-2 The sample PACF of the differenced series $\{Y_t\}$ in Example 5.1.1.

`inary Estimation` dialog box. (The MA order must be set to zero, but the AR order setting is immaterial.) Click `OK`, and the program will search through all the Yule–Walker AR(p) models, $p = 0, 1, \ldots, 27$, selecting the one with smallest AICC value. The minimum-AICC Yule–Walker AR model turns out to be the one defined by (5.1.14) with $p = 1$ and AICC value 74.541. □

Yule–Walker Estimation with $q > 0$; Moment Estimators

The Yule–Walker estimates for the parameters in an AR(p) model are examples of moment estimators: The autocovariances at lags $0, 1, \ldots, p$ are replaced by the corresponding sample estimates in the Yule–Walker equations (5.1.3), which are then solved for the parameters $\phi = (\phi_1, \ldots, \phi_p)'$ and σ^2. The analogous procedure for ARMA(p, q) models with $q > 0$ is easily formulated, but the corresponding equations are nonlinear in the unknown coefficients, leading to possible nonexistence and nonuniqueness of solutions for the required estimators.

From (3.2.5), the equations to be solved for $\phi_1, \ldots, \phi_p, \theta_1, \ldots, \theta_q$ and σ^2 are

$$\hat{\gamma}(k) - \phi_1\hat{\gamma}(k-1) - \cdots - \phi_p\hat{\gamma}(k-p) = \sigma^2 \sum_{j=k}^{q} \theta_j \psi_{j-k}, \quad 0 \le k \le p+q, \qquad (5.1.16)$$

where ψ_j must first be expressed in terms of ϕ and θ using the identity $\psi(z) = \theta(z)/\phi(z)$ ($\theta_0 := 1$ and $\theta_j = \psi_j = 0$ for $j < 0$).

Example 5.1.2 For the MA(1) model the equations (5.1.16) are equivalent to

$$\hat{\gamma}(0) = \hat{\sigma}^2\left(1 + \hat{\theta}_1^2\right), \qquad (5.1.17)$$

$$\hat{\rho}(1) = \frac{\hat{\theta}_1}{1 + \hat{\theta}_1^2}. \tag{5.1.18}$$

If $|\hat{\rho}(1)| > .5$, there is no real solution, so we define $\hat{\theta}_1 = \hat{\rho}(1)/|\hat{\rho}(1)|$. If $|\hat{\rho}(1)| \le .5$, then the solution of (5.1.17)–(5.1.18) (with $|\hat{\theta}| \le 1$) is

$$\hat{\theta}_1 = \left(1 - \left(1 - 4\hat{\rho}^2(1)\right)^{1/2}\right) / \left(2\hat{\rho}(1)\right),$$

$$\hat{\sigma}^2 = \hat{\gamma}(0) / \left(1 + \hat{\theta}_1^2\right).$$

For the overshort data of Example 3.2.8, $\hat{\rho}(1) = -0.5035$ and $\hat{\gamma}(0) = 3416$, so the fitted MA(1) model has parameters $\hat{\theta}_1 = -1.0$ and $\hat{\sigma}^2 = 1708$. □

Relative Efficiency of Estimators

The performance of two competing estimators is often measured by computing their asymptotic relative efficiency. In a general statistics estimation problem, suppose $\hat{\theta}_n^{(1)}$ and $\hat{\theta}_n^{(2)}$ are two estimates of the parameter θ in the parameter space Θ based on the observations $X_1, \ldots, X_n$. If $\hat{\theta}_n^{(i)}$ is approximately $\mathrm{N}\left(\theta, \sigma_i^2(\theta)\right)$ for large n, $i = 1, 2$, then the **asymptotic efficiency** of $\hat{\theta}_n^{(1)}$ relative to $\hat{\theta}_n^{(2)}$ is defined to be

$$e\left(\theta, \hat{\theta}^{(1)}, \hat{\theta}^{(2)}\right) = \frac{\sigma_2^2(\theta)}{\sigma_1^2(\theta)}.$$

If $e\left(\theta, \hat{\theta}^{(1)}, \hat{\theta}^{(2)}\right) \le 1$ for all $\theta \in \Theta$, then we say that $\hat{\theta}_n^{(2)}$ is a more efficient estimator of θ than $\hat{\theta}_n^{(1)}$ (strictly more efficient if in addition, $e\left(\theta, \hat{\theta}^{(1)}, \hat{\theta}^{(2)}\right) < 1$ for some $\theta \in \Theta$). For the MA(1) process the moment estimator $\theta_n^{(1)}$ discussed in Example 5.1.2 is approximately $\mathrm{N}\left(\theta_1, \sigma_1^2(\theta_1)/n\right)$ with

$$\sigma_1^2(\theta_1) = (1 + \theta_1^2 + 4\theta_1^4 + \theta_1^6 + \theta_1^8)/(1 - \theta_1^2)^2$$

(see TSTM, p. 254). On the other hand, the innovations estimator $\hat{\theta}_n^{(2)}$ discussed in the next section is distributed approximately as $\mathrm{N}\left(\theta_1, n^{-1}\right)$. Thus, $e\left(\theta_1, \hat{\theta}^{(1)}, \hat{\theta}^{(2)}\right) = \sigma_1^{-2}(\theta_1) \le 1$ for all $|\theta_1| < 1$, with strict inequality when $\theta \ne 1$. In particular,

$$e\left(\theta_1, \hat{\theta}^{(1)}, \hat{\theta}^{(2)}\right) = \begin{cases} .82, & \theta_1 = .25, \\ .37, & \theta_1 = .50, \\ .06, & \theta_1 = .75, \end{cases}$$

demonstrating the superiority, at least in terms of asymptotic relative efficiency, of $\hat{\theta}_n^{(2)}$ over $\hat{\theta}_n^{(1)}$. On the other hand (Section 5.2), the maximum likelihood estimator $\hat{\theta}_n^{(3)}$ of θ_1 is approximately $\mathrm{N}(\theta_1, (1 - \theta_1^2)/n)$. Hence,

$$e\left(\theta_1, \hat{\theta}^{(2)}, \hat{\theta}^{(3)}\right) = \begin{cases} .94, & \theta_1 = .25, \\ .75, & \theta_1 = .50, \\ .44, & \theta_1 = .75. \end{cases}$$

While $\hat{\theta}_n^{(3)}$ is more efficient, $\hat{\theta}_n^{(2)}$ has reasonably good efficiency, except when $|\theta_1|$ is close to 1, and can serve as initial value for the nonlinear optimization procedure in computing the maximum likelihood estimator.

While the method of moments is an effective procedure for fitting autoregressive models, it does not perform as well for ARMA models with $q > 0$. From a computational point of view, it requires as much computing time as the more efficient estimators based on either the innovations algorithm or the Hannan–Rissanen procedure and is therefore rarely used except when $q = 0$.

5.1.2 Burg's Algorithm

The Yule–Walker coefficients $\hat{\phi}_{p1}, \ldots, \hat{\phi}_{pp}$ are precisely the coefficients of the best linear predictor of X_{p+1} in terms of $\{X_p, \ldots, X_1\}$ under the assumption that the ACF of $\{X_t\}$ coincides with the sample ACF at lags $1, \ldots, p$.

Burg's algorithm estimates the PACF $\{\phi_{11}, \phi_{22}, \ldots\}$ by successively minimizing sums of squares of forward and backward one-step prediction errors with respect to the coefficients ϕ_{ii}. Given observations $\{x_1, \ldots, x_n\}$ of a stationary zero-mean time series $\{X_t\}$ we define $u_i(t), t = i+1, \ldots, n, 0 \le i < n$, to be the difference between $x_{n+1+i-t}$ and the best linear estimate of $x_{n+1+i-t}$ in terms of the preceding i observations. Similarly, we define $v_i(t), t = i + 1, \ldots, n, 0 \le i < n$, to be the difference between x_{n+1-t} and the best linear estimate of x_{n+1-t} in terms of the subsequent i observations. Then it can be shown (see Problem 5.6) that the **forward and backward prediction errors** $\{u_i(t)\}$ and $\{v_i(t)\}$ satisfy the recursions

$$u_0(t) = v_0(t) = x_{n+1-t},$$

$$u_i(t) = u_{i-1}(t-1) - \phi_{ii} v_{i-1}(t), \tag{5.1.19}$$

and

$$v_i(t) = v_{i-1}(t) - \phi_{ii} u_{i-1}(t-1). \tag{5.1.20}$$

Burg's estimate $\phi_{11}^{(B)}$ of ϕ_{11} is found by minimizing

$$\sigma_1^2 := \frac{1}{2(n-1)} \sum_{t=2}^{n} \left[u_1^2(t) + v_1^2(t)\right]$$

with respect to ϕ_{11}. This gives corresponding numerical values for $u_1(t)$ and $v_1(t)$ and σ_1^2 that can then be substituted into (5.1.19) and (5.1.20) with $i = 2$. Then we minimize

$$\sigma_2^2 := \frac{1}{2(n-2)} \sum_{t=3}^{n} \left[u_2^2(t) + v_2^2(t)\right]$$

with respect to ϕ_{22} to obtain the Burg estimate $\phi_{22}^{(B)}$ of ϕ_{22} and corresponding values of $u_2(t)$, $v_2(t)$, and σ_2^2. This process can clearly be continued to obtain estimates $\phi_{pp}^{(B)}$

and corresponding minimum values, $\sigma_p^{(B)2}$, $p \le n-1$. Estimates of the coefficients ϕ_{pj}, $1 \le j \le p-1$, in the best linear predictor

$$P_pX_{p+1} = \phi_{p1}X_p + \cdots + \phi_{pp}X_1$$

are then found by substituting the estimates $\phi_{ii}^{(B)}$, $i = 1, \ldots, p$, for ϕ_{ii} in the recursions (2.5.20)–(2.5.22). The resulting estimates of ϕ_{pj}, $j = 1, \ldots, p$, are the coefficient estimates of the Burg AR(p) model for the data $\{x_1, \ldots, x_n\}$. The Burg estimate of the white noise variance is the minimum value $\sigma_p^{(B)2}$ found in the determination of $\phi_{pp}^{(B)}$. The calculation of the estimates of ϕ_{pp} and σ_p^2 described above is equivalent (Problem 5.7) to solving the following recursions:

Burg's Algorithm:

$$d(1) = \sum_{t=2}^{n}(u_0^2(t-1) + v_0^2(t)),$$

$$\phi_{ii}^{(B)} = \frac{2}{d(i)} \sum_{t=i+1}^{n} v_{i-1}(t)u_{i-1}(t-1),$$

$$d(i+1) = \left(1 - \phi_{ii}^{(B)2}\right) d(i) - v_i^2(i+1) - u_i^2(n),$$

$$\sigma_i^{(B)2} = \left[\left(1 - \phi_{ii}^{(B)2}\right) d(i)\right] / [2(n-i)].$$

The large-sample distribution of the estimated coefficients for the Burg estimators of the coefficients of an AR(p) process is the same as for the Yule–Walker estimators, namely, $\mathrm{N}(\phi, n^{-1}\sigma^2\Gamma_p^{-1})$. Approximate large-sample confidence intervals for the coefficients can be found as in Section 5.1.1 by substituting estimated values for σ^2 and Γ_p.

Example 5.1.3 The Dow Jones Utilities Index

The fitting of AR models using Burg's algorithm in the program ITSM is completely analogous to the use of the Yule–Walker equations. Applying the same transformations as in Example 5.1.1 to the Dow Jones Utilities Index and selecting `Burg` instead of `Yule-Walker` in the `Preliminary Estimation` dialog box, we obtain the minimum AICC Burg model

$$X_t - 0.4371X_{t-1} = Z_t, \quad \{Z_t\} \sim \mathrm{WN}(0, 0.1423), \tag{5.1.21}$$

with AICC = 74.492. This is slightly different from the Yule–Walker AR(1) model fitted in Example 5.1.1, and it has a larger likelihood L, i.e., a smaller value of $-2\ln L$ (see Section 5.2). Although the two methods give estimators with the same *large-sample* distributions, for finite sample sizes the Burg model usually has smaller estimated white noise variance and larger Gaussian likelihood. From the ratio of the estimated coefficient to (1.96× standard error) displayed by ITSM, we obtain the 95% confidence bounds for ϕ: $0.4371 \pm 0.4371/2.1668 = (0.2354, 0.6388)$. □

Example 5.1.4 The lake data

This series $\{Y_t, t = 1, \ldots, 98\}$ has already been studied in Example 1.3.5. In this example we shall consider the problem of fitting an AR process directly to the data without first removing any trend component. A graph of the data was displayed in Figure 1.9. The sample ACF and PACF are shown in Figures 5.3 and 5.4, respectively.

The sample PACF shown in Figure 5.4 strongly suggests fitting an AR(2) model to the mean-corrected data $X_t = Y_t - 9.0041$. After clicking on the blue preliminary estimation button of ITSM select Yes to subtract the sample mean from $\{Y_t\}$. Then specify 2 for the AR order, 0 for the MA order, and Burg for estimation. Click OK to obtain the model

$$X_t - 1.0449X_{t-1} + 0.2456X_{t-2} = Z_t, \quad \{Z_t\} \sim \text{WN}(0, 0.4706),$$

with AICC value 213.55 and 95% confidence bounds

$$\phi_1 : 1.0449 \pm 1.0449/5.5295 = (0.8559, 1.2339),$$

$$\phi_2 : -0.2456 \pm 0.2456/1.2997 = (-0.4346, -0.0566).$$

Selecting the Yule–Walker method for estimation, we obtain the model

$$X_t - 1.0538X_{t-1} + 0.2668X_{t-2} = Z_t, \quad \{Z_t\} \sim \text{WN}(0, 0.4920),$$

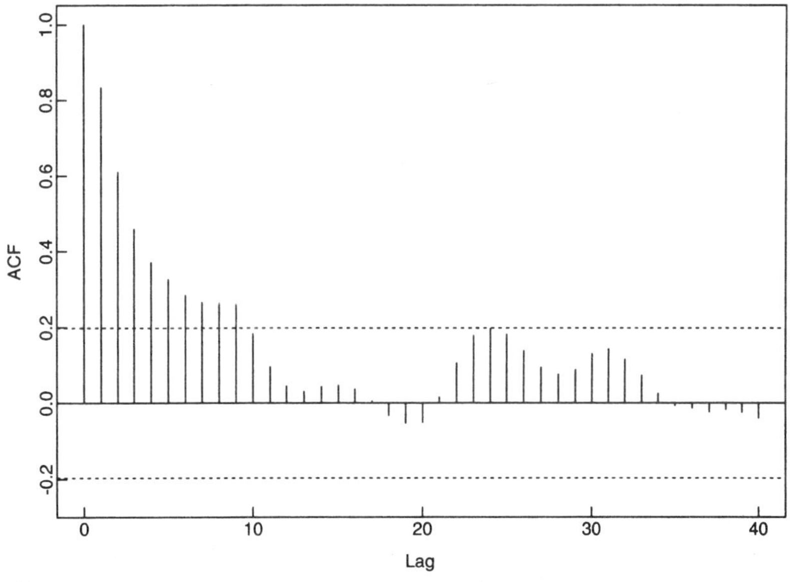

Figure 5-3 The sample ACF of the lake data in Example 5.1.4.

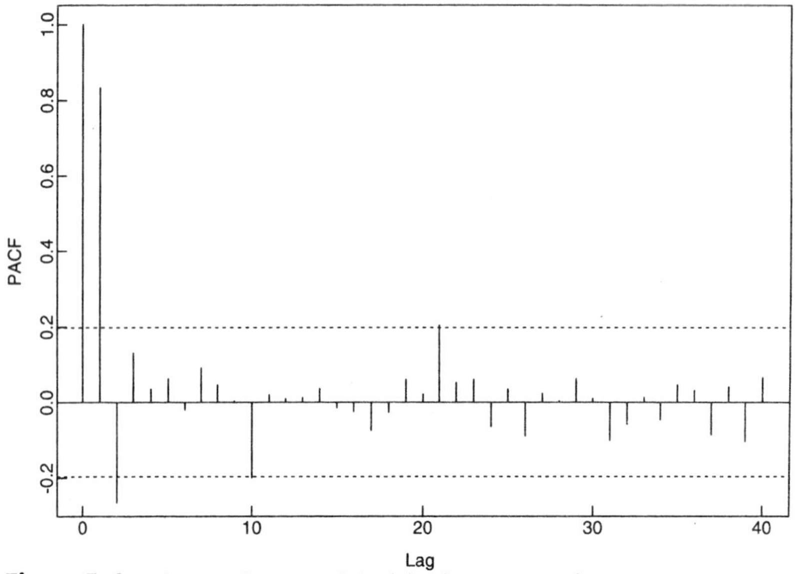

Figure 5-4 The sample PACF of the lake data in Example 5.1.4.

with AICC value 213.57 and 95% confidence bounds

$$\phi_1 : 1.0538 \pm 1.0538/5.5227 = (0.8630, 1.2446),$$

$$\phi_2 : -0.2668 \pm 0.2668/1.3980 = (-0.4576, -.0760).$$

We notice, as in Example 5.1.3, that the Burg model again has smaller white noise variance and larger Gaussian likelihood than the Yule–Walker model.

If we determine the minimum AICC Yule–Walker and Burg models, we find that they are both of order 2. Thus the order suggested by the sample PACF coincides again with the order obtained by AICC minimization. □

5.1.3 The Innovations Algorithm

Just as we can fit autoregressive models of orders $1, 2, \ldots$ to the data $\{x_1, \ldots, x_n\}$ by applying the Durbin–Levinson algorithm to the sample autocovariances, we can also fit moving average models

$$X_t = Z_t + \hat{\theta}_{m1} Z_{t-1} + \cdots + \hat{\theta}_{mm} Z_{t-m}, \quad \{Z_t\} \sim \mathrm{WN}\left(0, \hat{v}_m\right) \tag{5.1.22}$$

of orders $m = 1, 2, \ldots$ by means of the innovations algorithm (Section 2.5.2). The estimated coefficient vectors $\hat{\boldsymbol{\theta}}_m := \left(\hat{\theta}_{m1}, \ldots, \hat{\theta}_{mm}\right)'$ and white noise variances $\hat{v}_m$, $m = 1, 2, \ldots$, are specified in the following definition. (The justification for using estimators defined in this way is contained in Remark 1 following the definition.)

The **fitted innovations MA(m) model** is

$$X_t = Z_t + \hat{\theta}_{m1} Z_{t-1} + \cdots + \hat{\theta}_{mm} Z_{t-m}, \quad \{Z_t\} \sim \mathrm{WN}(0, \hat{v}_m),$$

where $\hat{\boldsymbol{\theta}}_m$ and $\hat{v}_m$ are obtained from the innovations algorithm with the ACVF replaced by the sample ACVF.

Remark 1. It can be shown (see Brockwell and Davis, 1988) that if $\{X_t\}$ is an invertible MA(q) process

$$X_t = Z_t + \theta_1 Z_{t-1} + \cdots + \theta_q Z_{t-q}, \quad \{Z_t\} \sim \mathrm{IID}\left(0, \sigma^2\right),$$

with $EZ_t^4 < \infty$, and if we define $\theta_0 = 1$ and $\theta_j = 0$ for $j > q$, then the innovation estimates have the following large-sample properties. If $n \to \infty$ and $m(n)$ is any sequence of positive integers such that $m(n) \to \infty$ but $n^{-1/3} m(n) \to 0$, then for each positive integer k the joint distribution function of

$$n^{1/2}\left(\hat{\theta}_{m1} - \theta_1, \hat{\theta}_{m2} - \theta_2, \ldots, \hat{\theta}_{mk} - \theta_k\right)'$$

converges to that of the multivariate normal distribution with mean $\mathbf{0}$ and covariance matrix $A = [a_{ij}]_{i,j=1}^k$, where

$$a_{ij} = \sum_{r=1}^{\min(i,j)} \theta_{i-r}\theta_{j-r}. \tag{5.1.23}$$

This result enables us to find approximate large-sample confidence intervals for the moving-average coefficients from the innovation estimates as described in the examples below. Moreover, the estimator $\hat{v}_m$ is **consistent** for σ^2 in the sense that for every $\epsilon > 0$, $P\left(\left|\hat{v}_m - \sigma^2\right| > \epsilon\right) \to 0$ as $m \to \infty$. □

Remark 2. Although the recursive fitting of moving-average models using the innovations algorithm is closely analogous to the recursive fitting of autoregressive models using the Durbin–Levinson algorithm, there is one important distinction. For an AR(p) process the Yule–Walker and Burg estimators $\hat{\phi}_p$ are consistent estimators of $(\phi_1, \ldots, \phi_p)'$ as the sample size $n \to \infty$. However, for an MA(q) process the estimator $\hat{\boldsymbol{\theta}}_q = (\theta_{q1}, \ldots, \theta_{qq})'$ is not consistent for $(\theta_1, \ldots, \theta_q)'$. For consistency it is necessary to use the estimators $(\theta_{m1}, \ldots, \theta_{mq})'$ with $m(n)$ satisfying the conditions of Remark 1. The choice of m for any fixed sample size can be made by increasing m until the vector $(\theta_{m1}, \ldots, \theta_{mq})'$ stabilizes. It is found in practice that there is a large range of values of m for which the fluctuations in θ_{mj} are small compared with the estimated asymptotic standard deviation $n^{-1/2}\left(\sum_{i=0}^{j-1} \hat{\theta}_{mi}^2\right)^{1/2}$ as found from (5.1.23) when the coefficients θ_j are replaced by their estimated values $\hat{\theta}_{mj}$. □

Order Selection

Three useful techniques for selecting an appropriate MA model are given below. The third is more systematic and extends beyond the narrow class of pure moving-average models.

- We know from Section 3.2.2 that for an MA(q) process the autocorrelations $\rho(m)$, $m > q$, are zero. Moreover, we know from Bartlett's formula (Section 2.4) that the sample autocorrelation $\hat{\rho}(m)$, $m > q$, is approximately normally distributed with mean $\rho(m) = 0$ and variance $n^{-1}\left[1 + 2\rho^2(1) + \cdots + 2\rho^2(q)\right]$. This result enables us to use the graph of $\hat{\rho}(m)$, $m = 1, 2, \ldots$, both to decide whether or not a given data set can be plausibly modeled by a moving-average process and also to obtain a preliminary estimate of the order q as the smallest value of m such that $\hat{\rho}(k)$ is not significantly different from zero for all $k > m$. For practical purposes "significantly different from zero" is often interpreted as "larger than $1.96/\sqrt{n}$ in absolute value" (cf. the corresponding approach to order selection for AR models based on the sample PACF and described in Section 5.1.1).

- If in addition to examining $\hat{\rho}(m), m = 1, 2, \ldots$, we examine the coefficient vectors $\hat{\theta}_m, m = 1, 2, \ldots$, we are able not only to assess the appropriateness of a moving-average model and estimate its order q, but at the same time to obtain preliminary estimates $\hat{\theta}_{m1}, \ldots, \hat{\theta}_{mq}$ of the coefficients. By inspecting the estimated coefficients $\hat{\theta}_{m1}, \ldots, \hat{\theta}_{mm}$ for $m = 1, 2, \ldots$ and the ratio of each coefficient estimate $\hat{\theta}_{mj}$ to 1.96 times its approximate standard deviation $\sigma_j = n^{-1/2}\left[\sum_{i=0}^{j-1} \hat{\theta}_{mi}^2\right]^{1/2}$, we can see which of the coefficient estimates are most significantly different from zero, estimate the order of the model to be fitted as the largest lag j for which the ratio is larger than 1 in absolute value, and at the same time read off estimated values for each of the coefficients. A default value of m is set by the program, but it may be altered manually. As m is increased the values $\hat{\theta}_{m1}, \ldots, \hat{\theta}_{mm}$ stabilize in the sense that the fluctuations in each component are of order $n^{-1/2}$, the asymptotic standard deviation of θ_{m1}.

- As for autoregressive models, a more systematic approach to order selection for moving-average models is to find the values of q and $\hat{\boldsymbol{\theta}}_q = \left(\hat{\theta}_{m1}, \ldots, \hat{\theta}_{mq}\right)'$ that minimize the AICC statistic

  $$\text{AICC} = -2 \ln L(\boldsymbol{\theta}_q, S(\boldsymbol{\theta}_q)/n) + 2(q+1)n/(n-q-2),$$

  where L is the Gaussian likelihood defined in (5.2.9) and S is defined in (5.2.11). (See Section 5.5 for further details.)

Confidence Regions for the Coefficients

Asymptotic confidence regions for the coefficient vector $\boldsymbol{\theta}_q$ and for its individual components can be found with the aid of the large-sample distribution specified in

Remark 1. For example, approximate 95% confidence bounds for θ_j are given by

$$\hat{\theta}_{mj} \pm 1.96n^{-1/2}\left(\sum_{i=0}^{j-1}\hat{\theta}_{mi}^2\right)^{1/2}. \tag{5.1.24}$$

Example 5.1.5 The Dow Jones Utilities Index

In Example 5.1.1 we fitted an AR(1) model to the differenced Dow Jones Utilities Index. The sample ACF of the differenced data shown in Figure 5.1 suggests that an MA(2) model might also provide a good fit to the data. To apply the innovation technique for preliminary estimation, we proceed as in Example 5.1.1 to difference the series DOWJ.TSM to obtain observations of the differenced series $\{Y_t\}$. We then select preliminary estimation by clicking on the blue PRE button and subtract the mean of the differences to obtain observations of the differenced and mean-corrected series $\{X_t\}$. In the `Preliminary Estimation` dialog box enter 0 for the AR order and 2 for the MA order, and select `Innovations` as the estimation method. We must then specify a value of m, which is set by default in this case to 17. If we accept the default value, the program will compute $\hat{\theta}_{17,1}, \ldots, \hat{\theta}_{17,17}$ and print out the first two values as the estimates of θ_1 and θ_2, together with the ratios of the estimated values to their estimated standard deviations. These are

```
MA COEFFICIENT
                          .4269      .2704
COEFFICIENT/(1.96*STANDARD ERROR)
                         1.9114     1.1133
```

The remaining parameter in the model is the white noise variance, for which two estimates are given:

```
WN VARIANCE ESTIMATE = (RESID SS)/N
                                    .1470
INNOVATION WN VARIANCE ESTIMATE
                                    .1122
```

The first of these is the average of the squares of the rescaled one-step prediction errors under the fitted MA(2) model, i.e., $\frac{1}{77}\sum_{j=1}^{77}\left(X_j - \hat{X}_j\right)^2/r_{j-1}$. The second value is the innovation estimate, $\hat{v}_{17}$. (By default ITSM retains the first value. If you wish instead to use the innovation estimate, you must change the white noise variance by selecting `Model>Specify` and setting the white noise value to the desired value.) The fitted model for $X_t (= Y_t - .1336)$ is thus

$$X_t = Z_t + 0.4269Z_{t-1} + 0.2704Z_{t-2}, \quad \{Z_t\} \sim \mathrm{WN}(0, 0.1470),$$

with AICC = 77.467.

To see all 17 estimated coefficients $\hat{\theta}_{17,j}$, $j = 1, \ldots, 17$, we repeat the preliminary estimation, this time fitting an MA(17) model with $m = 17$. The coefficients and ratios for the resulting model are found to be as follows:

MA COEFFICIENT

.4269	.2704	.1183	.1589	.1355	.1568	.1284	−.0060
.0148	−.0017	.1974	−.0463	.2023	.1285	−.0213	−.2575
.0760							

COEFFICIENT/(1.96*STANDARD ERROR)

1.9114	1.1133	.4727	.6314	.5331	.6127	.4969	−.0231
.0568	−.0064	.7594	−.1757	.7667	.4801	−.0792	−.9563
.2760							

The ratios indicate that the estimated coefficients most significantly different from zero are the first and second, reinforcing our original intention of fitting an MA(2) model to the data. Estimated coefficients $\hat{\theta}_{mj}$ for other values of m can be examined in the same way, and it is found that the values obtained for $m > 17$ change only slightly from the values tabulated above.

By fitting MA(q) models of orders $0, 1, 2, \ldots, 26$ using the innovations algorithm with the default settings for m, we find that the minimum AICC model is the one with $q = 2$ found above. Thus the model suggested by the sample ACF again coincides with the more systematically chosen minimum AICC model. □

Innovations Algorithm Estimates when $p > 0$ and $q > 0$

The causality assumption (Section 3.1) ensures that

$$X_t = \sum_{j=0}^{\infty} \psi_j Z_{t-j},$$

where the coefficients ψ_j satisfy

$$\psi_j = \theta_j + \sum_{i=1}^{\min(j,p)} \phi_i \psi_{j-i}, \quad j = 0, 1, \ldots, \tag{5.1.25}$$

and we define $\theta_0 := 1$ and $\theta_j := 0$ for $j > q$. To estimate $\psi_1, \ldots, \psi_{p+q}$ we can use the innovation estimates $\hat{\theta}_{m1}, \ldots, \hat{\theta}_{m,p+q}$, whose large-sample behavior is specified in Remark 1. Replacing ψ_j by $\hat{\theta}_{mj}$ in (5.1.25) and solving the resulting equations

$$\hat{\theta}_{mj} = \theta_j + \sum_{i=1}^{\min(j,p)} \phi_i \hat{\theta}_{m,j-i}, \quad j = 1, \ldots, p+q, \tag{5.1.26}$$

for ϕ and $\boldsymbol{\theta}$, we obtain initial parameter estimates $\hat{\phi}$ and $\hat{\boldsymbol{\theta}}$. To solve (5.1.26) we first find ϕ from the last q equations:

$$\begin{bmatrix} \hat{\theta}_{m,q+1} \\ \hat{\theta}_{m,q+2} \\ \vdots \\ \hat{\theta}_{m,q+p} \end{bmatrix} = \begin{bmatrix} \hat{\theta}_{mq} & \hat{\theta}_{m,q-1} & \cdots & \hat{\theta}_{m,q+1-p} \\ \hat{\theta}_{m,q+1} & \hat{\theta}_{m,q} & \cdots & \hat{\theta}_{m,q+2-p} \\ \vdots & \vdots & & \vdots \\ \hat{\theta}_{m,q+p-1} & \hat{\theta}_{m,q+p-2} & \cdots & \hat{\theta}_{m,q} \end{bmatrix} \begin{bmatrix} \phi_1 \\ \phi_2 \\ \vdots \\ \phi_p \end{bmatrix}. \tag{5.1.27}$$

Having solved (5.1.27) for $\hat{\phi}$ (which may not be causal), we can easily determine the estimate of θ from

$$\hat{\theta}_j = \hat{\theta}_{mj} - \sum_{i=1}^{\min(j,p)} \hat{\phi}_i \hat{\theta}_{m,j-i}, \quad j = 1, \ldots, q.$$

Finally, the white noise variance σ^2 is estimated by

$$\hat{\sigma}^2 = n^{-1} \sum_{t=1}^{n} \left(X_t - \hat{X}_t\right)^2 / r_{t-1},$$

where $\hat{X}_t$ is the one-step predictor of X_t computed from the fitted coefficient vectors $\hat{\phi}$ and $\hat{\theta}$, and r_{t-1} is defined in (3.3.8).

The above calculations can all be carried out by selecting the ITSM option `Model>Estimation>Preliminary`. This option also computes, if $p = q$, the ratio of each estimated coefficient to 1.96 times its estimated standard deviation. Approximate 95% confidence intervals can therefore easily be obtained in this case. If the fitted model is noncausal, it cannot be used to initialize the search for the maximum likelihood estimators, and so the autoregressive coefficients should be set to some causal values (e.g., all equal to .001) using the `Model>Specify` option. If both the innovation and Hannan–Rissanen algorithms give noncausal models, it is an indication (but not a conclusive one) that the assumed values of p and q may not be appropriate for the data.

Order Selection for Mixed Models

For models with $p > 0$ and $q > 0$, the sample ACF and PACF are difficult to recognize and are of far less value in order selection than in the special cases where $p = 0$ or $q = 0$. A systematic approach, however, is still available through minimization of the AICC statistic

$$\text{AICC} = -2 \ln L(\boldsymbol{\phi}_p, \boldsymbol{\theta}_q, S(\boldsymbol{\phi}_p, \boldsymbol{\theta}_q)/n) + 2(p+q+1)n/(n-p-q-2),$$

which is discussed in more detail in Section 5.5. For fixed p and q it is clear from the definition that the AICC value is minimized by the parameter values that maximize the likelihood. Hence, final decisions regarding the orders p and q that minimize AICC must be based on maximum likelihood estimation as described in Section 5.2.

Example 5.1.6 The lake data

In Example 5.1.4 we fitted AR(2) models to the mean corrected lake data using the Yule–Walker equations and Burg's algorithm. If instead we fit an ARMA(1,1) model using the innovations method in the option `Model>Estimation>Preliminary` of ITSM (with the default value $m = 17$), we obtain the model

$$X_t - 0.7234X_{t-1} = Z_t + 0.3596Z_{t-1}, \quad \{Z_t\} \sim \text{WN}(0, 0.4757),$$

for the mean-corrected series $X_t = Y_t - 9.0041$. The ratio of the two coefficient estimates ϕ and θ to 1.96 times their estimated standard deviations are given by ITSM as 3.2064 and 1.8513, respectively. The corresponding 95% confidence intervals are therefore

$$\phi : 0.7234 \pm 0.7234/3.2064 = (0.4978, 0.9490),$$

$$\theta : 0.3596 \pm 0.3596/1.8513 = (0.1654, 0.5538).$$

It is interesting to note that the value of AICC for this model is 212.89, which is smaller than the corresponding values for the Burg and Yule–Walker AR(2) models in Example 5.1.4. This suggests that an ARMA(1,1) model may be superior to a pure autoregressive model for these data. Preliminary estimation of a variety of ARMA(p, q) models shows that the minimum AICC value does in fact occur when $p = q = 1$. (Before committing ourselves to this model, however, we need to compare AICC values for the corresponding *maximum likelihood* models. We shall do this in Section 5.2.) □

5.1.4 The Hannan–Rissanen Algorithm

The defining equations for a causal AR(p) model have the form of a linear regression model with coefficient vector $\boldsymbol{\phi} = (\phi_1, \ldots, \phi_p)'$. This suggests the use of simple least squares regression for obtaining preliminary parameter estimates when $q = 0$. Application of this technique when $q > 0$ is complicated by the fact that in the general ARMA(p, q) equations X_t is regressed not only on $X_{t-1}, \ldots, X_{t-p}$, but also on the unobserved quantities $Z_{t-1}, \ldots, Z_{t-q}$. Nevertheless, it is still possible to apply least squares regression to the estimation of $\boldsymbol{\phi}$ and $\boldsymbol{\theta}$ by first replacing the unobserved quantities $Z_{t-1}, \ldots, Z_{t-q}$ in (5.1.1) by estimated values $\hat{Z}_{t-1}, \ldots, \hat{Z}_{t-q}$. The parameters $\boldsymbol{\phi}$ and $\boldsymbol{\theta}$ are then estimated by regressing X_t onto $X_{t-1}, \ldots, X_{t-p}, \hat{Z}_{t-1}, \ldots, \hat{Z}_{t-q}$. These are the main steps in the Hannan–Rissanen estimation procedure, which we now describe in more detail.

Step 1. A high-order AR(m) model (with $m > \max(p, q)$) is fitted to the data using the Yule–Walker estimates of Section 5.1.1. If $\left(\hat{\phi}_{m1}, \ldots, \hat{\phi}_{mm}\right)'$ is the vector of estimated coefficients, then the estimated residuals are computed from the equations

$$\hat{Z}_t = X_t - \hat{\phi}_{m1} X_{t-1} - \cdots - \hat{\phi}_{mm} X_{t-m}, \quad t = m + 1, \ldots, n.$$

Step 2. Once the estimated residuals $\hat{Z}_t$, $t = m + 1, \ldots, n$, have been computed as in Step 1, the vector of parameters, $\boldsymbol{\beta} = \left(\boldsymbol{\phi}', \boldsymbol{\theta}'\right)'$ is estimated by least squares linear regression of X_t onto $\left(X_{t-1}, \ldots, X_{t-p}, \hat{Z}_{t-1}, \ldots, \hat{Z}_{t-q}\right)$, $t = m + 1 + q, \ldots, n$, i.e., by minimizing the sum of squares

$$S(\boldsymbol{\beta}) = \sum_{t=m+1+q}^{n} \left(X_t - \phi_1 X_{t-1} - \cdots - \phi_p X_{t-p} - \theta_1 \hat{Z}_{t-1} - \cdots - \theta_q \hat{Z}_{t-q}\right)^2$$

with respect to β. This gives the Hannan–Rissanen estimator

$$\hat{\beta} = (Z'Z)^{-1}Z'\mathbf{X}_n,$$

where $\mathbf{X}_n = (X_{m+1+q}, \ldots, X_n)'$ and Z is the $(n-m-q) \times (p+q)$ matrix

$$Z = \begin{bmatrix} X_{m+q} & X_{m+q-1} & \cdots & X_{m+q+1-p} & \hat{Z}_{m+q} & \hat{Z}_{m+q-1} & \cdots & \hat{Z}_{m+1} \\ X_{m+q+1} & X_{m+q} & \cdots & X_{m+q+2-p} & \hat{Z}_{m+q+1} & \hat{Z}_{m+q} & \cdots & \hat{Z}_{m+2} \\ \vdots & \vdots & \cdots & \vdots & \vdots & \vdots & \cdots & \vdots \\ X_{n-1} & X_{n-2} & \cdots & X_{n-p} & \hat{Z}_{n-1} & \hat{Z}_{n-2} & \cdots & \hat{Z}_{n-q} \end{bmatrix}.$$

(If $p = 0$, Z contains only the last q columns.) The Hannan–Rissanen estimate of the white noise variance is

$$\hat{\sigma}^2_{\text{HR}} = \frac{S\left(\hat{\beta}\right)}{n-m-q}.$$

Example 5.1.7 The lake data

In Example 5.1.6 an ARMA(1,1) model was fitted to the mean corrected lake data using the innovations algorithm. We can fit an ARMA(1,1) model to these data using the Hannan–Rissanen estimates by selecting `Hannan-Rissanen` in the *Preliminary Estimation* dialog box of ITSM. The fitted model is

$$X_t - 0.6961X_{t-1} = Z_t + 0.3788Z_{t-1}, \quad \{Z_t\} \sim \text{WN}(0, 0.4774),$$

for the mean-corrected series $X_t = Y_t - 9.0041$. (Two estimates of the white noise variance are computed in ITSM for the Hannan–Rissanen procedure, $\hat{\sigma}^2_{\text{HR}}$ and $\sum_{j=1}^{n}(X_t - \hat{X}_{t-1})^2/n$. The latter is the one retained by the program.) The ratios of the two coefficient estimates to 1.96 times their standard deviation are 4.5289 and 1.3120, respectively. The corresponding 95% confidence bounds for ϕ and θ are

$$\phi : 0.6961 \pm 0.6961/4.5289 = (0.5424, 0.8498),$$

$$\theta : 0.3788 \pm 0.3788/1.3120 = (0.0901, 0.6675).$$

Clearly, there is little difference between this model and the one fitted using the innovations method in Example 5.1.6. (The AICC values are 213.18 for the current model and 212.89 for the model fitted in Example 5.1.6.) □

Hannan and Rissanen include a third step in their procedure to improve the estimates.

Step 3. Using the estimate $\hat{\beta} = \left(\hat{\phi}_1, \ldots, \hat{\phi}_p, \hat{\theta}_1, \ldots, \hat{\theta}_q\right)'$ from Step 2, set

$$\tilde{Z}_t = \begin{cases} 0, & \text{if } t \le \max(p, q), \\ X_t - \sum_{j=1}^{p} \hat{\phi}_j X_{t-j} - \sum_{j=1}^{q} \hat{\theta}_j \tilde{Z}_{t-j}, & \text{if } t > \max(p, q). \end{cases}$$

Now for $t = 1, \ldots, n$ put

$$V_t = \begin{cases} 0, & \text{if } t \le \max(p,q), \\ \sum_{j=1}^{p} \hat{\phi}_j V_{t-j} + \tilde{Z}_t, & \text{if } t > \max(p,q) \end{cases},$$

and

$$W_t = \begin{cases} 0, & \text{if } t \le \max(p,q), \\ -\sum_{j=1}^{p} \hat{\theta}_j W_{t-j} + \tilde{Z}_t, & \text{if } t > \max(p,q). \end{cases}$$

(Observe that both V_t and W_t satisfy the AR recursions $\hat{\phi}(B)V_t = \tilde{Z}_t$ and $\hat{\theta}(B)W_t = \tilde{Z}_t$ for $t = 1, \ldots, n$.) If $\hat{\beta}^\dagger$ is the regression estimate of β found by regressing $\tilde{Z}_t$ on $(V_{t-1}, \ldots, V_{t-p}, W_{t-1}, \ldots, W_{t-q})$, i.e., if $\hat{\beta}^\dagger$ minimizes

$$S^\dagger(\beta) = \sum_{t=\max(p,q)+1}^{n} \left(\tilde{Z}_t - \sum_{j=1}^{p} \beta_j V_{t-j} - \sum_{k=1}^{q} \beta_{k+p} W_{t-k} \right)^2,$$

then the improved estimate of β is $\tilde{\beta} = \hat{\beta}^\dagger + \hat{\beta}$. The new estimator $\tilde{\beta}$ then has the same asymptotic efficiency as the maximum likelihood estimator. In ITSM, however, we eliminate Step 3, using the model produced by Step 2 as the initial model for the calculation (by numerical maximization) of the maximum likelihood estimator itself.

5.2 Maximum Likelihood Estimation

Suppose that $\{X_t\}$ is a Gaussian time series with mean zero and autocovariance function $\kappa(i,j) = E(X_i X_j)$. Let $\mathbf{X}_n = (X_1, \ldots, X_n)'$ and let $\hat{\mathbf{X}}_n = (\hat{X}_1, \ldots, \hat{X}_n)'$, where $\hat{X}_1 = 0$ and $\hat{X}_j = E(X_j | X_1, \ldots, X_{j-1}) = P_{j-1}X_j$, $j \ge 2$. Let Γ_n denote the covariance matrix $\Gamma_n = E(\mathbf{X}_n \mathbf{X}_n')$, and assume that Γ_n is nonsingular.

The likelihood of $\mathbf{X}_n$ is

$$L(\Gamma_n) = (2\pi)^{-n/2} (\det \Gamma_n)^{-1/2} \exp\left(-\frac{1}{2} \mathbf{X}_n' \Gamma_n^{-1} \mathbf{X}_n \right). \tag{5.2.1}$$

As we shall now show, the direct calculation of $\det \Gamma_n$ and Γ_n^{-1} can be avoided by expressing this in terms of the one-step prediction errors $X_j - \hat{X}_j$ and their variances v_{j-1}, $j = 1, \ldots, n$, both of which are easily calculated recursively from the innovations algorithm (Section 2.5.2).

Let θ_{ij}, $j = 1, \ldots, i$; $i = 1, 2, \ldots$, denote the coefficients obtained when the innovations algorithm is applied to the autocovariance function κ of $\{X_t\}$, and let C_n be the $n \times n$ lower triangular matrix defined in Section 2.5.2. From (2.5.27) we have the identity

$$\mathbf{X}_n = C_n\left(\mathbf{X}_n - \hat{\mathbf{X}}_n\right). \tag{5.2.2}$$

We also know from Remark 5 of Section 2.5.2 that the components of $\mathbf{X}_n - \hat{\mathbf{X}}_n$ are uncorrelated. Consequently, by the definition of v_j, $\mathbf{X}_n - \hat{\mathbf{X}}_n$ has the diagonal covariance matrix

$$D_n = \text{diag}\{v_0, \ldots, v_{n-1}\}.$$

From (5.2.2) and (A.2.5) we conclude that

$$\Gamma_n = C_n D_n C_n'. \tag{5.2.3}$$

From (5.2.2) and (5.2.3) we see that

$$\mathbf{X}_n'\Gamma_n^{-1}\mathbf{X}_n = \left(\mathbf{X}_n - \hat{\mathbf{X}}_n\right)' D_n^{-1}\left(\mathbf{X}_n - \hat{\mathbf{X}}_n\right) = \sum_{j=1}^{n}\left(X_j - \hat{X}_j\right)^2/v_{j-1} \tag{5.2.4}$$

and

$$\det \Gamma_n = (\det C_n)^2(\det D_n) = v_0 v_1 \cdots v_{n-1}. \tag{5.2.5}$$

The likelihood (5.2.1) of the vector $\mathbf{X}_n$ therefore reduces to

$$L(\Gamma_n) = \frac{1}{\sqrt{(2\pi)^n v_0 \cdots v_{n-1}}}\exp\left\{-\frac{1}{2}\sum_{j=1}^{n}\left(X_j - \hat{X}_j\right)^2/v_{j-1}\right\}. \tag{5.2.6}$$

If Γ_n is expressible in terms of a finite number of unknown parameters $\beta_1, \ldots, \beta_r$ (as is the case when $\{X_t\}$ is an ARMA(p, q) process), the **maximum likelihood estimators** of the parameters are those values that maximize L for the given data set. When $X_1, X_2, \ldots, X_n$ are iid, it is known, under mild assumptions and for n large, that maximum likelihood estimators are approximately normally distributed with variances that are at least as small as those of other asymptotically normally distributed estimators (see, e.g., Lehmann, 1983).

Even if $\{X_t\}$ is not Gaussian, it still makes sense to regard (5.2.6) as a measure of goodness of fit of the model to the data, and to choose the parameters $\beta_1, \ldots, \beta_r$ in such a way as to maximize (5.2.6). We shall always refer to the estimators $\hat{\beta}_1, \ldots, \hat{\beta}_r$ so obtained as "maximum likelihood" estimators, even when $\{X_t\}$ is not Gaussian. Regardless of the joint distribution of $X_1, \ldots, X_n$, we shall refer to (5.2.1) and its algebraic equivalent (5.2.6) as the "likelihood" (or "Gaussian likelihood") of $X_1, \ldots, X_n$. A justification for using maximum Gaussian likelihood estimators of ARMA coefficients is that the large-sample distribution of the estimators is the same for $\{Z_t\} \sim \text{IID}(0, \sigma^2)$, regardless of whether or not $\{Z_t\}$ is Gaussian (see TSTM, Section 10.8).

The likelihood for data from an ARMA(p, q) process is easily computed from the innovations form of the likelihood (5.2.6) by evaluating the one-step predictors

$\hat{X}_{i+1}$ and the corresponding mean squared errors v_i. These can be found from the recursions (Section 3.3)

$$\hat{X}_{n+1} = \begin{cases} \sum_{j=1}^{n} \theta_{nj} \left(X_{n+1-j} - \hat{X}_{n+1-j} \right), & 1 \le n < m, \\ \phi_1 X_n + \cdots + \phi_p X_{n+1-p} + \sum_{j=1}^{q} \theta_{nj} \left(X_{n+1-j} - \hat{X}_{n+1-j} \right), & n \ge m, \end{cases} \tag{5.2.7}$$

and

$$E \left(X_{n+1} - \hat{X}_{n+1} \right)^2 = \sigma^2 E \left(W_{n+1} - \hat{W}_{n+1} \right)^2 = \sigma^2 r_n, \tag{5.2.8}$$

where θ_{nj} and r_n are determined by the innovations algorithm with κ as in (3.3.3) and $m = \max(p, q)$. Substituting in the general expression (5.2.6), we obtain the following:

The Gaussian Likelihood for an ARMA Process:

$$L \left(\boldsymbol{\phi}, \boldsymbol{\theta}, \sigma^2 \right) = \frac{1}{\sqrt{\left(2\pi\sigma^2\right)^n r_0 \cdots r_{n-1}}} \exp \left\{ -\frac{1}{2\sigma^2} \sum_{j=1}^{n} \frac{\left(X_j - \hat{X}_j \right)^2}{r_{j-1}} \right\}. \tag{5.2.9}$$

Differentiating $\ln L \left(\boldsymbol{\phi}, \boldsymbol{\theta}, \sigma^2 \right)$ partially with respect to σ^2 and noting that $\hat{X}_j$ and r_j are independent of σ^2, we find that the maximum likelihood estimators $\hat{\boldsymbol{\phi}}$, $\hat{\boldsymbol{\theta}}$, and $\hat{\sigma}^2$ satisfy the following equations (Problem 5.8):

Maximum Likelihood Estimators:

$$\hat{\sigma}^2 = n^{-1} S \left(\hat{\boldsymbol{\phi}}, \hat{\boldsymbol{\theta}} \right), \tag{5.2.10}$$

where

$$S \left(\hat{\boldsymbol{\phi}}, \hat{\boldsymbol{\theta}} \right) = \sum_{j=1}^{n} \left(X_j - \hat{X}_j \right)^2 / r_{j-1}, \tag{5.2.11}$$

and $\hat{\boldsymbol{\phi}}$, $\hat{\boldsymbol{\theta}}$ are the values of $\boldsymbol{\phi}$, $\boldsymbol{\theta}$ that minimize

$$\ell(\boldsymbol{\phi}, \boldsymbol{\theta}) = \ln \left(n^{-1} S(\boldsymbol{\phi}, \boldsymbol{\theta}) \right) + n^{-1} \sum_{j=1}^{n} \ln r_{j-1}. \tag{5.2.12}$$

Minimization of $\ell(\boldsymbol{\phi}, \boldsymbol{\theta})$ must be done numerically. Initial values for $\boldsymbol{\phi}$ and $\boldsymbol{\theta}$ can be obtained from ITSM using the methods described in Section 5.1. The program then searches systematically for the values of $\boldsymbol{\phi}$ and $\boldsymbol{\theta}$ that minimize the reduced likelihood (5.2.12) and computes the corresponding maximum likelihood estimate of σ^2 from (5.2.10).

Least Squares Estimation for Mixed Models

The least squares estimates $\tilde{\boldsymbol{\phi}}$ and $\tilde{\boldsymbol{\theta}}$ of $\boldsymbol{\phi}$ and $\boldsymbol{\theta}$ are obtained by minimizing the function S as defined in (5.2.11) rather than ℓ as defined in (5.2.12), subject to the constraints that the model be causal and invertible. The least squares estimate of σ^2 is

$$\tilde{\sigma}^2 = \frac{S\left(\tilde{\boldsymbol{\phi}}, \tilde{\boldsymbol{\theta}}\right)}{n-p-q}.$$

Order Selection

In Section 5.1 we introduced minimization of the AICC value as a major criterion for the selection of the orders p and q. This criterion is applied as follows:

AICC Criterion:

Choose p, q, $\boldsymbol{\phi}_p$, and $\boldsymbol{\theta}_q$ to minimize

$$\text{AICC} = -2\ln L(\boldsymbol{\phi}_p, \boldsymbol{\theta}_q, S(\boldsymbol{\phi}_p, \boldsymbol{\theta}_q)/n) + 2(p+q+1)n/(n-p-q-2).$$

For any fixed p and q it is clear that the AICC is minimized when $\boldsymbol{\phi}_p$ and $\boldsymbol{\theta}_q$ are the vectors that minimize $-2\ln L(\boldsymbol{\phi}_p, \boldsymbol{\theta}_q, S(\boldsymbol{\phi}_p, \boldsymbol{\theta}_q)/n)$, i.e., the maximum likelihood estimators. Final decisions with respect to order selection should therefore be made on the basis of maximum likelihood estimators (rather than the preliminary estimators of Section 5.1, which serve primarily as a guide). The AICC statistic and its justification are discussed in detail in Section 5.5.

One of the options in the program ITSM is `Model>Estimation>Autofit`. Selection of this option allows you to specify a range of values for both p and q, after which the program will automatically fit maximum likelihood ARMA(p, q) values for all p and q in the specified range, and select from these the model with smallest AICC value. This may be slow if a large range is selected (the maximum range is from 0 through 27 for both p and q), and once the model has been determined, it should be checked by preliminary estimation followed by maximum likelihood estimation to minimize the risk of the fitted model corresponding to a local rather than a global maximum of the likelihood. (For more details see Appendix D.3.1.)

Confidence Regions for the Coefficients

For large sample size the maximum likelihood estimator $\hat{\boldsymbol{\beta}}$ of $\boldsymbol{\beta} := (\phi_1, \ldots, \phi_p, \theta_1, \ldots, \theta_q)'$ is approximately normally distributed with mean $\boldsymbol{\beta}$ and covariance matrix $\left[n^{-1}V(\boldsymbol{\beta})\right]$ which can be approximated by $2H^{-1}(\boldsymbol{\beta})$, where H is the Hessian matrix $\left[\partial^2\ell(\beta)/\partial\beta_i\partial\beta_j\right]_{i,j=1}^{p+q}$. ITSM prints out the approximate standard deviations and correlations of the coefficient estimators based on the Hessian matrix evaluated numerically at $\hat{\beta}$ unless this matrix is not positive definite, in which case ITSM instead computes the theoretical asymptotic covariance matrix in Section 8.8 of TSTM. The resulting covariances can be used to compute confidence bounds for the parameters.

Large-Sample Distribution of Maximum Likelihood Estimators:

For a large sample from an ARMA(p, q) process,

$$\hat{\beta} \approx \mathrm{N}\left(\beta, n^{-1}V(\beta)\right).$$

The general form of $V(\beta)$ can be found in TSTM, Section 8.8. The following are several special cases.

Example 5.2.1 An AR(p) model

The asymptotic covariance matrix in this case is the same as that for the Yule–Walker estimates given by

$$V(\phi) = \sigma^2\Gamma_p^{-1}.$$

In the special cases $p = 1$ and $p = 2$, we have

$$\text{AR}(1): V(\phi) = \left(1 - \phi_1^2\right),$$

$$\text{AR}(2): V(\phi) = \begin{bmatrix} 1 - \phi_2^2 & -\phi_1(1 + \phi_2) \\ -\phi_1(1 + \phi_2) & 1 - \phi_2^2 \end{bmatrix}.$$ □

Example 5.2.2 An MA(q) model

Let Γ_q^* be the covariance matrix of $Y_1, \ldots, Y_q$, where $\{Y_t\}$ is the autoregressive process with autoregressive polynomial $\theta(z)$, i.e.,

$$Y_t + \theta_1 Y_{t-1} + \cdots + \theta_q Y_{t-q} = Z_t, \quad \{Z_t\} \sim \text{WN}(0, 1).$$

Then it can be shown that

$$V(\boldsymbol{\theta}) = \Gamma_q^{*-1}.$$

Inspection of the results of Example 5.2.1 and replacement of ϕ_i by $-\theta_i$) yields

$$\text{MA}(1): V(\boldsymbol{\theta}) = \left(1 - \theta_1^2\right),$$

$$\text{MA}(2): V(\boldsymbol{\theta}) = \begin{bmatrix} 1 - \theta_2^2 & \theta_1(1 - \theta_2) \\ \theta_1(1 - \theta_2) & 1 - \theta_2^2 \end{bmatrix}.$$ □

Example 5.2.3 An ARMA(1, 1) model

For a causal and invertible ARMA(1,1) process with coefficients ϕ and θ.

$$V(\phi, \theta) = \frac{1+\phi\theta}{(\phi+\theta)^2}\begin{bmatrix} (1-\phi^2)(1+\phi\theta) & -(1-\theta^2)(1-\phi^2) \\ -(1-\theta^2)(1-\phi^2) & (1-\theta^2)(1+\phi\theta) \end{bmatrix}.$$ □

Example 5.2.4 The Dow Jones Utilities Index

For the Burg and Yule–Walker AR(1) models derived for the differenced and mean-corrected series in Examples 5.1.1 and 5.1.3, the `Model>Estimation>Preliminary` option of ITSM gives $-2\ln(L) = 70.330$ for the Burg model and $-2\ln(L) = 70.378$ for the Yule–Walker model. Since maximum likelihood estimation attempts to minimize $-2\ln L$, the Burg estimate appears to be a slightly better initial estimate of ϕ. We therefore retain the Burg AR(1) model and then select `Model>Estimation>Max Likelihood` and click `OK`. The Burg coefficient estimates provide initial parameter values to start the search for the minimizing values. The model found on completion of the minimization is

$$Y_t - 0.4471Y_{t-1} = Z_t, \quad \{Z_t\} \sim \mathrm{WN}(0, 0.02117). \tag{5.2.13}$$

This model is different again from the Burg and Yule–Walker models. It has $-2\ln(L) = 70.321$, corresponding to a slightly higher likelihood. The standard error (or estimated standard deviation) of the estimator $\hat{\phi}$ is found from the program to be 0.1050. This is in good agreement with the estimated standard deviation $\sqrt{(1-(.4471)^2)/77} = .1019$, based on the large-sample approximation given in Example 5.2.1. Using the value computed from ITSM, approximate 95% confidence bounds for ϕ are $0.4471 \pm 1.96 \times 0.1050 = (0.2413, 0.6529)$. These are quite close to the bounds based on the Yule–Walker and Burg estimates found in Examples 5.1.1 and 5.1.3. To find the minimum-AICC model for the series $\{Y_t\}$, choose the option `Model>Estimation>Autofit`. Using the default range for both p and q, and clicking on `Start`, we quickly find that the minimum AICC ARMA(p, q) model with $p \le 5$ and $q \le 5$ is the AR(1) model defined by (5.2.13). The corresponding AICC value is 74.483. If we increase the upper limits for p and q, we obtain the same result. □

Example 5.2.5 The lake data

Using the option `Model>Estimation>Autofit` as in the previous example, we find that the minimum-AICC ARMA(p, q) model for the mean-corrected lake data, $X_t = Y_t - 9.0041$, of Examples 5.1.6 and 5.1.7 is the ARMA(1,1) model

$$X_t - 0.7446X_{t-1} = Z_t + 0.3213Z_{t-1}, \quad \{Z_t\} \sim \mathrm{WN}(0, 0.4750). \tag{5.2.14}$$

The estimated standard deviations of the two coefficient estimates $\hat{\phi}$ and $\hat{\theta}$ are found from ITSM to be 0.0773 and 0.1123, respectively. (The respective estimated standard deviations based on the large-sample approximation given in Example 5.2.3 are .0788 and .1119.) The corresponding 95% confidence bounds are therefore

$$\phi : 0.7446 \pm 1.96 \times 0.0773 = (0.5941, 0.8961),$$

$$\theta : 0.3208 \pm 1.96 \times 0.1123 = (0.1007, 0.5409).$$

The value of AICC for this model is 212.77, improving on the values for the preliminary models of Examples 5.1.4, 5.1.6, and 5.1.7. □

5.3 Diagnostic Checking

Typically, the goodness of fit of a statistical model to a set of data is judged by comparing the observed values with the corresponding predicted values obtained from the fitted model. If the fitted model is appropriate, then the residuals should behave in a manner that is consistent with the model.

When we fit an ARMA(p, q) model to a given series we determine the maximum likelihood estimators $\hat{\boldsymbol{\phi}}$, $\hat{\boldsymbol{\theta}}$, and $\hat{\sigma}^2$ of the parameters $\boldsymbol{\phi}$, $\boldsymbol{\theta}$, and σ^2. In the course of this procedure the predicted values $\hat{X}_t(\hat{\boldsymbol{\phi}}, \hat{\boldsymbol{\theta}})$ of X_t based on $X_1, \ldots, X_{t-1}$ are computed for the fitted model. The **residuals** are then defined, in the notation of Section 3.3, by

$$\hat{W}_t = \left(X_t - \hat{X}_t\left(\hat{\boldsymbol{\phi}}, \hat{\boldsymbol{\theta}}\right)\right) / \left(r_{t-1}\left(\hat{\boldsymbol{\phi}}, \hat{\boldsymbol{\theta}}\right)\right)^{1/2}, \quad t = 1, \ldots, n. \tag{5.3.1}$$

If we were to assume that the maximum likelihood ARMA(p, q) model is the *true* process generating $\{X_t\}$, then we could say that $\left\{\hat{W}_t\right\} \sim \mathrm{WN}\left(0, \hat{\sigma}^2\right)$. However, to check the appropriateness of an ARMA(p, q) model for the data we should assume only that $X_1, \ldots, X_n$ are generated by an ARMA(p, q) process with unknown parameters $\boldsymbol{\phi}$, $\boldsymbol{\theta}$, and σ^2, whose maximum likelihood *estimators* are $\hat{\boldsymbol{\phi}}$, $\hat{\boldsymbol{\theta}}$, and $\hat{\sigma}^2$, respectively. Then it is not true that $\left\{\hat{W}_t\right\}$ is white noise. Nonetheless $\hat{W}_t$, $t = 1, \ldots, n$, should have properties that are similar to those of the white noise sequence

$$W_t(\boldsymbol{\phi}, \boldsymbol{\theta}) = (X_t - \hat{X}_t(\boldsymbol{\phi}, \boldsymbol{\theta})) / (r_{t-1}(\boldsymbol{\phi}, \boldsymbol{\theta}))^{1/2}, \quad t = 1, \ldots, n.$$

Moreover, $W_t(\boldsymbol{\phi}, \boldsymbol{\theta})$ approximates the white noise term in the defining equation (5.1.1) in the sense that $E(W_t(\boldsymbol{\phi}, \boldsymbol{\theta}) - Z_t)^2 \to 0$ as $t \to \infty$ (TSTM, Section 8.11). Consequently, the properties of the residuals $\left\{\hat{W}_t\right\}$ should reflect those of the white noise sequence $\{Z_t\}$ generating the underlying ARMA(p, q) process. In particular, the sequence $\left\{\hat{W}_t\right\}$ should be approximately (i) uncorrelated if $\{Z_t\} \sim \mathrm{WN}\left(0, \sigma^2\right)$, (ii) independent if $\{Z_t\} \sim \mathrm{IID}\left(0, \sigma^2\right)$, and (iii) normally distributed if $Z_t \sim \mathrm{N}\left(0, \sigma^2\right)$.

The **rescaled residuals** $\hat{R}_t$, $t = 1, \ldots, n$, are obtained by dividing the residuals $\hat{W}_t$, $t = 1, \ldots, n$, by the estimate $\hat{\sigma} = \sqrt{\left(\sum_{t=1}^{n} W_t^2\right)/n}$ of the white noise standard deviation. Thus,

$$\hat{R}_t = \hat{W}_t / \hat{\sigma}. \tag{5.3.2}$$

If the fitted model is appropriate, the rescaled residuals should have properties similar to those of a WN(0, 1) sequence or of an iid(0,1) sequence if we make the stronger assumption that the white noise $\{Z_t\}$ driving the ARMA process is independent white noise.

The following diagnostic checks are all based on the expected properties of the residuals or rescaled residuals under the assumption that the fitted model is correct and that $\{Z_t\} \sim \text{IID}(0, \sigma^2)$. They are the same tests introduced in Section 1.6.

5.3.1 The Graph of $\{\hat{R}_t, t = 1, \ldots, n\}$

If the fitted model is appropriate, then the graph of the rescaled residuals $\{\hat{R}_t, t = 1, \ldots, n\}$ should resemble that of a white noise sequence with variance one. While it is difficult to identify the correlation structure of $\{\hat{R}_t\}$ (or any time series for that matter) from its graph, deviations of the mean from zero are sometimes clearly indicated by a trend or cyclic component and nonconstancy of the variance by fluctuations in $\hat{R}_t$, whose magnitude depends strongly on t.

The rescaled residuals obtained from the ARMA(1,1) model fitted to the mean-corrected lake data in Example 5.2.5 are displayed in Figure 5.5. The graph gives no indication of a nonzero mean or nonconstant variance, so on this basis there is no reason to doubt the compatibility of $\hat{R}_1, \ldots, \hat{R}_n$ with unit-variance white noise.

The next step is to check that the sample autocorrelation function of $\{\hat{W}_t\}$ (or equivalently of $\{\hat{R}_t\}$) behaves as it should under the assumption that the fitted model is appropriate.

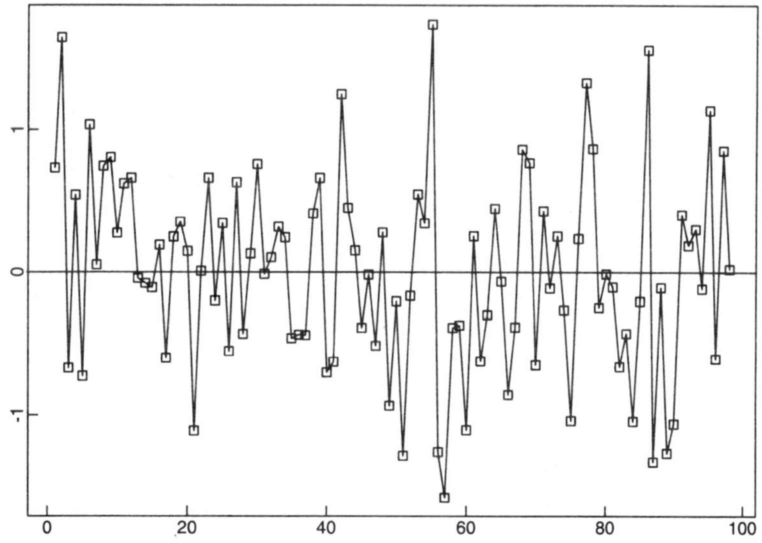

Figure 5-5 The rescaled residuals after fitting the ARMA(1,1) model of Example 5.2.5 to the lake data.

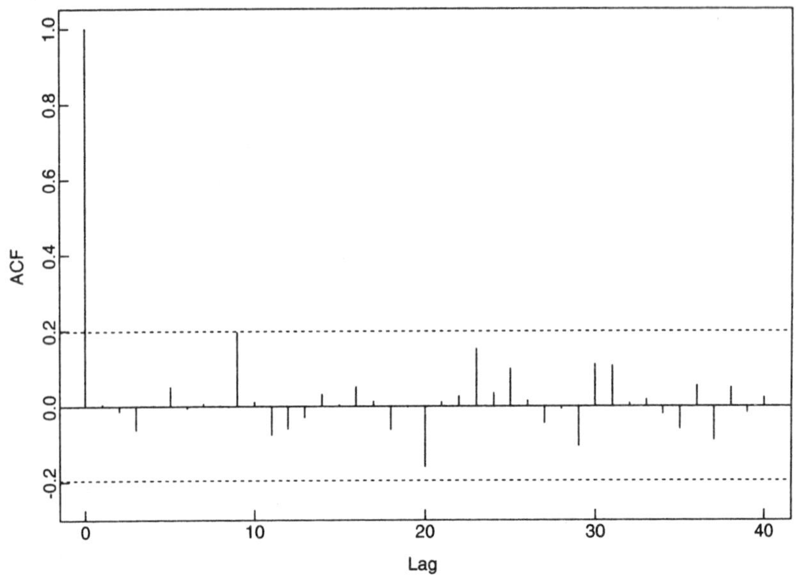

Figure 5-6 The sample ACF of the residuals after fitting the ARMA(1,1) model of Example 5.2.5 to the lake data.

5.3.2 The Sample ACF of the Residuals

We know from Section 1.6 that for large n the sample autocorrelations of an iid sequence $Y_1, \ldots, Y_n$ with finite variance are approximately iid with distribution $N(0, 1/n)$. We can therefore test whether or not the observed residuals are consistent with iid noise by examining the sample autocorrelations of the residuals and rejecting the iid noise hypothesis if more than two or three out of 40 fall outside the bounds $\pm 1.96/\sqrt{n}$ or if one falls far outside the bounds. (As indicated above, our *estimated* residuals will not be precisely iid even if the true model generating the data is as assumed. To correct for this the bounds $\pm 1.96/\sqrt{n}$ should be modified to give a more precise test as in Box and Pierce (1970) and TSTM, Section 9.4.) The sample ACF and PACF of the residuals and the bounds $\pm 1.96/\sqrt{n}$ can be viewed by pressing the second green button (`Plot ACF/PACF of residuals`) at the top of the ITSM window. Figure 5.6 shows the sample ACF of the residuals after fitting the ARMA(1,1) of Example 5.2.5 to the lake data. As can be seen from the graph, there is no cause to reject the fitted model on the basis of these autocorrelations.

5.3.3 Tests for Randomness of the Residuals

The tests (b), (c), (d), (e), and (f) of Section 1.6 can be carried out using the program ITSM by selecting `Statistics>Residual Analysis>Tests of Randomness`.

Applying these tests to the residuals from the ARMA(1,1) model for the mean-corrected lake data (Example 5.2.5), and using the default value $h = 22$ suggested for the portmanteau tests, we obtain the following results:

RANDOMNESS TEST STATISTICS
LJUNG-BOX PORTM. = 10.23 CHISQUR(20) p=.964
MCLEOD-LI PORTM. = 16.55 CHISQUR(22) p=.788
TURNING POINTS = 69 ANORMAL(64.0, 4.14**2) p=.227
DIFFERENCE-SIGN = 50 ANORMAL(48.5, 2.87**2) p=.602
RANK TEST = 2083 ANORMAL(2376, 488.7**2) p=.072
JARQUE-BERA=.285 CHISQUR(2) p=.867
ORDER OF MIN AICC YW MODEL FOR RESIDUALS = 0

This table shows the observed values of the statistics defined in Section 1.6, with each followed by its large-sample distribution under the null hypothesis of iid residuals, and the corresponding p-values. The observed values can thus be checked easily for compatibility with their distributions under the null hypothesis. Since all of the p-values are greater than .05, none of the test statistics leads us to reject the null hypothesis at this level. The order of the minimum AICC autoregressive model for the residuals also suggests the compatibility of the residuals with white noise.

A rough check for normality is provided by visual inspection of the histogram of the rescaled residuals, obtained by selecting the third green button at the top of the ITSM window. A Gaussian qq-plot of the residuals can also be plotted by selecting Statistics > Residual Analysis > QQ-Plot (normal). No obvious deviation from normality is apparent in either the histogram or the qq-plot. The Jarque-Bera statistic, $n[m_3^2/(6m_2^3) + (m_4/m_2^2 - 3)^2/24]$, where $m_r = \sum_{j=1}^{n}(Y_j - \bar{Y})^r/n$, is distributed asymptotically as $\chi^2(2)$ if $\{Y_t\} \sim$ IID N(μ, σ^2). This hypothesis is rejected if the statistic is sufficiently large (at level α if the p-value of the test is less than α). In this case the large p-value computed by ITSM provides no evidence for rejecting the normality hypothesis.

5.4 Forecasting

Once a model has been fitted to the data, forecasting future values of the time series can be carried out using the method described in Section 3.3. We illustrate this method with one of the examples from Section 3.2.

Example 5.4.1

For the overshort data $\{X_t\}$ of Example 3.2.8, selection of the ITSM option `Model>Estimation>Preliminary` and the innovations algorithm, followed by `Model>Estimation>Max likelihood`, leads to the maximum likelihood MA(1) model for $\{X_t\}$

$$X_t + 4.035 = Z_t - .818Z_{t-1}, \quad \{Z_t\} \sim \text{WN}(0, 2040.75). \tag{5.4.1}$$

To predict the next 7 days of overshorts, we treat (5.4.1) as the true model for the data, and use the results of Example 3.3.3 with $\phi = 0$. From (3.3.11), the predictors are given by

$$P_{57}X_{57+h} = -4.035 + \sum_{j=h}^{1} \theta_{57+h-1,j}\left(X_{57+h-j} - \hat{X}_{57+h-j}\right)$$

$$= \begin{cases} -4.035 + \theta_{57,1}\left(X_{57} - \hat{X}_{57}\right), & \text{if } h = 1, \\ -4.035, & \text{if } h > 1, \end{cases}$$

with mean squared error

$$E(X_{57+h} - P_{57}X_{57+h})^2 = \begin{cases} 2040.75r_{57}, & \text{if } h = 1, \\ 2040.75(1 + (-.818)^2), & \text{if } h > 1, \end{cases}$$

where $\theta_{57,1}$ and r_{57} are computed recursively from (3.3.9) with $\theta = -.818$.

These calculations are performed with ITSM by fitting the maximum likelihood model (5.4.1), selecting `Forecasting>ARMA`, and specifying the number of forecasts required. The 1-step, 2-step, ..., and 7-step forecasts of X_t are shown in Table 5.1. Notice that the predictor of X_t for $t \geq 59$ is equal to the sample mean, since under the MA(1) model $\{X_t, t \geq 59\}$ is uncorrelated with $\{X_t, t \leq 57\}$. □

Assuming that the innovations $\{Z_t\}$ are normally distributed, an approximate 95% prediction interval for X_{64} is given by

$$-4.0351 \pm 1.96 \times 58.3602 = (-118.42, 110.35).$$

The mean squared errors of prediction, as computed in Section 3.3 and the example above, are based on the assumption that the fitted model is in fact the true model for the data. As a result, they do not reflect the variability in the estimation of the model parameters. To illustrate this point, suppose the data $X_1, \ldots, X_n$ are generated from the causal AR(1) model

$$X_t = \phi X_{t-1} + Z_t, \quad \{Z_t\} \sim \text{iid}\left(0, \sigma^2\right).$$

Table 5.1 Forecasts of the next 7 observations of the overshort data of Example 3.2.8 using model (5.4.1).

#	XHAT	SQRT(MSE)	XHAT + MEAN
58	1.0097	45.1753	−3.0254
59	0.0000	58.3602	−4.0351
60	0.0000	58.3602	−4.0351
61	0.0000	58.3602	−4.0351
62	0.0000	58.3602	−4.0351
63	0.0000	58.3602	−4.0351
64	0.0000	58.3602	−4.0351

If $\hat{\phi}$ is the maximum likelihood estimate of ϕ, based on $X_1, \ldots, X_n$, then the one-step ahead forecast of X_{n+1} is $\hat{\phi}X_n$, which has mean squared error

$$E\left(X_{n+1}-\hat{\phi}X_n\right)^2 = E\left(\left(\phi-\hat{\phi}\right)X_n + Z_{n+1}\right)^2 = E((\phi-\hat{\phi})X_n)^2 + \sigma^2. \quad (5.4.2)$$

The second equality follows from the independence of Z_{n+1} and $\left(\hat{\phi}, X_n\right)'$. To evaluate the first term in (5.4.2), first condition on X_n and then use the approximations

$$E\left(\left(\phi-\hat{\phi}\right)^2 | X_n\right) \approx E\left(\phi-\hat{\phi}\right)^2 \approx \left(1-\phi^2\right)/n,$$

where the second relation comes from the formula for the asymptotic variance of $\hat{\phi}$ given by $\sigma^2\Gamma_1^{-1} = \left(1-\phi^2\right)$ (see Example 5.2.1). The one-step mean squared error is then approximated by

$$E\left(\phi-\hat{\phi}\right)^2 EX_n^2 + \sigma^2 \approx n^{-1}\left(1-\phi^2\right)\left(1-\phi^2\right)^{-1}\sigma^2 + \sigma^2 = \frac{n+1}{n}\sigma^2.$$

Thus, the error in parameter estimation contributes the term σ^2/n to the mean squared error of prediction. If the sample size is large, this factor is negligible, and so for the purpose of mean squared error computation, the estimated parameters can be treated as the true model parameters. On the other hand, for small sample sizes, ignoring parameter variability can lead to a severe underestimate of the actual mean squared error of the forecast.

5.5 Order Selection

Once the data have been transformed (e.g., by some combination of Box–Cox and differencing transformations or by removal of trend and seasonal components) to the point where the transformed series $\{X_t\}$ can potentially be fitted by a zero-mean ARMA model, we are faced with the problem of selecting appropriate values for the orders p and q.

It is not advantageous from a forecasting point of view to choose p and q arbitrarily large. Fitting a very high order model will generally result in a small estimated white noise variance, but when the fitted model is used for forecasting, the mean squared error of the forecasts will depend not only on the white noise variance of the fitted model but also on errors arising from estimation of the parameters of the model (see the paragraphs following Example 5.4.1). These will be larger for higher-order models. For this reason we need to introduce a "penalty factor" to discourage the fitting of models with too many parameters.

Many criteria based on such penalty factors have been proposed in the literature, since the problem of model selection arises frequently in statistics, particularly in regression analysis. We shall restrict attention here to a brief discussion of the FPE,

AIC, and BIC criteria of Akaike and a bias-corrected version of the AIC known as the AICC.

5.5.1 The FPE Criterion

The FPE criterion was developed by Akaike (1969) to select the appropriate order of an AR process to fit to a time series $\{X_1, \ldots, X_n\}$. Instead of trying to choose the order p to make the estimated white noise variance as small as possible, the idea is to choose the model for $\{X_t\}$ in such a way as to minimize the one-step mean squared error when the model fitted to $\{X_t\}$ is used to predict an independent realization $\{Y_t\}$ of the same process that generated $\{X_t\}$.

Suppose then that $\{X_1, \ldots, X_n\}$ is a realization of an AR(p) process with coefficients $\phi_1, \ldots, \phi_p$, $p < n$, and that $\{Y_1, \ldots, Y_n\}$ is an independent realization of the same process. If $\hat{\phi}_1, \ldots, \hat{\phi}_p$, are the maximum likelihood estimators of the coefficients based on $\{X_1, \ldots, X_n\}$ and if we use these to compute the one-step predictor $\hat{\phi}_1 Y_n + \cdots + \hat{\phi}_p Y_{n+1-p}$ of Y_{n+1}, then the mean square prediction error is

$$\begin{aligned} E&\left(Y_{n+1} - \hat{\phi}_1 Y_n - \cdots - \hat{\phi}_p Y_{n+1-p}\right)^2 \\ &= E\left[Y_{n+1} - \phi_1 Y_n - \cdots - \phi_p Y_{n+1-p} - \left(\hat{\phi}_1 - \phi_1\right) Y_n - \cdots - \left(\hat{\phi}_p - \phi_p\right) Y_{n+1-p}\right]^2 \\ &= \sigma^2 + E\left[\left(\hat{\phi}_p - \phi_p\right)' \left[Y_{n+1-i} Y_{n+1-j}\right]_{i,j=1}^p \left(\hat{\phi}_p - \phi\right)\right], \end{aligned}$$

where $\phi_p' = (\phi_1, \ldots, \phi_p)'$, $\hat{\phi}_p' = \left(\hat{\phi}_1, \ldots, \hat{\phi}_p\right)'$, and σ^2 is the white noise variance of the AR(p) model. Writing the last term in the preceding equation as the expectation of the conditional expectation given $X_1, \ldots, X_n$, and using the independence of $\{X_1, \ldots, X_n\}$ and $\{Y_1, \ldots, Y_n\}$, we obtain

$$E\left(Y_{n+1} - \hat{\phi}_1 Y_n - \cdots - \hat{\phi}_p Y_{n+1-p}\right)^2 = \sigma^2 + E\left[\left(\hat{\phi}_p - \phi_p\right)' \Gamma_p \left(\hat{\phi}_p - \phi\right)\right],$$

where $\Gamma_p = E[Y_i Y_j]_{i,j=1}^p$. We can approximate the last term by assuming that $n^{-1/2}\left(\hat{\phi}_p - \phi_p\right)$ has its large-sample distribution $\mathrm{N}(\mathbf{0}, \sigma^2 \Gamma_p^{-1})$ from Example 5.21. Using Problem 5.13, this gives

$$E\left(Y_{n+1} - \hat{\phi}_1 Y_n - \cdots - \hat{\phi}_p Y_{n+1-p}\right)^2 \approx \sigma^2 \left(1 + \frac{p}{n}\right). \tag{5.5.1}$$

If $\hat{\sigma}^2$ is the maximum likelihood estimator of σ^2, then for large n, $n\hat{\sigma}^2/\sigma^2$ is distributed approximately as chi-squared with $(n - p)$ degrees of freedom (see TSTM, Section 8.9). We therefore replace σ^2 in (5.5.1) by the estimator $n\hat{\sigma}^2/(n - p)$ to get the estimated mean square prediction error of Y_{n+1},

$$\mathrm{FPE}_p = \hat{\sigma}^2 \frac{n + p}{n - p}. \tag{5.5.2}$$

Table 5.2 $\hat{\sigma}_p^2$ and FPE_p for AR(p) models fitted to the lake data.

p	σ_p^2	FPE_p
0	1.7203	1.7203
1	0.5097	0.5202
2	0.4790	0.4989
3	0.4728	0.5027
4	0.4708	0.5109
5	0.4705	0.5211
6	0.4705	0.5318
7	0.4679	0.5399
8	0.4664	0.5493
9	0.4664	0.5607
10	0.4453	0.5465

To apply the FPE criterion for autoregressive order selection we therefore choose the value of p that minimizes FPE_p as defined in (5.5.2).

Example 5.5.1 FPE-based selection of an AR model for the lake data

In Example 5.1.4 we fitted AR(2) models to the mean-corrected lake data, the order 2 being suggested by the sample PACF shown in Figure 5.4. To use the FPE criterion to select p, we have shown in Table 5.2 the values of FPE for values of p from 0 to 10. These values were found using ITSM by fitting maximum likelihood AR models with the option `Model>Estimation>Max likelihood`. Also shown in the table are the values of the maximum likelihood estimates of σ^2 for the same values of p. Whereas $\hat{\sigma}_p^2$ decreases steadily with p, the values of FPE_p have a clear minimum at $p = 2$, confirming our earlier choice of $p = 2$ as the most appropriate for this data set. □

5.5.2 The AICC Criterion

A more generally applicable criterion for model selection than the FPE is the information criterion of Akaike (1973), known as the AIC. This was designed to be an approximately unbiased estimate of the Kullback–Leibler index of the fitted model relative to the true model (defined below). Here we use a bias-corrected version of the AIC, referred to as the AICC, suggested by Hurvich and Tsai (1989).

If $\mathbf{X}$ is an n-dimensional random vector whose probability density belongs to the family $\{f(\cdot;\psi), \psi \in \Psi\}$, the Kullback–Leibler discrepancy between $f(\cdot;\psi)$ and $f(\cdot;\theta)$ is defined as

$$d(\psi|\theta) = \Delta(\psi|\theta) - \Delta(\theta|\theta),$$

where

$$\Delta(\psi|\theta) = E_\theta(-2\ln f(\mathbf{X};\psi)) = \int_{\mathbb{R}^n} -2\ln(f(\mathbf{x};\psi))f(\mathbf{x};\theta)\,d\mathbf{x}$$

is the Kullback–Leibler index of $f(\cdot;\psi)$ relative to $f(\cdot;\theta)$. (Note that in general, $\Delta(\psi|\theta) \neq \Delta(\theta|\psi)$.) By Jensen's inequality (see, e.g., Mood et al., 1974),

$$\begin{aligned} d(\psi|\theta) &= \int_{\mathbb{R}^n} -2\ln\left(\frac{f(\mathbf{x};\psi)}{f(\mathbf{x};\theta)}\right) f(\mathbf{x};\theta)\,d\mathbf{x} \\ &\geq -2\ln\left(\int_{\mathbb{R}^n} \frac{f(\mathbf{x};\psi)}{f(\mathbf{x};\theta)} f(\mathbf{x};\theta)\,d\mathbf{x}\right) \\ &= -2\ln\left(\int_{\mathbb{R}^n} f(\mathbf{x};\psi)\,d\mathbf{x}\right) \\ &= 0, \end{aligned}$$

with equality holding if and only if $f(\mathbf{x};\psi) = f(\mathbf{x};\theta)$.

Given observations $X_1, \ldots, X_n$ of an ARMA process with unknown parameters $\theta = (\boldsymbol{\beta}, \sigma^2)$, the true model could be identified if it were possible to compute the Kullback–Leibler discrepancy between all candidate models and the true model. Since this is not possible, we *estimate* the Kullback–Leibler discrepancies and choose the model whose estimated discrepancy (or index) is minimum. In order to do this, we assume that the true model and the alternatives are all Gaussian. Then for any given $\theta = (\boldsymbol{\beta}, \sigma^2)$, $f(\cdot;\theta)$ is the probability density of $(Y_1, \ldots, Y_n)'$, where $\{Y_t\}$ is a Gaussian ARMA(p,q) process with coefficient vector $\boldsymbol{\beta}$ and white noise variance σ^2. (The dependence of θ on p and q is through the dimension of the autoregressive and moving-average coefficients in $\boldsymbol{\beta}$.)

Suppose, therefore, that our observations $X_1, \ldots, X_n$ are from a Gaussian ARMA process with parameter vector $\theta = (\boldsymbol{\beta}, \sigma^2)$ and assume for the moment that the true order is (p,q). Let $\hat{\theta} = (\hat{\boldsymbol{\beta}}, \hat{\sigma}^2)$ be the maximum likelihood estimator of θ based on $X_1, \ldots, X_n$ and let $Y_1, \ldots, Y_n$ be an independent realization of the true process (with parameter θ). Then

$$-2\ln L_Y\left(\hat{\boldsymbol{\beta}}, \hat{\sigma}^2\right) = -2\ln L_X\left(\hat{\boldsymbol{\beta}}, \hat{\sigma}^2\right) + \hat{\sigma}^{-2} S_Y\left(\hat{\boldsymbol{\beta}}\right) - n,$$

where L_X, L_Y, S_X, and S_Y are defined as in (5.2.9) and (5.2.11). Hence,

$$\begin{aligned} E_\theta(\Delta(\hat{\theta}|\theta)) &= E_{\boldsymbol{\beta},\sigma^2}\left(-2\ln L_Y\left(\hat{\boldsymbol{\beta}}, \hat{\sigma}^2\right)\right) \\ &= E_{\boldsymbol{\beta},\sigma^2}\left(-2\ln L_X\left(\hat{\boldsymbol{\beta}}, \hat{\sigma}^2\right)\right) + E_{\boldsymbol{\beta},\sigma^2}\left(\frac{S_Y\left(\hat{\boldsymbol{\beta}}\right)}{\hat{\sigma}^2}\right) - n. \qquad (5.5.3) \end{aligned}$$

It can be shown using large-sample approximations (see TSTM, Section 9.3 for details) that

$$E_{\beta,\sigma^2}\left(\frac{S_Y\left(\hat{\beta}\right)}{\hat{\sigma}^2}\right) \approx \frac{2(p+q+1)n}{n-p-q-2},$$

from which we see that $-2\ln L_X\left(\hat{\beta},\hat{\sigma}^2\right)+2(p+q+1)n/(n-p-q-2)$ is an approximately unbiased estimator of the expected Kullback–Leibler index $E_\theta\left(\Delta\left(\hat{\theta}|\theta\right)\right)$ in (5.5.3). Since the preceding calculations (and the maximum likelihood estimators $\hat{\beta}$ and $\hat{\sigma}^2$) are based on the assumption that the true order is (p,q), we therefore select the values of p and q for our fitted model to be those that minimize AICC$(\hat{\beta})$, where

$$\text{AICC}(\beta) := -2\ln L_X(\beta, S_X(\beta)/n) + 2(p+q+1)n/(n-p-q-2). \quad (5.5.4)$$

The AIC statistic, defined as

$$\text{AIC}(\beta) := -2\ln L_X(\beta, S_X(\beta)/n) + 2(p+q+1),$$

can be used in the same way. Both AICC$\left(\beta,\sigma^2\right)$ and AIC$\left(\beta,\sigma^2\right)$ can be defined for arbitrary σ^2 by replacing $S_X(\beta)/n$ in the preceding definitions by σ^2. The value $S_X(\beta)/n$ is used in (5.5.4), since AICC$\left(\beta,\sigma^2\right)$ (like AIC$\left(\beta,\sigma^2\right)$) is minimized for any given β by setting $\sigma^2 = S_X(\beta)/n$.

For fitting autoregressive models, Monte Carlo studies (Jones, 1975; Shibata, 1976) suggest that the AIC has a tendency to overestimate p. The penalty factors $2(p+q+1)n/(n-p-q-2)$ and $2(p+q+1)$ for the AICC and AIC statistics are asymptotically equivalent as $n\to\infty$. The AICC statistic, however, has a more extreme penalty for large-order models, which counteracts the overfitting tendency of the AIC. The BIC is another criterion that attempts to correct the overfitting nature of the AIC. For a zero-mean causal invertible ARMA(p,q) process, it is defined (Akaike, 1978) to be

$$\begin{aligned}\text{BIC} = {} & (n-p-q)\ln\left[n\hat{\sigma}^2/(n-p-q)\right] + n\left(1+\ln\sqrt{2\pi}\right) \\ & + (p+q)\ln\left[\left(\sum_{t=1}^{n} X_t^2 - n\hat{\sigma}^2\right)/(p+q)\right],\end{aligned} \quad (5.5.5)$$

where $\hat{\sigma}^2$ is the maximum likelihood estimate of the white noise variance.

The BIC is a consistent order-selection criterion in the sense that if the data $\{X_1,\ldots,X_n\}$ *are* in fact observations of an ARMA(p,q) process, and if $\hat{p}$ and $\hat{q}$ are the estimated orders found by minimizing the BIC, then $\hat{p}\to p$ and $\hat{q}\to q$ with probability 1 as $n\to\infty$ (Hannan, 1980). This property is not shared by the AICC or AIC. On the other hand, order selection by minimization of the AICC, AIC, or FPE is asymptotically efficient for autoregressive processes, while order selection by BIC minimization is not (Shibata, 1980; Hurvich and Tsai, 1989). Efficiency is a desirable property defined in terms of the one-step mean square prediction error achieved by the fitted model. For more details see TSTM, Section 9.3.

In the modeling of real data there is rarely such a thing as the "true order." For the process $X_t = \sum_{j=0}^{\infty} \psi_j Z_{t-j}$ there may be many polynomials $\theta(z)$, $\phi(z)$ such that the coefficients of z^j in $\theta(z)/\phi(z)$ closely approximate ψ_j for moderately small values of j. Correspondingly, there may be many ARMA processes with properties similar to $\{X_t\}$. This problem of identifiability becomes much more serious for multivariate processes. The AICC criterion does, however, provide us with a rational criterion for choosing among competing models. It has been suggested (Duong, 1984) that models with AIC values within c of the minimum value should be considered competitive (with $c = 2$ as a typical value). Selection from among the competitive models can then be based on such factors as whiteness of the residuals (Section 5.3) and model simplicity.

We frequently have occasion, particularly in analyzing seasonal data, to fit ARMA(p, q) models in which all except $m(\leq p+q)$ of the coefficients are constrained to be zero. In such cases the definition (5.5.4) is replaced by

$$\text{AICC}(\beta) := -2\ln L_X(\beta, S_X(\beta)/n) + 2(m+1)n/(n-m-2). \qquad (5.5.6)$$

Example 5.5.2 Models for the lake data

In Example 5.2.4 we found that the minimum-AICC ARMA(p, q) model for the mean-corrected lake data is the ARMA(1,1) model (5.2.14). For this model ITSM gives the values AICC = 212.77 and BIC = 216.86. A systematic check on ARMA(p, q) models for other values of p and q shows that the model (5.2.14) also minimizes the BIC statistic. The minimum-AICC AR(p) model is found to be the AR(2) model satisfying

$$X_t - 1.0441X_{t-1} + .2503X_{t-2} = Z_t, \quad \{Z_t\} \sim \text{WN}(0, 0.4789),$$

with AICC = 213.54 and BIC = 217.63. Both the AR(2) and ARMA(1,1) models pass the diagnostic checks of Section 5.3, and in view of the small difference between the AICC values there is no strong reason to prefer one model or the other. □

Problems

5.1. The sunspot numbers $\{X_t, t = 1, \ldots, 100\}$, filed as SUNSPOTS.TSM, have sample autocovariances $\hat{\gamma}(0) = 1382.2$, $\hat{\gamma}(1) = 1114.4$, $\hat{\gamma}(2) = 591.73$, and $\hat{\gamma}(3) = 96.216$. Use these values to find the Yule–Walker estimates of ϕ_1, ϕ_2, and σ^2 in the model

$$Y_t = \phi_1 Y_{t-1} + \phi_2 Y_{t-2} + Z_t, \quad \{Z_t\} \sim \text{WN}\left(0, \sigma^2\right),$$

for the mean-corrected series $Y_t = X_t - 46.93, t = 1, \ldots, 100$. Assuming that the data really are a realization of an AR(2) process, find 95% confidence intervals for ϕ_1 and ϕ_2.

5.2. From the information given in the previous problem, use the Durbin–Levinson algorithm to compute the sample partial autocorrelations $\hat{\phi}_{11}$, $\hat{\phi}_{22}$, and $\hat{\phi}_{33}$ of the sunspot series. Is the value of $\hat{\phi}_{33}$ compatible with the hypothesis that the data are generated by an AR(2) process? (Use significance level .05.)

5.3. Consider the AR(2) process $\{X_t\}$ satisfying

$$X_t - \phi X_{t-1} - \phi^2 X_{t-2} = Z_t, \quad \{Z_t\} \sim \text{WN}\left(0, \sigma^2\right).$$

a. For what values of ϕ is this a causal process?

b. The following sample moments were computed after observing $X_1, \ldots, X_{200}$:

$$\hat{\gamma}(0) = 6.06, \quad \hat{\rho}(1) = .687.$$

Find estimates of ϕ and σ^2 by solving the Yule–Walker equations. (If you find more than one solution, choose the one that is causal.)

5.4. Two hundred observations of a time series, $X_1, \ldots, X_{200}$, gave the following sample statistics:

sample mean:	$\bar{x}_{200} = 3.82;$
sample variance:	$\hat{\gamma}(0) = 1.15;$
sample ACF:	$\hat{\rho}(1) = .427;$
	$\hat{\rho}(2) = .475;$
	$\hat{\rho}(3) = .169.$

a. Based on these sample statistics, is it reasonable to suppose that $\{X_t - \mu\}$ is white noise?

b. Assuming that $\{X_t - \mu\}$ can be modeled as the AR(2) process

$$X_t - \mu - \phi_1(X_{t-1} - \mu) - \phi_2(X_{t-2} - \mu) = Z_t,$$

where $\{Z_t\} \sim \text{IID}\left(0, \sigma^2\right)$, find estimates of μ, ϕ_1, ϕ_2, and σ^2.

c. Would you conclude that $\mu = 0$?

d. Construct 95% confidence intervals for ϕ_1 and ϕ_2.

e. Assuming that the data were generated from an AR(2) model, derive estimates of the PACF for all lags $h \geq 1$.

5.5. Use the program ITSM to simulate and file 20 realizations of length 200 of the Gaussian MA(1) process

$$X_t = Z_t + \theta Z_{t-1}, \quad \{Z_t\} \sim \mathrm{WN}(0, 1),$$

with $\theta = 0.6$.

a. For each series find the moment estimate of θ as defined in Example 5.1.2.

b. For each series use the innovations algorithm in the ITSM option `Model>Estimation>Preliminary` to find an estimate of θ. (Use the default value of the parameter m.) As soon as you have found this preliminary estimate for a particular series, select `Model>Estimation>Max likelihood` to find the maximum likelihood estimate of θ for the series.

c. Compute the sample means and sample variances of your three sets of estimates.

d. Use the asymptotic formulae given at the end of Section 5.1.1 (with $n = 200$) to compute the variances of the moment, innovation, and maximum likelihood estimators of θ. Compare with the corresponding sample variances found in (c).

e. What do the results of (c) suggest concerning the relative merits of the three estimators?

5.6. Establish the recursions (5.1.19) and (5.1.20) for the forward and backward prediction errors $u_i(t)$ and $v_i(t)$ in Burg's algorithm.

5.7. Derive the recursions for the Burg estimates $\phi_{ii}^{(B)}$ and $\sigma_i^{(B)2}$.

5.8. From the innovation form of the likelihood (5.2.9) derive the equations (5.2.10), (5.2.11), and (5.2.12) for the maximum likelihood estimators of the parameters of an ARMA process.

5.9. Use equation (5.2.9) to show that for $n > p$, the likelihood of the observations $\{X_1, \ldots, X_n\}$ of the causal AR(p) process defined by

$$X_t = \phi_1 X_{t-1} + \cdots + \phi_p X_{t-p} + Z_t, \quad \{Z_t\} \sim \mathrm{WN}\left(0, \sigma^2\right),$$

is

$$L\left(\phi, \sigma^2\right) = \left(2\pi\sigma^2\right)^{-n/2} (\det G_p)^{-1/2}$$
$$\times \exp\left\{-\frac{1}{2\sigma^2}\left[\mathbf{X}_p' G_p^{-1} \mathbf{X}_p + \sum_{t=p+1}^{n} (X_t - \phi_1 X_{t-1} - \cdots - \phi_p X_{t-p})^2\right]\right\},$$

where $\mathbf{X}_p = (X_1, \ldots, X_p)'$ and $G_p = \sigma^{-2}\Gamma_p = \sigma^{-2}E(\mathbf{X}_p\mathbf{X}_p')$.

5.10. Use the result of Problem 5.9 to derive a pair of linear equations for the least squares estimates of ϕ_1 and ϕ_2 for a causal AR(2) process (with mean zero). Compare your equations with those for the Yule–Walker estimates. (Assume that the mean is known to be zero in writing down the latter equations, so that the sample autocovariances are $\hat{\gamma}(h) = \frac{1}{n}\sum_{t=1}^{n-h} X_{t+h}X_t$ for $h \geq 0$.)

5.11. Given two observations x_1 and x_2 from the causal AR(1) process satisfying

$$X_t = \phi X_{t-1} + Z_t, \quad \{Z_t\} \sim \mathrm{WN}\left(0, \sigma^2\right),$$

and assuming that $|x_1| \neq |x_2|$, find the maximum likelihood estimates of ϕ and σ^2.

5.12. Derive a cubic equation for the maximum likelihood estimate of the coefficient ϕ of a causal AR(1) process based on the observations $X_1, \ldots, X_n$.

5.13. Use the result of Problem A.7 and the approximate large-sample normal distribution of the maximum likelihood estimator $\hat{\phi}_p$ to establish the approximation (5.5.1).

6 Nonstationary and Seasonal Time Series Models

In this chapter we shall examine the problem of finding an appropriate model for a given set of observations $\{x_1, \ldots, x_n\}$ that are not necessarily generated by a stationary time series. If the data (a) exhibit no apparent deviations from stationarity and (b) have a rapidly decreasing autocovariance function, we attempt to fit an ARMA model to the mean-corrected data using the techniques developed in Chapter 5. Otherwise, we look first for a transformation of the data that generates a new series with the properties (a) and (b). This can frequently be achieved by differencing, leading us to consider the class of ARIMA (autoregressive integrated moving-average) models, defined in Section 6.1. We have in fact already encountered ARIMA processes. The model fitted in Example 5.1.1 to the Dow Jones Utilities Index was obtained by fitting an AR model to the differenced data, thereby effectively fitting an ARIMA model to the original series. In Section 6.1 we shall give a more systematic account of such models.

In Section 6.2 we discuss the problem of finding an appropriate transformation for the data and identifying a satisfactory ARMA(p, q) model for the transformed data. The latter can be handled using the techniques developed in Chapter 5. The sample ACF and PACF and the preliminary estimators $\hat{\phi}_m$ and $\hat{\theta}_m$ of Section 5.1 can provide useful guidance in this choice. However, our prime criterion for model selection will be the AICC statistic discussed in Section 5.5.2. To apply this criterion we compute maximum likelihood estimators of $\boldsymbol{\phi}$, $\boldsymbol{\theta}$, and σ^2 for a variety of competing p and q

values and choose the fitted model with smallest AICC value. Other techniques, in particular those that use the R and S arrays of Gray et al. (1978), are discussed in the survey of model identification by de Gooijer et al. (1985). If the fitted model is satisfactory, the residuals (see Section 5.3) should resemble white noise. Tests for this were described in Section 5.3 and should be applied to the minimum AICC model to make sure that the residuals are consistent with their expected behavior under the model. If they are not, then competing models (models with AICC value close to the minimum) should be checked until we find one that passes the goodness of fit tests. In some cases a small difference in AICC value (say less than 2) between two satisfactory models may be ignored in the interest of model simplicity. In Section 6.3 we consider the problem of testing for a unit root of either the autoregressive or moving-average polynomial. An autoregressive unit root suggests that the data require differencing, and a moving-average unit root suggests that they have been overdifferenced. Section 6.4 considers the prediction of ARIMA processes, which can be carried out using an extension of the techniques developed for ARMA processes in Sections 3.3 and 5.4. In Section 6.5 we examine the fitting and prediction of seasonal ARIMA (SARIMA) models, whose analysis, except for certain aspects of model identification, is quite analogous to that of ARIMA processes. Finally, we consider the problem of regression, allowing for dependence between successive residuals from the regression. Such models are known as regression models with time series residuals and often occur in practice as natural representations for data containing both trend and serially dependent errors.

6.1 ARIMA Models for Nonstationary Time Series

We have already discussed the importance of the class of ARMA models for representing stationary series. A generalization of this class, which incorporates a wide range of nonstationary series, is provided by the ARIMA processes, i.e., processes that reduce to ARMA processes when differenced finitely many times.

Definition 6.1.1

If d is a nonnegative integer, then $\{X_t\}$ is an **ARIMA(p,d,q) process** if $Y_t := (1-B)^d X_t$ is a causal ARMA(p,q) process.

This definition means that $\{X_t\}$ satisfies a difference equation of the form

$$\phi^*(B)X_t \equiv \phi(B)(1-B)^d X_t = \theta(B)Z_t, \quad \{Z_t\} \sim \text{WN}\left(0,\sigma^2\right), \qquad (6.1.1)$$

where $\phi(z)$ and $\theta(z)$ are polynomials of degrees p and q, respectively, and $\phi(z) \neq 0$ for $|z| \leq 1$. The polynomial $\phi^*(z)$ has a zero of order d at $z = 1$. The process $\{X_t\}$ is stationary if and only if $d = 0$, in which case it reduces to an ARMA(p,q) process.

Notice that if $d \geq 1$, we can add an arbitrary polynomial trend of degree $(d-1)$ to $\{X_t\}$ without violating the difference equation (6.1.1). ARIMA models are therefore useful for representing data with trend (see Sections 1.5 and 6.2). It should be noted, however, that ARIMA processes can also be appropriate for modeling series with no trend. Except when $d = 0$, the mean of $\{X_t\}$ is not determined by equation (6.1.1), and it can in particular be zero (as in Example 1.3.3). Since for $d \geq 1$, equation (6.1.1) determines the second-order properties of $\{(1 - B)^d X_t\}$ but not those of $\{X_t\}$ (Problem 6.1), estimation of ϕ, θ, and σ^2 will be based on the observed differences $(1 - B)^d X_t$. Additional assumptions are needed for prediction (see Section 6.4).

Example 6.1.1 $\{X_t\}$ is an ARIMA(1,1,0) process if for some $\phi \in (-1, 1)$,

$$(1 - \phi B)(1 - B)X_t = Z_t, \quad \{Z_t\} \sim \text{WN}\left(0, \sigma^2\right).$$

We can then write

$$X_t = X_0 + \sum_{j=1}^{t} Y_j, \quad t \geq 1,$$

where

$$Y_t = (1 - B)X_t = \sum_{j=0}^{\infty} \phi^j Z_{t-j}.$$

A realization of $\{X_1, \ldots, X_{200}\}$ with $X_0 = 0$, $\phi = 0.8$, and $\sigma^2 = 1$ is shown in Figure 6.1, with the corresponding sample autocorrelation and partial autocorrelation functions in Figures 6.2 and 6.3, respectively. □

A distinctive feature of the data that suggests the appropriateness of an ARIMA model is the slowly decaying positive sample autocorrelation function in Figure 6.2.

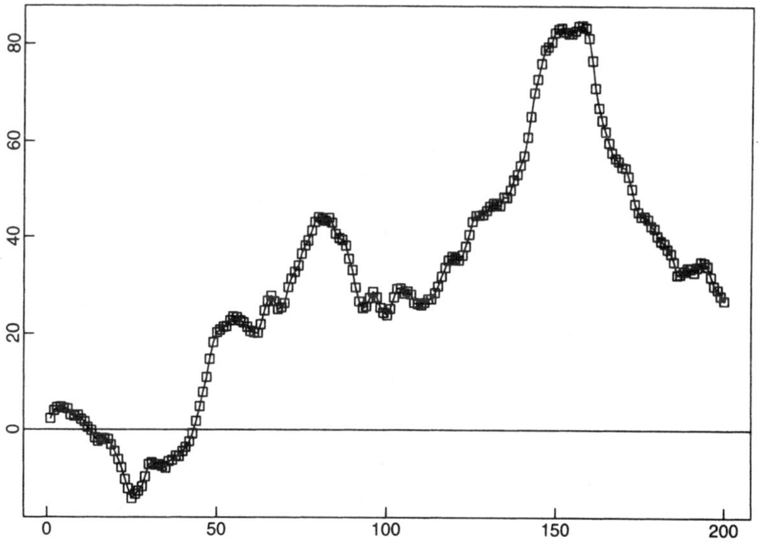

Figure 6-1 200 observations of the ARIMA(1,1,0) series X_t of Example 6.1.1.

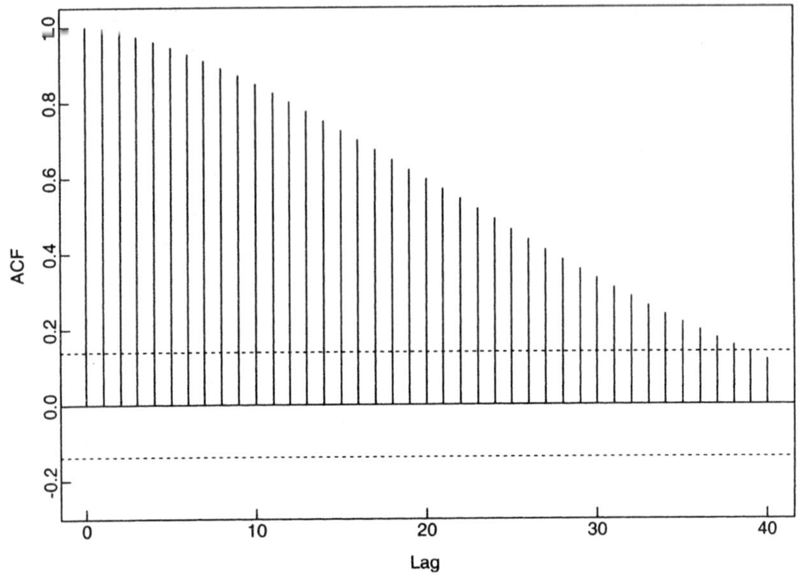

Figure 6-2 The sample ACF of the data in Figure 6.1.

If, therefore, we were given only the data and wished to find an appropriate model, it would be natural to apply the operator $\nabla = 1 - B$ repeatedly in the hope that for some j, $\{\nabla^j X_t\}$ will have a rapidly decaying sample autocorrelation function compatible with that of an ARMA process with no zeros of the autoregressive polynomial near the unit circle. For this particular time series, one application of the operator ∇ produces the realization shown in Figure 6.4, whose sample ACF and PACF (Figures 6.5 and

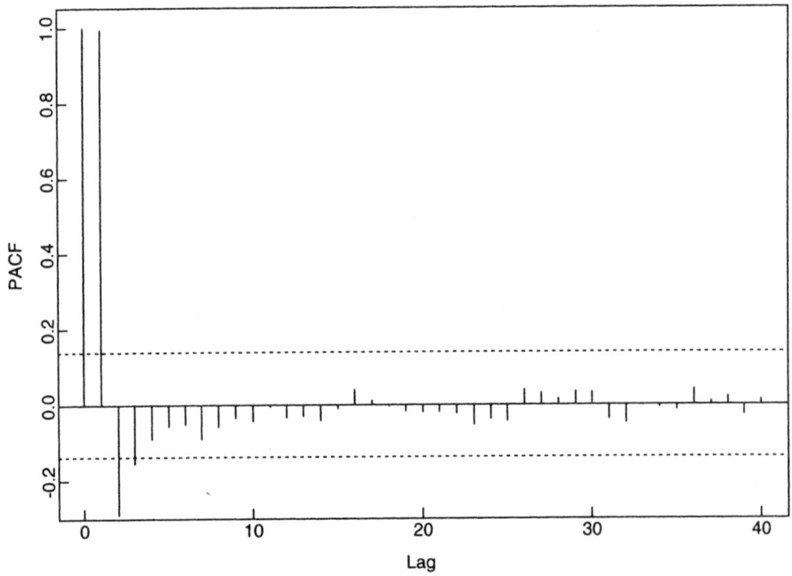

Figure 6-3 The sample PACF of the data in Figure 6.1.

6.6) suggest an AR(1) (or possibly AR(2)) model for $\{\nabla X_t\}$. The maximum likelihood estimates of ϕ and σ^2 obtained from ITSM under the assumption that $E(\nabla X_t) = 0$ (found by *not* subtracting the mean after differencing the data) are .808 and .978, respectively, giving the model

$$(1 - 0.808B)(1 - B)X_t = Z_t, \quad \{Z_t\} \sim \text{WN}(0, 0.978), \tag{6.1.2}$$

which bears a close resemblance to the true underlying process,

$$(1 - 0.8B)(1 - B)X_t = Z_t, \quad \{Z_t\} \sim \text{WN}(0, 1). \tag{6.1.3}$$

Instead of differencing the series in Figure 6.1 we could proceed more directly by attempting to fit an AR(2) process as suggested by the sample PACF of the original series in Figure 6.3. Maximum likelihood estimation, carried out using ITSM after fitting a preliminary model with Burg's algorithm and assuming that $EX_t = 0$, gives the model

$$(1 - 1.808B + 0.811B^2)X_t = (1 - 0.825B)(1 - .983B)X_t = Z_t,$$

$$\{Z_t\} \sim \text{WN}(0, 0.970), \tag{6.1.4}$$

which, although stationary, has coefficients closely resembling those of the true nonstationary process (6.1.3). (To obtain the model (6.1.4), two optimizations were carried out using the `Model>Estimation>Max likelihood` option of ITSM, the first with the default settings and the second after setting the accuracy parameter to 0.00001.)

From a sample of finite length it will be extremely difficult to distinguish between a nonstationary process such as (6.1.3), for which $\phi^*(1) = 0$, and a process such as

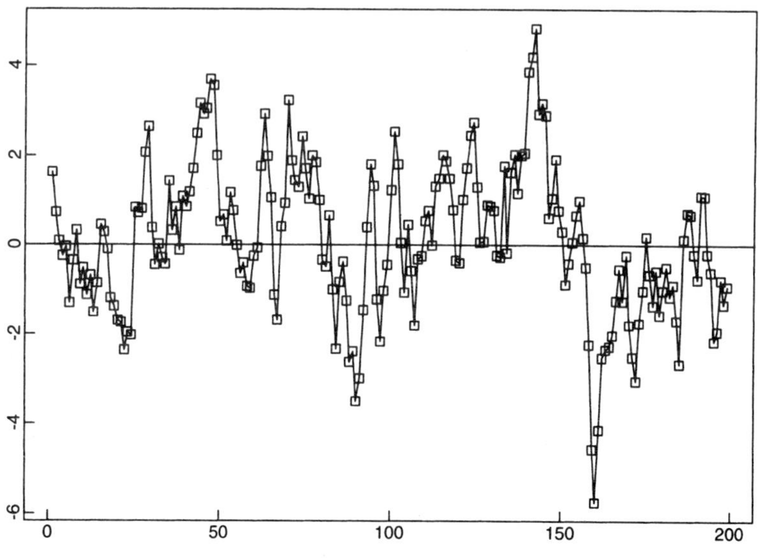

Figure 6-4 199 observations of the series $Y_t = \nabla X_t$ with $\{X_t\}$ as in Figure 6.1.

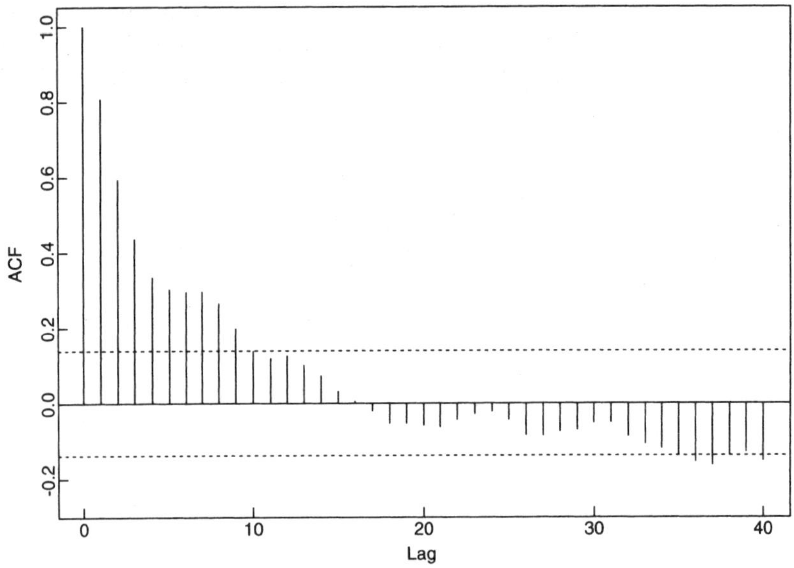

Figure 6-5 The sample ACF of the series $\{Y_t\}$ in Figure 6.4.

(6.1.4), which has very similar coefficients but for which ϕ^* has all of its zeros outside the unit circle. In either case, however, if it is possible by differencing to generate a series with rapidly decaying sample ACF, then the differenced data set can be fitted by a low-order ARMA process whose autoregressive polynomial ϕ^* has zeros that are comfortably outside the unit circle. This means that the fitted parameters will be well away from the boundary of the allowable parameter set. This is desirable

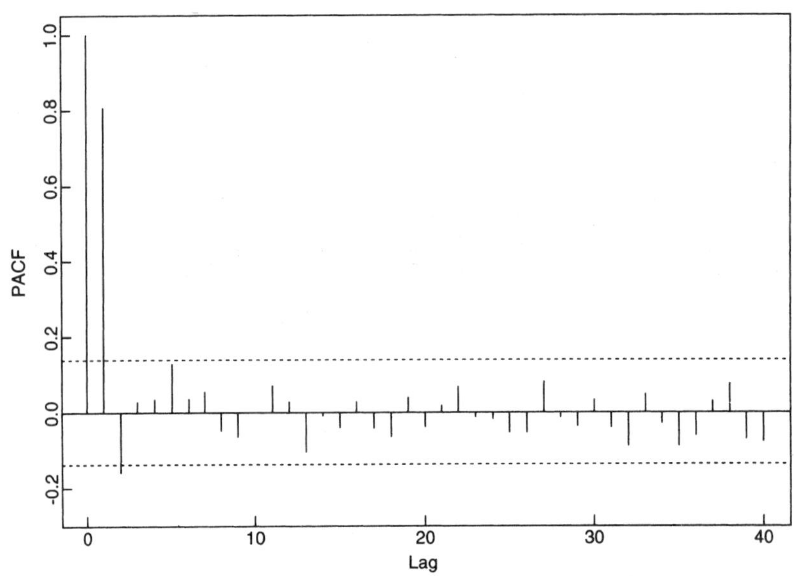

Figure 6-6 The sample PACF of the series $\{Y_t\}$ in Figure 6.4.

for numerical computation of parameter estimates and can be quite critical for some methods of estimation. For example, if we apply the Yule–Walker equations to fit an AR(2) model to the data in Figure 6.1, we obtain the model

$$(1 - 1.282B + 0.290B^2)X_t = Z_t, \quad \{Z_t\} \sim \text{WN}(0, 6.435), \tag{6.1.5}$$

which bears little resemblance to either the maximum likelihood model (6.1.4) or the true model (6.1.3). In this case the matrix $\hat{R}_2$ appearing in (5.1.7) is nearly singular.

An obvious limitation in fitting an ARIMA(p, d, q) process $\{X_t\}$ to data is that $\{X_t\}$ is permitted to be nonstationary only in a very special way, i.e., by allowing the polynomial $\phi^*(B)$ in the representation $\phi^*(B)X_t = Z_t$ to have a zero of multiplicity d at the point 1 on the unit circle. Such models are appropriate when the sample ACF is a slowly decaying positive function as in Figure 6.2, since sample autocorrelation functions of this form are associated with models $\phi^*(B)X_t = \theta(B)Z_t$ in which ϕ^* has a zero either at or close to 1.

Sample autocorrelations with slowly decaying oscillatory behavior as in Figure 6.8 are associated with models $\phi^*(B)X_t = \theta(B)Z_t$ in which ϕ^* has a zero close to $e^{i\omega}$ for some $\omega \in (-\pi, \pi]$ other than 0. Figure 6.8 is the sample ACF of the series of 200 observations in Figure 6.7, obtained from ITSM by simulating the AR(2) process

$$X_t - (2r^{-1}\cos\omega)X_{t-1} + r^{-2}X_{t-2} = Z_t, \quad \{Z_t\} \sim \text{WN}(0, 1), \tag{6.1.6}$$

with $r = 1.005$ and $\omega = \pi/3$, i.e.,

$$X_t - 0.9950X_{t-1} + 0.9901X_{t-2} = Z_t, \quad \{Z_t\} \sim \text{WN}(0, 1).$$

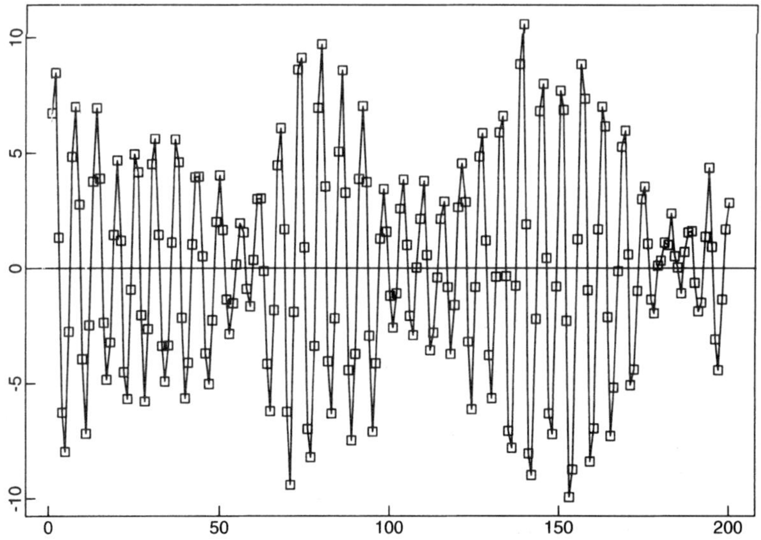

Figure 6-7 200 observations of the AR(2) process defined by (6.1.6) with $r = 1.005$ and $\omega = \pi/3$.

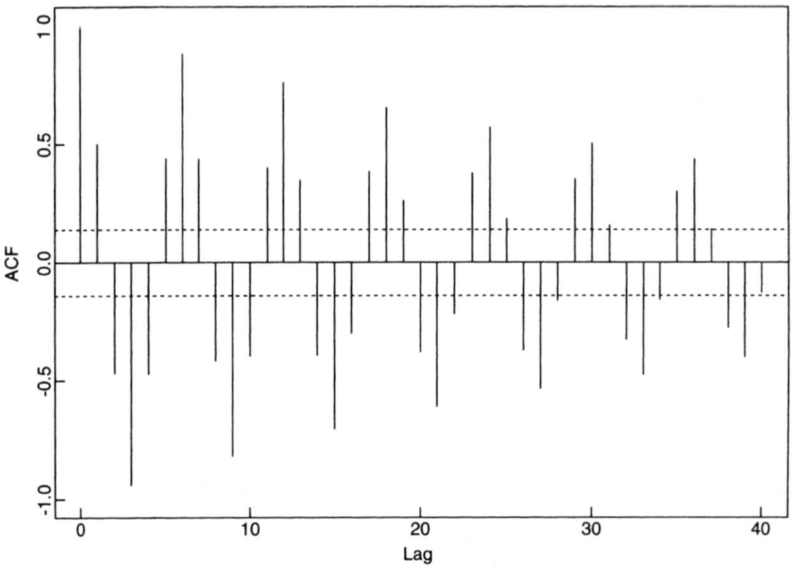

Figure 6-8 The sample ACF of the data in Figure 6.7.

The autocorrelation function of the model (6.1.6) can be derived by noting that

$$1 - \left(2r^{-1}\cos\omega\right)B + r^{-2}B^2 = \left(1 - r^{-1}e^{i\omega}B\right)\left(1 - r^{-1}e^{-i\omega}B\right) \tag{6.1.7}$$

and using (3.2.12). This gives

$$\rho(h) = r^{-h}\frac{\sin(h\omega + \psi)}{\sin\psi}, \quad h \geq 0, \tag{6.1.8}$$

where

$$\tan\psi = \frac{r^2 + 1}{r^2 - 1}\tan\omega. \tag{6.1.9}$$

It is clear from these equations that

$$\rho(h) \to \cos(h\omega) \text{ as } r \downarrow 1. \tag{6.1.10}$$

With $r = 1.005$ and $\omega = \pi/3$ as in the model generating Figure 6.7, the model ACF (6.1.8) is a damped sine wave with damping ratio $1/1.005$ and period 6. These properties are reflected in the sample ACF shown in Figure 6.8. For values of r closer to 1, the damping will be even slower as the model ACF approaches its limiting form (6.1.10).

If we were simply given the data shown in Figure 6.7, with no indication of the model from which it was generated, the slowly damped sinusoidal sample ACF with period 6 would suggest trying to make the sample ACF decay more rapidly by applying the operator (6.1.7) with $r = 1$ and $\omega = \pi/3$, i.e., $\left(1 - B + B^2\right)$. If it happens, as in this case, that the period $2\pi/\omega$ is close to some integer s (in this case 6), then the operator $1 - B^s$ can also be applied to produce a series with more rapidly decaying autocorrelation function (see also Section 6.5). Figures 6.9 and 6.10 show the sample autocorrelation functions obtained after applying the operators $1 - B + B^2$ and $1 - B^6$, respectively, to the data shown in Figure 6.7. For either one of these two differenced series, it is then not difficult to fit an ARMA model $\phi(B)X_t = \theta(B)Z_t$ for which the zeros of ϕ are well outside the unit circle. Techniques for identifying and determining such ARMA models have already been introduced in Chapter 5. For convenience we shall collect these together in the following sections with a number of illustrative examples.

6.2 Identification Techniques

(a) *Preliminary Transformations.* The estimation methods of Chapter 5 enable us to find, for given values of p and q, an ARMA(p, q) model to fit a given series of data. For this procedure to be meaningful it must be at least plausible that the data are in fact a realization of an ARMA process and in particular a realization of a stationary process. If the data display characteristics suggesting nonstationarity (e.g., trend and seasonality), then it may be necessary to make a transformation so as to produce a new series that is more compatible with the assumption of stationarity.

Deviations from stationarity may be suggested by the graph of the series itself or by the sample autocorrelation function or both.

Inspection of the graph of the series will occasionally reveal a strong dependence of variability on the level of the series, in which case the data should first be transformed to reduce or eliminate this dependence. For example, Figure 1.1 shows

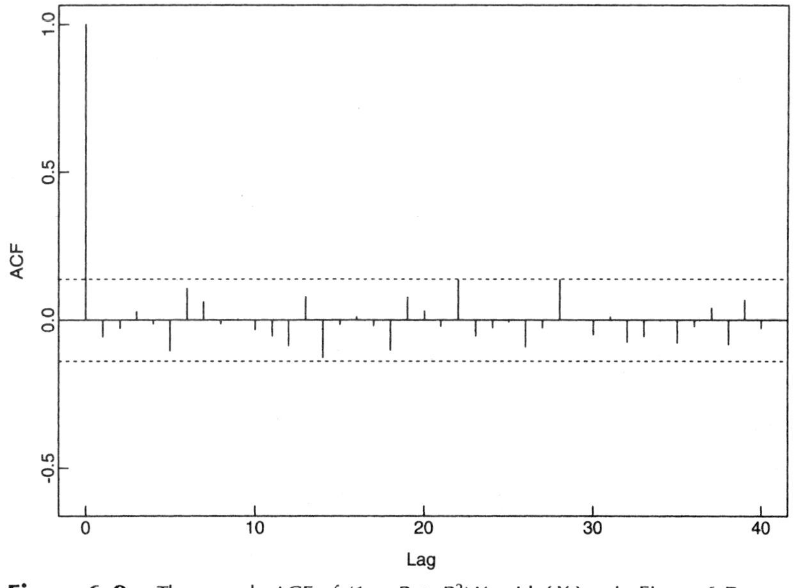

Figure 6-9 The sample ACF of $(1 - B + B^2)X_t$ with $\{X_t\}$ as in Figure 6.7.

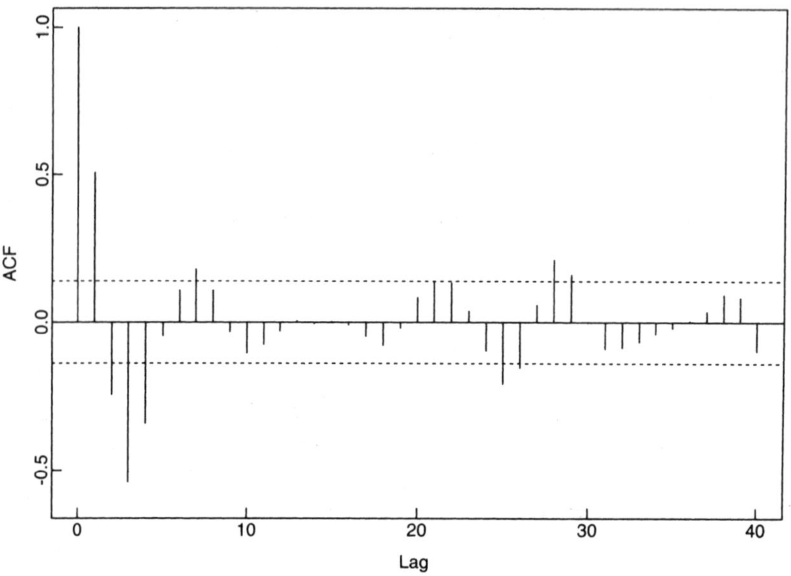

Figure 6-10 The sample ACF of $(1 - B^6)X_t$ with $\{X_t\}$ as in Figure 6.7.

the Australian monthly red wine sales from January 1980 through October 1991, and Figure 1.17 shows how the increasing variability with sales level is reduced by taking natural logarithms of the original series. The logarithmic transformation $V_t = \ln U_t$ used here is in fact appropriate whenever $\{U_t\}$ is a series whose standard deviation increases linearly with the mean. For a systematic account of a general class of variance-stabilizing transformations, we refer the reader to Box and Cox (1964). The defining equation for the general Box–Cox transformation f_λ is

$$f_\lambda(U_t) = \begin{cases} \lambda^{-1}(U_t^\lambda - 1), & U_t \geq 0, \lambda > 0, \\ \ln U_t, & U_t > 0, \lambda = 0, \end{cases}$$

and the program ITSM provides the option (`Transform>Box-Cox`) of applying f_λ (with $0 \leq \lambda \leq 1.5$) prior to the elimination of trend and/or seasonality from the data. In practice, if a Box–Cox transformation is necessary, it is often the case that either f_0 or $f_{0.5}$ is adequate.

Trend and seasonality are usually detected by inspecting the graph of the (possibly transformed) series. However, they are also characterized by autocorrelation functions that are slowly decaying and nearly periodic, respectively. The elimination of trend and seasonality was discussed in Section 1.5, where we described two methods:

i. "classical decomposition" of the series into a trend component, a seasonal component, and a random residual component, and

ii. differencing.

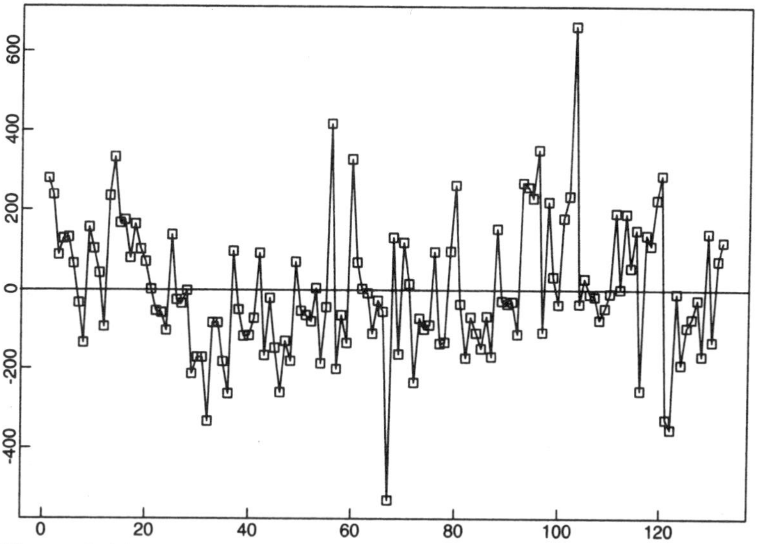

Figure 6-11 The Australian red wine data after taking natural logarithms and removing a seasonal component of period 12 and a linear trend.

The program ITSM (in the `Transform` option) offers a choice between these techniques. The results of applying methods (i) and (ii) to the transformed red wine data $V_t = \ln U_t$ in Figure 1.17 are shown in Figures 6.11 and 6.12, respectively. Figure 6.11 was obtained from ITSM by estimating and removing from $\{V_t\}$ a linear trend component and a seasonal component with period 12. Figure 6.12 was obtained by applying the operator $(1 - B^{12})$ to $\{V_t\}$. Neither of the two resulting series displays any apparent deviations from stationarity, nor do their sample autocorrelation functions. The sample ACF and PACF of $\{(1 - B^{12})V_t\}$ are shown in Figures 6.13 and 6.14, respectively.

After the elimination of trend and seasonality, it is still possible that the sample autocorrelation function may appear to be that of a nonstationary (or nearly nonstationary) process, in which case further differencing may be carried out.

In Section 1.5 we also mentioned a third possible approach:

iii. fitting a sum of harmonics and a polynomial trend to generate a noise sequence that consists of the residuals from the regression.

In Section 6.6 we discuss the modifications to classical least squares regression analysis that allow for dependence among the residuals from the regression. These modifications are implemented in the ITSM option `Regression>Estimation>Generalized LS`.

(b) *Identification and Estimation.* Let $\{X_t\}$ be the mean-corrected transformed series found as described in (a). The problem now is to find the most satisfactory ARMA(p, q) model to represent $\{X_t\}$. If p and q were known in advance, this would be a straightforward application of the estimation techniques described in Chapter 5.

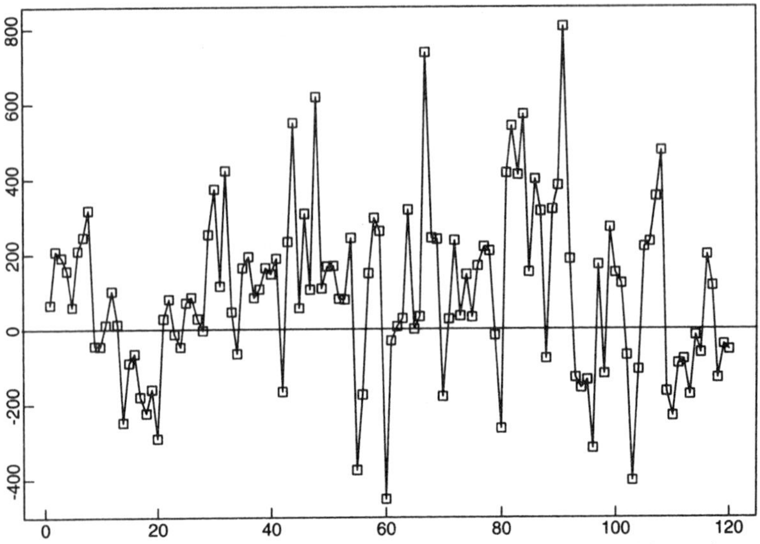

Figure 6-12 The Australian red wine data after taking natural logarithms and differencing at lag 12.

However, this is usually not the case, so it becomes necessary also to identify appropriate values for p and q.

It might appear at first sight that the higher the values chosen for p and q, the better the resulting fitted model will be. However, as pointed out in Section 5.5, estimation of too large a number of parameters introduces estimation errors that adversely affect the use of the fitted model for prediction as illustrated in Section 5.4. We therefore minimize one of the model selection criteria discussed in Section 5.5 in

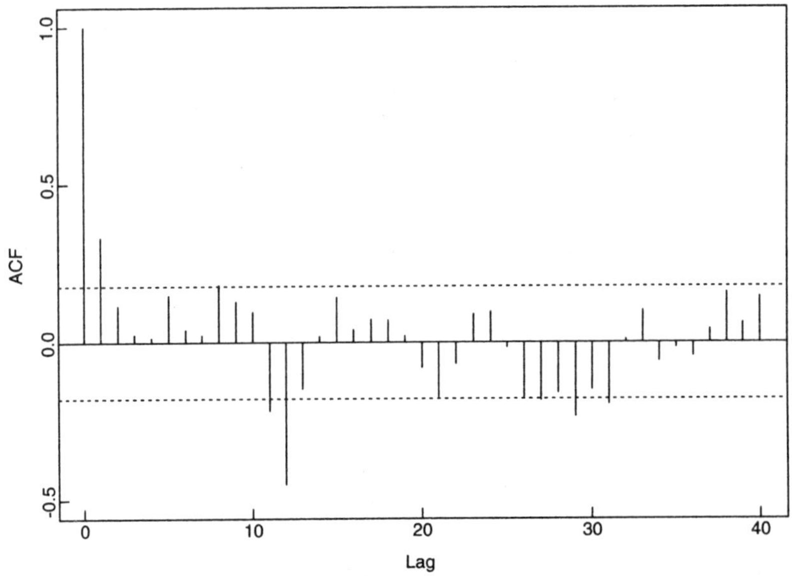

Figure 6-13 The sample ACF of the data in Figure 6.12.

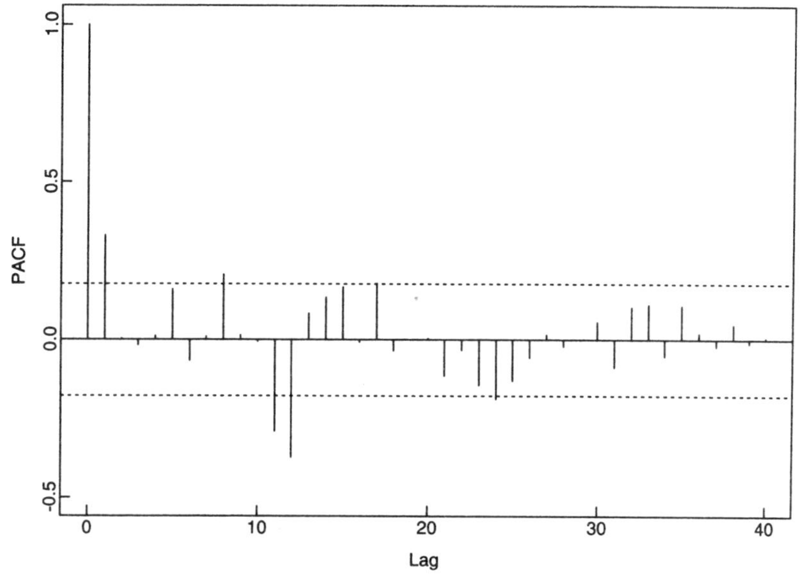

Figure 6-14 The sample PACF of the data in Figure 6.12.

order to choose the values of p and q. Each of these criteria includes a penalty term to discourage the fitting of too many parameters. We shall base our choice of p and q primarily on the minimization of the AICC statistic, defined as

$$\text{AICC}(\boldsymbol{\phi}, \boldsymbol{\theta}) = -2\ln L(\boldsymbol{\phi}, \boldsymbol{\theta}, S(\boldsymbol{\phi}, \boldsymbol{\theta})/n) + 2(p+q+1)n/(n-p-q-2), \quad (6.2.1)$$

where $L(\boldsymbol{\phi}, \boldsymbol{\theta}, \sigma^2)$ is the likelihood of the data under the Gaussian ARMA model with parameters $\left(\boldsymbol{\phi}, \boldsymbol{\theta}, \sigma^2\right)$, and $S(\boldsymbol{\phi}, \boldsymbol{\theta})$ is the residual sum of squares defined in (5.2.11). Once a model has been found that minimizes the AICC value, it is then necessary to check the model for goodness of fit (essentially by checking that the residuals are like white noise) as discussed in Section 5.3.

For any fixed values of p and q, the maximum likelihood estimates of $\boldsymbol{\phi}$ and $\boldsymbol{\theta}$ are the values that minimize the AICC. Hence, the minimum AICC model (over any given range of p and q values) can be found by computing the maximum likelihood estimators for each fixed p and q and choosing from these the maximum likelihood model with the smallest value of AICC. This can be done with the program ITSM by using the option `Model>Estimation>Autofit`. When this option is selected and upper and lower bounds for p and q are specified, the program fits maximum likelihood models for each pair (p, q) in the range specified and selects the model with smallest AICC value. If some of the coefficient estimates are small compared with their estimated standard deviations, maximum likelihood subset models (with those coefficients set to zero) can also be explored.

The steps in model identification and estimation can be summarized as follows:

- After transforming the data (if necessary) to make the fitting of an ARMA(p, q) model reasonable, examine the sample ACF and PACF to get some idea of potential p and q values. Preliminary estimation using the ITSM option `Model>Estimation>Preliminary` is also useful in this respect. Burg's algorithm with AICC minimization rapidly fits autoregressions of all orders up to 27 and selects the one with minimum AICC value. For preliminary estimation of models with $q > 0$, each pair (p, q) must be considered separately.
- Select the option `Model>Estimation>Autofit` of ITSM. Specify the required limits for p and q, and the program will then use maximum likelihood estimation to find the minimum AICC model with p and q in the range specified.
- Examination of the fitted coefficients and their standard errors may suggest that some of them can be set to zero. If this is the case, then a **subset model** can be fitted by clicking on the button `Constrain optimization` in the `Maximum Likelihood Estimation` dialog box and setting the selected coefficients to zero. Optimization will then give the maximum likelihood model with the chosen coefficients constrained to be zero. The constrained model is assessed by comparing its AICC value with those of the other candidate models.
- Check the candidate model(s) for goodness of fit as described in Section 5.3. These tests can be performed by selecting the option `Statistics>Residual Analysis`.

Example 6.2.1 The Australian red wine data

Let $\{X_1, \dots, X_{130}\}$ denote the series obtained from the red wine data of Example 1.1.1 after taking natural logarithms, differencing at lag 12, and subtracting the mean (0.0681) of the differences. The data prior to mean correction are shown in Figure 6.12. The sample PACF of $\{X_t\}$, shown in Figure 6.14, suggests that an AR(12) model might be appropriate for this series. To explore this possibility we use the ITSM option `Model>Estimation>Preliminary` with Burg's algorithm and AICC minimization. As anticipated, the fitted Burg models do indeed have minimum AICC when $p = 12$. The fitted model is

$$\begin{aligned}(1 - .245B - .069B^2 - .012B^3 - .021B^4 - .200B^5 + .025B^6 + .004B^7 \\ -.133B^8 + .010B^9 - .095B^{10} + .118B^{11} + .384B^{12})X_t = Z_t,\end{aligned}$$

with $\{Z_t\} \sim \text{WN}(0, 0.0135)$ and AICC value -158.77. Selecting the option `Model>Estimation>Max likelihood` then gives the maximum likelihood AR(12) model, which is very similar to the Burg model and has AICC value -158.87. Inspection of the standard errors of the coefficient estimators suggests the possibility of setting those at lags 2,3,4,6,7,9,10, and 11 equal to zero. If we do this by clicking on the `Constrain optimization` button in the `Maximum Likelihood Estimation` dialog box and then reoptimize, we obtain the model,

$$\left(1 - .270B - .224B^5 - .149B^8 + .099B^{11} + .353B^{12}\right)X_t = Z_t,$$

with $\{Z_t\} \sim \mathrm{WN}(0, 0.0138)$ and AICC value -172.49.

In order to check more general ARMA(p, q) models, select the option `Model>Estimation>Autofit` and specify the minimum and maximum values of p and q to be zero and 15, respectively. (The sample ACF and PACF suggest that these limits should be more than adequate to include the minimum AICC model.) In a few minutes (depending on the speed of your computer) the program selects an ARMA(1,12) model with AICC value -172.74, which is slightly better than the subset AR(12) model just found. Inspection of the estimated standard deviations of the MA coefficients at lags 1, 3, 4, 6, 7, 9, and 11 suggests setting them equal to zero and reestimating the values of the remaining coefficients. If we do this by clicking on the `Constrain optimization` button in the `Maximum Likelihood Estimation` dialog box, setting the required coefficients to zero and then reoptimizing, we obtain the model,

$$(1 - .286B)X_t = \left(1 + .127B^2 + .183B^5 + .177B^8 + .181B^{10} - .554B^{12}\right) Z_t,$$

with $\{Z_t\} \sim \mathrm{WN}(0, 0.0120)$ and AICC value -184.09.

The subset ARMA(1,12) model easily passes all the goodness of fit tests in the `Statistics>Residual Analysis` option. In view of this and its small AICC value, we accept it as a plausible model for the transformed red wine series. □

Example 6.2.2 The lake data

Let $\{Y_t, t = 1, \ldots, 99\}$ denote the lake data of Example 1.3.5. We have seen already in Example 5.2.5 that the ITSM option `Model>Estimation>Autofit` gives the minimum-AICC model

$$X_t - 0.7446X_{t-1} = Z_t + 0.3213Z_{t-1}, \quad \{Z_t\} \sim \mathrm{WN}(0, 0.4750),$$

for the mean-corrected series $X_t = Y_t - 9.0041$. The corresponding AICC value is 212.77. Since the model passes all the goodness of fit tests, we accept it as a reasonable model for the data. □

6.3 Unit Roots in Time Series Models

The unit root problem in time series arises when either the autoregressive or moving-average polynomial of an ARMA model has a root on or near the unit circle. A unit root in either of these polynomials has important implications for modeling. For example, a root near 1 of the autoregressive polynomial suggests that the data should be differenced before fitting an ARMA model, whereas a root near 1 of the moving-average polynomial indicates that the data were overdifferenced. In this section, we consider inference procedures for detecting the presence of a unit root in the autoregressive and moving-average polynomials.

6.3.1 Unit Roots in Autoregressions

In Section 6.1 we discussed the use of differencing to transform a nonstationary time series with a slowly decaying sample ACF and values near 1 at small lags into one with a rapidly decreasing sample ACF. The degree of differencing of a time series $\{X_t\}$ was largely determined by applying the difference operator repeatedly until the sample ACF of $\{\nabla^d X_t\}$ decays quickly. The differenced time series could then be modeled by a low-order ARMA(p, q) process, and hence the resulting ARIMA(p, d, q) model for the original data has an autoregressive polynomial $(1 - \phi_1 z - \cdots - \phi_p z^p)(1 - z)^d$ (see (6.1.1)) with d roots on the unit circle. In this subsection we discuss a more systematic approach to testing for the presence of a unit root of the autoregressive polynomial in order to decide whether or not a time series should be differenced. This approach was pioneered by Dickey and Fuller (1979).

Let $X_1, \ldots, X_n$ be observations from the AR(1) model

$$X_t - \mu = \phi_1(X_{t-1} - \mu) + Z_t, \qquad \{Z_t\} \sim \mathrm{WN}(0, \sigma^2), \tag{6.3.1}$$

where $|\phi_1| < 1$ and $\mu = EX_t$. For large n, the maximum likelihood estimator $\hat{\phi}_1$ of ϕ_1 is approximately $\mathrm{N}(\phi_1, (1-\phi_1^2)/n)$. For the unit root case, this normal approximation is no longer applicable, even asymptotically, which precludes its use for testing the unit root hypothesis $H_0 : \phi_1 = 1$ vs. $H_1 : \phi_1 < 1$. To construct a test of H_0, write the model (6.3.1) as

$$\nabla X_t = X_t - X_{t-1} = \phi_0^* + \phi_1^* X_{t-1} + Z_t, \qquad \{Z_t\} \sim \mathrm{WN}\left(0, \sigma^2\right), \tag{6.3.2}$$

where $\phi_0^* = \mu(1 - \phi_1)$ and $\phi_1^* = \phi_1 - 1$. Now let $\hat{\phi}_1^*$ be the ordinary least squares (OLS) estimator of ϕ_1^* found by regressing ∇X_t on 1 and X_{t-1}. The estimated standard error of $\hat{\phi}_1^*$ is

$$\widehat{\mathrm{SE}}\left(\hat{\phi}_1^*\right) = S\left(\sum_{t=2}^{n}\left(X_{t-1} - \bar{X}\right)^2\right)^{-1/2},$$

where $S^2 = \sum_{t=2}^{n}\left(\nabla X_t - \hat{\phi}_0^* - \hat{\phi}_1^* X_{t-1}\right)^2/(n-3)$ and $\bar{X}$ is the sample mean of $X_1, \ldots, X_{n-1}$. Dickey and Fuller derived the limit distribution as $n \to \infty$ of the t-ratio

$$\hat{\tau}_\mu := \hat{\phi}_1^* / \widehat{\mathrm{SE}}\left(\hat{\phi}_1^*\right) \tag{6.3.3}$$

under the unit root assumption $\phi_1^* = 0$, from which a test of the null hypothesis $H_0 : \phi_1 = 1$ can be constructed. The .01, .05, and .10 quantiles of the limit distribution of $\hat{\tau}_\mu$ (see Table 8.5.2 of Fuller, 1976) are -3.43, -2.86, and -2.57, respectively.

The augmented Dickey–Fuller test then rejects the null hypothesis of a unit root, at say, level .05 if $\hat{\tau}_\mu < -2.86$. Notice that the cutoff value for this test statistic is much smaller than the standard cutoff value of -1.645 obtained from the normal approximation to the t-distribution, so that the unit root hypothesis is less likely to be rejected using the correct limit distribution.

The above procedure can be extended to the case where $\{X_t\}$ follows the AR(p) model with mean μ given by

$$X_t - \mu = \phi_1 (X_{t-1} - \mu) + \cdots + \phi_p \left(X_{t-p} - \mu\right) + Z_t, \qquad \{Z_t\} \sim \mathrm{WN}\left(0, \sigma^2\right).$$

This model can be rewritten as (see Problem 6.2)

$$\nabla X_t = \phi_0^* + \phi_1^* X_{t-1} + \phi_2^* \nabla X_{t-1} + \cdots + \phi_p^* \nabla X_{t-p+1} + Z_t, \tag{6.3.4}$$

where $\phi_0 = \mu\left(1 - \phi_1 - \cdots - \phi_p\right)$, $\phi_1^* = \sum_{i=1}^p \phi_i - 1$, and $\phi_j^* = -\sum_{i=j}^p \phi_i$, $j = 2, \ldots, p$. If the autoregressive polynomial has a unit root at 1, then $0 = \phi(1) = -\phi_1^*$, and the differenced series $\{\nabla X_t\}$ is an AR($p-1$) process. Consequently, testing the hypothesis of a unit root at 1 of the autoregressive polynomial is equivalent to testing $\phi_1^* = 0$. As in the AR(1) example, ϕ_1^* can be estimated as the coefficient of X_{t-1} in the OLS regression of ∇X_t onto $1, X_{t-1}, \nabla X_{t-1}, \ldots, \nabla X_{t-p+1}$. For large n the t-ratio

$$\hat{\tau}_\mu := \hat{\phi}_1^* / \widehat{\mathrm{SE}}\left(\hat{\phi}_1^*\right), \tag{6.3.5}$$

where $\widehat{\mathrm{SE}}\left(\hat{\phi}_1^*\right)$ is the estimated standard error of $\hat{\phi}_1^*$, has the same limit distribution as the test statistic in (6.3.3). The augmented Dickey–Fuller test in this case is applied in exactly the same manner as for the AR(1) case using the test statistic (6.3.5) and the cutoff values given above.

Example 6.3.1

Consider testing the time series of Example 6.1.1 (see Figure 6.1) for the presence of a unit root in the autoregressive operator. The sample PACF in Figure 6.3 suggests fitting an AR(2) or possibly an AR(3) model to the data. Regressing ∇X_t on $1, X_{t-1}, \nabla X_{t-1}, \nabla X_{t-2}$ for $t = 4, \ldots, 200$ using OLS gives

$$\begin{aligned}\nabla X_t = \underset{(.1135)}{.1503} - \underset{(.0028)}{.0041} X_{t-1} + \underset{(.0707)}{.9335} \nabla X_{t-1} - \underset{(.0708)}{.1548} \nabla X_{t-2} + Z_t,\end{aligned}$$

where $\{Z_t\} \sim \mathrm{WN}(0, .9639)$. The test statistic for testing the presence of a unit root is

$$\hat{\tau}_\mu = \frac{-.0041}{.0028} = -1.464.$$

Since $-1.464 > -2.57$, the unit root hypothesis is not rejected at level .10. In contrast, if we had mistakenly used the t-distribution with 193 degrees of freedom as an approximation to $\hat{\tau}_\mu$, then we would have rejected the unit root hypothesis at the .10 level (p-value is .074). The t-ratios for the other coefficients, ϕ_0^*, ϕ_2^*, and ϕ_3^*, have an approximate t-distribution with 193 degrees of freedom. Based on these t-ratios, the intercept should be 0, while the coefficient of ∇X_{t-2} is barely significant. The evidence is much stronger in favor of a unit root if the analysis is repeated without a mean term. The fitted model without a mean term is

$$\nabla X_t = \underset{(.0018)}{.0012} X_{t-1} + \underset{(.0707)}{.9395} \nabla X_{t-1} - \underset{(.0709)}{.1585} \nabla X_{t-2} + Z_t,$$

where $\{Z_t\} \sim \mathrm{WN}(0, .9677)$. The .01, .05, and .10 cutoff values for the corresponding test statistic when a mean term is excluded from the model are -2.58, -1.95, and -1.62 (see Table 8.5.2 of Fuller, 1976). In this example, the test statistic is

$$\hat{\tau} = \frac{-.0012}{.0018} = -.667,$$

which is substantially larger than the .10 cutoff value of -1.62. □

Further extensions of the above test to AR models with $p = O\left(n^{1/3}\right)$ and to ARMA(p, q) models can be found in Said and Dickey (1984). However, as reported in Schwert (1987) and Pantula (1991), this test must be used with caution if the underlying model orders are not correctly specified.

6.3.2 Unit Roots in Moving Averages

A unit root in the moving-average polynomial can have a number of interpretations depending on the modeling application. For example, let $\{X_t\}$ be a causal and invertible ARMA(p, q) process satisfying the equations

$$\phi(B) X_t = \theta(B) Z_t, \qquad \{Z_t\} \sim \mathrm{WN}\left(0, \sigma^2\right).$$

Then the differenced series $Y_t := \nabla X_t$ is a noninvertible ARMA$(p, q+1)$ process with moving-average polynomial $\theta(z)(1-z)$. Consequently, testing for a unit root in the moving-average polynomial is equivalent to testing that the time series has been overdifferenced.

As a second application, it is possible to distinguish between the competing models

$$\nabla^k X_t = a + V_t$$

and

$$X_t = c_0 + c_1 t + \cdots + c_k t^k + W_t,$$

where $\{V_t\}$ and $\{W_t\}$ are invertible ARMA processes. For the former model the differenced series $\left\{\nabla^k X_t\right\}$ has no moving-average unit roots, while for the latter model $\{\nabla^k X_t\}$ has a multiple moving-average unit root of order k. We can therefore distinguish between the two models by using the observed values of $\left\{\nabla^k X_t\right\}$ to test for the presence of a moving-average unit root.

We confine our discussion of unit root tests to first-order moving-average models, the general case being considerably more complicated and not fully resolved. Let $X_1, \ldots, X_n$ be observations from the MA(1) model

$$X_t = Z_t + \theta Z_{t-1}, \qquad \{Z_t\} \sim \text{IID}\left(0, \sigma^2\right).$$

Davis and Dunsmuir (1996) showed that under the assumption $\theta = -1$, $n(\hat{\theta}+1)$ ($\hat{\theta}$ is the maximum likelihood estimator) converges in distribution. A test of $H_0 : \theta = -1$ vs. $H_1 : \theta > -1$ can be fashioned on this limiting result by rejecting H_0 when

$$\hat{\theta} > -1 + c_\alpha / n,$$

where c_α is the $(1 - \alpha)$ quantile of the limit distribution of $n\left(\hat{\theta} + 1\right)$. (From Table 3.2 of Davis, Chen, and Dunsmuir (1995), $c_{.01} = 11.93$, $c_{.05} = 6.80$, and $c_{.10} = 4.90$.) In particular, if $n = 50$, then the null hypothesis is rejected at level .05 if $\hat{\theta} > -1 + 6.80/50 = -.864$.

The likelihood ratio test can also be used for testing the unit root hypothesis. The likelihood ratio for this problem is $L(-1, S(-1)/n)/L\left(\hat{\theta}, \hat{\sigma}^2\right)$, where $L\left(\theta, \sigma^2\right)$ is the Gaussian likelihood of the data based on an MA(1) model, $S(-1)$ is the sum of squares given by (5.2.11) when $\theta = -1$, and $\hat{\theta}$ and $\hat{\sigma}^2$ are the maximum likelihood estimators of θ and σ^2. The null hypothesis is rejected at level α if

$$\lambda_n := -2 \ln \left(\frac{L(-1, S(-1)/n)}{L\left(\hat{\theta}, \hat{\sigma}^2\right)} \right) > c_{\text{LR},\alpha}$$

where the cutoff value is chosen such that $P_{\theta=-1}[\lambda_n > c_{\text{LR},\alpha}] = \alpha$. The limit distribution of λ_n was derived by Davis et al. (1995), who also gave selected quantiles of the limit. It was found that these quantiles provide a good approximation to their finite-sample counterparts for time series of length $n \geq 50$. The limiting quantiles for λ_n under H_0 are $c_{\text{LR},.01} = 4.41$, $c_{\text{LR},.05} = 1.94$, and $c_{\text{LR},.10} = 1.00$.

Example 6.3.2

For the overshort data $\{X_t\}$ of Example 3.2.8, the maximum likelihood MA(1) model for the mean corrected data $\{Y_t = X_t + 4.035\}$ was (see Example 5.4.1)

$$Y_t = Z_t - 0.818 Z_{t-1}, \quad \{Z_t\} \sim \text{WN}(0, 2040.75).$$

In the structural formulation of this model given in Example 3.2.8, the moving-average parameter θ was related to the measurement error variances σ_U^2 and σ_V^2 through the equation

$$\frac{\theta}{1 + \theta^2} = \frac{-\sigma_U^2}{2\sigma_U^2 + \sigma_V^2}.$$

(These error variances correspond to the daily measured amounts of fuel in the tank and the daily measured adjustments due to sales and deliveries.) A value of $\theta = -1$

indicates that there is no appreciable measurement error due to sales and deliveries (i.e., $\sigma_V^2 = 0$), and hence testing for a unit root in this case is equivalent to testing that $\sigma_U^2 = 0$. Assuming that the mean is known, the unit root hypothesis is rejected at $\alpha = .05$, since $-.818 > -1 + 6.80/57 = -.881$. The evidence against H_0 is stronger using the likelihood ratio statistic. Using ITSM and entering the MA(1) model $\theta = -1$ and $\sigma^2 = 2203.12$, we find that $-2\ln L(-1, 2203.12) = 604.584$, while $-2\ln L(\hat{\theta}, \hat{\sigma}^2) = 597.267$. Comparing the likelihood ratio statistic $\lambda_n = 604.584 - 597.267 = 7.317$ with the cutoff value $c_{\text{LR},.01}$, we reject H_0 at level $\alpha = .01$ and conclude that the measurement error associated with sales and deliveries is nonzero.

In the above example it was assumed that the mean was known. In practice, these tests should be adjusted for the fact that the mean is also being estimated.

Tanaka (1990) proposed a locally best invariant unbiased (LBIU) test for the unit root hypothesis. It was found that the LBIU test has slightly greater power than the likelihood ratio test for alternatives close to $\theta = -1$ but has less power for alternatives further away from -1 (see Davis et al., 1995). The LBIU test has been extended to cover more general models by Tanaka (1990) and Tam and Reinsel (1995). Similar extensions to tests based on the maximum likelihood estimator and the likelihood ratio statistic have been explored in Davis, Chen, and Dunsmuir (1996). □

6.4 Forecasting ARIMA Models

In this section we demonstrate how the methods of Section 3.3 and 5.4 can be adapted to forecast the future values of an ARIMA(p, d, q) process $\{X_t\}$. (The required numerical calculations can all be carried out using the program ITSM.)

If $d \geq 1$, the first and second moments EX_t and $E(X_{t+h}X_t)$ are not determined by the difference equations (6.1.1). We cannot expect, therefore, to determine best linear predictors for $\{X_t\}$ without further assumptions.

For example, suppose that $\{Y_t\}$ is a causal ARMA(p, q) process and that X_0 is any random variable. Define

$$X_t = X_0 + \sum_{j=1}^{t} Y_j, \quad t = 1, 2, \ldots.$$

Then $\{X_t, t \geq 0\}$ is an ARIMA$(p, 1, q)$ process with mean $EX_t = EX_0$ and autocovariances $E(X_{t+h}X_t) - (EX_0)^2$ that depend on $\text{Var}(X_0)$ and $\text{Cov}(X_0, Y_j)$, $j = 1, 2, \ldots$. The best linear predictor of X_{n+1} based on $\{1, X_0, X_1, \ldots, X_n\}$ is the same as the best linear predictor in terms of the set $\{1, X_0, Y_1, \ldots, Y_n\}$, since each linear combination of the latter is a linear combination of the former and vice versa. Hence, using P_n to denote best linear predictor in terms of either set and using the linearity of P_n, we can write

$$P_n X_{n+1} = P_n(X_0 + Y_1 + \cdots + Y_{n+1}) = P_n(X_n + Y_{n+1}) = X_n + P_n Y_{n+1}.$$

To evaluate $P_n Y_{n+1}$ it is necessary (see Section 2.5) to know $E(X_0 Y_j)$, $j = 1, \ldots, n+1$, and EX_0^2. However, if we assume that X_0 is uncorrelated with $\{Y_t, t \geq 1\}$, then $P_n Y_{n+1}$ is the same (Problem 6.5) as the best linear predictor $\hat{Y}_{n+1}$ of Y_{n+1} in terms of $\{1, Y_1, \ldots, Y_n\}$, which can be calculated as described in Section 3.3. The assumption that X_0 is uncorrelated with $Y_1, Y_2, \ldots$ therefore suffices to determine the best linear predictor $P_n X_{n+1}$ in this case.

Turning now to the general case, we shall assume that our observed process $\{X_t\}$ satisfies the difference equations

$$(1 - B)^d X_t = Y_t, \quad t = 1, 2, \ldots,$$

where $\{Y_t\}$ is a causal ARMA(p, q) process, and that the random vector $(X_{1-d}, \ldots, X_0)$ is uncorrelated with Y_t, $t > 0$. The difference equations can be rewritten in the form

$$X_t = Y_t - \sum_{j=1}^{d} \binom{d}{j} (-1)^j X_{t-j}, \quad t = 1, 2, \ldots. \tag{6.4.1}$$

It is convenient, by relabeling the time axis if necessary, to assume that we observe $X_{1-d}, X_{2-d}, \ldots, X_n$. (The observed values of $\{Y_t\}$ are then $Y_1, \ldots, Y_n$.) As usual, we shall use P_n to denote best linear prediction in terms of the observations up to time n (in this case $1, X_{1-d}, \ldots, X_n$ or equivalently $1, X_{1-d}, \ldots, X_0, Y_1, \ldots, Y_n$).

Our goal is to compute the best linear predictors $P_n X_{n+h}$. This can be done by applying the operator P_n to each side of (6.4.1) (with $t = n+h$) and using the linearity of P_n to obtain

$$P_n X_{n+h} = P_n Y_{n+h} - \sum_{j=1}^{d} \binom{d}{j} (-1)^j P_n X_{n+h-j}. \tag{6.4.2}$$

Now the assumption that $(X_{1-d}, \ldots, X_0)$ is uncorrelated with Y_t, $t > 0$, enables us to identify $P_n Y_{n+h}$ with the best linear predictor of Y_{n+h} in terms of $\{1, Y_1, \ldots, Y_n\}$, and this can be calculated as described in Section 3.3. The predictor $P_n X_{n+1}$ is obtained directly from (6.4.2) by noting that $P_n X_{n+1-j} = X_{n+1-j}$ for each $j \geq 1$. The predictor $P_n X_{n+2}$ can then be found from (6.4.2) using the previously calculated value of $P_n X_{n+1}$. The predictors $P_n X_{n+3}, P_n X_{n+4}, \ldots$ can be computed recursively in the same way.

To find the mean squared error of prediction it is convenient to express $P_n Y_{n+h}$ in terms of $\{X_j\}$. For $n \geq 0$ we denote the one-step predictors by $\hat{Y}_{n+1} = P_n Y_{n+1}$ and $\hat{X}_{n+1} = P_n X_{n+1}$. Then from (6.4.1) and (6.4.2) we have

$$X_{n+1} - \hat{X}_{n+1} = Y_{n+1} - \hat{Y}_{n+1}, \quad n \geq 1,$$

and hence from (3.3.12), if $n > m = \max(p, q)$ and $h \geq 1$, we can write

$$P_n Y_{n+h} = \sum_{i=1}^{p} \phi_i P_n Y_{n+h-i} + \sum_{j=h}^{q} \theta_{n+h-1,j} \left(X_{n+h-j} - \hat{X}_{n+h-j} \right). \tag{6.4.3}$$

Setting $\phi^*(z) = (1-z)^d \phi(z) = 1 - \phi_1^* z - \cdots - \phi_{p+d}^* z^{p+d}$, we find from (6.4.2) and (6.4.3) that

$$P_n X_{n+h} = \sum_{j=1}^{p+d} \phi_j^* P_n X_{n+h-j} + \sum_{j=h}^{q} \theta_{n+h-1,j} \left(X_{n+h-j} - \hat{X}_{n+h-j} \right), \tag{6.4.4}$$

which is analogous to the h-step prediction formula (3.3.12) for an ARMA process. As in (3.3.13), the mean squared error of the h-step predictor is

$$\sigma_n^2(h) = E(X_{n+h} - P_n X_{n+h})^2 = \sum_{j=0}^{h-1} \left(\sum_{r=0}^{j} \chi_r \theta_{n+h-r-1,j-r} \right)^2 v_{n+h-j-1}, \tag{6.4.5}$$

where $\theta_{n0} = 1$,

$$\chi(z) = \sum_{r=0}^{\infty} \chi_r z^r = \left(1 - \phi_1^* z - \cdots - \phi_{p+d}^* z^{p+d}\right)^{-1},$$

and

$$v_{n+h-j-1} = E\left(X_{n+h-j} - \hat{X}_{n+h-j}\right)^2 = E\left(Y_{n+h-j} - \hat{Y}_{n+h-j}\right)^2.$$

The coefficients χ_j can be found from the recursions (3.3.14) with ϕ_j^* replacing ϕ_j. For large n we can approximate (6.4.5), provided that $\theta(\cdot)$ is invertible, by

$$\sigma_n^2(h) = \sum_{j=0}^{h-1} \psi_j^2 \sigma^2, \tag{6.4.6}$$

where

$$\psi(z) = \sum_{j=0}^{\infty} \psi_j z^j = (\phi^*(z))^{-1} \theta(z).$$

6.4.1 The Forecast Function

Inspection of equation (6.4.4) shows that for fixed $n > m = \max(p, q)$, the h-step predictors

$$g(h) := P_n X_{n+h},$$

satisfy the homogeneous linear difference equations

$$g(h) - \phi_1^* g(h-1) - \cdots - \phi_{p+d}^* g(h-p-d) = 0, \quad h > q, \tag{6.4.7}$$

where $\phi_1^*, \ldots, \phi_{p+d}^*$ are the coefficients of $z, \ldots, z^{p+d}$ in

$$\phi^*(z) = (1 - z)^d \phi(z).$$

The solution of (6.4.7) is well known from the theory of linear difference equations (see TSTM, Section 3.6). If we assume that the zeros of $\phi(z)$ (denoted by $\xi_1, \ldots, \xi_p$) are all distinct, then the solution is

$$g(h) = a_0 + a_1 h + \cdots + a_d h^{d-1} + b_1 \xi_1^{-h} + \cdots + b_p \xi_p^{-h}, \quad h > q - p - d, \tag{6.4.8}$$

where the coefficients $a_1, \ldots, a_d$ and $b_1, \ldots, b_p$ can be determined from the $p + d$ equations obtained by equating the right-hand side of (6.4.8) for $q - p - d < h \leq q$ with the corresponding value of $g(h)$ computed numerically (for $h \leq 0$, $P_n X_{n+h} = X_{n+h}$, and for $1 \leq h \leq q$, $P_n X_{n+h}$ can be computed from (6.4.4) as already described). Once the constants a_i and b_i have been evaluated, the algebraic expression (6.4.8) gives the predictors for all $h > q - p - d$. In the case $q = 0$, the values of $g(h)$ in the equations for $a_0, \ldots, a_d, b_1, \ldots, b_p$ are simply the *observed* values $g(h) = X_{n+h}$, $-p - d \leq h \leq 0$, and the expression (6.4.6) for the mean squared error is exact.

The calculation of the forecast function is easily generalized to deal with more complicated ARIMA processes. For example, if the observations $X_{-13}, X_{-12}, \ldots, X_n$ are differenced at lags 12 and 1, and $(1 - B)(1 - B^{12})X_t$ is modeled as a causal invertible ARMA(p, q) process with mean μ and $\max(p, q) < n$, then $\{X_t\}$ satisfies an equation of the form

$$\phi(B)[(1 - B)(1 - B^{12})X_t - \mu] = \theta(B)Z_t, \quad \{Z_t\} \sim \text{WN}\left(0, \sigma^2\right), \tag{6.4.9}$$

and the forecast function $g(h) = P_n X_{n+h}$ satisfies the analogue of (6.4.7), namely,

$$\phi(B)(1 - B)(1 - B^{12})g(h) = \phi(1)\mu, \quad h > q. \tag{6.4.10}$$

To find the general solution of these inhomogeneous linear difference equations, it suffices (see TSTM, Section 3.6) to find one particular solution of (6.4.10) and then add to it the general solution of the same equations with the right-hand side set equal to zero. A particular solution is easily found (by trial and error) to be

$$g(h) = \frac{\mu h^2}{24},$$

and the general solution is therefore

$$g(h) = \frac{\mu h^2}{24} + a_0 + a_1 h + \sum_{j=1}^{11} c_j e^{ij\pi/6} + b_1 \xi_1^{-h} + \cdots + b_p \xi_p^{-h},$$

$$h > q - p - 13. \tag{6.4.11}$$

(The terms a_0 and $a_1 h$ correspond to the double root $z = 1$ of the equation $\phi(z)(1 - z)(1 - z^{12}) = 0$, and the subsequent terms to each of the other roots, which we assume to be distinct.) For $q - p - 13 < h \leq 0$, $g(h) = X_{n+h}$, and for $1 \leq h \leq q$, the values of $g(h) = P_n X_{n+h}$ can be determined resursively from the equations

$$P_n X_{n+h} = \mu + P_n X_{n-1} + P_n X_{n-12} - P_n X_{n-13} + P_n Y_{n+h},$$

where $\{Y_t\}$ is the ARMA process $Y_t = (1-B)\left(1-B^{12}\right)X_t - \mu$. Substituting these values of $g(h)$ into (6.4.11), we obtain a set of $p+13$ equations for the coefficients a_i, b_j, and c_k. Solving these equations then completes the determination of $g(h)$.

The large-sample approximation to the mean squared error is again given by (6.4.6), with ψ_j redefined as the coefficient of z^j in the power series expansion of $\theta(z)/\left[(1-z)\left(1-z^{12}\right)\phi(z)\right]$.

Example 6.4.1 An ARIMA(1,1,0) model

In Example 5.2.4 we found the maximum likelihood AR(1) model for the mean-corrected differences X_t of the Dow Jones Utilities Index (Aug. 28–Dec. 18, 1972). The model was

$$X_t - 0.4471 X_{t-1} = Z_t, \quad \{Z_t\} \sim \mathrm{WN}(0, 0.1455), \tag{6.4.12}$$

where $X_t = D_t - D_{t-1} - 0.1336$, $t = 1, \ldots, 77$, and $\{D_t, t = 0, 1, 2, \ldots, 77\}$ is the original series. The model for $\{D_t\}$ is thus

$$(1 - 0.4471B)[(1-B)D_t - 0.1336] = Z_t, \quad \{Z_t\} \sim \mathrm{WN}(0, 0.1455).$$

The recursions for $g(h)$ therefore take the form

$$(1 - 0.4471B)(1-B)g(h) = 0.5529 \times 0.1336 = 0.07387, \quad h > 0. \tag{6.4.13}$$

A particular solution of these equations is $g(h) = 0.1336h$, so the general solution is

$$g(h) = 0.1336h + a + b(.4471)^h, \quad h > -2. \tag{6.4.14}$$

Substituting $g(-1) = D_{76} = 122$ and $g(0) = D_{77} = 121.23$ in the equations with $h = -1$ and $h = 0$, and solving for a and b gives

$$g(h) = 0.1366h + 120.50 + 0.7331(.4471)^h.$$

Setting $h = 1$ and $h = 2$ gives

$$P_{77}D_{78} = 120.97 \quad \text{and} \quad P_{77}D_{79} = 120.94.$$

From (6.4.5) we find that the corresponding mean squared errors are

$$\sigma_{77}^2(1) = v_{77} = \sigma^2 = .1455$$

and

$$\sigma_{77}^2(2) = v_{78} + \phi_1^{*2} v_{77} = \sigma^2\left(1 + 1.4471^2\right) = .4502.$$

(Notice that the approximation (6.4.6) is exact in this case.) The predictors and their mean squared errors are easily obtained from the program ITSM by opening the file

DOWJ.TSM, differencing at lag 1, fitting a preliminary AR(1) model to the mean-corrected data with Burg's algorithm, and then selecting `Model>Estimation>Max likelihood` to find the maximum likelihood AR(1) model. The predicted values and their mean squared errors are then found using the option `Forecasting>ARMA`. □

6.5 Seasonal ARIMA Models

We have already seen how differencing the series $\{X_t\}$ at lag s is a convenient way of eliminating a seasonal component of period s. If we fit an ARMA(p,q) model $\phi(B)Y_t = \theta(B)Z_t$ to the differenced series $Y_t = (1-B^s)X_t$, then the model for the original series is $\phi(B)(1-B^s)X_t = \theta(B)Z_t$. This is a special case of the general seasonal ARIMA (SARIMA) model defined as follows.

Definition 6.5.1

If d and D are nonnegative integers, then $\{X_t\}$ is a **seasonal ARIMA$(p,d,q)\times(P,D,Q)_s$ process with period s** if the differenced series $Y_t = (1-B)^d(1-B^s)^D X_t$ is a causal ARMA process defined by

$$\phi(B)\Phi(B^s)Y_t = \theta(B)\Theta(B^s)Z_t, \qquad \{Z_t\} \sim \text{WN}\left(0,\sigma^2\right), \tag{6.5.1}$$

where $\phi(z) = 1-\phi_1 z - \cdots - \phi_p z^p$, $\Phi(z) = 1-\Phi_1 z - \cdots - \Phi_P z^P$, $\theta(z) = 1+\theta_1 z + \cdots + \theta_q z^q$, and $\Theta(z) = 1+\Theta_1 z + \cdots + \Theta_Q z^Q$.

Remark 1. Note that the process $\{Y_t\}$ is causal if and only if $\phi(z) \neq 0$ and $\Phi(z) \neq 0$ for $|z| \le 1$. In applications D is rarely more than one, and P and Q are typically less than three. □

Remark 2. The equation (6.5.1) satisfied by the differenced process $\{Y_t\}$ can be rewritten in the equivalent form

$$\phi^*(B)Y_t = \theta^*(B)Z_t, \tag{6.5.2}$$

where $\phi^*(\cdot)$, $\theta^*(\cdot)$ are polynomials of degree $p+sP$ and $q+sQ$, respectively, whose coefficients can all be expressed in terms of $\phi_1,\ldots,\phi_p$, $\Phi_1,\ldots,\Phi_P$, $\theta_1,\ldots,\theta_q$, and $\Theta_1,\ldots,\Theta_Q$. Provided that $p<s$ and $q<s$, the constraints on the coefficients of $\phi^*(\cdot)$ and $\theta^*(\cdot)$ can all be expressed as multiplicative relations

$$\phi^*_{is+j} = \phi^*_{is}\phi^*_j, \quad i=1,2,\ldots;\ j=1,\ldots,s-1,$$

and

$$\theta^*_{is+j} = \theta^*_{is}\theta^*_j, \quad i=1,2,\ldots;\ j=1,\ldots,s-1.$$

In Section 1.5 we discussed the classical decomposition model incorporating trend, seasonality, and random noise, namely, $X_t = m_t + s_t + Y_t$. In modeling real data it might not be reasonable to assume, as in the classical decomposition model, that the seasonal component s_t repeats itself precisely in the same way cycle after cycle. Seasonal ARIMA models allow for randomness in the seasonal pattern from one cycle to the next. □

Example 6.5.1

Suppose we have r years of monthly data, which we tabulate as follows:

Year/Month	1	2	...	12
1	Y_1	Y_2	...	Y_{12}
2	Y_{13}	Y_{14}	...	Y_{24}
3	Y_{25}	Y_{26}	...	Y_{36}
⋮	⋮	⋮	⋮	
r	$Y_{1+12(r-1)}$	$Y_{2+12(r-1)}$	...	$Y_{12+12(r-1)}$

Each column in this table may itself be viewed as a realization of a time series. Suppose that each one of these twelve time series is generated by the same ARMA(P, Q) model, or more specifically, that the series corresponding to the jth month, Y_{j+12t}, $t = 0, \ldots, r-1$, satisfies a difference equation of the form

$$\begin{aligned} Y_{j+12t} = {} & \Phi_1 Y_{j+12(t-1)} + \cdots + \Phi_P Y_{j+12(t-P)} + U_{j+12t} \\ & + \Theta_1 U_{j+12(t-1)} + \cdots + \Theta_Q U_{j+12(t-Q)}, \end{aligned} \tag{6.5.3}$$

where

$$\{U_{j+12t}, t = \ldots, -1, 0, 1, \ldots\} \sim \mathrm{WN}\left(0, \sigma_U^2\right). \tag{6.5.4}$$

Then since the same ARMA(P, Q) model is assumed to apply to each month, (6.5.3) holds for each $j = 1, \ldots, 12$. (Notice, however, that $E(U_t U_{t+h})$ is not necessarily zero except when h is an integer multiple of 12.) We can thus write (6.5.3) in the compact form

$$\Phi\left(B^{12}\right) Y_t = \Theta\left(B^{12}\right) U_t, \tag{6.5.5}$$

where $\Phi(z) = 1 - \Phi_1 z - \cdots - \Phi_P z^P$, $\Theta(z) = 1 + \Theta_1 z + \cdots + \Theta_Q z^Q$, and $\{U_{j+12t}, t = \ldots, -1, 0, 1, \ldots\} \sim \mathrm{WN}\left(0, \sigma_U^2\right)$ for each j. We refer to the model (6.5.5) as the between-year model. □

Example 6.5.2

Suppose $P = 0$, $Q = 1$, and $\Theta_1 = -0.4$ in (6.5.5). Then the series for any particular month is a moving-average of order 1. If $E(U_t U_{t+h}) = 0$ for all h, i.e., if the white noise sequences for different months are uncorrelated with each other, then the columns themselves are uncorrelated. The correlation function for such a process is shown in Figure 6.15. □

Example 6.5.3

Suppose $P = 1$, $Q = 0$, and $\Phi_1 = 0.7$ in (6.5.5). In this case the 12 series (one for each month) are AR(1) processes that are uncorrelated if the white noise sequences

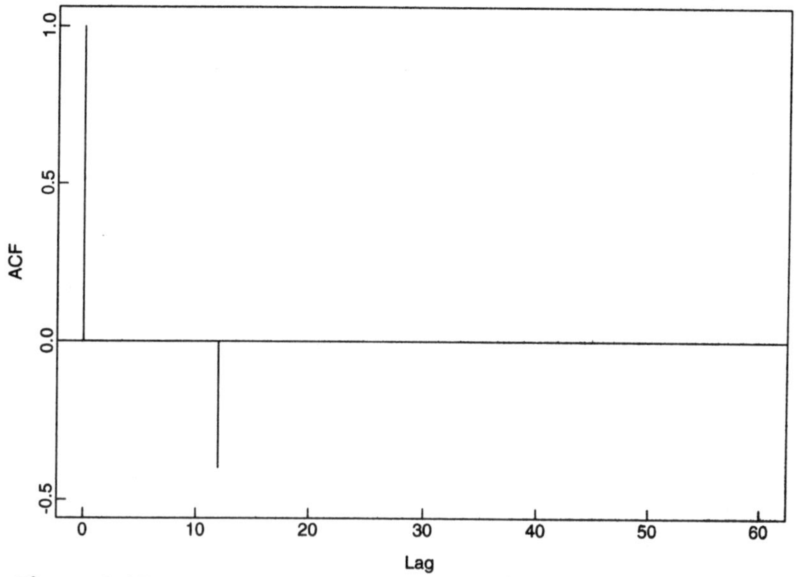

Figure 6-15 The ACF of the model $X_t = U_t - 0.4U_{t-12}$ of Example 6.5.2.

for different months are uncorrelated. A graph of the autocorrelation function of this process is shown in Figure 6.16. □

In each of the Examples 6.5.1, 6.5.2, and 6.5.3, the 12 series corresponding to the different months are uncorrelated. To incorporate dependence between these series

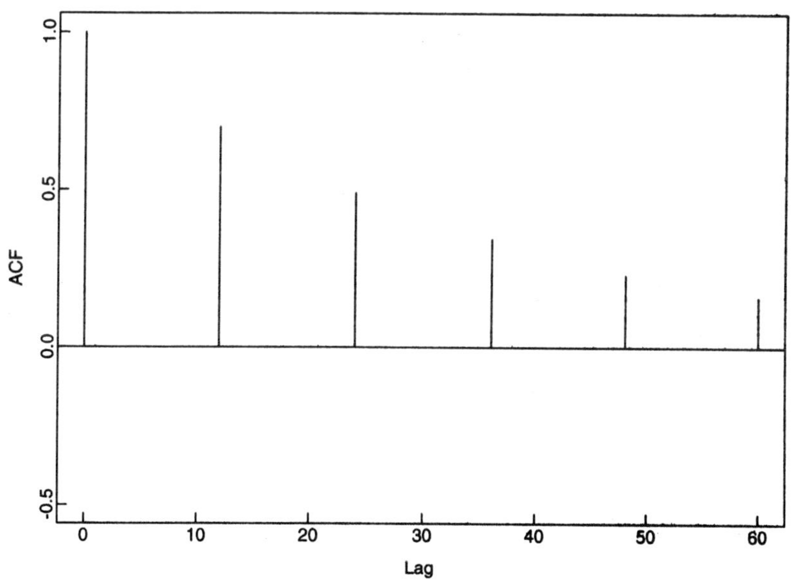

Figure 6-16 The ACF of the model $X_t - 0.7X_{t-12} = U_t$ of Example 6.5.3.

we allow the process $\{U_t\}$ in (6.5.5) to follow an ARMA(p, q) model,

$$\phi(B)U_t = \theta(B)Z_t, \qquad \{Z_t\} \sim \text{WN}\left(0, \sigma^2\right). \tag{6.5.6}$$

This assumption implies possible nonzero correlation not only between consecutive values of U_t, but also within the twelve sequences $\{U_{j+12t}, t = \ldots, -1, 0, 1, \ldots\}$, each of which was assumed to be uncorrelated in the preceding examples. In this case (6.5.4) may no longer hold; however, the coefficients in (6.5.6) will frequently have values such that $E(U_t U_{t+12j})$ is small for $j = \pm 1, \pm 2, \ldots$. Combining the two models (6.5.5) and (6.5.6) and allowing for possible differencing leads directly to Definition 6.5.1 of the general SARIMA model as given above.

The first steps in identifying SARIMA models for a (possibly transformed) data set are to find d and D so as to make the differenced observations

$$Y_t = (1 - B)^d (1 - B^s)^D X_t$$

stationary in appearance (see Sections 6.1–6.3). Next we examine the sample ACF and PACF of $\{Y_t\}$ at lags that are multiples of s for an indication of the orders P and Q in the model (6.5.5). If $\hat{\rho}(\cdot)$ is the sample ACF of $\{Y_t\}$, then P and Q should be chosen such that $\hat{\rho}(ks), k = 1, 2, \ldots$, is compatible with the ACF of an ARMA(P, Q) process. The orders p and q are then selected by trying to match $\hat{\rho}(1), \ldots, \hat{\rho}(s-1)$ with the ACF of an ARMA(p, q) process. Ultimately, the AICC criterion (Section 5.5) and the goodness of fit tests (Section 5.3) are used to select the best SARIMA model from competing alternatives.

For given values of p, d, q, P, D, and Q, the parameters $\boldsymbol{\phi}, \boldsymbol{\theta}, \boldsymbol{\Phi}, \boldsymbol{\Theta}$, and σ^2 can be found using the maximum likelihood procedure of Section 5.2. The differences $Y_t = (1 - B)^d \left(1 - B^s\right)^D X_t$ constitute an ARMA$(p + sP, q + sQ)$ process in which some of the coefficients are zero and the rest are functions of the $(p + P + q + Q)$-dimensional vector $\boldsymbol{\beta}' = (\boldsymbol{\phi}', \boldsymbol{\Phi}', \boldsymbol{\theta}', \boldsymbol{\Theta}')$. For any fixed $\boldsymbol{\beta}$ the reduced likelihood $\ell(\boldsymbol{\beta})$ of the differences $Y_{t+d+sD}, \ldots, Y_n$ is easily computed as described in Section 5.2. The maximum likelihood estimator of $\boldsymbol{\beta}$ is the value that minimizes $\ell(\boldsymbol{\beta})$, and the maximum likelihood estimate of σ^2 is given by (5.2.10). The estimates can be found using the program ITSM by specifying the required multiplicative relationships among the coefficients as given in Remark 2 above.

A more direct approach to modeling the differenced series $\{Y_t\}$ is simply to fit a subset ARMA model of the form (6.5.2) without making use of the multiplicative form of $\phi^*(\cdot)$ and $\theta^*(\cdot)$ in (6.5.1).

Example 6.5.4 Monthly accidental deaths

In Figure 1.27 we showed the series $\left\{Y_t = \left(1 - B^{12}\right)(1 - B)X_t\right\}$ obtained by differencing the accidental deaths series $\{X_t\}$ once at lag 12 and once at lag 1. The sample ACF of $\{Y_t\}$ is shown in Figure 6.17. □

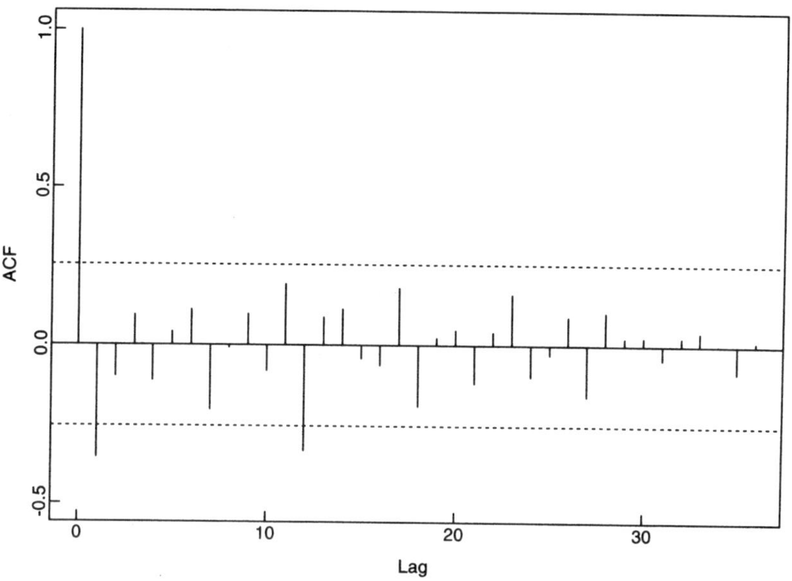

Figure 6-17 The sample ACF of the differenced accidental deaths $\{\nabla\nabla_{12}X_t\}$.

The values $\hat{\rho}(12) = -0.333$, $\hat{\rho}(24) = -0.099$, and $\hat{\rho}(36) = 0.013$ suggest a moving-average of order 1 for the between-year model (i.e., $P = 0$ and $Q = 1$). Moreover, inspection of $\hat{\rho}(1), \ldots, \hat{\rho}(11)$ suggests that $\rho(1)$ is the only short-term correlation different from zero, so we also choose a moving-average of order 1 for the between-month model (i.e., $p = 0$ and $q = 1$). Taking into account the sample mean (28.831) of the differences $\{Y_t\}$, we therefore arrive at the model

$$Y_t = 28.831 + (1 + \theta_1 B)(1 + \Theta_1 B^{12})Z_t, \quad \{Z_t\} \sim \text{WN}\left(0, \sigma^2\right), \qquad (6.5.7)$$

for the series $\{Y_t\}$. The maximum likelihood estimates of the parameters are obtained from ITSM by opening the file DEATHS.TSM and proceeding as follows. After differencing (at lags 1 and 12) and then mean-correcting the data, choose the option `Model>Specify`. In the dialog box enter an MA(13) model with $\theta_1 = -0.3$, $\theta_{12} = -0.3$, $\theta_{13} = 0.09$, and all other coefficients zero. (This corresponds to the initial guess $Y_t = (1 - 0.3B)\left(1 - 0.3B^{12}\right)Z_t$.) Then choose `Model>Estimation>Max likelihood` and click on the button `Constrain optimization`. Specify the number of multiplicative relations (one in this case) in the box provided and define the relationship by entering 1, 12, 13 to indicate that $\theta_1 \times \theta_{12} = \theta_{13}$. Click `OK` to return to the `Maximum Likelihood` dialog box. Click `OK` again to obtain the parameter estimates

$$\hat{\theta}_1 = -0.478,$$

$$\hat{\Theta}_1 = -0.591,$$

and

$$\hat{\sigma}^2 = 94255,$$

with AICC value 855.53. The corresponding fitted model for $\{X_t\}$ is thus the SARIMA $(0, 1, 1) \times (0, 1, 1)_{12}$ process

$$\nabla\nabla_{12}X_t = 28.831 + (1 - 0.478B)\left(1 - 0.588B^{12}\right)Z_t, \tag{6.5.8}$$

where $\{Z_t\} \sim \text{WN}(0, 94390)$.

If we adopt the alternative approach of fitting a subset ARMA model to $\{Y_t\}$ without seeking a multiplicative structure for the operators $\phi^*(B)$ and $\theta^*(B)$ in (6.5.2), we begin by fitting a preliminary MA(13) model (as suggested by Figure 6.17) to the series $\{Y_t\}$. We then fit a maximum likelihood MA(13) model and examine the standard errors of the coefficient estimators. This suggests setting the coefficients at lags 2, 3, 8, 10, and 11 equal to zero, since as these are all less than one standard error from zero. To do this select `Model>Estimation>Max likelihood` and click on the button `Constrain optimization`. Then highlight the coefficients to be set to zero and click on the button `Set to zero`. Click `OK` to return to the `Maximum Likelihood Estimation` dialog box and again to carry out the constrained optimization. The coefficients that have been set to zero will be held at that value, and the optimization will be with respect to the remaining coefficients. This gives a model with substantially smaller AICC than the unconstrained MA(13) model. Examining the standard errors again we see that the coefficients at lags 4, 5, and 7 are promising candidates to be set to zero, since each of them is less than one standard error from zero. Setting these coefficients to zero in the same way and reoptimizing gives a further reduction in AICC. Setting the coefficient at lag 9 to zero and reoptimizing again gives a further reduction in AICC (to 855.61) and the fitted model

$$\begin{aligned}\nabla\nabla_{12}X_t &= 28.831 + Z_t - 0.596Z_{t-1} - 0.407Z_{t-6} - 0.685Z_{t-12} + 0.460Z_{t-13},\\ &\{Z_t\} \sim \text{WN}(0, 71240).\end{aligned} \tag{6.5.9}$$

The AICC value 855.61 is quite close to the value 855.53 for the model (6.5.8). The residuals from the two models are also very similar, the randomness tests (with the exception of the difference-sign test) yielding high p-values for both.

6.5.1 Forecasting SARIMA Processes

Forecasting SARIMA processes is completely analogous to the forecasting of ARIMA processes discussed in Section 6.4. Expanding out the operator $(1 - B)^d\left(1 - B^s\right)^D$ in powers of B, rearranging the equation

$$(1 - B)^d (1 - B^s)^D X_t = Y_t,$$

and setting $t = n + h$ gives the analogue

$$X_{n+h} = Y_{n+h} + \sum_{j=1}^{d+Ds} a_j X_{n+h-j} \tag{6.5.10}$$

of equation (6.4.2). Under the assumption that the first $d+Ds$ observations $X_{-d-Ds+1}, \ldots, X_0$ are uncorrelated with $\{Y_t, t \geq 1\}$, we can determine the best linear predictors $P_n X_{n+h}$ of X_{n+h} based on $\{1, X_{-d-Ds+1}, \ldots, X_n\}$ by applying P_n to each side of (6.5.10) to obtain

$$P_n X_{n+h} = P_n Y_{n+h} + \sum_{j=1}^{d+Ds} a_j P_n X_{n+h-j}. \tag{6.5.11}$$

The first term on the right is just the best linear predictor of the (possibly nonzero-mean) ARMA process $\{Y_t\}$ in terms of $\{1, Y_1, \ldots, Y_n\}$, which can be calculated as described in Section 3.3. The predictors $P_n X_{n+h}$ can then be computed recursively for $h = 1, 2, \ldots$ from (6.5.11), if we note that $P_n X_{n+1-j} = X_{n+1-j}$ for each $j \geq 1$.

An argument analogous to the one leading to (6.4.5) gives the prediction mean squared error as

$$\sigma_n^2(h) = E(X_{n+h} - P_n X_{n+h})^2 = \sum_{j=0}^{h-1} \left(\sum_{r=0}^{j} \chi_r \theta_{n+h-r-1,j-r} \right)^2 v_{n+h-j-1}, \tag{6.5.12}$$

where θ_{nj} and v_n are obtained by applying the innovations algorithm to the differenced series $\{Y_t\}$ and

$$\chi(z) = \sum_{r=0}^{\infty} \chi_r z^r = \left[\phi(z)\Phi(z^s)(1-z)^d (1-z^s)^D \right]^{-1}, \quad |z| < 1.$$

For large n we can approximate (6.5.12), if $\theta(z)\Theta(z^s)$ is nonzero for all $|z| \leq 1$, by

$$\sigma_n^2(h) = \sum_{j=0}^{h-1} \psi_j^2 \sigma^2, \tag{6.5.13}$$

where

$$\psi(z) = \sum_{j=0}^{\infty} \psi_j z^j = \frac{\theta(z)\Theta(z^s)}{\phi(z)\Phi(z^s)(1-z)^d (1-z^s)^D}, \quad |z| < 1.$$

The required calculations can all be carried out with the aid of the program ITSM. The mean squared errors are computed from the large-sample approximation (6.5.13) if the fitted model is invertible. If the fitted model is not invertible, ITSM computes the mean squared errors by converting the model to the equivalent (in terms of Gaussian likelihood) invertible model and then using (6.5.13).

Table 6.1 Predicted values of the Accidental Deaths series for $t = 73, \ldots, 78$, the standard deviations σ_t of the prediction errors, and the corresponding observed values of X_t for the same period.

t	73	74	75	76	77	78
Model (6.5.8)						
Predictors	8441	7704	8549	8885	9843	10279
σ_t	308	348	383	415	445	474
Model (6.5.9)						
Predictors	8345	7619	8356	8742	9795	10179
σ_t	292	329	366	403	442	486
Observed values						
X_t	7798	7406	8363	8460	9217	9316

Example 6.5.5 Monthly accidental deaths

Continuing with Example 6.5.4, we next use ITSM to predict six future values of the Accidental Deaths series using the fitted models (6.5.8) and (6.5.9). First fit the desired model as described in Example 6.5.4 or enter the data and model directly by opening the file DEATHS.TSM, differencing at lags 12 and 1, subtracting the mean, and then entering the MA(13) coefficients and white noise variance using the option `Model>Specify`. Select `Forecasting>ARMA`, and you will see the `ARMA Forecast` dialog box. Enter 6 for the number of predicted values required. You will notice that the default options in the dialog box are set to generate predictors of the *original* series by reversing the transformations applied to the data. If for some reason you wish to predict the transformed data, these check marks can be removed. If you wish to include prediction bounds in the graph of the predictors, check the appropriate box and specify the desired coefficient (e.g., 95%). Click `OK`, and you will see a graph of the data with the six predicted values appended. For numerical values of the predictors and prediction bounds, right-click on the graph and then on `Info`. The prediction bounds are computed under the assumption that the white noise sequence in the ARMA model for the transformed data is Gaussian. Table 6.1 shows the predictors and standard deviations of the prediction errors under both models (6.5.8) and (6.5.9) for the Accidental Deaths series. □

6.6 Regression with ARMA Errors

6.6.1 OLS and GLS Estimation

In standard linear regression, the errors (or deviations of the observations from the regression function) are assumed to be independent and identically distributed. In many applications of regression analysis, however, this assumption is clearly violated, as can be seen by examination of the residuals from the fitted regression and their sample autocorrelations. It is often more appropriate to assume that the errors are observations of a zero-mean second-order stationary process. Since many autocorrelation functions can be well approximated by the autocorrelation function of a suitably chosen ARMA(p, q) process, it is of particular interest to consider the model

$$Y_t = \mathbf{x}_t'\boldsymbol{\beta} + W_t, \quad t = 1, \ldots, n, \tag{6.6.1}$$

or in matrix notation,

$$\mathbf{Y} = X\boldsymbol{\beta} + \mathbf{W}, \tag{6.6.2}$$

where $\mathbf{Y} = (Y_1, \ldots, Y_n)'$ is the vector of observations at times $t = 1, \ldots, n$, X is the design matrix whose tth row, $\mathbf{x}_t' = (x_{t1}, \ldots, x_{tk})$, consists of the values of the explanatory variables at time t, $\boldsymbol{\beta} = (\beta_1, \ldots, \beta_k)'$ is the vector of regression coefficients, and the components of $\mathbf{W} = (W_1, \ldots, W_n)'$ are values of a causal zero-mean ARMA(p, q) process satisfying

$$\phi(B)W_t = \theta(B)Z_t, \quad \{Z_t\} \sim \mathrm{WN}\left(0, \sigma^2\right). \tag{6.6.3}$$

The model (6.6.1) arises naturally in trend estimation for time series data. For example, the explanatory variables $x_{t1} = 1, x_{t2} = t$, and $x_{t3} = t^2$ can be used to estimate a quadratic trend, and the variables $x_{t1} = 1, x_{t2} = \cos(\omega t)$, and $x_{t3} = \sin(\omega t)$ can be used to estimate a sinusoidal trend with frequency ω. The columns of X are not necessarily simple functions of t as in these two examples. Any specified column of relevant variables, e.g., temperatures at times $t = 1, \ldots, n$, can be included in the design matrix X, in which case the regression is conditional on the observed values of the variables included in the matrix.

The **ordinary least squares** (OLS) estimator of $\boldsymbol{\beta}$ is the value, $\hat{\boldsymbol{\beta}}_{\text{OLS}}$, which minimizes the sum of squares

$$(\mathbf{Y} - X\boldsymbol{\beta})'(\mathbf{Y} - X\boldsymbol{\beta}) = \sum_{t=1}^{n} \left(Y_t - \mathbf{x}_t'\boldsymbol{\beta}\right)^2.$$

Equating to zero the partial derivatives with respect to each component of $\boldsymbol{\beta}$ and assuming (as we shall) that $X'X$ is nonsingular, we find that

$$\hat{\boldsymbol{\beta}}_{\text{OLS}} = (X'X)^{-1}X'\mathbf{Y}. \tag{6.6.4}$$

(If $X'X$ is singular, $\hat{\boldsymbol{\beta}}_{\text{OLS}}$ is not uniquely determined but still satisfies (6.6.4) with $(X'X)^{-1}$ any generalized inverse of $X'X$.) The OLS estimate also maximizes the likelihood of the observations when the errors $W_1, \ldots, W_n$ are iid and Gaussian. If the design matrix X is nonrandom, then even when the errors are non-Gaussian and dependent, the OLS estimator is unbiased (i.e., $E\left(\hat{\boldsymbol{\beta}}_{\text{OLS}}\right) = \boldsymbol{\beta}$) and its covariance matrix is

$$\text{Cov}(\hat{\boldsymbol{\beta}}_{\text{OLS}}) = \left(X'X\right)^{-1} X'\Gamma_n X \left(X'X\right)^{-1}, \tag{6.6.5}$$

where $\Gamma_n = E(\mathbf{W}\mathbf{W}')$ is the covariance matrix of $\mathbf{W}$.

The **generalized least squares** (GLS) estimator of β is the value $\hat{\beta}_{GLS}$ that minimizes the *weighted* sum of squares

$$(\mathbf{Y} - X\beta)' \Gamma_n^{-1} (\mathbf{Y} - X\beta). \tag{6.6.6}$$

Differentiating partially with respect to each component of β and setting the derivatives equal to zero, we find that

$$\hat{\beta}_{\text{GLS}} = \left(X'\Gamma_n^{-1}X\right)^{-1} X'\Gamma_n^{-1}\mathbf{Y}. \tag{6.6.7}$$

If the design matrix X is nonrandom, the GLS estimator is unbiased and has covariance matrix

$$\text{Cov}\left(\hat{\beta}_{\text{GLS}}\right) = \left(X'\Gamma_n^{-1}X\right)^{-1}. \tag{6.6.8}$$

It can be shown that the GLS estimator is the best linear unbiased estimator of β, i.e., for any k-dimensional vector $\mathbf{c}$ and for any unbiased estimator $\hat{\beta}$ of β that is a linear function of the observations $Y_1, \ldots, Y_n$,

$$\text{Var}\left(\mathbf{c}'\hat{\beta}_{\text{GLS}}\right) \le \text{Var}\left(\mathbf{c}'\hat{\beta}\right).$$

In this sense the GLS estimator is therefore superior to the OLS estimator. However, it can be computed only if ϕ and θ are known.

Let $V(\phi, \theta)$ denote the matrix $\sigma^{-2}\Gamma_n$ and let $T(\phi, \theta)$ be any square root of V^{-1} (i.e., a matrix such that $T'T = V^{-1}$). Then we can multiply each side of (6.6.2) by T to obtain

$$T\mathbf{Y} = TX\beta + T\mathbf{W}, \tag{6.6.9}$$

a regression equation with coefficient vector β, data vector $T\mathbf{Y}$, design matrix TX, and error vector $T\mathbf{W}$. Since the latter has uncorrelated, zero-mean components, each with variance σ^2, the best linear estimator of β in terms of $T\mathbf{Y}$ (which is clearly the same as the best linear estimator of β in terms of $\mathbf{Y}$, i.e., $\hat{\beta}_{\text{GLS}}$) can be obtained by applying OLS estimation to the transformed regression equation (6.6.9). This gives

$$\hat{\beta}_{\text{GLS}} = \left(X'T'TX\right)^{-1} X'T'T\mathbf{Y}, \tag{6.6.10}$$

which is clearly the same as (6.6.7). Cochrane and Orcutt (1949) pointed out that if $\{W_t\}$ is an AR(p) process satisfying

$$\phi(B)W_t = Z_t, \quad \{Z_t\} \sim \text{WN}\left(0, \sigma^2\right),$$

then application of $\phi(B)$ to each side of the regression equations (6.6.1) transforms them into regression equations with uncorrelated, zero-mean, constant-variance errors, so that ordinary least squares can again be used to compute best linear unbiased estimates of the components of β in terms of $Y_t^* = \phi(B)Y_t$, $t = p+1, \ldots, n$. This approach eliminates the need to compute the matrix T but suffers from the drawback that $\mathbf{Y}^*$ does not contain all the information in $\mathbf{Y}$. Cochrane and Orcutt's transformation can be improved, and at the same generalized to ARMA errors, as follows.

Instead of applying the operator $\phi(B)$ to each side of the regression equations (6.6.1), we multiply each side of equation (6.6.2) by the matrix $T(\phi, \boldsymbol{\theta})$ that maps $\{W_t\}$ into the residuals (see (5.3.1)) of $\{W_t\}$ from the ARMA model (6.6.3). We have already seen how to calculate these residuals using the innovations algorithm in Section 3.3. To see that T is a square root of the matrix V as defined in the previous paragraph, we simply recall that the residuals are uncorrelated with zero mean and variance σ^2, so that

$$\mathrm{Cov}(T\mathbf{W}) = T\Gamma_n T' = \sigma^2 I,$$

where I is the $n \times n$ identity matrix. Hence

$$T'T = \sigma^2\Gamma_n^{-1} = V^{-1}.$$

GLS estimation of $\boldsymbol{\beta}$ can therefore be carried out by multiplying each side of (6.6.2) by T and applying ordinary least squares to the transformed regression model. It remains only to compute $T\mathbf{Y}$ and TX.

Any data vector $\mathbf{d} = (d_1, \ldots, d_n)'$ can be left-multiplied by T simply by reading it into ITSM, entering the model (6.6.3), and pressing the green button labeled `RES`, which plots the residuals. (The calculations are performed using the innovations algorithm as described in Section 3.3.) The GLS estimator $\hat{\boldsymbol{\beta}}_{\mathrm{GLS}}$ is computed as follows. The data vector $\mathbf{Y}$ is left-multiplied by T to generate the transformed data vector $\mathbf{Y}^*$, and each column of the design matrix X is left-multiplied by T to generate the corresponding column of the transformed design matrix X^*. Then

$$\hat{\boldsymbol{\beta}}_{\mathrm{GLS}} = \left(X^{*\prime}X^*\right)^{-1} X^{*\prime}\mathbf{Y}^*. \tag{6.6.11}$$

The calculations of $\mathbf{Y}^*$, X^*, and hence of $\hat{\boldsymbol{\beta}}_{\mathrm{GLS}}$, are all carried out by the program ITSM in the option `Regression>Estimation>Generalized LS`.

6.6.2 ML Estimation

If (as is usually the case) the parameters of the ARMA(p, q) model for the errors are unknown, they can be estimated together with the regression coefficients by **maximizing the Gaussian likelihood**

$$L\left(\boldsymbol{\beta}, \phi, \boldsymbol{\theta}, \sigma^2\right) = (2\pi)^{-n/2}(\det\Gamma_n)^{-1/2}\exp\left\{-\frac{1}{2}(\mathbf{Y} - X\boldsymbol{\beta})'\Gamma_n^{-1}(\mathbf{Y} - X\boldsymbol{\beta})\right\},$$

where $\Gamma_n\left(\phi, \boldsymbol{\theta}, \sigma^2\right)$ is the covariance matrix of $\mathbf{W} = \mathbf{Y} - X\boldsymbol{\beta}$. Since $\{W_t\}$ is an ARMA(p, q) process with parameters $\left(\phi, \boldsymbol{\theta}, \sigma^2\right)$, the maximum likelihood estimators $\hat{\boldsymbol{\beta}}$, $\hat{\phi}$, and $\hat{\boldsymbol{\theta}}$ are found (as in Section 5.2) by minimizing

$$\ell(\boldsymbol{\beta}, \phi, \boldsymbol{\theta}) = \ln\left(n^{-1}S(\boldsymbol{\beta}, \phi, \boldsymbol{\theta})\right) + n^{-1}\sum_{t=1}^{n}\ln r_{t-1}, \tag{6.6.12}$$

where

$$S(\beta, \phi, \theta) = \sum_{t=1}^{n} \left(W_t - \hat{W}_t\right)^2 / r_{t-1},$$

$\hat{W}_t$ is the best one-step predictor of W_t, and $r_{t-1}\sigma^2$ is its mean squared error. The function $\ell(\beta, \phi, \theta)$ can be expressed in terms of the observations $\{Y_t\}$ and the parameters β, ϕ, and θ using the innovations algorithm (see Section 3.3) and minimized numerically to give the maximum likelihood estimators, $\hat{\beta}$, $\hat{\phi}$, and $\hat{\theta}$. The maximum likelihood estimator of σ^2 is then given, as in Section 5.2, by $\hat{\sigma}^2 = S\left(\hat{\beta}, \hat{\phi}, \hat{\theta}\right)/n$.

An extension of an iterative scheme, proposed by Cochrane and Orcutt (1949) for the case $q = 0$, simplifies the minimization considerably. It is based on the observation that for fixed ϕ and θ, the value of β that minimizes $\ell(\beta, \phi, \theta)$ is $\hat{\beta}_{\text{GLS}}(\phi, \theta)$, which can be computed algebraically from (6.6.11) instead of by searching numerically for the minimizing value. The scheme is as follows.

(i) Compute $\hat{\beta}_{\text{OLS}}$ and the estimated residuals $Y_t - \mathbf{x}_t'\hat{\beta}_{\text{OLS}}, \quad t = 1, \ldots, n$.

(ii) Fit an ARMA($p.q$) model by maximum Gaussian likelihood to the estimated residuals.

(iii) For the fitted ARMA model compute the corresponding estimator $\hat{\beta}_{\text{GLS}}$ from (6.6.11).

(iv) Compute the residuals $Y_t - \mathbf{x}_t'\hat{\beta}_{\text{GLS}}, \quad t = 1, \ldots, n$, and return to (ii), stopping when the estimators have stabilized.

If $\{W_t\}$ is a causal and invertible ARMA process, then under mild conditions on the explanatory variables $\mathbf{x}_t$, the maximum likelihood estimates are asymptotically multivariate normal (see Fuller, 1976). In addition, the estimated regression coefficients are asymptotically independent of the estimated ARMA parameters.

The large-sample covariance matrix of the ARMA parameter estimators, suitably normalized, has a complicated form that involves both the regression variables $\mathbf{x}_t$ and the covariance function of $\{W_t\}$. It is therefore convenient to estimate the covariance matrix as $-H^{-1}$, where H is the Hessian matrix of the observed log-likelihood evaluated at its maximum.

The OLS, GLS, and maximum likelihood estimators of the regression coefficients all have the same asymptotic covariance matrix, so in this sense the dependence does not play a major role. However, the asymptotic covariance of both the OLS and GLS estimators can be very inaccurate if the appropriate covariance matrix Γ_n is not used in the expressions (6.6.5) and (6.6.8). This point is illustrated in the following examples.

Remark 1. The use of the innovations algorithm for GLS and ML estimation extends to regression with ARIMA errors (see Example 6.6.3 below) and FARIMA errors (FARIMA processes are defined in Section 10.5).

Example 6.6.1 The overshort data

The analysis of the overshort data in Example 3.2.8 suggested the model

$$Y_t = \beta + W_t,$$

where $-\beta$ is interpreted as the daily leakage from the underground storage tank and $\{W_t\}$ is the MA(1) process

$$W_t = Z_t + \theta Z_{t-1}, \quad \{Z_t\} \sim \mathrm{WN}\left(0, \sigma^2\right).$$

(Here $k = 1$ and $x_{t1} = 1$.) The OLS estimate of β is simply the sample mean $\hat{\beta}_{\mathrm{OLS}} = \bar{Y}_n = -4.035$. Under the assumption that $\{W_t\}$ is iid noise, the estimated variance of the OLS estimator of β is $\hat{\gamma}_Y(0)/57 = 59.92$. However, since this estimate of the variance fails to take dependence into account, it is not reliable.

To find maximum Gaussian likelihood estimates of β and the parameters of $\{W_t\}$ using ITSM, open the file OSHORTS.TSM, select the option `Regression>Specify` and check the box marked `Include intercept term` only. Then press the blue GLS button and you will see the estimated value of β. (This is in fact the same as the OLS estimator since the default model in ITSM is WN(0,1).) Then select `Model>Estimation>Autofit` and press `Start`. The autofit option selects the minimum AICC model for the residuals,

$$W_t = Z_t - .818 Z_{t-1}, \quad \{Z_t\} \sim \mathrm{WN}(0, 2041), \tag{6.6.13}$$

and displays the estimated MA coefficient $\hat{\theta}_1^{(0)} = -.818$ and the corresponding GLS estimate $\hat{\beta}_{\mathrm{GLS}}^{(1)} = -4.745$, with a standard error of 1.188, in the `Regression estimates` window. (If we reestimate the variance of the OLS estimator, using (6.6.5) with Γ_{57} computed from the model (6.6.13), we obtain the value 2.214, a drastic reduction from the value 59.92 obtained when dependence is ignored. For a positively correlated time series, ignoring the dependence would lead to underestimation of the variance.)

Pressing the blue MLE button will reestimate the MA parameters using the residuals from the updated regression and at the same time reestimate the regression coefficient, printing the new parameters in the `Regression estimates` window. After this operation has been repeated several times, the parameters will stabilize, as shown in Table 6.2. Estimated 95% confidence bounds for β using the GLS estimate are $-4.75 \pm 1.96(1.408)^{1/2} = (-7.07, -2.43)$, strongly suggesting that the storage tank has a leak. Such a conclusion would not have been reached without taking into account the dependence in the data. □

Example 6.6.2 The lake data

In Examples 5.2.4 and 5.5.2 we found maximum likelihood ARMA(1,1) and AR(2) models for the mean-corrected lake data. Now let us consider fitting a linear trend to the data with AR(2) noise. The choice of an AR(2) model was suggested by an

Table 6.2 Estimates of β and θ_1 for the overshort data of Example 6.6.1.

Iteration i	$\hat{\theta}^{(i)}$	$\hat{\beta}_1^{(i)}$
0	0	−4.035
1	−.818	−4.745
2	−.848	−4.780
3	−.848	−4.780

analysis of the residuals obtained after removing a linear trend from the data using OLS. Our model now takes the form

$$Y_t = \beta_0 + \beta_1 t + W_t,$$

where $\{W_t\}$ is the AR(2) process satisfying

$$W_t = \phi_1 W_{t-1} + \phi_2 W_{t-2} + Z_t, \quad \{Z_t\} \sim \text{WN}\left(0, \sigma^2\right).$$

From Example 1.3.5, we find that the OLS estimate of $\boldsymbol{\beta}$ is $\hat{\boldsymbol{\beta}}_{\text{OLS}} = (10.202, -.0242)'$. If we ignore the correlation structure of the noise, the estimated covariance matrix Γ_n of $\mathbf{W}$ is $\hat{\gamma}(0)I$ (where I is the identity matrix). The corresponding estimated covariance matrix of $\hat{\boldsymbol{\beta}}_{\text{OLS}}$ is (from (6.6.5))

$$\hat{\gamma}_Y(0)\left(X'X\right)^{-1} = \hat{\gamma}_Y(0)\begin{bmatrix} n & \sum_{t=1}^{n} t \\ \sum_{t=1}^{n} t & \sum_{t=1}^{n} t^2 \end{bmatrix}^{-1} = \begin{bmatrix} .07203 & -.00110 \\ -.00110 & .00002 \end{bmatrix}. \qquad (6.6.14)$$

However, the estimated model for the noise process, found by fitting an AR(2) model to the residuals $Y_t - \hat{\boldsymbol{\beta}}'_{\text{OLS}}\mathbf{x}_t$, is

$$W_t = 1.008W_{t-1} - .295W_{t-2} + Z_t, \quad \{Z_t\} \sim \text{WN}(0, .4571).$$

Assuming that this is the true model for $\{W_t\}$, the GLS estimate is found to be $(10.091, -.0216)'$, in close agreement with the OLS estimate. The estimated covariance matrices for the OLS and GLS estimates are given by

$$\text{Cov}\left(\hat{\boldsymbol{\beta}}_{\text{OLS}}\right) = \begin{bmatrix} .22177 & -.00335 \\ -.00335 & .00007 \end{bmatrix}$$

and

$$\text{Cov}\left(\hat{\boldsymbol{\beta}}_{\text{GLS}}\right) = \begin{bmatrix} .21392 & -.00321 \\ -.00321 & .00006 \end{bmatrix}.$$

Notice how the estimated variances of the OLS and GLS estimators are nearly three times the magnitude of the corresponding variance estimates of the OLS calculated under the independence assumption (see (6.6.8)). Estimated 95% confidence bounds for the slope β_1 using the GLS estimate are $-.0216 \pm 1.96(.00006)^{1/2} = -.0216 \pm .0048$, indicating a significant decreasing trend in the level of Lake Huron during the years 1875–1972.

The iterative procedure described above was used to produce maximum likelihood estimates of the parameters. The calculations using ITSM are analogous to those in Example 6.6.1. The results from each iteration are summarized in Table 6.3. As in Example 6.6.1, the convergence of the estimates is very rapid. □

Example 6.6.3 Seat-belt legislation; SBL.TSM

Figure 6.18 shows the numbers of monthly deaths and serious injuries Y_t, $t = 1, \ldots, 120$, on UK roads for 10 years beginning in January 1975. They are filed as SBL.TSM. Seat-belt legislation was introduced in February 1983 in the hope of reducing the mean number of monthly "deaths and serious injuries," (from $t = 99$ onwards). In order to study whether or not there was a drop in mean from that time onwards, we consider the regression,

$$Y_t = a + bf(t) + W_t, \quad t = 1, \ldots, 120, \tag{6.6.15}$$

where $f_t = 0$ for $1 \leq t \leq 98$, and $f_t = 1$ for $t \geq 99$. The seat-belt legislation will be considered effective if the estimated value of the regression coefficient b is significantly negative. This problem also falls under the heading of *intervention analysis* (see Section 10.2).

OLS regression based on the model (6.6.15) suggests that the error sequence $\{W_t\}$ is highly correlated with a strong seasonal component of period 12. (To do the regression using ITSM proceed as follows. Open the file SBL.TSM, select `Regression>Specify`, check only `Include intercept term` and `Include auxiliary variables`, press the `Browse` button, and select the file SBLIN.TSM, which contains the function f_t of (6.6.15) and enter 1 for the number of columns. Then select `Regression>Estimation>Generalized LS`. The estimates of the coefficients a and b are displayed in the `Regression estimates` window, and the data become the

Table 6.3 Estimates of β and ϕ for the lake data after 3 iterations.

Iteration i	$\hat{\phi}_1^{(i)}$	$\hat{\phi}_2^{(i)}$	$\hat{\beta}_1^{(i)}$	$\hat{\beta}_2^{(i)}$
0	0	0	10.20	−.0242
1	1.008	−.295	10.09	−.0216
2	1.005	−.291	10.09	−.0216

estimates of the residuals $\{W_t\}$.) The graphs of the data and sample ACF clearly suggest a strong seasonal component with period 12. In order to transform the model (6.6.15) into one with stationary residuals, we therefore consider the differenced data $X_t = Y_t - Y_{t-12}$, which satisfy

$$X_t = bg_t + N_t, \ t = 13, \dots, 120, \tag{6.6.16}$$

where $g_t = 1$ for $99 \le t \le 110$, $g_t = 0$ otherwise, and $\{N_t = W_t - W_{t-12}\}$ is a stationary sequence to be represented by a suitably chosen ARMA model. The series $\{X_t\}$ is contained in the file SBLD.TSM, and the function g_t is contained in the file SBLDIN.TSM.

The next step is to perform ordinary least squares regression of X_t on g_t following steps analogous to those of the previous paragraph (but this thime checking *only* the box marked `Include auxiliary variables` in the `Regression Trend Function` dialog box) and again using the option `Regression>Estimation>Generalized LS` or pressing the blue GLS button. The model

$$X_t = -346.92g_t + N_t, \tag{6.6.17}$$

is then displayed in the `Regression estimates` window together with the assumed noise model (white noise in this case). Inspection of the sample ACF of the residuals suggests an MA(13) or AR(13) model for $\{N_t\}$. Fitting AR and MA models of order up to 13 (with no mean-correction) using the option `Model>Estimation>Autofit` gives an MA(12) model as the minimum AICC fit for the residuals. Once this model has been fitted, the model in the `Regression estimates` window is automatically

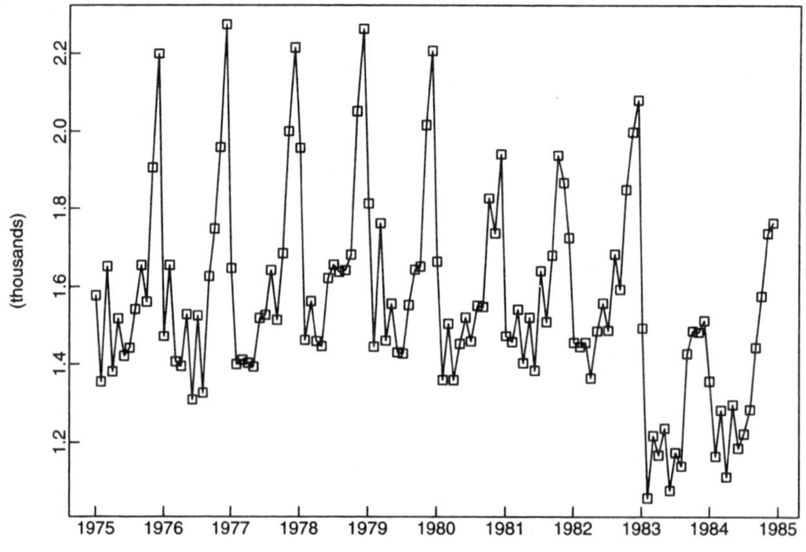

Figure 6-18 Monthly deaths and serious injuries $\{Y_t\}$ on UK roads, Jan., '75 - Dec., '84.

updated to

$$X_t = -328.45g_t + N_t, \tag{6.6.18}$$

with the fitted MA(12) model for the residuals also displayed. After several iterations (each iteration is performed by pressing the MLE button) we arrive at the model

$$X_t = -328.45g_t + N_t, \tag{6.6.19}$$

with

$$N_t = Z_t + .219Z_{t-1} + .098Z_{t-2} + .031Z_{t-3} + .064Z_{t-4} + .069Z_{t-5} + .111Z_{t-6}$$
$$+ .081Z_{t-7} + .057Z_{t-8} + .092Z_{t-9} - .028Z_{t-10} + .183Z_{t-11} - .627Z_{t-12},$$

where $\{Z_t\} \sim \text{WN}(0, 12, 581)$. The estimated standard deviation of the regression coefficient estimator is 49.41, so the estimated coefficient, −328.45, is very significantly negative, indicating the effectiveness of the legislation. The differenced data are shown in Figure 6.19 with the fitted regression function. □

Problems

6.1. Suppose that $\{X_t\}$ is an ARIMA(p, d, q) process satisfying the difference equations

$$\phi(B)(1 - B)^d X_t = \theta(B)Z_t, \quad \{Z_t\} \sim \text{WN}\left(0, \sigma^2\right).$$

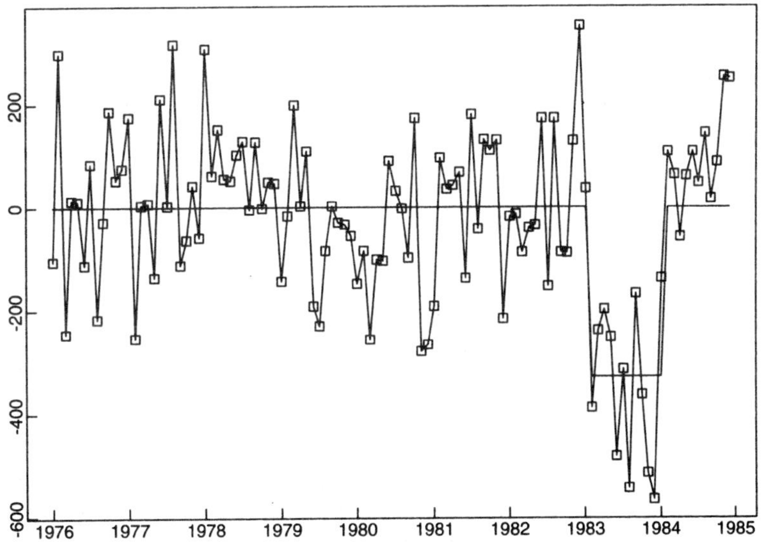

Figure 6-19 The differenced deaths and serious injuries on UK roads $\{X_t = Y_t - Y_{t-12}\}$, showing the fitted GLS regression line.

Show that these difference equations are also satisfied by the process $W_t = X_t + A_0 + A_1 t + \cdots + A_{d-1} t^{d-1}$, where $A_0, \ldots, A_{d-1}$ are arbitrary random variables.

6.2. Verify the representation given in (6.3.4).

6.3. Test the data in Example 6.3.1 for the presence of a unit root in an AR(2) model using the augmented Dickey–Fuller test.

6.4. Apply the augmented Dickey–Fuller test to the levels of Lake Huron data (LAKE.TSM). Perform two analyses assuming AR(1) and AR(2) models.

6.5. If $\{Y_t\}$ is a causal ARMA process (with zero mean) and if X_0 is a random variable with finite second moment such that X_0 is uncorrelated with Y_t for each $t = 1, 2, \ldots$, show that the best linear predictor of Y_{n+1} in terms of $1, X_0, Y_1, \ldots, Y_n$ is the same as the best linear predictor of Y_{n+1} in terms of $1, Y_1, \ldots, Y_n$.

6.6. Let $\{X_t\}$ be the ARIMA(2,1,0) process satisfying

$$\left(1 - 0.8B + 0.25B^2\right) \nabla X_t = Z_t, \quad \{Z_t\} \sim \mathrm{WN}(0, 1).$$

a. Determine the forecast function $g(h) = P_n X_{n+h}$ for $h > 0$.

b. Assuming that n is large, compute $\sigma_n^2(h)$ for $h = 1, \ldots, 5$.

6.7. Use a text editor to create a new data set ASHORT.TSM that consists of the data in AIRPASS.TSM with the last twelve values deleted. Use ITSM to find an ARIMA model for the logarithms of the data in ASHORT.TSM. Your analysis should include

a. a logical explanation of the steps taken to find the chosen model,

b. approximate 95% bounds for the components of ϕ and θ,

c. an examination of the residuals to check for whiteness as described in Section 1.6,

d. a graph of the series ASHORT.TSM showing forecasts of the next 12 values and 95% prediction bounds for the forecasts,

e. numerical values for the 12-step ahead forecast and the corresponding 95% prediction bounds,

f. a table of the actual forecast errors, i.e.,, the true value (deleted from AIRPASS.TSM) minus the forecast value, for each of the twelve forecasts.

Does the last value of AIRPASS.TSM lie within the corresponding 95% prediction bounds?

6.8. Repeat Problem 6.7, but instead of differencing, apply the classical decomposition method to the logarithms of the data in ASHORT.TSM by deseasonalizing, subtracting a quadratic trend, and then finding an appropriate ARMA model for the residuals. Compare the twelve forecast errors found from this approach with those found in Problem 6.7.

6.9. Repeat Problem 6.7 for the series BEER.TSM, deleting the last twelve values to create a file named BSHORT.TSM.

6.10. Repeat Problem 6.8 for the series BEER.TSM and the shortened series BSHORT.TSM.

6.11. A time series $\{X_t\}$ is differenced at lag 12, then at lag 1 to produce a zero-mean series $\{Y_t\}$ with the following sample ACF:

$$\hat{\rho}(12j) \approx (.8)^j, \qquad j = 0, \pm 1, \pm 2, \ldots,$$

$$\hat{\rho}(12j \pm 1) \approx (.4)(.8)^j, \quad j = 0, \pm 1, \pm 2, \ldots,$$

$$\hat{\rho}(h) \approx 0, \qquad \text{otherwise},$$

and $\hat{\gamma}(0) = 25$.

a. Suggest a SARIMA model for $\{X_t\}$ specifying all parameters.

b. For large n, express the one- and twelve-step linear predictors $P_n X_{n+1}$ and $P_n X_{n+12}$ in terms of X_t, $t = -12, -11, \ldots, n$, and $Y_t - \hat{Y}_t$, $t = 1, \ldots, n$.

c. Find the mean squared errors of the predictors in (b).

6.12. Use ITSM to verify the calculations of Examples 6.6.1, 6.6.2, and 6.6.3.

6.13. The file TUNDRA.TSM contains the average maximum temperature over the month of February for the years 1895-1993 in an area of the USA whose vegetation is characterized as tundra.

a. Fit a straight line to the data using OLS. Is the slope of the line significantly different from zero?

b. Find an appropriate ARMA model to the residuals from the OLS fit in (a).

c. Calculate the MLE estimates of the intercept and the slope of the line and the ARMA parameters in (a). Is the slope of the line significantly different from zero?

d. Use your model to forecast the average maximum temperature for the years 1994 to 2004.

7 Multivariate Time Series

Many time series arising in practice are best considered as components of some vector-valued (multivariate) time series $\{\mathbf{X}_t\}$ having not only serial dependence within each component series $\{X_{ti}\}$ but also interdependence between the different component series $\{X_{ti}\}$ and $\{X_{tj}\}$, $i \neq j$. Much of the theory of univariate time series extends in a natural way to the multivariate case; however, new problems arise. In this chapter we introduce the basic properties of multivariate series and consider the multivariate extensions of some of the techniques developed earlier. In Section 7.1 we introduce two sets of bivariate time series data for which we develop multivariate models later in the chapter. In Section 7.2 we discuss the basic properties of stationary multivariate time series, namely, the mean vector $\boldsymbol{\mu} = E\mathbf{X}_t$ and the covariance matrices $\Gamma(h) = E(\mathbf{X}_{t+h}\mathbf{X}_t') - \boldsymbol{\mu}\boldsymbol{\mu}'$, $h = 0, \pm 1, \pm 2, \ldots$, with reference to some simple examples, including multivariate white noise. Section 7.3 deals with estimation of $\boldsymbol{\mu}$ and $\Gamma(\cdot)$ and the question of testing for serial independence on the basis of observations of $\mathbf{X}_1, \ldots, \mathbf{X}_n$. In Section 7.4 we introduce multivariate ARMA processes and illustrate the problem of multivariate model identification with an example of a multivariate AR(1) process that also has an MA(1) representation. (Such examples do not exist in the univariate case.) The identification problem can be avoided by confining attention to multivariate autoregressive (or VAR) models. Forecasting multivariate time series with known second-order properties is discussed in Section 7.5, and in Section 7.6

we consider the modeling and forecasting of multivariate time series using the multivariate Yule–Walker equations and Whittle's generalization of the Durbin–Levinson algorithm. Section 7.7 contains a brief introduction to the notion of cointegrated time series.

7.1 Examples

In this section we introduce two examples of bivariate time series. A bivariate time series is a series of two-dimensional vectors $(X_{t1}, X_{t2})'$ observed at times t (usually $t = 1, 2, 3, \ldots$). The two component series $\{X_{t1}\}$ and $\{X_{t2}\}$ could be studied independently as univariate time series, each characterized, from a second-order point of view, by its own mean and autocovariance function. Such an approach, however, fails to take into account possible dependence *between* the two component series, and such cross-dependence may be of great importance, for example in predicting future values of the two component series.

We therefore consider the series of random vectors $\mathbf{X}_t = (X_{t1}, X_{t2})'$ and define the mean vector

$$\boldsymbol{\mu}_t := E\mathbf{X}_t = \begin{bmatrix} EX_{t1} \\ EX_{t2} \end{bmatrix}$$

and covariance matrices

$$\Gamma(t+h, t) := \mathrm{Cov}\big(\mathbf{X}_{t+h}, \mathbf{X}_t\big) = \begin{bmatrix} \mathrm{cov}(X_{t+h,1}, X_{t1}) & \mathrm{cov}(X_{t+h,1}, X_{t2}) \\ \mathrm{cov}(X_{t+h,2}, X_{t1}) & \mathrm{cov}(X_{t+h,2}, X_{t2}) \end{bmatrix}.$$

The bivariate series $\{\mathbf{X}_t\}$ is said to be **(weakly) stationary** if the moments $\boldsymbol{\mu}_t$ and $\Gamma(t+h, t)$ are both independent of t, in which case we use the notation

$$\boldsymbol{\mu} = E\mathbf{X}_t = \begin{bmatrix} EX_{t1} \\ EX_{t2} \end{bmatrix}$$

and

$$\Gamma(h) = \mathrm{Cov}\big(\mathbf{X}_{t+h}, \mathbf{X}_t\big) = \begin{bmatrix} \gamma_{11}(h) & \gamma_{12}(h) \\ \gamma_{21}(h) & \gamma_{22}(h) \end{bmatrix}.$$

The diagonal elements are the autocovariance functions of the univariate series $\{X_{t1}\}$ and $\{X_{t2}\}$ as defined in Chapter 2, while the off-diagonal elements are the covariances between $X_{t+h,i}$ and X_{tj}, $i \neq j$. Notice that $\gamma_{12}(h) = \gamma_{21}(-h)$.

A natural estimator of the mean vector $\boldsymbol{\mu}$ in terms of the observations $\mathbf{X}_1, \ldots, \mathbf{X}_n$ is the vector of sample means

$$\overline{\mathbf{X}}_n = \frac{1}{n}\sum_{t=1}^{n} \mathbf{X}_t,$$

and a natural estimator of $\Gamma(h)$ is

$$\hat{\Gamma}(h) = \begin{cases} n^{-1} \sum_{t=1}^{n-h} \left(\mathbf{X}_{t+h} - \overline{\mathbf{X}}_n\right)\left(\mathbf{X}_t - \overline{\mathbf{X}}_n\right)' & \text{for } 0 \le h \le n-1, \\ \hat{\Gamma}(-h)' & \text{for } -n+1 \le h < 0. \end{cases}$$

The correlation $\rho_{ij}(h)$ between $X_{t+h,i}$ and $X_{t,j}$ is estimated by

$$\hat{\rho}_{ij}(h) = \hat{\gamma}_{ij}(h)(\hat{\gamma}_{ii}(0)\hat{\gamma}_{jj}(0))^{-1/2}.$$

If $i = j$, then $\hat{\rho}_{ij}$ reduces to the sample autocorrelation function of the ith series. These estimators will be discussed in more detail in Section 7.2.

Example 7.1.1 Dow Jones and All Ordinaries Indices; DJAO2.TSM

Figure 7.1 shows the closing values $D_0, \ldots, D_{250}$ of the Dow Jones Index of stocks on the New York Stock Exchange and the closing values $A_0, \ldots, A_{250}$ of the Australian All Ordinaries Index of Share Prices, recorded at the termination of trading on 251 successive trading days up to August 26th, 1994. (Because of the time difference between Sydney and New York, the markets do not close simultaneously in both places; however, in Sydney the closing price of the Dow Jones index for the previous day is known before the opening of the market on any trading day.) The efficient market hypothesis suggests that these processes should resemble random walks with uncorrelated increments. In order to model the data as a stationary bivariate time series we first reexpress them as percentage relative price changes or **percentage**

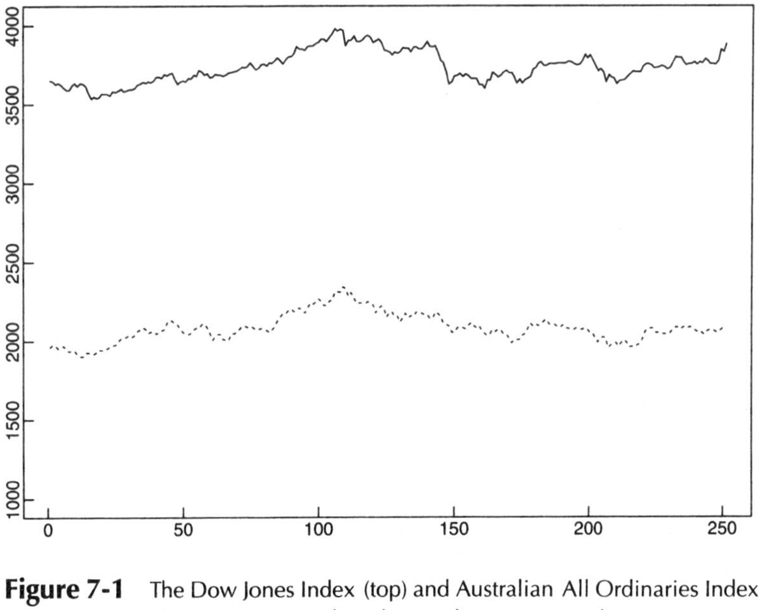

Figure 7-1 The Dow Jones Index (top) and Australian All Ordinaries Index (bottom) at closing on 251 trading days ending August 26th, 1994.

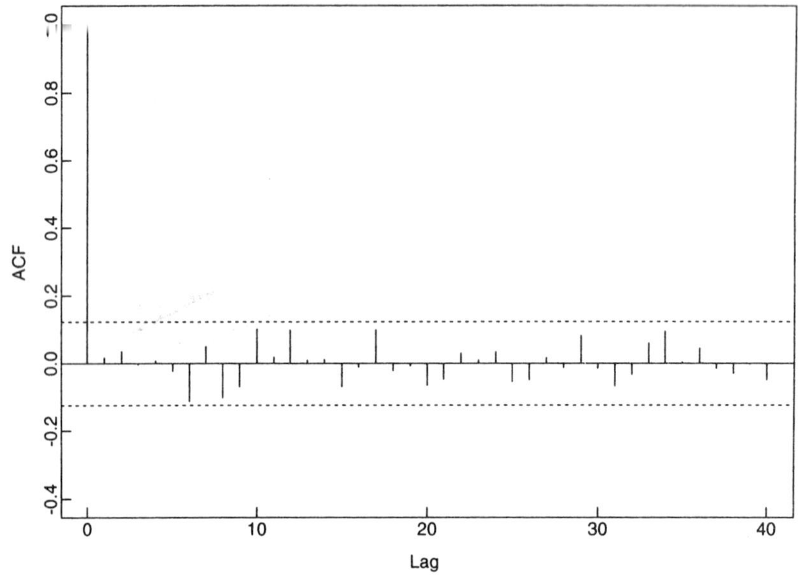

Figure 7-2 The sample ACF $\hat{\rho}_{11}$ of the observed values of $\{X_{t1}\}$ in Example 7.1.1, showing the bounds $\pm 1.96n^{-1/2}$.

returns (filed as DJAOPC2.TSM)

$$X_{t1} = 100\frac{(D_t - D_{t-1})}{D_{t-1}}, \qquad t = 1, \ldots, 250,$$

and

$$X_{t2} = 100\frac{(A_t - A_{t-1})}{A_{t-1}}, \qquad t = 1, \ldots, 250.$$

The estimators $\hat{\rho}_{11}(h)$ and $\hat{\rho}_{22}(h)$ of the autocorrelations of the two univariate series are shown in Figures 7.2 and 7.3. They are not significantly different from zero.

To compute the sample cross-correlations $\hat{\rho}_{12}(h)$ and $\hat{\rho}_{21}(h)$ using ITSM, select `File>Project>Open>Multivariate`. Then click `OK` and double-click on the file name DJAOPC2.TSM. You will see a dialog box in which `Number of columns` should be set to 2 (the number of components of the observation vectors). Then click OK, and the graphs of the two component series will appear. To see the correlations, press the middle yellow button at the top of the ITSM window. The correlation functions are plotted as a 2×2 array of graphs with $\hat{\rho}_{11}(h)$, $\hat{\rho}_{12}(h)$ in the top row and $\hat{\rho}_{21}(h)$, $\hat{\rho}_{22}(h)$ in the second row. We see from these graphs (shown in Figure 7.4) that although the autocorrelations $\hat{\rho}_{ii}(h)$, $i = 1, 2$, are all small, there is a much larger correlation between $X_{t-1,1}$ and $X_{t,2}$. This indicates the importance of considering the two series jointly as components of a bivariate time series. It also suggests that the value of $X_{t-1,1}$, i.e., the Dow Jones return on day $t - 1$, may be of assistance in predicting the value of $X_{t,2}$, the All Ordinaries return on day t. This last observation is supported by the scatterplot of the points $(x_{t-1,1}, x_{t,2})$, $t = 2, \ldots, 250$, shown in Figure 7.5. □

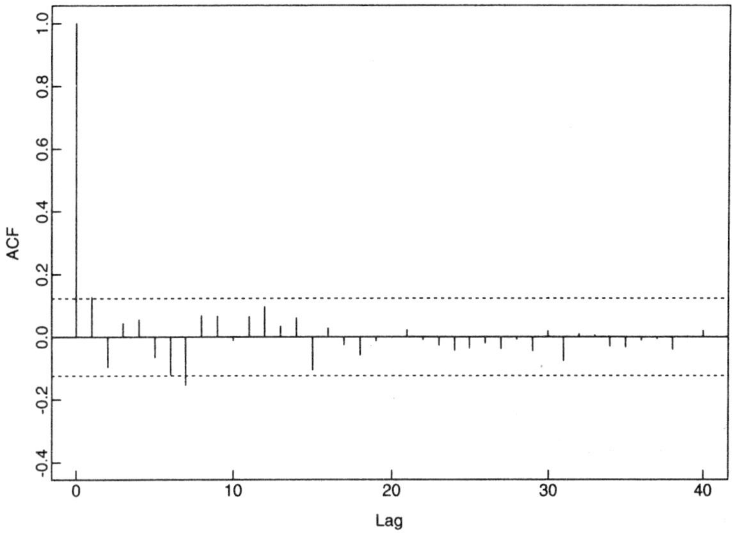

Figure 7-3 The sample ACF $\hat{\rho}_{22}$ of the observed values of $\{X_{t2}\}$ in Example 7.1.1, showing the bounds $\pm 1.96n^{-1/2}$.

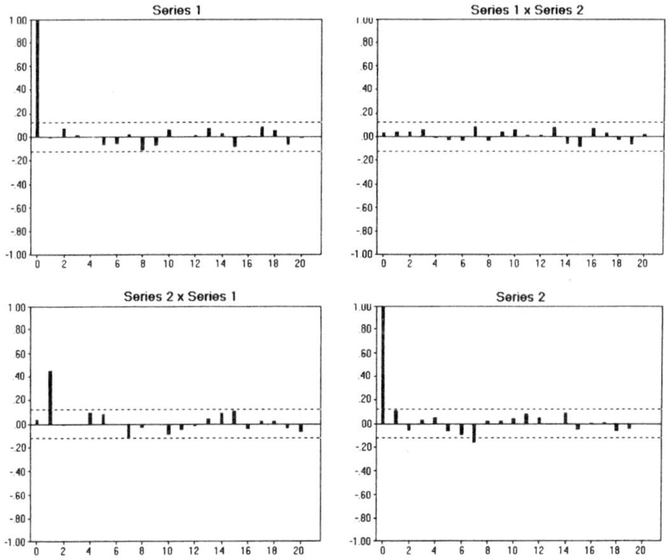

Figure 7-4 The sample correlations $\hat{\rho}_{ij}(h)$ between $X_{t+h,i}$ and $X_{t,j}$ for Example 7.1.1. ($\rho_{ij}(h)$ is plotted as the jth graph in the ith row, $i, j = 1, 2$. Series 1 and 2 consist of the daily Dow Jones and All Ordinaries percentage returns, respectively.)

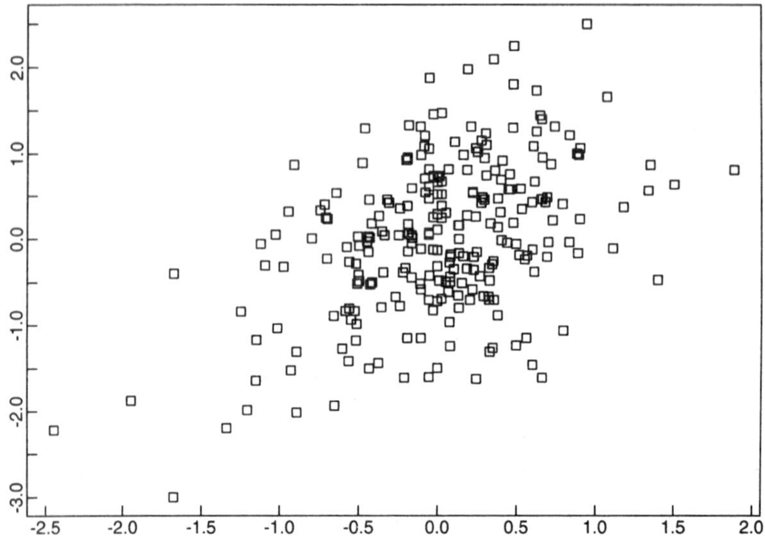

Figure 7-5 Scatterplot of $(x_{t-1,1}, x_{t,2})$, $t = 2, \ldots, 250$, for the data in Example 7.1.1.

Example 7.1.2 Sales with a leading indicator; LS2.TSM

In this example we consider the sales data $\{Y_{t2}, t = 1, \ldots, 150\}$ with leading indicator $\{Y_{t1}, t = 1, \ldots, 150\}$ given by Box and Jenkins (1976), p. 537. The two series are stored in the ITSM data files SALES.TSM and LEAD.TSM, respectively, and in bivariate format as LS2.TSM. The graphs of the two series and their sample autocorrelation functions strongly suggest that both series are nonstationary. Application of the operator $(1 - B)$ yields the two differenced series $\{D_{t1}\}$ and $\{D_{t2}\}$, whose properties are compatible with those of low-order ARMA processes. Using ITSM, we find that the models

$$D_{t1} - .0228 = Z_{t1} - .474Z_{t-1,1}, \quad \{Z_{t1}\} \sim \text{WN}(0, .0779), \tag{7.1.1}$$

$$D_{t2} - .838D_{t-1,2} - .0676 = Z_{t2} - .610Z_{t-1,2},$$

$$\{Z_{t2}\} \sim \text{WN}(0, 1.754), \tag{7.1.2}$$

provide good fits to the series $\{D_{t1}\}$ and $\{D_{t2}\}$.

The sample autocorrelations and cross-correlations of $\{D_{t1}\}$ and $\{D_{t2}\}$, are computed by opening the bivariate ITSM file LS2.TSM (as described in Example 7.1.1). The option `Transform>Difference`, with differencing lag equal to 1, generates the bivariate differenced series $\{(D_{t1}, D_{t2})\}$, and the correlation functions are then obtained as in Example 7.1.1 by clicking on the middle yellow button at the top of the ITSM screen. The sample auto- and cross-correlations $\hat{\rho}_{ij}(h)$, $i, j = 1, 2$, are shown in Figure 7.6. As we shall see in Section 7.3, care must be taken in interpreting the cross-correlations without first taking into account the autocorrelations of $\{D_{t1}\}$ and $\{D_{t2}\}$. □

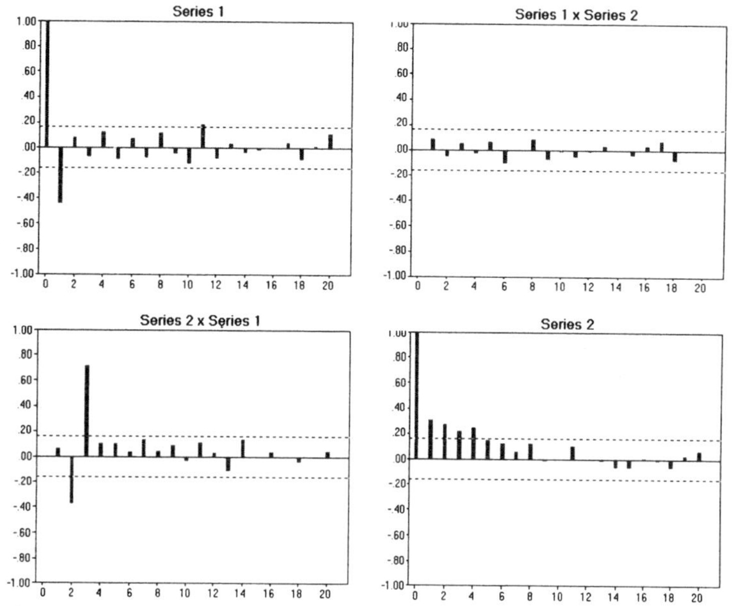

Figure 7-6 The sample correlations $\hat{\rho}_{ij}(h)$ of the series $\{D_{t1}\}$ and $\{D_{t2}\}$ of Example 7.1.2, showing the bounds $\pm 1.96n^{-1/2}$. ($\hat{\rho}_{ij}(h)$ is plotted as the jth graph in the ith row, $i, j = 1, 2$.)

7.2 Second-Order Properties of Multivariate Time Series

Consider m time series $\{X_{ti}, t = 0, \pm 1, \ldots, \}, i = 1, \ldots, m$, with $EX_{ti}^2 < \infty$ for all t and i. If all the finite-dimensional distributions of the random variables $\{X_{ti}\}$ were multivariate normal, then the distributional properties of $\{X_{ti}\}$ would be completely determined by the means

$$\mu_{ti} := EX_{ti} \tag{7.2.1}$$

and the covariances

$$\gamma_{ij}(t+h, t) := E[(X_{t+h,i} - \mu_{ti})(X_{tj} - \mu_{tj})]. \tag{7.2.2}$$

Even when the observations $\{X_{ti}\}$ do not have joint normal distributions, the quantities μ_{ti} and $\gamma_{ij}(t+h, t)$ specify the second-order properties, the covariances providing us with a measure of the dependence, not only between observations in the same series, but also between the observations in different series.

It is more convenient in dealing with m interrelated series to use vector notation. Thus we define

$$\mathbf{X}_t := \begin{bmatrix} X_{t1} \\ \vdots \\ X_{tm} \end{bmatrix}, \quad t = 0, \pm 1, \ldots. \tag{7.2.3}$$

The second-order properties of the multivariate time series $\{\mathbf{X}_t\}$ are then specified by the mean vectors

$$\boldsymbol{\mu}_t := E\mathbf{X}_t = \begin{bmatrix} \mu_{t1} \\ \vdots \\ \mu_{tm} \end{bmatrix} \tag{7.2.4}$$

and covariance matrices

$$\Gamma(t+h,t) := \begin{bmatrix} \gamma_{11}(t+h,t) & \cdots & \gamma_{1m}(t+h,t) \\ \vdots & \ddots & \vdots \\ \gamma_{m1}(t+h,t) & \cdots & \gamma_{mm}(t+h,t) \end{bmatrix}, \tag{7.2.5}$$

where

$$\gamma_{ij}(t+h,t) := \text{Cov}(X_{t+h,i}, X_{t,j}).$$

Remark 1. The matrix $\Gamma(t+h,t)$ can also be expressed as

$$\Gamma(t+h,t) := E[(\mathbf{X}_{t+h} - \boldsymbol{\mu}_{t+h})(\mathbf{X}_t - \boldsymbol{\mu}_t)'],$$

where as usual, the expected value of a random matrix A is the matrix whose components are the expected values of the components of A. □

As in the univariate case, a particularly important role is played by the class of **multivariate stationary time series**, defined as follows.

Definition 7.2.1

The m-variate series $\{\mathbf{X}_t\}$ is **(weakly) stationary** if

(i) $\boldsymbol{\mu}_X(t)$ is independent of t

and

(ii) $\Gamma_X(t+h,t)$ is independent of t for each h.

For a stationary time series we shall use the notation

$$\boldsymbol{\mu} := E\mathbf{X}_t = \begin{bmatrix} \mu_1 \\ \vdots \\ \mu_m \end{bmatrix} \tag{7.2.6}$$

and

$$\Gamma(h) := E[(\mathbf{X}_{t+h} - \boldsymbol{\mu})(\mathbf{X}_t - \boldsymbol{\mu})'] = \begin{bmatrix} \gamma_{11}(h) & \cdots & \gamma_{1m}(h) \\ \vdots & \ddots & \vdots \\ \gamma_{m1}(h) & \cdots & \gamma_{mm}(h) \end{bmatrix}. \tag{7.2.7}$$

We shall refer to $\boldsymbol{\mu}$ as the mean of the series and to $\Gamma(h)$ as the covariance matrix at lag h. Notice that if $\{\mathbf{X}_t\}$ is stationary with covariance matrix function $\Gamma(\cdot)$, then for each i, $\{X_{ti}\}$ is stationary with covariance function $\gamma_{ii}(\cdot)$. The function $\gamma_{ij}(\cdot)$, $i \neq j$, is called the cross-covariance function of the two series $\{X_{ti}\}$ and $\{X_{tj}\}$. It should be noted that $\gamma_{ij}(\cdot)$ is not in general the same as $\gamma_{ji}(\cdot)$. The correlation matrix function $R(\cdot)$ is defined by

$$R(h) := \begin{bmatrix} \rho_{11}(h) & \cdots & \rho_{1m}(h) \\ \vdots & \ddots & \vdots \\ \rho_{m1}(h) & \cdots & \rho_{mm}(h) \end{bmatrix}, \tag{7.2.8}$$

where $\rho_{ij}(h) = \gamma_{ij}(h)/[\gamma_{ii}(0)\gamma_{jj}(0)]^{1/2}$. The function $R(\cdot)$ is the covariance matrix function of the normalized series obtained by subtracting $\boldsymbol{\mu}$ from $\mathbf{X}_t$ and then dividing each component by its standard deviation.

Example 7.2.1 Consider the bivariate stationary process $\{\mathbf{X}_t\}$ defined by

$$X_{t1} = Z_t,$$

$$X_{t2} = Z_t + 0.75 Z_{t-10},$$

where $\{Z_t\} \sim \text{WN}(0, 1)$. Elementary calculations yield $\boldsymbol{\mu} = \mathbf{0}$,

$$\Gamma(-10) = \begin{bmatrix} 0 & 0.75 \\ 0 & 0.75 \end{bmatrix}, \quad \Gamma(0) = \begin{bmatrix} 1 & 1 \\ 1 & 1.5625 \end{bmatrix}, \quad \Gamma(10) = \begin{bmatrix} 0 & 0 \\ 0.75 & 0.75 \end{bmatrix},$$

and $\Gamma(j) = 0$ otherwise. The correlation matrix function is given by

$$R(-10) = \begin{bmatrix} 0 & 0.60 \\ 0 & 0.48 \end{bmatrix}, \quad R(0) = \begin{bmatrix} 1 & 0.8 \\ 0.8 & 1 \end{bmatrix}, \quad R(10) = \begin{bmatrix} 0 & 0 \\ 0.60 & 0.48 \end{bmatrix},$$

and $R(j) = 0$ otherwise. □

Basic Properties of $\boldsymbol{\Gamma}(\cdot)$:

1. $\Gamma(h) = \Gamma'(-h)$,
2. $|\gamma_{ij}(h)| \leq [\gamma_{ii}(0)\gamma_{jj}(0)]^{1/2}$, $i, j, = 1, \ldots, m$,
3. $\gamma_{ii}(\cdot)$ is an autocovariance function, $i = 1, \ldots, m$, and
4. $\sum_{j,k=1}^{n} \mathbf{a}_j' \Gamma(j-k) \mathbf{a}_k \geq 0$ for all $n \in \{1, 2, \ldots\}$ and $\mathbf{a}_1, \ldots, \mathbf{a}_n \in \mathbb{R}^m$.

Proof

The first property follows at once from the definition, the second from the fact that correlations cannot be greater than one in absolute value, and the third from the observation that $\gamma_{ii}(\cdot)$ is the autocovariance function of the stationary series $\{X_{ti}, t = 0, \pm 1, \ldots\}$. Property 4 is a statement of the obvious fact that

$$E\left(\sum_{j=1}^{n} \mathbf{a}_j'(\mathbf{X}_j - \boldsymbol{\mu})\right)^2 \geq 0. \qquad \blacksquare$$

Remark 2. The basic properties of the matrices $\Gamma(h)$ are shared also by the corresponding matrices of correlations $R(h) = [\rho_{ij}(h)]_{i,j=1}^{m}$, which have the additional property

$$\rho_{ii}(0) = 1 \quad \text{for all } i.$$

The correlation $\rho_{ij}(0)$ is the correlation between X_{ti} and X_{tj}, which is generally not equal to 1 if $i \neq j$ (see Example 7.2.1). It is also possible that $|\gamma_{ij}(h)| > |\gamma_{ij}(0)|$ if $i \neq j$ (see Problem 7.1). □

The simplest multivariate time series is multivariate white noise, the definition of which is quite analogous to that of univariate white noise.

Definition 7.2.2

The m-variate series $\{\mathbf{Z}_t\}$ is called **white noise with mean 0 and covariance matrix** Σ, written

$$\{\mathbf{Z}_t\} \sim \mathrm{WN}(\mathbf{0}, \Sigma), \tag{7.2.9}$$

if $\{\mathbf{Z}_t\}$ is stationary with mean vector $\mathbf{0}$ and covariance matrix function

$$\Gamma(h) = \begin{cases} \Sigma, & \text{if } h = 0, \\ 0, & \text{otherwise}. \end{cases} \tag{7.2.10}$$

Definition 7.2.3

The m-variate series $\{\mathbf{Z}_t\}$ is called **iid noise with mean 0 and covariance matrix** Σ, written

$$\{\mathbf{Z}_t\} \sim \mathrm{iid}(\mathbf{0}, \Sigma), \tag{7.2.11}$$

if the random vectors $\{\mathbf{Z}_t\}$ are independent and identically distributed with mean $\mathbf{0}$ and covariance matrix Σ.

Multivariate white noise $\{\mathbf{Z}_t\}$ is used as a building block from which can be constructed an enormous variety of multivariate time series. The linear processes are generated as follows.

Definition 7.2.4

The m-variate series $\{\mathbf{X}_t\}$ is a **linear process** if it has the representation

$$\mathbf{X}_t = \sum_{j=-\infty}^{\infty} C_j \mathbf{Z}_{t-j}, \quad \{\mathbf{Z}_t\} \sim \mathrm{WN}(\mathbf{0}, \Sigma), \tag{7.2.12}$$

where $\{C_j\}$ is a sequence of $m \times m$ matrices whose components are absolutely summable.

The linear process (7.2.12) is stationary (Problem 7.2) with mean **0** and covariance function

$$\Gamma(h) = \sum_{j=-\infty}^{\infty} C_{j+h} \Sigma C_j', \quad h = 0, \pm 1, \ldots. \tag{7.2.13}$$

An **MA(∞) process** is a linear process with $C_j = 0$ for $j < 0$. Thus $\{\mathbf{X}_t\}$ is an MA(∞) process if and only if there exists a white noise sequence $\{\mathbf{Z}_t\}$ and a sequence of matrices C_j with absolutely summable components such that

$$\mathbf{X}_t = \sum_{j=0}^{\infty} C_j \mathbf{Z}_{t-j}.$$

Multivariate ARMA processes will be discussed in Section 7.4, where it will be shown in particular that any causal ARMA(p, q) process can be expressed as an MA(∞) process, while any invertible ARMA(p, q) process can be expressed as an **AR(∞) process**, i.e.,, a process satisfying equations of the form

$$\mathbf{X}_t + \sum_{j=1}^{\infty} A_j \mathbf{X}_{t-j} = \mathbf{Z}_t,$$

in which the matrices A_j have absolutely summable components.

Second-Order Properties in the Frequency Domain

Provided that the components of the covariance matrix function $\Gamma(\cdot)$ have the property $\sum_{h=-\infty}^{\infty} |\gamma_{ij}(h)| < \infty, i, j = 1, \ldots, m$, then Γ has a **matrix-valued spectral density function**

$$f(\lambda) = \frac{1}{2\pi} \sum_{h=-\infty}^{\infty} e^{-i\lambda h} \Gamma(h), \quad -\pi \le \lambda \le \pi,$$

and Γ can be expressed in terms of f as

$$\Gamma(h) = \int_{-\pi}^{\pi} e^{i\lambda h} f(\lambda) d\lambda.$$

The second-order properties of the stationary process $\{\mathbf{X}_t\}$ can therefore be described equivalently in terms of $f(\cdot)$ rather than $\Gamma(\cdot)$. Similarly, $\{\mathbf{X}_t\}$ has a **spectral representation**

$$\mathbf{X}_t = \int_{-\pi}^{\pi} e^{i\lambda t} d\mathbf{Z}(\lambda),$$

where $\{\mathbf{Z}(\lambda), -\pi \le \lambda \le \pi\}$ is a process whose components are complex-valued processes satisfying

$$E\left(dZ_j(\lambda) d\overline{Z}_k(\mu)\right) = \begin{cases} f_{jk}(\lambda) d\lambda & \text{if } \lambda = \mu, \\ 0 & \text{if } \lambda \ne \mu, \end{cases}$$

and $\overline{Z}_k$ denotes the complex conjugate of Z_k. We shall not go into the spectral representation in this book. For details see TSTM.

7.3 Estimation of the Mean and Covariance Function

As in the univariate case, the estimation of the mean vector and covariances of a stationary multivariate time series plays an important role in describing and modeling the dependence structure of the component series. In this section we introduce estimators, for a stationary m-variate time series $\{\mathbf{X}_t\}$, of the components μ_j, $\gamma_{ij}(h)$, and $\rho_{ij}(h)$ of $\boldsymbol{\mu}$, $\Gamma(h)$, and $R(h)$, respectively. We also examine the large-sample properties of these estimators.

7.3.1 Estimation of $\boldsymbol{\mu}$

A natural unbiased estimator of the mean vector $\boldsymbol{\mu}$ based on the observations $\mathbf{X}_1, \ldots, \mathbf{X}_n$ is the vector of sample means

$$\overline{\mathbf{X}}_n = \frac{1}{n}\sum_{t=1}^{n}\mathbf{X}_t.$$

The resulting estimate of the mean of the jth time series is then the univariate sample mean $(1/n)\sum_{t=1}^{n} X_{tj}$. If each of the univariate autocovariance functions $\gamma_{ii}(\cdot)$, $i = 1, \ldots, m$, satisfies the conditions of Proposition 2.4.1, then the consistency of the estimator $\overline{\mathbf{X}}_n$ can be established by applying the proposition to each of the component time series $\{X_{ti}\}$. This immediately gives the following result.

Proposition 7.3.1

If $\{\mathbf{X}_t\}$ is a stationary multivariate time series with mean $\boldsymbol{\mu}$ and covariance function $\Gamma(\cdot)$, then as $n \to \infty$,

$$E\left(\overline{\mathbf{X}}_n - \boldsymbol{\mu}\right)'\left(\overline{\mathbf{X}}_n - \boldsymbol{\mu}\right) \to 0 \quad \text{if } \gamma_{ii}(n) \to 0, \quad 1 \le i \le m,$$

and

$$nE\left(\overline{\mathbf{X}}_n - \boldsymbol{\mu}\right)'\left(\overline{\mathbf{X}}_n - \boldsymbol{\mu}\right) \to \sum_{i=1}^{m}\sum_{h=-\infty}^{\infty}\gamma_{ii}(h) \quad \text{if } \sum_{h=-\infty}^{\infty}|\gamma_{ii}(h)| < \infty, \quad 1 \le i \le m.$$

Under more restrictive assumptions on the process $\{\mathbf{X}_t\}$ it can also be shown that $\overline{\mathbf{X}}_n$ is approximately normally distributed for large n. Determination of the covariance matrix of this distribution would allow us to obtain confidence regions for $\boldsymbol{\mu}$. However, this is quite complicated, and the following simple approximation is useful in practice.

For each i we construct a confidence interval for μ_i based on the sample mean $\overline{X}_i$ of the univariate series $X_{1i}, \ldots, X_{ti}$ and combine these to form a confidence region for $\boldsymbol{\mu}$. If $f_i(\omega)$ is the spectral density of the ith process $\{X_{ti}\}$ and if the sample size n is large, then we know, under the same conditions as in Section 2.4, that $\sqrt{n}\left(\overline{X}_i - \mu_i\right)$ is approximately normally distributed with mean zero and variance

$$2\pi f_i(0) = \sum_{k=-\infty}^{\infty} \gamma_{ii}(k).$$

It can also be shown (see, e.g., Anderson, 1971) that

$$2\pi \hat{f}_i(0) := \sum_{|h|\le r} \left(1 - \frac{|h|}{r}\right) \hat{\gamma}_{ii}(h)$$

is a consistent estimator of $2\pi f_i(0)$, provided that $r = r_n$ is a sequence of numbers depending on n in such a way that $r_n \to \infty$ and $r_n/n \to 0$ as $n \to \infty$. Thus if $\overline{X}_i$ denotes the sample mean of the ith process and Φ_α is the α-quantile of the standard normal distribution, then the bounds

$$\overline{X}_i \pm \Phi_{1-\alpha/2} \left(2\pi \hat{f}_i(0)/n\right)^{1/2}$$

are asymptotic $(1 - \alpha)$ confidence bounds for μ_i. Hence

$$P\left(|\mu_i - \overline{X}_i| \le \Phi_{1-\alpha/2} \left(2\pi \hat{f}_i(0)/n\right)^{1/2}, i = 1, \ldots, m\right)$$
$$\ge 1 - \sum_{i=1}^{m} P\left(\left|\mu_i - \overline{X}_i\right| > \Phi_{1-\alpha/2} \left(2\pi \hat{f}_i(0)/n\right)^{1/2}\right),$$

where the right-hand side converges to $1 - m\alpha$ as $n \to \infty$. Consequently, as $n \to \infty$, the set of m-dimensional vectors bounded by

$$\left\{x_i = \overline{X}_i \pm \Phi_{1-(\alpha/(2m))} \left(2\pi \hat{f}_i(0)/n\right)^{1/2}, i = 1, \ldots, m\right\} \tag{7.3.1}$$

has a confidence coefficient that converges to a value *greater than or equal to* $1 - \alpha$ (and substantially greater if m is large). Nevertheless, the region defined by (7.3.1) is easy to determine and is of reasonable size, provided that m is not too large.

7.3.2 Estimation of $\Gamma(h)$

As in the univariate case, a natural estimator of the covariance $\Gamma(h) = E\left[(\mathbf{X}_{t+h} - \boldsymbol{\mu})(\mathbf{X}_t - \boldsymbol{\mu})'\right]$ is

$$\hat{\Gamma}(h) = \begin{cases} n^{-1} \sum_{t=1}^{n-h} \left(\mathbf{X}_{t+h} - \overline{\mathbf{X}}_n\right)\left(\mathbf{X}_t - \overline{\mathbf{X}}_n\right)' & \text{for } 0 \le h \le n-1, \\ \hat{\Gamma}'(-h) & \text{for } -n+1 \le h < 0. \end{cases}$$

Writing $\hat{\gamma}_{ij}(h)$ for the (i, j)-component of $\hat{\Gamma}(h)$, $i, j = 1, 2, \ldots$, we estimate the cross-correlations by

$$\hat{\rho}_{ij}(h) = \hat{\gamma}_{ij}(h)(\hat{\gamma}_{ii}(0)\hat{\gamma}_{jj}(0))^{-1/2}.$$

If $i = j$, then $\hat{\rho}_{ij}$ reduces to the sample autocorrelation function of the ith series.

Derivation of the large-sample properties of $\hat{\gamma}_{ij}$ and $\hat{\rho}_{ij}$ is quite complicated in general. Here we shall simply note one result that is of particular importance for testing the independence of two component series. For details of the proof of this and related results, see TSTM.

Theorem 7.3.1 *Let $\{\mathbf{X}_t\}$ be the bivariate time series whose components are defined by*

$$X_{t1} = \sum_{k=-\infty}^{\infty} \alpha_k Z_{t-k,1}, \quad \{Z_{t1}\} \sim \text{IID}\left(0, \sigma_1^2\right),$$

and

$$X_{t2} = \sum_{k=-\infty}^{\infty} \beta_k Z_{t-k,2}, \quad \{Z_{t2}\} \sim \text{IID}\left(0, \sigma_2^2\right),$$

where the two sequences $\{Z_{t1}\}$ and $\{Z_{t2}\}$ are independent, $\sum_k |\alpha_k| < \infty$, and $\sum_k |\beta_k| < \infty$.

Then for all integers h and k with $h \neq k$, the random variables $n^{1/2}\hat{\rho}_{12}(h)$ and $n^{1/2}\hat{\rho}_{12}(k)$ are approximately bivariate normal with mean $\mathbf{0}$, variance $\sum_{j=-\infty}^{\infty} \rho_{11}(j)\rho_{22}(j)$, and covariance $\sum_{j=-\infty}^{\infty} \rho_{11}(j)\rho_{22}(j+k-h)$, for n large.

[For a related result that does not require the independence of the two series $\{X_{t1}\}$ and $\{X_{t2}\}$ see Theorem 7.3.2 below.]

Theorem 7.3.1 is useful in testing for correlation between two time series. If one of the two processes in the theorem is white noise, then it follows at once from the theorem that $\hat{\rho}_{12}(h)$ is approximately normally distributed with mean 0 and variance $1/n$, in which case it is straightforward to test the hypothesis that $\rho_{12}(h) = 0$. However, if neither process is white noise, then a value of $\hat{\rho}_{12}(h)$ that is large relative to $n^{-1/2}$ does not necessarily indicate that $\rho_{12}(h)$ is different from zero. For example, suppose that $\{X_{t1}\}$ and $\{X_{t2}\}$ are two independent AR(1) processes with $\rho_{11}(h) = \rho_{22}(h) = .8^{|h|}$. Then the large-sample variance of $\hat{\rho}_{12}(h)$ is $n^{-1}\left(1 + 2\sum_{k=1}^{\infty}(.64)^k\right) = 4.556n^{-1}$. It would therefore not be surprising to observe a value of $\hat{\rho}_{12}(h)$ as large as $3n^{-1/2}$ even though $\{X_{t1}\}$ and $\{X_{t2}\}$ are independent. If on the other hand, $\rho_{11}(h) = .8^{|h|}$ and $\rho_{22}(h) = (-.8)^{|h|}$, then the large-sample variance of $\hat{\rho}_{12}(h)$ is $.2195n^{-1}$, and an observed value of $3n^{-1/2}$ for $\hat{\rho}_{12}(h)$ would be very unlikely.

7.3.3 Testing for Independence of Two Stationary Time Series

Since by Theorem 7.3.1 the large-sample distribution of $\hat{\rho}_{12}(h)$ depends on both $\rho_{11}(\cdot)$ and $\rho_{22}(\cdot)$, any test for independence of the two component series cannot be based solely on estimated values of $\rho_{12}(h)$, $h = 0, \pm 1, \ldots$, without taking into account the nature of the two component series.

This difficulty can be circumvented by "prewhitening" the two series before computing the cross-correlations $\hat{\rho}_{12}(h)$, i.e.,, by transforming the two series to white noise by application of suitable filters. If $\{X_{t1}\}$ and $\{X_{t2}\}$ are invertible ARMA(p, q) processes, this can be achieved by the transformations

$$Z_{ti} = \sum_{j=0}^{\infty} \pi_j^{(i)} X_{t-j,i},$$

where $\sum_{j=0}^{\infty} \pi_j^{(i)} z^j = \phi^{(i)}(z)/\theta^{(i)}(z)$ and $\phi^{(i)}$, $\theta^{(i)}$ are the autoregressive and moving-average polynomials of the ith series, $i = 1, 2$.

Since in practice the true model is nearly always unknown and since the data X_{tj}, $t \leq 0$, are not available, it is convenient to replace the sequences $\{Z_{ti}\}$ by the residuals $\{\hat{W}_{ti}\}$ after fitting a maximum likelihood ARMA model to each of the component series (see (5.3.1)). If the fitted ARMA models were in fact the true models, the series $\{\hat{W}_{ti}\}$ would be white noise sequences for $i = 1, 2$.

To test the hypothesis H_0 that $\{X_{t1}\}$ and $\{X_{t2}\}$ are independent series, we observe that under H_0, the corresponding two prewhitened series $\{Z_{t1}\}$ and $\{Z_{t2}\}$ are also independent. Theorem 7.3.1 then implies that the sample cross-correlations $\hat{\rho}_{12}(h)$, $\hat{\rho}_{12}(k)$, $h \neq k$, of $\{Z_{t1}\}$ and $\{Z_{t2}\}$ are for large n approximately independent and normally distributed with means 0 and variances n^{-1}. An approximate test for independence can therefore be obtained by comparing the values of $|\hat{\rho}_{12}(h)|$ with $1.96n^{-1/2}$, exactly as in Section 5.3.2. If we prewhiten only one of the two original series, say $\{X_{t1}\}$, then under H_0 Theorem 7.3.1 implies that the sample cross-correlations $\tilde{\rho}_{12}(h)$, $\tilde{\rho}_{12}(k)$, $h \neq k$, of $\{Z_{t1}\}$ and $\{X_{t2}\}$ are for large n approximately normal with means 0, variances n^{-1} and covariance $n^{-1}\rho_{22}(k-h)$, where $\rho_{22}(\cdot)$ is the autocorrelation function of $\{X_{t2}\}$. Hence, for any fixed h, $\tilde{\rho}_{12}(h)$ also falls (under H_0) between the bounds $\pm 1.96n^{-1/2}$ with a probability of approximately 0.95.

Example 7.3.1

The sample correlation functions $\hat{\rho}_{ij}(\cdot)$, $i, j = 1, 2$, of the bivariate time series E731A.TSM (of length $n = 200$) are shown in Figure 7.7. Without taking into account the autocorrelations $\hat{\rho}_{ii}(\cdot)$, $i = 1, 2$, it is impossible to decide on the basis of the cross-correlations whether or not the two component processes are independent of each other. Notice that many of the sample cross-correlations $\hat{\rho}_{ij}(h)$, $i \neq j$, lie outside the bounds $\pm 1.96n^{-1/2} = \pm .139$. However, these bounds are relevant only if at least one of the component series is white noise. Since this is clearly not the case, a whitening transformation must be applied to at least one of the two component series. Analysis using ITSM leads to AR(1) models for each. The residuals from these maximum likelihood models are stored as a bivariate series in the file E731B.TSM, and their sample correlations, obtained from ITSM, are shown in Figure 7.8. All but two of the cross-correlations are between the bounds $\pm.139$, suggesting by Theorem 7.3.1 that the two residual series (and hence the two original series) are uncorrelated. The data for this example were in fact generated as two independent AR(1) series with $\phi = 0.8$ and $\sigma^2 = 1$. □

7.3.4 Bartlett's Formula

In Section 2.4 we gave Bartlett's formula for the large-sample distribution of the sample autocorrelation vector $\hat{\rho} = (\hat{\rho}(1), \dots, \hat{\rho}(k))'$ of a univariate time series. The following theorem gives a large-sample approximation to the covariances of the sample cross-correlations $\hat{\rho}_{12}(h)$ and $\hat{\rho}_{12}(k)$ of the bivariate time series $\{\mathbf{X}_t\}$ under the assumption that $\{\mathbf{X}_t\}$ is Gaussian. However, it is not assumed (as in Theorem 7.3.1) that $\{X_{t1}\}$ is independent of $\{X_{t2}\}$.

Bartlett's Formula:

If $\{\mathbf{X}_t\}$ is a bivariate Gaussian time series with covariances satisfying $\sum_{h=-\infty}^{\infty} |\gamma_{ij}(h)| < \infty$, $i, j = 1, 2$, then

$$\begin{aligned}\lim_{n\to\infty} n\mathrm{Cov}\big(\hat{\rho}_{12}(h), \hat{\rho}_{12}(k)\big) = \sum_{j=-\infty}^{\infty} \Big[&\rho_{11}(j)\rho_{22}(j+k-h) + \rho_{12}(j+k)\rho_{21}(j-h) \\ &- \rho_{12}(h)\{\rho_{11}(j)\rho_{12}(j+k) + \rho_{22}(j)\rho_{21}(j-k)\} \\ &- \rho_{12}(k)\{\rho_{11}(j)\rho_{12}(j+h) + \rho_{22}(j)\rho_{21}(j-h)\} \\ &+ \rho_{12}(h)\rho_{12}(k)\left\{\frac{1}{2}\rho_{11}^2(j) + \rho_{12}^2(j) + \frac{1}{2}\rho_{22}^2(j)\right\}\Big]\end{aligned}$$

Corollary 7.3.1 *If $\{\mathbf{X}_t\}$ satisfies the conditions for Bartlett's formula, if either $\{X_{t1}\}$ or $\{X_{t2}\}$ is white noise, and if*

$$\rho_{12}(h) = 0, \quad h \notin [a, b],$$

then

$$\lim_{n\to\infty} n\mathrm{Var}\big(\hat{\rho}_{12}(h)\big) = 1, \quad h \notin [a, b].$$

Example 7.3.2 Sales with a leading indicator

We consider again the differenced series $\{D_{t1}\}$ and $\{D_{t2}\}$ of Example 7.1.2, for which we found the maximum likelihood models (7.1.1) and (7.1.2) using ITSM. The residuals from the two models (which can be filed by ITSM) are the two "whitened" series

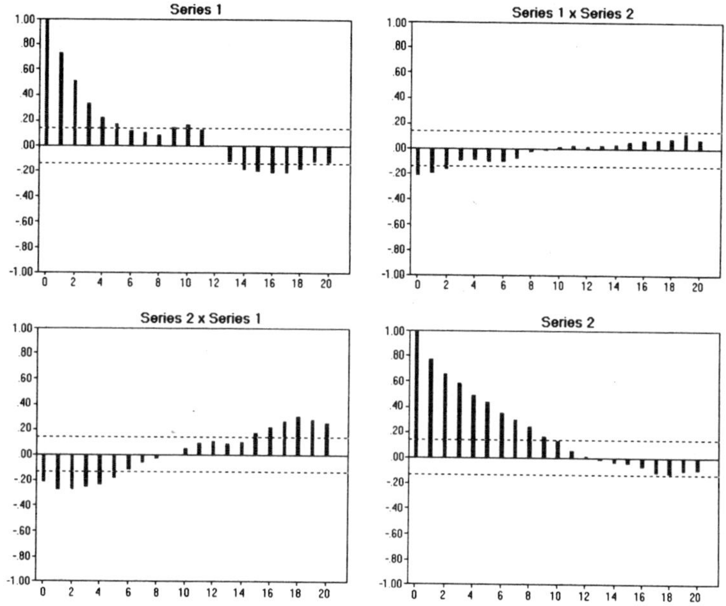

Figure 7-7 The sample correlations of the bivariate series E731A.TSM of Example 7.3.1, showing the bounds $\pm 1.96n^{-1/2}$.

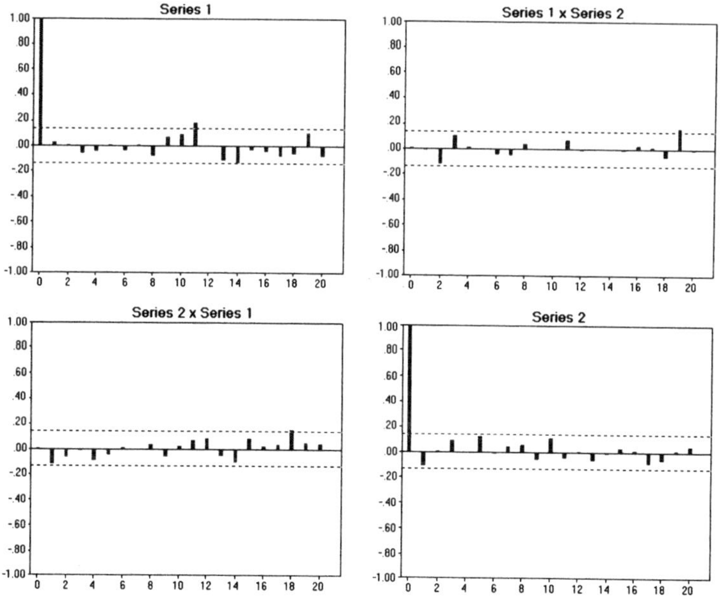

Figure 7-8 The sample correlations of the bivariate series of residuals E731B.TSM, whose components are the residuals from the AR(1) models fitted to each of the component series in E731A.TSM.

$\{\hat{W}_{t1}\}$ and $\{\hat{W}_{t2}\}$ with sample variances .0779 and 1.754, respectively. This bivariate series is contained in the file E732.TSM.

The sample auto- and cross-correlations of $\{D_{t1}\}$ and $\{D_{t2}\}$ were shown in Figure 7.6. Without taking into account the autocorrelations, it is not possible to draw any conclusions about the dependence between the two component series from the cross-correlations.

Examination of the sample cross-correlation function of the whitened series $\{\hat{W}_{t1}\}$ and $\{\hat{W}_{t2}\}$, on the other hand, is much more informative. From Figure 7.9 it is apparent that there is one large-sample cross-correlation (between $\hat{W}_{t+3,2}$ and $\hat{W}_{t,1}$), while the others are all between $\pm 1.96n^{-1/2}$. □

If $\{\hat{W}_{t1}\}$ and $\{\hat{W}_{t2}\}$ are assumed to be jointly Gaussian, Corollary 7.3.1 indicates the compatibility of the cross-correlations with a model for which

$$\rho_{12}(-3) \neq 0$$

and

$$\rho_{12}(h) = 0, \quad h \neq -3.$$

The value $\hat{\rho}_{12}(-3) = .969$ suggests the model

$$\hat{W}_{t2} = 4.74\hat{W}_{t-3,1} + N_t, \tag{7.3.2}$$

where the stationary noise $\{N_t\}$ has small variance compared with $\{\hat{W}_{t2}\}$ and $\{\hat{W}_{t1}\}$, and the coefficient 4.74 is the square root of the ratio of sample variances of $\{\hat{W}_{t2}\}$

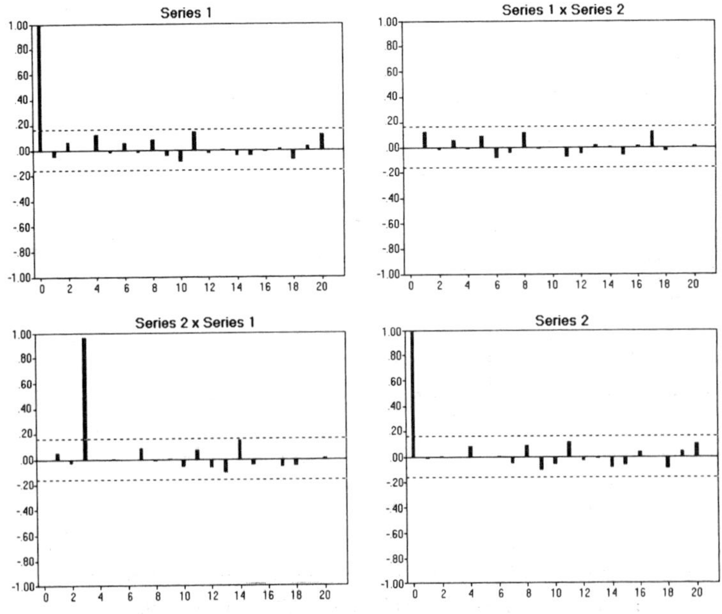

Figure 7-9 The sample correlations of the whitened series $\hat{W}_{t+h,1}$ and $\hat{W}_{t2}$ of Example 7.3.2, showing the bounds $\pm 1.96n^{-1/2}$.

and $\{\hat{W}_{t1}\}$. A study of the sample values of $\{\hat{W}_{t2} - 4.74\hat{W}_{t-3,1}\}$ suggests the model

$$(1 + .345B)N_t = U_t, \quad \{U_t\} \sim \text{WN}(0, .0782) \tag{7.3.3}$$

for $\{N_t\}$. Finally, replacing $\hat{W}_{t2}$ and $\hat{W}_{t-3,1}$ in (7.3.2) by Z_{t2} and $Z_{t-3,1}$, respectively, and then using (7.1.1) and (7.1.2) to express Z_{t2} and $Z_{t-3,1}$ in terms of $\{D_{t2}\}$ and $\{D_{t1}\}$, we obtain a model relating $\{D_{t1}\}$, $\{D_{t2}\}$, and $\{U_{t1}\}$, namely,

$$D_{t2} + .0773 = (1 - .610B)(1 - .838B)^{-1}[4.74(1 - .474B)^{-1}D_{t-3,1} + (1 + .345B)^{-1}U_t].$$

This model should be compared with the one derived later in Section 10.1 by the more systematic technique of transfer function modeling.

7.4 Multivariate ARMA Processes

As in the univariate case, we can define an extremely useful class of multivariate stationary processes $\{\mathbf{X}_t\}$ by requiring that $\{\mathbf{X}_t\}$ should satisfy a set of linear difference equations with constant coefficients. Multivariate white noise $\{\mathbf{Z}_t\}$ (see Definition 7.2.2) is a fundamental building block from which these ARMA processes are constructed.

Definition 7.4.1

$\{\mathbf{X}_t\}$ is an **ARMA(p, q) process** if $\{\mathbf{X}_t\}$ is stationary and if for every t,

$$\mathbf{X}_t - \Phi_1\mathbf{X}_{t-1} - \cdots - \Phi_p\mathbf{X}_{t-p} = \mathbf{Z}_t + \Theta_1\mathbf{Z}_{t-1} + \cdots + \Theta_q\mathbf{Z}_{t-q}, \tag{7.4.1}$$

where $\{\mathbf{Z}_t\} \sim \text{WN}(\mathbf{0}, \Sigma)$. ($\{\mathbf{X}_t\}$ is an **ARMA(p, q) process with mean μ** if $\{\mathbf{X}_t - \mu\}$ is an ARMA(p, q) process.)

Equations (7.4.1) can be written in the more compact form

$$\Phi(B)\mathbf{X}_t = \Theta(B)\mathbf{Z}_t, \quad \{\mathbf{Z}_t\} \sim \text{WN}(\mathbf{0}, \Sigma), \tag{7.4.2}$$

where $\Phi(z) := I - \Phi_1 z - \cdots - \Phi_p z^p$ and $\Theta(z) := I + \Theta_1 z + \cdots + \Theta_q z^q$ are matrix-valued polynomials, I is the $m \times m$ identity matrix, and B as usual denotes the backward shift operator. (Each component of the matrices $\Phi(z)$, $\Theta(z)$ is a polynomial with real coefficients and degree less than or equal to p, q, respectively.)

Example 7.4.1 The multivariate AR(1) process

Setting $p = 1$ and $q = 0$ in (7.4.1) gives the defining equations

$$\mathbf{X}_t = \Phi\mathbf{X}_{t-1} + \mathbf{Z}_t, \quad \{\mathbf{Z}_t\} \sim \text{WN}(\mathbf{0}, \Sigma), \tag{7.4.3}$$

for the multivariate AR(1) series $\{\mathbf{X}_t\}$. By exactly the same argument as used in Example 2.2.1, we can express $\mathbf{X}_t$ as

$$\mathbf{X}_t = \sum_{j=0}^{\infty} \Phi^j \mathbf{Z}_{t-j}, \tag{7.4.4}$$

provided that all the eigenvalues of Φ are less than 1 in absolute value, i.e.,, provided that

$$\det(I - z\Phi) \neq 0 \quad \text{for all } z \in \mathbb{C} \text{ such that } |z| \leq 1. \tag{7.4.5}$$

If this condition is satisfied, then the coefficients Φ^j are absolutely summable, and hence the series in (7.4.4) converges; i.e., each component of the matrix $\sum_{j=0}^{n} \Phi^j \mathbf{Z}_{t-j}$ converges (see Remark 1 of Section 2.2). The same argument as in Example 2.2.1 also shows that (7.4.4) is the unique stationary solution of (7.4.3). The condition that all the eigenvalues of Φ should be less than 1 in absolute value (or equivalently (7.4.5)) is just the multivariate analogue of the condition $|\phi| < 1$ required for the existence of a causal stationary solution of the univariate AR(1) equations (2.2.8). □

Causality and invertibility of a multivariate ARMA(p, q) process are defined precisely as in Section 3.1, except that the coefficients ψ_j, π_j in the representations $X_t = \sum_{j=0}^{\infty} \psi_j Z_{t-j}$ and $Z_t = \sum_{j=0}^{\infty} \pi_j X_{t-j}$ are replaced by $m \times m$ matrices Ψ_j and Π_j whose components are required to be absolutely summable. The following two theorems (proofs of which can be found in TSTM) provide us with criteria for causality and invertibility analogous to those of Section 3.1.

Causality:

An ARMA(p, q) process $\{\mathbf{X}_t\}$ is **causal**, or a **causal function of $\{\mathbf{Z}_t\}$**, if there exist matrices $\{\Psi_j\}$ with absolutely summable components such that

$$\mathbf{X}_t = \sum_{j=0}^{\infty} \Psi_j \mathbf{Z}_{t-j} \quad \text{for all } t. \tag{7.4.6}$$

Causality is equivalent to the condition

$$\det \Phi(z) \neq 0 \text{ for all } z \in \mathbb{C} \text{ such that } |z| \leq 1. \tag{7.4.7}$$

The matrices Ψ_j are found recursively from the equations

$$\Psi_j = \Theta_j + \sum_{k=1}^{\infty} \Phi_k \Psi_{j-k}, \quad j = 0, 1, \ldots, \tag{7.4.8}$$

where we define $\Theta_0 = I$, $\Theta_j = 0$ for $j > q$, $\Phi_j = 0$ for $j > p$, and $\Psi_j = 0$ for $j < 0$.

Invertibility:

An ARMA(p, q) process $\{\mathbf{X}_t\}$ is **invertible** if there exist matrices $\{\Pi_j\}$ with absolutely summable components such that

$$\mathbf{Z}_t = \sum_{j=0}^{\infty} \Pi_j \mathbf{X}_{t-j} \text{ for all } t. \tag{7.4.9}$$

Invertibility is equivalent to the condition

$$\det \Theta(z) \neq 0 \text{ for all } z \in \mathbb{C} \text{ such that } |z| \leq 1. \tag{7.4.10}$$

The matrices Π_j are found recursively from the equations

$$\Pi_j = -\Phi_j - \sum_{k=1}^{\infty} \Theta_k \Pi_{j-k}, \quad j = 0, 1, \ldots, \tag{7.4.11}$$

where we define $\Phi_0 = -I$, $\Phi_j = 0$ for $j > p$, $\Theta_j = 0$ for $j > q$, and $\Pi_j = 0$ for $j < 0$.

Example 7.4.2

For the multivariate AR(1) process defined by (7.4.3), the recursions (7.4.8) give

$$\Psi_0 = I,$$
$$\Psi_1 = \Phi\Psi_0 = \Phi,$$
$$\Psi_2 = \Phi\Psi_1 = \Phi^2,$$
$$\vdots$$
$$\Psi_j = \Phi\Psi_{j-1} = \Phi^j, \ j \geq 3,$$

as already found in Example 7.4.1. □

Remark 3. For the bivariate AR(1) process (7.4.3) with

$$\Phi = \begin{bmatrix} 0 & 0.5 \\ 0 & 0 \end{bmatrix}$$

it is easy to check that $\Psi_j = \Phi^j = 0$ for $j > 1$ and hence that $\{\mathbf{X}_t\}$ has the alternative representation

$$\mathbf{X}_t = \mathbf{Z}_t + \Phi \mathbf{Z}_{t-1}$$

as an MA(1) process. This example shows that it is not always possible to distinguish between multivariate ARMA models of different orders without imposing further restrictions. If, for example, attention is restricted to pure AR processes, the problem does not arise. For detailed accounts of the identification problem for general ARMA(p, q) models see Hannan and Deistler (1988) and Lütkepohl (1993). □

7.4.1 The Covariance Matrix Function of a Causal ARMA Process

From (7.2.13) we can express the covariance matrix $\Gamma(h) = E(\mathbf{X}_{t+h}\mathbf{X}'_t)$ of the causal process (7.4.6) as

$$\Gamma(h) = \sum_{j=0}^{\infty} \Psi_{h+j} \Sigma \Psi'_j, \quad h = 0, \pm 1, \ldots, \tag{7.4.12}$$

where the matrices Ψ_j are found from (7.4.8) and $\Psi_j := 0$ for $j < 0$.

The covariance matrices $\Gamma(h)$, $h = 0, \pm 1, \ldots$, can also be found by solving the Yule–Walker equations

$$\Gamma(j) - \sum_{r=1}^{p} \Phi_r \Gamma(j-r) = \sum_{j \le r \le q} \Theta_r \Sigma \Psi_{r-j}, \quad j = 0, 1, 2, \ldots, \tag{7.4.13}$$

obtained by postmultiplying (7.4.1) by $\mathbf{X}'_{t-j}$ and taking expectations. The first $p+1$ of the equations (7.4.13) can be solved for the components of $\Gamma(0), \ldots, \Gamma(p)$ using the fact that $\Gamma(-h) = \Gamma'(h)$. The remaining equations then give $\Gamma(p+1), \Gamma(p+2), \ldots$ recursively. An explicit form of the solution of these equations can be written down by making use of Kronecker products and the vec operator (see e.g., Lütkepohl, 1993).

Remark 4. If z_0 is the root of $\det \Phi(z) = 0$ with smallest absolute value, then it can be shown from the recursions (7.4.8) that $\Psi_j / r^j \to 0$ as $j \to \infty$ for all r such that $|z_0|^{-1} < r < 1$. Hence, there is a constant C such that each component of Ψ_j is smaller in absolute value than Cr^j. This implies in turn that there is a constant K such that each component of the matrix $\Psi_{h+j} \Sigma \Psi'_j$ on the right of (7.4.12) is bounded in absolute value by Kr^{2j}. Provided that $|z_0|$ is not very close to 1, this means that the series (7.4.12) converges rapidly, and the error incurred in each component by truncating the series after the term with $j = k-1$ is smaller in absolute value than $\sum_{j=k}^{\infty} Kr^{2j} = Kr^{2k} / \left(1 - r^2\right)$. □

7.5 Best Linear Predictors of Second-Order Random Vectors

Let $\{\mathbf{X}_t = (X_{t1}, \ldots, X_{tm})'\}$ be an m-variate time series with means $E\mathbf{X}_t = \boldsymbol{\mu}_t$ and covariance function given by the $m \times m$ matrices

$$K(i, j) = E\left(\mathbf{X}_i \mathbf{X}'_j\right) - \boldsymbol{\mu}_i \boldsymbol{\mu}'_j.$$

If $\mathbf{Y} = (Y_1, \ldots, Y_m)'$ is a random vector with finite second moments and $E\mathbf{Y} = \boldsymbol{\mu}$, we define

$$P_n(\mathbf{Y}) = (P_n Y_1, \ldots, P_n Y_m)', \tag{7.5.1}$$

where $P_n Y_j$ is the best linear predictor of the component Y_j of $\mathbf{Y}$ in terms of all of the components of the vectors $\mathbf{X}_t$, $t = 1, \ldots, n$, and the constant 1. It follows immediately from the properties of the prediction operator (Section 2.5) that

$$P_n(\mathbf{Y}) = \boldsymbol{\mu} + A_1(\mathbf{X}_n - \boldsymbol{\mu}_n) + \cdots + A_n(\mathbf{X}_1 - \boldsymbol{\mu}_1) \tag{7.5.2}$$

for some matrices $A_1, \ldots, A_n$, and that

$$\mathbf{Y} - P_n(\mathbf{Y}) \perp \mathbf{X}_{n+1-i}, \quad i = 1, \ldots, n, \tag{7.5.3}$$

where we say that two m-dimensional random vectors $\mathbf{X}$ and $\mathbf{Y}$ are orthogonal (written $\mathbf{X} \perp \mathbf{Y}$) if $E(\mathbf{X}\mathbf{Y}')$ is a matrix of zeros. The vector of best predictors (7.5.1) is uniquely determined by (7.5.2) and (7.5.3), although it is possible that there may be more than one possible choice for $A_1, \ldots, A_n$.

As a special case of the above, if $\{\mathbf{X}_t\}$ is a zero-mean time series, the best linear predictor $\hat{\mathbf{X}}_{n+1}$ of $\mathbf{X}_{n+1}$ in terms of $\mathbf{X}_1, \ldots, \mathbf{X}_n$ is obtained on replacing $\mathbf{Y}$ by $\mathbf{X}_{n+1}$ in (7.5.1). Thus

$$\hat{\mathbf{X}}_{n+1} = \begin{cases} \mathbf{0}, & \text{if } n = 0, \\ P_n(\mathbf{X}_{n+1}), & \text{if } n \geq 1. \end{cases}$$

Hence, we can write

$$\hat{\mathbf{X}}_{n+1} = \Phi_{n1}\mathbf{X}_n + \cdots + \Phi_{nn}\mathbf{X}_1, \quad n = 1, 2, \ldots, \tag{7.5.4}$$

where, from (7.5.3), the coefficients Φ_{nj}, $j = 1, \ldots, n$, are such that

$$E\left(\hat{\mathbf{X}}_{n+1}\mathbf{X}'_{n+1-i}\right) = E\left(\mathbf{X}_{n+1}\mathbf{X}'_{n+1-i}\right), \quad i = 1, \ldots, n, \tag{7.5.5}$$

i.e.,

$$\sum_{j=1}^{n} \Phi_{nj} K(n+1-j, n+1-i) = K(n+1, n+1-i), \quad i = 1, \ldots, n.$$

In the case where $\{\mathbf{X}_t\}$ is stationary with $K(i, j) = \Gamma(i-j)$, the prediction equations simplify to the m-dimensional analogues of (2.5.7), i.e.,

$$\sum_{j=1}^{n} \Phi_{nj}\Gamma(i-j) = \Gamma(i), \quad i = 1, \ldots, n. \tag{7.5.6}$$

Provided that the covariance matrix of the nm components of $\mathbf{X}_1, \ldots, \mathbf{X}_n$ is nonsingular for every $n \geq 1$, the coefficients $\{\Phi_{nj}\}$ can be determined recursively using a multivariate version of the Durbin–Levinson algorithm given by Whittle (1963) (for details see TSTM, Proposition 11.4.1). Whittle's recursions also determine the covariance matrices of the one-step prediction errors, namely, $V_0 = \Gamma(0)$ and, for $n \geq 1$,

$$\begin{aligned} V_n &= E(\mathbf{X}_{n+1} - \hat{\mathbf{X}}_{n+1})(\mathbf{X}_{n+1} - \hat{\mathbf{X}}_{n+1})' \\ &= \Gamma(0) - \Phi_{n1}\Gamma(-1) - \cdots - \Phi_{nn}\Gamma(-n). \end{aligned} \tag{7.5.7}$$

Remark 5. The innovations algorithm also has a multivariate version that can be used for prediction in much the same way as the univariate version described in Section 2.5.2 (for details see TSTM, Proposition 11.4.2). □

7.6 Modeling and Forecasting with Multivariate AR Processes

If $\{\mathbf{X}_t\}$ is any zero-mean second-order multivariate time series, it is easy to show from the results of Section 7.5 (Problem 7.4) that the one-step prediction errors $\mathbf{X}_j - \hat{\mathbf{X}}_j$, $j = 1, \ldots, n$, have the property

$$E\left(\mathbf{X}_j - \hat{\mathbf{X}}_j\right)\left(\mathbf{X}_k - \hat{\mathbf{X}}_k\right)' = 0 \text{ for } j \neq k. \tag{7.6.1}$$

Moreover, the matrix M such that

$$\begin{bmatrix} \mathbf{X}_1 - \hat{\mathbf{X}}_1 \\ \mathbf{X}_2 - \hat{\mathbf{X}}_2 \\ \mathbf{X}_3 - \hat{\mathbf{X}}_3 \\ \vdots \\ \mathbf{X}_n - \hat{\mathbf{X}}_n \end{bmatrix} = M \begin{bmatrix} \mathbf{X}_1 \\ \mathbf{X}_2 \\ \mathbf{X}_3 \\ \vdots \\ \mathbf{X}_n \end{bmatrix} \tag{7.6.2}$$

is lower triangular with ones on the diagonal and therefore has determinant equal to 1.

If the series $\{\mathbf{X}_t\}$ is also Gaussian, then (7.6.1) implies that the prediction errors $\mathbf{U}_j = \mathbf{X}_j - \hat{\mathbf{X}}_j$, $j = 1, \ldots, n$, are independent with covariance matrices $V_0, \ldots, V_{n-1}$, respectively (as specified in (7.5.7)). Consequently, the joint density of the prediction errors is the product

$$f(\mathbf{u}_1, \ldots, \mathbf{u}_n) = (2\pi)^{-nm/2}\left(\prod_{j=1}^{n} \det V_{j-1}\right)^{-1/2} \exp\left[-\frac{1}{2}\sum_{j=1}^{n} \mathbf{u}_j' V_{j-1}^{-1}\mathbf{u}_j\right].$$

Since the determinant of the matrix M in (7.6.2) is equal to 1, the joint density of the observations $\mathbf{X}_1, \ldots, \mathbf{X}_n$ at $\mathbf{x}_1, \ldots, \mathbf{x}_n$ is obtained on replacing $\mathbf{u}_1, \ldots, \mathbf{u}_n$ in the last expression by the values of $\mathbf{X}_j - \hat{\mathbf{X}}_j$ corresponding to the observations $\mathbf{x}_1, \ldots, \mathbf{x}_n$.

If we suppose that $\{\mathbf{X}_t\}$ is a zero-mean m-variate AR(p) process with coefficient matrices $\mathbf{\Phi} = \{\Phi_1, \ldots, \Phi_p\}$ and white noise covariance matrix Σ, we can therefore express the likelihood of the observations $\mathbf{X}_1, \ldots, \mathbf{X}_n$ as

$$L(\mathbf{\Phi}, \Sigma) = (2\pi)^{-nm/2}\left(\prod_{j=1}^{n} \det V_{j-1}\right)^{-1/2} \exp\left[-\frac{1}{2}\sum_{j=1}^{n} \mathbf{U}_j' V_{j-1}^{-1}\mathbf{U}_j\right],$$

where $\mathbf{U}_j = \mathbf{X}_j - \hat{\mathbf{X}}_j$, $j = 1, \ldots, n$, and $\hat{\mathbf{X}}_j$ and V_j are found from (7.5.4), (7.5.6), and (7.5.7).

Maximization of the Gaussian likelihood is much more difficult in the multivariate than in the univariate case because of the potentially large number of parameters involved and the fact that it is not possible to compute the maximum likelihood estimator of Φ independently of Σ as in the univariate case. In principle, maximum likelihood estimators can be computed with the aid of efficient nonlinear optimization algorithms, but it is important to begin the search with preliminary estimates that are reasonably close to the maximum. For pure AR processes good preliminary estimates can be obtained using Whittle's algorithm or a multivariate version of Burg's algorithm given by Jones (1978). We shall restrict our discussion here to the use of Whittle's algorithm (the multivariate option `AR-Model>Estimation>Yule-Walker` in ITSM), but Jones's multivariate version of Burg's algorithm is also available (`AR-Model>Estimation>Burg`). Other useful algorithms can be found in Lütkepohl (1993), in particular the method of conditional least squares and the method of Hannan and Rissanen (1982), the latter being useful also for preliminary estimation in the more difficult problem of fitting ARMA(p, q) models with $q > 0$. Spectral methods of estimation for multivariate ARMA processes are also frequently used. A discussion of these (as well as some time-domain methods) is given in Anderson (1980).

Order selection for multivariate autoregressive models can be made by minimizing a multivariate analogue of the univariate AICC statistic

$$\text{AICC} = -2\ln L(\Phi_1, \ldots, \Phi_p, \Sigma) + \frac{2(pm^2+1)nm}{nm - pm^2 - 2}. \tag{7.6.3}$$

7.6.1 Estimation for Autoregressive Processes Using Whittle's Algorithm

If $\{\mathbf{X}_t\}$ is the (causal) multivariate AR(p) process defined by the difference equations

$$\mathbf{X}_t = \Phi_1\mathbf{X}_{t-1} + \cdots + \Phi_p\mathbf{X}_{t-p} + \mathbf{Z}_t, \quad \{\mathbf{Z}_t\} \sim \text{WN}(\mathbf{0}, \Sigma), \tag{7.6.4}$$

then postmultiplying by $\mathbf{X}'_{t-j}$, $j = 0, \ldots, p$, and taking expectations gives the equations

$$\Sigma = \Gamma(0) - \sum_{j=1}^{p} \Phi_j\Gamma(-j) \tag{7.6.5}$$

and

$$\Gamma(i) = \sum_{j=1}^{n} \Phi_j\Gamma(i-j), \quad i = 1, \ldots, p. \tag{7.6.6}$$

Given the matrices $\Gamma(0), \ldots, \Gamma(p)$, equations (7.6.6) can be used to determine the coefficient matrices $\Phi_1, \ldots, \Phi_p$. The white noise covariance matrix Σ can then be found from (7.6.5). The solution of these equations for $\Phi_1, \ldots, \Phi_p$, and Σ is identical to the solution of (7.5.6) and (7.5.7) for the prediction coefficient matrices $\Phi_{p1}, \ldots, \Phi_{pp}$ and the corresponding prediction error covariance matrix V_p. Consequently, Whittle's algorithm can be used to carry out the algebra.

The Yule–Walker estimators $\hat{\Phi}_1, \ldots, \hat{\Phi}_p$, and $\hat{\Sigma}$ for the model (7.6.4) fitted to the data $\mathbf{X}_1, \ldots, \mathbf{X}_n$ are obtained by replacing $\Gamma(j)$ in (7.6.5) and (7.6.6) by $\hat{\Gamma}(j)$, $j = 0, \ldots, p$, and solving the resulting equations for $\Phi_1, \ldots, \Phi_p$, and Σ. The solution of these equations is obtained from ITSM by selecting the multivariate option `AR-Model>Estimation>Yule-Walker`. The mean vector of the fitted model is the sample mean of the data, and Whittle's algorithm is used to solve the equations (7.6.5) and (7.6.6) for the coefficient matrices and the white noise covariance matrix. The fitted model is displayed by ITSM in the form

$$\mathbf{X}_t = \phi_0 + \Phi_1 \mathbf{X}_{t-1} + \cdots + \Phi_p \mathbf{X}_{t-p} + \mathbf{Z}_t, \quad \{\mathbf{Z}_t\} \sim \mathrm{WN}(\mathbf{0}, \Sigma).$$

Note that the mean μ of this model is not the vector ϕ_0, but

$$\mu = (I - \Phi_1 - \cdots - \Phi_p)^{-1}\phi_0.$$

In fitting multivariate autoregressive models using ITSM, check the box `Find minimum AICC model` to find the AR(p) model with $0 \le p \le 20$ that minimizes the AICC value as defined in (7.6.3).

Analogous calculations using Jones's multivariate version of Burg's algorithm can be carried out by selecting `AR-Model>Estimation>Burg`.

Example 7.6.1 The Dow Jones and All Ordinaries Indices

To find the minimum AICC Yule–Walker model (of order less than or equal to 20) for the bivariate series $\{(X_{t1}, X_{t2})', t = 1, \ldots, 250\}$ of Example 7.1.1, proceed as follows. Select `File>Project>Open>Multivariate`, click `OK`, and then double-click on the file name, DJAOPC2.TSM. Check that `Number of columns` is set to 2, the dimension of the observation vectors, and click `OK` again to see graphs of the two component time series. No differencing is required (recalling from Example 7.1.1 that $\{X_{t1}\}$ and $\{X_{t2}\}$ are the daily percentage price changes of the original Dow Jones and All Ordinaries Indices). Select `AR-Model>Estimation>Yule-Walker`, check the box `Find minimum AICC Model`, click `OK`, and you will obtain the model

$$\begin{bmatrix} X_{t1} \\ X_{t2} \end{bmatrix} = \begin{bmatrix} .0288 \\ .00836 \end{bmatrix} + \begin{bmatrix} -.0148 & .0357 \\ .6589 & .0998 \end{bmatrix} \begin{bmatrix} X_{t-1,1} \\ X_{t-1,2} \end{bmatrix} + \begin{bmatrix} Z_{t1} \\ Z_{t2} \end{bmatrix},$$

where

$$\begin{bmatrix} Z_{t1} \\ Z_{t2} \end{bmatrix} \sim \mathrm{WN}\left(\begin{bmatrix} 0 \\ 0 \end{bmatrix}, \begin{bmatrix} .3653 & .0224 \\ .0224 & .6016 \end{bmatrix} \right).$$

□

Example 7.6.2 Sales with a leading indicator

The series $\{Y_{t1}\}$ (leading indicator) and $\{Y_{t2}\}$ (sales) are stored in bivariate form (Y_{t1} in column 1 and Y_{t2} in column 2) in the file LS2.TSM. On opening this file in ITSM you will see the graphs of the two component time series. Inspection of the graphs immediately suggests, as in Example 7.2.2, that the differencing operator

$\nabla = 1 - B$ should be applied to the data before a stationary AR model is fitted. Select `Transform>Difference` and specify 1 for the differencing lag. Click `OK` and you will see the graphs of the two differenced series. Inspection of the series and their correlation functions (obtained by pressing the second yellow button at the top of the ITSM window) suggests that no further differencing is necessary. The next step is to select `AR-model>Estimation>Yule-Walker` with the option `Find minimum AICC model`. The resulting model has order $p = 5$ and parameters $\phi_0 = (.0328\ \ .0156)'$,

$$\hat{\Phi}_1 = \begin{bmatrix} -.517 & .024 \\ -.019 & -.051 \end{bmatrix}, \hat{\Phi}_2 = \begin{bmatrix} -.192 & -.018 \\ .047 & .250 \end{bmatrix}, \hat{\Phi}_3 = \begin{bmatrix} -.073 & .010 \\ 4.678 & .207 \end{bmatrix},$$

$$\hat{\Phi}_4 = \begin{bmatrix} -.032 & -.009 \\ 3.664 & .004 \end{bmatrix}, \hat{\Phi}_5 = \begin{bmatrix} .022 & .011 \\ 1.300 & .029 \end{bmatrix}, \hat{\Sigma} = \begin{bmatrix} .076 & -.003 \\ -.003 & .095 \end{bmatrix},$$

with AICC=109.49. (Analogous calculations using Burg's algorithm give an AR(8) model for the differenced series.) The sample cross-correlations of the residual vectors $\hat{\mathbf{Z}}_t$ can be plotted by clicking on the last blue button at the top of the ITSM window. These are nearly all within the bounds $\pm 1.96/\sqrt{n}$, suggesting that the model is a good fit. The components of the residual vectors themselves are plotted by selecting `AR Model>Residual Analysis>Plot Residuals`. Simulated observations from the fitted model can be generated using the option `AR Model>Simulate`. The fitted model has the interesting property that the upper right component of each of the coefficient matrices is close to zero. This suggests that $\{X_{t1}\}$ can be effectively modeled independently of $\{X_{t2}\}$. In fact, the MA(1) model

$$X_{t1} = (1 - .474B)U_t, \quad \{U_t\} \sim \mathrm{WN}(0, .0779), \tag{7.6.7}$$

provides an adequate fit to the univariate series $\{X_{t1}\}$. Inspecting the bottom rows of the coefficient matrices and deleting small entries, we find that the relation between $\{X_{t1}\}$ and $\{X_{t2}\}$ can be expressed approximately as

$$X_{t2} = .250X_{t-2,2} + .207X_{t-3,2} + 4.678X_{t-3,1} + 3.664X_{t-4,1} + 1.300X_{t-5,1} + W_t,$$

or equivalently,

$$X_{t2} = \frac{4.678B^3(1 + .783B + .278B^2)}{1 - .250B^2 - .207B^3} X_{t1} + \frac{W_t}{1 - .250B^2 - .207B^3}, \tag{7.6.8}$$

where $\{W_t\} \sim \mathrm{WN}(0, .095)$. Moreover, since the estimated noise covariance matrix is essentially diagonal, it follows that the two sequences $\{X_{t1}\}$ and $\{W_t\}$ are uncorrelated. This reduced model defined by (7.6.7) and (7.6.8) is an example of a transfer function model that expresses the "output" series $\{X_{t2}\}$ as the output of a linear filter with "input" $\{X_{t1}\}$ plus added noise. A more direct approach to the fitting of transfer function models is given in Section 10.1 and applied to this same data set. □

7.6.2 Forecasting Multivariate Autoregressive Processes

The technique developed in Section 7.5 allows us to compute the minimum mean squared error one-step linear predictors $\hat{\mathbf{X}}_{n+1}$ for any multivariate stationary time series from the mean $\boldsymbol{\mu}$ and autocovariance matrices $\Gamma(h)$ by recursively determining the coefficients Φ_{ni}, $i = 1, \ldots, n$, and evaluating

$$\hat{\mathbf{X}}_{n+1} = \boldsymbol{\mu} + \Phi_{n1}(\mathbf{X}_n - \boldsymbol{\mu}) + \cdots + \Phi_{nn}(\mathbf{X}_1 - \boldsymbol{\mu}). \tag{7.6.9}$$

The situation is simplified when $\{\mathbf{X}_t\}$ is the causal AR(p) process defined by (7.6.4), since for $n \geq p$ (as is almost always the case in practice)

$$\hat{\mathbf{X}}_{n+1} = \Phi_1 \mathbf{X}_n + \cdots + \Phi_p \mathbf{X}_{n+1-p}. \tag{7.6.10}$$

To verify (7.6.10) it suffices to observe that the right-hand side has the required form (7.5.2) and that the prediction error

$$\mathbf{X}_{n+1} - \Phi_1 \mathbf{X}_n - \cdots - \Phi_p \mathbf{X}_{n+1-p} = \mathbf{Z}_{n+1}$$

is orthogonal to $\mathbf{X}_1, \ldots, \mathbf{X}_n$ in the sense of (7.5.3). (In fact, the prediction error is orthogonal to *all* $\mathbf{X}_j$, $-\infty < j \leq n$, showing that if $n \geq p$, then (7.6.10) is also the best linear predictor of $\mathbf{X}_{n+1}$ in terms of all components of $\mathbf{X}_j$, $-\infty < j \leq n$.) The covariance matrix of the one-step prediction error is clearly $E(\mathbf{Z}_{n+1}\mathbf{Z}'_{n+1}) = \Sigma$.

To compute the best h-step linear predictor $P_n \mathbf{X}_{n+h}$ based on all the components of $\mathbf{X}_1, \ldots, \mathbf{X}_n$ we apply the linear operator P_n to (7.6.4) to obtain the recursions

$$P_n \mathbf{X}_{n+h} = \Phi_1 P_n \mathbf{X}_{n+h-1} + \cdots + \Phi_p P_n \mathbf{X}_{n+h-p}. \tag{7.6.11}$$

These equations are easily solved recursively, first for $P_n \mathbf{X}_{n+1}$, then for $P_n \mathbf{X}_{n+2}$, $P_n \mathbf{X}_{n+3}$, ..., etc. If $n \geq p$, then the h-step predictors based on all components of $\mathbf{X}_j$, $-\infty < j \leq n$, also satisfy (7.6.11) and are therefore the same as the h-step predictors based on $\mathbf{X}_1, \ldots, \mathbf{X}_n$.

To compute the h-step error covariance matrices, recall from (7.4.6) that

$$\mathbf{X}_{n+h} = \sum_{j=0}^{\infty} \Psi_j \mathbf{Z}_{n+h-j}, \tag{7.6.12}$$

where the coefficient matrices Ψ_j are found from the recursions (7.4.8) with $q = 0$. From (7.6.12) we find that for $n \geq p$,

$$P_n \mathbf{X}_{n+h} = \sum_{j=h}^{\infty} \Psi_j \mathbf{Z}_{n+h-j}. \tag{7.6.13}$$

Subtracting (7.6.13) from (7.6.12) gives the h-step prediction error

$$\mathbf{X}_{n+h} - P_n \mathbf{X}_{n+h} = \sum_{j=0}^{h-1} \Psi_j \mathbf{Z}_{n+h-j}, \tag{7.6.14}$$

with covariance matrix

$$E\left[(\mathbf{X}_{n+h} - P_n\mathbf{X}_{n+h})(\mathbf{X}_{n+h} - P_n\mathbf{X}_{n+h})'\right] = \sum_{j=0}^{h-1} \Psi_j \Sigma \Psi_j', \quad n \geq p. \tag{7.6.15}$$

For the (not necessarily zero-mean) causal AR(p) process defined by

$$\mathbf{X}_t = \phi_0 + \Phi_1\mathbf{X}_{t-1} + \cdots + \Phi_p\mathbf{X}_{t-p} + \mathbf{Z}_t, \quad \{\mathbf{Z}_t\} \sim \text{WN}(\mathbf{0}, \Sigma),$$

equations (7.6.10) and (7.6.11) remain valid, provided that μ_0 is added to each of their right-hand sides. The error covariance matrices are the same as in the case $\phi_0 = \mathbf{0}$.

The above calculations are all based on the assumption that the AR(p) model for the series is known. However, in practice, the parameters of the model are usually estimated from the data, and the uncertainty in the predicted values of the series will be larger than indicated by (7.6.15) because of parameter estimation errors. See Lütkepohl (1993).

Example 7.6.3 The Dow Jones and All Ordinaries Indices

The VAR(1) model fitted to the series $\{\mathbf{X}_t, t = 1, \ldots, 250\}$ in Example 7.6.1 was

$$\begin{bmatrix} X_{t1} \\ X_{t2} \end{bmatrix} = \begin{bmatrix} .0288 \\ .00836 \end{bmatrix} + \begin{bmatrix} -.0148 & .0357 \\ .6589 & .0998 \end{bmatrix} \begin{bmatrix} X_{t-1,1} \\ X_{t-1,2} \end{bmatrix} + \begin{bmatrix} Z_{t1} \\ Z_{t2} \end{bmatrix},$$

where

$$\begin{bmatrix} Z_{t1} \\ Z_{t2} \end{bmatrix} \sim \text{WN}\left(\begin{bmatrix} 0 \\ 0 \end{bmatrix}, \begin{bmatrix} .3653 & .0224 \\ .0224 & .6016 \end{bmatrix}\right).$$

The one-step mean squared error for prediction of X_{t2}, assuming the validity of this model, is thus 0.6016. This is a substantial reduction from the estimated mean squared error $\hat{\gamma}_{22}(0) = .7712$ when the sample mean $\hat{\mu}_2 = .0309$ is used as the one-step predictor.

If we fit a univariate model to the series $\{X_{t2}\}$ using ITSM, we find that the autoregression with minimum AICC value (645.0) is

$$X_{t2} = .0273 + .1180X_{t-1,2} + Z_t, \quad \{Z_t\} \sim \text{WN}(0, .7604).$$

Assuming the validity of this model, we thus obtain a mean squared error for one-step prediction of .7604, which is slightly less than the estimated mean squared error (.7712) incurred when the sample mean is used for one-step prediction.

The preceding calculations suggest that there is little to be gained from the point of view of one-step prediction by fitting a univariate model to $\{X_{t2}\}$, while there is a substantial reduction achieved by the bivariate AR(1) model for $\{\mathbf{X}_t = (X_{t1}, X_{t2})'\}$.

To test the models fitted above, we consider the next forty values $\{\mathbf{X}_t, t = 251, \ldots, 290\}$, which are stored in the file DJAOPCF.TSM. We can use these values, in conjunction with the bivariate and univariate models fitted to the data for

$t = 1, \ldots, 250$, to compute one-step predictors of X_{t2}, $t = 251, \ldots, 290$. The results are as follows:

Predictor	Average Squared Error
$\hat{\mu} = 0.0309$	.4706
AR(1)	.4591
VAR(1)	.3962

It is clear from these results that the sample variance of the series $\{X_{t2}, t = 251, \ldots, 290\}$ is rather less than that of the series $\{X_{t2}, t = 1, \ldots, 250\}$, and consequently, the average squared errors of all three predictors are substantially less than expected from the models fitted to the latter series. Both the AR(1) and VAR(1) models show an improvement in one-step average squared error over the sample mean $\hat{\mu}$, but the improvement shown by the bivariate model is much more pronounced. □

The calculation of predictors and their error covariance matrices for multivariate ARIMA and SARIMA processes is analogous to the corresponding univariate calculation, so we shall simply state the pertinent results. Suppose that $\{\mathbf{Y}_t\}$ is a nonstationary process satisfying $D(B)\mathbf{Y}_t = \mathbf{U}_t$ where $D(z) = 1 - d_1 z - \cdots - d_r z^r$ is a polynomial with $D(1) = 0$ and $\{\mathbf{U}_t\}$ is a causal invertible ARMA process with mean $\boldsymbol{\mu}$. Then $\mathbf{X}_t = \mathbf{U}_t - \boldsymbol{\mu}$ satisfies

$$\Phi(B)\mathbf{X}_t = \Theta(B)\mathbf{Z}_t, \quad \{\mathbf{Z}_t\} \sim \mathrm{WN}(\mathbf{0}, \Sigma). \tag{7.6.16}$$

Under the assumption that the random vectors $\mathbf{Y}_{-r+1}, \ldots, \mathbf{Y}_0$ are uncorrelated with the sequence $\{\mathbf{Z}_t\}$, the best linear predictors $\tilde{P}_n\mathbf{Y}_j$ of $\mathbf{Y}_j$, $j > n > 0$, based on 1 and the components of $\mathbf{Y}_j$, $-r+1, \leq j \leq n$, are found as follows. Compute the observed values of $\mathbf{U}_t = D(B)\mathbf{Y}_t$, $t = 1, \ldots, n$, and use the ARMA model for $\mathbf{X}_t = \mathbf{U}_t - \boldsymbol{\mu}$ to compute predictors $P_n\mathbf{U}_{n+h}$. Then use the recursions

$$\tilde{P}_n\mathbf{Y}_{n+h} = P_n\mathbf{U}_{n+h} + \sum_{j=1}^{r} d_j \tilde{P}_n\mathbf{Y}_{n+h-j} \tag{7.6.17}$$

to compute successively $\tilde{P}_n\mathbf{Y}_{n+1}$, $\tilde{P}_n\mathbf{Y}_{n+2}$, $\tilde{P}_n\mathbf{Y}_{n+3}$, etc. The error covariance matrices are approximately (for large n)

$$E\left[(\mathbf{Y}_{n+h} - \tilde{P}_n\mathbf{Y}_{n+h})(\mathbf{Y}_{n+h} - \tilde{P}_n\mathbf{Y}_{n+h})'\right] = \sum_{j=0}^{h-1} \Psi_j^* \Sigma \Psi_j^{*\prime}, \tag{7.6.18}$$

where Ψ_j^* is the coefficient of z^j in the power series expansion

$$\sum_{j=0}^{\infty} \Psi_j^* z^j = D(z)^{-1}\Phi^{-1}(z)\Theta(z), \quad |z| < 1.$$

The matrices Ψ_j^* are most readily found from the recursions (7.4.8) after replacing Φ_j, $j = 1, \ldots, p$, by Φ_j^*, $j = 1, \ldots, p + r$, where Φ_j^* is the coefficient of z^j in $D(z)\Phi(z)$.

Remark 6. In the special case where $\Theta(z) = I$ (i.e., in the purely autoregressive case) the expression (7.6.18) for the h-step error covariance matrix is exact for all $n \geq p$ (i.e., if there are at least $p + r$ observed vectors) . The program ITSM allows differencing transformations and subtraction of the mean before fitting a multivariate autoregression. Predicted values for the original series and the standard deviations of the prediction errors can be determined using the multivariate option `Forecasting>AR Model`. □

Remark 7. In the multivariate case, simple differencing of the type discussed in this section where the same operator $D(B)$ is applied to all components of the random vectors is rather restrictive. It is useful to consider more general linear transformations of the data for the purpose of generating a stationary series. Such considerations lead to the class of **cointegrated models** discussed briefly in Section 7.7 below. □

Example 7.6.4 Sales with a leading indicator

Assume that the model fitted to the bivariate series $\{\mathbf{Y}_t, t = 0, \ldots, 149\}$ in Example 7.6.2 is correct, i.e., that

$$\Phi(B)\mathbf{X}_t = \mathbf{Z}_t, \quad \{\mathbf{Z}_t\} \sim \text{WN}\left(\mathbf{0}, \hat{\Sigma}\right),$$

where

$$\mathbf{X}_t = (1 - B)\mathbf{Y}_t - (.0228, .420)', \quad t = 1, \ldots, 149,$$

$\Phi(B) = I - \hat{\Phi}_1 B - \cdots - \hat{\Phi}_5 B^5$, and $\hat{\Phi}_1, \ldots, \hat{\Phi}_5, \hat{\Sigma}$ are the matrices found in Example 7.6.2. Then the one- and two-step predictors of $\mathbf{X}_{150}$ and $\mathbf{X}_{151}$ are obtained from (7.6.11) as

$$P_{149}\mathbf{X}_{150} = \hat{\Phi}_1\mathbf{X}_{149} + \cdots + \hat{\Phi}_5\mathbf{X}_{145} = \begin{bmatrix} .163 \\ -.217 \end{bmatrix}$$

and

$$P_{149}\mathbf{X}_{151} = \hat{\Phi}_1 P_{149}\mathbf{X}_{150} + \hat{\Phi}_2\mathbf{X}_{149} + \cdots + \hat{\Phi}_5\mathbf{X}_{146} = \begin{bmatrix} -.027 \\ .816 \end{bmatrix}$$

with error covariance matrices, from (7.6.15),

$$\hat{\Sigma} = \begin{bmatrix} .076 & -.003 \\ -.003 & .095 \end{bmatrix}$$

and

$$\hat{\Sigma} + \hat{\Phi}_1\hat{\Sigma}\hat{\Phi}_1' = \begin{bmatrix} .096 & -.002 \\ -.002 & .095 \end{bmatrix},$$

respectively.

Similarly, the one- and two-step predictors of $\mathbf{Y}_{150}$ and $\mathbf{Y}_{151}$ are obtained from (7.6.17) as

$$\tilde{P}_{149}\mathbf{Y}_{150} = \begin{bmatrix} .0228 \\ .420 \end{bmatrix} + P_{149}\mathbf{X}_{150} + \mathbf{Y}_{149} = \begin{bmatrix} 13.59 \\ 262.90 \end{bmatrix}$$

and

$$\tilde{P}_{149}\mathbf{Y}_{151} = \begin{bmatrix} .0228 \\ .420 \end{bmatrix} + P_{149}\mathbf{X}_{151} + \tilde{P}_{149}\mathbf{Y}_{150} = \begin{bmatrix} 13.59 \\ 264.14 \end{bmatrix}$$

with error covariance matrices, from (7.6.18),

$$\hat{\Sigma} = \begin{bmatrix} .076 & -.003 \\ -.003 & .095 \end{bmatrix}$$

and

$$\hat{\Sigma} + \left(I + \hat{\Phi}_1\right)\hat{\Sigma}\left(I + \hat{\Phi}_1\right)' = \begin{bmatrix} .094 & -.003 \\ -.003 & .181 \end{bmatrix},$$

respectively. The predicted values and the standard deviations of the predictors can easily be verified with the aid of the program ITSM. It is also of interest to compare the results with those obtained by fitting a transfer function model to the data as described in Section 10.1 below. □

7.7 Cointegration

We have seen that nonstationary univariate time series can frequently be made stationary by applying the differencing operator $\nabla = 1 - B$ repeatedly. If $\{\nabla^d X_t\}$ is stationary for some positive integer d but $\{\nabla^{d-1} X_t\}$ is nonstationary, we say that $\{X_t\}$ is **integrated of order *d***, or more concisely, $\{X_t\} \sim I(d)$. Many macroeconomic time series are found to be integrated of order 1.

If $\{\mathbf{X}_t\}$ is a k-variate time series, we define $\{\nabla^d \mathbf{X}_t\}$ to be the series whose jth component is obtained by applying the operator $(1-B)^d$ to the jth component of $\{\mathbf{X}_t\}$, $j = 1, \ldots, k$. The idea of a cointegrated multivariate time series was introduced by Granger (1981) and developed by Engle and Granger (1987). Here we use the slightly different definition of Lütkepohl (1993). We say that the k-dimensional time series $\{\mathbf{X}_t\}$ is integrated of order d (or $\{\mathbf{X}_t\} \sim I(d)$) if d is a positive integer, $\{\nabla^d \mathbf{X}_t\}$ is stationary, and $\{\nabla^{d-1} \mathbf{X}_t\}$ is nonstationary. The $I(d)$ process $\{\mathbf{X}_t\}$ is said to be **cointegrated with cointegration vector** $\boldsymbol{\alpha}$ if α is a $k \times 1$ vector such that $\{\alpha' \mathbf{X}_t\}$ is of order less than d.

Example 7.7.1

A simple example is provided by the bivariate process whose first component is the random walk

$$X_t = \sum_{j=1}^{t} Z_j, \quad t = 1, 2, \ldots, \quad \{Z_t\} \sim \text{IID}\left(0, \sigma^2\right),$$

and whose second component consists of noisy observations of the same random walk,

$$Y_t = X_t + W_t, \quad t = 1, 2, \ldots, \quad \{W_t\} \sim \text{IID}\left(0, \tau^2\right),$$

where $\{W_t\}$ is independent of $\{Z_t\}$. Then $\{(X_t, Y_t)'\}$ is integrated of order 1 and cointegrated with cointegration vector $\boldsymbol{\alpha} = (1, -1)'$.

The notion of cointegration captures the idea of univariate nonstationary time series "moving together." Thus, even though $\{X_t\}$ and $\{Y_t\}$ in Example 7.7.1 are both nonstationary, they are linked in the sense that they differ only by the stationary sequence $\{W_t\}$. Series that behave in a cointegrated manner are often encountered in economics. Engle and Granger (1991) give as an illustrative example the prices of tomatoes U_t and V_t in Northern and Southern California. These are linked by the fact that if one were to increase sufficiently relative to the other, the profitability of buying in one market and selling for a profit in the other would tend to push the prices $(U_t, V_t)'$ toward the straight line $v = u$ in $\mathbb{R}^2$. This line is said to be an **attractor** for $(U_t, V_t)'$, since although U_t and V_t may both vary in a nonstationary manner as t increases, the points $(U_t, V_t)'$ will exhibit relatively small random deviations from the line $v = u$. □

Example 7.7.2

If we apply the operator $\nabla = 1 - B$ to the bivariate process defined in Example 7.7.1 in order to render it stationary, we obtain the series $(U_t, V_t)'$, where

$$U_t = Z_t$$

and

$$V_t = Z_t + W_t - W_{t-1}.$$

The series $\{(U_t, V_t)'\}$ is clearly a stationary multivariate MA(1) process

$$\begin{bmatrix} U_t \\ V_t \end{bmatrix} = \begin{bmatrix} 1 & 0 \\ 0 & 1 \end{bmatrix} \begin{bmatrix} Z_t \\ Z_t + W_t \end{bmatrix} - \begin{bmatrix} 0 & 0 \\ -1 & 1 \end{bmatrix} \begin{bmatrix} Z_{t-1} \\ Z_{t-1} + W_{t-1} \end{bmatrix}.$$

However, the process $\{(U_t, V_t)'\}$ cannot be represented as an AR(∞) process, since the matrix $\left[\begin{smallmatrix} 1 & 0 \\ 0 & 1 \end{smallmatrix}\right] - z\left[\begin{smallmatrix} 0 & 0 \\ -1 & 1 \end{smallmatrix}\right]$ has zero determinant when $z = 1$, thus violating condition (7.4.10). Care is therefore needed in the estimation of parameters for such models (and the closely related error-correction models). We shall not go into the details here but refer the reader to Engle and Granger (1987) and Lütkepohl (1993). □

Problems

7.1. Let $\{Y_t\}$ be a stationary process and define the bivariate process $X_{t1} = Y_t$, $X_{t2} = Y_{t-d}$, where $d \neq 0$. Show that $\{(X_{t1}, X_{t2})'\}$ is stationary and express its cross-correlation function in terms of the autocorrelation function of $\{Y_t\}$. If $\rho_Y(h) \to 0$ as $h \to \infty$, show that there exists a lag k for which $\rho_{12}(k) > \rho_{12}(0)$.

7.2. Show that the covariance matrix function of the multivariate linear process defined by (7.2.12) is as specified in (7.2.13).

7.3. Let $\{\mathbf{X}_t\}$ be the bivariate time series whose components are the MA(1) processes defined by

$$X_{t1} = Z_{t,1} + .8Z_{t-1,1}, \quad \{Z_{t1}\} \sim \text{IID}\left(0, \sigma_1^2\right),$$

and

$$X_{t2} = Z_{t,2} - .6Z_{t-1,2}, \quad \{Z_{t2}\} \sim \text{IID}\left(0, \sigma_2^2\right),$$

where the two sequences $\{Z_{t1}\}$ and $\{Z_{t2}\}$ are independent.

a. Find a large-sample approximation to the variance of $n^{1/2}\hat{\rho}_{12}(h)$.

b. Find a large-sample approximation to the covariance of $n^{1/2}\hat{\rho}_{12}(h)$ and $n^{1/2}\hat{\rho}_{12}(k)$ for $h \neq k$.

7.4. Use the characterization (7.5.3) of the multivariate best linear predictor of $\mathbf{Y}$ in terms of $\{\mathbf{X}_1, \ldots \mathbf{X}_n\}$ to establish the orthogonality of the one-step prediction errors $\mathbf{X}_j - \hat{\mathbf{X}}_j$ and $\mathbf{X}_k - \hat{\mathbf{X}}_k$, $j \neq k$, as asserted in (7.6.1).

7.5. Determine the covariance matrix function of the ARMA(1,1) process satisfying

$$\mathbf{X}_t - \Phi\mathbf{X}_{t-1} = \mathbf{Z}_t + \Theta\mathbf{Z}_{t-1}, \quad \{\mathbf{Z}_t\} \sim \text{WN}(\mathbf{0}, I_2),$$

where I_2 is the 2×2 identity matrix and $\Phi = \Theta' = \begin{bmatrix} 0.5 & 0.5 \\ 0 & 0.5 \end{bmatrix}$.

7.6. a. Let $\{\mathbf{X}_t\}$ be a causal AR(p) process satisfying the recursions

$$\mathbf{X}_t = \Phi_1\mathbf{X}_{t-1} + \cdots + \Phi_p\mathbf{X}_{t-p} + \mathbf{Z}_t, \quad \{\mathbf{Z}_t\} \sim \text{WN}(\mathbf{0}, \Sigma).$$

For $n \geq p$ write down recursions for the predictors $P_n\mathbf{X}_{n+h}$, $h \geq 0$, and find explicit expressions for the error covariance matrices in terms of the AR coefficients and Σ when $h = 1, 2$, and 3.

b. Suppose now that $\{\mathbf{Y}_t\}$ is the multivariate ARIMA($p, 1, 0$) process satisfying $\nabla\mathbf{Y}_t = \mathbf{X}_t$, where $\{\mathbf{X}_t\}$ is the AR process in (a). Assuming that $E(\mathbf{Y}_0\mathbf{X}_t') = 0$, for $t \geq 1$, show (using (7.6.17) with $r = 1$ and $d = 1$) that

$$\tilde{P}_n(\mathbf{Y}_{n+h}) = \mathbf{Y}_n + \sum_{j=1}^{h} P_n\mathbf{X}_{n+j},$$

and derive the error covariance matrices when $h = 1, 2$, and 3. Compare these results with those obtained in Example 7.6.4.

7.7. Use the program ITSM to find the minimum AICC AR model of order less than or equal to 20 for the bivariate series $\{(X_{t1}, X_{t2})', t = 1, \ldots, 200\}$ with components filed as APPJK2.TSM. Use the fitted model to predict $(X_{t1}, X_{t2})'$, $t = 201, 202, 203$ and estimate the error covariance matrices of the predictors (assuming that the fitted model is appropriate for the data).

7.8. Let $\{X_{t1}, t = 1, \ldots, 63\}$ and $\{X_{t2}, t = 1, \ldots, 63\}$ denote the differenced series $\{\nabla \ln Y_{t1}\}$ and $\{\nabla \ln Y_{t2}\}$, where $\{Y_{t1}\}$ and $\{Y_{t2}\}$ are the annual mink and muskrat trappings filed as APPH.TSM and APPI.TSM, respectively).

a. Use ITSM to construct and save the series $\{X_{t1}\}$ and $\{X_{t2}\}$ as univariate data files X1.TSM and X2.TSM, respectively. (After making the required transformations press the red EXP button and save each transformed series to a file with the appropriate name.) To enter X1 and X2 as a bivariate series in ITSM, open X1 as a multivariate series with `Number of columns` equal to 1. Then open X2 as a univariate series. Click the project editor button (at the top left of the ITSM window), click on the plus signs next to the projects X1.TSM and X2.TSM, then click on the series that appears just below X2.TSM and drag it to the first line of the project X1.TSM. It will then be added as a second component, making X1.TSM a bivariate project consisting of the two component series X1 and X2. Click `OK` to close the project editor and close the ITSM window labeled X2.TSM. You will then see the graphs of X1 and X2. Press the second yellow button to see the correlation functions of $\{X_{t1}\}$ and $\{X_{t2}\}$. For more information on the project editor in ITSM select `Help>Contents>Project Editor`.

b. Conduct a for independence of the two series $\{X_{t1}\}$ and $\{X_{t1}\}$.

7.9. Use ITSM to open the data file STOCK7.TSM, which contains the daily returns on seven different stock market indices from April 27th, 1998, through April 9th, 1999. (Click on `Help>Contents>Data sets` for more information.) Fit a multivariate autoregression to the trivariate series consisting of the returns on the Dow Jones Industrials, All Ordinaries, and Nikkei indices. Check the model for goodness of fit and interpret the results.

8 State-Space Models

In recent years state-space representations and the associated Kalman recursions have had a profound impact on time series analysis and many related areas. The techniques were originally developed in connection with the control of linear systems (for accounts of this subject see Davis and Vinter, 1985, and Hannan and Deistler, 1988). An extremely rich class of models for time series, including and going well beyond the linear ARIMA and classical decomposition models considered so far in this book, can be formulated as special cases of the general state-space model defined below in Section 8.1. In econometrics the structural time series models developed by Harvey (1990) are formulated (like the classical decomposition model) directly in terms of components of interest such as trend, seasonal component, and noise. However, the rigidity of the classical decomposition model is avoided by allowing the trend and seasonal components to evolve randomly rather than deterministically. An introduction to these structural models is given in Section 8.2, and a state-space representation is developed for a general ARIMA process in Section 8.3. The Kalman recursions, which play a key role in the analysis of state-space models, are derived in Section 8.4. These recursions allow a unified approach to prediction and estimation for all processes that can be given a state-space representation. Following the development of the Kalman recursions we discuss estimation with structural models (Section 8.5) and the formulation of state-space models to deal with missing values (Section 8.6). In Section 8.7 we introduce the EM algorithm, an iterative procedure for maximizing the likelihood when only a subset of the complete data set is available. The EM algorithm is particularly well suited for estimation problems in the state-space framework. Generalized state-space models are introduced in Section 8.8. These are Bayesian models that can be used to represent time series of many different types, as demonstrated by two applications to time series of count data. Throughout the chapter we shall use the notation

$$\{\mathbf{W}_t\} \sim \mathrm{WN}(\mathbf{0}, \{R_t\})$$

to indicate that the random vectors $\mathbf{W}_t$ have mean $\mathbf{0}$ and that

$$E\left(\mathbf{W}_s\mathbf{W}_t'\right) = \begin{cases} R_t, & \text{if } s = t, \\ 0, & \text{otherwise.} \end{cases}$$

8.1 State-Space Representations

A state-space model for a (possibly multivariate) time series $\{\mathbf{Y}_t, t = 1, 2, \ldots\}$ consists of two equations. The first, known as the **observation equation**, expresses the w-dimensional observation $\mathbf{Y}_t$ as a linear function of a v-dimensional state variable $\mathbf{X}_t$ plus noise. Thus

$$\mathbf{Y}_t = G_t\mathbf{X}_t + \mathbf{W}_t, \quad t = 1, 2, \ldots, \tag{8.1.1}$$

where $\{\mathbf{W}_t\} \sim \mathrm{WN}(\mathbf{0}, \{R_t\})$ and $\{G_t\}$ is a sequence of $w \times v$ matrices. The second equation, called the **state equation**, determines the state $\mathbf{X}_{t+1}$ at time $t + 1$ in terms of the previous state $\mathbf{X}_t$ and a noise term. The state equation is

$$\mathbf{X}_{t+1} = F_t\mathbf{X}_t + \mathbf{V}_t, \quad t = 1, 2, \ldots, \tag{8.1.2}$$

where $\{F_t\}$ is a sequence of $v \times v$ matrices, $\{\mathbf{V}_t\} \sim \mathrm{WN}(\mathbf{0}, \{Q_t\})$, and $\{\mathbf{V}_t\}$ is uncorrelated with $\{\mathbf{W}_t\}$ (i.e., $E(\mathbf{W}_t\mathbf{V}_s') = 0$ for all s and t). To complete the specification, it is assumed that the initial state $\mathbf{X}_1$ is uncorrelated with all of the noise terms $\{\mathbf{V}_t\}$ and $\{\mathbf{W}_t\}$.

Remark 1. A more general form of the state-space model allows for correlation between $\mathbf{V}_t$ and $\mathbf{W}_t$ (see TSTM, Chapter 12) and for the addition of a control term $H_t\mathbf{u}_t$ in the state equation. In control theory, $H_t\mathbf{u}_t$ represents the effect of applying a "control" $\mathbf{u}_t$ at time t for the purpose of influencing $\mathbf{X}_{t+1}$. However, the system defined by (8.1.1) and (8.1.2) with $E\left(\mathbf{W}_t\mathbf{V}_s'\right) = 0$ for all s and t will be adequate for our purposes. □

Remark 2. In many important special cases, the matrices F_t, G_t, Q_t, and R_t will be independent of t, in which case the subscripts will be suppressed. □

Remark 3. It follows from the observation equation (8.1.1) and the state equation (8.1.2) that $\mathbf{X}_t$ and $\mathbf{Y}_t$ have the functional forms, for $t = 2, 3, \ldots$,

$$\begin{aligned} \mathbf{X}_t &= F_{t-1}\mathbf{X}_{t-1} + \mathbf{V}_{t-1} \\ &= F_{t-1}(F_{t-2}\mathbf{X}_{t-2} + \mathbf{V}_{t-2}) + \mathbf{V}_{t-1} \\ &\ \vdots \\ &= (F_{t-1}\cdots F_1)\mathbf{X}_1 + (F_{t-1}\cdots F_2)\mathbf{V}_1 + \cdots + F_{t-1}\mathbf{V}_{t-2} + \mathbf{V}_{t-1} \\ &= f_t(\mathbf{X}_1, \mathbf{V}_1, \ldots, \mathbf{V}_{t-1}) \end{aligned} \tag{8.1.3}$$

and

$$\mathbf{Y}_t = g_t(\mathbf{X}_1, \mathbf{V}_1, \ldots, \mathbf{V}_{t-1}, \mathbf{W}_t). \tag{8.1.4}$$

□

Remark 4. From Remark 3 and the assumptions on the noise terms, it is clear that

$$E\left(\mathbf{V}_t\mathbf{X}_s'\right) = 0, \qquad E\left(\mathbf{V}_t\mathbf{Y}_s'\right) = 0, \quad 1 \le s \le t,$$

and

$$E\left(\mathbf{W}_t\mathbf{X}_s'\right) = 0, \quad 1 \le s \le t, \qquad E(\mathbf{W}_t\mathbf{Y}_s') = 0, \quad 1 \le s < t.$$ □

Definition 8.1.1

A time series $\{\mathbf{Y}_t\}$ has a **state-space representation** if there exists a state-space model for $\{\mathbf{Y}_t\}$ as specified by equations (8.1.1) and (8.1.2).

As already indicated, it is possible to find a state-space representation for a large number of time-series (and other) models. It is clear also from the definition that neither $\{\mathbf{X}_t\}$ nor $\{\mathbf{Y}_t\}$ is necessarily stationary. The beauty of a state-space representation, when one can be found, lies in the simple structure of the state equation (8.1.2), which permits relatively simple analysis of the process $\{\mathbf{X}_t\}$. The behavior of $\{\mathbf{Y}_t\}$ is then easy to determine from that of $\{\mathbf{X}_t\}$ using the observation equation (8.1.1). If the sequence $\{\mathbf{X}_1, \mathbf{V}_1, \mathbf{V}_2, \ldots\}$ is independent, then $\{\mathbf{X}_t\}$ has the Markov property; i.e., the distribution of $\mathbf{X}_{t+1}$ given $\mathbf{X}_t, \ldots, \mathbf{X}_1$ is the same as the distribution of $\mathbf{X}_{t+1}$ given $\mathbf{X}_t$. This is a property possessed by many physical systems, provided that we include sufficiently many components in the specification of the state $\mathbf{X}_t$ (for example, we may choose the state vector in such a way that $\mathbf{X}_t$ includes components of $\mathbf{X}_{t-1}$ for each t).

Example 8.1.1 An AR(1) process

Let $\{Y_t\}$ be the causal AR(1) process given by

$$Y_t = \phi Y_{t-1} + Z_t, \quad \{Z_t\} \sim \mathrm{WN}\left(0, \sigma^2\right). \tag{8.1.5}$$

In this case, a state-space representation for $\{Y_t\}$ is easy to construct. We can, for example, define a sequence of state variables X_t by

$$X_{t+1} = \phi X_t + V_t, \quad t = 1, 2, \ldots, \tag{8.1.6}$$

where $X_1 = Y_1 = \sum_{j=0}^{\infty} \phi^j Z_{1-j}$ and $V_t = Z_{t+1}$. The process $\{Y_t\}$ then satisfies the observation equation

$$Y_t = X_t,$$

which has the form (8.1.1) with $G_t = 1$ and $W_t = 0$. □

Example 8.1.2 An ARMA(1,1) process

Let $\{Y_t\}$ be the causal and invertible ARMA(1,1) process satisfying the equations

$$Y_t = \phi Y_{t-1} + Z_t + \theta Z_{t-1}, \quad \{Z_t\} \sim \mathrm{WN}\left(0, \sigma^2\right). \tag{8.1.7}$$

Although the existence of a state-space representation for $\{Y_t\}$ is not obvious, we can find one by observing that

$$Y_t = \theta(B) X_t = \begin{bmatrix} \theta & 1 \end{bmatrix} \begin{bmatrix} X_{t-1} \\ X_t \end{bmatrix}, \tag{8.1.8}$$

where $\{X_t\}$ is the causal AR(1) process satisfying

$$\phi(B) X_t = Z_t,$$

or the equivalent equation

$$\begin{bmatrix} X_t \\ X_{t+1} \end{bmatrix} = \begin{bmatrix} 0 & 1 \\ 0 & \phi \end{bmatrix} \begin{bmatrix} X_{t-1} \\ X_t \end{bmatrix} + \begin{bmatrix} 0 \\ Z_{t+1} \end{bmatrix}. \tag{8.1.9}$$

Noting that $X_t = \sum_{j=0}^{\infty} \phi^j Z_{t-j}$, we see that equations (8.1.8) and (8.1.9) for $t = 1, 2, \ldots$ furnish a state-space representation of $\{Y_t\}$ with

$$\mathbf{X}_t = \begin{bmatrix} X_{t-1} \\ X_t \end{bmatrix} \text{ and } \mathbf{X}_1 = \begin{bmatrix} \sum_{j=0}^{\infty} \phi^j Z_{-j} \\ \sum_{j=0}^{\infty} \phi^j Z_{1-j} \end{bmatrix}.$$

The extension of this state-space representation to general ARMA and ARIMA processes is given in Section 8.3. □

In subsequent sections we shall give examples that illustrate the versatility of state-space models. (More examples can be found in Aoki, 1987, Hannan and Deistler, 1988, Harvey, 1990, and West and Harrison, 1989.) Before considering these, we need a slight modification of (8.1.1) and (8.1.2), which allows for series in which the time index runs from $-\infty$ to ∞. This is a more natural formulation for many time series models.

State-Space Models with $t \in \{0, \pm 1, \ldots\}$

Consider the observation and state equations

$$\mathbf{Y}_t = G\mathbf{X}_t + \mathbf{W}_t, \quad t = 0, \pm 1, \ldots, \tag{8.1.10}$$

$$\mathbf{X}_{t+1} = F\mathbf{X}_t + \mathbf{V}_t, \quad t = 0, \pm 1, \ldots, \tag{8.1.11}$$

where F and G are $v \times v$ and $w \times v$ matrices, respectively, $\{\mathbf{V}_t\} \sim \mathrm{WN}(\mathbf{0}, Q)$, $\{\mathbf{W}_t\} \sim \mathrm{WN}(\mathbf{0}, R)$, and $E(\mathbf{V}_s\mathbf{W}_t') = 0$ for all s, and t.

The state equation (8.1.11) is said to be **stable** if the matrix F has all its eigenvalues in the interior of the unit circle, or equivalently if $\det(I - Fz) \neq 0$ for all z complex such that $|z| \leq 1$. The matrix F is then also said to be stable.

In the stable case the equations (8.1.11) have the unique stationary solution (Problem 8.1) given by

$$\mathbf{X}_t = \sum_{j=0}^{\infty} F^j \mathbf{V}_{t-j-1}.$$

The corresponding sequence of observations

$$\mathbf{Y}_t = \mathbf{W}_t + \sum_{j=0}^{\infty} GF^j \mathbf{V}_{t-j-1}$$

is also stationary.

8.2 The Basic Structural Model

A structural time series model, like the classical decomposition model defined by (1.5.1), is specified in terms of components such as trend, seasonality, and noise, which are of direct interest in themselves. The deterministic nature of the trend and seasonal components in the classical decomposition model, however, limits its applicability. A natural way in which to overcome this deficiency is to permit random variation in these components. This can be very conveniently done in the framework of a state-space representation, and the resulting rather flexible model is called a structural model. Estimation and forecasting with this model can be encompassed in the general procedure for state-space models made possible by the Kalman recursions of Section 8.4.

Example 8.2.1 The random walk plus noise model

One of the simplest structural models is obtained by adding noise to a random walk. It is suggested by the nonseasonal classical decomposition model

$$Y_t = M_t + W_t, \quad \text{where } \{W_t\} \sim \mathrm{WN}\left(0, \sigma_w^2\right), \tag{8.2.1}$$

and $M_t = m_t$, the deterministic "level" or "signal" at time t. We now introduce randomness into the level by supposing that M_t is a random walk satisfying

$$M_{t+1} = M_t + V_t, \quad \text{and} \quad \{V_t\} \sim \text{WN}\left(0, \sigma_v^2\right), \tag{8.2.2}$$

with initial value $M_1 = m_1$. Equations (8.2.1) and (8.2.2) constitute the "local level" or "random walk plus noise" model. Figure 8.1 shows a realization of length 100 of this model with $M_1 = 0, \sigma_v^2 = 4$, and $\sigma_w^2 = 8$. (The realized values m_t of M_t are plotted as a solid line, and the observed data are plotted as square boxes.) The differenced data

$$D_t := \nabla Y_t = Y_t - Y_{t-1} = V_{t-1} + W_t - W_{t-1}, \quad t \geq 2,$$

constitute a stationary time series with mean 0 and ACF

$$\rho_D(h) = \begin{cases} \dfrac{-\sigma_w^2}{2\sigma_w^2 + \sigma_v^2}, & \text{if } |h| = 1, \\ 0, & \text{if } |h| > 1. \end{cases}$$

Since $\{D_t\}$ is 1-correlated, we conclude from Proposition 2.1.1 that $\{D_t\}$ is an MA(1) process and hence that $\{Y_t\}$ is an ARIMA(0,1,1) process. More specifically,

$$D_t = Z_t + \theta Z_{t-1}, \quad \{Z_t\} \sim \text{WN}\left(0, \sigma^2\right), \tag{8.2.3}$$

where θ and σ^2 are found by solving the equations

$$\frac{\theta}{1+\theta^2} = \frac{-\sigma_w^2}{2\sigma_w^2 + \sigma_v^2} \quad \text{and} \quad \theta\sigma^2 = -\sigma_w^2.$$

For the process $\{Y_t\}$ generating the data in Figure 8.1, the parameters θ and σ^2 of

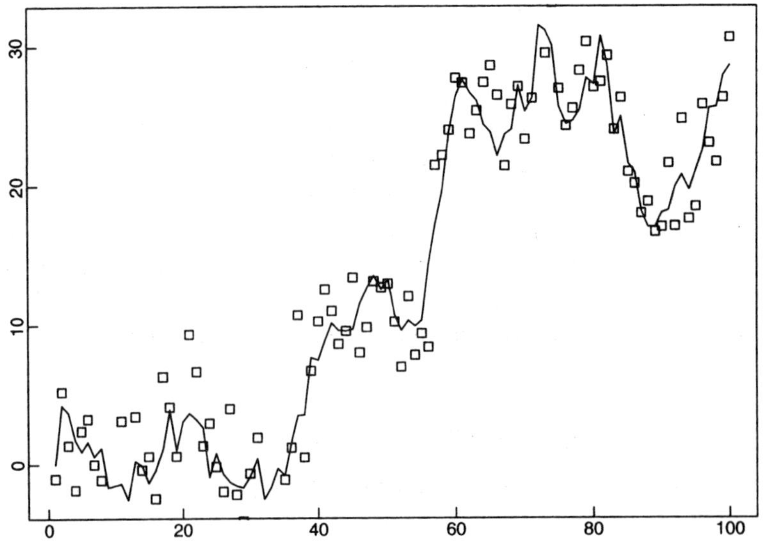

Figure 8-1 Realization from a random walk plus noise model. The random walk is represented by the solid line and the data are represented by boxes.

the differenced series $\{D_t\}$ satisfy $\theta/(1+\theta^2) = -.4$ and $\theta\sigma^2 = -8$. Solving these equations for θ and σ^2, we find that $\theta = -.5$ and $\sigma^2 = 16$ (or $\theta = -2$ and $\sigma^2 = 4$). The sample ACF of the observed differences D_t of the realization of $\{Y_t\}$ in Figure 8.1 is shown in Figure 8.2.

The local level model is often used to represent a measured characteristic of the output of an industrial process for which the unobserved process level $\{M_t\}$ is intended to be within specified limits (to meet the design specifications of the manufactured product). To decide whether or not the process requires corrective attention, it is important to be able to test the hypothesis that the process level $\{M_t\}$ is constant. From the state equation, we see that $\{M_t\}$ is constant (and equal to m_1) when $V_t = 0$ or equivalently when $\sigma_v^2 = 0$. This in turn is equivalent to the moving-average model (8.2.3) for $\{D_t\}$ being noninvertible with $\theta = -1$ (see Problem 8.2). Tests of the unit root hypothesis $\theta = -1$ were discussed in Section 6.3.2. □

The local level model can easily be extended to incorporate a locally linear trend with slope β_t at time t. Equation (8.2.2) is replaced by

$$M_t = M_{t-1} + B_{t-1} + V_{t-1}, \tag{8.2.4}$$

where $B_{t-1} = \beta_{t-1}$. Now if we introduce randomness into the slope by replacing it with the random walk

$$B_t = B_{t-1} + U_{t-1}, \quad \text{where } \{U_t\} \sim \text{WN}\left(0, \sigma_u^2\right), \tag{8.2.5}$$

we obtain the "local linear trend" model.

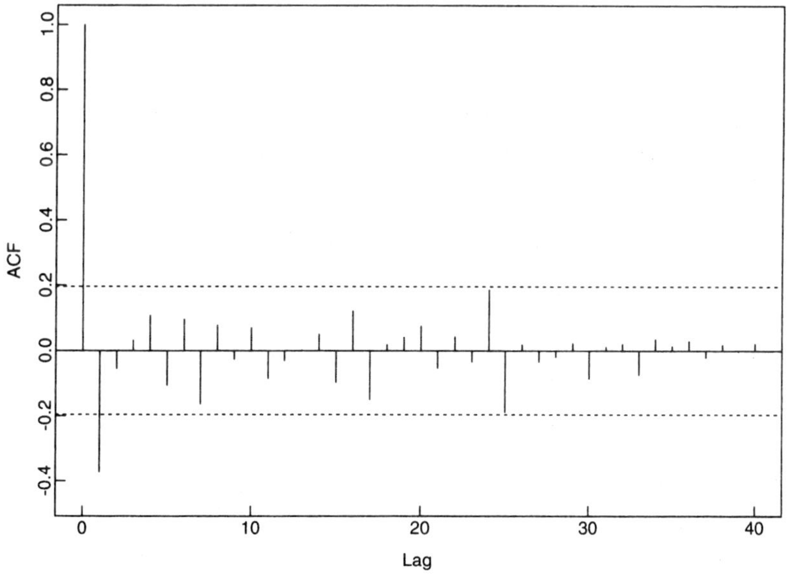

Figure 8-2 Sample ACF of the series obtained by differencing the data in Figure 8.1.

To express the local linear trend model in state-space form we introduce the state vector

$$\mathbf{X}_t = (M_t, B_t)'.$$

Then (8.2.4) and (8.2.5) can be written in the equivalent form

$$\mathbf{X}_{t+1} = \begin{bmatrix} 1 & 1 \\ 0 & 1 \end{bmatrix} \mathbf{X}_t + \mathbf{V}_t, \quad t = 1, 2, \ldots, \tag{8.2.6}$$

where $\mathbf{V}_t = (V_t, U_t)'$. The process $\{Y_t\}$ is then determined by the observation equation

$$Y_t = [1 \quad 0]\, \mathbf{X}_t + W_t. \tag{8.2.7}$$

If $\{\mathbf{X}_1, U_1, V_1, W_1, U_2, V_2, W_2, \ldots\}$ is an uncorrelated sequence, then equations (8.2.6) and (8.2.7) constitute a state-space representation of the process $\{Y_t\}$, which is a model for data with randomly varying trend and added noise. For this model we have $v = 2$, $w = 1$,

$$F = \begin{bmatrix} 1 & 1 \\ 0 & 1 \end{bmatrix}, \quad G = [1 \quad 0], \quad Q = \begin{bmatrix} \sigma_v^2 & 0 \\ 0 & \sigma_u^2 \end{bmatrix}, \quad \text{and } R = \sigma_w^2.$$

Example 8.2.2 A seasonal series with noise

The classical decomposition (1.5.11) expressed the time series $\{X_t\}$ as a sum of trend, seasonal, and noise components. The seasonal component (with period d) was a sequence $\{s_t\}$ with the properties $s_{t+d} = s_t$ and $\sum_{t=1}^{d} s_t = 0$. Such a sequence can be generated, for *any* values of $s_1, s_0, \ldots, s_{-d+3}$, by means of the recursions

$$s_{t+1} = -s_t - \cdots - s_{t-d+2}, \quad t = 1, 2, \ldots. \tag{8.2.8}$$

A somewhat more general seasonal component $\{Y_t\}$, allowing for random deviations from strict periodicity, is obtained by adding a term S_t to the right side of (8.2.8), where $\{V_t\}$ is white noise with mean zero. This leads to the recursion relations

$$Y_{t+1} = -Y_t - \cdots - Y_{t-d+2} + S_t, \quad t = 1, 2, \ldots. \tag{8.2.9}$$

To find a state-space representation for $\{Y_t\}$ we introduce the $(d-1)$-dimensional state vector

$$\mathbf{X}_t = (Y_t, Y_{t-1}, \ldots, Y_{t-d+2})'.$$

The series $\{Y_t\}$ is then given by the observation equation

$$Y_t = [1 \quad 0 \quad 0 \cdots 0]\, \mathbf{X}_t, \quad t = 1, 2, \ldots, \tag{8.2.10}$$

where $\{\mathbf{X}_t\}$ satisfies the state equation

$$\mathbf{X}_{t+1} = F\mathbf{X}_t + \mathbf{V}_t, \quad t = 1, 2 \ldots, \tag{8.2.11}$$

$\mathbf{V}_t = (S_t, 0, \ldots, 0)'$, and

$$F = \begin{bmatrix} -1 & -1 & \cdots & -1 & -1 \\ 1 & 0 & \cdots & 0 & 0 \\ 0 & 1 & \cdots & 0 & 0 \\ \vdots & \vdots & \ddots & \vdots & \vdots \\ 0 & 0 & \cdots & 1 & 0 \end{bmatrix}. \quad \square$$

Example 8.2.3 A randomly varying trend with random seasonality and noise

A series with randomly varying trend, random seasonality and noise can be constructed by adding the two series in Examples 8.2.1 and 8.2.2. (Addition of series with state-space representations is in fact always possible by means of the following construction. See Problem 8.9.) We introduce the state vector

$$\mathbf{X}_t = \begin{bmatrix} \mathbf{X}_t^1 \\ \mathbf{X}_t^2 \end{bmatrix},$$

where $\mathbf{X}_t^1$ and $\mathbf{X}_t^2$ are the state vectors in (8.2.6) and (8.2.11). We then have the following representation for $\{Y_t\}$, the sum of the two series whose state-space representations were given in (8.2.6)–(8.2.7) and (8.2.10)–(8.2.11). The state equation is

$$\mathbf{X}_{t+1} = \begin{bmatrix} F_1 & 0 \\ 0 & F_2 \end{bmatrix} \mathbf{X}_t + \begin{bmatrix} \mathbf{V}_t^1 \\ \mathbf{V}_t^2 \end{bmatrix}, \tag{8.2.12}$$

where F_1, F_2 are the coefficient matrices and $\{\mathbf{V}_t^1\}$, $\{\mathbf{V}_t^2\}$ are the noise vectors in the state equations (8.2.6) and (8.2.11), respectively. The observation equation is

$$Y_t = [1 \quad 0 \quad 1 \quad 0 \cdots 0]\,\mathbf{X}_t + W_t, \tag{8.2.13}$$

where $\{W_t\}$ is the noise sequence in (8.2.7). If the sequence of random vectors $\{\mathbf{X}_1, \mathbf{V}_1^1, \mathbf{V}_1^2, W_1, \mathbf{V}_2^1, \mathbf{V}_2^2, W_2, \ldots\}$ is uncorrelated, then equations (8.2.12) and (8.2.13) constitute a state-space representation for $\{Y_t\}$. □

8.3 State-Space Representation of ARIMA Models

We begin by establishing a state-space representation for the causal AR(p) process and then build on this example to find representations for the general ARMA and ARIMA processes.

Example 8.3.1 State-space representation of a causal AR(p) process

Consider the AR(p) process defined by

$$Y_{t+1} = \phi_1 Y_t + \phi_2 Y_{t-1} + \cdots + \phi_p Y_{t-p+1} + Z_{t+1}, \quad t = 0, \pm 1, \ldots, \tag{8.3.1}$$

where $\{Z_t\} \sim \mathrm{WN}(0, \sigma^2)$, and $\phi(z) := 1 - \phi_1 z - \cdots - \phi_p z^p$ is nonzero for $|z| \le 1$. To express $\{Y_t\}$ in state-space form we simply introduce the state vectors

$$\mathbf{X}_t = \begin{bmatrix} Y_{t-p+1} \\ Y_{t-p+2} \\ \vdots \\ Y_t \end{bmatrix}, \quad t = 0, \pm 1, \ldots. \tag{8.3.2}$$

From (8.3.1) and (8.3.2) the observation equation is

$$Y_t = [0 \quad 0 \quad 0 \cdots 1]\mathbf{X}_t, \quad t = 0, \pm 1, \ldots, \tag{8.3.3}$$

while the state equation is given by

$$\mathbf{X}_{t+1} = \begin{bmatrix} 0 & 1 & 0 & \cdots & 0 \\ 0 & 0 & 1 & \cdots & 0 \\ \vdots & \vdots & \vdots & \ddots & \vdots \\ 0 & 0 & 0 & \cdots & 1 \\ \phi_p & \phi_{p-1} & \phi_{p-2} & \cdots & \phi_1 \end{bmatrix} \mathbf{X}_t + \begin{bmatrix} 0 \\ 0 \\ \vdots \\ 0 \\ 1 \end{bmatrix} Z_{t+1}, \quad t = 0, \pm 1, \ldots. \tag{8.3.4}$$

These equations have the required forms (8.1.10) and (8.1.11) with $\mathbf{W}_t = \mathbf{0}$ and $\mathbf{V}_t = (0, 0, \ldots, Z_{t+1})'$, $t = 0, \pm 1, \ldots$. □

Remark 1. In Example 8.3.1 the causality condition $\phi(z) \ne 0$ for $|z| \le 1$ is equivalent to the condition that the state equation (8.3.4) is stable, since the eigenvalues of the coefficient matrix in (8.3.4) are simply the reciprocals of the zeros of $\phi(z)$ (Problem 8.3). □

Remark 2. If equations (8.3.3) and (8.3.4) are postulated to hold only for $t = 1, 2, \ldots$, and if $\mathbf{X}_1$ is a random vector such that $\{\mathbf{X}_1, Z_1, Z_2, \ldots\}$ is an uncorrelated sequence, then we have a state-space representation for $\{Y_t\}$ of the type defined earlier by (8.1.1) and (8.1.2). The resulting process $\{Y_t\}$ is well-defined, regardless of whether or not the state equation is stable, but it will not in general be stationary. It will be stationary if the state equation is stable and if $\mathbf{X}_1$ is defined by (8.3.2) with $Y_t = \sum_{j=0}^{\infty} \psi_j Z_{t-j}$, $t = 1, 0, \ldots, 2 - p$, and $\psi(z) = 1/\phi(z)$, $|z| \le 1$. □

Example 8.3.2 State-space form of a causal ARMA(p, q) process

State-space representations are not unique. Here we shall give one of the (infinitely many) possible representations of a causal ARMA(p,q) process that can easily be derived from Example 8.3.1. Consider the ARMA(p,q) process defined by

$$\phi(B)Y_t = \theta(B)Z_t, \quad t = 0, \pm 1, \ldots, \tag{8.3.5}$$

where $\{Z_t\} \sim \mathrm{WN}(0, \sigma^2)$ and $\phi(z) \ne 0$ for $|z| \le 1$. Let

$$r = \max(p, q + 1), \quad \phi_j = 0 \quad \text{for } j > p, \quad \theta_j = 0 \quad \text{for } j > q, \quad \text{and} \quad \theta_0 = 1.$$

If $\{U_t\}$ is the causal AR(p) process satisfying

$$\phi(B)U_t = Z_t, \tag{8.3.6}$$

then $Y_t = \theta(B)U_t$, since

$$\phi(B)Y_t = \phi(B)\theta(B)U_t = \theta(B)\phi(B)U_t = \theta(B)Z_t.$$

Consequently,

$$Y_t = [\theta_{r-1} \quad \theta_{r-2} \quad \cdots \quad \theta_0]\mathbf{X}_t, \tag{8.3.7}$$

where

$$\mathbf{X}_t = \begin{bmatrix} U_{t-r+1} \\ U_{t-r+2} \\ \vdots \\ U_t \end{bmatrix}. \tag{8.3.8}$$

But from Example 8.3.1 we can write

$$\mathbf{X}_{t+1} = \begin{bmatrix} 0 & 1 & 0 & \cdots & 0 \\ 0 & 0 & 1 & \cdots & 0 \\ \vdots & \vdots & \vdots & \ddots & \vdots \\ 0 & 0 & 0 & \cdots & 1 \\ \phi_r & \phi_{r-1} & \phi_{r-2} & \cdots & \phi_1 \end{bmatrix} \mathbf{X}_t + \begin{bmatrix} 0 \\ 0 \\ \vdots \\ 0 \\ 1 \end{bmatrix} Z_{t+1}, \quad t = 0, \pm 1, \ldots. \tag{8.3.9}$$

Equations (8.3.7) and (8.3.9) are the required observation and state equations. As in Example 8.3.1, the observation and state noise vectors are again $\mathbf{W}_t = \mathbf{0}$ and $\mathbf{V}_t = (0, 0, \ldots, Z_{t+1})'$, $t = 0, \pm 1, \ldots$. □

Example 8.3.3 State-space representation of an ARIMA(p, d, q) process

If $\{Y_t\}$ is an ARIMA(p, d, q) process with $\{\nabla^d Y_t\}$ satisfying (8.3.5), then by the preceding example $\{\nabla^d Y_t\}$ has the representation

$$\nabla^d Y_t = G\mathbf{X}_t, \quad t = 0, \pm 1, \ldots, \tag{8.3.10}$$

where $\{\mathbf{X}_t\}$ is the unique stationary solution of the state equation

$$\mathbf{X}_{t+1} = F\mathbf{X}_t + \mathbf{V}_t,$$

F and G are the coefficients of $\mathbf{X}_t$ in (8.3.9) and (8.3.7), respectively, and $\mathbf{V}_t = (0, 0, \ldots, Z_{t+1})'$. Let A and B be the $d \times 1$ and $d \times d$ matrices defined by $A = B = 1$ if $d = 1$ and

$$A = \begin{bmatrix} 0 \\ 0 \\ \vdots \\ 0 \\ 1 \end{bmatrix}, \quad B = \begin{bmatrix} 0 & 1 & 0 & \cdots & 0 \\ 0 & 0 & 1 & \cdots & 0 \\ \vdots & \vdots & \vdots & \ddots & \vdots \\ 0 & 0 & 0 & \cdots & 1 \\ (-1)^{d+1}\binom{d}{d} & (-1)^{d}\binom{d}{d-1} & (-1)^{d-1}\binom{d}{d-2} & \cdots & d \end{bmatrix}$$

if $d > 1$. Then since

$$Y_t = \nabla^d Y_t - \sum_{j=1}^{d} \binom{d}{j} (-1)^j Y_{t-j}, \tag{8.3.11}$$

the vector

$$\mathbf{Y}_{t-1} := (Y_{t-d}, \dots, Y_{t-1})'$$

satisfies the equation

$$\mathbf{Y}_t = A\nabla^d Y_t + B\mathbf{Y}_{t-1} = AG\mathbf{X}_t + B\mathbf{Y}_{t-1}.$$

Defining a new state vector $\mathbf{T}_t$ by stacking $\mathbf{X}_t$ and $\mathbf{Y}_{t-1}$, we therefore obtain the state equation

$$\mathbf{T}_{t+1} := \begin{bmatrix} \mathbf{X}_{t+1} \\ \mathbf{Y}_t \end{bmatrix} = \begin{bmatrix} F & 0 \\ AG & B \end{bmatrix} \mathbf{T}_t + \begin{bmatrix} \mathbf{V}_t \\ \mathbf{0} \end{bmatrix}, \quad t = 1, 2, \dots, \tag{8.3.12}$$

and the observation equation, from (8.3.10) and (8.3.11),

$$Y_t = \begin{bmatrix} G & (-1)^{d+1}\binom{d}{d} & (-1)^d \binom{d}{d-1} & (-1)^{d-1}\binom{d}{d-2} & \cdots & d \end{bmatrix} \begin{bmatrix} \mathbf{X}_t \\ \mathbf{Y}_{t-1} \end{bmatrix},$$

$$t = 1, 2, \dots, \tag{8.3.13}$$

with initial condition

$$\mathbf{T}_1 = \begin{bmatrix} \mathbf{X}_1 \\ \mathbf{Y}_0 \end{bmatrix} = \begin{bmatrix} \sum_{j=0}^{\infty} F^j \mathbf{V}_{-j} \\ \mathbf{Y}_0 \end{bmatrix}, \tag{8.3.14}$$

and the assumption

$$E(\mathbf{Y}_0 Z_t') = 0, \quad t = 0, \pm 1, \dots, \tag{8.3.15}$$

where $\mathbf{Y}_0 = (Y_{1-d}, Y_{2-d}, \dots, Y_0)'$. The conditions (8.3.15), which are satisfied in particular if $\mathbf{Y}_0$ is considered to be nonrandom and equal to the vector of *observed* values $(y_{1-d}, y_{2-d}, \dots, y_0)'$, are imposed to ensure that the assumptions of a state-space model given in Section 8.1 are satisfied. They also imply that $E\left(\mathbf{X}_1 \mathbf{Y}_0'\right) = 0$ and $E(\mathbf{Y}_0 \nabla^d Y_t') = 0$, $t \geq 1$, as required earlier in Section 6.4 for prediction of ARIMA processes.

State-space models for more general ARIMA processes (e.g., $\{Y_t\}$ such that $\{\nabla\nabla_{12} Y_t\}$ is an ARMA(p, q) process) can be constructed in the same way. See Problem 8.4. □

For the ARIMA(1, 1, 1) process defined by

$$(1 - \phi B)(1 - B)Y_t = (1 + \theta B)Z_t, \quad \{Z_t\} \sim \mathrm{WN}\left(0, \sigma^2\right),$$

the vectors $\mathbf{X}_t$ and $\mathbf{Y}_{t-1}$ reduce to $\mathbf{X}_t = (X_{t-1}, X_t)'$ and $\mathbf{Y}_{t-1} = Y_{t-1}$. From (8.3.12) and (8.3.13) the state-space representation is therefore (Problem 8.8)

$$Y_t = \begin{bmatrix} \theta & 1 & 1 \end{bmatrix} \begin{bmatrix} X_{t-1} \\ X_t \\ Y_{t-1} \end{bmatrix}, \tag{8.3.16}$$

where

$$\begin{bmatrix} X_t \\ X_{t+1} \\ Y_t \end{bmatrix} = \begin{bmatrix} 0 & 1 & 0 \\ 0 & \phi & 0 \\ \theta & 1 & 1 \end{bmatrix} \begin{bmatrix} X_{t-1} \\ X_t \\ Y_{t-1} \end{bmatrix} + \begin{bmatrix} 0 \\ Z_{t+1} \\ 0 \end{bmatrix}, \quad t = 1, 2, \ldots, \tag{8.3.17}$$

and

$$\begin{bmatrix} X_0 \\ X_1 \\ Y_0 \end{bmatrix} = \begin{bmatrix} \sum_{j=0}^{\infty} \phi^j Z_{-j} \\ \sum_{j=0}^{\infty} \phi^j Z_{1-j} \\ Y_0 \end{bmatrix}. \tag{8.3.18}$$

8.4 The Kalman Recursions

In this section we shall consider three fundamental problems associated with the state-space model defined by (8.1.1) and (8.1.2) in Section 8.1. These are all concerned with finding best (in the sense of minimum mean square error) linear estimates of the state-vector $\mathbf{X}_t$ in terms of the observations $\mathbf{Y}_1, \mathbf{Y}_2, \ldots$, and a random vector $\mathbf{Y}_0$ that is orthogonal to $\mathbf{V}_t$ and $\mathbf{W}_t$ for all $t \geq 1$. In many cases $\mathbf{Y}_0$ will be the constant vector $(1, 1, \ldots, 1)'$. Estimation of $\mathbf{X}_t$ in terms of:

a. $\mathbf{Y}_0, \ldots, \mathbf{Y}_{t-1}$ defines the **prediction problem**,
b. $\mathbf{Y}_0, \ldots, \mathbf{Y}_t$ defines the **filtering problem**,
c. $\mathbf{Y}_0, \ldots, \mathbf{Y}_n$ $(n > t)$ defines the **smoothing problem**.

Each of these problems can be solved recursively using an appropriate set of Kalman recursions, which will be established in this section.

In the following definition of best linear predictor (and throughout this chapter) it should be noted that we do not automatically include the constant 1 among the predictor variables as we did in Sections 2.5 and 7.5. (It can, however, be included by choosing $\mathbf{Y}_0 = (1, 1, \ldots, 1)'$.)

Definition 8.4.1

For the random vector $\mathbf{X} = (X_1, \ldots, X_v)'$,

$$P_t(\mathbf{X}) := (P_t(X_1), \ldots, P_t(X_v))',$$

where $P_t(X_i) := P(X_i|\mathbf{Y}_0, \mathbf{Y}_1, \ldots, \mathbf{Y}_t)$, is the best linear predictor of X_i in terms of all components of $\mathbf{Y}_0, \mathbf{Y}_1, \ldots, \mathbf{Y}_t$.

Remark 1. By the definition of the best predictor of each component X_i of $\mathbf{X}$, $P_t(\mathbf{X})$ is the unique random vector of the form

$$P_t(\mathbf{X}) = A_0\mathbf{Y}_0 + \cdots + A_t\mathbf{Y}_t$$

with $v \times w$ matrices $A_0, \ldots, A_t$ such that

$$[\mathbf{X} - P_t(\mathbf{X})] \perp \mathbf{Y}_s, \quad s = 0, \ldots, t$$

(cf. (7.5.2) and (7.5.3)). Recall that two random vectors $\mathbf{X}$ and $\mathbf{Y}$ are orthogonal (written $\mathbf{X} \perp \mathbf{Y}$) if $E(\mathbf{X}\mathbf{Y}')$ is a matrix of zeros. □

Remark 2. If all the components of $\mathbf{X}, \mathbf{Y}_1, \ldots, \mathbf{Y}_t$ are jointly normally distributed and $\mathbf{Y}_0 = (1, \ldots, 1)'$, then

$$P_t(\mathbf{X}) = E(\mathbf{X}|\mathbf{Y}_1, \ldots, \mathbf{Y}_t), \quad t \geq 1.$$ □

Remark 3. P_t is linear in the sense that if A is any $k \times v$ matrix and $\mathbf{X}, \mathbf{V}$ are two v-variate random vectors with finite second moments, then (Problem 8.10)

$$P_t(A\mathbf{X}) = AP_t(\mathbf{X})$$

and

$$P_t(\mathbf{X} + \mathbf{V}) = P_t(\mathbf{X}) + P_t(\mathbf{V}).$$ □

Remark 4. If $\mathbf{X}$ and $\mathbf{Y}$ are random vectors with v and w components, respectively, each with finite second moments, then

$$P(\mathbf{X}|\mathbf{Y}) = M\mathbf{Y},$$

where M is a $v \times w$ matrix, $M = E(\mathbf{X}\mathbf{Y}')[E(\mathbf{Y}\mathbf{Y}')]^{-1}$ with $[E(\mathbf{Y}\mathbf{Y}')]^{-1}$ any generalized inverse of $E(\mathbf{Y}\mathbf{Y}')$. (A generalized inverse of a matrix S is a matrix S^{-1} such that $SS^{-1}S = S$. Every matrix has at least one. See Problem 8.11.)

In the notation just developed, the prediction, filtering, and smoothing problems (a), (b), and (c) formulated above reduce to the determination of $P_{t-1}(\mathbf{X}_t)$, $P_t(\mathbf{X}_t)$, and $P_n(\mathbf{X}_t)$ $(n > t)$, respectively. We deal first with the prediction problem. □

Kalman Prediction:

For the state-space model (8.1.1)–(8.1.2), the one-step predictors $\hat{\mathbf{X}}_t := P_{t-1}(\mathbf{X}_t)$ and their error covariance matrices $\Omega_t = E\left[(\mathbf{X}_t - \hat{\mathbf{X}}_t)(\mathbf{X}_t - \hat{\mathbf{X}}_t)'\right]$ are uniquely determined by the initial conditions

$$\hat{\mathbf{X}}_1 = P(\mathbf{X}_1|\mathbf{Y}_0), \qquad \Omega_1 = E\left[(\mathbf{X}_1 - \hat{\mathbf{X}}_1)(\mathbf{X}_1 - \hat{\mathbf{X}}_1)'\right]$$

and the recursions, for $t = 1, \ldots,$

$$\hat{\mathbf{X}}_{t+1} = F_t\hat{\mathbf{X}}_t + \Theta_t\Delta_t^{-1}\left(\mathbf{Y}_t - G_t\hat{\mathbf{X}}_t\right), \tag{8.4.1}$$

$$\Omega_{t+1} = F_t\Omega_t F_t' + Q_t - \Theta_t\Delta_t^{-1}\Theta_t', \tag{8.4.2}$$

where

$$\Delta_t = G_t\Omega_t G_t' + R_t,$$

$$\Theta_t = F_t\Omega_t G_t',$$

and Δ_t^{-1} is any generalized inverse of Δ_t.

Proof We shall make use of the **innovations** $\mathbf{I}_t$ defined by $\mathbf{I}_0 = \mathbf{Y}_0$ and

$$\mathbf{I}_t = \mathbf{Y}_t - P_{t-1}\mathbf{Y}_t = \mathbf{Y}_t - G_t\hat{\mathbf{X}}_t = G_t\left(\mathbf{X}_t - \hat{\mathbf{X}}_t\right) + \mathbf{W}_t, \quad t = 1, 2, \ldots.$$

The sequence $\{\mathbf{I}_t\}$ is orthogonal by Remark 1. Using Remarks 3 and 4 and the relation

$$P_t(\cdot) = P_{t-1}(\cdot) + P(\cdot|\mathbf{I}_t) \tag{8.4.3}$$

(see Problem 8.12), we find that

$$\begin{aligned}\hat{\mathbf{X}}_{t+1} &= P_{t-1}(\mathbf{X}_{t+1}) + P(\mathbf{X}_{t+1}|\mathbf{I}_t) = P_{t-1}(F_t\mathbf{X}_t + \mathbf{V}_t) + \Theta_t\Delta_t^{-1}\mathbf{I}_t \\ &= F_t\hat{\mathbf{X}}_t + \Theta_t\Delta_t^{-1}\mathbf{I}_t,\end{aligned} \tag{8.4.4}$$

where

$$\Delta_t = E(\mathbf{I}_t\,\mathbf{I}_t') = G_t\Omega_t G_t' + R_t,$$

$$\begin{aligned}\Theta_t &= E(\mathbf{X}_{t+1}\mathbf{I}_t') = E\left[(F_t\mathbf{X}_t + \mathbf{V}_t)\left(\left[\mathbf{X}_t - \hat{\mathbf{X}}_t\right]' G_t' + \mathbf{W}_t'\right)\right] \\ &= F_t\Omega_t G_t'.\end{aligned}$$

To verify (8.4.2), we observe from the definition of Ω_{t+1} that

$$\Omega_{t+1} = E\left(\mathbf{X}_{t+1}\mathbf{X}_{t+1}'\right) - E\left(\hat{\mathbf{X}}_{t+1}\hat{\mathbf{X}}_{t+1}'\right).$$

With (8.1.2) and (8.4.4) this gives

$$\Omega_{t+1} = F_t E(\mathbf{X}_t\mathbf{X}_t')F_t' + Q_t - F_t E\left(\hat{\mathbf{X}}_t\hat{\mathbf{X}}_t'\right) F_t' - \Theta_t\Delta_t^{-1}\Theta_t'$$

$$= F_t\Omega_t F_t' + Q_t - \Theta_t\Delta_t^{-1}\Theta_t'.$$

■

h-step Prediction of $\{\mathbf{Y}_t\}$ Using the Kalman Recursions

The Kalman prediction equations lead to a very simple algorithm for recursive calculation of the best linear mean square predictors $P_t\mathbf{Y}_{t+h}$, $h = 1, 2, \ldots$. From (8.4.4), (8.1.1), (8.1.2), and Remark 3 in Section 8.1, we find that

$$P_t\mathbf{X}_{t+1} = F_t P_{t-1}\mathbf{X}_t + \Theta_t\Delta_t^{-1}(\mathbf{Y}_t - P_{t-1}\mathbf{Y}_t), \tag{8.4.5}$$

$$\begin{aligned} P_t\mathbf{X}_{t+h} &= F_{t+h-1}P_t\mathbf{X}_{t+h-1} \\ &\ \vdots \\ &= (F_{t+h-1}F_{t+h-2}\cdots F_{t+1})\,P_t\mathbf{X}_{t+1}, \quad h = 2, 3, \ldots, \end{aligned} \tag{8.4.6}$$

and

$$P_t\mathbf{Y}_{t+h} = G_{t+h}P_t\mathbf{X}_{t+h}, \quad h = 1, 2, \ldots. \tag{8.4.7}$$

From the relation

$$\mathbf{X}_{t+h} - P_t\mathbf{X}_{t+h} = F_{t+h-1}(\mathbf{X}_{t+h-1} - P_t\mathbf{X}_{t+h-1}) + \mathbf{V}_{t+h-1}, \quad h = 2, 3, \ldots,$$

we find that $\Omega_t^{(h)} := E[(\mathbf{X}_{t+h} - P_t\mathbf{X}_{t+h})(\mathbf{X}_{t+h} - P_t\mathbf{X}_{t+h})']$ satisfies the recursions

$$\Omega_t^{(h)} = F_{t+h-1}\Omega_t^{(h-1)}F_{t+h-1}' + Q_{t+h-1}, \quad h = 2, 3, \ldots, \tag{8.4.8}$$

with $\Omega_t^{(1)} = \Omega_{t+1}$. Then from (8.1.1) and (8.4.7), $\Delta_t^{(h)} := E[(\mathbf{Y}_{t+h} - P_t\mathbf{Y}_{t+h})(\mathbf{Y}_{t+h} - P_t\mathbf{Y}_{t+h})']$ is given by

$$\Delta_t^{(h)} = G_{t+h}\Omega_t^{(h)}G_{t+h}' + R_{t+h}, \quad h = 1, 2, \ldots. \tag{8.4.9}$$

Example 8.4.1 Consider the random walk plus noise model of Example 8.2.1 defined by

$$Y_t = X_t + W_t, \quad \{W_t\} \sim \mathrm{WN}\left(0, \sigma_w^2\right),$$

where the local level X_t follows the random walk

$$X_{t+1} = X_t + V_t, \quad \{V_t\} \sim \mathrm{WN}\left(0, \sigma_v^2\right).$$

Applying the Kalman prediction equations with $Y_0 := 1$, $R = \sigma_w^2$, and $Q = \sigma_v^2$, we obtain

$$\begin{aligned} \hat{Y}_{t+1} = P_t Y_{t+1} &= \hat{X}_t + \frac{\Theta_t}{\Delta_t}\left(Y_t - \hat{Y}_t\right) \\ &= (1 - a_t)\hat{Y}_t + a_t Y_t \end{aligned}$$

where

$$a_t = \frac{\Theta_t}{\Delta_t} = \frac{\Omega_t}{\Omega_t + \sigma_w^2}.$$

For a state-space model (like this one) with time-independent parameters, the solution of the Kalman recursions (8.4.2) is called a **steady-state solution** if Ω_t is independent of t. If $\Omega_t = \Omega$ for all t, then from (8.4.2)

$$\Omega_{t+1} = \Omega = \Omega + \sigma_v^2 - \frac{\Omega^2}{\Omega + \sigma_w^2} = \frac{\Omega\sigma_w^2}{\Omega + \sigma_w^2} + \sigma_v^2.$$

Solving this quadratic equation for Ω and noting that $\Omega \geq 0$, we find that

$$\Omega = \frac{1}{2}\left(\sigma_v^2 + \sqrt{\sigma_v^4 + 4\sigma_v^2\sigma_w^2}\right)$$

Since $\Omega_{t+1} - \Omega_t$ is a continuous function of Ω_t on $\Omega_t \geq 0$, positive at $\Omega_t = 0$, negative for large Ω_t, and zero only at $\Omega_t = \Omega$, it is clear that $\Omega_{t+1} - \Omega_t$ is negative for $\Omega_t > \Omega$ and positive for $\Omega_t < \Omega$. A similar argument shows (Problem 8.14) that $(\Omega_{t+1} - \Omega)(\Omega_t - \Omega) \geq 0$ for all $\Omega_t \geq 0$. These observations imply that Ω_{t+1} always falls between Ω and Ω_t. Consequently, regardless of the value of Ω_1, Ω_t converges to Ω, the unique solution of $\Omega_{t+1} = \Omega_t$. For *any* initial predictors $\hat{Y}_1 = \hat{X}_1$ and any initial mean squared error $\Omega_1 = E\left(X_1 - \hat{X}_1\right)^2$, the coefficients $a_t := \Omega_t / \left(\Omega_t + \sigma_w^2\right)$ converge to

$$a = \frac{\Omega}{\Omega + \sigma_w^2},$$

and the mean squared errors of the predictors defined by

$$\hat{Y}_{t+1} = (1 - a_t)\hat{Y}_t + a_t Y_t$$

converge to $\Omega + \sigma_w^2$.

If, as is often the case, we do not know Ω_1, then we cannot determine the sequence $\{a_t\}$. It is natural, therefore, to consider the behavior of the predictors defined by

$$\hat{Y}_{t+1} = (1 - a)\hat{Y}_t + aY_t$$

with a as above and arbitrary $\hat{Y}_1$. It can be shown (Problem 8.16) that this sequence of predictors is also asymptotically optimal in the sense that the mean squared error converges to $\Omega + \sigma_w^2$ as $t \to \infty$.

As shown in Example 8.2.1, the differenced process $D_t = Y_t - Y_{t-1}$ is the MA(1) process

$$D_t = Z_t + \theta Z_{t-1}, \ \{Z_t\} \sim \text{WN}\left(0, \sigma^2\right),$$

where $\theta/\left(1+\theta^2\right) = -\sigma_w^2/\left(2\sigma_w^2+\sigma_v^2\right)$. Solving this equation for θ (Problem 8.15), we find that

$$\theta = -\frac{1}{2\sigma_w^2}\left(2\sigma_w^2+\sigma_v^2-\sqrt{\sigma_v^4+4\sigma_v^2\sigma_w^2}\right)$$

and that $\theta = a-1$.

It is instructive to derive the exponential smoothing formula for $\hat{Y}_t$ directly from the ARIMA(0,1,1) structure of $\{Y_t\}$. For $t \geq 2$, we have from Section 6.5 that

$$\hat{Y}_{t+1} = Y_t + \theta_{t1}(Y_t - \hat{Y}_t) = -\theta_{t1}\hat{Y}_t + (1+\theta_{t1})Y_t$$

for $t \geq 2$, where θ_{t1} is found by application of the innovations algorithm to an MA(1) process with coefficient θ. It follows that $1-a_t = -\theta_{t1}$, and since $\theta_{t1} \to \theta$ (see Remark 1 of Section 3.3) and a_t converges to the steady-state solution a, we conclude that

$$1-a = \lim_{t\to\infty}(1-a_t) = -\lim_{t\to\infty}\theta_{t1} = -\theta.$$

□

Kalman Filtering:

The filtered estimates $\mathbf{X}_{t|t} = P_t(\mathbf{X}_t)$ and their error covariance matrices $\Omega_{t|t} = E[(\mathbf{X}_t - \mathbf{X}_{t|t})(\mathbf{X}_t - \mathbf{X}_{t|t})']$ are determined by the relations

$$P_t\mathbf{X}_t = P_{t-1}\mathbf{X}_t + \Omega_t G_t'\Delta_t^{-1}\left(\mathbf{Y}_t - G_t\hat{\mathbf{X}}_t\right) \tag{8.4.10}$$

and

$$\Omega_{t|t} = \Omega_t - \Omega_t G_t'\Delta_t^{-1}G_t\Omega_t'. \tag{8.4.11}$$

Proof From (8.4.3) it follows that

$$P_t\mathbf{X}_t = P_{t-1}\mathbf{X}_t + M\mathbf{I}_t,$$

where

$$M = E(\mathbf{X}_t\mathbf{I}_t')[E(\mathbf{I}_t\mathbf{I}_t')]^{-1} = E\left[\mathbf{X}_t(G_t(\mathbf{X}_t-\hat{\mathbf{X}}_t)+W_t)'\right]\Delta_t^{-1} = \Omega_t G_t'\Delta_t^{-1}. \tag{8.4.12}$$

To establish (8.4.11) we write

$$\mathbf{X}_t - P_{t-1}\mathbf{X}_t = \mathbf{X}_t - P_t\mathbf{X}_t + P_t\mathbf{X}_t - P_{t-1}\mathbf{X}_t = \mathbf{X}_t - P_t\mathbf{X}_t + M\mathbf{I}_t.$$

Using (8.4.12) and the orthogonality of $\mathbf{X}_t - P_t\mathbf{X}_t$ and $M\mathbf{I}_t$, we find from the last equation that

$$\Omega_t = \Omega_{t|t} + \Omega_t G_t'\Delta_t^{-1}G_t\Omega_t',$$

as required. ■

Kalman Fixed-Point Smoothing:

The smoothed estimates $\mathbf{X}_{t|n} = P_n\mathbf{X}_t$ and the error covariance matrices $\Omega_{t|n} = E[(\mathbf{X}_t - \mathbf{X}_{t|n})(\mathbf{X}_t - \mathbf{X}_{t|n})']$ are determined for fixed t by the following recursions, which can be solved successively for $n = t, t+1, \ldots$:

$$P_n\mathbf{X}_t = P_{n-1}\mathbf{X}_t + \Omega_{t,n}G_n'\Delta_n^{-1}\left(\mathbf{Y}_n - G_n\hat{\mathbf{X}}_n\right), \tag{8.4.13}$$

$$\Omega_{t,n+1} = \Omega_{t,n}[F_n - \Theta_n\Delta_n^{-1}G_n]', \tag{8.4.14}$$

$$\Omega_{t|n} = \Omega_{t|n-1} - \Omega_{t,n}G_n'\Delta_n^{-1}G_n\Omega_{t,n}', \tag{8.4.15}$$

with initial conditions $P_{t-1}\mathbf{X}_t = \hat{\mathbf{X}}_t$ and $\Omega_{t,t} = \Omega_{t|t-1} = \Omega_t$ (found from Kalman prediction).

Proof

Using (8.4.3) we can write $P_n\mathbf{X}_t = P_{n-1}\mathbf{X}_t + C\mathbf{I}_n$, where $\mathbf{I}_n = G_n\left(\mathbf{X}_n - \hat{\mathbf{X}}_n\right) + \mathbf{W}_n$. By Remark 4 above,

$$C = E\left[\mathbf{X}_t(G_n\left(\mathbf{X}_n - \hat{\mathbf{X}}_n\right) + \mathbf{W}_n)'\right]\left[E\left(\mathbf{I}_n\mathbf{I}_n'\right)\right]^{-1} = \Omega_{t,n}G_n'\Delta_n^{-1}, \tag{8.4.16}$$

where $\Omega_{t,n} := E\left[(\mathbf{X}_t - \hat{\mathbf{X}}_t)(\mathbf{X}_n - \hat{\mathbf{X}}_n)'\right]$. It follows now from (8.1.2), (8.4.5), the orthogonality of $\mathbf{V}_n$ and $\mathbf{W}_n$ with $\mathbf{X}_t - \hat{\mathbf{X}}_t$, and the definition of $\Omega_{t,n}$ that

$$\Omega_{t,n+1} = E\left[\left(\mathbf{X}_t - \hat{\mathbf{X}}_t\right)\left(\mathbf{X}_n - \hat{\mathbf{X}}_n\right)'\left(F_n - \Theta_n\Delta_n^{-1}G_n\right)'\right] = \Omega_{t,n}\left[F_n - \Theta_n\Delta_n^{-1}G_n\right]',$$

thus establishing (8.4.14). To establish (8.4.15) we write

$$\mathbf{X}_t - P_n\mathbf{X}_t = \mathbf{X}_t - P_{n-1}\mathbf{X}_t - C\mathbf{I}_n.$$

Using (8.4.16) and the orthogonality of $\mathbf{X}_t - P_n\mathbf{X}_t$ and $\mathbf{I}_n$, the last equation then gives

$$\Omega_{t|n} = \Omega_{t|n-1} - \Omega_{t,n}G_n'\Delta_n^{-1}G_n\Omega_{t,n}', \quad n = t, t+1, \ldots,$$

as required. ∎

8.5 Estimation For State-Space Models

Consider the state-space model defined by equations (8.1.1) and (8.1.2) and suppose that the model is completely parameterized by the components of the vector $\boldsymbol{\theta}$. The maximum likelihood estimate of $\boldsymbol{\theta}$ is found by maximizing the likelihood of the observations $\mathbf{Y}_1, \ldots, \mathbf{Y}_n$ with respect to the components of the vector $\boldsymbol{\theta}$. If the conditional probability density of $\mathbf{Y}_t$ given $\mathbf{Y}_{t-1} = \mathbf{y}_{t-1}, \ldots, \mathbf{Y}_0 = \mathbf{y}_0$ is $f_t(\cdot|\mathbf{y}_{t-1}, \ldots, \mathbf{y}_0)$, then the likelihood of $\mathbf{Y}_t, t = 1, \ldots, n$ (conditional on $\mathbf{Y}_0$), can immediately be written as

$$L(\boldsymbol{\theta}; \mathbf{Y}_1, \ldots, \mathbf{Y}_n) = \prod_{t=1}^{n} f_t(\mathbf{Y}_t|\mathbf{Y}_{t-1}, \ldots, \mathbf{Y}_0). \tag{8.5.1}$$

The calculation of the likelihood for any fixed numerical value of $\boldsymbol{\theta}$ is extremely complicated in general, but is greatly simplified if $\mathbf{Y}_0, \mathbf{X}_1$ and $\mathbf{W}_t, \mathbf{V}_t, t = 1, 2, \ldots,$ are assumed to be jointly Gaussian. The resulting likelihood is called the Gaussian likelihood and is widely used in time series analysis (cf. Section 5.2) whether the time series is truly Gaussian or not. As before, we shall continue to use the term *likelihood* to mean Gaussian likelihood.

If $\mathbf{Y}_0, \mathbf{X}_1$ and $\mathbf{W}_t, \mathbf{V}_t, t = 1, 2, \ldots,$ are jointly Gaussian, then the conditional densities in (8.5.1) are given by

$$f_t(\mathbf{Y}_t|\mathbf{Y}_{t-1}, \ldots, \mathbf{Y}_0) = (2\pi)^{-w/2} (\det\Delta_t)^{-1/2} \exp\left[-\frac{1}{2}\mathbf{I}_t'\Delta_t^{-1}\mathbf{I}_t\right],$$

where $\mathbf{I}_t = \mathbf{Y}_t - P_{t-1}\mathbf{Y}_t = \mathbf{Y}_t - G\hat{\mathbf{X}}_t$, $P_{t-1}\mathbf{Y}_t$, and Δ_t, $t \geq 1$, are the one-step predictors and error covariance matrices found from the Kalman prediction recursions. The likelihood of the observations $\mathbf{Y}_1, \ldots, \mathbf{Y}_n$ (conditional on $\mathbf{Y}_0$) can therefore be expressed as

$$L(\boldsymbol{\theta}; \mathbf{Y}_1, \ldots, \mathbf{Y}_n) = (2\pi)^{-nw/2} \left(\prod_{j=1}^{n} \det\Delta_j\right)^{-1/2} \exp\left[-\frac{1}{2}\sum_{j=1}^{n} \mathbf{I}_j'\Delta_j^{-1}\mathbf{I}_j\right]. \quad (8.5.2)$$

Given the observations $\mathbf{Y}_1, \ldots, \mathbf{Y}_n$, the distribution of $\mathbf{Y}_0$ (see Section 8.4), and a particular parameter value $\boldsymbol{\theta}$, the numerical value of the likelihood L can be computed from the previous equation with the aid of the Kalman recursions of Section 8.4. To find maximum likelihood estimates of the components of $\boldsymbol{\theta}$, a nonlinear optimization algorithm must be used to search for the value of $\boldsymbol{\theta}$ that maximizes the value of L.

Having estimated the parameter vector $\boldsymbol{\theta}$, we can compute forecasts based on the fitted state-space model and estimated mean squared errors by direct application of equations (8.4.7) and (8.4.9).

Application to Structural Models

The general structural model for a univariate time series $\{Y_t\}$ of which we gave examples in Section 8.2 has the form

$$Y_t = G\mathbf{X}_t + W_t, \quad \{W_t\} \sim \mathrm{WN}\left(0, \sigma_w^2\right), \quad (8.5.3)$$

$$\mathbf{X}_{t+1} = F\mathbf{X}_t + \mathbf{V}_t, \quad \{\mathbf{V}_t\} \sim \mathrm{WN}(0, Q), \quad (8.5.4)$$

for $t = 1, 2, \ldots,$ where F and G are assumed known. We set $Y_0 = 1$ in order to include constant terms in our predictors and complete the specification of the model by prescribing the mean and covariance matrix of the initial state $\mathbf{X}_1$. A simple and convenient assumption is that $\mathbf{X}_1$ is equal to a deterministic but unknown parameter $\boldsymbol{\mu}$ and that $\hat{\mathbf{X}}_1 = \boldsymbol{\mu}$, so that $\Omega_1 = 0$. The parameters of the model are then $\boldsymbol{\mu}$, Q, and σ_w^2.

Direct maximization of the likelihood (8.5.2) is difficult if the dimension of the state vector is large. The maximization can, however, be simplified by the following stepwise procedure. For fixed Q we find $\hat{\mu}(Q)$ and $\sigma_w^2(Q)$ that maximize the likelihood $L\left(\mu, Q, \sigma_w^2\right)$. We then maximize the "reduced likelihood" $L\left(\hat{\mu}(Q), Q, \hat{\sigma}_w^2(Q)\right)$ with respect to Q.

To achieve this we define the mean-corrected state vectors, $\mathbf{X}_t^* = \mathbf{X}_t - F^{t-1}\mu$, and apply the Kalman prediction recursions to $\{\mathbf{X}_t^*\}$ with initial condition $\mathbf{X}_1^* = \mathbf{0}$. This gives, from (8.4.1),

$$\hat{\mathbf{X}}_{t+1}^* = F\hat{\mathbf{X}}_t^* + \Theta_t\Delta_t^{-1}\left(Y_t - G\hat{\mathbf{X}}_t^*\right), \quad t = 1, 2, \ldots, \tag{8.5.5}$$

with $\hat{\mathbf{X}}_1^* = \mathbf{0}$. Since $\hat{\mathbf{X}}_t$ also satisfies (8.5.5), but with initial condition $\hat{\mathbf{X}}_t = \mu$, it follows that

$$\hat{\mathbf{X}}_t = \hat{\mathbf{X}}_t^* + C_t\mu \tag{8.5.6}$$

for some $v \times v$ matrices C_t. (Note that although $\hat{\mathbf{X}}_t = P(\mathbf{X}_t | Y_0, Y_1, \ldots, Y_t)$, the quantity $\hat{\mathbf{X}}_t^*$ is not the corresponding predictor of $\mathbf{X}_t^*$.) The matrices C_t can be determined recursively from (8.5.5), (8.5.6), and (8.4.1). Substituting (8.5.6) into (8.5.5) and using (8.4.1), we have

$$\begin{aligned}
\hat{\mathbf{X}}_{t+1}^* &= F\left(\hat{\mathbf{X}}_t - C_t\mu\right) + \Theta_t\Delta_t^{-1}\left(Y_t - G\left(\hat{\mathbf{X}}_t - C_t\mu\right)\right) \\
&= F\hat{\mathbf{X}}_t + \Theta_t\Delta_t^{-1}\left(Y_t - G\hat{\mathbf{X}}_t\right) - \left(F - \Theta_t\Delta_t^{-1}G\right)C_t\mu \\
&= \hat{\mathbf{X}}_{t+1} - \left(F - \Theta_t\Delta_t^{-1}G\right)C_t\mu,
\end{aligned}$$

so that

$$C_{t+1} = \left(F - \Theta_t\Delta_t^{-1}G\right)C_t \tag{8.5.7}$$

with C_1 equal to the identity matrix. The quadratic form in the likelihood (8.5.2) is therefore

$$S(\mu, Q, \sigma_w^2) = \sum_{t=1}^{n} \frac{\left(Y_t - G\hat{\mathbf{X}}_t\right)^2}{\Delta_t} \tag{8.5.8}$$

$$= \sum_{t=1}^{n} \frac{\left(Y_t - G\hat{\mathbf{X}}_t^* - GC_t\mu\right)^2}{\Delta_t}. \tag{8.5.9}$$

Now let $Q^* := \sigma_w^{-2}Q$ and define L^* to be the likelihood function with this new parameterization, i.e., $L^*\left(\mu, Q^*, \sigma_w^2\right) = L\left(\mu, \sigma_w^2 Q^*, \sigma_w^2\right)$. Writing $\Delta_t^* = \sigma_w^{-2}\Delta_t$ and $\Omega_t^* = \sigma_w^{-2}\Omega_t$, we see that the predictors $\hat{X}_t^*$ and the matrices C_t in (8.5.7) depend on the parameters only through Q^*. Thus,

$$S\left(\mu, Q, \sigma_w^2\right) = \sigma_w^{-2}S\left(\mu, Q^*, 1\right),$$

so that

$$-2\ln L^*\left(\mu, Q^*, \sigma_w^2\right) = n\ln(2\pi) + \sum_{t=1}^{n}\ln\Delta_t + \sigma_w^{-2}S(\mu, Q^*, 1)$$

$$= n\ln(2\pi) + \sum_{t=1}^{n}\ln\Delta_t^* + n\ln\sigma_w^2 + \sigma_w^{-2}S(\mu, Q^*, 1).$$

For Q^* fixed, it is easy to show (see Problem 8.18) that this function is minimized when

$$\hat{\mu} = \hat{\mu}(Q^*) = \left[\sum_{t=1}^{n}\frac{C_t'G'GC_t}{\Delta_t^*}\right]^{-1}\sum_{t=1}^{n}\frac{C_t'G'\left(Y_t - G\hat{\mathbf{X}}_t^*\right)}{\Delta_t^*} \tag{8.5.10}$$

and

$$\hat{\sigma}_w^2 = \hat{\sigma}_w^2(Q^*) = n^{-1}\sum_{t=1}^{n}\frac{\left(Y_t - G\hat{\mathbf{X}}_t^* - GC_t\hat{\mu}\right)^2}{\Delta_t^*}. \tag{8.5.11}$$

Replacing μ and σ_w^2 by these values in $-2\ln L^*$ and ignoring constants, the reduced likelihood becomes

$$\ell(Q^*) = \ln\left(n^{-1}\sum_{t=1}^{n}\frac{\left(Y_t - G\hat{\mathbf{X}}_t^* - GC_t\hat{\mu}\right)^2}{\Delta_t^*}\right) + n^{-1}\sum_{t=1}^{n}\ln\left(\det\Delta_t^*\right). \tag{8.5.12}$$

If $\hat{Q}^*$ denotes the minimizer of (8.5.12), then the maximum likelihood estimator of the parameters μ, Q, σ_w^2 are $\hat{\mu}$, $\hat{\sigma}_w^2\hat{Q}^*$, $\hat{\sigma}_w^2$, where $\hat{\mu}$ and $\hat{\sigma}_w^2$ are computed from (8.5.10) and (8.5.11) with Q^* replaced by $\hat{Q}^*$.

We can now summarize the steps required for computing the maximum likelihood estimators of μ, Q, and σ_w^2 for the model (8.5.3)–(8.5.4).

1. For a fixed Q^*, apply the Kalman prediction recursions with $\hat{\mathbf{X}}_1^* = \mathbf{0}$, $\Omega_1 = 0$, $Q = Q^*$, and $\sigma_w^2 = 1$ to obtain the *predictors* $\hat{\mathbf{X}}_t^*$. Let Δ_t^* denote the one-step prediction error produced by these recursions.
2. Set $\hat{\mu} = \hat{\mu}(Q^*) = \left[\sum_{t=1}^{n} C_t'G'GC_t/\Delta_t\right]^{-1}\sum_{t=1}^{n} C_t'G'(Y_t - G\hat{\mathbf{X}}_t^*)/\Delta_t^*$.
3. Let $\hat{Q}^*$ be the minimizer of (8.5.12).
4. The maximum likelihood estimators of μ, Q, and σ_w^2 are then given by $\hat{\mu}$, $\hat{\sigma}_w^2\hat{Q}^*$, and $\hat{\sigma}_w^2$, respectively, where $\hat{\mu}$ and $\hat{\sigma}_w^2$ are found from (8.5.10) and (8.5.11) evaluated at $\hat{Q}^*$.

Example 8.5.1 Random walk plus noise model

In Example 8.2.1, 100 observations were generated from the structural model

$$Y_t = M_t + W_t, \quad \{W_t\} \sim \text{WN}\left(0, \sigma_w^2\right),$$

$$M_{t+1} = M_t + V_t, \quad \{V_t\} \sim \text{WN}\left(0, \sigma_v^2\right),$$

with initial values $\mu = M_1 = 0$, $\sigma_w^2 = 8$, and $\sigma_v^2 = 4$. The maximum likelihood estimates of the parameters are found by first minimizing (8.5.12) with $\hat{\mu}$ given by (8.5.10). Substituting these values into (8.5.11) gives $\hat{\sigma}_w^2$. The resulting estimates are $\hat{\mu} = .906$, $\hat{\sigma}_v^2 = 5.351$, and $\hat{\sigma}_w^2 = 8.233$, which are in reasonably close agreement with the true values. □

Example 8.5.2 International airline passengers, 1949–1960; AIRPASS.TSM

The monthly totals of international airline passengers from January 1949 to December 1960 (Box and Jenkins, 1976) are displayed in Figure 8.3. The data exhibit both a strong seasonal pattern and a nearly linear trend. Since the variability of the data $Y_1, \ldots, Y_{144}$ increases for larger values of Y_t, it may be appropriate to consider a logarithmic transformation of the data. For the purpose of this illustration, however, we will fit a structural model incorporating a randomly varying trend and seasonal and noise components (see Example 8.2.3) to the raw data. This model has the form

$$
\begin{aligned}
Y_t &= G\mathbf{X}_t + W_t, \quad \{W_t\} \sim \mathrm{WN}\left(0, \sigma_w^2\right), \\
\mathbf{X}_{t+1} &= F\mathbf{X}_t + \mathbf{V}_t, \quad \{\mathbf{V}_t\} \sim \mathrm{WN}(0, Q),
\end{aligned}
$$

where $\mathbf{X}_t$ is a 13-dimensional state-vector,

$$
F = \begin{bmatrix}
1 & 1 & 0 & 0 & \cdots & 0 & 0 \\
0 & 1 & 0 & 0 & \cdots & 0 & 0 \\
0 & 0 & -1 & -1 & \cdots & -1 & -1 \\
0 & 0 & 1 & 0 & \cdots & 0 & 0 \\
0 & 0 & 0 & 1 & \cdots & 0 & 0 \\
\vdots & \vdots & \vdots & \vdots & \ddots & \vdots & \vdots \\
0 & 0 & 0 & 0 & \cdots & 1 & 0
\end{bmatrix},
$$

$$
G = [1 \quad 0 \quad 1 \quad 0 \quad \cdots \quad 0],
$$

and

$$
Q = \begin{bmatrix}
\sigma_1^2 & 0 & 0 & 0 & \cdots & 0 \\
0 & \sigma_2^2 & 0 & 0 & \cdots & 0 \\
0 & 0 & \sigma_3^2 & 0 & \cdots & 0 \\
0 & 0 & 0 & 0 & \cdots & 0 \\
\vdots & \vdots & \vdots & \vdots & \ddots & \vdots \\
0 & 0 & 0 & 0 & \cdots & 0
\end{bmatrix}.
$$

The parameters of the model are $\boldsymbol{\mu}, \sigma_1^2, \sigma_2^2, \sigma_3^2$, and σ_w^2, where $\boldsymbol{\mu} = \mathbf{X}_1$. Minimizing (8.5.12) with respect to Q^* we find from (8.5.11) and (8.5.12) that

$$
\left(\hat{\sigma}_1^2, \hat{\sigma}_2^2, \hat{\sigma}_3^2, \hat{\sigma}_w^2\right) = (170.63, .00000, 11.338, .014179)
$$

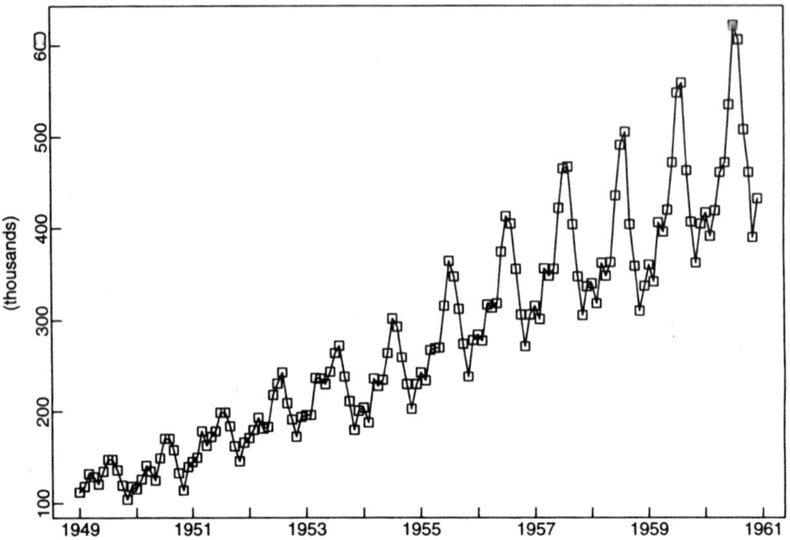

Figure 8-3 International airline passengers; monthly totals from January 1949 to December 1960.

and from (8.5.10) that $\hat{\mu} = (146.9, 2.171, -34.92, -34.12, -47.00, -16.98, 22.99, 53.99, 58.34, 33.65, 2.204, -4.053, -6.894)'$. The first component, X_{t1}, of the state vector corresponds to the local linear trend with slope X_{t2}. Since $\hat{\sigma}_2^2 = 0$, the slope at time t, which satisfies

$$X_{t2} = X_{t-1,2} + V_{t2},$$

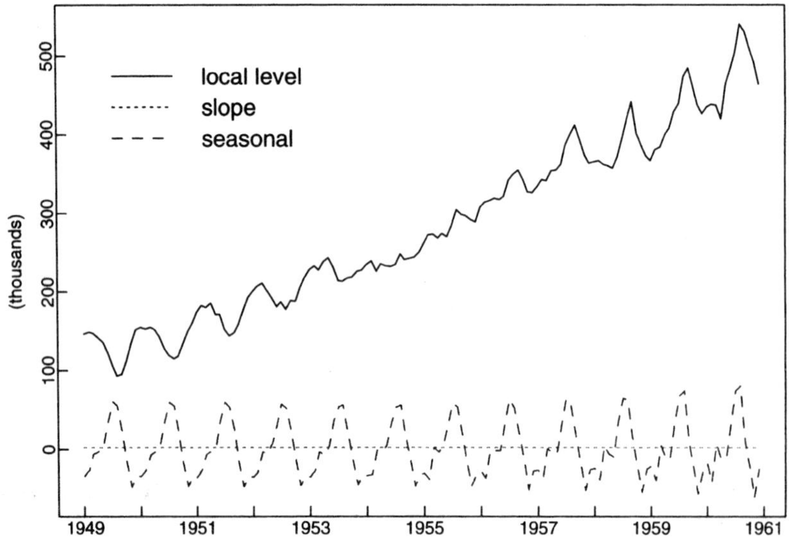

Figure 8-4 The one-step predictors $\left(\hat{X}_{t1}, \hat{X}_{t2}, \hat{X}_{t3}\right)'$ for the airline passenger data in Example 8.5.2.

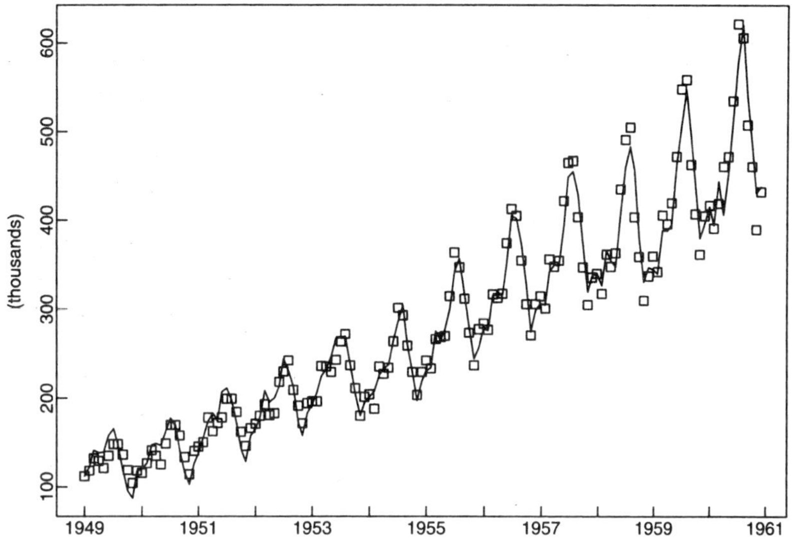

Figure 8-5 The one-step predictors $\hat{Y}_t$ for the airline passenger data (solid line) and the actual data (square boxes).

must be nearly constant and equal to $\hat{X}_{12} = 2.171$. The first three components of the predictors $\hat{\mathbf{X}}_t$ are plotted in Figure 8.4. Notice that the first component varies like a random walk around a straight line, while the second component is nearly constant as a result of $\hat{\sigma}_2^2 \approx 0$. The third component, corresponding to the seasonal component, exhibits a clear seasonal cycle that repeats roughly the same pattern throughout the 12 years of data. The one-step predictors $\hat{X}_{t1} + \hat{X}_{t3}$ of Y_t are plotted in Figure 8.5 (solid line) together with the actual data (square boxes). For this model the predictors follow the movement of the data quite well. □

8.6 State-Space Models with Missing Observations

State-space representations and the associated Kalman recursions are ideally suited to the analysis of data with missing values, as was pointed out by Jones (1980) in the context of maximum likelihood estimation for ARMA processes. In this section we shall deal with two missing-value problems for state-space models. The first is the evaluation of the (Gaussian) likelihood based on $\{\mathbf{Y}_{i_1}, \ldots, \mathbf{Y}_{i_r}\}$, where $i_1, i_2, \ldots, i_r$ are positive integers such that $1 \le i_1 < i_2 < \cdots < i_r \le n$. (This allows for observation of the process $\{\mathbf{Y}_t\}$ at irregular intervals, or equivalently for the possibility that $(n-r)$ observations are missing from the sequence $\{\mathbf{Y}_1, \ldots, \mathbf{Y}_n\}$.) The solution of this problem will, in particular, enable us to carry out maximum likelihood estimation for ARMA and ARIMA processes with missing values. The second problem to be considered is the minimum mean squared error estimation of the missing values themselves.

The Gaussian Likelihood of $\{\mathbf{Y}_{i_1},\ldots,\mathbf{Y}_{i_r}\}$, $1 \le i_1 < i_2 < \cdots < i_r \le n$

Consider the state-space model defined by equations (8.1.1) and (8.1.2) and suppose that the model is completely parameterized by the components of the vector $\boldsymbol{\theta}$. If there are no missing observations, i.e., if $r = n$ and $i_j = j$, $j = 1, \ldots, n$, then the likelihood of the observations $\{\mathbf{Y}_1, \ldots, \mathbf{Y}_n\}$ is easily found as in Section 8.5 to be

$$L(\boldsymbol{\theta}; \mathbf{Y}_1, \ldots, \mathbf{Y}_n) = (2\pi)^{-nw/2} \left(\prod_{j=1}^{n} \det\Delta_j\right)^{-1/2} \exp\left[-\frac{1}{2}\sum_{j=1}^{n} \mathbf{I}_j' \Delta_j^{-1} \mathbf{I}_j\right],$$

where $\mathbf{I}_j = \mathbf{Y}_j - P_{j-1}\mathbf{Y}_j$ and Δ_j, $j \ge 1$, are the one-step predictors and error covariance matrices found from (8.4.7) and (8.4.9) with $\mathbf{Y}_0 = \mathbf{1}$.

To deal with the more general case of possibly irregularly spaced observations $\{\mathbf{Y}_{i_1}, \ldots, \mathbf{Y}_{i_r}\}$, we introduce a new series $\{\mathbf{Y}_t^*\}$, related to the process $\{\mathbf{X}_t\}$ by the modified observation equation

$$\mathbf{Y}_t^* = G_t^* \mathbf{X}_t + \mathbf{W}_t^*, \quad t = 1, 2, \ldots, \tag{8.6.1}$$

where

$$G_t^* = \begin{cases} G_t & \text{if } t \in \{i_1, \ldots, i_r\}, \\ 0 & \text{otherwise,} \end{cases} \qquad \mathbf{W}_t^* = \begin{cases} \mathbf{W}_t & \text{if } t \in \{i_1, \ldots, i_r\}, \\ \mathbf{N}_t & \text{otherwise,} \end{cases} \tag{8.6.2}$$

and $\{\mathbf{N}_t\}$ is iid with

$$\mathbf{N}_t \sim \mathrm{N}(\mathbf{0}, I_{w\times w}), \quad \mathbf{N}_s \perp \mathbf{X}_1, \quad \mathbf{N}_s \perp \begin{bmatrix} \mathbf{V}_t \\ \mathbf{W}_t \end{bmatrix}, \quad s, t = 0, \pm 1, \ldots. \tag{8.6.3}$$

Equations (8.6.1) and (8.1.2) constitute a state-space representation for the new series $\{\mathbf{Y}_t^*\}$, which coincides with $\{\mathbf{Y}_t\}$ at each $t \in \{i_1, i_2, \ldots, i_r\}$, and at other times takes random values that are independent of $\{\mathbf{Y}_t\}$ with a distribution independent of $\boldsymbol{\theta}$.

Let $L_1(\boldsymbol{\theta}; \mathbf{y}_{i_1}, \ldots, \mathbf{y}_{i_r})$ be the Gaussian likelihood based on the observed values $\mathbf{y}_{i_1}, \ldots, \mathbf{y}_{i_r}$ of $\mathbf{Y}_{i_1}, \ldots, \mathbf{Y}_{i_r}$ under the model defined by (8.1.1) and (8.1.2). Corresponding to these observed values, we define a new sequence, $\mathbf{y}_1^*, \ldots, \mathbf{y}_n^*$, by

$$\mathbf{y}_t^* = \begin{cases} \mathbf{y}_t & \text{if } t \in \{i_1, \ldots, i_r\}, \\ \mathbf{0} & \text{otherwise.} \end{cases} \tag{8.6.4}$$

Then it is clear from the preceding paragraph that

$$L_1(\boldsymbol{\theta}; \mathbf{y}_{i_1}, \ldots, \mathbf{y}_{i_r}) = (2\pi)^{(n-r)w/2} L_2(\boldsymbol{\theta}; \mathbf{y}_1^*, \ldots, \mathbf{y}_n^*), \tag{8.6.5}$$

where L_2 denotes the Gaussian likelihood under the model defined by (8.6.1) and (8.1.2).

In view of (8.6.5) we can now compute the required likelihood L_1 of the realized values $\{\mathbf{y}_t, t = i_1, \ldots, i_r\}$ as follows:

i. Define the sequence $\{\mathbf{y}_t^*, t = 1, \ldots, n\}$ as in (8.6.4).

ii. Find the one-step predictors $\hat{\mathbf{Y}}_t^*$ of $\mathbf{Y}_t^*$, and their error covariance matrices Δ_t^*, using Kalman prediction and equations (8.4.7) and (8.4.9) applied to the state-space representation (8.6.1) and (8.1.2) of $\{\mathbf{Y}_t^*\}$. Denote the realized values of the predictors, based on the observation sequence $\{\mathbf{y}_t^*\}$, by $\{\hat{\mathbf{y}}_t^*\}$.

iii. The required Gaussian likelihood of the irregularly spaced observations $\{\mathbf{y}_{i_1}, \ldots, \mathbf{y}_{i_r}\}$ is then, by (8.6.5),

$$L_1(\boldsymbol{\theta}; \mathbf{y}_{i_1}, \ldots, \mathbf{y}_{i_r}) = (2\pi)^{-rw/2} \left(\prod_{j=1}^{n} \det \Delta_j^* \right)^{-1/2} \exp\left\{ -\frac{1}{2} \sum_{j=1}^{n} \mathbf{i}_j^{*\prime} \Delta_j^{*-1} \mathbf{i}_j^* \right\},$$

where $\mathbf{i}_j^*$ denotes the observed innovation $\mathbf{y}_j^* - \hat{\mathbf{y}}_j^*$, $j = 1, \ldots, n$.

Example 8.6.1 An AR(1) series with one missing observation

Let $\{Y_t\}$ be the causal AR(1) process defined by

$$Y_t - \phi Y_{t-1} = Z_t, \qquad \{Z_t\} \sim \mathrm{WN}\left(0, \sigma^2\right).$$

To find the Gaussian likelihood of the observations y_1, y_3, y_4, and y_5 of Y_1, Y_3, Y_4, and Y_5 we follow the steps outlined above.

i. Set $y_i^* = y_i$, $i = 1, 3, 4, 5$ and $y_2^* = 0$.

ii. We start with the state-space model for $\{Y_t\}$ from Example 8.1.1, i.e., $Y_t = X_t$, $X_{t+1} = \phi X_t + Z_{t+1}$. The corresponding model for $\{Y_t^*\}$ is then, from (8.6.1),

$$Y_t^* = G_t^* X_t + W_t^*, \ t = 1, 2, \ldots,$$

where

$$X_{t+1} = F_t X_t + V_t, \ t = 1, 2, \ldots,$$

$$F_t = \phi, \quad G_t^* = \begin{cases} 1 & \text{if } t \neq 2, \\ 0 & \text{if } t = 2, \end{cases} \quad V_t = Z_{t+1}, \quad W_t^* = \begin{cases} 0 & \text{if } t \neq 2, \\ N_t & \text{if } t = 2, \end{cases}$$

$$Q_t = \sigma^2, \qquad R_t^* = \begin{cases} 0 & \text{if } t \neq 2, \\ 1 & \text{if } t = 2, \end{cases} \qquad S_t^* = 0,$$

and $X_1 = \sum_{j=0}^{\infty} \phi^j Z_{1-j}$. Starting from the initial conditions

$$\hat{X}_1 = 0, \qquad \Omega_1 = \sigma^2 / \left(1 - \phi^2\right),$$

and applying the recursions (8.4.1) and (8.4.2), we find (Problem 8.19) that

$$\Theta_t \Delta_t^{-1} = \begin{cases} \phi & \text{if } t = 1, 3, 4, 5, \\ 0 & \text{if } t = 2, \end{cases} \qquad \Omega_t = \begin{cases} \sigma^2/\left(1-\phi^2\right) & \text{if } t = 1, \\ \sigma^2\left(1+\phi^2\right) & \text{if } t = 3, \\ \sigma^2 & \text{if } t = 2, 4, 5, \end{cases}$$

and

$$\hat{X}_1 = 0, \quad \hat{X}_2 = \phi Y_1, \quad \hat{X}_3 = \phi^2 Y_1, \quad \hat{X}_4 = \phi Y_3, \quad \hat{X}_5 = \phi Y_4.$$

From (8.4.7) and (8.4.9) with $h = 1$, we find that

$$\hat{Y}_1^* = 0, \quad \hat{Y}_2^* = 0, \quad \hat{Y}_3^* = \phi^2 Y_1, \quad \hat{Y}_4^* = \phi Y_3, \quad \hat{Y}_5^* = \phi Y_4,$$

with corresponding mean squared errors

$$\Delta_1^* = \sigma^2/\left(1-\phi^2\right), \quad \Delta_2^* = 1, \quad \Delta_3^* = \sigma^2\left(1+\phi^2\right), \quad \Delta_4^* = \sigma^2, \quad \Delta_5^* = \sigma^2.$$

iii. From the preceding calculations we can now write the likelihood of the original data as

$$L_1(\phi, \sigma^2;\ y_1, y_3, y_4, y_5) = \sigma^{-4}(2\pi)^{-2}\left[\left(1-\phi^2\right)/\left(1+\phi^2\right)\right]^{1/2}$$
$$\times \exp\left\{-\frac{1}{2\sigma^2}\left[y_1^2\left(1-\phi^2\right) + \frac{(y_3-\phi^2 y_1)^2}{1+\phi^2} + (y_4-\phi y_3)^2 + (y_5-\phi y_4)^2\right]\right\}. \square$$

Remark 1. If we are given observations $y_{1-d}, y_{2-d}, \ldots, y_0, y_{i_1}, y_{i_2}, \ldots, y_{i_r}$ of an ARIMA(p, d, q) process at times $1-d, 2-d, \ldots, 0, i_1, \ldots, i_r$, where $1 \le i_1 < i_2 < \cdots < i_r \le n$, a similar argument can be used to find the Gaussian likelihood of $y_{i_1}, \ldots, y_{i_r}$ *conditional on* $Y_{1-d} = y_{1-d}, Y_{2-d} = y_{2-d}, \ldots, Y_0 = y_0$. Missing values among the first d observations $y_{1-d}, y_{2-d}, \ldots, y_0$ can be handled by treating them as unknown parameters for likelihood maximization. For more on ARIMA series with missing values see TSTM and Ansley and Kohn (1985). $\square$

Estimation of Missing Values for State-Space Models

Given that we observe only $\mathbf{Y}_{i_1}, \mathbf{Y}_{i_2}, \ldots, \mathbf{Y}_{i_r}$, $1 \le i_1 < i_2 < \cdots < i_r \le n$, where $\{\mathbf{Y}_t\}$ has the state-space representation (8.1.1) and (8.1.2), we now consider the problem of finding the minimum mean squared error estimators $P\left(\mathbf{Y}_t | \mathbf{Y}_0, \mathbf{Y}_{i_1}, \ldots, \mathbf{Y}_{i_r}\right)$ of $\mathbf{Y}_t$, $1 \le t \le n$, where $\mathbf{Y}_0 = \mathbf{1}$. To handle this problem we again use the modified process $\{\mathbf{Y}_t^*\}$ defined by (8.6.1) and (8.1.2) with $\mathbf{Y}_0^* = \mathbf{1}$. Since $\mathbf{Y}_s^* = \mathbf{Y}_s$ for $s \in \{i_1, \ldots, i_r\}$ and $\mathbf{Y}_s^* \perp \mathbf{X}_t, \mathbf{Y}_0$ for $1 \le t \le n$ and $s \notin \{0, i_1, \ldots, i_r\}$, we immediately obtain the minimum mean squared error state estimators

$$P\left(\mathbf{X}_t | \mathbf{Y}_0, \mathbf{Y}_{i_1}, \ldots, \mathbf{Y}_{i_r}\right) = P\left(\mathbf{X}_t | \mathbf{Y}_0^*, \mathbf{Y}_1^*, \ldots, \mathbf{Y}_n^*\right), \quad 1 \le t \le n. \tag{8.6.6}$$

The right-hand side can be evaluated by application of the Kalman fixed-point smoothing algorithm to the state-space model (8.6.1) and (8.1.2). For computational purposes the observed values of $\mathbf{Y}_t^*$, $t \notin \{0, i_1, \dots, i_r\}$, are quite immaterial. They may, for example, all be set equal to zero, giving the sequence of *observations* of $\mathbf{Y}_t^*$ defined in (8.6.4).

To evaluate $P(\mathbf{Y}_t|\mathbf{Y}_0, \mathbf{Y}_{i_1}, \dots, \mathbf{Y}_{i_r})$, $1 \le t \le n$, we use (8.6.6) and the relation

$$\mathbf{Y}_t = G_t\mathbf{X}_t + \mathbf{W}_t. \tag{8.6.7}$$

Since $E(\mathbf{V}_t\mathbf{W}_t') = S_t = 0$, $\quad t = 1, \dots, n$, we find from (8.6.7) that

$$P(\mathbf{Y}_t|\mathbf{Y}_0, \mathbf{Y}_{i_1}, \dots, \mathbf{Y}_{i_r}) = G_t P(\mathbf{X}_t|\mathbf{Y}_0^*, \mathbf{Y}_1^*, \dots, \mathbf{Y}_n^*). \tag{8.6.8}$$

Example 8.6.2 An AR(1) series with one missing observation

Consider the problem of estimating the missing value Y_2 in Example 8.6.1 in terms of $Y_0 = 1, Y_1, Y_3, Y_4$, and Y_5. We start from the state-space model $X_{t+1} = \phi X_t + Z_{t+1}$, $Y_t = X_t$, for $\{Y_t\}$. The corresponding model for $\{Y_t^*\}$ is the one used in Example 8.6.1. Applying the Kalman smoothing equations to the latter model, we find that

$$\begin{aligned} &P_1X_2 = \phi Y_1, \qquad P_2X_2 = \phi Y_1, \qquad P_3X_2 = \frac{\phi(Y_1+Y_3)}{(1+\phi^2)}, \\ &P_4X_2 = P_3X_2, \quad P_5X_2 = P_3X_2, \\ &\Omega_{2,2} = \sigma^2, \qquad \Omega_{2,3} = \phi\sigma^2, \qquad \Omega_{2,t} = 0, \quad t \ge 4, \end{aligned}$$

and

$$\Omega_{2|1} = \sigma^2, \quad \Omega_{2|2} = \sigma^2, \quad \Omega_{2|t} = \frac{\sigma^2}{(1+\phi^2)}, \qquad t \ge 3,$$

where $P_t(\cdot)$ here denotes $P(\cdot|Y_0^*, \dots, Y_t^*)$ and $\Omega_{t,n}$, $\Omega_{t|n}$ are defined correspondingly. We deduce from (8.6.8) that the minimum mean squared error estimator of the missing value Y_2 is

$$P_5Y_2 = P_5X_2 = \frac{\phi(Y_1+Y_3)}{(1+\phi^2)},$$

with mean squared error

$$\Omega_{2|5} = \frac{\sigma^2}{(1+\phi^2)}.$$

□

Remark 2. Suppose we have observations $Y_{1-d}, Y_{2-d}, \dots, Y_0, Y_{i_1}, \dots, Y_{i_r}$ $(1 \le i_1 < i_2 \cdots < i_r \le n)$ of an ARIMA(p, d, q) process. Determination of the best linear estimates of the missing values Y_t, $t \notin \{i_1, \dots, i_r\}$, in terms of Y_t, $t \in \{i_1, \dots, i_r\}$, and the components of $\mathbf{Y}_0 := (Y_{1-d}, Y_{2-d}, \dots, Y_0)'$ can be carried out as in Example 8.6.2 using the state-space representation of the ARIMA series $\{Y_t\}$ from Example 8.3.3 and the Kalman recursions for the corresponding state-space model for $\{Y_t^*\}$ defined by (8.6.1) and (8.1.2). See TSTM for further details. □

We close this section with a brief discussion of a direct approach to estimating missing observations. This approach is often more efficient than the methods just described, especially if the number of missing observations is small and we have a simple (e.g., autoregressive) model. Consider the general problem of computing $E(\mathbf{X}|\mathbf{Y})$ when the random vector $(\mathbf{X}', \mathbf{Y}')'$ has a multivariate normal distribution with mean $\mathbf{0}$ and covariance matrix Σ. (In the missing observation problem, think of $\mathbf{X}$ as the vector of the missing observations and $\mathbf{Y}$ as the vector of observed values.) Then the joint probability density function of $\mathbf{X}$ and $\mathbf{Y}$ can be written as

$$f_{\mathbf{X},\mathbf{Y}}(\mathbf{x},\mathbf{y}) = f_{\mathbf{X}|\mathbf{Y}}(\mathbf{x}|\mathbf{y}) f_{\mathbf{Y}}(\mathbf{y}), \tag{8.6.9}$$

where $f_{\mathbf{X}|\mathbf{Y}}(\mathbf{x}|\mathbf{y})$ is a multivariate normal density with mean $E(\mathbf{X}|\mathbf{Y})$ and covariance matrix $\Sigma_{\mathbf{X}|\mathbf{Y}}$ (see Proposition A.3.1). In particular,

$$f_{\mathbf{X}|\mathbf{Y}}(\mathbf{x}|\mathbf{y}) = \frac{1}{\sqrt{(2\pi)^q \det \Sigma_{\mathbf{X}|\mathbf{Y}}}} \exp\left\{-\frac{1}{2}(\mathbf{x} - E(\mathbf{X}|\mathbf{y}))'\Sigma_{\mathbf{X}|\mathbf{Y}}^{-1}(\mathbf{x} - E(\mathbf{X}|\mathbf{y}))\right\}, \tag{8.6.10}$$

where $q = \dim(\mathbf{X})$. It is clear from (8.6.10) that $f_{\mathbf{X}|\mathbf{Y}}(\mathbf{x}|\mathbf{y})$ (and also $f_{\mathbf{X},\mathbf{Y}}(\mathbf{x},\mathbf{y})$) is maximum when $\mathbf{x} = E(\mathbf{X}|\mathbf{y})$. Thus, the best estimator of $\mathbf{X}$ in terms of $\mathbf{Y}$ can be found by maximizing the joint density of $\mathbf{X}$ and $\mathbf{Y}$ with respect to $\mathbf{x}$. For autoregressive processes it is relatively straightforward to carry out this optimization, as shown in the following example.

Example 8.6.3 Estimating missing observations in an AR process

Suppose $\{Y_t\}$ is the AR(p) process defined by

$$Y_t = \phi_1 Y_{t-1} + \cdots + \phi_p Y_{t-p} + Z_t, \quad \{Z_t\} \sim \mathrm{WN}\left(0, \sigma^2\right),$$

and $\mathbf{Y} = (Y_{i_1}, \ldots, Y_{i_r})'$, with $1 \le i_1 < \cdots < i_r \le n$, are the observed values. If there are no missing observations in the first p observations, then the best estimates of the missing values are found by minimizing

$$\sum_{t=p+1}^{n} (Y_t - \phi_1 Y_{t-1} - \cdots - \phi_p Y_{t-p})^2 \tag{8.6.11}$$

with respect to the missing values (see Problem 8.20). For the AR(1) model in Example 8.6.2, minimization of (8.6.11) is equivalent to minimizing

$$(Y_2 - \phi Y_1)^2 + (Y_3 - \phi Y_2)^2$$

with respect to Y_2. Setting the derivative of this expression with respect to Y_2 equal to 0 and solving for Y_2 we obtain $E(Y_2|Y_1, Y_3, Y_4, Y_5) = \phi(Y_1 + Y_3)/\left(1 + \phi^2\right)$. □

8.7 The EM Algorithm

The expectation-maximization (EM) algorithm is an iterative procedure for computing the maximum likelihood estimator when only a subset of the complete data set is available. Dempster, Laird, and Rubin (1977) demonstrated the wide applicability of the EM algorithm and are largely responsible for popularizing this method in statistics. Details regarding the convergence and performance of the EM algorithm can be found in Wu (1983).

In the usual formulation of the EM algorithm, the "complete" data vector $\mathbf{W}$ is made up of "observed" data $\mathbf{Y}$ (sometimes called incomplete data) and "unobserved" data $\mathbf{X}$. In many applications, $\mathbf{X}$ consists of values of a "latent" or unobserved process occurring in the specification of the model. For example, in the state-space model of Section 8.1, $\mathbf{Y}$ could consist of the observed vectors $\mathbf{Y}_1, \ldots, \mathbf{Y}_n$ and $\mathbf{X}$ of the unobserved state vectors $\mathbf{X}_1, \ldots, \mathbf{X}_n$. The EM algorithm provides an iterative procedure for computing the maximum likelihood estimator based only on the observed data $\mathbf{Y}$. Each iteration of the EM algorithm consists of two steps. If $\theta^{(i)}$ denotes the estimated value of the parameter θ after i iterations, then the two steps in the $(i+1)$th iteration are

E–step. Calculate $Q(\theta|\theta^{(i)}) = E_{\theta^{(i)}}\left[\ell(\theta; \mathbf{X}, \mathbf{Y})|\mathbf{Y}\right]$

and

M–step. Maximize $Q(\theta|\theta^{(i)})$ with respect to θ.

Then $\theta^{(i+1)}$ is set equal to the maximizer of Q in the M-step. In the E-step, $\ell(\theta; \mathbf{x}, \mathbf{y}) = \ln f(\mathbf{x}, \mathbf{y}; \theta)$, and $E_{\theta^{(i)}}(\cdot|\mathbf{Y})$ denotes the conditional expectation relative to the conditional density $f\left(\mathbf{x}|\mathbf{y}; \theta^{(i)}\right) = f\left(\mathbf{x}, \mathbf{y}; \theta^{(i)}\right)/f\left(\mathbf{y}; \theta^{(i)}\right)$.

It can be shown that $\ell\left(\theta^{(i)}; \mathbf{Y}\right)$ is nondecreasing in i, and a simple heuristic argument shows that if $\theta^{(i)}$ has a limit $\hat{\theta}$ then $\hat{\theta}$ must be a solution of the likelihood equations $\ell'\left(\hat{\theta}; \mathbf{Y}\right) = 0$. To see this, observe that $\ln f(\mathbf{x}, \mathbf{y}; \theta) = \ln f(\mathbf{x}|\mathbf{y}; \theta) + \ell(\theta; \mathbf{y})$, from which we obtain

$$Q\left(\theta|\theta^{(i)}\right) = \int (\ln f(\mathbf{x}|\mathbf{Y}; \theta))\, f\left(\mathbf{x}|\mathbf{Y}; \theta^{(i)}\right) d\mathbf{x} + \ell(\theta; \mathbf{Y})$$

and

$$Q'(\theta|\theta^{(i)}) = \int \left[\frac{\partial}{\partial\theta} f(\mathbf{x}|\mathbf{Y}; \theta)\right] / f(\mathbf{x}|\mathbf{Y}; \theta)\, f\left(\mathbf{x}|\mathbf{Y}; \theta^{(i)}\right) d\mathbf{x} + \ell'(\theta; \mathbf{Y}).$$

Now replacing θ with $\theta^{(i+1)}$, noticing that $Q'(\theta^{(i+1)}|\theta^{(i)}) = 0$, and letting $i \to \infty$, we find that

$$0 = \int \frac{\partial}{\partial\theta} \left[f(\mathbf{x}|\mathbf{Y}; \theta)\right]_{\theta=\hat{\theta}} d\mathbf{x} + \ell'\left(\hat{\theta}; \mathbf{Y}\right) = \ell'\left(\hat{\theta}; \mathbf{Y}\right).$$

The last equality follows from the fact that

$$0 = \frac{\partial}{\partial \theta}(1) = \frac{\partial}{\partial \theta}\left[\int (f(\mathbf{x}|\mathbf{Y};\theta)\,d\mathbf{x}\right]_{\theta=\hat{\theta}} = \int \left[\frac{\partial}{\partial \theta} f(\mathbf{x}|\mathbf{Y};\theta)\right]_{\theta=\hat{\theta}} d\mathbf{x}.$$

The computational advantage of the EM algorithm over direct maximization of the likelihood is most pronounced when the calculation and maximization of the exact likelihood is difficult as compared with the maximization of Q in the M-step. (There are some applications in which the maximization of Q can easily be carried out explicitly.)

Missing Data

The EM algorithm is particularly useful for estimation problems in which there are missing observations. Suppose the complete data set consists of $Y_1, \ldots, Y_n$ of which r are observed and $n-r$ are missing. Denote the observed and missing data by $\mathbf{Y} = (Y_{i_1}, \ldots, Y_{i_r})'$ and $\mathbf{X} = (Y_{j_1}, \ldots, Y_{j_{n-r}})'$, respectively. Assuming that $\mathbf{W} = (\mathbf{X}', \mathbf{Y}')'$ has a multivariate normal distribution with mean $\mathbf{0}$ and covariance matrix Σ, which depends on the parameter $\boldsymbol{\theta}$, the log-likelihood of the complete data is given by

$$\ell(\boldsymbol{\theta}; \mathbf{W}) = -\frac{n}{2}\ln(2\pi) - \frac{1}{2}\ln\det(\Sigma) - \frac{1}{2}\mathbf{W}'\Sigma\mathbf{W}.$$

The E-step requires that we compute the expectation of $\ell(\boldsymbol{\theta}; \mathbf{W})$ with respect to the conditional distribution of $\mathbf{W}$ given $\mathbf{Y}$ with $\boldsymbol{\theta} = \boldsymbol{\theta}^{(i)}$. Writing $\Sigma(\boldsymbol{\theta})$ as the block matrix

$$\Sigma = \begin{bmatrix} \Sigma_{11} & \Sigma_{12} \\ \Sigma_{21} & \Sigma_{22} \end{bmatrix},$$

which is conformable with $\mathbf{X}$ and $\mathbf{Y}$, the conditional distribution of $\mathbf{W}$ given $\mathbf{Y}$ is multivariate normal with mean $\begin{bmatrix}\hat{\mathbf{X}} \\ \mathbf{Y}\end{bmatrix}$ and covariance matrix $\begin{bmatrix}\Sigma_{11|2}(\boldsymbol{\theta}) & 0 \\ 0 & 0\end{bmatrix}$, where $\hat{\mathbf{X}} = E_{\boldsymbol{\theta}}(\mathbf{X}|\mathbf{Y}) = \Sigma_{12}\Sigma_{22}^{-1}\mathbf{Y}$ and $\Sigma_{11|2}(\boldsymbol{\theta}) = \Sigma_{11} - \Sigma_{12}\Sigma_{22}^{-1}\Sigma_{21}$ (see Proposition A.3.1). Using Problem A.8, we have

$$E_{\boldsymbol{\theta}^{(i)}}\left[(\mathbf{X}', \mathbf{Y}')\Sigma^{-1}(\boldsymbol{\theta})(\mathbf{X}', \mathbf{Y}')'|\mathbf{Y}\right] = \operatorname{trace}\left(\Sigma_{11|2}(\boldsymbol{\theta}^{(i)})\Sigma_{11|2}^{-1}(\boldsymbol{\theta})\right) + \hat{\mathbf{W}}'\Sigma^{-1}(\boldsymbol{\theta})\hat{\mathbf{W}},$$

where $\hat{\mathbf{W}} = \left(\hat{\mathbf{X}}', \mathbf{Y}'\right)'$. It follows that

$$Q\left(\boldsymbol{\theta}|\boldsymbol{\theta}^{(i)}\right) = \ell\left(\boldsymbol{\theta}, \hat{\mathbf{W}}\right) - \frac{1}{2}\operatorname{trace}\left(\Sigma_{11|2}\left(\boldsymbol{\theta}^{(i)}\right)\Sigma_{11|2}^{-1}(\boldsymbol{\theta})\right).$$

The first term on the right is the log-likelihood based on the complete data, but with $\mathbf{X}$ replaced by its "best estimate" $\hat{\mathbf{X}}$ calculated from the previous iteration. If the increments $\boldsymbol{\theta}^{(i+1)} - \boldsymbol{\theta}^{(i)}$ are small, then the second term on the right is nearly constant ($\approx n-r$) and can be ignored. For ease of computation in this application we shall use the modified version

$$\tilde{Q}\left(\boldsymbol{\theta}|\boldsymbol{\theta}^{(i)}\right) = \ell\left(\boldsymbol{\theta}; \hat{\mathbf{W}}\right).$$

With this adjustment, the steps in the EM algorithm are as follows:

E-step. Calculate $E_{\theta^{(i)}}(\mathbf{X}|\mathbf{Y})$ (e.g., with the Kalman fixed-point smoother) and form $\ell(\theta; \hat{\mathbf{W}})$.

M-step. Find the maximum likelihood estimator for the "complete" data problem, i.e., maximize $\ell(\theta : \hat{\mathbf{W}})$. For ARMA processes, ITSM can be used directly, with the missing values replaced with their best estimates computed in the E-step.

Example 8.7.1 The lake data

It was found in Example 5.2.5 that the AR(2) model

$$W_t - 1.0415W_{t-1} + 0.2494W_{t-2} = Z_t, \quad \{Z_t\} \sim \text{WN}(0, .4790)$$

was a good fit to the mean-corrected lake data $\{W_t\}$. To illustrate the use of the EM algorithm for missing data, consider fitting an AR(2) model to the mean-corrected data assuming that there are 10 missing values at times $t = 17, 24, 31, 38, 45, 52, 59, 66, 73$, and 80. We start the algorithm at iteration 0 with $\hat{\phi}_1^{(0)} = \hat{\phi}_2^{(0)} = 0$. Since this initial model represents white noise, the first E-step gives, in the notation used above, $\hat{W}_{17} = \cdots = \hat{W}_{80} = 0$. Replacing the "missing" values of the mean-corrected lake data with 0 and fitting a mean-zero AR(2) model to the resulting complete data set using the maximum likelihood option in ITSM, we find that $\hat{\phi}_1^{(1)} = .7252$, $\hat{\phi}_2^{(1)} = .0236$. (Examination of the plots of the ACF and PACF of this new data set suggests an AR(1) as a better model. This is also borne out by the small estimated value of ϕ_2.) The updated missing values at times $t = 17, 24, \ldots, 80$ are found (see Section 8.6 and Problem 8.21) by minimizing

$$\sum_{j=0}^{2} \left(W_{t+j} - \hat{\phi}_1^{(1)} W_{t+j-1} - \hat{\phi}_2^{(1)} W_{t+j-2} \right)^2$$

with respect to W_t. The solution is given by

$$\hat{W}_t = \frac{\hat{\phi}_2^{(1)}(W_{t-2} + W_{t+2}) + \left(\hat{\phi}_1^{(1)} - \hat{\phi}_1^{(1)}\hat{\phi}_2^{(1)}\right)(W_{t-1} + W_{t+1})}{1 + \left(\hat{\phi}_1^{(1)}\right)^2 + \left(\hat{\phi}_2^{(1)}\right)^2}.$$

The M-step of iteration 1 is then carried out by fitting an AR(2) model using ITSM applied to the updated data set. As seen in the summary of the results reported in Table 8.1, the EM algorithm converges in four iterations with the final parameter estimates reasonably close to the fitted model based on the complete data set. (In Table 8.1, estimates of the missing values are recorded only for the first three.) Also notice how $-2\ell\left(\theta^{(i)}, \mathbf{W}\right)$ decreases at every iteration. The standard errors of the parameter estimates produced from the last iteration of ITSM are based on a "complete" data set and, as such, underestimate the true sampling errors. Formulae for adjusting the

Table 8.1 Estimates of the missing observations at times $t = 17$, 24, 31 and the AR estimates using the EM algorithm in Example 8.7.1.

iteration i	$\hat{W}_{17}$	$\hat{W}_{24}$	$\hat{W}_{31}$	$\hat{\phi}_1^{(i)}$	$\hat{\phi}_2^{(i)}$	$-2\ell\,(\theta^{(i)}, \mathbf{W})$
0				0	0	322.60
1	0	0	0	.7252	.0236	244.76
2	.534	.205	.746	1.0729	−.2838	203.57
3	.458	.393	.821	1.0999	−.3128	202.25
4	.454	.405	.826	1.0999	−.3128	202.25

standard errors to reflect the true sampling error based on the observed data can be found in Dempster, Laird, and Rubin (1977). □

8.8 Generalized State-Space Models

As in Section 8.1, we consider a sequence of state variables $\{X_t,\ t \geq 1\}$ and a sequence of observations $\{Y_t,\ t \geq 1\}$. For simplicity, we consider only one-dimensional state and observation variables, since extensions to higher dimensions can be carried out with little change. Throughout this section it will be convenient to write $\mathbf{Y}^{(t)}$ and $\mathbf{X}^{(t)}$ for the t dimensional column vectors $\mathbf{Y}^{(t)} = (Y_1, Y_2, \ldots, Y_t)'$ and $\mathbf{X}^{(t)} = (X_1, X_2, \ldots, X_t)'$.

There are two important types of state-space models, "parameter driven" and "observation driven," both of which are frequently used in time series analysis. The observation equation is the same for both, but the state vectors of a parameter-driven model evolve independently of the past history of the observation process, while the state vectors of an observation-driven model depend on past observations.

8.8.1 Parameter-Driven Models

In place of the observation and state equations (8.1.1) and (8.1.2), we now make the assumptions that Y_t given $\left(X_t, \mathbf{X}^{(t-1)}, \mathbf{Y}^{(t-1)}\right)$ is independent of $\left(\mathbf{X}^{(t-1)}, \mathbf{Y}^{(t-1)}\right)$ with conditional probability density

$$p(y_t|x_t) := p\left(y_t|x_t, \mathbf{x}^{(t-1)}, \mathbf{y}^{(t-1)}\right), \quad t = 1, 2, \ldots, \tag{8.8.1}$$

and that X_{t+1} given $\left(X_t, \mathbf{X}^{(t-1)}, \mathbf{Y}^{(t)}\right)$ is independent of $\left(\mathbf{X}^{(t-1)}, \mathbf{Y}^{(t)}\right)$ with conditional density function

$$p(x_{t+1}|x_t) := p\left(x_{t+1}|x_t, \mathbf{x}^{(t-1)}, \mathbf{y}^{(t)}\right) \quad t = 1, 2, \ldots. \tag{8.8.2}$$

We shall also assume that the initial state X_1 has probability density p_1. The joint density of the observation and state variables can be computed directly from (8.8.1)–(8.8.2) as

$$\begin{aligned} p(y_1, \ldots, y_n, x_1, \ldots, x_n) &= p\left(y_n|x_n, \mathbf{x}^{(n-1)}, \mathbf{y}^{(n-1)}\right) p\left(x_n, \mathbf{x}^{(n-1)}, \mathbf{y}^{(n-1)}\right) \\ &= p(y_n|x_n) p\left(x_n|\mathbf{x}^{(n-1)}, \mathbf{y}^{(n-1)}\right) p\left(\mathbf{y}^{(n-1)}, \mathbf{x}^{(n-1)}\right) \\ &= p(y_n|x_n) p(x_n|x_{n-1}) p\left(\mathbf{y}^{(n-1)}, \mathbf{x}^{(n-1)}\right) \\ &= \cdots \\ &= \left(\prod_{j=1}^{n} p(y_j|x_j)\right)\left(\prod_{j=2}^{n} p(x_j|x_{j-1})\right) p_1(x_1), \end{aligned}$$

and since (8.8.2) implies that $\{X_t\}$ is Markov (see Problem 8.22),

$$p(y_1, \ldots, y_n|x_1, \ldots, x_n) = \left(\prod_{j=1}^{n} p(y_j|x_j)\right). \tag{8.8.3}$$

We conclude that $Y_1, \ldots, Y_n$ are conditionally independent given the state variables $X_1, \ldots, X_n$, so that the dependence structure of $\{Y_t\}$ is inherited from that of the state process $\{X_t\}$. The sequence of state variables $\{X_t\}$ is often referred to as the **hidden** or **latent** generating process associated with the observed process.

In order to solve the **filtering** and **prediction** problems in this setting, we shall determine the conditional densities $p\left(x_t|\mathbf{y}^{(t)}\right)$ of X_t given $\mathbf{Y}^{(t)}$, and $p\left(x_t|\mathbf{y}^{(t-1)}\right)$ of X_t given $\mathbf{Y}^{(t-1)}$, respectively. The minimum mean squared error estimates of X_t based on $\mathbf{Y}^{(t)}$ and $\mathbf{Y}^{(t-1)}$ can then be computed as the conditional expectations, $E\left(X_t|\mathbf{Y}^{(t)}\right)$ and $E\left(X_t|\mathbf{Y}^{(t-1)}\right)$.

An application of Bayes's theorem, using the assumption that the distribution of Y_t given $\left(X_t, \mathbf{X}^{(t-1)}, \mathbf{Y}^{(t-1)}\right)$ does not depend on $\left(\mathbf{X}^{(t-1)}, \mathbf{Y}^{(t-1)}\right)$, yields

$$p\left(x_t|\mathbf{y}^{(t)}\right) = p(y_t|x_t) p\left(x_t|\mathbf{y}^{(t-1)}\right) / p\left(y_t|\mathbf{y}^{(t-1)}\right) \tag{8.8.4}$$

and

$$p\left(x_{t+1}|\mathbf{y}^{(t)}\right) = \int p\left(x_t|\mathbf{y}^{(t)}\right) p(x_{t+1}|x_t)\, d\mu(x_t). \tag{8.8.5}$$

(The integral relative to $d\mu(x_t)$ in (8.8.4) is interpreted as the integral relative to dx_t in the continuous case and as the sum over all values of x_t in the discrete case.) The initial condition needed to solve these recursions is

$$p\left(x_1|\mathbf{y}^{(0)}\right) := p_1(x_1). \tag{8.8.6}$$

The factor $p\left(y_t|\mathbf{y}^{(t-1)}\right)$ appearing in the denominator of (8.8.4) is just a scale factor, determined by the condition $\int p\left(x_t|\mathbf{y}^{(t)}\right)\, d\mu(x_t) = 1$. In the generalized state-space setup, prediction of a future state variable is less important than forecasting a future value of the observations. The relevant forecast density can be computed from (8.8.5) as

$$p\left(y_{t+1}|\mathbf{y}^{(t)}\right) = \int p(y_{t+1}|x_{t+1})p\left(x_{t+1}|\mathbf{y}^{(t)}\right)\, d\mu(x_{t+1}). \tag{8.8.7}$$

Equations (8.8.1)–(8.8.2) can be regarded as a Bayesian model specification. A classical Bayesian model has two key assumptions. The first is that the data $Y_1, \ldots, Y_t$, given an unobservable parameter ($\mathbf{X}^{(t)}$ in our case), are independent with specified conditional distribution. This corresponds to (8.8.3). The second specifies a **prior distribution** for the parameter value. This corresponds to (8.8.2). The **posterior distribution** is then the conditional distribution of the parameter given the data. In the present setting the posterior distribution of the component X_t of $\mathbf{X}^{(t)}$ is determined by the solution (8.8.4) of the filtering problem.

Example 8.8.1

Consider the simplified version of the linear state-space model of Section 8.1,

$$Y_t = GX_t + W_t, \quad \{W_t\} \sim \text{iid N}(0, R), \tag{8.8.8}$$

$$X_{t+1} = FX_t + V_t, \quad \{V_t\} \sim \text{iid N}(0, Q), \tag{8.8.9}$$

where the noise sequences $\{W_t\}$ and $\{V_t\}$ are independent of each other. For this model the probability densities in (8.8.1)–(8.8.2) become

$$p_1(x_1) = n(x_1;\, EX_1, \text{Var}(X_1)), \tag{8.8.10}$$

$$p(y_t|x_t) = n(y_t;\, Gx_t, R), \tag{8.8.11}$$

$$p(x_{t+1}|x_t) = n(x_{t+1};\, Fx_t, Q), \tag{8.8.12}$$

where $n\left(x; \mu, \sigma^2\right)$ is the normal density with mean μ and variance σ^2 defined in Example (a) of Section A.1.

To solve the filtering and prediction problems in this new framework, we first observe that the filtering and prediction densities in (8.8.4) and (8.8.5) are both normal. We shall write them, using the notation of Section 8.4, as

$$p\left(x_t|\mathbf{Y}^{(t)}\right) = n(x_t;\, X_{t|t}, \Omega_{t|t}) \tag{8.8.13}$$

and

$$p\left(x_{t+1}|\mathbf{Y}^{(t)}\right) = n\left(x_{t+1};\, \hat{X}_{t+1}, \Omega_{t+1}\right). \tag{8.8.14}$$

From (8.8.5), (8.8.12), (8.8.13), and (8.8.14), we find that

$$\begin{aligned}\hat{X}_{t+1} &= \int_{-\infty}^{\infty} x_{t+1} p(x_{t+1}|\mathbf{Y}^{(t)}) dx_{t+1} \\ &= \int_{-\infty}^{\infty} x_{t+1} \int_{-\infty}^{\infty} p(x_t|\mathbf{Y}^{(t)}) p(x_{t+1}|x_t)\, dx_t\, dx_{t+1} \\ &= \int_{-\infty}^{\infty} p(x_t|\mathbf{Y}^{(t)}) \left[\int_{-\infty}^{\infty} x_{t+1} p(x_{t+1}|x_t)\, dx_{t+1}\right] dx_t \\ &= \int_{-\infty}^{\infty} F x_t p(x_t|\mathbf{Y}^{(t)})\, dx_t \\ &= F X_{t|t}\end{aligned}$$

and (see Problem 8.23)

$$\Omega_{t+1} = F^2 \Omega_{t|t} + Q.$$

Substituting the corresponding densities (8.8.11) and (8.8.14) into (8.8.4), we find by equating the coefficient of x_t^2 on both sides of (8.8.4) that

$$\Omega_{t|t}^{-1} = G^2 R^{-1} + \Omega_t^{-1} = G^2 R^{-1} + (F^2 \Omega_{t-1|t-1} + Q)^{-1}$$

and

$$X_{t|t} = \hat{X}_t + \Omega_{t|t} G R^{-1} \left(Y_t - G\hat{X}_t\right).$$

Also, from (8.8.4) with $p\left(x_1|\mathbf{y}^{(0)}\right) = n(x_1; EX_1, \Omega_1)$ we obtain the initial conditions

$$X_{1|1} = EX_1 + \Omega_{1|1} G R^{-1}(Y_1 - GEX_1)$$

and

$$\Omega_{1|1}^{-1} = G^2 R^{-1} + \Omega_1^{-1}.$$

The Kalman prediction and filtering recursions of Section 8.4 give the same results for $\hat{X}_t$ and $X_{t|t}$, since for Gaussian systems best linear mean square estimation is equivalent to best mean square estimation. □

Example 8.8.2 A non-Gaussian example

In general, the solution of the recursions (8.8.4) and (8.8.5) presents substantial computational problems. Numerical methods for dealing with non-Gaussian models are discussed by Sorenson and Alspach (1971) and Kitagawa (1987). Here we shall illustrate the recursions (8.8.4) and (8.8.5) in a very simple special case. Consider the state equation

$$X_t = aX_{t-1}, \tag{8.8.15}$$

with observation density

$$p(y_t|x_t) = \frac{(\pi x_t)^{y_t} e^{-\pi x_t}}{y_t!}, \quad y_t = 0, 1, \ldots, \tag{8.8.16}$$

where π is a constant between 0 and 1. The relationship in (8.8.15) implies that the transition density (in the discrete sense—see the comment after (8.8.5)) for the state variables is

$$p(x_{t+1}|x_t) = \begin{cases} 1, & \text{if } x_{t+1} = ax_t, \\ 0, & \text{otherwise.} \end{cases}$$

We shall assume that X_1 has the gamma density function

$$p_1(x_1) = g(x_1; \alpha, \lambda) = \frac{\lambda^\alpha x_1^{\alpha-1} e^{-\lambda x_1}}{\Gamma(\alpha)}, \quad x_1 > 0.$$

(This is a simplified model for the evolution of the number X_t of individuals at time t infected with a rare disease, in which X_t is treated as a continuous rather than an integer-valued random variable. The observation Y_t represents the number of infected individuals observed in a random sample consisting of a small fraction π of the population at time t.) Because the transition distribution of $\{X_t\}$ is not continuous, we use the integrated version of (8.8.5) to compute the prediction density. Thus,

$$\begin{aligned} P\left(X_t \le x|\mathbf{y}^{(t-1)}\right) &= \int_0^\infty P(X_t \le x|x_{t-1}) p\left(x_{t-1}|\mathbf{y}^{(t-1)}\right) dx_{t-1} \\ &= \int_0^{x/a} p\left(x_{t-1}|\mathbf{y}^{(t-1)}\right) dx_{t-1}. \end{aligned}$$

Differentiation with respect to x gives

$$p\left(x_t|\mathbf{y}^{(t-1)}\right) = a^{-1} p_{X_{t-1}|\mathbf{Y}^{(t-1)}}\left(a^{-1}x_t|\mathbf{y}^{(t-1)}\right). \tag{8.8.17}$$

Now applying (8.8.4), we find that

$$\begin{aligned} p(x_1|y_1) &= p(y_1|x_1)p_1(x_1)/p(y_1) \\ &= \left(\frac{(\pi x_1)^{y_1} e^{-\pi x_1}}{y_1!}\right)\left(\frac{\lambda^\alpha x_1^{\alpha-1} e^{-\lambda x_1}}{\Gamma(\alpha)}\right)\left(\frac{1}{p(y_1)}\right) \\ &= c(y_1) x_1^{\alpha+y_1-1} e^{-(\pi+\lambda)x_1}, \quad x_1 > 0, \end{aligned}$$

where $c(y_1)$ is an integration factor ensuring that $p(\cdot|y_1)$ integrates to 1. Since $p(\cdot|y_1)$ has the form of a gamma density, we deduce (see Example (d) of Section A.1) that

$$p(x_1|y_1) = g(x_1; \alpha_1, \lambda_1), \tag{8.8.18}$$

where $\alpha_1 = \alpha + y_1$ and $\lambda_1 = \lambda + \pi$. The prediction density, calculated from (8.8.5) and (8.8.18), is

$$\begin{aligned} p\left(x_2|\mathbf{y}^{(1)}\right) &= a^{-1} p_{X_1|\mathbf{Y}^{(1)}}\left(a^{-1}x_2|\mathbf{y}^{(1)}\right) \\ &= a^{-1} g\left(a^{-1}x_2; \alpha_1, \lambda_1\right) \\ &= g(x_2; \alpha_1, \lambda_1/a). \end{aligned}$$

Iterating the recursions (8.8.4) and (8.8.5) and using (8.8.17), we find that for $t \geq 1$,

$$p\left(x_t|\mathbf{y}^{(t)}\right) = g(x_t; \alpha_t, \lambda_t) \tag{8.8.19}$$

and

$$\begin{aligned} p\left(x_{t+1}|\mathbf{y}^{(t)}\right) &= a^{-1} g\left(a^{-1}x_{t+1}; \alpha_t, \lambda_t\right) \\ &= g(x_{t+1}; \alpha_t, \lambda_t/a), \end{aligned} \tag{8.8.20}$$

where $\alpha_t = \alpha_{t-1} + y_t = \alpha + y_1 + \cdots + y_t$ and $\lambda_t = \lambda_{t-1}/a + \pi = \lambda a^{1-t} + \pi\left(1 - a^{-t}\right)/(1 - a^{-1})$. In particular, the minimum mean squared error estimate of x_t based on $\mathbf{y}^{(t)}$ is the conditional expectation α_t/λ_t with conditional variance α_t/λ_t^2. From (8.8.7) the probability density of Y_{t+1} given $\mathbf{Y}^{(t)}$ is

$$\begin{aligned} p(y_{t+1}|\mathbf{y}^{(t)}) &= \int_0^\infty \left(\frac{(\pi x_{t+1})^{y_{t+1}} e^{-\pi x_{t+1}}}{y_{t+1}!}\right) g(x_{t+1}; \alpha_t, \lambda_t/a)\, dx_{t+1} \\ &= \frac{\Gamma(\alpha_t + y_{t+1})}{\Gamma(\alpha_t)\Gamma(y_{t+1}+1)} \left(1 - \frac{\pi}{\lambda_{t+1}}\right)^{\alpha_t} \left(\frac{\pi}{\lambda_{t+1}}\right)^{y_{t+1}} \\ &= nb(y_{t+1}; \alpha_t, 1 - \pi/\lambda_{t+1}), \quad y_{t+1} = 0, 1, \ldots, \end{aligned}$$

where $nb(y; \alpha, p)$ is the negative binomial density defined in example (i) of Section A.1. Conditional on $\mathbf{Y}^{(t)}$, the best one-step predictor of Y_{t+1} is therefore the mean, $\alpha_t\pi/(\lambda_{t+1} - \pi)$, of this negative binomial distribution. The conditional mean squared error of the predictor is $\text{Var}\left(Y_{t+1}|\mathbf{Y}^{(t)}\right) = \alpha_t\pi\lambda_{t+1}/(\lambda_{t+1} - \pi)^2$ (see Problem 8.25). □

Example 8.8.3 A model for time series of counts

We often encounter time series in which the observations represent count data. One such example is the monthly number of newly recorded cases of poliomyelitis in the U.S. for the years 1970–1983 plotted in Figure 8.6. Unless the actual counts are large and can be approximated by continuous variables, Gaussian and linear time series models are generally inappropriate for analyzing such data. The parameter-driven specification provides a flexible class of models for modeling count data. We now discuss a specific model based on a Poisson observation density. This model is similar to the one presented by Zeger (1988) for analyzing the polio data. The observation density is assumed to be Poisson with mean $\exp\{x_t\}$, i.e.,

$$p(y_t|x_t) = \frac{e^{x_t y_t} e^{-e^{x_t}}}{y_t!}, \qquad y_t = 0, 1, \ldots, \tag{8.8.21}$$

while the state variables are assumed to follow a regression model with Gaussian AR(1) noise. If $\mathbf{u}_t = (u_{t1}, \ldots, u_{tk})'$ are the regression variables, then

$$X_t = \boldsymbol{\beta}'\mathbf{u}_t + W_t, \tag{8.8.22}$$

where $\boldsymbol{\beta}$ is a k-dimensional regression parameter and

$$W_t = \phi W_{t-1} + Z_t, \quad \{Z_t\} \sim \text{IID N}\left(0, \sigma^2\right).$$

The transition density function for the state variables is then

$$p(x_{t+1}|x_t) = n(x_{t+1}; \boldsymbol{\beta}'\mathbf{u}_{t+1} + \phi\left(x_t - \boldsymbol{\beta}'\mathbf{u}_t\right), \sigma^2\right). \tag{8.8.23}$$

The case $\sigma^2 = 0$ corresponds to a log-linear model with Poisson noise.

Estimation of the parameters $\boldsymbol{\theta} = \left(\boldsymbol{\beta}', \phi, \sigma^2\right)'$ in the model by direct numerical maximization of the likelihood function is difficult, since the likelihood cannot be written down in closed form. (From (8.8.3) the likelihood is the n-fold integral,

$$\int_{-\infty}^{\infty} \cdots \int_{-\infty}^{\infty} \exp\left\{\sum_{t=1}^{n}\left(x_t y_t - e^{x_t}\right)\right\} L\left(\boldsymbol{\theta}; \mathbf{x}^{(n)}\right) (dx_1 \cdots dx_n) \Big/ \prod_{i=1}^{n}(y_i!),$$

where $L(\boldsymbol{\theta}; \mathbf{x})$ is the likelihood based on $X_1, \ldots, X_n$.) To overcome this difficulty, Chan and Ledolter (1995) proposed an algorithm, called Monte Carlo EM (MCEM), whose iterates $\theta^{(i)}$ converge to the maximum likelihood estimate. To apply this algorithm, first note that the conditional distribution of $\mathbf{Y}^{(n)}$ given $\mathbf{X}^{(n)}$ does not depend

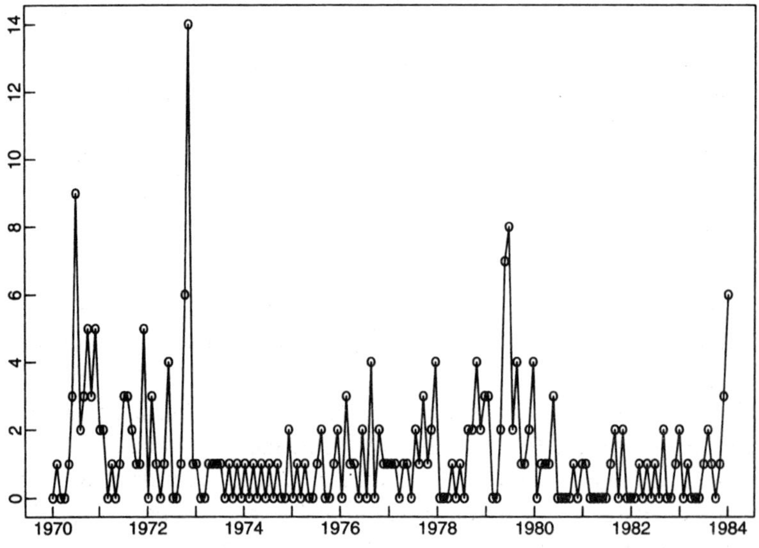

Figure 8-6 Monthly number of U.S. cases of polio, Jan. '70–Dec. '83.

on $\boldsymbol{\theta}$, so that the likelihood based on the complete data $\left(\mathbf{X}^{(n)\prime}, \mathbf{Y}^{(n)\prime}\right)'$ is given by

$$L\left(\boldsymbol{\theta}; \mathbf{X}^{(n)}, \mathbf{Y}^{(n)}\right) = f\left(\mathbf{Y}^{(n)}|\mathbf{X}^{(n)}\right) L\left(\boldsymbol{\theta}; \mathbf{X}^{(n)}\right).$$

The E-step of the algorithm (see Section 8.7) requires calculation of

$$\begin{aligned} Q(\boldsymbol{\theta}|\boldsymbol{\theta}^{(i)}) &= E_{\boldsymbol{\theta}^{(i)}}\left(\ln L(\boldsymbol{\theta}; \mathbf{X}^{(n)}, \mathbf{Y}^{(n)})|\mathbf{Y}^{(n)}\right) \\ &= E_{\boldsymbol{\theta}^{(i)}}\left(\ln f(\mathbf{Y}^{(n)}|\mathbf{X}^{(n)})|\mathbf{Y}^{(n)}\right) + E_{\boldsymbol{\theta}^{(i)}}\left(\ln L(\boldsymbol{\theta}; \mathbf{X}^{(n)})|\mathbf{Y}^{(n)}\right). \end{aligned}$$

We delete the first term from the definition of Q, since it is independent of $\boldsymbol{\theta}$ and hence plays no role in the M-step of the EM algorithm. The new Q is redefined as

$$Q(\boldsymbol{\theta}|\boldsymbol{\theta}^{(i)}) = E_{\boldsymbol{\theta}^{(i)}}\left(\ln L(\boldsymbol{\theta}; \mathbf{X}^{(n)})|\mathbf{Y}^{(n)}\right). \tag{8.8.24}$$

Even with this simplification, direct calculation of Q is still intractable. Suppose for the moment that it is possible to generate replicates of $\mathbf{X}^{(n)}$ from the conditional distribution of $\mathbf{X}^{(n)}$ given $\mathbf{Y}^{(n)}$ when $\boldsymbol{\theta} = \boldsymbol{\theta}^{(i)}$. If we denote m independent replicates of $\mathbf{X}^{(n)}$ by $\mathbf{X}_1^{(n)}, \ldots, \mathbf{X}_m^{(n)}$, then a Monte Carlo approximation to Q in (8.8.24) is given by

$$Q_m\left(\boldsymbol{\theta}|\boldsymbol{\theta}^{(i)}\right) = \frac{1}{m}\sum_{j=1}^{m} \ln L\left(\boldsymbol{\theta}; \mathbf{X}_j^{(n)}\right).$$

The M-step is easy to carry out using Q_m in place of Q (especially if we condition on $X_1 = 0$ in all the simulated replicates), since L is just the Gaussian likelihood of the regression model with AR(1) noise treated in Section 6.6. The difficult steps in the algorithm are the generation of replicates of $\mathbf{X}^{(n)}$ given $\mathbf{Y}^{(n)}$ and the choice of m. Chan and Ledolter (1995) discuss the use of the Gibb's sampler for generating the desired replicates and give some guidelines on the choice of m.

In their analyses of the polio data, Zeger (1988) and Chan and Ledolter (1995) included as regression components an intercept, a slope, and harmonics at periods of 6 and 12 months. Specifically, they took

$$\mathbf{u}_t = (1, t/1000, \cos(2\pi t/12), \sin(2\pi t/12), \cos(2\pi t/6), \sin(2\pi t/6))'.$$

The implementation of Chan and Ledolter's MCEM method by Kuk and Cheng (1994) gave estimates $\hat{\boldsymbol{\beta}} = (.247, -3.871, .162, -.482, .414, -.011)'$, $\hat{\phi} = .648$, and $\hat{\sigma}^2 = .281$. The estimated trend function $\hat{\boldsymbol{\beta}}'\mathbf{u}_t$ is displayed in Figure 8.7. The negative coefficient of $t/1000$ indicates a slight downward trend in the monthly number of polio cases. □

8.8.2 Observation-Driven Models

In an observation-driven model it is again assumed that Y_t, conditional on $\left(X_t, \mathbf{X}^{(t-1)}, \mathbf{Y}^{(t-1)}\right)$, is independent of $\left(\mathbf{X}^{(t-1)}, \mathbf{Y}^{(t-1)}\right)$. The model is specified by the conditional densities

$$p(y_t|x_t) = p\left(y_t|\mathbf{x}^{(t)}, \mathbf{y}^{(t-1)}\right), \quad t = 1, 2, \ldots, \tag{8.8.25}$$

$$p\left(x_{t+1}|\mathbf{y}^{(t)}\right) = p_{X_{t+1}|\mathbf{Y}^{(t)}}\left(x_{t+1}|\mathbf{y}^{(t)}\right), \quad t = 0, 1, \ldots, \tag{8.8.26}$$

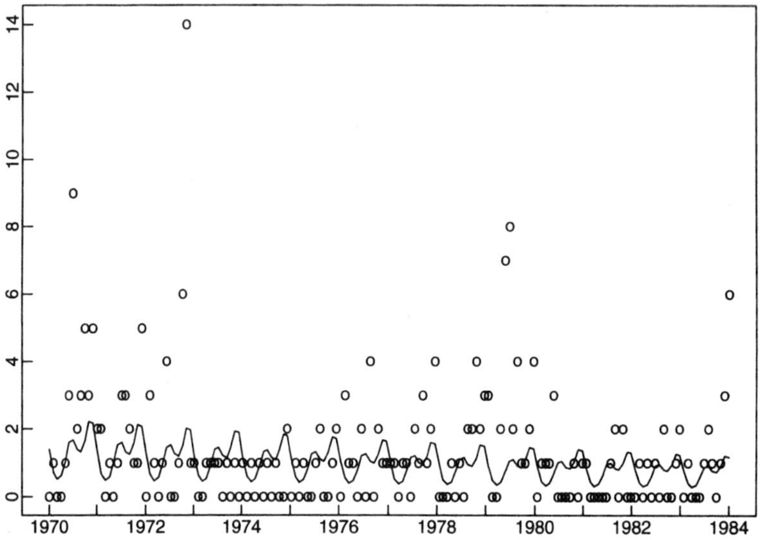

Figure 8-7 Trend estimate for the monthly number of U.S. cases of polio, Jan. '70–Dec. '83.

where $p\left(x_1|\mathbf{y}^{(0)}\right) := p_1(x_1)$ for some prespecified initial density $p_1(x_1)$. The advantage of the observation-driven state equation (8.8.26) is that the posterior distribution of X_t given $\mathbf{Y}^{(t)}$ can be computed directly from (8.8.4) without the use of the updating formula (8.8.5). This then allows for easy computation of the forecast function in (8.8.7) and hence of the joint density function of $(Y_1, \ldots, Y_n)'$,

$$p(y_1, \ldots, y_n) = \prod_{t=1}^{n} p\left(y_t|\mathbf{y}^{(t-1)}\right). \tag{8.8.27}$$

On the other hand, the mechanism by which the state X_{t-1} makes the transition to X_t is not explicitly defined. In fact, without further assumptions there may be state sequences $\{X_t\}$ and $\{X_t^*\}$ with different distributions for which both (8.8.25) and (8.8.26) hold (see Example 8.8.6). Both sequences, however, lead to the same joint distribution, given by (8.8.27), for $Y_1, \ldots, Y_n$. The ambiguity in the specification of the distribution of the state variables can be removed by assuming that X_{t+1} given $\left(\mathbf{X}^{(t)}, \mathbf{Y}^{(t)}\right)$ is independent of $\mathbf{X}^{(t)}$, with conditional distribution (8.8.26), i.e.,

$$p\left(x_{t+1}|\mathbf{x}^{(t)}, \mathbf{y}^{(t)}\right) = p_{X_{t+1}|\mathbf{Y}^{(t)}}\left(x_{t+1}|\mathbf{y}^{(t)}\right). \tag{8.8.28}$$

With this modification, the joint density of $\mathbf{Y}^{(n)}$ and $\mathbf{X}^{(n)}$ is given by (cf. (8.8.3))

$$\begin{aligned} p\left(\mathbf{y}^{(n)}, \mathbf{x}^{(n)}\right) &= p(y_n|x_n)p\left(x_n|\mathbf{y}^{(n-1)}\right)p\left(\mathbf{y}^{(n-1)}, \mathbf{x}^{(n-1)}\right) \\ &= \cdots \\ &= \prod_{t=1}^{n}\left(p(y_t|x_t)p\left(x_t|\mathbf{y}^{(t-1)}\right)\right). \end{aligned}$$

Example 8.8.4 An AR(1) process

An AR(1) process with iid noise can be expressed as an observation driven model. Suppose $\{Y_t\}$ is the AR(1) process

$$Y_t = \phi Y_{t-1} + Z_t,$$

where $\{Z_t\}$ is an iid sequence of random variables with mean 0 and some probability density function $f(x)$. Then with $X_t := Y_{t-1}$ we have

$$p(y_t|x_t) = f(y_t - \phi x_t)$$

and

$$p\left(x_{t+1}|\mathbf{y}^{(t)}\right) = \begin{cases} 1, & \text{if } x_{t+1} = y_t, \\ 0, & \text{otherwise.} \end{cases}$$

□

Example 8.8.5 Suppose the observation-equation density is given by

$$p(y_t|x_t) = \frac{x_t^{y_t} e^{-x_t}}{y_t!}, \quad y_t = 0, 1, \ldots, \tag{8.8.29}$$

and the state equation (8.8.26) is

$$p\left(x_{t+1}|\mathbf{y}^{(t)}\right) = g(x_t; \alpha_t, \lambda_t), \tag{8.8.30}$$

where $\alpha_t = \alpha + y_1 + \cdots + y_t$ and $\lambda_t = \lambda + t$. It is possible to give a parameter-driven specification that gives rise to the same state equation (8.8.30). Let $\{X_t^*\}$ be the parameter-driven state variables, where $X_t^* = X_{t-1}^*$ and X_1^* has a gamma distribution with parameters α and λ. (This corresponds to the model in Example 8.8.2 with $\pi = a = 1$.) Then from (8.8.19) we see that $p\left(x_t^*|\mathbf{y}^{(t)}\right) = g(x_t^*; \alpha_t, \lambda_t)$, which coincides with the state equation (8.8.30). If $\{X_t\}$ are the state variables whose joint distribution is specified through (8.8.28), then $\{X_t\}$ and $\{X_t^*\}$ cannot have the same joint distributions. To see this, note that

$$p\left(x_{t+1}^*|x_t^*\right) = \begin{cases} 1, & \text{if } x_{t+1}^* = x_t^*, \\ 0, & \text{otherwise,} \end{cases}$$

while

$$p\left(x_{t+1}|\mathbf{x}^{(t)}, \mathbf{y}^{(t)}\right) = p\left(x_{t+1}|\mathbf{y}^{(t)}\right) = g(x_t; \alpha_t, \lambda_t).$$

If the two sequences had the same joint distribution, then the latter density could take only the values 0 and 1, which contradicts the continuity (as a function of x_t) of this density. □

Exponential Family Models

The exponential family of distributions provides a large and flexible class of distributions for use in the observation equation. The density in the observation equation is said to belong to an **exponential family** (in natural parameterization) if

$$p(y_t|x_t) = \exp\{y_t x_t - b(x_t) + c(y_t)\}, \tag{8.8.31}$$

where $b(\cdot)$ is a twice continuously differentiable function and $c(y_t)$ does not depend on x_t. This family includes the normal, exponential, gamma, Poisson, binomial, and many other distributions frequently encountered in statistics. Detailed properties of the exponential family can be found in Barndorff-Nielsen (1978), and an excellent treatment of its use in the analysis of linear models is given by McCullagh and Nelder (1989). We shall need only the following important facts:

$$e^{b(x_t)} = \int \exp\{y_t x_t + c(y_t)\}\, \nu(dy_t), \tag{8.8.32}$$

$$b'(x_t) = E(Y_t|x_t), \tag{8.8.33}$$

$$b''(x_t) = \mathrm{Var}(Y_t|x_t) := \int y_t^2 p(y_x|x_t)\, \nu(dy_t) - \left[b'(x_t)\right]^2, \tag{8.8.34}$$

where integration with respect to $\nu(dy_t)$ means integration with respect to dy_t in the continuous case and summation over all values of y_t in the discrete case.

Proof of (8.8.32)–(8.8.34)
The first relation is simply the statement that $p(y_t|x_t)$ integrates to 1. The second relation is established by differentiating both sides of (8.8.32) with respect to x_t and then multiplying through by $e^{-b(x_t)}$ (for justification of the differentiation under the integral sign see Barndorff-Nielson (1978)). The last relation is obtained by differentiating (8.8.32) twice with respect to x_t and simplifying. ■

Example 8.8.6 The Poisson case

If the observation Y_t, given $X_t = x_t$, has a Poisson distribution of the form (8.8.21), then

$$p(y_t|x_t) = \exp\left\{y_t x_t - e^{x_t} - \ln y_t!\right\}, \quad y_t = 0, 1, \ldots, \tag{8.8.35}$$

which has the form (8.8.31) with $b(x_t) = e^{x_t}$ and $c(y_t) = -\ln y_t!$. From (8.8.33) we easily find that $E(Y_t|x_t) = b'(x_t) = e^{x_t}$. This parameterization is slightly different from the one used in Examples 8.8.2 and 8.8.5, where the conditional mean of Y_t given x_t was πx_t and not e^{x_t}. For this observation equation, define the family of densities

$$f(x; \alpha, \lambda) = \exp\{\alpha x - \lambda b(x) + A(\alpha, \lambda)\}, \quad -\infty < x < \infty, \tag{8.8.36}$$

where $\alpha > 0$ and $\lambda > 0$ are parameters and $A(\alpha, \lambda) = -\ln\Gamma(\alpha) + \alpha \ln \lambda$. Now consider state densities of the form

$$p(x_{t+1}|\mathbf{y}^{(t)}) = f(x_{t+1}; \alpha_{t+1|t}, \lambda_{t+1|t}), \tag{8.8.37}$$

where $\alpha_{t+1|t}$ and $\lambda_{t+1|t}$ are, for the moment, unspecified functions of $\mathbf{y}^{(t)}$. (The subscript $t+1|t$ on the parameters is a shorthand way to indicate dependence on the conditional distribution of X_{t+1} given $\mathbf{Y}^{(t)}$.) With this specification of the state densities, the parameters $\alpha_{t+1|t}$ are related to the best one-step predictor of Y_t through the formula

$$\alpha_{t+1|t}/\lambda_{t+1|t} = \hat{Y}_{t+1} := E\left(Y_{t+1}|\mathbf{y}^{(t)}\right). \tag{8.8.38}$$

Proof We have from (8.8.7) and (8.8.33) that

$$\begin{aligned} E(Y_{t+1}|\mathbf{y}^{(t)}) &= \sum_{y_{t+1}=0}^{\infty} \int_{-\infty}^{\infty} y_{t+1} p(y_{t+1}|x_{t+1}) p\left(x_{t+1}|\mathbf{y}^{(t)}\right) dx_{t+1} \\ &= \int_{-\infty}^{\infty} b'(x_{t+1}) p\left(x_{t+1}|\mathbf{y}^{(t)}\right) dx_{t+1}. \end{aligned}$$

Addition and subtraction of $\alpha_{t+1|t}/\lambda_{t+1|t}$ then gives

$$\begin{aligned} E(Y_{t+1}|\mathbf{y}^{(t)}) &= \int_{-\infty}^{\infty} \left(b'(x_{t+1}) - \frac{\alpha_{t+1|t}}{\lambda_{t+1|t}}\right) p\left(x_{t+1}|\mathbf{y}^{(t)}\right) dx_{t+1} + \frac{\alpha_{t+1|t}}{\lambda_{t+1|t}} \\ &= \int_{-\infty}^{\infty} -\lambda_{t+1|t}^{-1} p'\left(x_{t+1}|\mathbf{y}^{(t)}\right) dx_{t+1} + \frac{\alpha_{t+1|t}}{\lambda_{t+1|t}} \\ &= \left[-\lambda_{t+1|t}^{-1} p\left(x_{t+1}|\mathbf{y}^{(t)}\right)\right]_{x_{t+1}=-\infty}^{x_{t+1}=\infty} + \frac{\alpha_{t+1|t}}{\lambda_{t+1|t}} \\ &= \frac{\alpha_{t+1|t}}{\lambda_{t+1|t}}. \end{aligned}$$

■

Letting $A_{t|t-1} = A(\alpha_{t|t-1}, \lambda_{t|t-1})$, we can write the posterior density of X_t given $\mathbf{Y}^{(t)}$ as

$$\begin{aligned} p\left(x_t|\mathbf{y}^{(t)}\right) &= \exp\{y_t x_t - b(x_t) + c(y_t)\} \exp\{\alpha_{t|t-1} x_t - \lambda_{t|t-1} b(x_t) \\ &\quad + A_{t|t-1}\}/p\left(y_t|\mathbf{y}^{(t-1)}\right) \\ &= \exp\{\lambda_{t|t}\left(\alpha_{t|t} x_t - b(x_t)\right) - A_{t|t}\}, \\ &= f(x_t; \alpha_t, \lambda_t), \end{aligned}$$

where we find, by equating coefficients of x_t and $b(x_t)$, that the coefficients λ_t and α_t are determined by

$$\lambda_t = 1 + \lambda_{t|t-1}, \tag{8.8.39}$$

$$\alpha_t = y_t + \alpha_{t|t-1}. \tag{8.8.40}$$

The family of prior densities in (8.8.37) is called a **conjugate family of priors** for the observation equation (8.8.35), since the resulting posterior densities are again members of the same family.

As mentioned earlier, the parameters $\alpha_{t|t-1}$ and $\lambda_{t|t-1}$ can be quite arbitrary: Any nonnegative functions of $\mathbf{y}^{(t-1)}$ will lead to a consistent specification of the state densities. One convenient choice is to link these parameters with the corresponding parameters of the posterior distribution at time $t-1$ through the relations

$$\lambda_{t+1|t} = \delta\lambda_t \left(= \delta(1 + \lambda_{t|t-1})\right), \tag{8.8.41}$$

$$\alpha_{t+1|t} = \delta\alpha_t \left(= \delta(y_t + \alpha_{t|t-1})\right), \tag{8.8.42}$$

where $0 < \delta < 1$ (see Remark 4 below). Iterating the relation (8.8.41), we see that

$$\begin{aligned}\lambda_{t+1|t} &= \delta(1 + \lambda_{t|t-1}) = \delta + \delta\lambda_{t|t-1} \\ &= \delta + \delta(\delta + \delta\lambda_{t-2|t-2}) \\ &= \cdots \\ &= \delta + \delta^2 + \cdots + \delta^t + \delta^t\lambda_{1|0} \\ &\to \delta/(1-\delta)\end{aligned} \tag{8.8.43}$$

as $t \to \infty$. Similarly,

$$\begin{aligned}\alpha_{t+1|t} &= \delta y_t + \delta\alpha_{t|t-1} \\ &= \cdots \\ &= \delta y_t + \delta^2 y_{t-1} + \cdots + \delta^t y_1 + \delta^t\alpha_{1|0}.\end{aligned} \tag{8.8.44}$$

For large t, we have the approximations

$$\lambda_{t+1|t} = \delta/(1-\delta) \tag{8.8.45}$$

and

$$\alpha_{t+1|t} = \delta\sum_{j=0}^{t-1}\delta^j y_{t-j}, \tag{8.8.46}$$

which are exact if $\lambda_{1|0} = \delta/(1-\delta)$ and $\alpha_{1|0} = 0$. From (8.8.38) the one-step predictors are linear and given by

$$\hat{Y}_{t+1} = \frac{\alpha_{t+1|t}}{\lambda_{t+1|t}} = \frac{\sum_{j=0}^{t-1}\delta^j y_{t-j} + \delta^{t-1}\alpha_{1|0}}{\sum_{j=0}^{t-1}\delta^j + \delta^{t-1}\lambda_{1|0}}. \tag{8.8.47}$$

Replacing the denominator with its limiting value, or starting with $\lambda_{1|0} = \delta/(1-\delta)$, we find that $\hat{Y}_{t+1}$ is the solution of the recursions

$$\hat{Y}_{t+1} = (1-\delta)y_t + \delta\hat{Y}_t, \quad t = 1, 2, \ldots, \tag{8.8.48}$$

with initial condition $\hat{Y}_1 = (1-\delta)\delta^{-1}\alpha_{1|0}$. In other words, under the restrictions of (8.8.41) and (8.8.42), the best one-step predictors can be found by exponential smoothing. □

Remark 1. The preceding analysis for the Poisson-distributed observation equation holds, almost verbatim, for the general family of exponential densities (8.8.31). (One only needs to take care in specifying the correct range for x and the allowable parameter space for α and λ in (8.8.37).) The relations (8.8.43)–(8.8.44), as well as the exponential smoothing formula (8.8.48), continue to hold even in the more general setting, provided that the parameters $\alpha_{t|t-1}$ and $\lambda_{t|t-1}$ satisfy the relations (8.8.41)–(8.8.42). □

Remark 2. Equations (8.8.41)–(8.8.42) are equivalent to the assumption that the prior density of X_t given $\mathbf{y}^{(t-1)}$ is proportional to the δ-power of the posterior distribution of X_{t-1} given $\mathbf{Y}^{(t-1)}$, or more succinctly that

$$
\begin{aligned}
f(x_t; \alpha_{t|t-1}, \lambda_{t|t-1}) &= f(x_t; \delta\alpha_{t-1|t-1}, \delta\lambda_{t-1|t-1}) \\
&\propto f^{\delta}(x_t; \alpha_{t-1|t-1}, \lambda_{t-1|t-1}).
\end{aligned}
$$

This power relationship is sometimes referred to as the **power steady model** (Grunwald, Raftery, and Guttorp, 1993, and Smith, 1979). □

Remark 3. The transformed state variables $W_t = e^{X_t}$ have a gamma state density given by

$$p\left(w_{t+1}|\mathbf{y}^{(t)}\right) = g(w_{t+1}; \alpha_{t+1|t}, \lambda_{t+1|t})$$

(see Problem 8.26). The mean and variance of this conditional density are

$$E\left(W_{t+1}|\mathbf{y}^{(t)}\right) = \alpha_{t+1|t} \quad \text{and} \quad \operatorname{Var}\left(W_{t+1}|\mathbf{y}^{(t)}\right) = \alpha_{t+1|t}/\lambda^2_{t+1|t}. \quad □$$

Remark 4. If we regard the random walk plus noise model of Example 8.2.1 as the prototypical state-space model, then from the calculations in Example 8.8.1 with $G = F = 1$, we have

$$E\left(X_{t+1}|\mathbf{Y}^{(t)}\right) = E\left(X_t|\mathbf{Y}^{(t)}\right)$$

and

$$\operatorname{Var}\left(X_{t+1}|\mathbf{Y}^{(t)}\right) = \operatorname{Var}\left(X_t|\mathbf{Y}^{(t)}\right) + Q > \operatorname{Var}\left(X_t|\mathbf{Y}^{(t)}\right).$$

The first of these equations implies that the best estimate of the next state is the same as the best estimate of the current state, while the second implies that the variance increases. Under the conditions (8.8.41), and (8.8.42), the same is also true for the state variables in the above model (see Problem 8.26). This was, in part, the rationale behind these conditions given in Harvey and Fernandes (1989). □

Remark 5. While the calculations work out neatly for the power steady model, Grunwald, Hyndman, and Hamza (1994) have shown that such processes have degenerate sample paths for large t. In the Poisson example above, they argue that the observations Y_t converge to 0 as $t \to \infty$ (see Figure 8.12). Although such models may still be useful in practice for modeling series of moderate length, the efficacy of using such models for describing long-term behavior is doubtful. □

Example 8.8.7 Goals scored by England against Scotland

The time series of the number of goals scored by England against Scotland in soccer matches played at Hampden Park in Glasgow is graphed in Figure 8.8. The matches have been played nearly every second year, with interruptions during the war years. We will treat the data $y_1, \ldots, y_{52}$ as coming from an equally spaced time series model $\{Y_t\}$. Since the number of goals scored is small (see the frequency histogram in Figure 8.9), a model based on the Poisson distribution might be deemed appropriate. The observed relative frequencies and those based on a Poisson distribution with mean equal to $\bar{y}_{52} = 1.269$ are contained in Table 8.2. The standard chi-squared goodness of fit test, comparing the observed frequencies with expected frequencies based on a Poisson model, has a p-value of .02. The lack of fit with a Poisson distribution is hardly unexpected, since the sample variance (1.652) is much larger than the sample mean, while the mean and variance of the Poisson distribution are equal. In this case the data are said to be *overdispersed* in the sense that there is more variability in the data than one would expect from a sample of independent Poisson-distributed variables. Overdispersion can sometimes be explained by serial dependence in the data.

Dependence in count data can often be revealed by estimating the probabilities of transition from one state to another. Table 8.3 contains estimates of these probabilities, computed as the average number of one-step transitions from state y_t to state y_{t+1}. If the data were independent, then in each column the entries should be nearly the same. This is certainly not the case in Table 8.3. For example, England is very unlikely to be shut out or score 3 or more goals in the next match after scoring at least 3 goals in the previous encounter.

Harvey and Fernandes (1989) model the dependence in this data using an observation-driven model of the type described in Example 8.8.6. Their model assumes a

Table 8.2 Relative frequency and fitted Poisson distribution of goals scored by England against Scotland

	Number of goals					
	0	1	2	3	4	5
Relative frequency	.288	.423	.154	.019	.096	.019
Poisson distribution	.281	.356	.226	.096	.030	.008

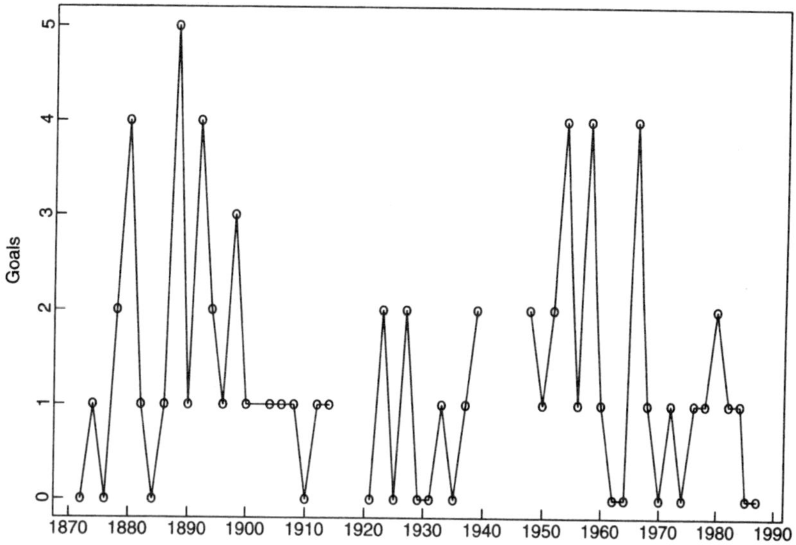

Figure 8-8 Goals scored by England against Scotland at Hampden Park, Glasgow, 1872–1987.

Poisson observation equation and a log-gamma state equation:

$$p(y_t|x_t) = \frac{\exp\{y_t x_t - e^{x_t}\}}{y_t!}, \quad y_t = 0, 1, \ldots,$$

$$p\left(x_t|\mathbf{y}^{(t-1)}\right) = f(x_t; \alpha_{t|t-1}, \lambda_{t|t-1}), \quad -\infty < x < \infty,$$

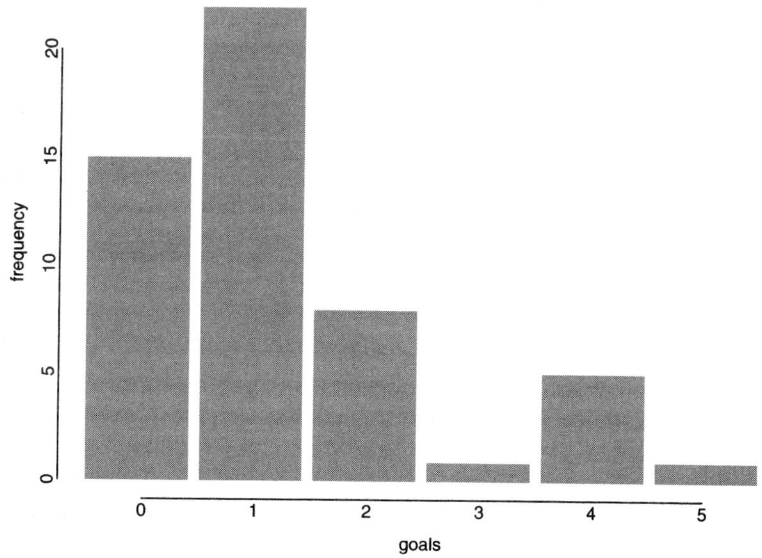

Figure 8-9 Histogram of the data in Figure 8.8.

Table 8.3 Transition probabilities for the number of goals scored by England against Scotland.

		y_{t+1}			
$p(y_{t+1}\|y_t)$		0	1	2	≥ 3
	0	.214	.500	.214	.072
y_t	1	.409	.272	.136	.182
	2	.250	.375	.125	.250
	≥ 3	0	.857	.143	0

for $t = 1, 2, \ldots,$ where f is given by (8.8.36) and $\alpha_{1|0} = 0, \lambda_{1|0} = 0$. The power steady conditions (8.8.41)–(8.8.42) are assumed to hold for $\alpha_{t|t-1}$ and $\lambda_{t|t-1}$. The only unknown parameter in the model is δ. The log-likelihood function for δ based on the conditional distribution of $y_1, \ldots, y_{52}$ given y_1 is given by (see (8.8.27))

$$\ell\left(\delta, \mathbf{y}^{(n)}\right) = \sum_{t=1}^{n-1} \ln p\left(y_{t+1} | \mathbf{y}^{(t)}\right), \tag{8.8.49}$$

where $p\left(y_{t+1}|\mathbf{y}^{(t)}\right)$ is the negative binomial density (see Problem 8.25(c))

$$p\left(y_{t+1}|\mathbf{y}^{(t)}\right) = nb\left(y_{t+1}; \alpha_{t+1|t}, (1 + \lambda_{t+1|t})^{-1}\right),$$

with $\alpha_{t+1|t}$ and $\lambda_{t+1|t}$ as defined in (8.8.44) and (8.8.43). (For the goal data, $y_1 = 0$, which implies $\alpha_{2|1} = 0$ and hence that $p\left(y_2|y^{(1)}\right)$ is a degenerate density with unit mass at $y_2 = 0$. Harvey and Fernandes avoid this complication by conditioning the likelihood on $y^{(\tau)}$, where τ is the time of the first nonzero data value.)

Maximizing this likelihood with respect to δ, we obtain $\hat{\delta} = .844$. (Starting the equations (8.8.43)–(8.8.44) with $\alpha_{1|0} = 0$ and $\lambda_{1|0} = \delta/(1-\delta)$, we obtain $\hat{\delta} = .732$.) With .844 as our estimate of δ, the prediction density of the next observation Y_{53} given $\mathbf{y}^{(52)}$ is $nb(y_{53}; \alpha_{53|52}, (1+\lambda_{53|52})^{-1}$. The first five values of this distribution are given in Table 8.4. Under this model, the probability that England will be held scoreless in the next match is .471. The one-step predictors, $\hat{Y}_1 = 0, \hat{Y}_2, \ldots, Y_{52}$ are graphed in Figure 8.10. (This graph can be obtained by using the ITSM option `Smooth>Exponential` with $\alpha = 0.154$.)

Figures 8.11 and 8.12 contain two realizations from the fitted model for the goal data. The general appearance of the first realization is somewhat compatible with the goal data, while the second realization illustrates the convergence of the sample path to 0 in accordance with the result of Grunwald et al. (1994). □

Table 8.4 Prediction density of Y_{53} given $\mathbf{Y}^{(52)}$ for data in Figure 8.7.

	Number of goals					
	0	1	2	3	4	5
$p(y_{53}\|\mathbf{y}^{(52)})$	.472	.326	.138	.046	.013	.004

Example 8.8.8 The exponential case

Suppose Y_t given X_t has an exponential density with mean $-1/X_t$ ($X_t < 0$). The observation density is given by

$$p(y_t|x_t) = \exp\{y_t x_t + \ln(-x_t)\}, \quad y_t > 0,$$

which has the form (8.8.31) with $b(x) = -\ln(-x)$ and $c(y) = 0$. The state densities corresponding to the family of conjugate priors (see (8.8.37)) are given by

$$p\left(x_{t+1}|\mathbf{y}^{(t)}\right) = \exp\{\alpha_{t+1|t}x_{t+1} - \lambda_{t+1|t}b(x_{t+1}) + A_{t+1|t}\}, \quad -\infty < x < 0.$$

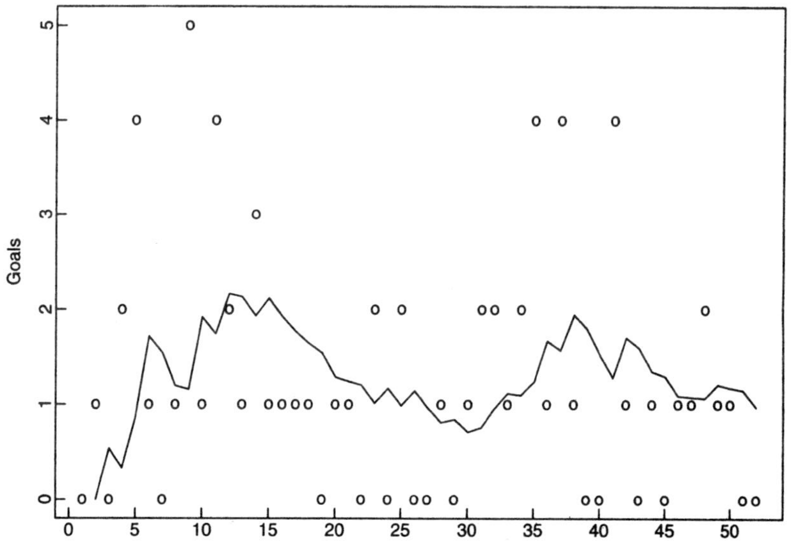

Figure 8-10 One-step predictors of the goal data.

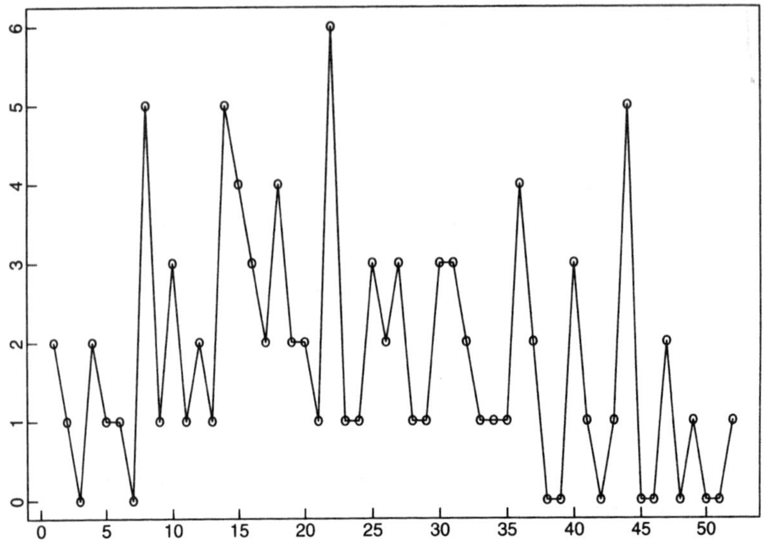

Figure 8-11 A simulated time series from the fitted model to the goal data.

(Here $p(x_{t+1}|\mathbf{y}^{(t)})$ is a probability density when $\alpha_{t+1|t} > 0$ and $\lambda_{t+1|t} > -1$.) The one-step prediction density is

$$p\left(y_{t+1}|\mathbf{y}^{(t)}\right) = \int_{-\infty}^{0} e^{x_{t+1}y_{t+1}+\ln(-x_{t+1})+\alpha_{t+1|t}x-\lambda_{t+1|t}b(x)+A_{t+1|t}}\,dx_{t+1}$$

$$= (\lambda_{t+1|t}+1)\alpha_{t+1|t}^{\lambda_{t+1|t}+1}(y_{t+1}+\alpha_{t+1|t})^{-\lambda_{t+1|t}-2}, \quad y_{t+1} > 0$$

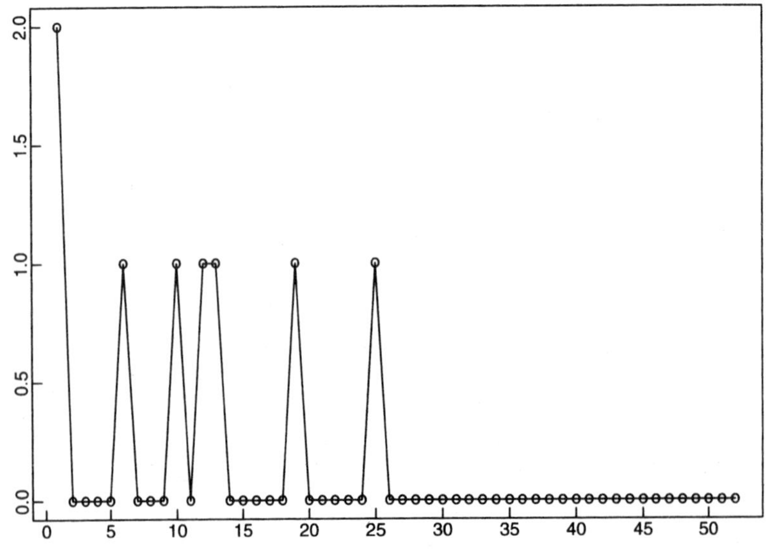

Figure 8-12 A second simulated time series from the fitted model to the goal data.

(see Problem 8.28). While $E(Y_{t+1}|\mathbf{y}^{(t)}) = \alpha_{t+1|t}/\lambda_{t+1|t}$, the conditional variance is finite if and only if $\lambda_{t+1|t} > 1$. Under assumptions (8.8.41)–(8.8.42), and starting with $\lambda_{1|0} = \delta/(1-\delta)$, the exponential smoothing formula (8.8.48) remains valid. □

Problems

8.1. Show that if all the eigenvalues of F are less than 1 in absolute value (or equivalently that $F^k \to 0$ as $k \to \infty$), the unique stationary solution of equation (8.1.11) is given by the infinite series

$$\mathbf{X}_t = \sum_{j=0}^{\infty} F^j V_{t-j-1}$$

and that the corresponding observation vectors are

$$\mathbf{Y}_t = \mathbf{W}_t + \sum_{j=0}^{\infty} GF^j \mathbf{V}_{t-j-1}.$$

Deduce that $\{(\mathbf{X}_t', \mathbf{Y}_t')'\}$ is a multivariate stationary process. (Hint: Use a vector analogue of the argument in Example 2.2.1.)

8.2. In Example 8.2.1, show that $\theta = -1$ if and only if $\sigma_v^2 = 0$, which in turn is equivalent to the signal M_t being constant.

8.3. Let F be the coefficient of $\mathbf{X}_t$ in the state equation (8.3.4) for the causal AR(p) process

$$X_t - \phi_1 X_{t-1} - \cdots - \phi_p X_{t-p} = Z_t, \quad \{Z_t\} \sim \mathrm{WN}\left(0, \sigma^2\right).$$

Establish the stability of (8.3.4) by showing that

$$\det(zI - F) = z^p \phi\left(z^{-1}\right),$$

and hence that the eigenvalues of F are the reciprocals of the zeros of the autoregressive polynomial $\phi(z) = 1 - \phi_1 z - \cdots - \phi_p z^p$.

8.4. By following the argument in Example 8.3.3, find a state-space model for $\{Y_t\}$ when $\{\nabla\nabla_{12} Y_t\}$ is an ARMA(p, q) process.

8.5. For the local linear trend model defined by equations (8.2.6)–(8.2.7), show that $\nabla^2 Y_t = (1-B)^2 Y_t$ is a 2-correlated sequence and hence, by Proposition 2.1.1, is an MA(2) process. Show that this MA(2) process is noninvertible if $\sigma_u^2 = 0$.

8.6. a. For the seasonal model of Example 8.2.2, show that $\nabla_d Y_t = Y_t - Y_{t-d}$ is an MA(1) process.

b. Show that $\nabla\nabla_d Y_t$ is an MA$(d+1)$ process where $\{Y_t\}$ follows the seasonal model with a local linear trend as described in Example 8.2.3.

8.7. Let $\{Y_t\}$ be the MA(1) process

$$Y_t = Z_t + \theta Z_{t-1}, \quad \{Z_t\} \sim \text{WN}\left(0, \sigma^2\right).$$

Show that $\{Y_t\}$ has the state-space representation

$$Y_t = [1 \quad 0]\mathbf{X}_t,$$

where $\{\mathbf{X}_t\}$ is the unique stationary solution of

$$\mathbf{X}_{t+1} = \begin{bmatrix} 0 & 1 \\ 0 & 0 \end{bmatrix}\mathbf{X}_t + \begin{bmatrix} 1 \\ \theta \end{bmatrix} Z_{t+1}.$$

In particular, show that the state vector $\mathbf{X}_t$ can written as

$$\mathbf{X}_t = \begin{bmatrix} 1 & \theta \\ \theta & 0 \end{bmatrix}\begin{bmatrix} Z_t \\ Z_{t-1} \end{bmatrix}.$$

8.8. Verify equations (8.3.16)–(8.3.18) for an ARIMA(1,1,1) process.

8.9. Consider the two state-space models

$$\begin{cases} \mathbf{X}_{t+1,1} = F_1\mathbf{X}_{t1} + \mathbf{V}_{t1}, \\ \mathbf{Y}_{t1} \quad = G_1\mathbf{X}_{t1} + \mathbf{W}_{t1}, \end{cases}$$

and

$$\begin{cases} \mathbf{X}_{t+1,2} = F_2\mathbf{X}_{t2} + \mathbf{V}_{t2}, \\ \mathbf{Y}_{t2} \quad = G_2\mathbf{X}_{t2} + \mathbf{W}_{t2}, \end{cases}$$

where $\{(\mathbf{V}'_{t1}, \mathbf{W}'_{t1}, \mathbf{V}'_{t2}, \mathbf{W}'_{t2})'\}$ is white noise. Derive a state-space representation for $\{(\mathbf{Y}'_{t1}, \mathbf{Y}'_{t2})'\}$.

8.10. Use Remark 1 of Section 8.4 to establish the linearity properties of the operator P_t stated in Remark 3.

8.11. a. Show that if the matrix equation $XS = B$ can be solved for X, then $X = BS^{-1}$ is a solution for *any* generalized inverse S^{-1} of S.

b. Use the result of (a) to derive the expression for $P(\mathbf{X}|\mathbf{Y})$ in Remark 4 of Section 8.4.

8.12. In the notation of the Kalman prediction equations, show that every vector of the form

$$\mathbf{Y} = A_1\mathbf{X}_1 + \cdots + A_t\mathbf{X}_t$$

can be expressed as

$$\mathbf{Y} = B_1\mathbf{X}_1 + \cdots + B_{t-1}\mathbf{X}_{t-1} + C_t\mathbf{I}_t,$$

where $B_1, \ldots, B_{t-1}$ and C_t are matrices that depend on the matrices $A_1, \ldots, A_t$. Show also that the converse is true. Use these results and the fact that $E(\mathbf{X}_s\mathbf{I}_t) = 0$ for all $s < t$ to establish (8.4.3).

8.13. In Example 8.4.1, verify that the steady-state solution of the Kalman recursions (8.1.2) is given by $\Omega_t = \left(\sigma_v^2 + \sqrt{\sigma_v^4 + 4\sigma_v^2\sigma_w^2}\right)/2$.

8.14. Show from the difference equations for Ω_t in Example 8.4.1 that $(\Omega_{t+1} - \Omega)(\Omega_t - \Omega) \geq 0$ for all $\Omega_t \geq 0$, where Ω is the steady-state solution for Ω_t given in Problem 8.13.

8.15. Show directly that for the MA(1) model (8.2.3), the parameter θ is equal to $-\left(2\sigma_w^2 + \sigma_v^2 - \sqrt{\sigma_v^4 + 4\sigma_v^2\sigma_w^2}\right)/\left(2\sigma_w^2\right)$, which in turn is equal to $-\sigma_w^2/(\Omega + \sigma_w^2)$, where Ω is the steady-state solution for Ω_t given in Problem 8.13.

8.16. Use the ARMA(0,1,1) representation of the series $\{Y_t\}$ in Example 8.4.1 to show that the predictors defined by

$$\hat{Y}_{n+1} = aY_n + (1-a)\hat{Y}_n, \quad n = 1, 2, \ldots,$$

where $a = \Omega/(\Omega + \sigma_w^2)$, satisfy

$$Y_{n+1} - \hat{Y}_{n+1} = Z_{n+1} + (1-a)^n\left(Y_0 - Z_0 - \hat{Y}_1\right).$$

Deduce that if $0 < a < 1$, the mean squared error of $\hat{Y}_{n+1}$ converges to $\Omega + \sigma_w^2$ for any initial predictor $\hat{Y}_1$ with finite mean squared error.

8.17. a. Using equations (8.4.1) and (8.4.10), show that $\hat{\mathbf{X}}_{t+1} = F_t\mathbf{X}_{t|t}$.

b. From (a) and (8.4.10) show that $\mathbf{X}_{t|t}$ satisfies the recursions

$$\mathbf{X}_{t|t} = F_{t-1}\mathbf{X}_{t-1|t-1} + \Omega_t G_t'\Delta_t^{-1}(\mathbf{Y}_t - G_t F_{t-1}\mathbf{X}_{t-1|t-1})$$

for $t = 2, 3, \ldots$, with $\mathbf{X}_{1|1} = \hat{\mathbf{X}}_1 + \Omega_1 G_1'\Delta_1^{-1}\left(\mathbf{Y}_1 - G_1\hat{\mathbf{X}}_1\right)$.

8.18. In Section 8.5, show that for fixed Q^*, $-2\ln L\left(\mu, Q^*, \sigma_w^2\right)$ is minimized when μ and σ_w^2 are given by (8.5.10) and (8.5.11), respectively.

8.19. Verify the calculation of $\Theta_t\Delta_t^{-1}$ and Ω_t in Example 8.6.1.

8.20. Verify that the best estimates of missing values in an AR(p) process are found by minimizing (8.6.11) with respect to the missing values.

8.21. Suppose that $\{Y_t\}$ is the AR(2) process

$$Y_t = \phi_1 Y_{t-1} + \phi_2 Y_{t-2} + Z_t, \quad \{Z_t\} \sim \text{WN}\left(0, \sigma^2\right),$$

and that we observe $Y_1, Y_2, Y_4, Y_5, Y_6, Y_7$. Show that the best estimator of Y_3 is

$$(\phi_2(Y_1 + Y_5) + (\phi_1 - \phi_1\phi_2)(Y_2 + Y_4)) \,/\, \left(1 + \phi_1^2 + \phi_2^2\right).$$

8.22. Let X_t be the state at time t of a parameter-driven model (see (8.8.2)). Show that $\{X_t\}$ is a Markov chain and that (8.8.3) holds.

8.23. For the generalized state-space model of Example 8.8.1, show that $\Omega_{t+1} = F^2\Omega_{t|t} + Q$.

8.24. If Y and X are random variables, show that

$$\mathrm{Var}(Y) = E(\mathrm{Var}(Y|X)) + \mathrm{Var}(E(Y|X)).$$

8.25. Suppose that Y and X are two random variables such that the distribution of Y given X is Poisson with mean πX, $0 < \pi \le 1$, and X has the gamma density $g(x; \alpha, \lambda)$.

a. Show that the posterior distribution of X given Y also has a gamma density and determine its parameters.

b. Compute $E(X|Y)$ and $\mathrm{Var}(X|Y)$.

c. Show that Y has a negative binomial density and determine its parameters.

d. Use (c) to compute $E(Y)$ and $\mathrm{Var}(Y)$.

e. Verify in Example 8.8.2 that $E\left(Y_{t+1}|\mathbf{Y}^{(t)}\right) = \alpha_t\pi/(\lambda_{t+1} - \pi)$ and $\mathrm{Var}\left(Y_{t+1}|\mathbf{Y}^{(t)}\right) = \alpha_t\pi\lambda_{t+1}/(\lambda_{t+1} - \pi)^2$.

8.26. For the model of Example 8.8.6, show that

a. $E\left(X_{t+1}|\mathbf{Y}^{(t)}\right) = E\left(X_t|\mathbf{Y}^{(t)}\right)$, $\mathrm{Var}\left(X_{t+1}|\mathbf{Y}^{(t)}\right) > \mathrm{Var}\left(X_t|\mathbf{Y}^{(t)}\right)$, and

b. the transformed sequence $W_t = e^{X_t}$ has a gamma state density.

8.27. Let $\{V_t\}$ be a sequence of independent exponential random variables with $EV_t = t^{-1}$ and suppose that $\{X_t, t \ge 1\}$ and $\{Y_t, t \ge 1\}$ are the state and observation random variables, respectively, of the parameter-driven state-space system

$$X_1 = V_1,$$

$$X_t = X_{t-1} + V_t, \quad t = 2, 3, \ldots,$$

where the distribution of the observation Y_t, conditional on the random variables $Y_1, Y_2, \ldots, Y_{t-1}, X_t$, is Poisson with mean X_t.

a. Determine the observation and state transition density functions $p(y_t|x_t)$ and $p(x_{t+1}|x_t)$ in the parameter-driven model for $\{Y_t\}$.

b. Show, using (8.8.4)–(8.8.6), that

$$p(x_1|y_1) = g(x_1; y_1 + 1, 2)$$

and

$$p(x_2|y_1) = g(x_2; y_1 + 2, 2),$$

where $g(x; \alpha, \lambda)$ is the gamma density function (see Example (d) of Section A.1).

c. Show that

$$p\left(x_t|\mathbf{y}^{(t)}\right) = g(x_t; \alpha_t + t, t + 1)$$

and

$$p\left(x_{t+1}|\mathbf{y}^{(t)}\right) = g(x_{t+1}; \alpha_t + t + 1, t + 1),$$

where $\alpha_t = y_1 + \cdots + y_t$.

d. Conclude from (c) that the minimum mean squared error estimates of X_t and X_{t+1} based on $Y_1, \ldots, Y_t$ are

$$X_{t|t} = \frac{t + Y_1 + \cdots + Y_t}{t + 1}$$

and

$$\hat{X}_{t+1} = \frac{t + 1 + Y_1 + \cdots + Y_t}{t + 1},$$

respectively.

8.28. Let Y and X be two random variables such that Y given X is exponential with mean $1/X$, and X has the gamma density function with

$$g(x; \lambda + 1, \alpha) = \frac{\alpha^{\lambda+1} x^{\lambda} \exp\{-\alpha x\}}{\Gamma(\lambda + 1)}, \qquad x > 0,$$

where $\lambda > -1$ and $\alpha > 0$.

a. Determine the posterior distribution of X given Y.

b. Show that Y has a Pareto distribution

$$p(y) = (\lambda + 1)\alpha^{\lambda+1}(y + \alpha)^{-\lambda-2}, \qquad y > 0.$$

c. Find the mean of variance of Y. Under what conditions on α and λ does the latter exist?

d. Verify the calculation of $p\left(y_{t+1}|\mathbf{y}^{(t)}\right)$ and $E\left(Y_{t+1}|\mathbf{y}^{(t)}\right)$ for the model in Example 8.8.8.

8.29. Consider an observation-driven model in which Y_t given X_t is binomial with parameters n and X_t, i.e.,

$$p(y_t|x_t) = \binom{n}{y_t} x_t^{y_t}(1 - x_t)^{n-y_t}, \qquad y_t = 0, 1, \ldots, n.$$

a. Show that the observation equation with state variable transformed by the logit transformation $W_t = \ln(X_t/(1 - X_t))$ follows an exponential family

$$p(y_t|w_t) = \exp\{y_t w_t - b(w_t) + c(y_t)\}.$$

Determine the functions $b(\cdot)$ and $c(\cdot)$.

b. Suppose that the state X_t has the beta density

$$p(x_{t+1}|\mathbf{y}^{(t)}) = f(x_{t+1}; \alpha_{t+1|t}, \lambda_{t+1|t}),$$

where

$$f(x; \alpha, \lambda) = [B(\alpha, \lambda)]^{-1} x^{\alpha-1}(1 - x)^{\lambda-1}, \quad 0 < x < 1,$$

$B(\alpha, \lambda) := \Gamma(\alpha)\Gamma(\lambda)/\Gamma(\alpha+\lambda)$ is the beta function, and $\alpha, \lambda > 0$. Show that the posterior distribution of X_t given Y_t is also beta and express its parameters in terms of y_t and $\alpha_{t|t-1}, \lambda_{t|t-1}$.

c. Under the assumptions made in (b), show that $E(X_t|\mathbf{Y}^{(t)}) = E(X_{t+1}|\mathbf{Y}^{(t)})$ and $\mathrm{Var}(X_t|\mathbf{Y}^{(t)}) < \mathrm{Var}(X_{t+1}|\mathbf{Y}^{(t)})$.

d. Assuming that the parameters in (b) satisfy (8.8.41)–(8.8.42), show that the one-step prediction density $p(y_{t+1}|\mathbf{y}^{(t)})$ is beta-binomial,

$$p(y_{t+1}|\mathbf{y}^{(t)}) = \frac{B(\alpha_{t+1|t} + y_{t+1}, \lambda_{t+1|t} + n - y_{t+1})}{(n+1)B(y_{t+1}+1, n - y_{t+1} + 1)B(\alpha_{t+1|t}, \lambda_{t+1|t})},$$

and verify that $\hat{Y}_{t+1}$ is given by (8.8.47).

9 Forecasting Techniques

We have focused until now on the construction of time series models for stationary and nonstationary series and the determination, assuming the appropriateness of these models, of minimum mean squared error predictors. If the observed series had in fact been generated by the fitted model, this procedure would give minimum mean squared error forecasts. In this chapter we discuss three forecasting techniques that have less emphasis on the explicit construction of a model for the data. Each of the three selects, from a limited class of algorithms, the one that is optimal according to specified criteria.

The three techniques have been found in practice to be effective on wide ranges of real data sets (for example, the economic time series used in the forecasting competition described by Makridakis et al., 1984).

The ARAR algorithm described in Section 9.1 is an adaptation of the ARARMA algorithm (Newton and Parzen, 1984; Parzen, 1982) in which the idea is to apply automatically selected "memory-shortening" transformations (if necessary) to the data and then to fit an ARMA model to the transformed series. The ARAR algorithm we describe is a version of this in which the ARMA fitting step is replaced by the fitting of a subset AR model to the transformed data.

The Holt–Winters (HW) algorithm described in Section 9.2 uses a set of simple recursions that generalize the exponential smoothing recursions of Section 1.5.1 to generate forecasts of series containing a locally linear trend.

The Holt–Winters seasonal (HWS) algorithm extends the HW algorithm to handle data in which there are both trend and seasonal variation of known period. It is described in Section 9.3.

The algorithms can be applied to specific data sets with the aid of the ITSM options `Forecasting>ARAR`, `Forecasting>Holt-Winters` and `Forecasting> Seasonal Holt-Winters`.

9.1 The ARAR Algorithm

9.1.1 Memory Shortening

Given a data set $\{Y_t, t = 1, 2, \ldots, n\}$, the first step is to decide whether the underlying process is "long-memory," and if so to apply a memory-shortening transformation before attempting to fit an autoregressive model. The differencing operations permitted under the option `Transform` of ITSM are examples of memory-shortening transformations; however, the ones from which the option `Forecasting>ARAR` selects are members of a more general class. There are two types allowed:

$$\tilde{Y}_t = Y_t - \hat{\phi}\left(\hat{\tau}\right) Y_{t-\hat{\tau}} \tag{9.1.1}$$

and

$$\tilde{Y}_t = Y_t - \hat{\phi}_1 Y_{t-1} - \hat{\phi}_2 Y_{t-2}. \tag{9.1.2}$$

With the aid of the five-step algorithm described below, we classify $\{Y_t\}$ and take one of the following three courses of action:

- **L.** Declare $\{Y_t\}$ to be long-memory and form $\left\{\tilde{Y}_t\right\}$ using (9.1.1).
- **M.** Declare $\{Y_t\}$ to be moderately long-memory and form $\left\{\tilde{Y}_t\right\}$ using (9.1.2).
- **S.** Declare $\{Y_t\}$ to be short-memory.

If the alternative L or M is chosen, then the transformed series $\left\{\tilde{Y}_t\right\}$ is again checked. If it is found to be long-memory or moderately long-memory, then a further transformation is performed. The process continues until the transformed series is classified as short-memory. At most three memory-shortening transformations are performed, but it is very rare to require more than two. The algorithm for deciding among L, M, and S can be described as follows:

1. For each $\tau = 1, 2, \ldots, 15$, we find the value $\hat{\phi}(\tau)$ of ϕ that minimizes

$$\text{ERR}(\phi, \tau) = \frac{\sum_{t=\tau+1}^{n} [Y_t - \phi Y_{t-\tau}]^2}{\sum_{t=\tau+1}^{n} Y_t^2}.$$

We then define

$$\text{Err}(\tau) = \text{ERR}\big(\hat{\phi}(\tau), \tau\big)$$

and choose the lag $\hat{\tau}$ to be the value of τ that minimizes $\text{Err}(\tau)$.

2. If $\text{Err}(\hat{\tau}) \le 8/n$, go to L.

3. If $\hat{\phi}(\hat{\tau}) \ge .93$ and $\hat{\tau} > 2$, go to L.

4. If $\hat{\phi}(\hat{\tau}) \ge .93$ and $\hat{\tau} = 1$ or 2, determine the values $\hat{\phi}_1$ and $\hat{\phi}_2$ of ϕ_1 and ϕ_2 that minimize $\sum_{t=3}^{n}[Y_t - \phi_1 Y_{t-1} - \phi_2 Y_{t-2}]^2$; then go to M.

5. If $\hat{\phi}(\hat{\tau}) < .93$, go to S.

9.1.2 Fitting a Subset Autoregression

Let $\{S_t, t = k+1, \dots, n\}$ denote the memory-shortened series derived from $\{Y_t\}$ by the algorithm of the previous section and let $\overline{S}$ denote the sample mean of $S_{k+1}, \dots, S_n$.

The next step in the modeling procedure is to fit an autoregressive process to the mean-corrected series

$$X_t = S_t - \overline{S}, \quad t = k+1, \dots, n.$$

The fitted model has the form

$$X_t = \phi_1 X_{t-1} + \phi_{l_1} X_{t-l_1} + \phi_{l_2} X_{t-l_2} + \phi_{l_3} X_{t-l_3} + Z_t,$$

where $\{Z_t\} \sim \text{WN}\left(0, \sigma^2\right)$, and for given lags, l_1, l_2, and l_3, the coefficients ϕ_j and the white noise variance σ^2 are found from the Yule–Walker equations

$$\begin{bmatrix} 1 & \hat{\rho}(l_1-1) & \hat{\rho}(l_2-1) & \hat{\rho}(l_3-1) \\ \hat{\rho}(l_1-1) & 1 & \hat{\rho}(l_2-l_1) & \hat{\rho}(l_3-l_1) \\ \hat{\rho}(l_2-1) & \hat{\rho}(l_2-l_1) & 1 & \hat{\rho}(l_3-l_2) \\ \hat{\rho}(l_3-1) & \hat{\rho}(l_3-l_1) & \hat{\rho}(l_3-l_2) & 1 \end{bmatrix} \begin{bmatrix} \phi_1 \\ \phi_{l_1} \\ \phi_{l_2} \\ \phi_{l_3} \end{bmatrix} = \begin{bmatrix} \hat{\rho}(1) \\ \hat{\rho}(l_1) \\ \hat{\rho}(l_2) \\ \hat{\rho}(l_3) \end{bmatrix}$$

and

$$\sigma^2 = \hat{\gamma}(0)\left[1 - \phi_1\hat{\rho}(1) - \phi_{l_1}\hat{\rho}(l_1) - \phi_{l_2}\hat{\rho}(l_2) - \phi_{l_3}\hat{\rho}(l_3)\right],$$

where $\hat{\gamma}(j)$ and $\hat{\rho}(j)$, $j = 0, 1, 2, \dots$, are the sample autocovariances and autocorrelations of the series $\{X_t\}$.

The program computes the coefficients ϕ_j for each set of lags such that

$$1 < l_1 < l_2 < l_3 \le m,$$

where m can be chosen to be either 13 or 26. It then selects the model for which the Yule–Walker estimate σ^2 is minimal and prints out the lags, coefficients, and white noise variance for the fitted model.

A slower procedure chooses the lags and coefficients (computed from the Yule–Walker equations as above) that maximize the Gaussian likelihood of the observations. For this option the maximum lag m is 13.

The options are displayed in the `ARAR Forecasting` dialog box, which appears on the screen when the option `Forecasting>ARAR` is selected. It allows you also to bypass memory shortening and fit a subset AR to the original (mean-corrected) data.

9.1.3 Forecasting

If the memory-shortening filter found in the first step has coefficients $\psi_0(=1)$, $\psi_1, \ldots, \psi_k$ $(k \geq 0)$, then the memory-shortened series can be expressed as

$$S_t = \psi(B)Y_t = Y_t + \psi_1 Y_{t-1} + \cdots + \psi_k Y_{t-k}, \tag{9.1.3}$$

where $\psi(B)$ is the polynomial in the backward shift operator,

$$\psi(B) = 1 + \psi_1 B + \cdots + \psi_k B^k.$$

Similarly, if the coefficients of the subset autoregression found in the second step are $\phi_1, \phi_{l_1}, \phi_{l_2}$, and ϕ_{l_3}, then the subset AR model for the mean-corrected series $\left\{X_t = S_t - \overline{S}\right\}$ is

$$\phi(B)X_t = Z_t, \tag{9.1.4}$$

where $\{Z_t\} \sim \mathrm{WN}\left(0, \sigma^2\right)$ and

$$\phi(B) = 1 - \phi_1 B - \phi_{l_1} B^{l_1} - \phi_{l_2} B^{l_2} - \phi_{l_3} B^{l_3}.$$

From (9.1.3) and (9.1.4) we obtain the equations

$$\xi(B)Y_t = \phi(1)\overline{S} + Z_t, \tag{9.1.5}$$

where

$$\xi(B) = \psi(B)\phi(B) = 1 + \xi_1 B + \cdots + \xi_{k+l_3} B^{k+l_3}.$$

Assuming that the fitted model (9.1.5) is appropriate and that the white noise term Z_t is uncorrelated with $\{Y_j, j < t\}$ for each t, we can determine the minimum mean squared error linear predictors $P_n Y_{n+h}$ of Y_{n+h} in terms of $\{1, Y_1, \ldots, Y_n\}$, for $n > k + l_3$, from the recursions

$$P_n Y_{n+h} = -\sum_{j=1}^{k+l_3} \xi_j P_n Y_{n+h-j} + \phi(1)\overline{S}, \quad h \geq 1, \tag{9.1.6}$$

with the initial conditions

$$P_n Y_{n+h} = Y_{n+h}, \quad \text{for } h \leq 0. \tag{9.1.7}$$

The mean squared error of the predictor $P_n Y_{n+h}$ is found to be (Problem 9.1)

$$E\left[(Y_{n+h} - P_n Y_{n+h})^2\right] = \sum_{j=1}^{h-1} \tau_j^2 \sigma^2, \tag{9.1.8}$$

where $\sum_{j=0}^{\infty} \tau_j z^j$ is the Taylor expansion of $1/\xi(z)$ in a neighborhood of $z = 0$. Equivalently the sequence $\{\tau_j\}$ can be found from the recursion

$$\tau_0 = 1, \sum_{j=0}^{n} \tau_j \xi_{n-j} = 0, \quad n = 1, 2, \ldots. \tag{9.1.9}$$

9.1.4 Application of the ARAR Algorithm

To determine an ARAR model for a given data set $\{Y_t\}$ using ITSM, select `Forecasting>ARAR` and choose the appropriate options in the resulting dialog box. These include specification of the number of forecasts required, whether or not you wish to include the memory-shortening step, whether you require prediction bounds, and which of the optimality criteria is to be used. Once you have made these selections, click `OK`, and the forecasts will be plotted with the original data. Right-click on the graph and then `Info` to see the coefficients $1, \psi_1, \ldots, \psi_k$ of the memory-shortening filter $\psi(B)$, the lags and coefficients of the subset autoregression

$$X_t - \phi_1 X_{t-1} - \phi_{l_1} X_{t-l_1} - \phi_{l_2} X_{t-l_2} - \phi_{l_3} X_{t-l_3} = Z_t,$$

and the coefficients ξ_j of B^j in the overall whitening filter

$$\xi(B) = \left(1 + \psi_1 B + \cdots + \psi_k B^k\right)\left(1 - \phi_1 B - \phi_{l_1} B^{l_1} - \phi_{l_2} B^{l_2} - \phi_{l_3} B^{l_3}\right).$$

The numerical values of the predictors, their root mean squared errors, and the prediction bounds are also printed.

Example 9.1.1

To use the ARAR algorithm to predict 24 values of the accidental deaths data, open the file DEATHS.TSM and proceed as described above. Selecting `Minimize WN variance [max lag=26]` gives the graph of the data and predictors shown in Figure 9.1. Right-clicking on the graph and then `Info`, we find that the selected memory-shortening filter is $\left(1 - .9779B^{12}\right)$. The fitted subset autoregression and the coefficients ξ_j of the overall whitening filter $\xi(B)$ are shown below:

```
Optimal lags              1         3        12        13
Optimal coeffs        .5915     -.3822    -.3022     .2970
WN Variance:    .12314E+06
COEFFICIENTS OF OVERALL WHITENING FILTER:
1.0000    -.5915     .0000    -.2093     .0000
 .0000     .0000     .0000     .0000     .0000
 .0000     .0000    -.6757     .2814     .0000
 .2047     .0000     .0000     .0000     .0000
 .0000     .0000     .0000     .0000    -.2955
 .2904
```

□

In Table 9.1 we compare the predictors of the next six values of the accidental deaths series with the actual observed values. The predicted values obtained from ARAR as described in the example are shown together with the predictors obtained by fitting ARIMA models as described in Chapter 6 (see Table 9.1). The observed root mean squared errors (i.e., $\sqrt{\sum_{h=1}^{6}(Y_{72+h} - P_{72}Y_{72+h})^2/6}$) for the three prediction methods are easily calculated to be 253 for ARAR, 583 for the ARIMA model (6.5.8), and 501 for the ARIMA model (6.5.9). The ARAR algorithm thus performs very well here. Notice that in this particular example the ARAR algorithm effectively fits a causal AR model to the data, but this is not always the case.

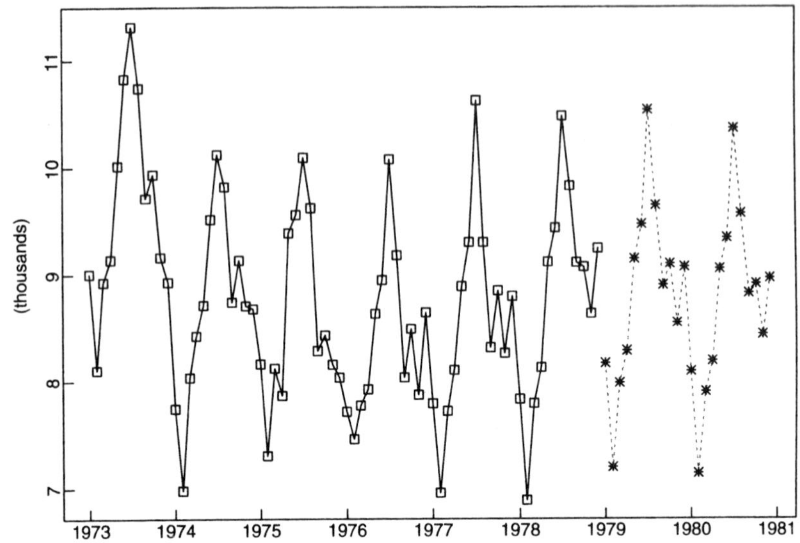

Figure 9-1 The data set DEATHS.TSM with 24 values predicted by the ARAR algorithm.

9.2 The Holt–Winters Algorithm

9.2.1 The Algorithm

Given observations $Y_1, Y_2, \ldots, Y_n$ from the "trend plus noise" model (1.5.2), the exponential smoothing recursions (1.5.7) allowed us to compute estimates $\hat{m}_t$ of the trend at times $t = 1, 2, \ldots, n$. If the series is stationary, then m_t is constant and the exponential smoothing forecast of Y_{n+h} based on the observations $Y_1, \ldots, Y_n$ is

$$P_n Y_{n+h} = \hat{m}_n, \quad h = 1, 2, \ldots. \tag{9.2.1}$$

If the data have a (nonconstant) trend, then a natural generalization of the forecast function (9.2.1) that takes this into account is

$$P_n Y_{n+h} = \hat{a}_n + \hat{b}_n h, \quad h = 1, 2, \ldots, \tag{9.2.2}$$

where $\hat{a}_n$ and $\hat{b}_n$ can be thought of as estimates of the "level" a_n and "slope" b_n of the trend function at time n. Holt (1957) suggested a recursive scheme for computing

Table 9.1 Predicted and observed values of the accidental deaths series for $t = 73, \ldots, 78$.

t	73	74	75	76	77	78
Observed Y_t	7798	7406	8363	8460	9217	9316
Predicted by ARAR	8168	7196	7982	8284	9144	9465
Predicted by (6.5.8)	8441	7704	8549	8885	9843	10279
Predicted by (6.5.9)	8345	7619	8356	8742	9795	10179

the quantities $\hat{a}_n$ and $\hat{b}_n$ in (9.2.2). Denoting by $\hat{Y}_{n+1}$ the one-step forecast $P_n Y_{n+1}$, we have from (9.2.2)

$$\hat{Y}_{n+1} = \hat{a}_n + \hat{b}_n.$$

Now, as in exponential smoothing, we suppose that the estimated level at time $n+1$ is a linear combination of the observed value at time $n+1$ and the forecast value at time $n+1$. Thus,

$$\hat{a}_{n+1} = \alpha Y_{n+1} + (1-\alpha)\left(\hat{a}_n + \hat{b}_n\right). \tag{9.2.3}$$

We can then estimate the slope at time $n+1$ as a linear combination of $\hat{a}_{n+1} - \hat{a}_n$ and the estimated slope $\hat{b}_n$ at time n. Thus,

$$\hat{b}_{n+1} = \beta\left(\hat{a}_{n+1} - \hat{a}_n\right) + (1-\beta)\hat{b}_n. \tag{9.2.4}$$

In order to solve the recursions (9.2.3) and (9.2.4) we need initial conditions. A natural choice is to set

$$\hat{a}_2 = Y_2 \tag{9.2.5}$$

and

$$\hat{b}_2 = Y_2 - Y_1. \tag{9.2.6}$$

Then (9.2.3) and (9.2.4) can be solved successively for $\hat{a}_i$ and $\hat{b}_i$, $i = 3, \ldots, n$, and the predictors $P_n Y_{n+h}$ found from (9.2.2).

The forecasts depend on the "smoothing parameters" α and β. These can either be prescribed arbitrarily (with values between 0 and 1) or chosen in a more systematic way to minimize the sum of squares of the one-step errors $\sum_{i=3}^{n}(Y_i - P_{i-1}Y_i)^2$, obtained when the algorithm is applied to the already observed data. Both choices are available in the ITSM option `Forecasting>Holt-Winters`.

Before illustrating the use of the Holt–Winters forecasting procedure, we discuss the connection between the recursions (9.2.3)–(9.2.4) and the steady-state solution of the Kalman filtering equations for a local linear trend model. Suppose $\{Y_t\}$ follows the local linear structural model with observation equation

$$Y_t = M_t + W_t$$

and state equation

$$\begin{bmatrix} M_{t+1} \\ B_{t+1} \end{bmatrix} = \begin{bmatrix} 1 & 1 \\ 0 & 1 \end{bmatrix} \begin{bmatrix} M_t \\ B_t \end{bmatrix} + \begin{bmatrix} V_t \\ U_t \end{bmatrix}$$

(see (8.2.4)–(8.2.7)). Now define $\hat{a}_n$ and $\hat{b}_n$ to be the filtered estimates of M_n and B_n, respectively, i.e.,

$$\hat{a}_n = M_{n|n} := P_n M_n,$$

$$\hat{b}_n = B_{n|n} := P_n B_n.$$

Using Problem 8.17 and the Kalman recursion (8.4.10), we find that

$$\begin{bmatrix} \hat{a}_{n+1} \\ \hat{b}_{n+1} \end{bmatrix} = \begin{bmatrix} \hat{a}_n + \hat{b}_n \\ \hat{b}_n \end{bmatrix} + \Delta_n^{-1}\Omega_n G' \left(Y_n - \hat{a}_n - \hat{b}_n\right), \tag{9.2.7}$$

where $G = \begin{bmatrix} 1 & 0 \end{bmatrix}$. Assuming that $\Omega_n = \Omega_1 = [\Omega_{ij}]_{i,j=1}^2$ is the steady-state solution of (8.4.2) for this model, then $\Delta_n = \Omega_{11} + \sigma_w^2$ for all n, so that (9.2.7) simplifies to the equations

$$\hat{a}_{n+1} = \hat{a}_n + \hat{b}_n + \frac{\Omega_{11}}{\Omega_{11} + \sigma_w^2}\left(Y_n - \hat{a}_n - \hat{b}_n\right) \tag{9.2.8}$$

and

$$\hat{b}_{n+1} = \hat{b}_n + \frac{\Omega_{12}}{\Omega_{11} + \sigma_w^2}\left(Y_n - \hat{a}_n - \hat{b}_n\right). \tag{9.2.9}$$

Solving (9.2.8) for $\left(Y_n - \hat{a}_n - \hat{b}_n\right)$ and substituting into (9.2.9), we find that

$$\hat{a}_{n+1} = \alpha Y_{n+1} + (1-\alpha)\left(\hat{a}_n + \hat{b}_n\right), \tag{9.2.10}$$

$$\hat{b}_{n+1} = \beta\left(\hat{a}_{n+1} - \hat{a}_n\right) + (1-\beta)\hat{b}_n \tag{9.2.11}$$

with $\alpha = \Omega_{11}/\left(\Omega_{11} + \sigma_w^2\right)$ and $\beta = \Omega_{21}/\Omega_{11}$. These equations coincide with the Holt–Winters recursions (9.2.3)–(9.2.4). Equations relating α and β to the variances σ_u^2, σ_v^2, and σ_w^2 can be found in Harvey (1990).

Example 9.2.1

To predict 24 values of the accidental deaths series using the Holt–Winters algorithm, open the file DEATHS.TSM and select `Forecasting>Holt-Winters`. In the resulting dialog box specify 24 for the number of predictors and check the box marked `Optimize coefficients` for automatic selection of the smoothing coefficients α and β. Click `OK`, and the forecasts will be plotted with the original data as shown in Figure 9.2. Right-click on the graph and then `Info` to see the numerical values of the predictors, their root mean squared errors, and the optimal values of α and β. □

The root mean squared error $\left(\sqrt{\sum_{h=1}^{6}(Y_{72+h} - P_{72}Y_{72+h})^2/6}\right)$ for the nonseasonal Holt–Winters forecasts is found to be 1143. Not surprisingly, since we have not taken seasonality into account, this is a much larger value than for the three sets of forecasts shown in Table 9.1. In the next section we show how to modify the Holt–Winters algorithm to allow for seasonality.

9.2.2 Holt–Winters and ARIMA Forecasting

The one-step forecasts obtained by exponential smoothing with parameter α (defined by (1.5.7) and (9.2.1)) satisfy the relations

$$P_n Y_{n+1} = Y_n - (1-\alpha)(Y_n - P_{n-1}Y_n), \quad n \geq 2. \tag{9.2.12}$$

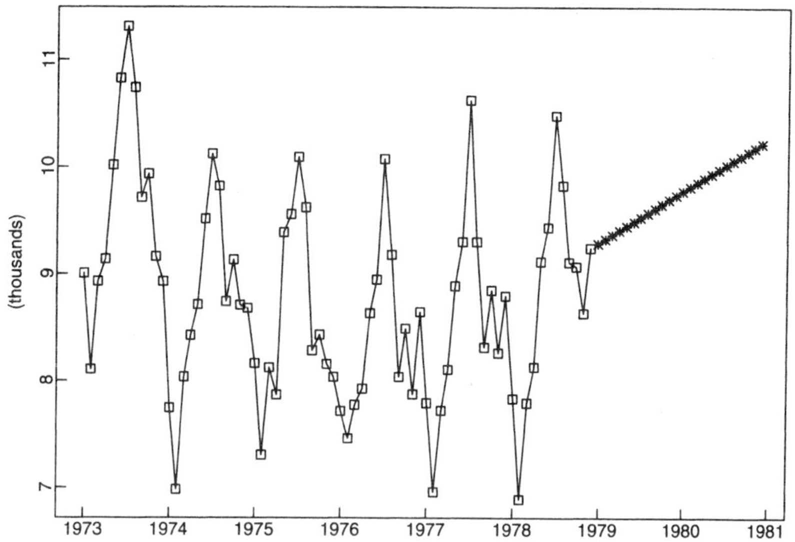

Figure 9-2 The data set DEATHS.TSM with 24 values predicted by the nonseasonal Holt–Winters algorithm.

But these are the same relations satisfied by the large-sample minimum mean squared error forecasts of the invertible ARIMA(0,1,1) process

$$Y_t = Y_{t-1} + Z_t - (1-\alpha)Z_{t-1}, \quad \{Z_t\} \sim \text{WN}\left(0, \sigma^2\right). \tag{9.2.13}$$

Forecasting by exponential smoothing with optimal α can therefore be viewed as fitting a member of the two-parameter family of ARIMA processes (9.2.13) to the data and using the corresponding large-sample forecast recursions initialized by $P_0Y_1 = Y_1$. In ITSM, the optimal α is found by minimizing the average squared error of the one-step forecasts of the *observed* data $Y_2, \ldots, Y_n$, and the parameter σ^2 is estimated by this average squared error. This algorithm could easily be modified to minimize other error measures such as average absolute one-step error and average 12-step squared error.

In the same way it can be shown that Holt–Winters forecasting can be viewed as fitting a member of the three-parameter family of ARIMA processes,

$$(1-B)^2Y_t = Z_t - (2-\alpha-\alpha\beta)Z_{t-1} + (1-\alpha)Z_{t-2}, \tag{9.2.14}$$

Table 9.2 Predicted and observed values of the accidental deaths series for $t = 73, \ldots, 78$ from the (nonseasonal) Holt–Winters algorithm.

t	73	74	75	76	77	78
Observed Y_t	7798	7406	8363	8460	9217	9316
Predicted by HW	9281	9322	9363	9404	9445	9486

where $\{Z_t\} \sim \text{WN}(0, \sigma^2)$. The coefficients α and β are selected as described after (9.2.6), and the estimate of σ^2 is the average squared error of the one-step forecasts of $Y_3, \ldots, Y_n$ obtained from the large-sample forecast recursions corresponding to (9.2.14).

9.3 The Holt–Winters Seasonal Algorithm

9.3.1 The Algorithm

If the series $Y_1, Y_2, \ldots, Y_n$ contains not only trend, but also seasonality with period d (as in the model (1.5.11)), then a further generalization of the forecast function (9.2.2) that takes this into account is

$$P_n Y_{n+h} = \hat{a}_n + \hat{b}_n h + \hat{c}_{n+h}, \quad h = 1, 2, \ldots, \tag{9.3.1}$$

where $\hat{a}_n$, $\hat{b}_n$, and $\hat{c}_n$ can be thought of as estimates of the "trend level" a_n, "trend slope" b_n, and "seasonal component" c_n at time n. If k is the smallest integer such that $n + h - kd \le n$, then we set

$$\hat{c}_{n+h} = \hat{c}_{n+h-kd}, \quad h = 1, 2, \ldots, \tag{9.3.2}$$

while the values of $\hat{a}_i, \hat{b}_i$, and $\hat{c}_i$, $i = d+2, \ldots, n$, are found from recursions analogous to (9.2.3) and (9.2.4), namely,

$$\hat{a}_{n+1} = \alpha\left(Y_{n+1} - \hat{c}_{n+1-d}\right) + (1-\alpha)\left(\hat{a}_n + \hat{b}_n\right), \tag{9.3.3}$$

$$\hat{b}_{n+1} = \beta\left(\hat{a}_{n+1} - \hat{a}_n\right) + (1-\beta)\hat{b}_n, \tag{9.3.4}$$

and

$$\hat{c}_{n+1} = \gamma(Y_{n+1} - \hat{a}_{n+1}) + (1-\gamma)\hat{c}_{n+1-d}, \tag{9.3.5}$$

with initial conditions

$$\hat{a}_{d+1} = Y_{d+1}, \tag{9.3.6}$$

$$\hat{b}_{d+1} = (Y_{d+1} - Y_1)/d, \tag{9.3.7}$$

and

$$\hat{c}_i = Y_i - \left(Y_1 + \hat{b}_{d+1}(i-1)\right), \quad i = 1, \ldots, d+1. \tag{9.3.8}$$

Then (9.3.3)–(9.3.5) can be solved successively for $\hat{a}_i$, $\hat{b}_i$, and $\hat{c}_i$, $i = d+1, \ldots, n$, and the predictors $P_n Y_{n+h}$ found from (9.3.1).

As in the nonseasonal case of Section 9.2, the forecasts depend on the parameters α, β, and γ. These can either be prescribed arbitrarily (with values between 0 and 1) or chosen in a more systematic way to minimize the sum of squares of the one-step errors $\sum_{i=d+2}^{n}(Y_i - P_{i-1}Y_i)^2$, obtained when the algorithm is applied to the already

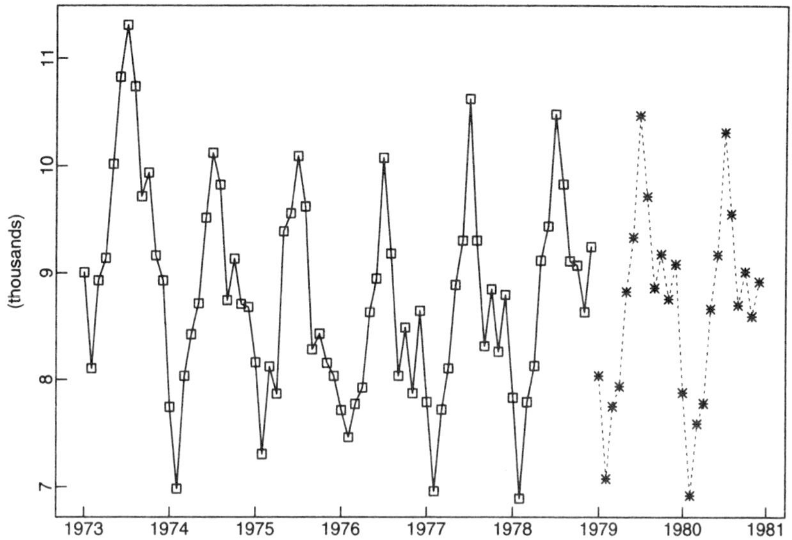

Figure 9-3 The data set DEATHS.TSM with 24 values predicted by the seasonal Holt–Winters algorithm.

observed data. Seasonal Holt–Winters forecasts can be computed by selecting the ITSM option `Forecasting>Seasonal Holt-Winters`.

Example 9.3.1

As in Example 9.2.1, open the file DEATHS.TSM, but this time select `Forecasting>Seasonal Holt-Winters`. Specify 24 for the number of predicted values required, 12 for the period of the seasonality, and check the box marked `Optimize Coefficients`. Click `OK`, and the graph of the data and predicted values shown in Figure 9.3 will appear. Right-click on the graph and then on `Info` and you will see the numerical values of the predictors and the optimal values of the coefficients α, β, and γ (minimizing the observed one-step average squared error $\sum_{i=14}^{72}(Y_i - P_{i-1}Y_i)^2/59$). Table 9.3 compares the predictors of $Y_{73}, \ldots, Y_{78}$ with the corresponding observed values. □

The root mean squared error $(\sqrt{\sum_{h=1}^{6}(Y_{72+h} - P_{72}Y_{72+h})^2/6}\ )$ for the seasonal Holt–Winters forecasts is found to be 401. This is not as good as the value 253 achieved by the ARAR model for this example but is substantially better than the

Table 9.3 Predicted and observed values of the accidental deaths series for $t = 73, \ldots, 78$ from the seasonal Holt–Winters algorithm.

t	73	74	75	76	77	78
Observed Y_t	7798	7406	8363	8460	9217	9316
Predicted by HWS	8039	7077	7750	7941	8824	9329

values achieved by the nonseasonal Holt–Winters algorithm (1143) and the ARIMA models (6.5.8) and (6.5.9) (583 and 501, respectively).

9.3.2 Holt–Winters Seasonal and ARIMA Forecasting

As in Section 9.2.2, the Holt–Winters seasonal recursions with seasonal period d correspond to the large-sample forecast recursions of an ARIMA process, in this case defined by

$$\begin{aligned}(1-B)(1-B^d)Y_t = {} & Z_t + \cdots + Z_{t-d+1} + \gamma(1-\alpha)(Z_{t-d} - Z_{t-d-1}) \\ & - (2 - \alpha - \alpha\beta)(Z_{t-1} + \cdots + Z_{t-d}) \\ & + (1-\alpha)(Z_{t-2} + \cdots + Z_{t-d-1}),\end{aligned}$$

where $\{Z_t\} \sim \text{WN}(0, \sigma^2)$. Holt–Winters seasonal forecasting with optimal α, β, and γ can therefore be viewed as fitting a member of this four-parameter family of ARIMA models and using the corresponding large-sample forecast recursions.

9.4 Choosing a Forecasting Algorithm

Real data are rarely if ever generated by a simple mathematical model such as an ARIMA process. Forecasting methods that are predicated on the assumption of such a model are therefore not necessarily the best, even in the mean squared error sense. Nor is the measurement of error in terms of mean squared error necessarily always the most appropriate one in spite of its mathematical convenience. Even within the framework of minimum mean squared-error forecasting, we may ask (for example) whether we wish to minimize the one-step, two-step, or twelve-step mean squared error.

The use of more heuristic algorithms such as those discussed in this chapter is therefore well worth serious consideration in practical forecasting problems. But how do we decide which method to use? A relatively simple solution to this problem, given the availability of a substantial historical record, is to choose among competing algorithms by comparing the relevant errors when the algorithms are applied to the data already observed (e.g., by comparing the mean absolute percentage errors of the twelve-step predictors of the historical data if twelve-step prediction is of primary concern).

It is extremely difficult to make general theoretical statements about the relative merits of the various techniques we have discussed (ARIMA modeling, exponential smoothing, ARAR, and HW methods). For the series DEATHS.TSM we found on the basis of average mean squared error for predicting the series at times 73–78 that the ARAR method was best, followed by the seasonal Holt–Winters algorithm, and then the ARIMA models fitted in Chapter 6. This ordering is by no means universal. For example, if we consider the natural logarithms $\{Y_t\}$ of the first 130 observations in the series WINE.TSM (Figure 1.1) and compare the average mean squared errors of the forecasts of $Y_{131}, \ldots, Y_{142}$, we find (Problem 9.2) that an MA(12) model fitted to the mean corrected differenced series $\{Y_t - Y_{t-12}\}$ does better than seasonal Holt–Winters (with period 12), which in turn does better than ARAR and (not surprisingly) dramatically better than nonseasonal Holt–Winters. An interesting empirical comparison of these and other methods applied to a variety of economic time series is contained in Makridakis et al. (1998).

The versions of the Holt–Winters algorithms we have discussed in Sections 9.2 and 9.3 are referred to as "additive," since the seasonal and trend components enter the forecasting function in an additive manner. "Multiplicative" versions of the algorithms can also be constructed to deal directly with processes of the form

$$Y_t = m_t s_t Z_t, \tag{9.4.1}$$

where m_t, s_t, and Z_t are trend, seasonal, and noise factors, respectively (see, e.g., Makridakis et al., 1983). An alternative approach (provided that $Y_t > 0$ for all t) is to apply the linear Holt–Winters algorithms to $\{\ln Y_t\}$ (as in the case of WINE.TSM in the preceding paragraph). Because of the rather general memory shortening permitted by the ARAR algorithm, it gives reasonable results when applied directly to series of the form (9.4.1), even without preliminary transformations. In particular, if we consider the first 132 observations in the series AIRPASS.TSM and apply the ARAR algorithm to predict the last 12 values in the series, we obtain (Problem 9.4) an observed root mean squared error of 18.21. On the other hand if we use the same data take logarithms, difference at lag 12, subtract the mean and then fit an AR(13) model by maximum likelihood using ITSM and use it to predict the last 12 values, we

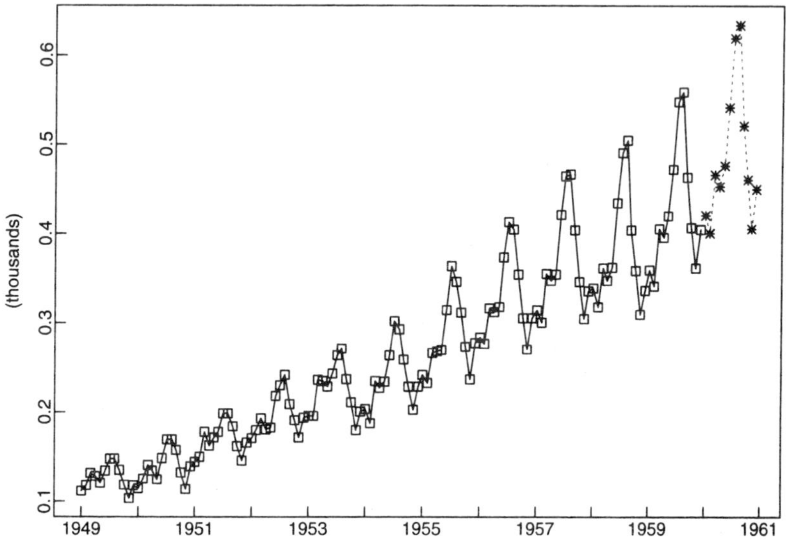

Figure 9-4 The first 132 values of the data set AIRPASS.TSM and predictors of the last 12 values obtained by direct application of the ARAR algorithm.

obtain an observed root mean squared error of 21.67. The data and predicted values from the ARAR algorithm are shown in Figure 9.4.

Problems

9.1. Establish the formula (9.1.8) for the mean squared error of the h-step forecast based on the ARAR algorithm.

9.2. Let $\{X_1, \ldots, X_{142}\}$ denote the data in the file WINE.TSM and let $\{Y_1, \ldots, Y_{142}\}$ denote their natural logarithms. Denote by m the sample mean of the differenced series $\{Y_t - Y_{t-12}, t = 13, \ldots, 130\}$.

a. Use the program ITSM to find the maximum likelihood MA(12) model for the differenced and mean-corrected series $\{Y_t - Y_{t-12} - m, t = 13, \ldots, 130\}$.

b. Use the model in (a) to compute forecasts of $\{X_{131}, \ldots, X_{142}\}$.

c. Tabulate the forecast errors $\{X_t - P_{130}X_t, t = 131, \ldots, 142\}$.

d. Compute the average squared error for the 12 forecasts.

e. Repeat steps (b), (c), and (d) for the corresponding forecasts obtained by applying the ARAR algorithm to the series $\{X_t, t = 1, \ldots, 130\}$.

f. Repeat steps (b), (c), and (d) for the corresponding forecasts obtained by applying the seasonal Holt–Winters algorithm (with period 12) to the logged data $\{Y_t, t = 1, \ldots, 130\}$. (Open the file WINE.TSM, select `Transform>Box-Cox` with parameter $\lambda = 0$, then select `Forecasting>Seasonal Holt-Winters`, and check `Apply to original data` in the dialog box.)

g. Repeat steps (b), (c), and (d) for the corresponding forecasts obtained by applying the nonseasonal Holt–Winters algorithm to the logged data $\{Y_t, t = 1, \ldots, 130\}$. (The procedure is analogous to that described in part (f).)

h. Compare the average squared errors obtained by the four methods.

9.3. In equations (9.2.10)–(9.2.11), show that $\alpha = \Omega_{11}/(\Omega_{11} + \sigma_w^2)$ and $\beta = \Omega_{21}/\Omega_{11}$.

9.4. Verify the assertions made in the last paragraph of Section 9.4, comparing the forecasts of the last 12 values of the series AIRPASS.TSM obtained from the ARAR algorithm (with no log transformation) and the corresponding forecasts obtained by taking logarithms of the original series, then differencing at lag 12, mean-correcting, and fitting an AR(13) model to the transformed series.

10 Further Topics

In this final chapter we touch on a variety of topics of special interest. In Section 10.1 we consider transfer function models, designed to exploit for predictive purposes the relationship between two time series when one acts as a leading indicator for the other. Section 10.2 deals with intervention analysis, which allows for possible changes in the mechanism generating a time series, causing it to have different properties over different time intervals. In Section 10.3 we introduce the very fast growing area of nonlinear time series analysis, and in Section 10.4 we briefly discuss continuous-time ARMA processes, which, besides being of interest in their own right, are very useful also for modeling irregularly spaced data. In Section 10.5 we discuss fractionally integrated ARMA processes, sometimes called "long-memory" processes on account of the slow rate of convergence of their autocorrelation functions to zero as the lag increases.

10.1 Transfer Function Models

In this section we consider the problem of estimating the transfer function of a linear filter when the output includes added uncorrelated noise. Suppose that $\{X_{t1}\}$ and $\{X_{t2}\}$

are, respectively, the input and output of the transfer function model

$$X_{t2} = \sum_{j=0}^{\infty} \tau_j X_{t-j,1} + N_t, \tag{10.1.1}$$

where $T = \{\tau_j, j = 0, 1, \ldots\}$ is a causal time-invariant linear filter and $\{N_t\}$ is a zero-mean stationary process, uncorrelated with the input process $\{X_{t1}\}$. We further assume that $\{X_{t1}\}$ is a zero-mean stationary time series. Then the bivariate process $\{(X_{t1}, X_{t2})'\}$ is also stationary. Multiplying each side of (10.1.1) by $X_{t-k,1}$ and then taking expectations gives the equation

$$\gamma_{21}(k) = \sum_{j=0}^{\infty} \tau_j \gamma_{11}(k-j). \tag{10.1.2}$$

Equation (10.1.2) simplifies a great deal if the input process happens to be white noise. For example, if $\{X_{t1}\} \sim \mathrm{WN}(0, \sigma_1^2)$, then we can immediately identify t_k from (10.1.2) as

$$\tau_k = \gamma_{21}(k)/\sigma_1^2. \tag{10.1.3}$$

This observation suggests that "prewhitening" of the input process might simplify the identification of an appropriate transfer function model and at the same time provide simple preliminary estimates of the coefficients t_k.

If $\{X_{t1}\}$ can be represented as an invertible ARMA(p, q) process

$$\phi(B)X_{t1} = \theta(B)Z_t, \qquad \{Z_t\} \sim \mathrm{WN}\left(0, \sigma_Z^2\right), \tag{10.1.4}$$

then application of the filter $\pi(B) = \phi(B)\theta^{-1}(B)$ to $\{X_{t1}\}$ will produce the whitened series $\{Z_t\}$. Now applying the operator $\pi(B)$ to each side of (10.1.1) and letting $Y_t = \pi(B)X_{t2}$, we obtain the relation

$$Y_t = \sum_{j=0}^{\infty} \tau_j Z_{t-j} + N_t',$$

where

$$N_t' = \pi(B)N_t,$$

and $\{N_t'\}$ is a zero-mean stationary process, uncorrelated with $\{Z_t\}$. The same arguments that led to (10.1.3) therefore yield the equation

$$\tau_j = \rho_{YZ}(j)\sigma_Y/\sigma_Z, \tag{10.1.5}$$

where ρ_{YZ} is the cross-correlation function of $\{Y_t\}$ and $\{Z_t\}$, $\sigma_Z^2 = \mathrm{Var}(Z_t)$, and $\sigma_Y^2 = \mathrm{Var}(Y_t)$.

Given the observations $\{(X_{t1}, X_{t2})', t = 1, \ldots, n\}$, the results of the previous paragraph suggest the following procedure for estimating $\{\tau_j\}$ and analyzing the noise $\{N_t\}$ in the model (10.1.1):

1. Fit an ARMA model to $\{X_{t1}\}$ and file the residuals $(\hat{Z}_1, \ldots, \hat{Z}_n)$ (using the `Export` button in ITSM to copy them to the clipboard and then pasting them into the first column of an Excel file). Let $\hat{\phi}$ and $\hat{\theta}$ denote the maximum likelihood estimates of the autoregressive and moving-average parameters and let $\hat{\sigma}_Z^2$ be the maximum likelihood estimate of the variance of $\{Z_t\}$.
2. Apply the operator $\hat{\pi}(B) = \hat{\phi}(B)\hat{\theta}^{-1}(B)$ to $\{X_{t2}\}$ to obtain the series $\left(\hat{Y}_1, \ldots, \hat{Y}_n\right)$. (After fitting the ARMA model as in Step 1 above, highlight the window containing the graph of $\{X_t\}$ and replace $\{X_t\}$ by $\{Y_t\}$ using the option `File>Import`. The residuals are then automatically replaced by the residuals of $\{Y_t\}$ under the model already fitted to $\{X_t\}$.) Export the new residuals to the clipboard, paste them into the second column of the Excel file created in Step 1, and save this as a text file, FNAME.TSM. The file FNAME.TSM then contains the bivariate series$\{(Z_t, Y_t)\}$.) Let $\hat{\sigma}_Y^2$ denote the sample variance of $\hat{Y}_t$.
3. Compute the sample auto- and cross-correlation functions of $\{Z_t\}$ and $\{Y_t\}$ by opening the bivariate project FNAME.TSM in ITSM and clicking on the second yellow button at the top of the ITSM window. Comparison of $\hat{\rho}_{YZ}(h)$ with the bounds $\pm 1.96n^{-1/2}$ gives a preliminary indication of the lags h at which $\rho_{YZ}(h)$ is significantly different from zero. A more refined check can be carried out by using Bartlett's formula in Section 7.3.4 for the asymptotic variance of $\hat{\rho}_{YZ}(h)$. Under the assumptions that $\left\{\hat{Z}_t\right\} \sim \text{WN}\left(0, \hat{\sigma}_Z^2\right)$ and $\left\{\left(\hat{Y}_t, \hat{Z}_t\right)'\right\}$ is a stationary Gaussian process,

$$n\text{Var}(\hat{\rho}_{YZ}(h)) \sim 1 - \rho_{YZ}^2(h)\left[1.5 - \sum_{k=-\infty}^{\infty}\left(\rho_{YZ}^2(k) + \rho_{YY}^2(k)/2\right)\right] + \sum_{k=-\infty}^{\infty}\left[\rho_{YZ}(h+k)\rho_{YZ}(h-k) - 2\rho_{YZ}(h)\rho_{YZ}(k+h)\rho_{YY}^2(k)\right].$$

In order to check the hypothesis H_0 that $\rho_{YZ}(h) = 0, h \notin [a, b]$, where a and b are integers, we note from Corollary 7.3.1 that under H_0,

$$\text{Var}\left(\hat{\rho}_{YZ}(h)\right) \sim n^{-1} \qquad \text{for } h \notin [a, b].$$

We can therefore check the hypothesis H_0 by comparing $\hat{\rho}_{YZ}, h \notin [a, b]$, with the bounds $\pm\, 1.96n^{-1/2}$. Observe that $\rho_{ZY}(h)$ should be zero for $h > 0$ if the model (10.1.1) is valid.
4. Preliminary estimates of τ_h for the lags h at which $\hat{\rho}_{YZ}(h)$ is significantly different from zero are

$$\hat{\tau}_h = \hat{\rho}_{YZ}(h)\hat{\sigma}_Y/\hat{\sigma}_Z.$$

For other values of h the preliminary estimates are $\hat{\tau}_h = 0$. The numerical values of the cross-correlations $\hat{\rho}_{YZ}(h)$ are found by right-clicking on the graphs of the sample correlations plotted in Step 3 and then on `Info`. The values of $\hat{\sigma}_Z$ and $\hat{\sigma}_Y$ are found by doing the same with the graphs of the series themselves. Let $m \geq 0$

be the largest value of j such that $\hat{\tau}_j$ is nonzero and let $b \geq 0$ be the smallest such value. Then b is known as the *delay parameter* of the filter $\{\hat{\tau}_j\}$. If m is very large and if the coefficients $\{\hat{\tau}_j\}$ are approximately related by difference equations of the form

$$\hat{\tau}_j - v_1\hat{\tau}_{j-1} - \cdots - v_p\hat{\tau}_{j-p} = 0, \qquad j \geq b + p,$$

then $\hat{T}(B) = \sum_{j=b}^{m} \hat{\tau}_j B^j$ can be represented approximately, using fewer parameters, as

$$\hat{T}(B) = w_0(1 - v_1 B - \cdots - v_p B_p)^{-1} B^b.$$

In particular, if $\hat{\tau}_j = 0$, $j < b$, and $\hat{\tau}_j = w_0 v_1^{j-b}$, $j \geq b$, then

$$\hat{T}(B) = w_0(1 - v_1 B)^{-1} B^b. \tag{10.1.6}$$

Box and Jenkins (1976) recommend choosing $\hat{T}(B)$ to be a ratio of two polynomials. However, the degrees of the polynomials are often difficult to estimate from $\{\hat{\tau}_j\}$. The primary objective at this stage is to find a parametric function that provides an adequate approximation to $\hat{T}(B)$ without introducing too large a number of parameters. If $\hat{T}(B)$ is represented as $\hat{T}(B) = B^b w(B) v^{-1}(B) = B^b \left(w_0 + w_1 B + \cdots + w_q B^q\right)\left(1 - v_1 B - \cdots - v_p B^p\right)^{-1}$ with $v(z) \neq 0$ for $|z| \leq 1$, then we define $m = \max(q + b, p)$.

5. The noise sequence $\{N_t, t = m + 1, \ldots, n\}$ is estimated as

$$\hat{N}_t = X_{t2} - \hat{T}(B) X_{t1}.$$

(We set $\hat{N}_t = 0$, $t \leq m$, in order to compute $\hat{N}_t$, $t > m = \max(b+q, p)$). The calculations are done in ITSM by opening the bivariate file containing $\{(X_{t1}, X_{t2})\}$, selecting `Transfer>Specify Model`, and entering the preliminary model found in Step 4. Click on the fourth green button to see a graph of the residuals $\{N_t\}$. These should then be filed as, say, NOISE.TSM.

6. Preliminary identification of a suitable model for the noise sequence is carried out by fitting a causal invertible ARMA model

$$\phi^{(N)}(B) N_t = \theta^{(N)}(B) W_t, \qquad \{W_t\} \sim \mathrm{WN}\left(0, \sigma_W^2\right), \tag{10.1.7}$$

to the estimated noise $\hat{N}_{m+1}, \ldots, \hat{N}_n$ filed as NOISE.TSM in Step 5.

7. At this stage we have the preliminary model

$$\phi^{(N)}(B) v(B) X_{t2} = B^b \phi^{(N)}(B) w(B) X_{t1} + \theta^{(N)}(B) v(B) W_t,$$

where $\hat{T}(B) = B^b w(B) v^{-1}(B)$ as in step (4). For this model we can compute $\hat{W}_t\left(\mathbf{w}, \mathbf{v}, \boldsymbol{\phi}^{(N)}, \boldsymbol{\theta}^{(N)}\right)$, $t > m^* = \max(p_2 + p, b + p_2 + q)$, by setting $\hat{W}_t = 0$ for $t \leq m^*$. The parameters $\mathbf{w}$, $\mathbf{v}$, $\boldsymbol{\phi}^{(N)}$, and $\boldsymbol{\theta}^{(N)}$ can then be reestimated (more efficiently) by minimizing the sum of squares

$$\sum_{t=m^*+1}^{n} \hat{W}_t^2\left(\mathbf{w}, \mathbf{v}, \boldsymbol{\phi}^{(N)}, \boldsymbol{\theta}^{(N)}\right).$$

(The calculations are performed in ITSM by opening the bivariate project $\{(X_{t1}, X_{t2})\}$, selecting `Transfer>Specify model`, entering the preliminary model, and clicking `OK`. Then choose `Transfer>Estimation`, click `OK`, and the least squares estimates of the parameters will be computed. Pressing the fourth green button at the top of the screen will give a graph of the estimated residuals $\hat{W}_t$.)

8. To test for goodness of fit, the estimated residuals $\left\{\hat{W}_t, t > m^*\right\}$ and $\left\{\hat{Z}_t.t > m^*\right\}$ should be filed as a bivariate series and the auto- and cross correlations compared with the bounds $\pm 1.96/\sqrt{n}$ in order to check the hypothesis that the two series are uncorrelated white noise sequences. Alternative models can be compared using the AICC value that is printed with the estimated parameters in Step 7. It is computed from the exact Gaussian likelihood, which is computed using a state-space representation of the model, described in TSTM, Section 13.1.

Example 10.1.1 Sales with a leading indicator

In this example we fit a transfer function model to the bivariate time series of Example 7.1.2. Let

$$X_{t1} = (1 - B)Y_{t1} - .0228, \quad t = 2, \ldots, 150,$$

$$X_{t2} = (1 - B)Y_{t2} - .420, \quad t = 2, \ldots, 150,$$

where $\{Y_{t1}\}$ and $\{Y_{t2}\}$, $t = 1, \ldots, 150$, are the leading indicator and sales data, respectively. It was found in Example 7.1.2 that $\{X_{t1}\}$ and $\{X_{t2}\}$ can be modeled as low-order zero-mean ARMA processes. In particular, we fitted the model

$$X_{t1} = (1 - .474B)Z_t, \qquad \{Z_t\} \sim \text{WN}(0, .0779),$$

to the series $\{X_{t1}\}$. We can therefore whiten the series by application of the filter $\hat{\pi}(B) = (1 - .474B)^{-1}$. Applying $\hat{\pi}(B)$ to both $\{X_{t1}\}$ and $\{X_{t2}\}$ we obtain

$$\hat{Z}_t = (1 - .474B)^{-1}X_{t1}, \quad \hat{\sigma}_Z^2 = .0779,$$

$$\hat{Y}_t = (1 - .474B)^{-1}X_{t2}, \quad \hat{\sigma}_Y^2 = 4.0217.$$

These calculations and the filing of the series $\left\{\hat{Z}_t\right\}$ and $\left\{\hat{Y}_t\right\}$ were carried out using ITSM as described in steps (1) and (2). Their sample auto- and cross-correlations, found as described in step (3), are shown in Figure 10.1. The cross-correlations $\hat{\rho}_{ZY}(h)$ (top right) and $\hat{\rho}_{YZ}(h)$ (bottom left), when compared with the bounds $\pm 1.96(149)^{-1/2} = \pm .161$, strongly suggest a transfer function model for $\{X_{t2}\}$ in terms of $\{X_{t1}\}$ with delay parameter 3. Since $\hat{\tau}_j = \hat{\rho}_{YZ}(j)\hat{\sigma}_Y/\hat{\sigma}_Z$ is decreasing approximately geometrically for $j \geq 3$, we take $T(B)$ to have the form (10.1.6), i.e.,

$$T(B) = w_0(1 - v_1 B)^{-1}B^3.$$

The preliminary estimates of w_0 and v_1 are $\hat{w}_0 = \hat{\tau}_3 = 4.86$ and $\hat{v}_1 = \hat{\tau}_4/\hat{\tau}_3 = .698$, the coefficients τ_j being estimated as described in step (4). The estimated noise sequence is determined and filed using ITSM as described in step (5). It satisfies the equations

$$\hat{N}_t = X_{t2} - 4.86B^3(1 - .698B)^{-1}X_{t1}, \qquad t = 5, 6, \ldots, 150.$$

Analysis of this univariate series with ITSM gives the MA(1) model

$$N_t = (1 - .364B)W_t, \qquad \{W_t\} \sim \mathrm{WN}(0, .0590).$$

Substituting these preliminary noise and transfer function models into equation (10.1.1) then gives

$$X_{t2} = 4.86B^3(1 - .698B)^{-1}X_{t1} + (1 - .364B)W_t, \quad \{W_t\} \sim \mathrm{WN}(0, .0590).$$

Now minimizing the sum of squares (10.1.7) with respect to the parameters $\left(w_0, v_1, \theta_1^{(N)}\right)$ as described in step (7), we obtain the least squares model

$$X_{t2} = 4.717B^3(1 - .724B)^{-1}X_{t1} + (1 - .582B)W_t, \tag{10.1.8}$$

where $\{W_t\} \sim \mathrm{WN}(0, .0486)$ and

$$X_{t1} = (1 - .474B)Z_t, \quad \{Z_t\} \sim \mathrm{WN}(0, .0779).$$

Notice the reduced white noise variance of $\{W_t\}$ in the least squares model as compared with the preliminary model.

The sample auto- and cross-correlation functions of the series $\hat{Z}_t$ and $\hat{W}_t$, $t = 5, \ldots, 150$, are shown in Figure 10.2. All of the correlations lie between the bounds $\pm 1.96/\sqrt{144}$, supporting the assumption underlying the fitted model that the residuals are uncorrelated white noise sequences. □

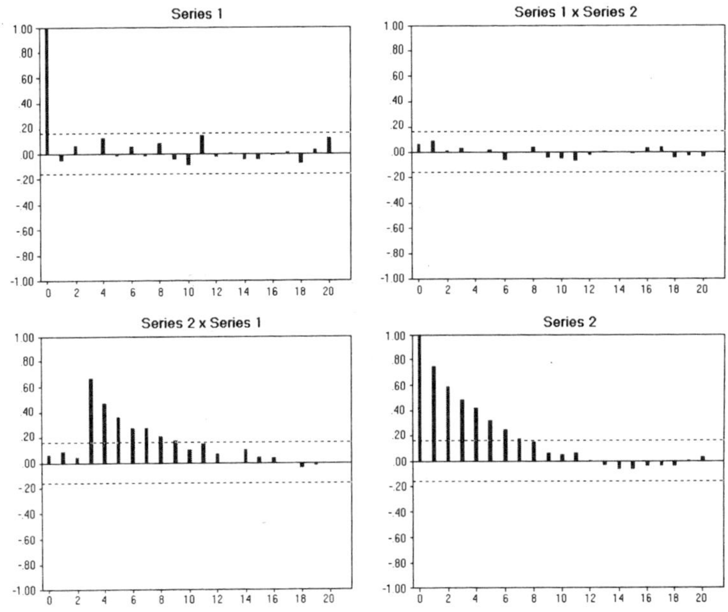

Figure 10-1 The sample correlation functions $\hat{\rho}_{ij}(h)$, of Example 10.1.1. Series 1 is $\{\hat{Z}_t\}$ and Series 2 is $\{\hat{Y}_t\}$.

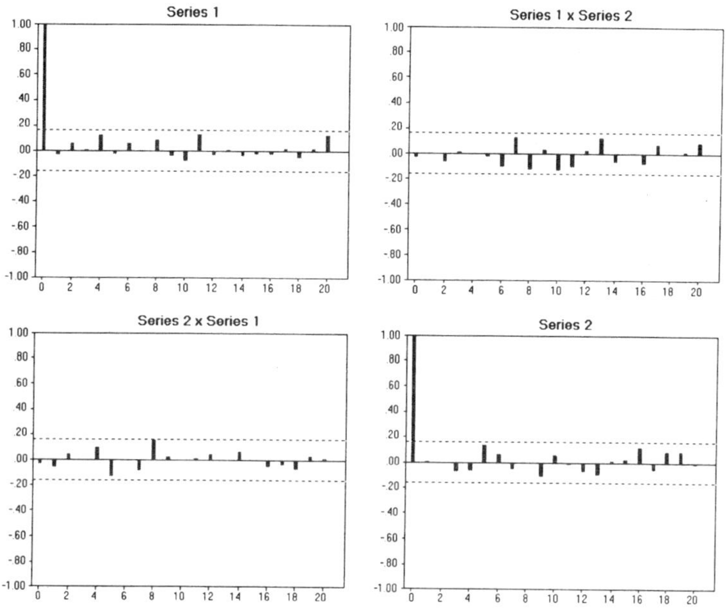

Figure 10-2 The sample correlation functions of the estimated residuals from the model fitted in Example 10.1.1. Series 1 is $\{\hat{Z}_t\}$ and Series 2 is $\{\hat{W}_t\}$.

10.1.1 Prediction Based on a Transfer Function Model

When predicting $X_{n+h,2}$ on the basis of the transfer function model defined by (10.1.1), (10.1.4), and (10.1.7), with observations of X_{t1} and X_{t2}, $t = 1, \ldots, n$, our aim is to find the linear combination of $1, X_{11}, \ldots, X_{n1}, X_{12}, \ldots, X_{n2}$ that predicts $X_{n+h,2}$ with minimum mean squared error. The exact solution of this problem can be found with the help of the Kalman recursions (see TSTM, Section 13.1 for details). The program ITSM uses these recursions to compute the predictors and their mean squared errors.

In order to provide a little more insight, we give here the predictors $\tilde{P}_n X_{n+h}$ and mean squared errors based on infinitely many past observations X_{t1} and X_{t2}, $-\infty < t \leq n$. These predictors and their mean squared errors will be close to those based on X_{t1} and X_{t2}, $1 \leq t \leq n$, if n is sufficiently large.

The transfer function model defined by (10.1.1), (10.1.4), and (10.1.7) can be rewritten as

$$X_{t2} = T(B)X_{t1} + \beta(B)W_t, \tag{10.1.9}$$

$$X_{t1} = \theta(B)\phi^{-1}(B)Z_t, \tag{10.1.10}$$

where $\beta(B) = \theta^{(N)}(B)/\phi^{(N)}(B)$. Eliminating X_{t1} gives

$$X_{t2} = \sum_{j=0}^{\infty} \alpha_j Z_{t-j} + \sum_{j=0}^{\infty} \beta_j W_{t-j}, \tag{10.1.11}$$

where $\alpha(B) = T(B)\theta(B)/\phi(B)$.

Noting that each limit of linear combinations of $\{X_{t1}, X_{t2}, -\infty < t \le n\}$ is a limit of linear combinations of $\{Z_t, W_t, -\infty < t \le n\}$ and conversely and that $\{Z_t\}$ and $\{W_t\}$ are uncorrelated, we see at once from (10.1.11) that

$$\tilde{P}_n X_{n+h,2} = \sum_{j=h}^{\infty} \alpha_j Z_{n+h-j} + \sum_{j=h}^{\infty} \beta_j W_{n+h-j}. \tag{10.1.12}$$

Setting $t = n + h$ in (10.1.11) and subtracting (10.1.12) gives the mean squared error

$$E\left(X_{n+h,2} - \tilde{P}_n X_{n+h,2}\right)^2 = \sigma_Z^2 \sum_{j=0}^{h-1} \alpha_j^2 + \sigma_W^2 \sum_{j=0}^{h-1} \beta_j^2. \tag{10.1.13}$$

To compute the predictors $\tilde{P}_n X_{n+h,2}$ we proceed as follows. Rewrite (10.1.9) as

$$A(B)X_{t2} = B^b U(B) X_{t1} + V(B) W_t, \tag{10.1.14}$$

where A, U, and V are polynomials of the form

$$A(B) = 1 - A_1 B - \cdots - A_a B^a,$$

$$U(B) = U_0 + U_1 B + \cdots + U_u B^u,$$

$$V(B) = 1 + V_1 B + \cdots + V_v B^v.$$

Applying the operator $\tilde{P}_n$ to equation (10.1.14) with $t = n + h$, we obtain

$$\tilde{P}_n X_{n+h,2} = \sum_{j=1}^{a} A_j \tilde{P}_n X_{n+h-j,2} + \sum_{j=0}^{u} U_j \tilde{P}_n X_{n+h-b-j,1} + \sum_{j=h}^{v} V_j W_{n+h-j}, \tag{10.1.15}$$

where the last sum is zero if $h > v$.

Since $\{X_{t1}\}$ is uncorrelated with $\{W_t\}$, the predictors appearing in the second sum in (10.1.15) are therefore obtained by predicting the univariate series $\{X_{t1}\}$ as described in Section 3.3 using the model (10.1.10). In keeping with our assumption that n is large, we can replace $\tilde{P}_n X_{j1}$ for each j by the finite-past predictor obtained from the program ITSM. The values W_j, $j \le n$, are replaced by their estimated values $\hat{W}_j$ from the least squares estimation in step (7) of the modeling procedure.

Equations (10.1.15) can now be solved recursively for the predictors $\tilde{P}_n X_{n+1,2}$, $\tilde{P}_n X_{n+2,2}$, $\tilde{P}_n X_{n+3,2}$, ...

Example 10.1.2 Sales with a leading indicator

Applying the preceding results to the series $\{X_{t1}, X_{t2}, 2 \le t \le 150\}$ of Example 10.1.1, and using the values $X_{148,1} = -.093$, $X_{150,2} = .08$, $\hat{W}_{150} = -.0706$, $\hat{W}_{149} = .1449$, we find from (10.1.8) and (10.1.15) that

$$\tilde{P}_{150} X_{151,2} = .724 X_{150,2} + 4.717 X_{148,1} - 1.306 W_{150} + .421 W_{149} = -.228$$

and, using the value $X_{149,1} = .237$, that

$$\tilde{P}_{150} X_{152,2} = .724 \tilde{P}_{150} X_{151,2} + 4.717 X_{149,1} + .421 W_{150} = .923.$$

In terms of the original sales data $\{Y_{t2}\}$ we have $Y_{149,2} = 262.7$ and

$$Y_{t2} = Y_{t-1,2} + X_{t2} + .420.$$

Hence the predictors of actual sales are

$$P_{150}^{*} Y_{151,2} = 262.70 - .228 + .420 = 262.89,$$

$$P_{150}^{*} Y_{152,2} = 262.89 + .923 + .420 = 264.23,$$

where P_{149}^{*} is based on $\{1, Y_{11}, Y_{12}, X_{s1}, X_{s2}, -\infty < s \le 150\}$, and it is assumed that Y_{11} and Y_{12} are uncorrelated with $\{X_{s1}\}$ and with $\{X_{s2}\}$. The predicted values are in close agreement with those based on the finite number of available observations that are computed by ITSM. Since our model for the sales data is

$$(1 - B)Y_{t2} = .420 + 4.717B^3(1 - .474B)(1 - .724B)^{-1}Z_t + (1 - .582B)W_t,$$

it can be shown, using an argument analogous to that which gave (10.1.13), that the mean squared errors are given by

$$E(Y_{150+h,2} - P_{150}Y_{150+h,2})^2 = \sigma_Z^2 \sum_{j=0}^{h-1} \alpha_j^{*2} + \sigma_W^2 \sum_{j=0}^{h-1} \beta_j^{*2},$$

where

$$\sum_{j=0}^{\infty} \alpha_j^* z^j = 4.717z^3(1 - .474z)(1 - .724z)^{-1}(1 - z)^{-1}$$

and

$$\sum_{j=0}^{\infty} \beta_j^* z^j = (1 - .582z)(1 - z)^{-1}.$$

For $h = 1$ and 2 we obtain

$$E(Y_{151,2} - P_{150}^{*}Y_{151,2})^2 = .0486,$$

$$E(Y_{152,2} - P_{150}^{*}Y_{152,2})^2 = .0570,$$

in close agreement with the finite-past mean squared errors obtained by ITSM.

It is interesting to examine the improvement obtained by using the transfer function model rather than fitting a univariate model to the sales data alone. If we adopt the latter course, we obtain the model

$$X_{t2} - .249X_{t-1,2} - .199X_{t-2,2} = U_t,$$

where $\{U_t\} \sim \text{WN}(0, 1.794)$ and $X_{t2} = Y_{t2} - Y_{t-1,2} - .420$. The corresponding predictors of $Y_{151,2}$ and $Y_{152,2}$ are easily found from the program ITSM to be 263.14 and 263.58 with mean squared errors 1.794 and 4.593, respectively. These mean squared errors are dramatically worse than those obtained using the transfer function model. □

10.2 Intervention Analysis

During the period for which a time series is observed, it is sometimes the case that a change occurs that affects the level of the series. A change in the tax laws may, for example, have a continuing effect on the daily closing prices of shares on the stock market. In the same way construction of a dam on a river may have a dramatic effect on the time series of streamflows below the dam. In the following we shall assume that the time T at which the change (or "intervention") occurs is known.

To account for such changes, Box and Tiao (1975) introduced a model for intervention analysis that has the same form as the transfer function model

$$Y_t = \sum_{j=0}^{\infty} \tau_j X_{t-j} + N_t, \tag{10.2.1}$$

except that the input series $\{X_t\}$ is not a random series but a deterministic function of t. It is clear from (10.2.1) that $\sum_{j=0}^{\infty} \tau_j X_{t-j}$ is then the mean of Y_t. The function $\{X_t\}$ and the coefficients $\{\tau_j\}$ are therefore chosen in such a way that the changing level of the observations of $\{Y_t\}$ is well represented by the sequence $\sum_{j=0}^{\infty} \tau_j X_{t-j}$. For a series $\{Y_t\}$ with $EY_t = 0$ for $t \le T$ and $EY_t \to 0$ as $t \to \infty$, a suitable input series is

$$X_t = I_t(T) = \begin{cases} 1 & \text{if } t = T, \\ 0 & \text{if } t \ne T. \end{cases} \tag{10.2.2}$$

For a series $\{Y_t\}$ with $EY_t = 0$ for $t \le T$ and $EY_t \to a \ne 0$ as $t \to \infty$, a suitable input series is

$$X_t = H_t(T) = \sum_{k=T}^{\infty} I_t(k) = \begin{cases} 1 & \text{if } t \ge T, \\ 0 & \text{if } t < T. \end{cases} \tag{10.2.3}$$

(Other deterministic input functions $\{X_t\}$ can also be used, for example when interventions occur at more than one time.) The function $\{X_t\}$ having been selected by inspection of the data, the determination of the coefficients $\{\tau_j\}$ in (10.2.1) then reduces to a regression problem in which the errors $\{N_t\}$ constitute an ARMA process. This problem can be solved using the program ITSM as described below.

The goal of intervention analysis is to estimate the effect of the intervention as indicated by the term $\sum_{j=0}^{\infty} \tau_j X_{t-j}$ and to use the resulting model (10.2.1) for forecasting. For example, Wichern and Jones (1978) used intervention analysis to investigate the effect of the American Dental Association's endorsement of Crest toothpaste on Crest's market share. Other applications of intervention analysis can be found in Box and Tiao (1975), Atkins (1979), and Bhattacharyya and Layton (1979). A more general approach can also be found in West and Harrison (1989), Harvey (1990), and Pole, West, and Harrison (1994).

As in the case of transfer function modeling, once $\{X_t\}$ has been chosen (usually as either (10.2.2) or (10.2.3)), estimation of the linear filter $\{\tau_j\}$ in (10.2.1) is simplified by approximating the operator $T(B) = \sum_{j=0}^{\infty} \tau_j B^j$ with a rational operator of the form

$$T(B) = \frac{B^b W(B)}{V(B)}, \tag{10.2.4}$$

where b is the delay parameter and $W(B)$ and $V(B)$ are polynomials of the form

$$W(B) = w_0 + w_1 B + \cdots + w_q B^q$$

and

$$V(B) = 1 - v_1 B - \cdots - v_p B^p.$$

By suitable choice of the parameters b, q, p and the coefficients w_i and v_j, the intervention term $T(B)X_t$ can made to take a great variety of functional forms.

For example, if $T(B) = wB^2/(1 - vB)$ and $X_t = I_t(T)$ as in (10.2.2), the resulting intervention term is

$$\frac{wB^2}{(1 - vB)} I_t(T) = \sum_{j=0}^{\infty} v^j w I_{t-j-2}(T) = \sum_{j=0}^{\infty} v^j w I_t(T + 2 + j),$$

a series of pulses of sizes $v^j w$ at times $T+2+j$, $j = 0, 1, 2, \ldots$. If $|v| < 1$, the effect of the intervention is to add a series of pulses with size w at time $T + 2$, decreasing to zero at a geometric rate depending on v as $t \to \infty$. Similarly, with $X_t = H_t(T)$ as in (10.2.3),

$$\frac{wB^2}{(1 - vB)} H_t(T) = \sum_{j=0}^{\infty} v^j w H_{t-j-2}(T) = \sum_{j=0}^{\infty} (1 + v + \cdots + v^j) w I_t(T + 2 + j),$$

a series of pulses of sizes $(1 + v + \cdots + v^j)w$ at times $T + 2 + j$, $j = 0, 1, 2, \ldots$. If $|v| < 1$, the effect of the intervention is to bring about a shift in level of the series X_t, the size of the shift converging to $w/(1 - v)$ as $t \to \infty$.

An appropriate form for X_t and possible values of b, q, and p having been chosen by inspection of the data, the estimation of the parameters in (10.2.4) and the fitting of the model for $\{N_t\}$ can be carried out using steps (6)–(8) of the transfer function modeling procedure described in Section 10.1. Start with step (7) and assume that $\{N_t\}$ is white noise to get preliminary estimates of the coefficients w_i and v_j by least squares. The residuals are filed and used as estimates of $\{N_t\}$. Then go to step (6) and continue exactly as for transfer function modeling with input series $\{X_t\}$ and output series $\{Y_t\}$.

Example 10.2.1 Seat-belt legislation

In this example we reanalyze the seat-belt legislation data, SBL.TSM of Example 6.6.3 from the point of view of intervention analysis. For this purpose the bivariate series $\{(f_t, Y_t)\}$ consisting of the series filed as SBLIN.TSM and SBL.TSM respectively has been saved in the file SBL2.TSM. The *input* series $\{f_t\}$ is the deterministic

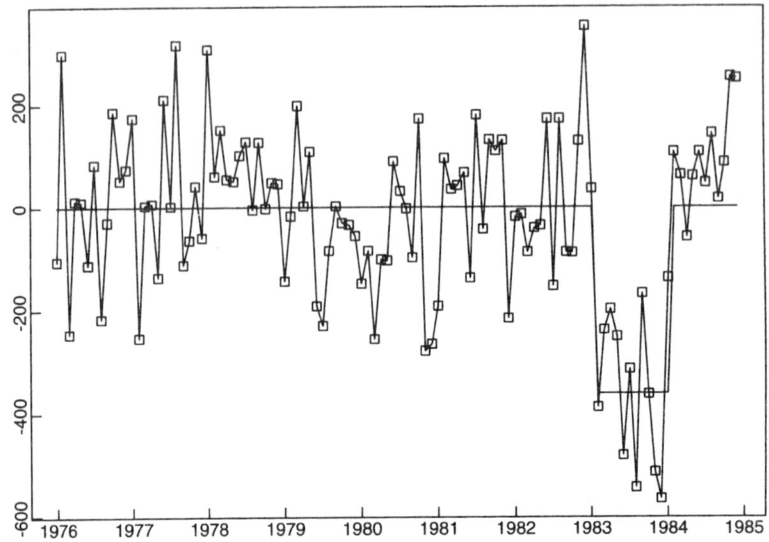

Figure 10-3 The differenced series of Example 10.2.1 (showing also the fitted intervention term accounting for the seat-belt legislation of 1983).

step-function defined in Example 6.6.3 and Y_t is the number of deaths and serious injuries on UK roads in month t, $t = 1, \ldots, 120$, corresponding to the 10 years beginning with January 1975.

To account for the seat-belt legislation, we use the same model (6.6.15) as in Example 6.6.3 and, because of the apparent non-stationarity of the residuals, we again difference both $\{f_t\}$ and $\{Y_t\}$ at lag 12 to obtain the model (6.6.16), i.e.,

$$X_t = bg_t + N_t, \tag{10.2.4}$$

where $X_t = \nabla_{12}Y_t$, $g_t = \nabla_{12}f_t$, and $\{N_t\}$ is a zero-mean stationary time series. This is a particularly simple example of the general intervention model (10.2.1) for the series $\{X_t\}$ with intervention $\{bg_t\}$. Our aim is to find a suitable model for $\{N_t\}$ and at the same time to estimate b, taking into account the autocorrelation function of the model for $\{N_t\}$. To apply intervention analysis to this problem using ITSM, we proceed as follows:

(1) Open the bivariate project SBL2.TSM and difference the series at lag 12.

(2) Select `Transfer>Specify model` and you will see that the default input and noise are white noise, while the default transfer model relating the input g_t to the output X_t is $X_t = bg_t$ with $b = 1$. Click `OK`, leaving these settings as they are. The input model is irrelevant for intervention analysis and estimation of the transfer function with the default noise model will give us the ordinary least squares estimate of b in the model (10.2.4), with the residuals providing estimates of N_t. Now selection `Transfer>Estimation` and click `OK`. You will then see the estimated value -346.9 for b. Finally, press the red Export button (top right in the ITSM window) to export the residuals (estimated values of N_t) to a file and call it, say, NOISE.TSM.

(3) Without closing the bivariate project, open the univariate project NOISE.TSM. The sample ACF and PACF of the series suggests either an MA(13) or AR(13) model. Fitting AR and MA models of order up to 13 (with no mean-correction) using the option `Model>Estimation>Autofit` gives an MA(12) model as the minimum AICC fit.

(4) Return to the bivariate project by highlighting the window labeled SBL2.TSM and select `Transfer>Specify model`. The transfer model will now show the estimated value −346.9 for b. Click on the `Residual Model` tab, enter 12 for the MA order and click `OK`. Select `Transfer>Estimation` and again click `OK`. The parameters in both the noise and transfer models will then be estimated and printed on the screen. Repeating the minimization with decreasing step-sizes, .1, .01 and then .001, gives the model,

$$X_t = -362.5g_t + N_t,$$

where $N_t = W_t + .207W_{t-1} + .311W_{t-2} + .105W_{t-3} + .040W_{t-4} + .194W_{t-5} + .100W_{t-6} + .299W_{t-7} + .080W_{t-8} + .125W_{t-9} + .210W_{t-10} + .109W_{t-11} + .501W_{t-12}$, and $\{W_t\} \sim \text{WN}(0{,}17289)$. File the residuals (which are now estimates of $\{W_t\}$) as RES.TSM. The differenced series $\{X_t\}$ and the fitted intervention term, $-362.5g_t$, are shown in Figure 10.3.

(5) Open the univariate project RES.TSM and apply the usual tests for randomness by selecting `Statistics>Residual Analysis`. The tests are all passed at level .05, leading us to conclude that the model found in step (4) is satisfactory. The sample ACF of the residuals is shown in Figure 10.4. □

10.3 Nonlinear Models

A time series of the form

$$X_t = \sum_{j=0}^{\infty} \psi_j Z_{t-j}, \quad \{Z_t\} \sim \text{IID}\left(0, \sigma^2\right), \tag{10.3.1}$$

where Z_t is expressible as a mean square limit of linear combinations of $\{X_s, \infty < s \le t\}$, has the property that the best mean square predictor $E(X_{t+h}|X_s, -\infty < s \le t)$ and the best linear predictor $\tilde{P}_t X_{t+h}$ in terms of $\{X_s, -\infty < s \le t\}$ are identical. It can be shown that if iid is replaced by WN in (10.3.1), then the two predictors are identical if and only if $\{Z_t\}$ is a **martingale difference sequence** relative to $\{X_t\}$, i.e., if and only if $E(Z_t|X_s, -\infty < s \le t) = 0$ for all t.

The Wold decomposition (Section 2.6) ensures that every purely nondeterministic stationary process can be expressed in the form (10.3.1) with $\{Z_t\} \sim \text{WN}\left(0, \sigma^2\right)$. The

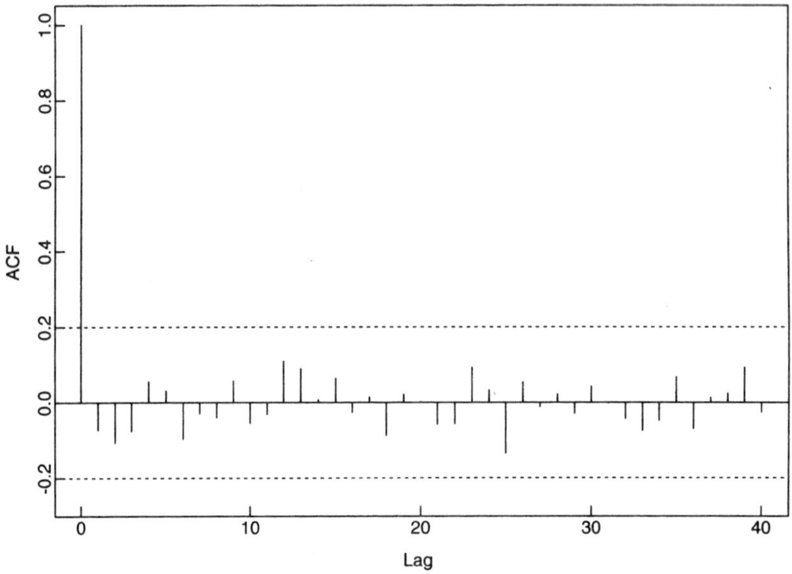

Figure 10-4 The sample ACF of the residuals from the model in Example 10.2.1

process $\{Z_t\}$ in the Wold decomposition, however, is generally not an iid sequence, and the best mean square predictor of X_{t+h} may be quite different from the best linear predictor.

In the case where $\{X_t\}$ is a purely nondeterministic Gaussian stationary process, the sequence $\{Z_t\}$ in the Wold decomposition is Gaussian and therefore iid. Every stationary purely nondeterministic Gaussian process can therefore be generated by applying a causal linear filter to an iid Gaussian sequence. We shall therefore refer to such a process as a **Gaussian linear process**.

In this section we shall use the term linear process to mean a process $\{X_t\}$ of the form (10.3.1). This is a more restrictive use of the term than in Definition 2.2.1.

10.3.1 Deviations from Linearity

Many of the time series encountered in practice exhibit characteristics not shown by linear processes, and so to obtain good models and predictors it is necessary to look to models more general than those satisfying (10.3.1) with iid noise. As indicated above, this will mean that the minimum mean squared error predictors are not, in general, linear functions of the past observations.

Gaussian linear processes have a number of properties that are often found to be violated by observed time series. The former are reversible in the sense that $(X_{t_1}, \cdots, X_{t_n})'$ has the same distribution as $(X_{t_n}, \cdots, X_{t_1})'$. (Except in a few special cases, ARMA processes are reversible if and only if they are Gaussian (Breidt and Davis, 1992).) Deviations from this property by observed time series are suggested by sample paths that rise to their maxima and fall away at different rates (see, for example, the sunspot numbers filed as SUNSPOTS.TSM). Bursts of outlying values are frequently observed in practical time series and are seen also in the sample paths of nonlinear (and infinite-variance) models. They are rarely seen, however, in the sample paths of Gaussian linear processes. Other characteristics suggesting deviation from a Gaussian linear model are discussed by Tong (1990).

Many observed time series, particularly financial time series, exhibit periods during which they are "less predictable" (or "more volatile"), depending on the past history of the series. This dependence of the predictability (i.e., the size of the prediction mean squared error) on the past of the series cannot be modeled with a linear time series, since for a linear process the minimum h-step mean squared error is independent of the past history. Linear models thus fail to take account of the possibility that certain past histories may permit more accurate forecasting than others, and cannot identify the circumstances under which more accurate forecasts can be expected. Nonlinear models, on the other hand, do allow for this. The ARCH and GARCH models considered below are in fact constructed around the dependence of the conditional variance of the process on its past history.

10.3.2 Chaotic Deterministic Sequences

To distinguish between linear and nonlinear processes, we need to be able to decide in particular when a white noise sequence is also iid. Sequences generated by nonlinear deterministic difference equations can exhibit sample correlation functions that are very close to those of samples from a white noise sequence. However, the deterministic nature of the recursions implies the strongest possible dependence between successive observations. For example, the celebrated logistic equation (see May, 1976, and Tong,

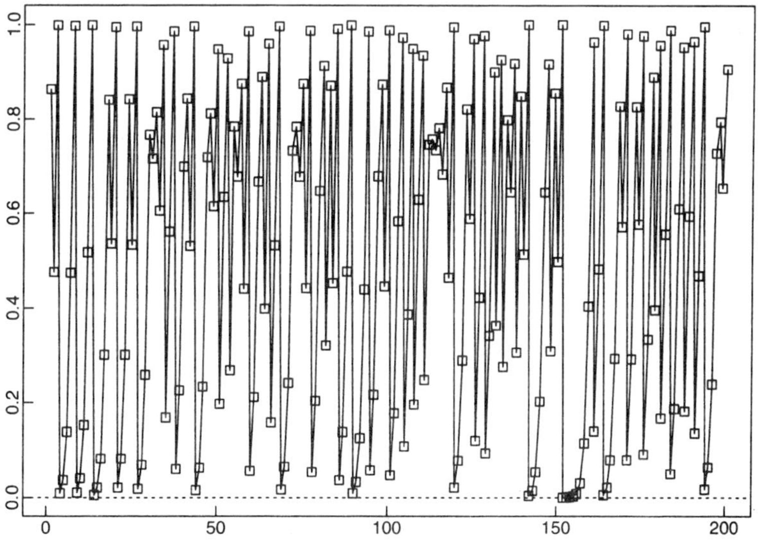

Figure 10-5 A sequence generated by the recursions $x_n = 4x_{n-1}(1 - x_{n-1})$.

1990) defines a sequence $\{x_n\}$, for any given x_0, via the equations

$$x_n = 4x_{n-1}(1 - x_{n-1}), \quad 0 < x_0 < 1.$$

The values of x_n are, for even moderately large values of n, extremely sensitive to small changes in x_0. This is clear from the fact that the sequence can be expressed explicitly as

$$x_n = \sin^2\left(2^n \arcsin\left(\sqrt{x_0}\right)\right), \quad n = 0, 1, 2, \ldots.$$

A very small change δ in $\arcsin\left(\sqrt{x_0}\right)$ leads to a change $2^n\delta$ in the argument of the sine function defining x_n. If we generate a sequence numerically, the generated sequence will, for most values of x_0 in the interval (0,1), be random in appearance, with a sample autocorrelation function similar to that of a sample from white noise. The data file CHAOS.TSM contains the sequence $x_1, \ldots, x_{200}$ (correct to nine decimal places) generated by the logistic equation with $x_0 = \pi/10$. The calculation requires specification of x_0 to at least 70 decimal places and the use of correspondingly high precision arithmetic. The series and its sample autocorrelation function are shown in Figures 10.5 and 10.6. The sample ACF and the AICC criterion both suggest white noise with mean .4954 as a model for the series. Under this model the best linear predictor of X_{201} would be .4954. However, the best predictor of X_{201} to nine decimal places is, in fact, $4x_{200}(1 - x_{200}) = 0.016286669$, with zero mean squared error.

Distinguishing between iid and non-iid white noise is clearly not possible on the basis of second-order properties. For insight into the dependence structure we can examine sample moments of order higher than two. For example, the dependence in the data in CHAOS.TSM is reflected by a significantly nonzero sample autocorre-

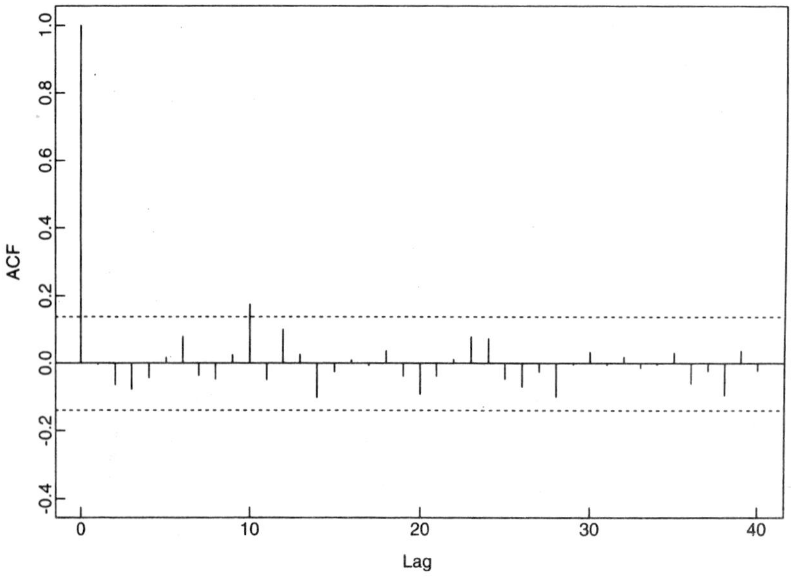

Figure 10-6 The sample autocorrelation function of the sequence in Figure 10.5.

lation at lag 1 of the *squared* data. In the following paragraphs we consider several approaches to this problem.

10.3.3 Distinguishing Between White Noise and iid Sequences

If $\{X_t\} \sim \text{WN}\left(0, \sigma^2\right)$ and $E|X_t|^4 < \infty$, a useful tool for deciding whether or not $\{X_t\}$ is iid is the ACF $\rho_{X^2}(h)$ of the process $\left\{X_t^2\right\}$. If $\{X_t\}$ is iid, then $\rho_{X^2}(h) = 0$ for all $h \neq 0$, whereas this is not necessarily the case otherwise. This is the basis for the test of McLeod and Li described in Section 1.6.

Now suppose that $\{X_t\}$ is a strictly stationary time series such that $E|X_t|^k \le K < \infty$ for some integer $k \ge 3$. The kth-order cumulant $C_k(r_1, \ldots, r_{k-1})$ of $\{X_t\}$ is then defined as the joint cumulant of the random variables, $X_t, X_{t+r_1}, \ldots, X_{t+r_{k-1}}$, i.e., as the coefficient of $i^k z_1 z_2 \cdots z_k$ in the Taylor expansion about $(0, \ldots, 0)$ of

$$\chi(z_1, \ldots, z_k) := \ln E[\exp(iz_1 X_t + iz_2 X_{t+r_1} + \cdots + iz_k X_{t+r_{k-1}})]. \quad (10.3.2)$$

(Since $\{X_t\}$ is strictly stationary, this quantity does not depend on t.) In particular, the third-order cumulant function C_3 of $\{X_t\}$ coincides with the third-order central moment function, i.e.,

$$C_3(r, s) = E[(X_t - \mu)(X_{t+r} - \mu)(X_{t+s} - \mu)], \qquad r, s \in \{0, \pm 1, \ldots\},$$

where $\mu = EX_t$. If $\sum_r \sum_s |C_3(r, s)| < \infty$, we define the third-order polyspectral density (or bispectral density) of $\{X_t\}$ to be the Fourier transform

$$f_3(\omega_1, \omega_2) = \frac{1}{(2\pi)^2} \sum_{r=-\infty}^{\infty} \sum_{s=-\infty}^{\infty} C_3(r, s) e^{-ir\omega_1 - is\omega_2}, \qquad -\pi \le \omega_1, \omega_2 \le \pi,$$

in which case

$$C_3(r, s) = \int_{-\pi}^{\pi} \int_{-\pi}^{\pi} e^{ir\omega_1 + is\omega_2} f_3(\omega_1, \omega_2) d\omega_1\, d\omega_2.$$

[More generally, if the kth order cumulants $C_k(r_1, \cdots, r_{k-1})$, of $\{X_t\}$ are absolutely summable, we define the kth order polyspectral density as the Fourier transform of C_k. For details see Rosenblatt (1985) and Priestley (1988).]

If $\{X_t\}$ is a Gaussian linear process, it follows from Problem 10.3 that the cumulant function C_3 of $\{X_t\}$ is identically zero. (The same is also true of all the cumulant functions C_k with $k > 3$.) Consequently, $f_3(\omega_1, \omega_2) = 0$ for all $\omega_1, \omega_2 \in [-\pi, \pi]$. Appropriateness of a Gaussian linear model for a given data set can therefore be checked by using the data to test the null hypothesis $f_3 = 0$. For details of such a test, see Subba-Rao and Gabr (1984).

If $\{X_t\}$ is a linear process of the form (10.3.1) with $E|Z_t|^3 < \infty$, $EZ_t^3 = \eta$, and $\sum_{j=0}^{\infty} |\psi_j| < \infty$, it can be shown from (10.3.2) (see Problem 10.3) that the third-order cumulant function of $\{X_t\}$ is given by

$$C_3(r,s) = \eta \sum_{i=-\infty}^{\infty} \psi_i \psi_{i+r} \psi_{i+s} \tag{10.3.3}$$

(with $\psi_j = 0$ for $j < 0$), and hence that $\{X_t\}$ has bispectral density

$$f_3(\omega_1,\omega_2) = \frac{\eta}{4\pi^2} \psi\left(e^{i(\omega_1+\omega_2)}\right) \psi\left(e^{-i\omega_1}\right) \psi\left(e^{-i\omega_2}\right), \tag{10.3.4}$$

where $\psi(z) := \sum_{j=0}^{\infty} \psi_j z^j$. By Proposition 4.3.1, the spectral density of $\{X_t\}$ is

$$f(\omega) = \frac{\sigma^2}{2\pi} \left|\psi\left(e^{-i\omega}\right)\right|^2.$$

Hence,

$$\phi(\omega_1,\omega_2) := \frac{|f_3(\omega_1,\omega_2)|^2}{f(\omega_1)f(\omega_2)f(\omega_1+\omega_2)} = \frac{\eta^2}{2\pi\sigma^6}.$$

Appropriateness of the linear process (10.3.1) for modeling a given data set can therefore be checked by using the data to test for constancy of $\phi(\omega_1,\omega_2)$ (see Subba-Rao and Gabr, 1984).

10.3.4 Three Useful Classes of Nonlinear Models

If it is decided that a linear Gaussian model is not appropriate, there is a choice of several families of nonlinear processes that have been found useful for modeling purposes. These include bilinear models, autoregressive models with random coefficients, and threshold models. Excellent accounts of these are available in Subba-Rao and Gabr (1984), Nicholls and Quinn (1982), and Tong (1990), respectively.

The bilinear model of order (p,q,r,s) is defined by the equations

$$X_t = Z_t + \sum_{i=1}^{p} a_i X_{t-i} + \sum_{j=1}^{q} b_j Z_{t-j} + \sum_{i=1}^{r}\sum_{j=1}^{s} c_{ij} X_{t-i} Z_{t-j},$$

where $\{Z_t\} \sim \text{iid}\left(0,\sigma^2\right)$. A sufficient condition for the existence of a strictly stationary solution of these equations is given by Liu and Brockwell (1988).

A random coefficient autoregressive process $\{X_t\}$ of order p satisfies an equation of the form

$$X_t = \sum_{i=1}^{p} \left(\phi_i + U_t^{(i)}\right) X_{t-i} + Z_t,$$

where $\{Z_t\} \sim \text{IID}\left(0,\sigma^2\right)$, $\left\{U_t^{(i)}\right\} \sim \text{IID}\left(0,\nu^2\right)$, $\{Z_t\}$ is independent of $\left\{U_t\right\}$, and $\phi_1,\ldots,\phi_p \in \mathbb{R}$.

Threshold models can be regarded as piecewise linear models in which the linear relationship varies with the values of the process. For example, if $R^{(i)}$, $i = 1,\ldots,k$, is a partition of $\mathbb{R}^p$, and $\{Z_t\} \sim \text{IID}(0, 1)$, then the k difference equations

$$X_t = \sigma^{(i)} Z_t + \sum_{j=1}^{p} \phi_j^{(i)} X_{t-j}, \quad (X_{t-1}, \cdots, X_{t-p}) \in R^{(i)}, \quad i = 1, \cdots, k, \quad (10.3.5)$$

define a threshold AR(p) model. Model identification and parameter estimation for threshold models can be carried out in a manner similar to that for linear models using maximum likelihood and the AIC criterion.

10.3.5 Modeling Volatility

For modeling changing volatility as discussed above under deviations from linearity, Engle (1982) introduced the **ARCH(p) process** $\{X_t\}$ as a solution of the equations

$$Z_t = \sqrt{h_t} e_t, \; \{e_t\} \sim \text{IID N}(0, 1), \quad (10.3.6)$$

where h_t is the (positive) function of $\{Z_s, s < t\}$, defined by

$$h_t = \alpha_0 + \sum_{i=1}^{p} \alpha_i Z_{t-i}^2, \quad (10.3.7)$$

with $\alpha_0 > 0$ and $\alpha_j \geq 0$, $j = 1, \ldots, p$. The name ARCH signifies autoregressive conditional heteroscedasticity. h_t is the conditional variance of Z_t given $\{Z_s, s < t\}$.

The simplest such process is the ARCH(1) process. In this case the recursions (10.3.6) and (10.3.7) give

$$\begin{aligned} Z_t^2 &= \alpha_0 e_t^2 + \alpha_1 Z_{t-1}^2 e_t^2 \\ &= \alpha_0 e_t^2 + \alpha_1 \alpha_0 e_t^2 e_{t-1}^2 + \alpha_1^2 Z_{t-2}^2 e_t^2 e_{t-1}^2 \\ &= \cdots \\ &= \alpha_0 \sum_{j=0}^{n} \alpha_1^j e_t^2 e_{t-1}^2 \cdots e_{t-j}^2 + \alpha_1^{n+1} Z_{t-n-1}^2 e_t^2 e_{t-1}^2 \cdots e_{t-n}^2. \end{aligned}$$

If $|\alpha_1| < 1$ and $\{Z_t\}$ is stationary and causal (i.e., Z_t is a function of $\{e_s, s \leq t\}$), then the last term has expectation $\alpha^{n+1} E Z_t^2$ and consequently (by the Borel-Cantelli lemma) converges to zero with probability one as $n \to \infty$. The first term converges with probability one by Proposition 3.1.1 of TSTM, and hence

$$Z_t^2 = \alpha_0 \sum_{j=0}^{\infty} \alpha_1^j e_t^2 e_{t-1}^2 \cdots e_{t-j}^2. \quad (10.3.8)$$

From (10.3.8) we immediately find that

$$E Z_t^2 = \alpha_0 / (1 - \alpha_1). \quad (10.3.9)$$

Since

$$Z_t = e_t \sqrt{\alpha_0 \left(1 + \sum_{j=1}^{\infty} \alpha_1^j e_{t-1}^2 \cdots e_{t-j}^2\right)}, \tag{10.3.10}$$

it is clear that $\{Z_t\}$ is strictly stationary and hence, since $EZ_t^2 < \infty$, also stationary in the weak sense. We have now established the following result.

Solution of the ARCH(1) Equations:

If $|\alpha_1| < 1$, the unique causal stationary solution of the ARCH(1) equations is given by (10.3.10). It has the properties

$$E(Z_t) = E(E(Z_t|e_s, s < t)) = 0,$$

$$\text{Var}(Z_t) = \alpha_0/(1 - \alpha_1),$$

and

$$E(Z_{t+h}Z_t) = E(E(Z_{t+h}Z_t|e_s, s < t + h)) = 0 \text{ for } h > 0.$$

Thus the ARCH(1) process with $|\alpha_1| < 1$ is strictly stationary white noise. However, it is not an iid sequence, since from (10.3.6) and (10.3.7),

$$E(Z_t^2|Z_{t-1}) = (\alpha_0 + \alpha_1 Z_{t-1}^2)E(e_t^2|Z_{t-1}) = \alpha_0 + \alpha_1 Z_{t-1}^2.$$

This also shows that $\{Z_t\}$ is not Gaussian, since strictly stationary Gaussian white noise is necessarily iid. From (10.3.10) it is clear that the distribution of Z_t is symmetric, i.e., that Z_t and $-Z_t$ have the same distribution. From (10.3.8) it is easy to calculate $E(Z_t^4)$ (Problem 10.4) and hence to show that $E(Z_t^4)$ is finite if and only if $3\alpha_1^2 < 1$. More generally (see Engle, 1982), it can be shown that for every α_1 in the interval (0, 1), $E(Z^{2k}) = \infty$ for some positive integer k. This indicates the "heavy-tailed" nature of the marginal distribution of Z_t. If $EZ_t^4 < \infty$, the squared process $Y_t = Z_t^2$ has the same ACF as the AR(1) process $W_t = \alpha_1 W_{t-1} + e_t$, a result that extends also to ARCH(p) processes (see Problem 10.5).

The ARCH(p) process is conditionally Gaussian, in the sense that for given values of $\{Z_s, s = t-1, t-2, \ldots, t-p\}$, Z_t is Gaussian with known distribution. This makes it easy to write down the likelihood of $Z_{p+1}, \ldots, Z_n$ conditional on $\{Z_1, \ldots, Z_p\}$ and hence, by numerical maximization, to compute conditional maximum likelihood estimates of the parameters. For example, the conditional likelihood of observations $\{z_2, \ldots, z_n\}$ of the ARCH(1) process given $Z_1 = z_1$ is

$$L = \prod_{t=2}^{n} \frac{1}{\sqrt{2\pi\left(\alpha_0 + \alpha_1 z_{t-1}^2\right)}} \exp\left\{-\frac{z_t^2}{2(\alpha_0 + \alpha_1 z_{t-1}^2)}\right\}.$$

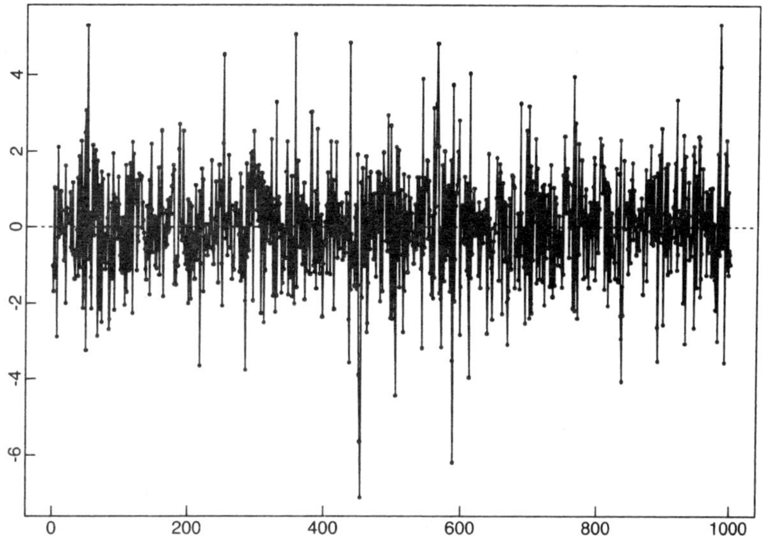

Figure 10-7 A realization of the process $Z_t = e_t\sqrt{1 + 0.5Z_{t-1}^2}$.

Example 10.3.1 An ARCH(1) series

Figure 10.7 shows a realization of the ARCH(1) process with $\alpha_0 = 1$ and $\alpha_1 = 0.5$. The graph of the realization and the sample autocorrelation function shown in Figure 10.8 suggest that the process is white noise. This conclusion is correct from a second-order point of view.

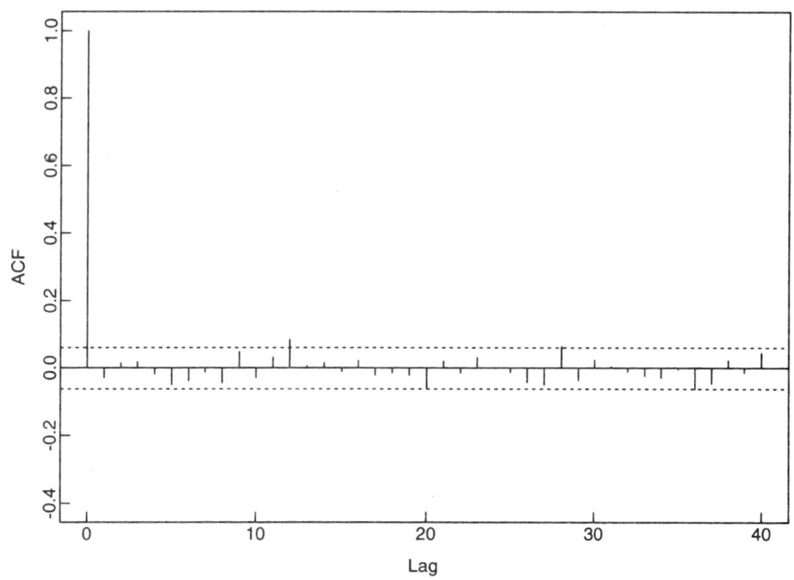

Figure 10-8 The sample autocorrelation function of the series in Figure 10.7.

However, the fact that the series is not a realization of iid noise is very strongly indicated by Figure 10.9, which shows the sample autocorrelation function of the series $\{Z_t^2\}$. (The sample ACF of $\{|Z_t|\}$ and that of $\{Z_t^2\}$ can be plotted in ITSM by selecting `Statistics>Residual Analysis>ACF abs values/Squares`.)

It is instructive to apply the Ljung–Box and McLeod–Li portmanteau tests for white noise to this series (see Section 1.6). To do this using ITSM, open the file ARCH.TSM, and then select `Statistics>Residual Analysis>Tests of Randomness`. We find (with $h = 20$) that the Ljung–Box test (and all the others except for the McLeod–Li test) are passed comfortably at level .05. However, the McLeod–Li test gives a p-value of 0 to five decimal places, clearly rejecting the hypothesis that the series is iid. □

The **GARCH(p, q) process** (see Bollerslev, 1986) is a generalization of the ARCH(p) process in which the variance equation (10.3.7) is replaced by

$$h_t = \alpha_0 + \sum_{i=1}^{p} \alpha_i Z_{t-i}^2 + \sum_{j=1}^{q} \beta_j h_{t-j}^2, \tag{10.3.11}$$

with $\alpha_0 > 0$ and $\alpha_j, \beta_j \geq 0$, $j = 1, 2, \ldots$.

In the analysis of empirical financial data such as percentage daily stock returns (defined as $100 \ln(P_t/P_{t-1})$, where P_t is the closing price on trading day t), it is usually found that better fits to the data are obtained by relaxing the Gaussian assumption in (10.3.6) and supposing instead that the distribution of Z_t given $\{Z_s, s < t\}$ has a heavier-tailed zero-mean distribution such as Student's t-distribution. To incorporate such distributions we can define a general GARCH(p, q) process as a stationary

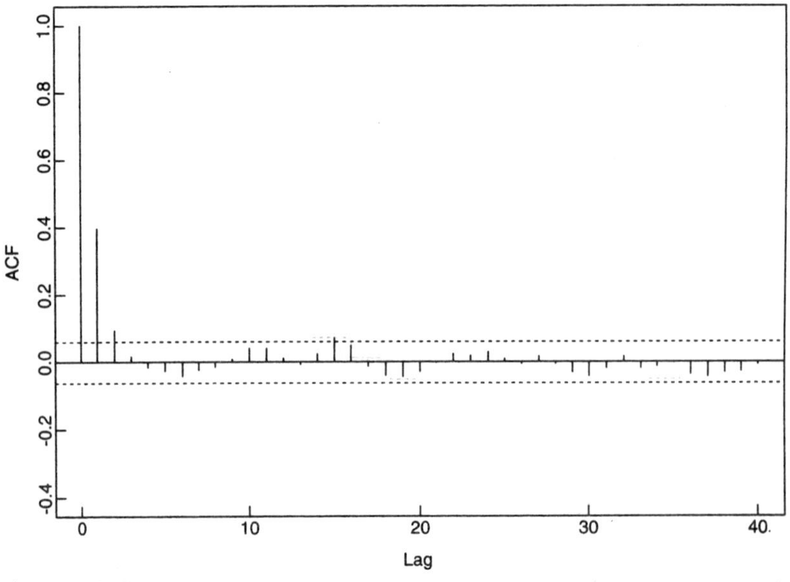

Figure 10-9 The sample autocorrelation function of the squares of the data shown in Figure 10.7.

process $\{Z_t\}$ satisfying (10.3.11) and the generalized form of (10.3.6),

$$Z_t = \sqrt{h_t}e_t, \quad \{e_t\} \sim \text{IID}(0, 1). \tag{10.3.12}$$

For modeling purposes it is usually assumed in addition that either

$$e_t \sim N(0, 1), \tag{10.3.13}$$

(as in (10.3.6)) or that

$$\sqrt{\frac{\nu}{\nu - 2}}e_t \sim t_\nu, \quad \nu > 2, \tag{10.3.14}$$

where t_ν denotes Student's t-distribution with ν degrees of freedom. (The scale factor on the left of (10.3.14) is introduced to make the variance of e_t equal to 1.) Other distributions for e_t can also be used.

One of the striking features of stock return data that is reflected by GARCH models is the "persistence of volatility," or the phenomenon that large (small) fluctuations in the data tend to be followed by fluctuations of comparable magnitude. GARCH models reflect this by incorporating correlation in the sequence $\{h_t\}$ of conditional variances.

Example 10.3.2 Fitting GARCH models to stock data

The top graph in Figure 10.10 shows the percentage daily returns of the Dow Jones Industrial Index for the period July 1st, 1997, through April 9th, 1999, contained in the file E1032.TSM. The graph suggests that there are sustained periods of both high volatility (in October, 1997, and August, 1998) and of low volatility. The sample autocorrelation function of this series, like that Example 10.3.1, has very small values, however the sample autocorrelations of the absolute values and squares of the data (like those in Example 10.3.1) are significantly different from zero, indicating dependence in spite of the lack of autocorrelation. (The sample autocorrelations of the absolute values and squares of the residuals (or of the data if no transformations have been made and no model fitted) can be seen by clicking on the third green button at the top of the ITSM window.) These properties suggest that an ARCH or GARCH model might be appropriate for this series.

The model

$$Y_t = a + Z_t, \tag{10.3.15}$$

where $\{Z_t\}$ is the GARCH(p, q) process defined by (10.3.11), (10.3.12) and (10.3.13), can be fitting using ITSM as follows. Open the project E1032.TSM and click on the red button labeled GAR at the top of the ITSM screen. In the resulting dialog box enter the desired values of p and q, e.g., 1 and 1 if you wish to fit a GARCH(1,1) model. You may also enter initial values for the coefficients $a_0, \ldots, a_p$, and $\beta_1, \ldots, \beta_q$, or alternatively use the default values specified by the program. Make sure that `Use normal noise` is selected, click on `OK` and then click on the red MLE button. You will

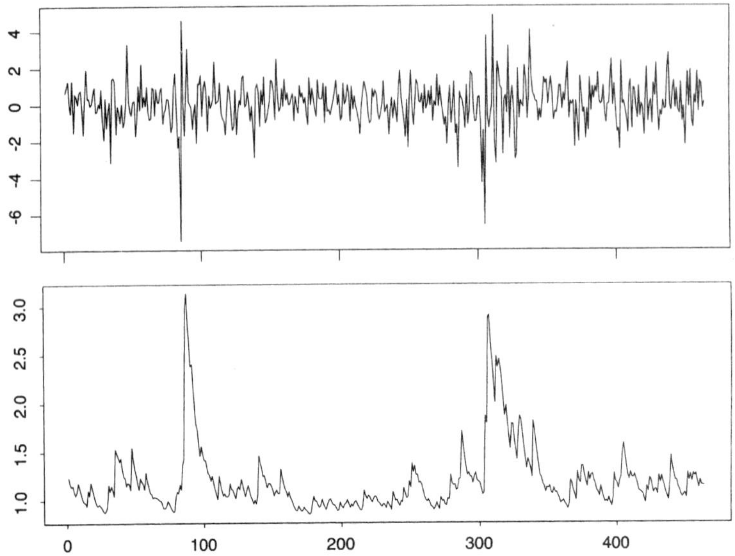

Figure 10-10 The daily percentage returns of the Dow Jones Industrial Index (E1032.TSM) from July 1, 1997, through April 9,1999 (above), and the estimates of $\sigma_t = \sqrt{h_t}$ for the conditional Gaussian GARCH(1,1) model of Example 10.3.2.

be advised to subtract the sample mean (unless you wish to assume that the parameter a in (10.3.15) is zero). If you subtract the sample mean it will be used as the estimate of a in the model (10.3.15). The `GARCH Maximum Likelihood Estimation` box will then open. When you click on `OK` the optimization will proceed. Denoting by $\{\tilde{Z}_t\}$ the (possibly) mean-corrected observations, the GARCH coefficients are estimated by numerically maximizing the likelihood of $\tilde{Z}_{p+1}, \ldots, \tilde{Z}_n$ conditional on the known values $\tilde{Z}_1, \ldots, \tilde{Z}_p$, and with assumed values 0 for each $\tilde{Z}_t$, $t \le 0$, and $\hat{\sigma}^2$ for each h_t, $t \le 0$, where $\hat{\sigma}^2$ is the sample variance of $\{\tilde{Z}_1, \ldots, \tilde{Z}_n\}$. In other words the program maximizes

$$L(\alpha_0, \ldots, \alpha_p, \beta_1, \ldots, \beta_q) = \prod_{t=p+1}^{n} \frac{1}{\sigma_t}\phi\left(\frac{\tilde{Z}_t}{\sigma_t}\right), \tag{10.3.16}$$

with respect to the coefficients $\alpha_0, \ldots, \alpha_p$ and $\beta_1, \ldots, \beta_q$, where ϕ denotes the standard normal density, and the standard deviations $\sigma_t = \sqrt{h_t}$, $t \ge 1$, are computed recursively from (10.3.11) with Z_t replaced by $\tilde{Z}_t$, and with $\tilde{Z}_t = 0$ and $h_t = \hat{\sigma}^2$ for $t \le 0$. To find the minimum of $-2\ln(L)$ it is advisable to repeat the optimization by clicking on the red MLE button and then on `OK` several times until the result stabilizes. It is also useful to try other initial values for $\alpha_0, \ldots, \alpha_p$, and $\beta_1, \ldots, \beta_q$, to minimize the chance of finding only a local minimum of $-2\ln(L)$. Note that the optimization is constrained so that the estimated parameters are all non-negative with

$$\hat{\alpha}_1 + \cdots + \hat{\alpha}_p + \hat{\beta}_1 + \cdots + \hat{\beta}_q < 1, \tag{10.3.17}$$

and $\hat{\alpha}_0 > 0$. Condition (10.3.17) is necessary and sufficient for the corresponding GARCH equations to have a causal weakly stationary solution.

Comparison of models with different orders p and q can be made with the aid of the AICC, which is defined in terms of the conditional likelihood L as

$$\text{AICC} := -2\frac{n}{n-p}\ln L + 2(p+q+2)n/(n-p-q-3). \tag{10.3.18}$$

The factor $n/(n-p)$ multiplying the first term on the right has been introduced to correct for the fact that the number of factors in (10.3.16) is only $n-p$. Notice also that the GARCH(p, q) model has $p+q+1$ coefficients.

The estimated mean is $\hat{a} = 0.0608$ and the minimum-AICC GARCH model (with Gaussian noise) for the residuals, $\tilde{Z}_t = Y_t - \hat{a}$, is found to be the GARCH(1,1) with estimated parameter values

$$\hat{\alpha}_0 = 0.1300, \hat{\alpha}_1 = 0.1266, \hat{\beta}_1 = 0.7922,$$

and an AICC value (defined by (10.3.18)) of 1469.02. The bottom graph in Figure 10.10 shows the corresponding estimated conditional standard deviations, $\hat{\sigma}_t$, which clearly reflect the changing volatility of the series $\{Y_t\}$. This graph is obtained from ITSM by clicking on the red SV (stochastic volatility) button. Under the model defined by (10.3.11), (10.3.12), (10.3.13) and (10.3.15), the GARCH residuals, $\{\tilde{Z}_t/\hat{\sigma}_t\}$, should be approximately IID N(0,1). A check on the independence is provided by the sample ACF of the absolute values and squares of the residuals, which is obtained by clicking on the fifth red button at the top of the ITSM window. These are found to be not significantly different from zero. To check for normality, select `Garch>Garch residuals>QQ-Plot(normal)`. If the model is appropriate the resulting graph should approximate a straight line through the origin with slope 1. It is found that the deviations from the expected line are quite large for large values of $|\tilde{Z}_t|$, suggesting the need for a heavier-tailed model, e.g., a model with conditional t-distribution as defined by (10.3.14).

To fit the GARCH model defined by (10.3.11), (10.3.12), (10.3.14) and (10.3.15) (i.e., with conditional t-distribution), we proceed in the same way, but with the conditional likelihood replaced by

$$L(\alpha_0, \ldots, \alpha_p, \beta_1, \ldots, \beta_q, \nu) = \prod_{t=p+1}^{n} \frac{\sqrt{\nu}}{\sigma_t\sqrt{\nu-2}} t_\nu \left(\frac{\tilde{Z}_t\sqrt{\nu}}{\sigma_t\sqrt{\nu-2}}\right). \tag{10.3.19}$$

Maximization is now carried out with respect to the coefficients, $\alpha_0, \ldots, \alpha_p, \beta_1, \ldots, \beta_q$ and the degrees of freedom ν of the t-density, t_ν. The optimization can be performed using ITSM in exactly the same way as described for the GARCH model with Gaussian noise, except that the option `Use t-distribution for noise` should be checked in each of the dialog boxes where it appears. In order to locate the minimum of $-2\ln(L)$ it is often useful to initialize the coefficients of the model by first fitting a GARCH model with Gaussian noise and then carrying out the optimization using t-distributed noise.

The estimated mean is $\hat{a} = 0.0608$ as before and the minimum-AICC GARCH model for the residuals, $\tilde{Z}_t = Y_t - \hat{a}$, is the GARCH(1,1) with estimated parameter values

$$\hat{\alpha}_0 = 0.1324, \quad \hat{\alpha}_1 = 0.0672, \quad \hat{\beta}_1 = 0.8400, \quad \hat{\nu} = 5.714,$$

and an AICC value (as in (10.3.18) with q replaced by $q+1$) of 1437.89. Thus from the point of view of AICC, the model with conditional t-distribution is substantially better than the conditional Gaussian model. The sample ACF of the absolute values and squares of the GARCH residuals are much the same as those found using Gaussian noise, but the qq plot (obtained by clicking on the red QQ button and based on the t-distribution with 5.714 degrees of freedom) is closer to the expected line than was the case for the model with Gaussian noise.

There are many important and interesting theoretical questions associated with the existence and properties of stationary solutions of the GARCH equations and their moments and of the sampling properties of these processes. As indicated above, in maximizing the conditional likelihood, ITSM constrains the GARCH coefficients to be non-negative and to satisfy the condition (10.3.17) with $\hat{\alpha}_0 > 0$. These conditions are sufficient for the process defined by the GARCH equations to be stationary. It is frequently found in practice that the estimated values of $\alpha_1, \ldots, \alpha_p$ and $\beta_1, \ldots, \beta_q$ have a sum which is very close to 1. A GARCH(p,q) model with $\alpha_1 + \cdots + \alpha_p + \beta_1 + \cdots \beta_q = 1$ is called I-GARCH. Many generalizations of GARCH processes (ARCH-M, E-GARCH, I-GARCH, T-GARCH, FI-GARCH, etc., as well as ARMA models driven by GARCH noise, and regression models with GARCH errors) can now be found in the econometrics literature.

ITSM can be used to fit ARMA and regression models with GARCH noise by using the procedures described in Example 10.3.2 to fit a GARCH model to the residuals $\{\tilde{Z}_t\}$ from the ARMA (or regression) fit.

Example 10.3.3 Fitting ARMA models driven by GARCH noise

If we open the data file SUNSPOTS.TSM, subtract the mean and use the option `Model>Estimation>Autofit` with the default ranges for p and q, we obtain an ARMA(3,4) model for the mean-corrected data. Clicking on the second green button at the top of the ITSM window, we see that the sample ACF of the ARMA residuals is compatible with iid noise. However the sample autocorrelation functions of the absolute values and squares of the residuals (obtained by clicking on the third green button) indicate that they are not independent. To fit a Gaussian GARCH(1,1) model to the ARMA residuals click on the red GAR button, enter the value 1 for both p and q and click `OK`. Then click on the red MLE button, click `OK` in the dialog box, and the `GARCH ML Estimates` window will open, showing the estimated parameter values. Repeat the steps in the previous sentence two more times and the window will display the following ARMA(3,4) model for the mean-corrected sunspot data and the fitted GARCH model for the ARMA noise process $\{Z_t\}$.

$$X_t = 2.463Z_{t-1} - 2.248Z_{t-2} + .757Z_{t-3} + Z_t - .948Z_{t-1}$$
$$- .296Z_{t-2} + .313Z_{t-3} + .136Z_{t-4},$$

where

$$Z_t = \sqrt{h_t} e_t$$

and

$$h_t = 31.152 + .223 Z_{t-1}^2 + .596 h_{t-1}.$$

The AICC value for the GARCH fit (805.12) should be used for comparing alternative GARCH models for the ARMA residuals. The AICC value adjusted for the ARMA fit (821.70) should be used for comparison with alternative ARMA models (with or without GARCH noise). Standard errors of the estimated coefficients are also displayed.

Simulation using the fitted ARMA(3,4) model with GARCH (1,1) noise can be carried out by selecting `Garch>Simulate Garch process`. If you retain the settings in the ARMA Simulation dialog box and click `OK` you will see a simulated realization of the model for the *original* data in SUNSPOTS.TSM. □

Some useful references for extensions and further properties of GARCH models are Weiss (1986), Engle (1995), Shephard (1996), and Gouriéroux (1997).

10.4 Continuous-Time Models

Discrete time series are often obtained by observing a continuous-time process at a discrete sequence of observation times. It is then natural, even though the observations are made at discrete times, to model the underlying process as a continuous-time series. Even if there is no underlying continuous-time process, it may still be advantageous to model the data as observations of a continuous-time process at discrete times. The analysis of time series data observed at irregularly spaced times can be handled very conveniently via continuous-time models, as pointed out by Jones (1980).

Continuous-time ARMA processes are defined in terms of stochastic differential equations analogous to the difference equations that are used to define discrete-time ARMA processes. Here we shall confine attention to the continuous-time AR(1) process, which is defined as a stationary solution of the first-order stochastic differential equation

$$DX(t) + aX(t) = \sigma DB(t) + b, \tag{10.4.1}$$

where the operator D denotes differentiation with respect to t, $\{B(t)\}$ is standard Brownian motion, and a, b, and σ are parameters. The derivative $DB(t)$ does not exist in the usual sense, so equation (10.4.1) is interpreted as an Itô differential equation

$$dX(t) + aX(t)dt = \sigma dB(t) + b\,dt, \quad t > 0, \tag{10.4.2}$$

with $dX(t)$ and $dB(t)$ denoting the increments of X and B in the time interval $(t, t+dt)$ and $X(0)$ a random variable with finite variance, independent of $\{B(t)\}$ (see, e.g.,

Chung and Williams, 1990, Karatzas and Shreve, 1991, and Oksendal, 1992). The solution of (10.4.2) can be written as

$$X(t) = e^{-at}X(0) + \sigma \int_0^t e^{-a(t-u)}\, dB(u) + b \int_0^t e^{-a(t-u)}\, du,$$

or equivalently,

$$X(t) = e^{-at}X(0) + e^{-at}I(t) + be^{-at} \int_0^t e^{au}\, du, \qquad (10.4.3)$$

where $I(t) = \sigma \int_0^t e^{au} dB(u)$ is an Itô integral (see Chung and Williams, 1990) satisfying $E(I(t)) = 0$ and $\text{Cov}(I(t+h), I(t)) = \sigma^2 \int_0^t e^{2au}\, du$ for all $t \geq 0$ and $h \geq 0$.

If $a > 0$ and $X(0)$ has mean b/a and variance $\sigma^2/(2a)$, it is easy to check (Problem 10.9) that $\{X(t)\}$ as defined by (10.4.3) is stationary with

$$E(X(t)) = \frac{b}{a} \quad \text{and} \quad \text{Cov}(X(t+h), X(t)) = \frac{\sigma^2}{2a}e^{-ah}, \quad t, h \geq 0. \qquad (10.4.4)$$

Conversely, if $\{X(t)\}$ is stationary, then by equating the variances of both sides of (10.4.3), we find that $\left(1 - e^{-2at}\right)\text{Var}(X(0)) = \sigma^2 \int_0^t e^{-2au}\, du$ for all $t \geq 0$, and hence that $a > 0$ and $\text{Var}(X(0)) = \sigma^2/(2a)$. Equating the means of both sides of (10.4.3) then gives $E(X(0)) = b/a$. Necessary and sufficient conditions for $\{X(t)\}$ to be stationary are therefore $a > 0$, $E(X(0)) = b/a$, and $\text{Var}(X(0)) = \sigma^2/(2a)$. If $a > 0$ and $X(0)$ is $\text{N}(b/a, \sigma^2/(2a))$, then the CAR(1) process will also be Gaussian and strictly stationary.

If $a > 0$ and $0 \leq s \leq t$, it follows from (10.4.3) that $X(t)$ can be expressed as

$$X(t) = e^{-a(t-s)}X(s) + \frac{b}{a}\left(1 - e^{-a(t-s)}\right) + e^{-at}(I(t) - I(s)). \qquad (10.4.5)$$

This shows that the process is Markovian, i.e., that the distribution of $X(t)$ given $X(u), u \leq s$, is the same as the distribution of $X(t)$ given $X(s)$. It also shows that the conditional mean and variance of $X(t)$ given $X(s)$ are

$$E(X(t)|X(s)) = e^{-a(t-s)}X(s) + b/a\left(1 - e^{-a(t-s)}\right)$$

and

$$\text{Var}(X(t)|X(s)) = \frac{\sigma^2}{2a}\left[1 - e^{-2a(t-s)}\right].$$

We can now use the Markov property and the moments of the stationary distribution to write down the Gaussian likelihood of observations $x(t_1), \ldots, x(t_n)$ at times $t_1, \ldots, t_n$ of a CAR(1) process satisfying (10.4.1). This is just the joint density of $(X(t_1), \ldots, X(t_n))'$ at $(x(t_1), \ldots, x(t_n))'$, which can be expressed as the product of the stationary density at $x(t_1)$ and the transition densities of $X(t_i)$ given $X(t_{i-1}) = x(t_{i-1})$,

$i = 2, \ldots, n$. The joint density g is therefore given by

$$g\left(x(t_1), \ldots, x(t_n); a, b, \sigma^2\right) = \prod_{i=1}^{n} \frac{1}{\sqrt{v_i}} f\left(\frac{x(t_i) - m_i}{\sqrt{v_i}}\right), \tag{10.4.6}$$

where $f(x) = n(x; 0, 1)$ is the standard normal density, $m_1 = b/a$, $v_1 = \sigma^2/(2a)$, and for $i > 1$,

$$m_i = e^{-a(t_i - t_{i-1})} x(t_{i-1}) + \frac{b}{a}\left(1 - e^{-a(t_i - t_{i-1})}\right)$$

and

$$v_i = \frac{\sigma^2}{2a}\left[1 - e^{-2a(t_i - t_{i-1})}\right].$$

The maximum likelihood estimators of a, b, and σ^2 are the values that maximize $g\left(x(t_1), \ldots, x(t_n); a, b, \sigma^2\right)$. These can be found with the aid of a nonlinear maximization algorithm. Notice that the times t_i appearing in (10.4.6) are quite arbitrarily spaced. It is this feature that makes the CAR(1) process so useful for modeling irregularly spaced data.

If the observations are regularly spaced, say $t_i = i$, $i = 1, \ldots, n$, then the joint density g is exactly the same as the joint density of observations of the discrete-time Gaussian AR(1) process

$$Y_n - \frac{b}{a} = e^{-a}\left(Y_{n-1} - \frac{b}{a}\right) + Z_n, \quad \{Z_t\} \sim \mathrm{WN}\left(0, \frac{\sigma^2\left(1 - e^{-2a}\right)}{2a}\right).$$

This shows that the "embedded" discrete-time process $\{X(i), i = 1, 2, \ldots\}$ of the CAR(1) process is a discrete-time AR(1) process with coefficient e^{-a}. This coefficient is clearly positive, immediately raising the question of whether there is a continuous-time ARMA process for which the embedded process is a discrete-time AR(1) process with negative coefficient. It can be shown (Chan and Tong, 1987) that the answer is yes and that given a discrete-time AR(1) process with negative coefficient, it can always be embedded in a suitably chosen continuous-time ARMA(2,1) process.

We define a zero-mean CARMA(p, q) process $\{Y(t)\}$ (with $0 \le q < p$) to be a stationary solution of the pth-order linear differential equation

$$\begin{aligned} &D^p Y(t) + a_1 D^{p-1} Y(t) + \cdots + a_p Y(t) \\ &\quad = b_0 D B(t) + b_1 D^2 B(t) + \cdots + b_q D^{q+1} B(t), \end{aligned} \tag{10.4.7}$$

where $D^{(j)}$ denotes j-fold differentiation with respect to t, $\{B(t)\}$ is standard Brownian motion, and $a_1, \ldots, a_p$, $b_0, \ldots, b_q$, and c are constants. We assume that $b_q \neq 0$ and define $b_j := 0$ for $j > q$. Since the derivatives $D^j B(t)$, $j > 0$, do not exist in the usual sense, we interpret (10.4.7) as being equivalent to the *observation* and *state* equations

$$Y(t) = \mathbf{b}'\mathbf{X}(t), \quad t \ge 0, \tag{10.4.8}$$

and

$$d\mathbf{X}(t) = A\mathbf{X}(t)\,dt + \mathbf{e}\,dB(t), \tag{10.4.9}$$

where

$$A = \begin{bmatrix} 0 & 1 & 0 & \cdots & 0 \\ 0 & 0 & 1 & \cdots & 0 \\ \vdots & \vdots & \vdots & \ddots & \vdots \\ 0 & 0 & 0 & \cdots & 1 \\ -a_p & -a_{p-1} & -a_{p-2} & \cdots & -a_1 \end{bmatrix},$$

$\mathbf{e} = \begin{bmatrix} 0 & 0 & \cdots & 0 & 1 \end{bmatrix}'$, $\mathbf{b} = \begin{bmatrix} b_0 & b_1 & \cdots & b_{p-2} & b_{p-1} \end{bmatrix}'$, and (10.4.8) is an Itô differential equation for the state vector $\mathbf{X}(t)$. (We assume also that $\mathbf{X}(0)$ is independent of $\{B(t)\}$.)

The solution of (10.4.9) can be written as

$$\mathbf{X}(t) = e^{At}\mathbf{X}(0) + \int_0^t e^{A(t-u)}\mathbf{e}\,dB(u),$$

which is stationary if and only if

$$E(\mathbf{X}(0)) = \begin{bmatrix} 0 & 0 & \cdots & 0 \end{bmatrix}',$$

$$\operatorname{Cov}(\mathbf{X}(0)) = \int_0^\infty e^{Ay}\mathbf{e}\mathbf{e}'e^{A'y}\,dy,$$

and all the eigenvalues of A (i.e., the roots of $z^p + a_1 z^{p-1} + \cdots + a_p = 0$) have negative real parts.

Then $\{Y(t), t \geq 0\}$ is said to be a zero-mean CARMA(p, q) process with parameters $(a_1, \ldots, a_p, b_0, \ldots, b_q, \sigma, c)$ if

$$Y(t) = \begin{bmatrix} b_0 & b_1 & \cdots & b_{p-2} & b_{p-1} \end{bmatrix}\mathbf{X}(t),$$

where $\{\mathbf{X}(t)\}$ is a stationary solution of (10.4.9) and $b_j := 0$ for $j > q$.

The autocovariance function of the process $\mathbf{X}(t)$ at lag h is easily found to be

$$\operatorname{Cov}(\mathbf{X}(t+h), \mathbf{X}(t)) = e^{Ah}\Sigma, \quad h \geq 0,$$

where

$$\Sigma := \int_0^\infty e^{Ay}\mathbf{e}\,\mathbf{e}'e^{A'y}dy.$$

The mean and autocovariance function of the CARMA(p, q) process $\{Y(t)\}$ are therefore given by

$$EY(t) = 0$$

and

$$\text{Cov}(Y(t+h), Y(t)) = \mathbf{b}' e^{Ah} \Sigma \mathbf{b}.$$

Inference for continuous-time ARMA processes is more complicated than for continuous-time AR(1) processes because higher-order processes are not Markovian, so the simple calculation that led to (10.4.6) must be modified. However, the likelihood of observations at times $t_1, \ldots, t_n$ can still easily be computed using the discrete-time Kalman recursions (see Jones, 1980).

Continuous-time ARMA processes with thresholds constitute a useful class of nonlinear time series models. For example, the continuous-time threshold AR(1) process with threshold at r is defined as a solution of the stochastic differential equations

$$dX(t) + a_1 X(t)dt = b_1\, dt + \sigma_1 dB(t), \qquad X(t) \le r,$$

and

$$dX(t) + a_2 X(t)dt = b_2\, dt + \sigma_2 dB(t), \qquad X(t) > r.$$

For a detailed discussion of such processes, see Stramer, Brockwell, and Tweedie (1996). Continuous-time threshold ARMA processes are discussed in Brockwell (1994) and non-Gaussian CARMA(p, q) processes in Brockwell (2001). For more on continuous-time models see Bergstrom (1990) and Harvey (1990).

10.5 Long-Memory Models

The autocorrelation function $\rho(\cdot)$ of an ARMA process at lag h converges rapidly to zero as $h \to \infty$ in the sense that there exists $r > 1$ such that

$$r^h \rho(h) \to 0 \qquad \text{as} \quad h \to \infty. \tag{10.5.1}$$

Stationary processes with much more slowly decreasing autocorrelation function, known as **fractionally integrated ARMA processes**, or more precisely as ARIMA (p, d, q) processes with $0 < |d| < 0.5$, satisfy difference equations of the form

$$(1 - B)^d \phi(B) X_t = \theta(B) Z_t, \tag{10.5.2}$$

where $\phi(z)$ and $\theta(z)$ are polynomials of degrees p and q, respectively, satisfying

$$\phi(z) \ne 0 \quad \text{and} \quad \theta(z) \ne 0 \quad \text{for all } z \text{ such that } |z| \le 1,$$

B is the backward shift operator, and $\{Z_t\}$ is a white noise sequence with mean 0 and variance σ^2. The operator $(1 - B)^d$ is defined by the binomial expansion

$$(1 - B)^d = \sum_{j=0}^{\infty} \pi_j B^j,$$

where $n_0 = 1$ and

$$\pi_j = \prod_{0<k\le j} \frac{k-1-d}{k}, \qquad j = 1, 2, \ldots.$$

The autocorrelation $\rho(h)$ at lag h of an ARIMA(p, d, q) process with $0 < |d| < 0.5$ has the property

$$\rho(h)h^{1-2d} \to c \qquad \text{as} \quad h \to \infty. \tag{10.5.3}$$

This implies (see (10.5.1)) that $\rho(h)$ converges to zero as $h \to \infty$ at a much slower rate than $\rho(h)$ for an ARMA process. Consequently, fractionally integrated ARMA processes are said to have "long memory." In contrast, stationary processes whose ACF converges to 0 rapidly, such as ARMA processes, are said to have "short memory."

A fractionally integrated ARIMA(p, d, q) process can be regarded as an ARMA (p, q) process driven by fractionally integrated noise; i.e., we can replace equation (10.5.2) by the two equations

$$\phi(B)X_t = \theta(B)W_t \tag{10.5.4}$$

and

$$(1-B)^d W_t = Z_t. \tag{10.5.5}$$

The process $\{W_t\}$ is called **fractionally integrated white noise** and can be shown (see, e.g., TSTM, Section 13.2) to have variance and autocorrelations given by

$$\gamma_W(0) = \sigma^2 \frac{\Gamma(1-2d)}{\Gamma^2(1-d)} \tag{10.5.6}$$

and

$$\rho_W(h) = \frac{\Gamma(h+d)\Gamma(1-d)}{\Gamma(h-d+1)\Gamma(d)} = \prod_{0<k\le h} \frac{k-1+d}{k-d}, \qquad h = 1, 2, \ldots, \tag{10.5.7}$$

where $\Gamma(\cdot)$ is the gamma function (see Example (*d*) of Section A.1). The exact autocovariance function of the ARIMA(p, d, q) process $\{X_t\}$ defined by (10.5.2) can therefore be expressed, by Proposition 2.2.1, as

$$\gamma_X(h) = \sum_{j=0}^{\infty}\sum_{k=0}^{\infty} \psi_j \psi_k \gamma_W(h+j-k), \tag{10.5.8}$$

where $\sum_{i=0}^{\infty} \psi_i z^i = \theta(z)/\phi(z)$, $|z| \le 1$, and $\gamma_W(\cdot)$ is the autocovariance function of fractionally integrated white noise with parameters d and σ^2, i.e.,

$$\gamma_W(h) = \gamma_W(0)\rho_W(h),$$

with $\gamma_W(0)$ and $\rho_W(h)$ as in (10.5.6) and (10.5.7). The series (10.5.8) converges rapidly as long as $\phi(z)$ does not have zeros with absolute value close to 1.

The spectral density of $\{X_t\}$ is given by

$$f(\lambda) = \frac{\sigma^2}{2\pi} \frac{\left|\theta(e^{-i\lambda})\right|^2}{\left|\phi(e^{-i\lambda})\right|^2} \left|1 - e^{-i\lambda}\right|^{-2d}. \tag{10.5.9}$$

Calculation of the exact Gaussian likelihood of observations $\{x_1, \ldots, x_n\}$ of a fractionally integrated ARMA process is very slow and demanding in terms of computer memory. Instead of estimating the parameters $d, \phi_1, \ldots, \phi_p, \theta_1, \ldots, \theta_q$, and σ^2 by maximizing the exact Gaussian likelihood, it is much simpler to maximize the Whittle approximation L_W, defined by

$$-2\ln(L_W) = n\ln(2\pi) + 2n\ln\sigma + \sigma^{-2}\sum_j \frac{I_n(\omega_j)}{g(\omega_j)} + \sum_j \ln g(\omega_j), \tag{10.5.10}$$

where I_n is the periodogram, $\sigma^2 g/(2\pi)(= f)$ is the model spectral density, and $\sum_j$ denotes the sum over all nonzero Fourier frequencies $\omega_j = 2\pi j/n \in (-\pi, \pi]$. The program ITSM estimates parameters for ARIMA(p, d, q) models in this way. It can also be used to predict and simulate fractionally integrated ARMA series and to compute the autocovariance function of any specified fractionally integrated ARMA model.

Example 10.5.1 Annual Minimum Water Levels; NILE.TSM

The data file NILE.TSM consists of the annual minimum water levels of the Nile river as measured at the Roda gauge near Cairo for the years 622-871. These values are plotted in Figure 10.11 with the corresponding sample autocorrelations shown in Figure 10.12. The rather slow decay of the sample autocorrelation function suggests the possibility of a fractionally intergrated model for the mean-corrected series $Y_t = X_t - 1119$.

The ARMA model with minimum (exact) AICC value for the mean-corrected series $\{Y_t\}$ is found, using `Model>Estimation>Autofit`, to be

$$\begin{aligned} Y_t = &-.323Y_{t-1} - .060Y_{t-2} + .633Y_{t-3} + .069Y_{t-4} + .248Y_{t-5} \\ &+ Z_t + .702Z_{t-1} + .350Z_{t-2} - .419Z_{t-3}, \end{aligned} \tag{10.5.11}$$

with $\{Z_t\} \sim \text{WN}(0, 5663.6)$ and AICC$= 2889.9$.

To fit a fractionally integrated ARMA model to this series, select the option `Model>Specify`, check the box marked `Fractionally integrated model`, and click on `OK`. Then select `Model>Estimation>Autofit`, and click on `Start`. This estimation procedure is relatively slow so the specified ranges for p and q should be small (the default is from 0 to 2). When models have been fitted for each value of (p, q), the fractionally integrated model with the smallest modified AIC value is found to be

$$(1-B)^{.3830}(1 - .1694B + .9704B^2)Y_t = (1 - .1800B + .9278B^2)Z_t, \tag{10.5.12}$$

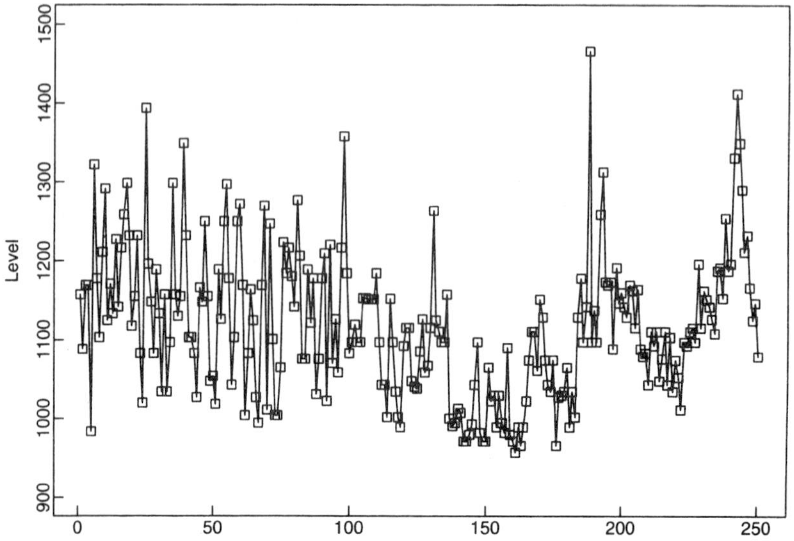

Figure 10-11 Annual minimum water levels of the Nile river for the years 622-871.

with $\{Z_t\} \sim \text{WN}(0, 5827.4)$ and modified AIC= 2884.94. (The modified AIC statistic for estimating the parameters of a fractionally integrated ARMA(p, q) process is defined in terms of the Whittle likelihood L_W as $-2\ln L_W + 2(p+q+2)$ if d is estimated, and $-2\ln L_W + 2(p+q+1)$ otherwise. The Whittle likelihood was defined in (10.5.10).)

In order to compare the models (10.5.11) and (10.5.12), the modified AIC value for (10.5.11) is found as follows. After fitting the model as described above, select

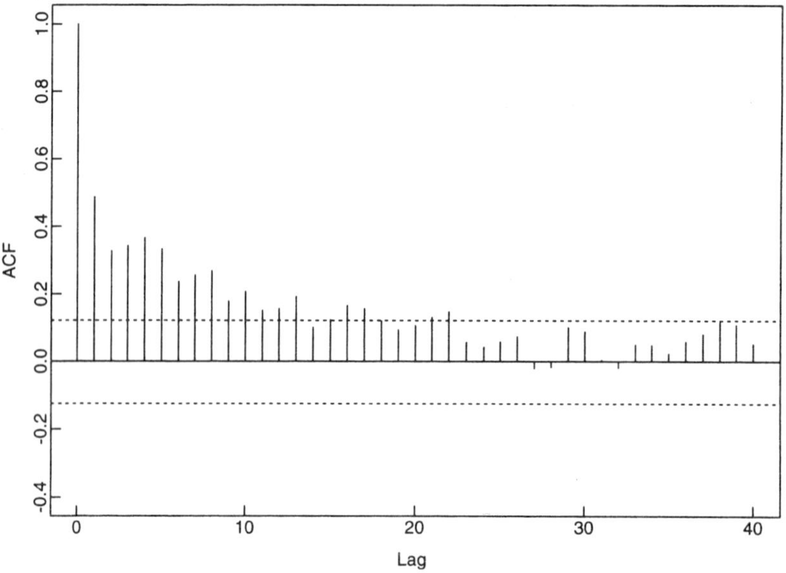

Figure 10-12 The sample correlation function of the data in Figure 10.11.

`Model>Specify`, check the box marked `Fractionally integrated model`, set $d = 0$ and click on `OK`. The next step is to choose `Model>Estimation>Max likelihood`, check `No optimization` and click on `OK`. You will then see the modified AIC value, 2884.58, displayed in the `ML estimates` window together with the value 2866.58 of $-2\ln L_W$.

The ARMA(5,3) model is slightly better in terms of modified AIC than the fractionally integrated model and its ACF is closer to the sample ACF of the data than is the ACF of the fractionally integrated model. (The sample and model autocorrelation functions can be compared by clicking on the third yellow button at the top of the ITSM window.) The residuals from both models pass all of the ITSM tests for randomness.

Figure 10.13 shows the graph of $\{x_{200}, \ldots, x_{250}\}$ with predictors of the next 20 values obtained from the model (10.5.12) for the mean-corrected series. □

Problems

10.1. Find a transfer function model relating the input and output series X_{t1} and X_{t2}, $t = 1, \ldots, 200$, contained in the ITSM data files APPJ.TSM and APPK.TSM, respectively. Use the fitted model to predict $X_{201,2}$, $X_{202,2}$, and $X_{203,2}$. Compare the predictors and their mean squared errors with the corresponding predictors and mean squared errors obtained by modeling $\{X_{t2}\}$ as a univariate ARMA process and with the results of Problem 7.7.

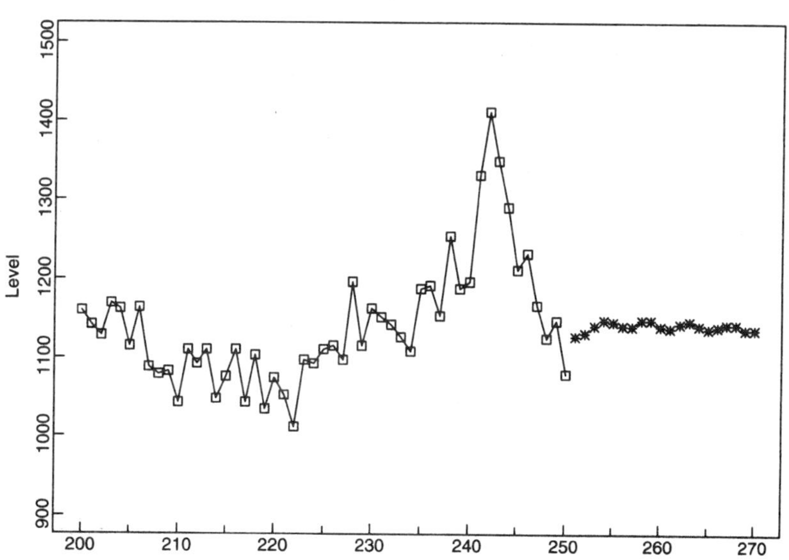

Figure 10-13 The minimum annual Nile river levels for the years 821–871, with 20 forecasts based on the model (10.5.12).

10.2. Verify the calculations of Example 10.2.1 to fit an intervention model to the series SB.TSM.

10.3. If $\{X_t\}$ is the linear process (10.3.1) with $\{Z_t\} \sim \text{IID}\left(0, \sigma^2\right)$ and $\eta = EZ_t^3$, how that the third-order cumulant function of $\{X_t\}$ is given by

$$C_3(r, s) = \eta \sum_{i=-\infty}^{\infty} \psi_i \psi_{i+r} \psi_{i+s}.$$

Use this result to establish equation (10.3.4). Conclude that if $\{X_t\}$ is a Gaussian linear process, then $C_3(r, s) \equiv 0$ and $f_3(\omega_1, \omega_2) \equiv 0$.

10.4. Evaluate EZ_t^4 for the ARCH(1) process (10.3.10) with $0 < \alpha_1 < 1$ and $\{e_t\} \sim$ IID N(0, 1). Deduce that $EX_t^4 < \infty$ if and only if $3\alpha_1^2 < 1$.

10.5. Let $\{Z_t\}$ be a causal stationary solution of the ARCH(p) equations (10.3.6) and (10.3.7) with $EZ_t^4 < \infty$. Assuming that such a process exists, show that $Y_t = Z_t^2/\alpha_0$ satisfies the equations

$$Y_t = e_t^2 \left(1 + \sum_{i=1}^{p} \alpha_i Y_{t-i}\right)$$

and deduce that $\{Y_t\}$ has the same autocorrelation function as the AR(p) process

$$W_t = \sum_{i=1}^{p} \alpha_i W_{t-i} + e_t, \quad \{e_t\} \sim \text{WN}(0, 1).$$

(In the case $p = 1$, a necessary and sufficient condition for existence of a causal stationary solution of (10.3.6) and (10.3.7) with $EZ_t^4 < \infty$ is $3\alpha_1^2 < 1$, as shown by the results of Section 10.3 and Problem 10.4.)

10.6. Suppose that $\{Z_t\}$ is a causal stationary GARCH(p, q) process $Z_t = \sqrt{h_t} e_t$, where $\{e_t\} \sim$ IID(0,1), $\sum_{i=1}^{p} a_i + \sum_{j=1}^{q} B_j < 1$ and

$$h_t = \alpha_0 + \alpha_1 Z_{t-1}^2 + \cdots + \alpha_p Z_{t-p}^2 + \beta_1 h_{t-1} + \cdots + \beta_q h_{t-q}.$$

a. Show that $E(Z_t^2 | Z_{t-1}^2, Z_{t-2}^2, \ldots) = h_t$.

b. Show that the squared process $\{Z_t^2\}$ is an ARMA(m, q) process satisfying the equations

$$Z_t^2 = \alpha_0 + (\alpha_1 + \beta_1) Z_{t-1}^2 + \cdots + (\alpha_m + \beta_m) Z_{t-m}^2 + U_t - \beta_1 U_{t-1} - \cdots - \beta_q U_{t-q},$$

where $m = \max\{p, q\}$, $\alpha_j = 0$ for $j > p$, $\beta_j = 0$ for $j > q$, and $U_t = Z_t^2 - h_t$ is white noise if $EZ_t^4 < \infty$.

c. For $p \geq 1$, show that the conditional variance process $\{h_t\}$ is an ARMA$(m, p-1)$ process satisfying the equations

$$h_t = \alpha_0 + (\alpha_1 + \beta_1)h_{t-1} + \cdots + (\alpha_m + \beta_m)h_{t-m}$$
$$+ V_t + \alpha_1^* V_{t-1} + \cdots + \alpha_p^* V_{t-p-1},$$

where $V_t = \alpha_1^{-1} U_{t-1}$ and $\alpha_j^* = \alpha_{j+1}/\alpha_1$ for $j = 1, \ldots, p-1$.

10.7. To each of the seven components of the multivariate time series filed as STOCK7.TSM, fit an ARMA model driven by GARCH noise. Compare the fitted models for the various series and comment on the differences. (For exporting components of a multivariate time series to a univariate project, see the ITSM `Help` topic, `Project editor`.)

10.8. If $a > 0$ and $X(0)$ has mean b/a and variance $\sigma^2/(2a)$, show that the process defined by (10.4.3) is stationary and evaluate its mean and autocovariance function.

10.9. The file TRINGS.TSM contains normalized tree-ring widths of a Colorado pine for the years 525–774 (Donald Graybill, 1984) from the file CO522.DAT at http://www-personal.buseco.monash.edu.au/hyndman/TSDL/.

a. Fit a fractionally integrated ARMA model to the first 230 tree-ring widths and use the model to generate forecasts and 95% prediction bounds for the last 20 observations (corresponding to $t = 231, \ldots, 250$). Plot the entire data set with the forecasts and prediction bounds superposed on the graph of the data.

b. Repeat part (a), but this time fitting an appropriate ARMA model. Compare the performance of the two sets of predictors.

10.10. The tent map with parameter $s \in (1, \infty)$ is the function

$$g(x) = sxI_{[0,1/s)}(x) + \frac{s}{s-1}(1-x)I_{[1/s,1]}(x), \quad x \in [0, 1],$$

where I_A denotes the indicator function of the set A. If X_0 has the uniform distribution on $[0, 1]$ (written more concisely as $X_0 \sim U$) and if $\{X_n\}$ is the sequence defined by $X_n = g(X_{n-1})$, $n = 1, 2, \ldots$, then $\{X_n\}$ is a Markov chain and $X_n \sim U$ for all $n \in \{0, 1, 2, \ldots\}$, so that $\{X_n\}$ is strictly (and weakly) stationary.

a. Show that in the symmetric case ($s = 2$), $\{X_n\} \sim \text{WN}(0, 1/12)$.

b. In the general case, $X_n - 0.5 = \phi(X_{n-1} - 0.5) + Z_n$, $n = 1, 2, \ldots$, where $\phi = (2/s) - 1$ and $\{Z_n\}$ is an uncorrelated (but strongly dependent) sequence of random variables with mean zero and variance $(1 - \phi^2)/12$. (See Sakai and Tokumaru, 1980.)

A Random Variables and Probability Distributions

A.1 Distribution Functions and Expectation

The distribution function F of a random variable X is defined by

$$F(x) = P[X \leq x] \tag{A.1.1}$$

for all real x. The following properties are direct consequences of (A.1.1):

1. F is nondecreasing, i.e., $F(x) \leq F(y)$ if $x \leq y$.
2. F is right continuous, i.e., $F(y) \downarrow F(x)$ as $y \downarrow x$.
3. $F(x) \to 1$ and $F(y) \to 0$ as $x \to \infty$ and $y \to -\infty$, respectively.

Conversely, any function that satisfies properties 1–3 is the distribution function of some random variable.

Most of the commonly encountered distribution functions F can be expressed either as

$$F(x) = \int_{-\infty}^{x} f(y)dy \tag{A.1.2}$$

or

$$F(x) = \sum_{j:x_j \leq x} p(x_j), \tag{A.1.3}$$

where $\{x_0, x_1, x_2, \ldots\}$ is a finite or countably infinite set. In the case (A.1.2) we shall say that the random variable X is **continuous**. The function f is called the **probability density function** (pdf) of X and can be found from the relation

$$f(x) = F'(x).$$

In case (A.1.3), the possible values of X are restricted to the set $\{x_0, x_1, \ldots\}$, and we shall say that the random variable X is **discrete**. The function p is called the **probability mass function** (pmf) of X, and F is constant except for upward jumps of size $p(x_j)$ at the points x_j. Thus $p(x_j)$ is the size of the jump in F at x_j, i.e.,

$$p(x_j) = F(x_j) - F(x_j^-) = P[X = x_j],$$

where $F(x_j^-) = \lim_{y \uparrow x_j} F(y)$.

Examples of Continuous Distributions

(a) *The normal distribution with mean μ and variance σ^2.* We say that a random variable X has the normal distribution with mean μ and variance σ^2 (written more concisely as $X \sim N(\mu, \sigma^2)$) if X has the pdf given by

$$n\left(x; \mu, \sigma^2\right) = (2\pi)^{-1/2}\sigma^{-1}e^{-(x-\mu)^2/(2\sigma^2)} \qquad -\infty < x < \infty.$$

It follows then that $Z = (X - \mu)/\sigma \sim N(0, 1)$ and that

$$P[X \le x] = P\left[Z \le \frac{x-\mu}{\sigma}\right] = \Phi\left(\frac{x-\mu}{\sigma}\right),$$

where $\Phi(x) = \int_{-\infty}^{x}(2\pi)^{-1/2}e^{-\frac{1}{2}z^2}\,dz$ is known as the **standard normal distribution function**. The significance of the terms *mean* and *variance* for the parameters μ and σ^2 is explained below (see Example A.1.1).

(b) *The uniform distribution on* $[a,b]$. The pdf of a random variable uniformly distributed on the interval $[a, b]$ is given by

$$u(x; a, b) = \begin{cases} \dfrac{1}{b-a}, & \text{if } a \le x \le b, \\ 0, & \text{otherwise.} \end{cases}$$

(c) *The exponential distribution with parameter λ.* The pdf of an exponentially distributed random variable with parameter $\lambda > 0$ is

$$e(x; \lambda) = \begin{cases} 0, & \text{if } x < 0, \\ \lambda e^{-\lambda x}, & \text{if } x \ge 0. \end{cases}$$

The corresponding distribution function is

$$F(x) = \begin{cases} 0, & \text{if } x < 0, \\ 1 - e^{-\lambda x}, & \text{if } x \ge 0. \end{cases}$$

(d) *The gamma distribution with parameters α and λ.* The pdf of a gamma-distributed random variable is

$$g(x;\alpha,\lambda)=\begin{cases}0, & \text{if } x<0,\\ x^{\alpha-1}\lambda^{\alpha}e^{-\lambda x}/\Gamma(\alpha), & \text{if } x\geq 0,\end{cases}$$

where the parameters α and λ are both positive and Γ is the gamma function defined as

$$\Gamma(\alpha)=\int_0^{\infty} x^{\alpha-1}e^{-x}\,dx.$$

Note that f is the exponential pdf when $\alpha=1$ and that when α is a positive integer

$$\Gamma(\alpha)=(\alpha-1)!\text{ with }0!\text{ defined to be }1.$$

(e) *The chi-squared distribution with ν degrees of freedom.* For each positive integer ν, the chi-squared distribution with ν degrees of freedom is defined to be the distribution of the sum

$$X=Z_1^2+\cdots+Z_\nu^2,$$

where $Z_1,\ldots,Z_\nu$ are independent normally distributed random variables with mean 0 and variance 1. This distribution is the same as the gamma distribution with parameters $\alpha=\nu/2$ and $\lambda=\frac{1}{2}$.

Examples of Discrete Distributions

(f) *The binomial distribution with parameters n and p.* The pmf of a binomially distributed random variable X with parameters n and p is

$$b(j;n,p)=P[X=j]=\binom{n}{j}p^j(1-p)^{n-j},\qquad j=0,1,\ldots,n,$$

where n is a positive integer and $0\leq p\leq 1$.

(g) *The uniform distribution on* $\{1,2,\ldots,k\}$. The pmf of a random variable X uniformly distributed on $\{1,2,\ldots,k\}$ is

$$p(j)=P[X=j]=\frac{1}{k},\qquad j=1,2\ldots,k,$$

where k is a positive integer.

(h) *The Poisson distribution with parameter λ.* A random variable X is said to have a Poisson distribution with parameter $\lambda>0$ if

$$p(j;\lambda)=P[X=j]=\frac{\lambda^j}{j!}e^{-\lambda},\qquad j=0,1,\ldots.$$

We shall see in Example A.1.2 below that λ is the mean of X.

(i) *The negative binomial distribution with parameters α and p.* The random variable X is said to have a negative binomial distribution with parameters $\alpha > 0$ and $p \in [0, 1]$ if it has pmf

$$nb(j; \alpha, p) = \left(\prod_{k=1}^{j} \frac{k-1+\alpha}{k}\right)(1-p)^j p^\alpha, \qquad j = 0, 1, \ldots,$$

where the product is defined to be 1 if $j = 0$.

Not all random variables can be neatly categorized as either continuous or discrete. For example, consider the time you spend waiting to be served at a checkout counter and suppose that the probability of finding no customers ahead of you is $\frac{1}{2}$. Then the time you spend waiting for service can be expressed as

$$W = \begin{cases} 0, & \text{with probability } \dfrac{1}{2}, \\ W_1, & \text{with probability } \dfrac{1}{2}, \end{cases}$$

where W_1 is a continuous random variable. If the distribution of W_1 is exponential with parameter 1, then the distribution function of W is

$$F(x) = \begin{cases} 0, & \text{if } x < 0, \\ \dfrac{1}{2} + \dfrac{1}{2}\left(1 - e^{-x}\right) = 1 - \dfrac{1}{2}e^{-x}, & \text{if } x \geq 0. \end{cases}$$

This distribution function is neither continuous (since it has a discontinuity at $x = 0$) nor discrete (since it increases continuously for $x > 0$). It is expressible as a *mixture*,

$$F = pF_{\mathrm{d}} + (1-p)F_{\mathrm{c}},$$

with $p = \frac{1}{2}$, of a discrete distribution function

$$F_{\mathrm{d}} = \begin{cases} 0, & x < 0, \\ 1, & x \geq 0, \end{cases}$$

and a continuous distribution function

$$F_{\mathrm{c}} = \begin{cases} 0, & x < 0, \\ 1 - e^{-x}, & x \geq 0. \end{cases}$$

Every distribution function can in fact be expressed in the form

$$F = p_1 F_{\mathrm{d}} + p_2 F_{\mathrm{c}} + p_3 F_{\mathrm{sc}},$$

where $0 \leq p_1, p_2, p_3 \leq 1$, $p_1 + p_2 + p_3 = 1$, F_{d} is discrete, F_{c} is continuous, and F_{sc} is *singular continuous* (continuous but not of the form A.1.2). Distribution functions with a singular continuous component are rarely encountered.

Expectation, Mean, and Variance

The **expectation** of a function g of a random variable X is defined by

$$E\left(g(X)\right) = \int g(x)\, dF(x),$$

where

$$\int g(x)\, dF(x) := \begin{cases} \int_{-\infty}^{\infty} g(x) f(x)\, dx & \text{in the continuous case,} \\ \sum_{j=0}^{\infty} g(x_j) p(x_j) & \text{in the discrete case,} \end{cases}$$

and g is any function such that $E|g(x)| < \infty$. (If F is the mixture $F = pF_c + (1-p)F_d$, then $E(g(X)) = p\int g(x)\, dF_c(x) + (1-p)\int g(x)\, dF_d(x)$.) The **mean** and **variance** of X are defined as $\mu = EX$ and $\sigma^2 = E(X-\mu)^2$, respectively. They are evaluated by setting $g(x) = x$ and $g(x) = (x-\mu)^2$ in the definition of $E(g(X))$.

It is clear from the definition that expectation has the **linearity property**

$$E(aX + b) = aE(X) + b$$

for any real constants a and b (provided that $E|X| < \infty$).

Example A.1.1 The normal distribution

If X has the normal distribution with pdf $n\left(x; \mu, \sigma^2\right)$ as defined in Example (a) above, then

$$E(X-\mu) = \int_{-\infty}^{\infty} (x-\mu) n\left(x; \mu, \sigma^2\right)\, dx = -\sigma^2 \int_{-\infty}^{\infty} n'\left(x : \mu, \sigma^2\right)\, dx = 0.$$

This shows, with the help of the linearity property of E, that

$$E(X) = \mu,$$

i.e., that the parameter μ *is* in fact the mean of the normal distribution defined in Example (a). Similarly,

$$E(X-\mu)^2 = \int_{-\infty}^{\infty} (x-\mu)^2 n\left(x; \mu, \sigma^2\right)\, dx = -\sigma^2 \int_{-\infty}^{\infty} (x-\mu) n'\left(x; \mu, \sigma^2\right)\, dx.$$

Integrating by parts and using the fact that f is a pdf, we find that the variance of X is

$$E(X-\mu)^2 = \sigma^2 \int_{-\infty}^{\infty} n\left(x; \mu, \sigma^2\right)\, dx = \sigma^2. \qquad \square$$

Example A.1.2 The Poisson distribution

The mean of the Poisson distribution with parameter λ (see Example (h) above) is given by

$$\mu = \sum_{j=0}^{\infty} \frac{j\lambda^j}{j!} e^{-\lambda} = \sum_{j=1}^{\infty} \frac{\lambda\lambda^{j-1}}{(j-1)!} e^{-\lambda} = \lambda e^{\lambda} e^{-\lambda} = \lambda.$$

A similar calculation shows that the variance is also equal to λ (see Problem A.2). □

Remark. Functions and parameters associated with a random variable X will be labeled with the subscript X whenever it is necessary to identify the particular random variable to which they refer. For example, the distribution function, pdf, mean, and variance of X will be written as F_X, f_X, μ_X, and σ_X^2, respectively, whenever it is necessary to distinguish them from the corresponding quantities F_Y, f_Y, μ_Y, and σ_Y^2 associated with a different random variable Y. □

A.2 Random Vectors

An n-dimensional random vector is a column vector $\mathbf{X} = (X_1, \ldots, X_n)'$ each of whose components is a random variable. The distribution function F of $\mathbf{X}$, also called the **joint distribution** of $X_1, \ldots, X_n$, is defined by

$$F(x_1, \ldots, x_n) = P[X_1, \le x_1, \ldots, X_n \le x_n] \tag{A.2.1}$$

for all real numbers $x_1, \ldots, x_n$. This can be expressed in a more compact form as

$$F(\mathbf{x}) = P[\mathbf{X} \le \mathbf{x}], \quad \mathbf{x} = (x_1, \ldots, x_n)',$$

for all real vectors $\mathbf{x} = (x_1, \ldots, x_n)'$. The joint distribution of any subcollection $X_{i_1}, \ldots, X_{i_k}$ of these random variables can be obtained from F by setting $x_j = \infty$ in (A.2.1) for all $j \notin \{i_1, \ldots, i_k\}$. In particular, the distributions of X_1 and $(X_1, X_n)'$ are given by

$$F_{X_1}(x_1) = P[X_1 \le x_1] = F(x_1, \infty, \ldots, \infty)$$

and

$$F_{X_1,X_n}(x_1, x_n) = P[X_1 \le x_1, X_n \le x_n] = F(x_1, \infty, \ldots, \infty, x_n).$$

As in the univariate case, a random vector with distribution function F is said to be continuous if F has a density function, i.e., if

$$F(x_1, \ldots, x_n) = \int_{-\infty}^{x_n} \cdots \int_{-\infty}^{x_2} \int_{-\infty}^{x_1} f(y_1, \ldots, y_n)\, dy_1\, dy_2 \cdots dy_n.$$

The probability density of $\mathbf{X}$ is then found from

$$f(x_1, \ldots, x_n) = \frac{\partial^n F(x_1, \ldots, x_n)}{\partial x_1 \cdots \partial x_n}.$$

The random vector $\mathbf{X}$ is said to be discrete if there exist real-valued vectors $\mathbf{x}_0, \mathbf{x}_1, \ldots$ and a probability mass function $p(\mathbf{x}_j) = P[\mathbf{X} = \mathbf{x}_j]$ such that

$$\sum_{j=0}^{\infty} p(\mathbf{x}_j) = 1.$$

The expectation of a function g of a random vector $\mathbf{X}$ is defined by

$$E(g(\mathbf{X})) = \int g(\mathbf{x})\, dF(\mathbf{x}) = \int g(x_1, \ldots, x_n)\, dF(x_1, \ldots, x_n),$$

where

$$\int g(x_1, \ldots, x_n)\, dF(x_1, \ldots, x_n)$$
$$= \begin{cases} \displaystyle\int \cdots \int g(x_1, \ldots, x_n) f(x_1, \ldots, x_n)\, dx_1 \cdots dx_n, & \text{in the continuous case,} \\ \displaystyle\sum_{j_1} \cdots \sum_{j_n} g(x_{j_1}, \ldots, x_{j_n}) p(x_{j_1}, \ldots, x_{j_n}), & \text{in the discrete case,} \end{cases}$$

and g is any function such that $E|g(\mathbf{X})| < \infty$.

The random variables $X_1, \ldots, X_n$ are said to be **independent** if

$$P[X_1 \le x_1, \ldots, X_n \le x_n] = P[X_1 \le x_1] \cdots P[X_n \le x_n],$$

i.e.,

$$F(x_1, \ldots, x_n) = F_{X_1}(x_1) \cdots F_{X_n}(x_n)$$

for all real numbers $x_1, \ldots, x_n$. In the continuous and discrete cases, independence is equivalent to the factorization of the joint density function or probability mass function into the product of the respective marginal densities or mass functions, i.e.,

$$f(x_1, \ldots, x_n) = f_{X_1}(x_1) \cdots f_{X_n}(x_n) \tag{A.2.2}$$

or

$$p(x_1, \ldots, x_n) = p_{X_1}(x_1) \cdots p_{X_n}(x_n). \tag{A.2.3}$$

For two random vectors $\mathbf{X} = (X_1, \ldots, X_n)'$ and $\mathbf{Y} = (Y_1, \ldots, Y_m)'$ with joint density function $f_{\mathbf{X},\mathbf{Y}}$, the conditional density of $\mathbf{Y}$ given $\mathbf{X} = \mathbf{x}$ is

$$f_{\mathbf{Y}|\mathbf{X}}(\mathbf{y}|\mathbf{x}) = \begin{cases} \dfrac{f_{\mathbf{X},\mathbf{Y}}(\mathbf{x}, \mathbf{y})}{f_{\mathbf{X}}(\mathbf{x})}, & \text{if } f_{\mathbf{X}}(\mathbf{x}) > 0, \\ f_{\mathbf{Y}}(\mathbf{y}), & \text{if } f_{\mathbf{X}}(\mathbf{x}) = 0. \end{cases}$$

The conditional expectation of $g(\mathbf{Y})$ given $\mathbf{X} = \mathbf{x}$ is then

$$E(g(\mathbf{Y})|\mathbf{X} = \mathbf{x}) = \int_{-\infty}^{\infty} g(\mathbf{y}) f_{\mathbf{Y}|\mathbf{X}}(\mathbf{y}|\mathbf{x})\, d\mathbf{y}.$$

If $\mathbf{X}$ and $\mathbf{Y}$ are independent, then $f_{\mathbf{Y}|\mathbf{X}}(\mathbf{y}|\mathbf{x}) = f_{\mathbf{Y}}(\mathbf{y})$ by (A.2.2), and so the conditional expectation of $g(\mathbf{Y})$ given $\mathbf{X} = \mathbf{x}$ is

$$E(g(\mathbf{Y})|\mathbf{X} = \mathbf{x}) = E(g(\mathbf{Y})),$$

which, as expected, does not depend on $\mathbf{x}$. The same ideas hold in the discrete case with the probability mass function assuming the role of the density function.

Means and Covariances

If $E|X_i| < \infty$ for each i, then we define the mean or expected value of $\mathbf{X} = (X_1, \ldots, X_n)'$ to be the column vector

$$\mu_X = E\mathbf{X} = (EX_1, \ldots, EX_n)'.$$

In the same way we define the expected value of any array whose elements are random variables (e.g., a matrix of random variables) to be the same array with each random variable replaced by its expected value (if the expectation exists).

If $\mathbf{X} = (X_1, \ldots, X_n)'$ and $\mathbf{Y} = (Y_1, \ldots, Y_m)'$ are random vectors such that each X_i and Y_j has a finite variance, then the **covariance matrix** of $\mathbf{X}$ and $\mathbf{Y}$ is defined to be the matrix

$$\begin{aligned}\Sigma_{\mathbf{XY}} &= \mathrm{Cov}(\mathbf{X}, \mathbf{Y}) = E[(\mathbf{X} - E\mathbf{X})(\mathbf{Y} - E\mathbf{Y})'] \\ &= E(\mathbf{XY}') - (E\mathbf{X})(E\mathbf{Y})'.\end{aligned}$$

The (i, j) element of $\Sigma_{\mathbf{XY}}$ is the covariance $\mathrm{Cov}(X_i, Y_j) = E(X_iY_j) - E(X_i)E(Y_j)$. In the special case where $\mathbf{Y} = \mathbf{X}$, $\mathrm{Cov}(\mathbf{X}, \mathbf{Y})$ reduces to the covariance matrix of the random vector $\mathbf{X}$.

Now suppose that $\mathbf{Y}$ and $\mathbf{X}$ are linearly related through the equation

$$\mathbf{Y} = \mathbf{a} + B\mathbf{X},$$

where $\mathbf{a}$ is an m-dimensional column vector and B is an $m \times n$ matrix. Then $\mathbf{Y}$ has mean

$$E\mathbf{Y} = \mathbf{a} + BE\mathbf{X} \tag{A.2.4}$$

and covariance matrix

$$\Sigma_{\mathbf{YY}} = B\Sigma_{\mathbf{XX}}B' \tag{A.2.5}$$

(see Problem A.3).

Proposition A.2.1

The covariance matrix $\Sigma_{\mathbf{XX}}$ of a random vector $\mathbf{X}$ is symmetric and nonnegative definite, i.e., $\mathbf{b}'\Sigma_{\mathbf{XX}}\mathbf{b} \geq 0$ for all vectors $\mathbf{b} = (b_1, \ldots, b_n)'$ with real components.

Proof

Since the (i, j) element of $\Sigma_{\mathbf{XX}}$ is $\text{Cov}(X_i, X_j) = \text{Cov}(X_j, X_i)$, it is clear that $\Sigma_{\mathbf{XX}}$ is symmetric. To prove nonnegative definiteness, let $\mathbf{b} = (b_1, \ldots, b_n)'$ be an arbitrary vector. Then applying (A.2.5) with $\mathbf{a} = \mathbf{0}$ and $B = \mathbf{b}$, we have

$$\mathbf{b}'\Sigma_{\mathbf{XX}}\mathbf{b} = \text{Var}(\mathbf{b}'\mathbf{X}) = \text{Var}(b_1X_1 + \cdots + b_nX_n) \geq 0. \qquad \blacksquare$$

Proposition A.2.2 *Every $n \times n$ covariance matrix Σ can be factorized as*

$$\Sigma = P\Lambda P'$$

where P is an orthogonal matrix (i.e., $P' = P^{-1}$) whose columns are an orthonormal set of right eigenvectors corresponding to the (nonnegative) eigenvalues $\lambda_1, \ldots, \lambda_n$ of Σ, and Λ is the diagonal matrix

$$\Lambda = \begin{bmatrix} \lambda_1 & 0 & \cdots & 0 \\ 0 & \lambda_2 & \cdots & 0 \\ \vdots & \vdots & \ddots & \vdots \\ 0 & 0 & \cdots & \lambda_n \end{bmatrix}.$$

In particular, Σ is nonsingular if and only if all the eigenvalues are strictly positive.

Proof

Every covariance matrix is symmetric and nonnegative definite by Proposition A.2.1, and for such matrices the specified factorization is a standard result (see Graybill, 1983 for a proof). The determinant of an orthogonal matrix is 1, so that $\det(\Sigma) = \det(P)\det(\Lambda)\det(P) = \lambda_1 \cdots \lambda_n$. It follows that Σ is nonsingular if and only if $\lambda_i > 0$ for all i. $\blacksquare$

Remark. Given a covariance matrix Σ, it is sometimes useful to be able to find a square root $A = \Sigma^{1/2}$ with the property that $AA' = \Sigma$. It is clear from Proposition A.2.2 and the orthogonality of P that one such matrix is given by

$$A = \Sigma^{1/2} = P\Lambda^{1/2}P'.$$

If Σ is nonsingular, then we can define

$$\Sigma^s = P\Lambda^s P', \qquad -\infty < s < \infty.$$

The matrix $\Sigma^{-1/2}$ defined in this way is then a square root of Σ^{-1} and also the inverse of $\Sigma^{1/2}$. $\square$

A.3 The Multivariate Normal Distribution

The multivariate normal distribution is one of the most commonly encountered and important distributions in statistics. It plays a key role in the modeling of time series data. Let $\mathbf{X} = (X_1, \ldots, X_n)'$ be a random vector.

Definition A.3.1

> $\mathbf{X}$ has a **multivariate normal distribution** with mean $\boldsymbol{\mu}$ and nonsingular covariance matrix $\Sigma = \Sigma_{\mathbf{XX}}$, written as $\mathbf{X} \sim \mathrm{N}(\boldsymbol{\mu}; \Sigma)$, if
>
> $$f_{\mathbf{X}}(\mathbf{x}) = (2\pi)^{-n/2}(\det \Sigma)^{-1/2} \exp\left\{-\frac{1}{2}(\mathbf{x}-\boldsymbol{\mu})'\Sigma^{-1}(\mathbf{x}-\boldsymbol{\mu})\right\}.$$

If $\mathbf{X} \sim \mathrm{N}(\boldsymbol{\mu}, \Sigma)$, we can define a *standardized* random vector $\mathbf{Z}$ by applying the linear transformation

$$\mathbf{Z} = \Sigma^{-1/2}(\mathbf{X}-\boldsymbol{\mu}), \tag{A.3.1}$$

where $\Sigma^{-1/2}$ is defined as in the remark of Section A.2. Then by (A.2.4) and (A.2.5), $\mathbf{Z}$ has mean $\mathbf{0}$ and covariance matrix $\Sigma_{\mathbf{ZZ}} = \Sigma^{-1/2}\Sigma\Sigma^{-1/2} = I_n$, where I_n is the $n \times n$ identity matrix. Using the change of variables formula for probability densities (see Mood, Graybill, and Boes, 1974), we find that the probability density of $\mathbf{Z}$ is

$$\begin{aligned} f_{\mathbf{Z}}(\mathbf{z}) &= (\det \Sigma)^{1/2} f_{\mathbf{X}}\left(\Sigma^{1/2}\mathbf{z}+\boldsymbol{\mu}\right) \\ &= (\det \Sigma)^{1/2}(2\pi)^{-n/2}(\det \Sigma)^{-1/2} \exp\left\{-\frac{1}{2}(\Sigma^{-1/2}\mathbf{z})'\Sigma^{-1}\Sigma^{-1/2}\mathbf{z}\right\} \\ &= (2\pi)^{-n/2} \exp\left\{-\frac{1}{2}\mathbf{z}'\mathbf{z}\right\} \\ &= \left((2\pi)^{-1/2} \exp\left\{-\frac{1}{2}z_1^2\right\}\right)\cdots\left((2\pi)^{-1/2} \exp\left\{-\frac{1}{2}z_n^2\right\}\right), \end{aligned}$$

showing, by (A.2.2), that $Z_1, \ldots, Z_n$ are independent N(0, 1) random variables. Thus the standardized random vector $\mathbf{Z}$ defined by (A.3.1) has independent standard normal random components. Conversely, given any $n \times 1$ mean vector $\boldsymbol{\mu}$, a nonsingular $n \times n$ covariance matrix Σ, and an $n \times 1$ vector of standard normal random variables, we can construct a normally distributed random vector with mean $\boldsymbol{\mu}$ and covariance matrix Σ by defining

$$\mathbf{X} = \Sigma^{1/2}\mathbf{Z} + \boldsymbol{\mu}. \tag{A.3.2}$$

(See Problem A.4.)

Remark 1. The multivariate normal distribution with mean $\boldsymbol{\mu}$ and covariance matrix Σ can be defined, even when Σ is singular, as the distribution of the vector $\mathbf{X}$ in (A.3.2). The **singular multivariate normal distribution** does not have a joint density, since the possible values of $\mathbf{X} - \boldsymbol{\mu}$ are constrained to lie in a subspace of $\mathbb{R}^n$ with dimension equal to rank(Σ). □

Remark 2. If $\mathbf{X} \sim \mathrm{N}(\boldsymbol{\mu}, \Sigma)$, B is an $m \times n$ matrix, and $\mathbf{a}$ is a real $m \times 1$ vector, then the random vector

$$\mathbf{Y} = \mathbf{a} + B\mathbf{X}$$

is also multivariate normal (see Problem A.5). Note that from (A.2.4) and (A.2.5), $\mathbf{Y}$ has mean $\mathbf{a} + B\boldsymbol{\mu}$ and covariance matrix $B\Sigma B'$. In particular, by taking B to be the row vector $\mathbf{b}' = (b_1, \ldots, b_n)$, we see that any linear combination of the components of a multivariate normal random vector is normal. Thus $\mathbf{b}'\mathbf{X} = b_1 X_1 + \cdots + b_n X_n \sim \mathrm{N}(\mathbf{b}'\boldsymbol{\mu}_{\mathbf{X}}, \mathbf{b}'\Sigma_{\mathbf{XX}}\mathbf{b})$. □

Example A.3.1 The bivariate normal distribution

Suppose that $\mathbf{X} = (X_1, X_2)'$ is a bivariate normal random vector with mean $\boldsymbol{\mu} = (\mu_1, \mu_2)'$ and covariance matrix

$$\Sigma = \begin{bmatrix} \sigma_1^2 & \rho\sigma_1\sigma_2 \\ \rho\sigma_1\sigma_2 & \sigma_2^2 \end{bmatrix}, \quad \sigma > 0, \sigma_2 > 0, \ -1 < \rho < 1. \tag{A.3.3}$$

The parameters σ_1, σ_2, and ρ are the standard deviations and correlation of the components X_1 and X_2. Every nonsingular 2-dimensional covariance matrix can be expressed in the form (A.3.3). The inverse of Σ is

$$\Sigma^{-1} = \left(1 - \rho^2\right)^{-1} \begin{bmatrix} \sigma_1^{-2} & -\rho\sigma_1^{-1}\sigma_2^{-1} \\ -\rho\sigma_1^{-1}\sigma_2^{-1} & \sigma_2^{-2} \end{bmatrix},$$

and so the pdf of $\mathbf{X}$ is given by

$$f_{\mathbf{X}}(\mathbf{x}) = \left(2\pi\sigma_1\sigma_2\left(1 - \rho^2\right)^{1/2}\right)^{-1} \times \exp\left\{\frac{-1}{2\left(1-\rho^2\right)}\left[\left(\frac{x_1 - \mu_1}{\sigma_1}\right)^2 - 2\rho\left(\frac{x_1 - \mu_1}{\sigma_1}\right)\left(\frac{x_2 - \mu_2}{\sigma_2}\right) + \left(\frac{x_2 - \mu_2}{\sigma_2}\right)^2\right]\right\}.$$ □

Multivariate normal random vectors have the important property that the conditional distribution of any set of components, given any other set, is again multivariate normal. In the following proposition we shall suppose that the nonsingular normal random vector $\mathbf{X}$ is partitioned into two subvectors

$$\mathbf{X} = \begin{bmatrix} \mathbf{X}^{(1)} \\ \mathbf{X}^{(2)} \end{bmatrix}.$$

Correspondingly, we shall write the mean and covariance matrix of $\mathbf{X}$ as

$$\mu = \begin{bmatrix} \mu^{(1)} \\ \mu^{(2)} \end{bmatrix} \quad \text{and} \quad \Sigma = \begin{bmatrix} \Sigma_{11} & \Sigma_{12} \\ \Sigma_{21} & \Sigma_{22} \end{bmatrix},$$

where $\mu^{(i)} = E\mathbf{X}^{(i)}$ and $\Sigma_{ij} = E\left(\mathbf{X}^{(i)} - \mu^{(i)}\right)\left(\mathbf{X}^{(j)} - \mu^{(i)}\right)'$.

Proposition A.3.1

i. *$\mathbf{X}^{(1)}$ and $\mathbf{X}^{(2)}$ are independent if and only if $\Sigma_{12} = 0$.*
ii. *The conditional distribution of $\mathbf{X}^{(1)}$ given $\mathbf{X}^{(2)} = \mathbf{x}^{(2)}$ is $\mathrm{N}\left(\mu^{(1)} + \Sigma_{12}\Sigma_{22}^{-1}\left(\mathbf{x}^{(2)} - \mu^{(2)}\right), \Sigma_{11} - \Sigma_{12}\Sigma_{22}^{-1}\Sigma_{21}\right)$. In particular,*

$$E\left(\mathbf{X}^{(1)}|\mathbf{X}^{(2)} = \mathbf{x}^{(2)}\right) = \mu^{(1)} + \Sigma_{12}\Sigma_{22}^{-1}\left(\mathbf{x}^{(2)} - \mu^{(2)}\right).$$

The proof of this proposition involves routine algebraic manipulations of the multivariate normal density function and is left as an exercise (see Problem A.6).

Example A.3.2

For the bivariate normal random vector $\mathbf{X}$ in Example A.3.1, we immediately deduce from Proposition A.3.1 that X_1 and X_2 are independent if and only if $\rho\sigma_1\sigma_2 = 0$ (or $\rho = 0$, since σ_1 and σ_2 are both positive). The conditional distribution of X_1 given $X_2 = x_2$ is normal with mean

$$E(X_1|X_2 = x_2) = \mu_1 + \rho\sigma_1\sigma_2^{-1}(x_2 - \mu_2)$$

and variance

$$\mathrm{Var}(X_1|X_2 = x_2) = \sigma_1^2\left(1 - \rho^2\right).$$

□

Definition A.3.2

$\{X_t\}$ is a **Gaussian time series** if all of its joint distributions are multivariate normal, i.e., if for any collection of integers $i_1, \ldots, i_n$, the random vector $(X_{i_1}, \ldots, X_{i_n})'$ has a multivariate normal distribution.

Remark 3. If $\{X_t\}$ is a Gaussian time series, then all of its joint distributions are completely determined by the mean function $\mu(t) = EX_t$ and the autocovariance function $\kappa(s,t) = \mathrm{Cov}(X_s, X_t)$. If the process also happens to be stationary, then the mean function is constant ($\mu_t = \mu$ for all t) and $\kappa(t+h, t) = \gamma(h)$ for all t. In this case, the joint distribution of $X_1, \ldots, X_n$ is the same as that of $X_{1+h}, \ldots, X_{n+h}$ for all integers h and $n > 0$. Hence for a Gaussian time series strict stationarity is equivalent to weak stationarity (see Section 2.1). □

Problems

A.1. Let X have a negative binomial distribution with parameters α and p, where $\alpha > 0$ and $0 \le p < 1$.

a. Show that the probability generating function of X (defined as $M(s) = E(s^X)$) is

$$M(s) = p^\alpha (1 - s + sp)^{-\alpha}, \quad 0 \le s \le 1.$$

b. Using the property that $M'(1) = E(X)$ and $M''(1) = E(X^2) - E(X)$, show that

$$E(X) = \alpha(1-p)/p \quad \text{and} \quad \text{Var}(X) = \alpha(1-p)/p^2.$$

A.2. If X has the Poisson distribution with mean λ, show that the variance of X is also λ.

A.3. Use the linearity of the expectation operator for real-valued random variables to establish (A.2.4) and (A.2.5).

A.4. If Σ is an $n \times n$ covariance matrix, $\Sigma^{1/2}$ is the square root of Σ defined in the remark of Section A.2, and $\mathbf{Z}$ is an n-vector whose components are independent normal random variables with mean 0 and variance 1, show that

$$X = \Sigma^{1/2}\mathbf{Z} + \boldsymbol{\mu}$$

is a normally distributed random vector with mean $\boldsymbol{\mu}$ and covariance matrix Σ.

A.5. Show that if $\mathbf{X}$ is an n-dimensional random vector such that $\mathbf{X} \sim \text{N}(\boldsymbol{\mu}, \Sigma)$, B is a real $m \times n$ matrix, and $\mathbf{a}$ is a real-valued m-vector, then

$$\mathbf{Y} = \mathbf{a} + B\mathbf{X}$$

is a multivariate normal random vector. Specify the mean and covariance matrix of $\mathbf{Y}$.

A.6. Prove Proposition A.3.1.

A.7. Suppose that $\mathbf{X} = (X_1, \ldots, X_n)' \sim \text{N}(\mathbf{0}, \Sigma)$ with Σ nonsingular. Using the fact that $\mathbf{Z}$, as defined in (A.3.1), has independent standard normal components, show that $(\mathbf{X} - \boldsymbol{\mu})'\Sigma^{-1}(\mathbf{X} - \boldsymbol{\mu})$ has the chi-squared distribution with n degrees of freedom (Section A.1, Example (e)).

A.8. Suppose that $\mathbf{X} = (X_1, \ldots, X_n)' \sim \text{N}(\boldsymbol{\mu}, \Sigma)$ with Σ nonsingular. If A is a symmetric $n \times n$ matrix, show that $E(\mathbf{X}'A\mathbf{X}) = \text{trace}(A\Sigma) + \boldsymbol{\mu}'\Sigma\boldsymbol{\mu}$.

A.9. Suppose that $\{X_t\}$ is a stationary Gaussian time series with mean 0 and autocovariance function $\gamma(h)$. Find $E(X_t | X_s)$ and $\text{Var}(X_t | X_s)$, $s \ne t$.

B Statistical Complements

B.1 Least Squares Estimation

Consider the problem of finding the "best" straight line

$$y = \theta_0 + \theta_1 x$$

to approximate observations $y_1, \ldots, y_n$ of a dependent variable y taken at fixed values $x_1, \ldots, x_n$ of the independent variable x. The **(ordinary) least squares estimates** $\hat{\theta}_0$, $\hat{\theta}_1$ are defined to be values of θ_0, θ_1 that minimize the sum

$$S(\theta_0, \theta_1) = \sum_{i=1}^{n} (y_i - \theta_0 - \theta_1 x_i)^2$$

of squared deviations of the observations y_i from the fitted values $\theta_0 + \theta_1 x_i$. (The "sum of squares" $S(\theta_0, \theta_1)$ is identical to the Euclidean squared distance between $\mathbf{y}$ and $\theta_0\mathbf{1} + \theta_1\mathbf{x}$, i.e.,

$$S(\theta_0, \theta_1) = \|\mathbf{y} - \theta_0\mathbf{1} - \theta_1\mathbf{x}\|^2,$$

where $\mathbf{x} = (x_1, \ldots, x_n)'$, $\mathbf{1} = (1, \ldots, 1)'$, and $\mathbf{y} = (y_1, \ldots, y_n)'$.) Setting the partial derivatives of S with respect to θ_0 and θ_1 both equal to zero shows that the vector

$\hat{\boldsymbol{\theta}} = (\hat{\theta}_0, \hat{\theta}_1)'$ satisfies the "normal equations"

$$X'X\hat{\boldsymbol{\theta}} = X'\mathbf{y},$$

where X is the $n \times 2$ matrix $X = [\mathbf{1}, \mathbf{x}]$. Since $0 \le S(\boldsymbol{\theta})$ and $S(\boldsymbol{\theta}) \to \infty$ as $\|\boldsymbol{\theta}\| \to \infty$, the normal equations have at least one solution. If $\hat{\boldsymbol{\theta}}^{(1)}$ and $\hat{\boldsymbol{\theta}}^{(2)}$ are two solutions of the normal equations, then a simple calculation shows that

$$\left(\hat{\boldsymbol{\theta}}^{(1)} - \hat{\boldsymbol{\theta}}^{(2)}\right)' X'X \left(\hat{\boldsymbol{\theta}}^{(1)} - \hat{\boldsymbol{\theta}}^{(2)}\right) = 0,$$

i.e., that $X\hat{\boldsymbol{\theta}}^{(1)} = X\hat{\boldsymbol{\theta}}^{(2)}$. The solution of the normal equations is unique if and only if the matrix $X'X$ is nonsingular. But the preceding calculations show that even if $X'X$ is singular, the vector $\hat{\mathbf{y}} = X\hat{\boldsymbol{\theta}}$ of fitted values is the same for *any* solution $\hat{\boldsymbol{\theta}}$ of the normal equations.

The argument just given applies equally well to least squares estimation for the general linear model. Given a set of data points

$$(x_{i1}, x_{i2}, \ldots, x_{im}, y_i), \qquad i = 1, \ldots, n \text{ with } m \le n,$$

the least squares estimate, $\hat{\boldsymbol{\theta}} = \left(\hat{\theta}_1, \ldots, \hat{\theta}_m\right)'$ of $\boldsymbol{\theta} = (\theta_1, \ldots, \theta_m)'$ minimizes

$$S(\boldsymbol{\theta}) = \sum_{i=1}^{n} (y_i - \theta_1 x_{i1} - \cdots - \theta_m x_{im})^2 = \left\|\mathbf{y} - \theta_1 \mathbf{x}^{(1)} - \cdots - \theta_m \mathbf{x}^{(m)}\right\|^2,$$

where $\mathbf{y} = (y_1, \ldots, y_n)'$ and $\mathbf{x}^{(j)} = (x_{1j}, \ldots, x_{nj})'$, $j = 1, \ldots, m$. As in the previous special case, $\hat{\boldsymbol{\theta}}$ satisfies the equations

$$X'X\hat{\boldsymbol{\theta}} = X'\mathbf{y},$$

where X is the $n \times m$ matrix $X = \left[\mathbf{x}^{(1)}, \ldots, \mathbf{x}^{(m)}\right]$. The solution of this equation is unique if and only if $X'X$ nonsingular, in which case

$$\hat{\boldsymbol{\theta}} = (X'X)^{-1}X'\mathbf{y}.$$

If $X'X$ is singular, there are infinitely many solutions $\hat{\boldsymbol{\theta}}$, but the vector of fitted values $X\hat{\boldsymbol{\theta}}$ is the same for all of them.

Example B.1.1 To illustrate the general case, let us fit a quadratic function

$$y = \theta_0 + \theta_1 x + \theta_2 x^2$$

to the data

x	0	1	2	3	4
y	1	0	3	5	8

The matrix X for this problem is

$$X = \begin{bmatrix} 1 & 0 & 0 \\ 1 & 1 & 1 \\ 1 & 2 & 4 \\ 1 & 3 & 9 \\ 1 & 4 & 16 \end{bmatrix}, \text{ giving } (X'X)^{-1} = \frac{1}{140}\begin{bmatrix} 124 & -108 & 20 \\ -108 & 174 & -40 \\ 20 & -40 & 10 \end{bmatrix}.$$

The least squares estimate $\hat{\boldsymbol{\theta}} = \left(\hat{\theta}_0, \hat{\theta}_1, \hat{\theta}_2\right)'$ is therefore unique and given by

$$\hat{\boldsymbol{\theta}} = (X'X)^{-1}X'\mathbf{y} = \begin{bmatrix} 0.6 \\ -0.1 \\ 0.5 \end{bmatrix}.$$

The vector of fitted values is given by

$$\hat{\mathbf{y}} = X\hat{\boldsymbol{\theta}} = (0.6, 1, 2.4, 4.8, 8.2)'$$

as compared with the observed values

$$\mathbf{y} = (1, 0, 3, 5, 8)'.$$

□

B.1.1 The Gauss–Markov Theorem

Suppose now that the observations $y_1, \ldots, y_n$ are realized values of random variables $Y_1, \ldots, Y_n$ satisfying

$$Y_i = \theta_1 x_{i1} + \cdots + \theta_m x_{im} + Z_i,$$

where $Z_i \sim \text{WN}\left(0, \sigma^2\right)$. Letting $\mathbf{Y} = (Y_1, \ldots, Y_n)'$ and $\mathbf{Z} = (Z_1, \ldots, Z_n)'$, we can write these equations as

$$\mathbf{Y} = X\boldsymbol{\theta} + \mathbf{Z}.$$

Assume for simplicity that the matrix $X'X$ is nonsingular (for the general case see, e.g., Silvey, 1975). Then the least squares estimator of $\boldsymbol{\theta}$ is, as above,

$$\hat{\boldsymbol{\theta}} = (X'X)^{-1}X'\mathbf{Y},$$

and the least squares estimator of the parameter σ^2 is the unbiased estimator

$$\hat{\sigma}^2 = \frac{1}{n-m}\left\|\mathbf{Y} - X\hat{\boldsymbol{\theta}}\right\|^2.$$

It is easy to see that $\hat{\boldsymbol{\theta}}$ is also unbiased, i.e., that

$$E\left(\hat{\boldsymbol{\theta}}\right) = \boldsymbol{\theta}.$$

It follows at once that if $\mathbf{c}'\boldsymbol{\theta}$ is any linear combination of the parameters θ_i, $i = 1, \ldots, m$, then $\mathbf{c}'\hat{\boldsymbol{\theta}}$ is an unbiased estimator of $\mathbf{c}'\boldsymbol{\theta}$. The Gauss–Markov theorem says that of all unbiased estimators of $\mathbf{c}'\boldsymbol{\theta}$ of the form $\sum_{i=1}^{n} a_i Y_i$, the estimator $\mathbf{c}'\hat{\boldsymbol{\theta}}$ has the smallest variance.

In the special case where $Z_1, \ldots, Z_n$ are IID $\mathrm{N}(0, \sigma^2)$, the least squares estimator $\hat{\boldsymbol{\theta}}$ has the distribution $\mathrm{N}(\boldsymbol{\theta}, \sigma^2(X'X)^{-1})$, and $(n-m)\hat{\sigma}^2/\sigma^2$ has the χ^2 distribution with $n-m$ degrees of freedom.

B.1.2 Generalized Least Squares

The Gauss–Markov theorem depends on the assumption that the errors $Z_1, \ldots, Z_n$ are uncorrelated with constant variance. If, on the other hand, $\mathbf{Z} = (Z_1, \ldots, Z_n)'$ has mean $\mathbf{0}$ and nonsingular covariance matrix $\sigma^2\Sigma$ where $\Sigma \neq I$, we consider the transformed observation vector $U = R^{-1}\mathbf{Y}$, where R is a nonsingular matrix such that $RR' = \Sigma$. Then

$$\mathbf{U} = R^{-1}X\boldsymbol{\theta} + \mathbf{W} = M\boldsymbol{\theta} + \mathbf{W},$$

where $M = R^{-1}X$ and $\mathbf{W}$ has mean $\mathbf{0}$ and covariance matrix $\sigma^2 I$. The Gauss–Markov theorem now implies that the best linear estimate of any linear combination $\mathbf{c}'\boldsymbol{\theta}$ is $\mathbf{c}'\hat{\boldsymbol{\theta}}$, where $\hat{\boldsymbol{\theta}}$ is the **generalized least squares estimator**, which minimizes

$$\|\mathbf{U} - M\boldsymbol{\theta}\|^2.$$

In the special case where $Z_1, \ldots, Z_n$ are uncorrelated and Z_i has mean 0 and variance $\sigma^2 r_i^2$, the generalized least squares estimator minimizes the weighted sum of squares

$$\sum_{i=1}^{n} \frac{1}{r_i^2}(Y_i - \theta_1 x_{i1} - \cdots - \theta_m x_{im})^2.$$

In the general case, if $X'X$ and Σ are both nonsingular, the generalized least squares estimator is given by

$$\hat{\boldsymbol{\theta}} = (M'M)^{-1}M'\mathbf{U}.$$

Although the least squares estimator $(X'X)^{-1}X'\mathbf{Y}$ is unbiased if $E(\mathbf{Z}) = \mathbf{0}$, even when the covariance matrix of $\mathbf{Z}$ is not equal to $\sigma^2 I$, the variance of the corresponding estimate of any linear combination of $\theta_1, \ldots, \theta_m$ is greater than or equal to the estimator based on the generalized least squares estimator.

B.2 Maximum Likelihood Estimation

The method of least squares has an appealing intuitive interpretation. Its application depends on knowledge only of the means and covariances of the observations. Maximum likelihood estimation depends on the assumption of a particular distributional form for the observations, known apart from the values of parameters $\theta_1, \ldots, \theta_m$. We can regard the estimation problem as that of selecting the most appropriate value of a parameter vector $\boldsymbol{\theta}$, taking values in a subset Θ of $\mathbb{R}^m$. We suppose that these distributions have probability densities $p(\mathbf{x}; \boldsymbol{\theta})$, $\boldsymbol{\theta} \in \Theta$. For a fixed vector of observations

x, the function $L(\boldsymbol{\theta}) = p(\mathbf{x}; \boldsymbol{\theta})$ on Θ is called the **likelihood function**. A maximum likelihood estimate $\hat{\boldsymbol{\theta}}(\mathbf{x})$ of $\boldsymbol{\theta}$ is a value of $\boldsymbol{\theta} \in \Theta$ that maximizes the value of $L(\boldsymbol{\theta})$ for the given observed value **x**, i.e.,

$$L(\hat{\boldsymbol{\theta}}) = p\left(x; \hat{\boldsymbol{\theta}}(\mathbf{x})\right) = \max_{\boldsymbol{\theta} \in \Theta} p(\mathbf{x}; \boldsymbol{\theta}).$$

Example B.2.1

If $\mathbf{x} = (x_1, \ldots, x_n)'$ is a vector of observations of independent $\mathrm{N}(\mu, \sigma^2)$ random variables, the likelihood function is

$$L\left(\mu, \sigma^2\right) = \frac{1}{\left(2\pi\sigma^2\right)^{n/2}} \exp\left[-\frac{1}{2\sigma^2}\sum_{i=1}^{n}(x_i - \mu)^2\right], \quad -\infty < \mu < \infty, \quad \sigma > 0.$$

Maximization of L with respect to μ and σ is equivalent to minimization of

$$-2\ln L\left(\mu, \sigma^2\right) = n\ln(2\pi) + 2n\ln(\sigma) + \frac{1}{\sigma^2}\sum_{i=1}^{n}(x_i - \mu)^2.$$

Setting the partial derivatives of $-2\ln L$ with respect to μ and σ both equal to zero gives the maximum likelihood estimates

$$\hat{\mu} = \bar{x} = \frac{1}{n}\sum_{i=1}^{n} x_i \quad \text{and} \quad \hat{\sigma}^2 = \frac{1}{n}\sum_{i=1}^{n}(x_i - \bar{x})^2. \quad \square$$

B.2.1 Properties of Maximum Likelihood Estimators

The Gauss–Markov theorem lent support to the use of least squares estimation by showing its property of minimum variance among unbiased linear estimators. Maximum likelihood estimators are not generally unbiased, but in particular cases they can be shown to have small mean squared error relative to other competing estimators. Their main justification, however, lies in their good large-sample behavior.

For independent and identically distributed observations with true probability density $p(\cdot; \boldsymbol{\theta}_0)$ satisfying certain regularity conditions, it can be shown that the maximum likelihood estimator $\hat{\boldsymbol{\theta}}$ of $\boldsymbol{\theta}_0$ converges in probability to $\boldsymbol{\theta}_0$ and that the distribution of $\sqrt{n}\left(\hat{\boldsymbol{\theta}} - \boldsymbol{\theta}_0\right)$ is approximately normal with mean 0 and covariance matrix $I(\boldsymbol{\theta}_0)^{-1}$, where $I(\boldsymbol{\theta})$ is Fisher's information matrix with (i, j) component

$$E_{\boldsymbol{\theta}}\left[\frac{\partial \ln p(X; \boldsymbol{\theta})}{\partial \theta_i} \frac{\partial \ln p(X; \boldsymbol{\theta})}{\partial \theta_j}\right].$$

In time series analysis the situation is rather more complicated than in the case of iid observations. "Likelihood" in the time series context is almost always used in the sense of Gaussian likelihood, i.e., the likelihood computed under the (possibly false) assumption that the series is Gaussian. Nevertheless, estimators of ARMA coefficients computed by maximization of the Gaussian likelihood have good large-sample properties analogous to those described in the preceding paragraph. For details see TSTM, Section 10.8.

B.3 Confidence Intervals

Estimation of a parameter or parameter vector by least squares or maximum likelihood leads to a particular value, often referred to as a **point estimate**. It is clear that this will rarely be exactly equal to the true value, and so it is important to convey some idea of the probable accuracy of the estimator. This can be done using the notion of confidence interval, which specifies a random set covering the true parameter value with some specified (high) probability.

Example B.3.1

If $\mathbf{X} = (X_1, \ldots, X_n)'$ is a vector of independent $\mathrm{N}(\mu, \sigma^2)$ random variables, we saw in Section B.2 that the random variable $\overline{X}_n = \frac{1}{n}\sum_{i=1}^n X_i$ is the maximum likelihood estimator of μ. This is a point estimator of μ. To construct a confidence interval for μ from $\overline{X}_n$, we observe that the random variable

$$\frac{\overline{X}_n - \mu}{S/\sqrt{n}}$$

has Student's t-distribution with $n-1$ degrees of freedom, where S is the sample standard deviation, i.e., $S^2 = \frac{1}{n-1}\sum_{i=1}^n \left(X_i - \overline{X}_n\right)^2$. Hence,

$$P\left[-t_{1-\alpha/2} < \frac{\overline{X}_n - \mu}{S/\sqrt{n}} < t_{1-\alpha/2}\right] = 1 - \alpha,$$

where $t_{1-\alpha/2}$ denotes the $(1-\alpha/2)$ quantile of the t-distribution with $n-1$ degrees of freedom. This probability statement can be expressed in the form

$$P\left[\overline{X}_n - t_{1-\alpha/2}S/\sqrt{n} < \mu < \overline{X}_n + t_{1-\alpha/2}S/\sqrt{n}\right] = 1 - \alpha,$$

which shows that the random interval bounded by $\overline{X}_n \pm t_{1-\alpha/2}S/\sqrt{n}$ includes the true value μ with probability $1-\alpha$. This interval is called a $(1-\alpha)$ confidence interval for the mean μ. □

B.3.1 Large-Sample Confidence Regions

Many estimators of a vector-valued parameter $\boldsymbol{\theta}$ are approximately normally distributed when the sample size n is large. For example, under mild regularity conditions, the maximum likelihood estimator $\hat{\boldsymbol{\theta}}(\mathbf{X})$ of $\boldsymbol{\theta} = (\theta_1, \ldots, \theta_m)'$ is approximately $\mathrm{N}\left(\mathbf{0}, \frac{1}{n}I(\hat{\boldsymbol{\theta}})^{-1}\right)$, where $I(\boldsymbol{\theta})$ is the Fisher information defined in Section B.2. Consequently,

$$n\left(\hat{\boldsymbol{\theta}} - \boldsymbol{\theta}\right)' I\left(\hat{\boldsymbol{\theta}}\right)\left(\hat{\boldsymbol{\theta}} - \boldsymbol{\theta}\right)$$

is approximately distributed as χ^2 with m degrees of freedom, and the random set of $\boldsymbol{\theta}$-values defined by

$$n\left(\boldsymbol{\theta} - \hat{\boldsymbol{\theta}}\right)' I\left(\hat{\boldsymbol{\theta}}\right)\left(\boldsymbol{\theta} - \hat{\boldsymbol{\theta}}\right) \le \chi^2_{1-\alpha}(m)$$

covers the true value of $\boldsymbol{\theta}$ with probability approximately equal to $1-\alpha$.

Example B.3.2

For iid observations $X_1, \ldots, X_n$ from $\mathrm{N}(\mu, \sigma^2)$, a straightforward calculation gives, for $\boldsymbol{\theta} = (\mu, \sigma^2)'$,

$$I(\theta) = \begin{bmatrix} \sigma^{-2} & 0 \\ 0 & \sigma^{-4}/2 \end{bmatrix}.$$

Thus we obtain the large-sample confidence region for $(\mu, \sigma^2)'$,

$$n\left(\mu - \overline{X}_n\right)^2 / \hat{\sigma}^2 + n(\sigma^2 - \hat{\sigma}^2)^2 / \left(2\hat{\sigma}^4\right) \le \chi^2_{1-\alpha}(2),$$

which covers the true value of $\boldsymbol{\theta}$ with probability approximately equal to $1 - \alpha$. This region is an ellipse centered at $\left(\overline{X}_n, \hat{\sigma}^2\right)$. □

B.4 Hypothesis Testing

Parameter estimation can be regarded as choosing one from infinitely many possible decisions regarding the value of a parameter vector $\boldsymbol{\theta}$. Hypothesis testing, on the other hand, involves a choice between two alternative hypotheses, a "null" hypothesis H_0 and an "alternative" hypothesis H_1, regarding the parameter vector $\boldsymbol{\theta}$. The hypotheses H_0 and H_1 correspond to subsets Θ_0 and Θ_1 of the parameter set Θ. The problem is to decide, on the basis of an observed data vector $\mathbf{X}$, whether or not we should reject the null hypothesis H_0. A statistical test of H_0 can therefore be regarded as a partition of the *sample* space into one set of values of $\mathbf{X}$ for which we reject H_0 and another for which we do not. The problem is to specify a test (i.e., a subset of the sample space called the "rejection region") for which the corresponding decision rule performs well in practice.

Example B.4.1

If $\mathbf{X} = (X_1, \ldots, X_n)'$ is a vector of independent $\mathrm{N}(\mu, 1)$ random variables, we may wish to test the null hypothesis H_0: $\mu = 0$ against the alternative H_1: $\mu \ne 0$. A plausible choice of rejection region in this case is the set of all samples $\mathbf{X}$ for which $\left|\overline{X}_n\right| > c$ for some suitably chosen constant c. We shall return to this example after considering those factors that should be taken into account in the systematic selection of a "good" rejection region. □

B.4.1 Error Probabilities

There are two types of error that may be incurred in the application of a statistical test:

- type I error is the rejection of H_0 when it is true.
- type II error is the acceptance of H_0 when it is false.

For a given test (i.e., for a given rejection region R), the probabilities of error can both be found from the **power function** of the test, defined as

$$P_{\boldsymbol{\theta}}(R), \quad \boldsymbol{\theta} \in \Theta,$$

where $P_{\boldsymbol{\theta}}$ is the distribution of $\mathbf{X}$ when the true parameter value is $\boldsymbol{\theta}$. The probabilities of a type I error are

$$\alpha(\boldsymbol{\theta}) = P_{\boldsymbol{\theta}}(R), \quad \boldsymbol{\theta} \in \Theta_0,$$

and the probabilities of a type II error are

$$\beta(\boldsymbol{\theta}) = 1 - P_{\boldsymbol{\theta}}(R), \quad \boldsymbol{\theta} \in \Theta_1.$$

It is not generally possible to find a test that simultaneously minimizes $\alpha(\boldsymbol{\theta})$ and $\beta(\boldsymbol{\theta})$ for all values of their arguments. Instead, therefore, we seek to limit the probability of type I error and then, subject to this constraint, to minimize the probability of type II error uniformly on Θ_1. Given a **significance level** α, an optimum level-α test is a test satisfying

$$\alpha(\boldsymbol{\theta}) \leq \alpha, \quad \text{for all } \boldsymbol{\theta} \in \Theta_0,$$

that minimizes $\beta(\boldsymbol{\theta})$ for every $\boldsymbol{\theta} \in \Theta_1$. Such a test is called a **uniformly most powerful (U.M.P.) test of level α**. The quantity $\sup_{\boldsymbol{\theta}\in\Theta_0} \alpha(\boldsymbol{\theta})$ is called the **size** of the test.

In the special case of a simple hypothesis vs. a simple hypothesis, e.g., H_0: $\boldsymbol{\theta} = \boldsymbol{\theta}_0$ vs. H_1: $\boldsymbol{\theta} = \boldsymbol{\theta}_1$, an optimal test based on the likelihood ratio statistic can be constructed (see Silvey, 1975). Unfortunately, it is usually not possible to find a uniformly most powerful test of a simple hypothesis against a composite (more than one value of $\boldsymbol{\theta}$) alternative. This problem can sometimes be solved by searching for uniformly most powerful tests within the smaller classes of unbiased or invariant tests. For further information see Lehmann (1986).

B.4.2 Large-Sample Tests Based on Confidence Regions

There is a natural link between the testing of a simple hypothesis H_0: $\boldsymbol{\theta} = \boldsymbol{\theta}_0$ vs. H_1: $\boldsymbol{\theta} \neq \boldsymbol{\theta}_0$ and the construction of confidence regions. To illustrate this connection, suppose that $\hat{\boldsymbol{\theta}}$ is an estimator of $\boldsymbol{\theta}$ whose distribution is approximately $N(\boldsymbol{\theta}, n^{-1}I^{-1}(\boldsymbol{\theta}))$, where $I(\boldsymbol{\theta})$ is a positive definite matrix. This is usually the case, for example, when $\hat{\boldsymbol{\theta}}$ is a maximum likelihood estimator and $I(\boldsymbol{\theta})$ is the Fisher information. As in Section

B.3.1, we have

$$P_\theta\left(n\left(\theta-\hat{\theta}\right)' I\left(\hat{\theta}\right)\left(\theta-\hat{\theta}\right) \leq \chi^2_{1-\alpha}(m)\right) \approx 1-\alpha.$$

Consequently, an approximate α-level test is to reject H_0 if

$$n\left(\theta_0-\hat{\theta}\right)' I\left(\hat{\theta}\right)\left(\theta_0-\hat{\theta}\right) > \chi^2_{1-\alpha}(m),$$

or equivalently, if the confidence region determined by those $\boldsymbol{\theta}$'s satisfying

$$n\left(\theta-\hat{\theta}\right)' I\left(\hat{\theta}\right)\left(\theta-\hat{\theta}\right) \leq \chi^2_{1-\alpha}(m)$$

does not include $\boldsymbol{\theta}_0$.

Example B.4.2

Consider again the problem described in Example B.4.1. Since $\overline{X}_n \sim N\left(\mu, n^{-1}\right)$, the hypothesis H_0: $\mu = 0$ is rejected at level α if

$$n\left(\overline{X}_n\right)^2 > \chi^2_{1-\alpha,1},$$

or equivalently, if

$$\left|\overline{X}_n\right| > \frac{\Phi_{1-\alpha/2}}{n^{1/2}}.$$

□

C Mean Square Convergence

The sequence S_n of random variables is said to converge in mean square to the random variable S if

$$E(S_n - S)^2 \to 0 \quad \text{as } n \to \infty.$$

In particular, we say that the sum $\sum_{k=1}^{n} X_k$ converges (in mean square) if there exists a random variable S such that $E\left(\sum_{k=1}^{n} X_k - S\right)^2 \to 0$ as $n \to \infty$. If this is the case, then we use the notation $S = \sum_{k=1}^{\infty} X_k$.

C.1 The Cauchy Criterion

For a given sequence S_n of random variables to converge in mean square to *some* random variable, it is necessary and sufficient that

$$E(S_m - S_n)^2 \to 0 \quad \text{as } m, n \to \infty$$

(for a proof of this see TSTM, Chapter 2). The point of the criterion is that it permits checking for mean square convergence without having to identify the limit of the sequence.

Example C.1.1

Consider the sequence of partial sums $S_n = \sum_{t=-n}^{n} a_t Z_t$, $n = 1, 2, \ldots$, where $\{Z_t\} \sim \text{WN}\left(0, \sigma^2\right)$. Under what conditions on the coefficients a_i does this sequence converge in mean square? To answer this question we apply the Cauchy criterion as follows. For $n > m > 0$,

$$E(S_n - S_m)^2 = E\left(\sum_{m<|i|\le n} a_i Z_i\right)^2 = \sigma^2 \sum_{m<|i|\le n} a_i^2.$$

Consequently, $E(S_n - S_m)^2 \to 0$ if and only if $\sum_{m<|i|\le n} a_i^2 \to 0$. Since the Cauchy criterion applies also to real-valued sequences, this last condition is equivalent to convergence of the sequence $\sum_{i=-n}^{n} a_i^2$, or equivalently to the condition

$$\sum_{i=-\infty}^{\infty} a_i^2 < \infty.$$ □

Properties of Mean Square Convergence:

If $X_n \to X$ and $Y_n \to Y$, in mean square as $n \to \infty$, then

(a) $E(X_n^2) \to E(X^2)$,

(b) $E(X_n) \to E(X)$,

and

(c) $E(X_n Y_n) \to E(XY)$.

Proof See TSTM, Proposition 2.1.2. ■

D An ITSM Tutorial

The package ITSM2000, the student version of which is included with this book, requires an IBM-compatible PC operating under Windows 95, NT, version 4.0 or a later version of either of these operating systems. To install the package, copy the folder ITSM2000 from the CD-ROM to any convenient location on your hard disk. To run the program, you can either double-click on the icon ITSM.EXE in the folder ITSM2000 or, on the Windows task bar, left-click on Start, select Run, enter the location and name of the file ITSM.EXE (e.g. C:\ITSM2000\ITSM.EXE) and click on `OK`. You may find it convenient to create a shortcut on your desktop by right-clicking on the ITSM.EXE icon and selecting `Create shortcut`. Then right-click on the shortcut icon, drag it to your desktop, and select `Move here`. The program can then be run at any time by double-clicking on the shortcut icon. The program can also be run directly from the CD-ROM by opening the folder ITSM2000 and double-clicking on the icon ITSM.EXE. The package ITSM2000 supersedes earlier versions of the package ITSM distributed with this book.

D.1 Getting Started

D.1.1 Running ITSM

Double-click on the icon labeled ITSM.EXE, and the ITSM window will open. Selecting the option `Help>Contents` will show you the topics for which explanations and examples are provided. Clicking on `Index` at the top of the Help window will allow you to find more specific topics. Close the Help window by clicking on the X at its top right corner. To begin analyzing one of the data sets provided, select `File>Project>Open` at the top left corner of the ITSM window.

There are several distinct functions of the program ITSM. The first is to analyze and display the properties of time series data, the second is to compute and display the properties of time series models, and the third is to combine these functions in order to fit models to data. The last of these includes checking that the properties of the fitted model match those of the data in a suitable sense. Having found an appropriate model, we can (for example) then use it in conjunction with the data to forecast future values of the series. Sections D.2–D.5 of this appendix deal with the modeling and analysis of data, while Section D.6 is concerned with model properties. Section D.7 explains how to open multivariate projects in ITSM. Examples of the analysis of multivariate time series are given in Chapter 7.

It is important to keep in mind the distinction between data and model properties and not to confuse the data with the model. In any one project ITSM stores one data set and one model (which can be identified by highlighting the project window and pressing the red INFO button at the top of the ITSM window). Until a model is entered by the user, ITSM stores the default model of white noise with variance 1. If the data are transformed (e.g., differenced and mean-corrected), then the data are replaced in ITSM by the transformed data. (The original data can, however, be restored by inverting the transformations.) Rarely (if ever) is a real time series generated by a model as simple as those used for fitting purposes. In model fitting the objective is to develop a model that mimics important features of the data, but is still simple enough to be used with relative ease.

The following sections constitute a tutorial that illustrates the use of some of the features of ITSM by leading you through a complete analysis of the well-known airline passenger series of Box and Jenkins (1976) filed as AIRPASS.TSM in the ITSM2000 folder.

D.2 Preparing Your Data for Modeling

The observed values of your time series should be available in a single-column ASCII file (or two columns for a bivariate series). The file, like those provided with the package, should be given a name with suffix .TSM. You can then begin model fitting with ITSM. The program will read your data from the file, plot it on the screen, compute sample statistics, and allow you to make a number of transformations designed to make your transformed data representable as a realization of a zero-mean stationary process.

Example D.2.1

To illustrate the analysis we shall use the file AIRPASS.TSM, which contains the number of international airline passengers (in thousands) for each month from January, 1949, through December, 1960. □

D.2.1 Entering Data

Once you have opened the ITSM window as described above under Getting Started, select the options `File>Project>Open`, and you will see a dialog box in which you can check either `Univariate` or `Multivariate`. Since the data set for this example is univariate, make sure that the univariate option is checked and then click `OK`. A window labeled `Open File` will then appear, in which you can either type the name AIRPASS.TSM and click `Open`, or else locate the icon for AIRPASS.TSM in the Open File window and double-click on it. You will then see a graph of the monthly international airline passenger totals (measured in thousands) $X_1, \ldots, X_n$, with $n = 144$. Directly behind the graph is a window containing data summary statistics.

An additional, second, project can be opened by repeating the procedure described in the preceding paragraph. Alternatively, the data can be *replaced* in the current project using the option `File>Import File`. This option is useful if you wish to examine how well a fitted model represents a different data set. (See the entry `Project Editor` in the ITSM Help Files for information on multiple project management. Each ITSM project has its own data set and model.) For the purpose of this introduction we shall open only one project.

D.2.2 Information

If, with the window labeled AIRPASS.TSM highlighted, you press the red INFO button at the top of the ITSM window, you will see the sample mean, sample variance, estimated standard deviation of the sample mean, and the current model (white noise with variance 1).

Example D.2.2

Go through the steps in Entering Data to open the project AIRPASS.TSM and use the INFO button to determine the sample mean and variance of the series. □

D.2.3 Filing Data

You may wish to transform your data using ITSM and then store it in another file. At any time before or after transforming the data in ITSM, the data can be exported to a file by clicking on the red `Export` button, selecting `Time Series` and `File`, clicking

`OK`, and specifying a new file name. The numerical values of the series can also be pasted to the clipboard (and from there into another document) in the same way by choosing `Clipboard` instead of `File`. Other quantities computed by the program (e.g., the residuals from the current model) can be filed or pasted to the clipboard in the same way by making the appropriate selection in the Export dialog box. Graphs can also be pasted to the clipboard by right-clicking on them and selecting `Copy to Clipboard`.

Example D.2.3
Copy the series AIRPASS.TSM to the clipboard, open Wordpad or some convenient screen editor, and choose `Edit>Paste` to insert the series into your new document. Then copy the graph of the series to the clipboard and insert it into your document in the same way.

D.2.4 Plotting Data

A time series graph is automatically plotted when you open a data file (with time measured in units of the interval between observations, i.e., $t = 1, 2, 3, \ldots$). To see a histogram of the data press the rightmost yellow button at the top of the ITSM screen. If you wish to adjust the number of bins in the histogram, select `Statistics>Histogram>Set Bin Count` and specify the number of bins required. The histogram will then be replotted accordingly.

To insert any of the ITSM graphs into a text document, right-click on the graph concerned, select `Copy to Clipboard`, and the graph will be copied to the clipboard. It can then be pasted into a document opened by any standard text editor such as MS-Word or Wordpad using the `Edit>Paste` option in the screen editor. The graph can also be sent directly to a printer by right-clicking on the graph and selecting `Print`. Another useful graphics feature is provided by the white Zoom buttons at the top of the ITSM screen. The first and second of these enable you to enlarge a designated segment or box, respectively, of any of the graphs. The third button restores the original graph.

Example D.2.4
Continuing with our analysis of AIRPASS.TSM, press the yellow histogram button to see a histogram of the data. Replot the histogram with 20 bins by selecting `Statistics>Histogram>Set Bin Count`. □

D.2.5 Transforming Data

Transformations are applied in order to produce data that can be successfully modeled as "stationary time series." In particular, they are used to eliminate trend and cyclic components and to achieve approximate constancy of level and variability with time.

Example D.2.5
The airline passenger data (see Figure 9.4) are clearly not stationary. The level and variability both increase with time, and there appears to be a large seasonal component

(with period 12). They must therefore be transformed in order to be represented as a realization of a stationary time series using one or more of the transformations available for this purpose in ITSM. □

Box–Cox Transformations

Box–Cox transformations are performed by selecting `Transform>Box-Cox` and specifying the value of the Box–Cox parameter λ. If the original observations are $Y_1, Y_2, \ldots, Y_n$, the Box–Cox transformation f_λ converts them to $f_\lambda(Y_1), f_\lambda(Y_2), \ldots, f_\lambda(Y_n)$, where

$$f_\lambda(y) = \begin{cases} \dfrac{y^\lambda - 1}{\lambda}, & \lambda \neq 0, \\ \log(y), & \lambda = 0. \end{cases}$$

These transformations are useful when the variability of the data increases or decreases with the level. By suitable choice of λ, the variability can often be made nearly constant. In particular, for positive data whose standard deviation increases linearly with level, the variability can be stabilized by choosing $\lambda = 0$.

The choice of λ can be made visually by watching the graph of the data when you click on the pointer in the Box–Cox dialog box and drag it back and forth along the scale, which runs from zero to 1.5. Very often it is found that no transformation is needed or that the choice $\lambda = 0$ is satisfactory.

Example D.2.6

For the series AIRPASS.TSM, the variability increases with level, and the data are strictly positive. Taking natural logarithms (i.e., choosing a Box–Cox transformation with $\lambda = 0$) gives the transformed data shown in Figure D.1.

Notice how the amplitude of the fluctuations no longer increases with the level of the data. However, the seasonal effect remains, as does the upward trend. These will be removed shortly. The data stored in ITSM now consist of the natural logarithms of the original data. □

Classical Decompositon

There are two methods provided in ITSM for the elimination of trend and seasonality. These are:

i. "classical decomposition" of the series into a trend component, a seasonal component, and a random residual component, and
ii. differencing.

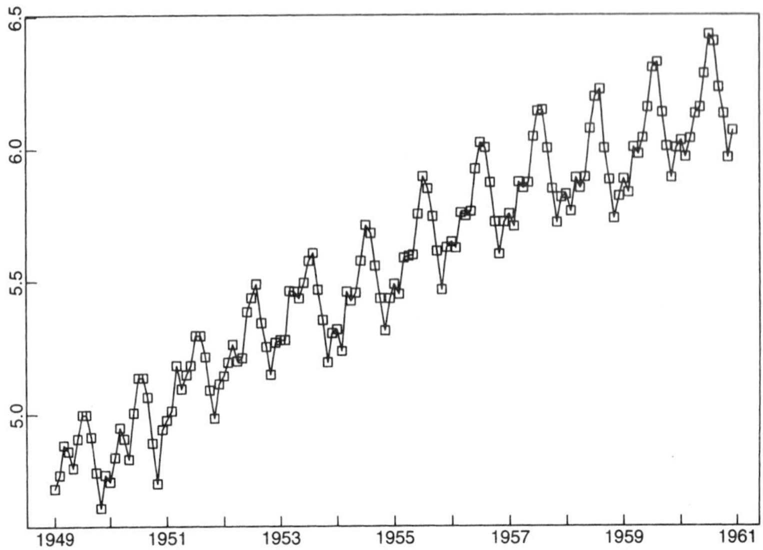

Figure D-1 The series AIRPASS.TSM after taking logs.

Classical decomposition of the series $\{X_t\}$ is based on the model

$$X_t = m_t + s_t + Y_t,$$

where X_t is the observation at time t, m_t is a "trend component," s_t is a "seasonal component," and Y_t is a "random noise component," which is stationary with mean zero. The objective is to estimate the components m_t and s_t and subtract them from the data to generate a sequence of residuals (or estimated noise) that can then be modeled as a stationary time series.

To achieve this, select `Transform>Classical` and you will see the Classical Decomposition dialog box. To remove a seasonal component and trend, check the `Seasonal Fit` and `Polynomial Fit` boxes, enter the period of the seasonal component, and choose between the alternatives `Quadratic Trend` and `Linear Trend`. Click `OK`, and the trend and seasonal components will be estimated and removed from the data, leaving the estimated noise sequence stored as the current data set.

The estimated noise sequence automatically replaces the previous data stored in ITSM.

Example D.2.7

The logged airline passenger data have an apparent seasonal component of period 12 (corresponding to the month of the year) and an approximately quadratic trend. Remove these using the option `Transform>Classical` as described above. (An alternative approach is to use the option `Regression`, which allows the specification and fitting of polynomials of degree up to 10 and a linear combination of up to 4 sine waves.)

Figure D.2 shows the transformed data (or residuals) Y_t, obtained by removal of trend and seasonality from the logged AIRPASS.TSM series by classical decom-

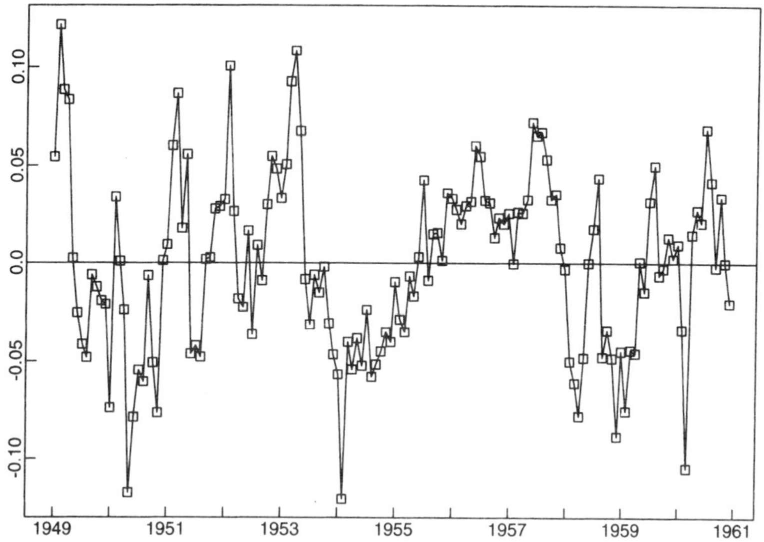

Figure D-2 The logged AIRPASS.TSM series after removal of trend and seasonal components by classical decomposition.

position. $\{Y_t\}$ shows no obvious deviations from stationarity, and it would now be reasonable to attempt to fit a stationary time series model to this series. To see how well the estimated seasonal and trend components fit the data, select `Transform>Show Classical Fit`. We shall not pursue this approach any further here, but turn instead to the **differencing** approach. (You should have no difficulty in later returning to this point and completing the classical decomposition analysis by fitting a stationary time series model to $\{Y_t\}$.) □

Differencing

Differencing is a technique that can also be used to remove seasonal components and trends. The idea is simply to consider the differences between pairs of observations with appropriate time separations. For example, to remove a seasonal component of period 12 from the series $\{X_t\}$, we generate the transformed series

$$Y_t = X_t - X_{t-12}.$$

It is clear that all seasonal components of period 12 are eliminated by this transformation, which is called **differencing at lag 12**. A linear trend can be eliminated by differencing at lag 1, and a quadratic trend by differencing twice at lag 1 (i.e., differencing once to get a new series, then differencing the new series to get a second new series). Higher-order polynomials can be eliminated analogously. It is worth noting that differencing at lag 12 eliminates not only seasonal components with period 12 but also any linear trend.

Data are differenced in ITSM by selecting `Transform>Difference` and entering the required lag in the resulting dialog box.

Example D.2.8

Restore the original airline passenger data using the option `File>Import File` and selecting AIRPASS.TSM. We take natural logarithms as in Example D.2.6 by selecting `Transform>Box-Cox` and setting $\lambda = 0$. The transformed series can now be deseasonalized by differencing at lag 12. To do this select `Transform>Difference`, enter the lag 12 in the dialog box, and click `OK`. Inspection of the graph of the deseasonalized series suggests a further differencing at lag 1 to eliminate the remaining trend. To do this, repeat the previous step with lag equal to 1 and you will see the transformed and twice-differenced series shown in Figure D.3. □

Subtracting the Mean

The term *ARMA model* is used in ITSM to denote a *zero-mean* ARMA process (see Definition 3.1.1). To fit such a model to data, the sample mean of the data should therefore be small. Once the apparent deviations from stationarity of the data have been removed, we therefore (in most cases) subtract the sample mean of the transformed data from each observation to generate a series to which we then fit a zero-mean stationary model. Effectively we are estimating the mean of the model by the sample mean, then fitting a (zero-mean) ARMA model to the "mean-corrected" transformed data. If we know a priori that the observations are from a process with zero mean, then this process of mean correction is omitted. ITSM keeps track of all the transformations (including mean correction) that are made. When it comes time to predict the original series, ITSM will invert all these transformations automatically.

Example D.2.9

Subtract the mean of the transformed and twice-differenced series AIRPASS.TSM by selecting `Transform>Subtract Mean`. To check the current model status press the

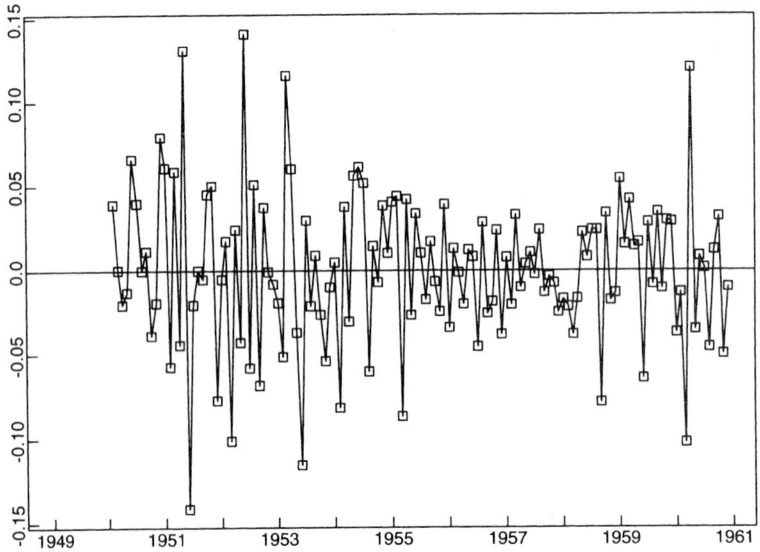

Figure D-3 The series AIRPASS.TSM after taking logs and differencing at lags 12 and 1.

red INFO button, and you will see that the current model is white noise with variance 1, since no model has yet been entered. □

D.3 Finding a Model for Your Data

After transforming the data (if necessary) as described above, we are now in a position to fit an ARMA model. ITSM uses a variety of tools to guide us in the search for an appropriate model. These include the sample ACF (autocorrelation function), the sample PACF (partial autocorrelation function), and the AICC statistic, a bias-corrected form of Akaike's AIC statistic (see Section 5.5.2).

D.3.1 Autofit

Before discussing the considerations that go into the selection, fitting, and checking of a stationary time series model, we first briefly describe an automatic feature of ITSM that searches through ARMA(p, q) models with p and q between specified limits (less than or equal to 27) and returns the model with smallest AICC value (see Sections 5.5.2 and D.3.5). Once the data set is judged to be representable by a stationary model, select `Model>Estimation>Autofit`. A dialog box will appear in which you must specify the upper and lower limits for p and q. Since the number of maximum likelihood models to be fitted is the product of the number of p-values and the number of q-values, these ranges should not be chosen to be larger than necessary. Once the limits have been specified, press `Start`, and the search will begin. You can watch the progress of the search in the dialog box that continually updates the values of p and q and the best model found so far. This option does not consider models in which the coefficients are required to satisfy constraints (other than causality) and consequently does not always lead to the optimal representation of the data. However, like the tools described below, it provides valuable information on which to base the selection of an appropriate model.

D.3.2 The Sample ACF and PACF

Pressing the second yellow button at the top of the ITSM window will produce graphs of the sample ACF and PACF for values of the lag h from 1 up to 40. For higher lags choose `Statistics>ACF/PACF>Specify Lag`, enter the maximum lag required, and click `OK`. Pressing the second yellow button repeatedly then rotates the display through ACF, PACF, and side-by-side graphs of both. Values of the ACF that decay rapidly as h increases indicate short-term dependency in the time series, while slowly decaying values indicate long-term dependency. For ARMA fitting it is desirable to have a sample ACF that decays fairly rapidly. A sample ACF that is positive and very slowly decaying suggests that the data may have a trend. A sample ACF with very slowly damped periodicity suggests the presence of a periodic seasonal component. In either of these two cases you may need to transform your data before continuing.

As a rule of thumb, the sample ACF and PACF are good estimates of the ACF and PACF of a stationary process for lags up to about a third of the sample size. It is clear from the definition of the sample ACF, $\hat{\rho}(h)$, that it will be a very poor estimator of $\rho(h)$ for h close to the sample size n.

The horizontal lines on the graphs of the sample ACF and PACF are the bounds $\pm 1.96/\sqrt{n}$. If the data constitute a large sample from an independent white noise sequence, approximately 95% of the sample autocorrelations should lie between these bounds. Large or frequent excursions from the bounds suggest that we need a model to explain the dependence and sometimes to suggest the kind of model we need (see below). To obtain numerical values of the sample ACF and PACF, right-click on the graphs and select `Info`.

The graphs of the sample ACF and PACF sometimes suggest an appropriate ARMA model for the data. As a rough guide, if the sample ACF falls between the plotted bounds $\pm 1.96/\sqrt{n}$ for lags $h > q$, then an MA(q) model is suggested, while if the sample PACF falls between the plotted bounds $\pm 1.96/\sqrt{n}$ for lags $h > p$, then an AR(p) model is suggested.

If neither the sample ACF nor PACF "cuts off" as in the previous paragraph, a more refined model selection technique is required (see the discussion of the AICC statistic in Section 5.5.2). Even if the sample ACF or PACF does cut off at some lag, it is still advisable to explore models other than those suggested by the sample ACF and PACF values.

Example D.3.1

Figure D.4 shows the sample ACF of the AIRPASS.TSM series after taking logarithms, differencing at lags 12 and 1, and subtracting the mean. Figure D.5 shows the corresponding sample PACF. These graphs suggest that we consider an MA model of order 12 (or perhaps 23) with a large number of zero coefficients, or alternatively an AR model of order 12. □

D.3.3 Entering a Model

A major function of ITSM is to find an ARMA model whose properties reflect to a high degree those of an observed (and possibly transformed) time series. Any particular causal ARMA(p, q) model with $p \leq 27$ and $q \leq 27$ can be entered directly by choosing `Model>Specify`, entering the values of p, q, the coefficients, and the white noise variance, and clicking `OK`. If there is a data set already open in ITSM, a quick way of entering a reasonably appropriate model is to use the option `Model>Estimation>Preliminary`, which estimates the coefficients and white noise variance of an ARMA model after you have specified the orders p and q and selected one of the four preliminary estimation algorithms available. An optimal preliminary AR model can also be fitted by checking `Find AR model with min AICC` in the

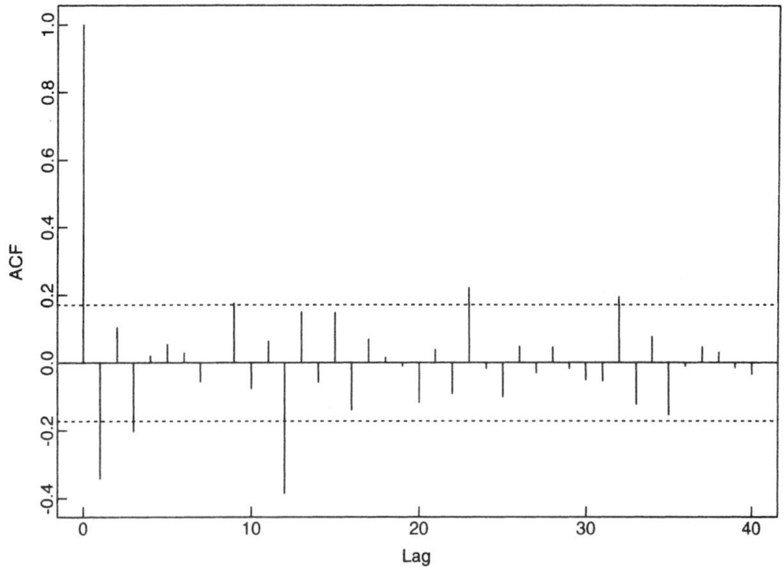

Figure D-4 The sample ACF of the transformed AIRPASS.TSM series.

`Preliminary Estimation` dialog box. If no model is entered or estimated, ITSM assumes the default ARMA(0,0), or white noise, model

$$X_t = Z_t,$$

where $\{Z_t\}$ is an uncorrelated sequence of random variables with mean zero and variance 1.

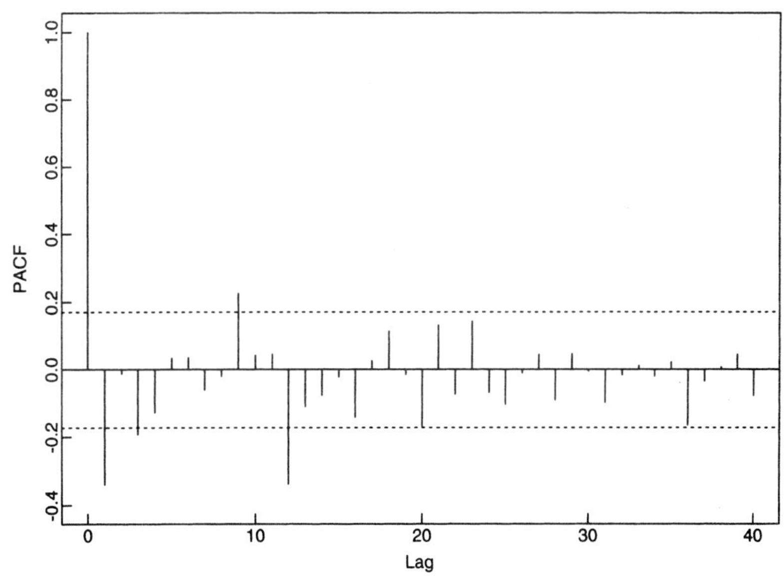

Figure D-5 The sample PACF of the transformed AIRPASS.TSM series.

If you have data and no particular ARMA model in mind, it is advisable to use the option Model>Estimation>Preliminary or equivalently to press the blue PRE button at the top of the ITSM window.

Sometimes you may wish to try a model found in a previous session or a model suggested by someone else. In that case choose Model>Specify and enter the required model. You can save both the model and data from any project by selecting File>Project>Save as and specifying the name for the new file. When the new file is opened, both the model and the data will be imported. To create a project with this model and a new data set select File>Import File and enter the name of the file containing the new data. (This file must contain data only. If it also contains a model, then the model will be imported with the data and the model previously in ITSM will be overwritten.)

D.3.4 Preliminary Estimation

The option Model>Estimation>Preliminary contains fast (but not the most efficient) model-fitting algorithms. They are useful for suggesting the most promising models for the data, but should be followed by maximum likelihood estimation using Model>Estimation>Max likelihood. The fitted preliminary model is generally used as an initial approximation with which to start the nonlinear optimization carried out in the course of maximizing the (Gaussian) likelihood.

To fit an ARMA model of specified order, first enter the values of p and q (see Section 2.6.1). For pure AR models $q = 0$, and the preliminary estimation option offers a choice between the Burg and Yule–Walker estimates. (The Burg estimates frequently give higher values of the Gaussian likelihood than the Yule–Walker estimates.) If $q = 0$, you can also check the box Find AR model with min AICC to allow the program to fit AR models of orders $0, 1, \ldots, 27$ and select the one with smallest AICC value (Section 5.5.2). For models with $q > 0$, ITSM provides a choice between two preliminary estimation methods, one based on the Hannan–Rissanen procedure and the other on the innovations algorithm. If you choose the innovations option, a default value of m will be displayed on the screen. This parameter was defined in Section 5.1.3. The standard choice is the default value computed by ITSM. The Hannan–Rissanen algorithm is recommended when p and q are both greater than 0, since it tends to give causal models more frequently than the innovations method. The latter is recommended when $p = 0$.

Once the required entries in the Preliminary Estimation dialog box have been completed, click OK, and ITSM will quickly estimate the parameters of the selected model and display a number of diagnostic statistics. (If p and q are both greater than 0, it is possible that the fitted model may be noncausal, in which case ITSM sets all the coefficients to .001 to ensure the causality required for subsequent maximum likelihood estimation. It will also give you the option of fitting a model of different order.)

Provided that the fitted model is causal, the estimated parameters are given with the ratio of each estimate to 1.96 times its standard error. The denominator (1.96 × standard error) is the critical value (at level .05) for the coefficient. Thus, if the ratio is greater than 1 in absolute value, we may conclude (at level .05) that the corresponding coefficient is different from zero. On the other hand, a ratio less than 1 in absolute value suggests the possibility that the corresponding coefficient in the model may be zero. (If the innovations option is chosen, the ratios of estimates to 1.96 × standard error are displayed only when $p = q$ or $p = 0$.) In the Preliminary Estimates window you will also see one or more estimates of the white noise variance (the residual sum of squares divided by the sample size is the estimate retained by ITSM) and some further diagnostic statistics. These are $-2\ln L(\hat{\boldsymbol{\phi}}, \hat{\boldsymbol{\theta}}, \hat{\sigma}^2)$, where L denotes the Gaussian likelihood (5.2.9), and the AICC statistic

$$-2\ln L + 2(p+q+1)n/(n-p-q-2)$$

(see Section 5.5.2).

Our eventual aim is to find a model with as small an AICC value as possible. Smallness of the AICC value computed in the preliminary estimation phase is indicative of a good model, but should be used only as a rough guide. Final decisions between models should be based on maximum likelihood estimation, carried out using the option `Model>Estimation>Max likelihood`, since for fixed p and q, the values of $\boldsymbol{\phi}$, $\boldsymbol{\theta}$, and σ^2 that minimize the AICC statistic are the maximum likelihood estimates, not the preliminary estimates. After completing preliminary estimation, ITSM stores the estimated model coefficients and white noise variance. The stored estimate of the white noise variance is the sum of squares of the residuals (or one-step prediction errors) divided by the number of observations.

A variety of models should be explored using the preliminary estimation algorithms, with a view to finding the most likely candidates for minimizing AICC when the parameters are reestimated by maximum likelihood.

Example D.3.2

To find the minimum-AICC Burg AR model for the logged, differenced, and mean-corrected series AIRPASS.TSM currently stored in ITSM, press the blue PRE button, set the MA order equal to zero, select `Burg` and `Find AR model with min AICC`, and then click `OK`. The minimum-AICC AR model is of order 12 with an AICC value of −458.13. To fit a preliminary MA(25) model to the same data, press the blue PRE button again, but this time set the AR order to 0, the MA order to 25, select `Innovations`, and click `OK`.

The ratios (estimated coefficient)/(1.96×standard error) indicate that the coefficients at lags 1 and 12 are nonzero, as suggested by the sample ACF. The estimated coefficients at lags 3 and 23 also look substantial even though the corresponding ratios are less than 1 in absolute value. The displayed values are as follows:

MA COEFFICIENTS

−.3568	.0673	−.1629	−.0415	.1268
.0264	.0283	−.0648	.1326	−.0762
−.0066	−.4987	.1789	−.0318	.1476
−.1461	.0440	−.0226	−.0749	−.0456
−.0204	−.0085	.2014	−.0767	−.0789

RATIO OF COEFFICIENTS TO (1.96*STANDARD ERROR)

−2.0833	.3703	−.8941	−.2251	.6875
.1423	.1522	−.3487	.7124	−.4061
−.0353	−2.6529	.8623	−.1522	.7068
−.6944	.2076	−.1065	−.3532	−.2147
−.0960	−.0402	.9475	−.3563	−.3659

The estimated white noise variance is .00115 and the AICC value is −440.93, which is not as good as that of the AR(12) model. Later we shall find a subset MA(25) model that has a smaller AICC value than both of these models. □

D.3.5 The AICC Statistic

The AICC statistic for the model with parameters p, q, ϕ, and θ is defined (see Section 5.2.2) as

$$\mathrm{AICC}(\phi, \theta) = -2 \ln L(\phi, \theta, S(\phi, \theta)/n) + 2(p+q+1)n/(n-p-q-2),$$

and a model chosen according to the AICC criterion minimizes this statistic.

Model-selection statistics other than AICC are also available in ITSM. A Bayesian modification of the AIC statistic known as the BIC statistic is also computed in the option `Model>Estimation>Max likelihood`. It is used in the same way as the AICC.

An exhaustive search for a model with minimum AICC or BIC value can be very slow. For this reason the sample ACF and PACF and the preliminary estimation techniques described above are useful in narrowing down the range of models to be considered more carefully in the maximum likelihood estimation stage of model fitting.

D.3.6 Changing Your Model

The model currently stored by the program can be checked at any time by selecting `Model>Specify`. Any parameter can be changed in the resulting dialog box, including the white noise variance. The model can be filed together with the data for later use by selecting `File>Project>Save as` and specifying a file name with suffix .TSM.

Example D.3.3
We shall now set some of the coefficients in the current model to zero. To do this choose `Model>Specify` and click on the box containing the value −.35676 of Theta(1). Press `Enter`, and the value of Theta(2) will appear in the box. Set this to zero. Press `Enter` again, and the value of Theta(3) will appear. Continue to work through the coefficients, setting all except Theta(1), Theta(3), Theta(12), and Theta(23) equal to zero. When you have reset the parameters, click `OK`, and the new model stored in ITSM will be the subset MA(23) model

$$X_t = Z_t - .357Z_{t-1} - .163Z_{t-3} - .499Z_{t-12} + .201Z_{t-23},$$

where $\{Z_t\} \sim \text{WN}(0, .00115)$. □

D.3.7 Maximum Likelihood Estimation

Once you have specified values of p and q and possibly set some coefficients to zero, you can carry out efficient parameter estimation by selecting `Model>Estimation>Max likelihood` or equivalently by pressing the blue MLE button.

The resulting dialog box displays the default settings, which in most cases will not need to be modified. However, if you wish to compute the likelihood without maximizing it, check the box labeled `No optimization`. The remaining information concerns the optimization settings. (With the default settings, any coefficients that are set to zero will be treated as fixed values and not as parameters. Coefficients to be optimized must therefore not be set exactly to zero. If you wish to impose further constraints on the optimization, press the `Constrain optimization` button. This allows you to fix certain coefficients or to impose multiplicative relationships on the coefficients during optimization.)

To find the maximum likelihood estimates of your parameters, click `OK`, and the estimated parameters will be displayed. To refine the estimates, repeat the estimation, specifying a smaller value of the accuracy parameter in the `Maximum Likelihood` dialog box.

Example D.3.4
To find the maximum likelihood estimates of the parameters in the model for the logged, differenced, and mean-corrected airline passenger data currently stored in ITSM, press the blue MLE button and click `OK`. The following estimated parameters and diagnostic statistics will then be displayed:

ARMA MODEL:
$X(t) = Z(t) + (-.355) * Z(t-1) + (-.201) * Z(t-3) + (-.523) * Z(t-12) + (.242) * Z(t-23)$

WN Variance = .001250

MA Coefficients
THETA(1)= -.355078 THETA(3)= -.201125
THETA(12)= -.523423 THETA(23)= .241527

Standard Error of MA Coefficients
THETA(1): .059385 THETA(3): .059297
THETA(12): .058011 THETA(23): .055828

(Residual SS)/N = .125024E-02
AICC = -.486037E+03
BIC = -.487622E+03

-2 Ln(Likelihood)= -.496517E+03

Accuracy parameter = .00205000

Number of iterations = 5

Number of function evaluations = 46

Optimization stopped within accuracy level.

The last message indicates that the minimum of $-2 \ln L$ has been located with the specified accuracy. If you see the message

```
Iteration limit exceeded,
```

then the minimum of $-2 \ln L$ could not be located with the number of iterations (50) allowed. You can continue the search (starting from the point at which the iterations were interrupted) by pressing the MLE button to continue the minimization and possibly increasing the maximum number of iterations from 50 to 100. □

D.3.8 Optimization Results

After maximizing the Gaussian likelihood, ITSM displays the model parameters (coefficients and white noise variance), the values of $-2 \ln L$, AICC, BIC, and information regarding the computations.

Example D.3.5

The next stage of the analysis is to consider a variety of competing models and to select the most suitable. The following table shows the AICC statistics for a variety of subset moving average models of order less than 24.

			Lags			*AICC*
1	3		12		23	−486.04
1	3		12	13	23	−485.78
1	3	5	12		23	−489.95
1	3		12	13		−482.62
1			12			−475.91

The best of these models from the point of view of AICC value is the one with nonzero coefficients at lags 1, 3, 5, 12, and 23. To obtain this model from the one currently stored in ITSM, select `Model>Specify`, change the value of THETA(5) from zero to .001, and click `OK`. Then reoptimize by pressing the blue MLE button and clicking `OK`. You should obtain the noninvertible model

$$X_t = Z_t - .434Z_{t-1} - .305Z_{t-3} + .238Z_{t-5} - .656Z_{t-12} + .351Z_{t-23},$$

where $\{Z_t\} \sim \text{WN}(0, .00103)$. For future reference, file the model and data as AIR-PASS2.TSM using the option `File>Project>Save as`. □

The next step is to check our model for goodness of fit.

D.4 Testing Your Model

Once we have a model, it is important to check whether it is any good or not. Typically this is judged by comparing observations with corresponding predicted values obtained from the fitted model. If the fitted model is appropriate then the prediction errors should behave in a manner that is consistent with the model. The **residuals** are the rescaled one-step prediction errors,

$$\hat{W}_t = (X_t - \hat{X}_t)/\sqrt{r_{t-1}},$$

where $\hat{X}_t$ is the best linear mean-square predictor of X_t based on the observations up to time $t-1$, $r_{t-1} = E(X_t - \hat{X}_t)^2/\sigma^2$ and σ^2 is the white noise variance of the fitted model.

If the data were truly generated by the fitted ARMA(p, q) model with white noise sequence $\{Z_t\}$, then for large samples the properties of $\{\hat{W}_t\}$ should reflect those of $\{Z_t\}$. To check the appropriateness of the model we therefore examine the residual series $\{\hat{W}_t\}$, and check that it resembles a realization of a white noise sequence.

ITSM provides a number of tests for doing this in the Residuals Menu, which is obtained by selecting the option `Statistics>Residual Analysis`. Within this option are the suboptions

Plot
QQ-Plot (normal)
QQ-Plot (t-distr)
Histogram
ACF/PACF
ACF Abs vals/Squares
Tests of randomness

D.4.1 Plotting the Residuals

Select `Statistics>Residual Analysis>Histogram`, and you will see a histogram of the **rescaled residuals**, defined as

$$\hat{R}_t = \hat{W}_t / \hat{\sigma},$$

where $n\hat{\sigma}^2$ is the sum of the squared residuals. If the fitted model is appropriate, the histogram of the rescaled residuals should have mean close to zero. If in addition the data are Gaussian, this will be reflected in the shape of the histogram, which should then resemble a normal density with mean zero and variance 1.

Select `Statistics>Residual Analysis>Plot` and you will see a graph of $\hat{R}_t$ vs. t. If the fitted model is appropriate, this should resemble a realization of a white noise sequence. Look for trends, cycles, and nonconstant variance, any of which suggest that the fitted model is inappropriate. If substantially more than 5% of the rescaled residuals lie outside the bounds ± 1.96 or if there are rescaled residuals far outside these bounds, then the fitted model should not be regarded as Gaussian.

Compatibility of the distribution of the residuals with either the normal distribution or the t-distribution can be checked by inspecting the corresponding qq plots and checking for approximate linearity. To test for normality, the Jarque-Bera statistic is also computed.

Example D.4.1

The histogram of the rescaled residuals from our model for the logged, differenced, and mean-corrected airline passenger series is shown in Figure D.6. The mean is close to zero, and the shape suggests that the assumption of Gaussian white noise is not unreasonable in our proposed model.

The graph of $\hat{R}_t$ vs. t is shown in Figure D.7. A few of the rescaled residuals are greater in magnitude than 1.96 (as is to be expected), but there are no obvious indications here that the model is inappropriate. The approximate linearity of the normal qq plot and the Jarque-Bera test confirm the approximate normality of the residuals. □

D.4.2 ACF/PACF of the Residuals

If we were to assume that our fitted model is the true process generating the data, then the observed residuals would be realized values of a white noise sequence.

In particular, the sample ACF and PACF of the observed residuals should lie within the bounds $\pm 1.96/\sqrt{n}$ roughly 95% of the time. These bounds are displayed on the graphs of the ACF and PACF. If substantially more than 5% of the correlations are outside these limits, or if there are a few very large values, then we should look for a better-fitting model. (More precise bounds, due to Box and Pierce, can be found in TSTM Section 9.4.)

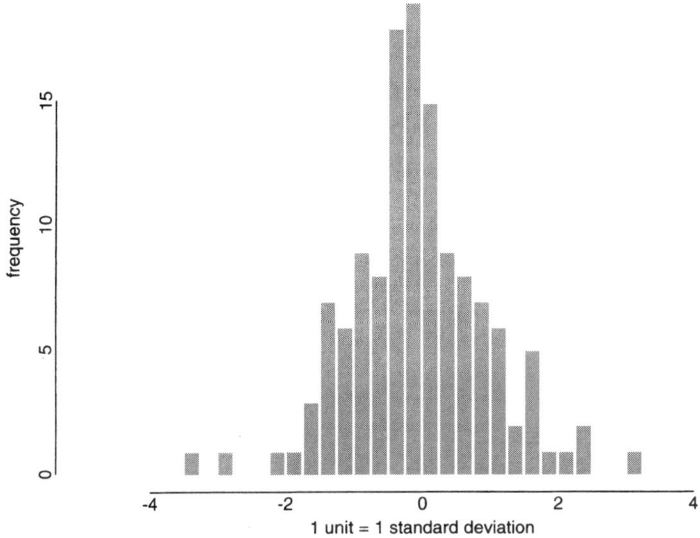

Figure D-6 Histogram of the rescaled residuals from AIRPASS.MOD.

Example D.4.2

Choose `Statistics>Residual Analysis>ACF/PACF`, or equivalently press the middle green button at the top of the ITSM window. The sample ACF and PACF of the residuals will then appear as shown in Figures D.8 and D.9. No correlations are outside the bounds in this case. They appear to be compatible with the hypothesis that the residuals are in fact observations of a white noise sequence. To check for independence of the residuals, the sample autocorrelation functions of their absolute values and squares can be plotted by clicking on the third green button. □

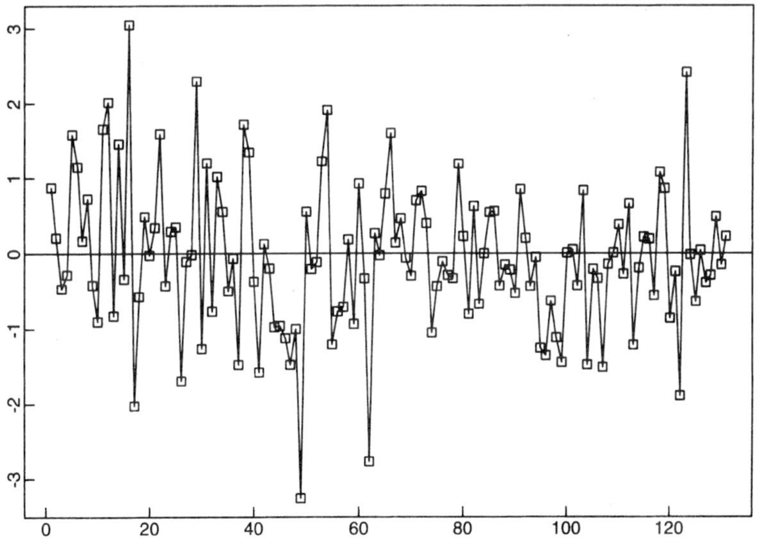

Figure D-7 Time plot of the rescaled residuals from AIRPASS.MOD.

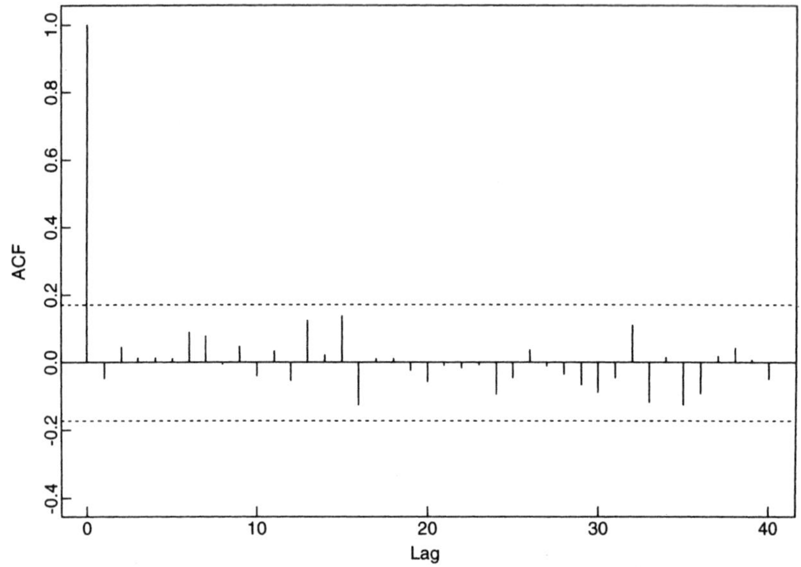

Figure D-8 Sample ACF of the residuals from AIRPASS.MOD.

D.4.3 Testing for Randomness of the Residuals

The option `Statistics>Residual Analysis>Tests of Randomness` carries out the six tests for randomness of the residuals described in Section 5.3.3.

Example D.4.3

The residuals from our model for the logged, differenced, and mean-corrected series AIRPASS.TSM are checked by selecting the option indicated above and selecting

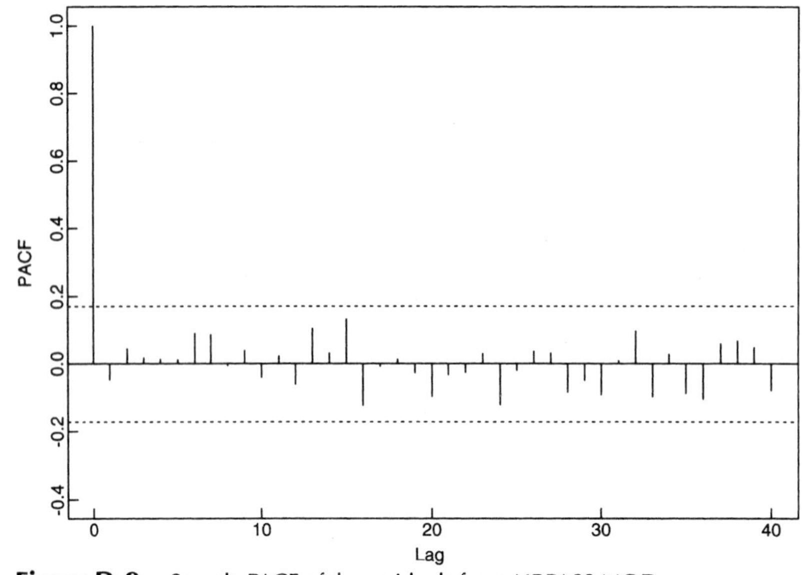

Figure D-9 Sample PACF of the residuals from AIRPASS.MOD.

the parameter h for the portmanteau tests. Adopting the value $h = 25$ suggested by ITSM, we obtain the following results:

RANDOMNESS TEST STATISTICS (see Section 5.3.3)

LJUNG-BOX PORTM.= 13.76	CHISQUR(20),	p-value = 0.843
MCLEOD-LI PORTM.= 17.39	CHISQUR(25),	p-value = 0.867
TURNING POINTS = 87.	ANORMAL(86.00, 4.79**2),	p-value = 0.835
DIFFERENCE-SIGN = 65.	ANORMAL(65.00, 3.32**2),	p-value = 1.000
RANK TEST = 3934.	ANORMAL(4257.50, 251.3**2),	p-value = 0.198
JARQUE-BERA = 4.33	CHISQUR(2)	p-value = 0.115
ORDER OF MIN AICC	YW MODEL FOR RESIDUALS = 0	

Every test is easily passed by our fitted model (with significance level $\alpha = .05$), and the order of the minimum-AICC AR model for the residuals supports the compatibility of the residuals with white noise. For later use, file the residuals by pressing the red EXP button and exporting the residuals to a file with the name AIRRES.TSM. □

D.5 Prediction

One of the main purposes of time series modeling is the prediction of future observations. Once you have found a suitable model for your data, you can predict future values using the option `Forecasting>ARMA`. (The other options listed under `Forecasting` refer to the methods of Chapter 9.)

D.5.1 Forecast Criteria

Given observations $X_1, \ldots, X_n$ of a series that we assume to be appropriately modeled as an ARMA(p, q) process, ITSM predicts future values of the series X_{n+h} from the data and the model by computing the linear combination $P_n(X_{n+h})$ of $X_1, \ldots, X_n$ that minimizes the mean squared error $E(X_{n+h} - P_n(X_{n+h}))^2$.

D.5.2 Forecast Results

Assuming that the current data set has been adequately fitted by the current ARMA(p, q) model, choose `Forecasting>ARMA`, and you will see the `ARMA Forecast` dialog box.

You will be asked for the number of forecasts required, which of the transformations you wish to invert (the default settings are to invert all of them so as to obtain forecasts of the *original* data), whether or not you wish to plot prediction bounds (assuming normality), and if so, the confidence level required, e.g., 95%. After providing this information, click `OK`, and the data will be plotted with the forecasts (and possibly prediction bounds) appended. As is to be expected, the separation of the prediction bounds increases with the lead time h of the forecast.

Right-click on the graph, select `Info`, and the numerical values of the predictors and prediction bounds will be printed.

Example D.5.1

We left our logged, differenced, and mean-corrected airline passenger data stored in ITSM with the subset MA(23) model found in Example D.3.5. To predict the next 24 values of the original series, select `Forecasting>ARMA` and accept the default settings in the dialog box by clicking `OK`. You will then see the graph shown in Figure D.10. Numerical values of the forecasts are obtained by right-clicking on the graph and selecting `Info`. The ARMA `Forecast` dialog box also permits using a model constructed from a subset of the data to obtain forecasts and prediction bounds for the remaining observed values of the series. □

D.6 Model Properties

ITSM can be used to analyze the properties of a specified ARMA process without reference to any data set. This enables us to explore and compare the properties

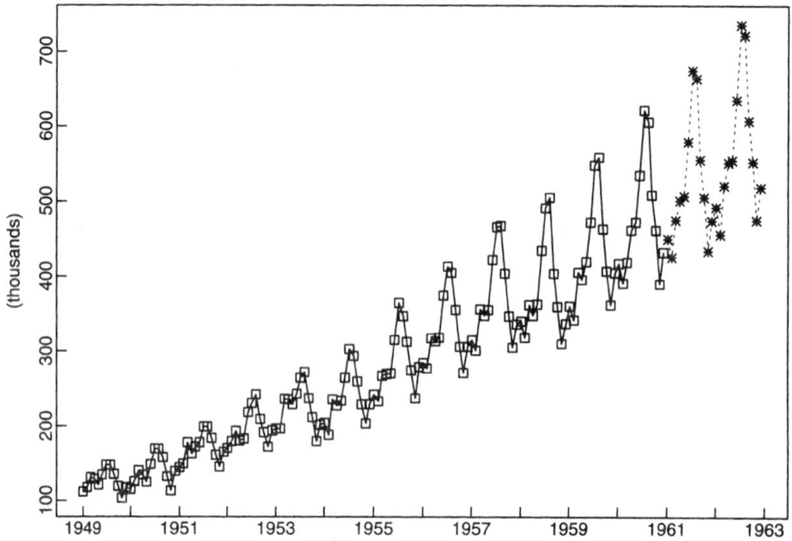

Figure D-10 The original AIRPASS data with 24 forecasts appended.

of different ARMA models in order to gain insight into which models might best represent particular features of a given data set.

For any ARMA(p, q) process or fractionally integrated ARMA(p, q) process with $p \le 27$ and $q \le 27$, ITSM allows you to compute the autocorrelation and partial autocorrelation functions, the spectral density and distribution functions, and the MA(∞) and AR(∞) representations of the process. It also allows you to generate simulated realizations of the process driven by either Gaussian or non-Gaussian noise. The use of these options is described in this section.

Example D.6.1

We shall illustrate the use of ITSM for model analysis using the model for the transformed series AIRPASS.TSM that is currently stored in the program. □

D.6.1 ARMA Models

For modeling zero-mean stationary time series, ITSM uses the class of ARMA (and fractionally integrated ARMA) processes. ITSM Enables you to compute characteristics of the causal ARMA model defined by

$$X_t = \phi_1 X_{t-1} + \phi_2 X_{t-2} + \cdots + \phi_p X_{t-p} + Z_t + \theta_1 Z_{t-1} + \theta_2 Z_{t-2} + \cdots + \theta_q Z_{t-q},$$

or more concisely $\phi(B)X_t = \theta(B)Z_t$, where $\{Z_t\} \sim \text{WN}\left(0, \sigma^2\right)$ and the parameters are all specified. (Characteristics of the fractionally integrated ARIMA(p, d, q) process defined by

$$(1 - B)^d \phi(B) X_t = \theta(B) Z_t, \quad |d| < 0.5,$$

can also be computed.)

ITSM works exclusively with causal models. It will not permit you to enter a model for which $1 - \phi_1 z - \cdots - \phi_p z^p$ has a zero inside or on the unit circle, nor does it generate fitted models with this property. From the point of view of second-order properties, this represents no loss of generality (Section 3.1). If you are trying to enter an ARMA(p, q) model manually, the simplest way to ensure that your model is causal is to set all the autoregressive coefficients close to zero (e.g., .001). ITSM will not accept a noncausal model.

ITSM does not restrict models to be invertible. You can check whether or not the current model is invertible by choosing `Model>Specify` and pressing the button labeled Causal/Invertible in the resulting dialog box. If the model is noninvertible, i.e., if the moving-average polynomial $1 + \theta_1 z + \cdots + \theta_q z^q$ has a zero inside or on the unit circle, the message `Non-invertible` will appear beneath the box containing the moving-average coefficients. (A noninvertible model can be converted to an invertible model with the same autocovariance function by choosing `Model>Switch to invertible`. If the model is already invertible, the program will tell you.)

D.6.2 Model ACF, PACF

The *model* ACF and PACF are plotted using `Model>ACF/PACF>Model`. If you wish to change the maximum lag from the default value of 40, select `Model>ACF/PACF>Specify Lag` and enter the required maximum lag. (It can be much larger than 40, e.g., 10000). The graph will then be modified, showing the correlations up to the specified maximum lag.

If there is a data file open as well as a model in ITSM, the model ACF and PACF can be compared with the sample ACF and PACF by pressing the third yellow button at the top of the ITSM window. The model correlations will then be plotted in red, with the corresponding sample correlations shown in the same graph but plotted in green.

Example D.6.2

The sample and model ACF and PACF for the current model and transformed series AIRPASS.TSM are shown in Figures D.11 and D.12. They are obtained by pressing the third yellow button at the top of the ITSM window. The vertical lines represent the model values, and the squares are the sample ACF/PACF. The graphs show that the data and the model ACF both have large values at lag 12, while the sample and model partial autocorrelation functions both tend to die away geometrically after the peak at lag 12. The similarities between the graphs indicate that the model is capturing some of the important features of the data. □

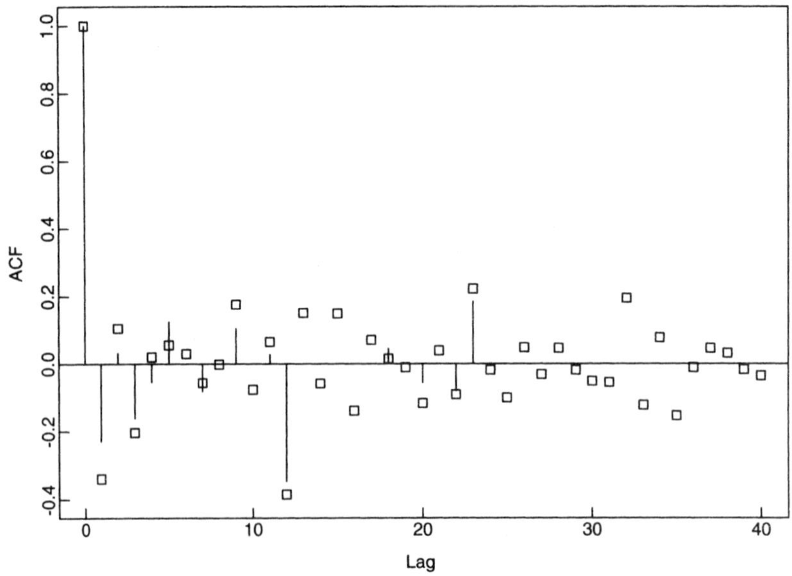

Figure D-11 The ACF of the model in Example D.3.5 together with the sample ACF of the transformed AIRPASS.TSM series.

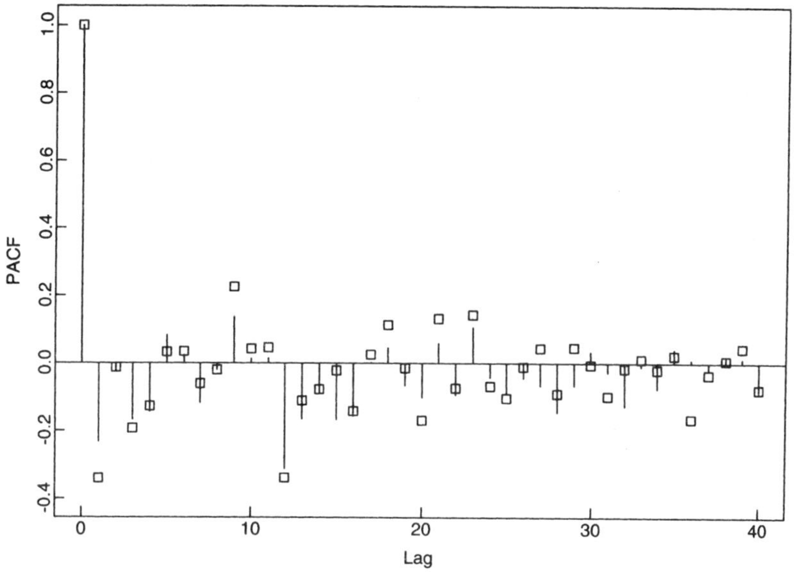

Figure D-12 The PACF of the model in Example D.3.5 together with the sample PACF of the transformed AIRPASS.TSM series.

D.6.3 Model Representations

As indicated in Section 3.1, if $\{X_t\}$ is a causal ARMA process, then it has an MA(∞) representation

$$X_t = \sum_{j=0}^{\infty} \psi_j Z_{t-j}, \quad t = 0, \pm1, \pm2, \ldots,$$

where $\sum_{j=0}^{\infty} |\psi_j| < \infty$ and $\psi_0 = 1$.

Similarly, if $\{X_t\}$ is an invertible ARMA process, then it has an AR(∞) representation

$$Z_t = \sum_{j=0}^{\infty} \pi_j X_{t-j}, \quad t = 0, \pm1, \pm2, \ldots,$$

where $\sum_{j=0}^{\infty} |\pi_j| < \infty$ and $\pi_0 = 1$.

For any specified causal ARMA model you can determine the coefficients in these representations by selecting the option `Model>AR/MA Infinity`. (If the model is not invertible, you will see only the MA(∞) coefficients, since the AR(∞) representation does not exist in this case.)

Example D.6.3

The current subset MA(23) model for the transformed series AIRPASS.TSM does not have an AR(∞) representation, since it is not invertible. However, we can replace the model with an invertible one having the same autocovariance function by selecting `Model>Switch to Invertible`. For this model we can then find an AR(∞) representation by selecting `Model>AR Infinity`. This gives 50 coefficients, the first 20 of which are shown below.

MA-Infinity	*AR − Infinity*	
j	*psi(j)*	*pi(j)*
0	1.00000	1.00000
1	−.36251	.36251
2	.01163	.11978
3	−.26346	.30267
4	−.06924	.27307
5	.15484	−.00272
6	−.02380	.05155
7	−.06557	.16727
8	−.04487	.10285
9	.01921	.01856
10	−.00113	.07947
11	.01882	.07000
12	−.57008	.58144
13	.00617	.41683
14	.00695	.23490
15	.03188	.37200
16	.02778	.38961
17	.01417	.10918
18	.02502	.08776
19	.00958	.22791

□

D.6.4 Generating Realizations of a Random Series

ITSM can be used to generate realizations of a random time series defined by the currently stored model.

To generate such a realization, select the option `Model>Simulate`, and you will see the ARMA Simulation dialog box. You will be asked to specify the number of observations required, the white noise variance (if you wish to change it from the current value), and an integer-valued random number seed (by specifying and recording this integer with up to nine digits you can reproduce the same realization at a later date by reentering the same seed). You will also have the opportunity to add a specified mean to the simulated ARMA values. If the current model has been fitted to transformed data, then you can also choose to apply the inverse transformations to the simulated ARMA to generate a simulated version of the *original* series. The default distribution for the white noise is Gaussian. However, by pressing the button `Change noise distribution` you can select from a variety of alternative distributions or by checking the box `Use Garch model for noise process` you can generate an ARMA process driven by GARCH noise. Finally, you can choose whether the simulated data will overwrite the data set in the current project or whether they will be used to create a new project. Once you are satisfied with your choices, click `OK`, and the simulated series will be generated.

Example D.6.4

To generate a simulated realization of the series AIRPASS.TSM using the current model and transformed data set, select the option `Model>Simulate`. The default options in the dialog box are such as to generate a realization of the *original* series as a new project, so it suffices to click `OK`. You will then see a graph of the simulated series that should resemble the original series AIRPASS.TSM. □

D.6.5 Spectral Properties

Spectral properties of both data and fitted ARMA models can also be computed and plotted with the aid of ITSM. The spectral density of the *model* is determined by selecting the option `Spectrum>Model`. Estimation of the spectral density from observations of a stationary series can be carried out in two ways, either by fitting an ARMA model as already described and computing the spectral density of the fitted model (Section 4.4) or by computing the periodogram of the data and smoothing (Section 4.2). The latter method is applied by selecting the option `Spectrum>Smoothed Periodogram`. Examples of both approaches are given in Chapter 4.

D.7 Multivariate Time Series

Observations $\{\mathbf{x}_1, \ldots, \mathbf{x}_n\}$ of an m-component time series must be stored as an ASCII file with n rows and m columns, with at least one space between entries in the same row. To open a multivariate series for analysis, select `File>Project>Open>Multivariate` and click `OK`. Then double-click on the file containing the data, and you will be asked to enter the number of columns (m) in the data file. After doing this, click `OK`, and you will see graphs of each component of the series, with the multivariate tool bar at the top of the ITSM screen. For examples of the application of ITSM to the analysis of multivariate series, see Chapter 7.

References

Akaike, H. (1969), Fitting autoregressive models for prediction, *Annals of the Institute of Statistical Mathematics*, *21*, 243–247.

Akaike, H. (1973), Information theory and an extension of the maximum likelihood principle, *2nd International Symposium on Information Theory*, B.N. Petrov and F. Csaki (eds.), Akademiai Kiado, Budapest, 267–281.

Akaike, H. (1978), Time series analysis and control through parametric models, *Applied Time Series Analysis*, D.F. Findley (ed.), Academic Press, New York.

Anderson, T.W. (1971), *The Statistical Analysis of Time Series*, John Wiley, New York.

Anderson, T.W. (1980), Maximum likelihood estimation for vector autoregressive moving-average models, *Directions in Time Series*, D.R. Brillinger and G.C. Tiao (eds.), Institute of Mathematical Statistics, 80–111.

Ansley, C.F. (1979), An algorithm for the exact likelihood of a mixed autoregressive-moving-average process, *Biometrika*, *66*, 59–65.

Ansley, C.F. and Kohn, R. (1985), On the estimation of ARIMA models with missing values, *Time Series Analysis of Irregularly Observed Data*, E. Parzen (ed.), Springer Lecture Notes in Statistics, *25*, 9–37.

Aoki, M. (1987), *State Space Modeling of Time Series*, Springer-Verlag, Berlin.

Atkins, Stella M. (1979), Case study on the use of intervention analysis applied to traffic accidents, *J. Opns Res. Soc.*, *30*, 7, 651–659.

Barndorff-Nielsen, O. (1978), *Information and Exponential Families in Statistical Theory*, John Wiley, New York.

Bergstrom, A.R. (1990), *Continuous Time Econometric Modelling*, Oxford University Press, Oxford.

Bhattacharyya, M.N. and Layton, A.P. (1979), Effectiveness of seat belt legislation on the Queensland road toll—an Australian case study in intervention analysis, *J. Amer. Stat. Assoc.*, *74*, 596–603.

Bloomfield, P. (2000), *Fourier Analysis of Time Series: An Introduction*, 2nd edition, John Wiley, New York.

Bollerslev, T. (1986), Generalized autoregressive conditional heteroskedasticity, *J. Econometrics*, *31*, 307–327.

Box, G.E.P. and Cox, D.R. (1964), An analysis of transformations (with discussion), *J. R. Stat. Soc. B 26*, 211–252.

Box, G.E.P. and Jenkins, G.M. (1976), *Time Series Analysis: Forecasting and Control, Revised Edition*, Holden-Day, San Francisco.

Box, G.E.P. and Pierce, D.A. (1970), Distribution of residual autocorrelations in autoregressive-integrated moving-average time series models, *J. Amer. Stat. Assoc. 65*, 1509–1526.

Box, G.E.P. and Tiao, G.C. (1975), Intervention analysis with applications to economic and environmental problems, *J. Amer. Stat. Assoc. 70*, 70–79.

Breidt, F.J. and Davis, R.A. (1992), Time reversibility, identifiability and independence of innovations for stationary time series, *J. Time Series Anal. 13*, 377–390.

Brockwell, P.J. (1994), On continuous time threshold ARMA processes, *J. Statistical Planning and Inference 39*, 291–304.

Brockwell, P.J. (2001), Continuous-time ARMA processes, *Handbook of Statistics*, Vol. 19, D. N. Shanbhag and C. R. Rao (eds.), Elsevier, Amsterdam, 249–276.

Brockwell, P.J. and Davis, R.A. (1988), Applications of innovation representations in time series analysis, *Probability and Statistics, Essays in Honor of Franklin A. Graybill*, J.N. Srivastava (ed.), Elsevier, Amsterdam, 61–84.

Brockwell, P.J. and Davis, R.A. (1991), *Time Series: Theory and Methods, 2nd Edition*, Springer-Verlag, New York.

Brockwell, P.J. and Davis, R.A. (1994), *ITSM for Windows*, Springer-Verlag, New York.

Chan, K.S. and Ledolter, J. (1995), Monte Carlo EM estimation for time series models involving counts, *J. Amer. Stat. Assoc. 90*, 242–252.

Chan, K.S. and Tong, H. (1987), A note on embedding a discrete parameter ARMA model in a continuous parameter ARMA model, *J. Time Series Anal., 8*, 277–281.

Chung, K.L. and Williams, R.J. (1990), *Introduction to Stochastic Integration, 2nd Edition*, Birkhäuser, Boston.

Cochran, D. and Orcutt, G.H. (1949), Applications of least squares regression to relationships containing autocorrelated errors, *J. Amer. Stat. Assoc., 44*, 32–61.

Davis, M.H.A. and Vinter, R.B. (1985), *Stochastic Modelling and Control*, Chapman and Hall, London.

Davis, R.A., Chen, M., and Dunsmuir, W.T.M. (1995), Inference for MA(1) processes with a root on or near the unit circle, *Probability and Mathematical Statistics, 15*, 227–242.

Davis, R.A., Chen, M., and Dunsmuir, W.T.M. (1996), Inference for seasonal moving-average models with a unit root. "Athens Conference on Applied Probability and Time Series, Volume 2: Time Series Analysis", Lecture Notes in Statistics, Vol. 115, Springer-Verlag, Berlin, 160–176.

Davis, R.A. and Dunsmuir, W.T.M. (1996), Maximum likelihood estimation for MA(1) processes with a root on or near the unit circle, *Econometric Theory, 12*, 1–29.

Dempster, A.P., Laird, N.M., and Rubin, D.B. (1977), Maximum likelihood from incomplete data via the EM algorithm, *J. R. Stat. Soc. B*, *39*, 1–38.

Dickey, D.A. and Fuller, W.A. (1979), Distribution of the estimators for autoregressive time series with a unit root, *J. Amer. Stat. Assoc.*, *74*, 427–431.

Duong, Q.P. (1984), On the choice of the order of autoregressive models: a ranking and selection approach, *J. Time Series Anal.*, *5*, 145–157.

Engle, R.F. (1982), Autoregressive conditional heteroscedasticity with estimates of the variance of UK inflation, *Econometrica*, *50*, 987–1007.

Engle, R.F. (1995), *Arch: Selected Readings*, Advanced Texts in Econometrics, Oxford Univerity Press, Oxford.

Engle, R.F. and Granger, C.W.J. (1987), Co-integration and error correction: representation, estimation and testing, *Econometrica*, *55*, 251–276.

Engle, R.F. and Granger, C.W.J. (1991), *Long-run Economic Relationships*, Advanced Texts in Econometrics, Oxford University Press, Oxford.

Fuller, W.A. (1976), *Introduction to Statistical Time Series*, John Wiley, New York.

de Gooijer, J.G., Abraham, B., Gould, A., and Robinson, L. (1985), Methods of determining the order of an autoregressive-moving-average process: A survey, *Int. Stat., Review*, *53*, 301–329.

Granger, C.W.J. (1981), Some properties of time series data and their use in econometric model specification, *J. Econometrics*, *16*, 121–130.

Gray, H.L., Kelley, G.D., and McIntire, D.D. (1978), A new approach to ARMA modeling, *Comm. Stat.*, *B7*, 1–77.

Graybill, F.A. (1983), *Matrices with Applications in Statistics*, Wadsworth, Belmont, California.

Grunwald, G.K., Hyndman, R.J., and Hamza, K. (1994), Some properties and generalizations of nonnegative Bayesian time series models, *Technical Report*, Statistics Dept., Melbourne Univeristy, Parkville, Australia.

Grunwald, G.K., Raftery, A.E., and Guttorp, P. (1993), Prediction rule for exponential family state space models, *J. R. Stat. Soc. B*, *55*, 937–943.

Hannan, E.J. (1980), The estimation of the order of an ARMA process, *Ann. Stat.*, *8*, 1071–1081.

Hannan, E.J. and Deistler, M. (1988), *The Statistical Theory of Linear Systems*, John Wiley, New York.

Hannan, E.J. and Rissanen, J. (1982), Recursive estimation of mixed autoregressive moving-average order, *Biometrika*, *69*, 81–94.

Harvey, A.C. (1990), *Forecasting, Structural Time Series Models and the Kalman Filter*, Cambridge University Press, Cambridge.

Harvey, A.C. and Fernandes, C. (1989), Time Series models for count data of qualitative observations, *J. Business and Economic Statistics*, *7*, 407–422.

Holt, C.C. (1957), Forecasting seasonals and trends by exponentially weighted moving-averages, *ONR Research Memorandum 52*, Carnegie Institute of Technology, Pittsburgh, Pennsylvania.

Hurvich, C.M. and Tsai, C.L. (1989), Regression and time series model selection in small samples, *Biometrika*, *76*, 297–307.

Jarque, C.M. and Bera, A.K. (1980), Efficient tests for normality, heteroscedasticity and serial independence of regression residuals, *Economics Letters*, *6*, 255–259.

Jones, R.H. (1975), Fitting autoregressions, *J. Amer. Stat. Assoc.*, *70*, 590–592.

Jones, R.H. (1978), Multivariate autoregression estimation using residuals, *Applied Time Series Analysis*, David F. Findley (ed.), Academic Press, New York, 139–162.

Jones, R.H. (1980), Maximum likelihood fitting of ARMA models to time series with missing observations, *Technometrics*, *22*, 389–395.

Karatzas, I. and Shreve, S.E. (1991), *Brownian Motion and Stochastic Calculus, 2nd Edition*, Springer-Verlag, New York.

Kendall, M.G. and Stuart, A. (1976), *The Advanced Theory of Statistics, Vol. 3*, Griffin, London.

Kitagawa, G. (1987), Non-Gaussian state-space modeling of non-stationary time series, *J. Amer. Stat. Assoc.*, *82* (with discussion), 1032–1063.

Kuk, A.Y.C. and Cheng, Y.W. (1994), The Monte Carlo Newton-Raphson algorithm, *Technical Report S94-10*, Department of Statistics, U. New South Wales, Sydney, Australia.

Lehmann, E.L. (1983), *Theory of Point Estimation*, John Wiley, New York.

Lehmann, E.L. (1986), *Testing Statistical Hypotheses, 2nd Edition*, John Wiley, New York.

Liu, J. and Brockwell, P.J. (1988), The general bilinear time series model, *J. Appl. Probability* *25*, 553–564.

Ljung, G.M. and Box, G.E.P. (1978), On a measure of lack of fit in time series models, *Biometrika*, *65*, 297–303.

Lütkepohl, H. (1993), *Introduction to Multiple Time Series Analysis, 2nd Edition*, Springer-Verlag, Berlin.

McCullagh, P., and Nelder, J.A. (1989), *Generalized Linear Models, 2nd Edition*, Chapman and Hall, London.

McLeod, A.I. and Li, W.K. (1983), Diagnostic checking ARMA time series models using squared-residual autocorrelations, *J. Time Series Anal.*, *4*, 269–273.

Mage, D.T. (1982), An objective graphical method for testing normal distributional assumptions using probability plots, *Amer. Stat.*, *36*, 116–120.

Makridakis, S., Andersen, A., Carbone, R., Fildes, R., Hibon, M., Lewandowski, R., Newton, J., Parzen, E., and Winkler, R. (1984), *The Forecasting Accuracy of Major Time Series Methods*, John Wiley, New York.

Makridakis, S., Wheelwright, S.C., and Hyndman, R.J. (1997), *Forecasting: Methods and Applications*, John Wiley, New York.

May, R.M. (1976), Simple mathematical models with very complicated dynamics, *Nature*, *261*, 459–467.

Mendenhall, W., Wackerly, D.D., and Scheaffer, D.L. (1990), *Mathematical Statistics with Applications, 4th Edition*, Duxbury, Belmont.

Mood, A.M., Graybill, F.A., and Boes, D.C. (1974), *Introduction to the Theory of Statistics*, McGraw-Hill, New York.

Newton, H.J. and Parzen, E. (1984), Forecasting and time series model types of 111 economic time series, *The Forecasting Accuracy of Major Time Series Methods*, S. Makridakis et al. (eds.), John Wiley and Sons, Chichester.

Nicholls, D.F. and Quinn, B.G. (1982), *Random Coefficient Autoregressive Models: An Introduction*, Springer Lecture Notes in Statistics, *11*.

Oksendal, B. (1992), *Stochastic Differential Equations: An Introduction with Applications, 3rd Edition*, Springer-Verlag, New York.

Pantula, S. (1991), Asymptotic distributions of unit-root tests when the process is nearly stationary, *J. Business and Economic Statistics*, *9*, 63–71.

Parzen, E. (1982), ARARMA models for time series analysis and forecasting, *J. Forecasting*, *1*, 67–82.

Pole, A., West, M., and Harrison, J. (1994), *Applied Bayesian Forecasting and Time Series Analysis*, Chapman and Hall, New York.

Priestley, M.B. (1988), *Non-linear and Non-stationary Time Series Analysis*, Academic Press, London.

Rosenblatt, M. (1985), *Stationary Sequences and Random Fields*, Birkhäuser, Boston.

Said, S.E. and Dickey, D.A. (1984), Testing for unit roots in autoregressive moving-average models with unknown order, *Biometrika*, *71*, 599–607.

Sakai, H. and Tokumaru, H. (1980). Autocorrelations of a certain chaos. *IEEE Transactions on Acoustics, Speech and Signal Processing* *28*, 588–590.

Schwert, G.W. (1987), Effects of model specification on tests for unit roots in macroeconomic data, *J. Monetary Economics*, *20*, 73–103.

Shapiro, S.S. and Francia, R.S. (1972), An approximate analysis of variance test for normality, *J. Amer. Stat. Assoc.*, *67*, 215–216.

Shibata, R. (1976), Selection of the order of an autoregressive model by Akaike's information criterion, *Biometrika*, *63*, 117–126.

Shibata, R. (1980), Asymptotically efficient selection of the order of the model for estimating parameters of a linear process, *Ann. Stat.*, *8*, 147–164.

Silvey, S.D. (1975), *Statistical Inference*, Halsted, New York.

Smith, J.Q. (1979), A Generalization of the Bayesian steady forecasting model, *J. R. Stat. Soc. B*, *41*, 375–387.

Sorenson, H.W. and Alspach, D.L. (1971), Recursive Bayesian estimation using Gaussian sums, *Automatica*, *7*, 465–479.

Stramer, O., Brockwell, P.J., and Tweedie, R.L. (1995), Existence and stability of continuous time threshold ARMA processes, *Statistica Sinica.*

Subba-Rao, T. and Gabr, M.M. (1984), *An Introduction to Bispectral Analysis and Bilinear Time Series Models*, Springer Lecture Notes in Statistics, *24*.

Tam, W.K. and Reinsel, G.C. (1995), Tests for seasonal moving-average unit root in ARIMA models, *Preprint, University of Wisconsin-Madison.*

Tanaka, K. (1990), Testing for a moving-average unit root, *Econometric Theory*, *9*, 433–444.

Tong, H. (1990), *Non-linear Time Series: A Dynamical Systems Approach*, Oxford University Press, Oxford.

Venables, W.N. and Ripley, B.D. (1994), *Modern Applied Statistics with S-Plus*, Springer-Verlag, New York.

West, M. and Harrison, P.J. (1989), *Bayesian Forecasting and Dynamic Models*, Springer-Verlag, New York.

Whittle, P. (1963), On the fitting of multivariate autoregressions and the approximate canonical factorization of a spectral density matrix, *Biometrika*, *40*, 129–134.

Wichern, D. and Jones, R.H. (1978), Assessing the impact of market disturbances using intervention analysis, *Management Science*, *24*, 320–337.

Wu, C.F.J. (1983), On the convergence of the EM algorithm, *Ann. Stat.*, *11*, 95–103.

Zeger, S.L. (1988), A regression model for time series of counts, *Biometrika*, *75*, 621–629.

Index

A

B

C

T

U

V

W

Y

Z

Installation of ITSM2000.

1. Place the ITSM2000 CD-ROM in your CD drive.

2. On the desktop, double-click on the icon labelled ``My Computer''. A window with the title "My Computer" will appear.

3. In the "My Computer" window, double-click on the icon for your CD drive. In the CD window you will then see the icon for the folder ITSM2000, which contains the program ITSM.EXE, the help file ITSM.HLP and the data sets.

4. Copy and paste the folder ITSM2000 to any convenient location on your hard drive. For example, to copy and paste it to the C: drive,

   (a) highlight the icon for the ITSM2000 folder in the CD window (by left-clicking on it),

   (b) select Edit=>Copy from the menu of the CD window,

   (c) open the C: drive window by double-clicking on its icon in the "My Computer'' window,

   (d) select Edit=>Paste from the menu of the C: drive window.

The ITSM2000 folder, together with its contents, will then have been copied from the CD drive to the C: drive.

5. To run the program, either

   (a) double-click on the icon ITSM.EXE in the folder ITSM2000

   or

   (b) on the Windows task bar, click on Start, select Run, enter the location and name of the program (e.g. C:\ITSM2000\ITSM.EXE) and click on OK.

(The program can also be run directly from the CD-ROM by opening the folder ITSM2000 and double-clicking on the icon ITSM.EXE. For further information see Appendix D.)